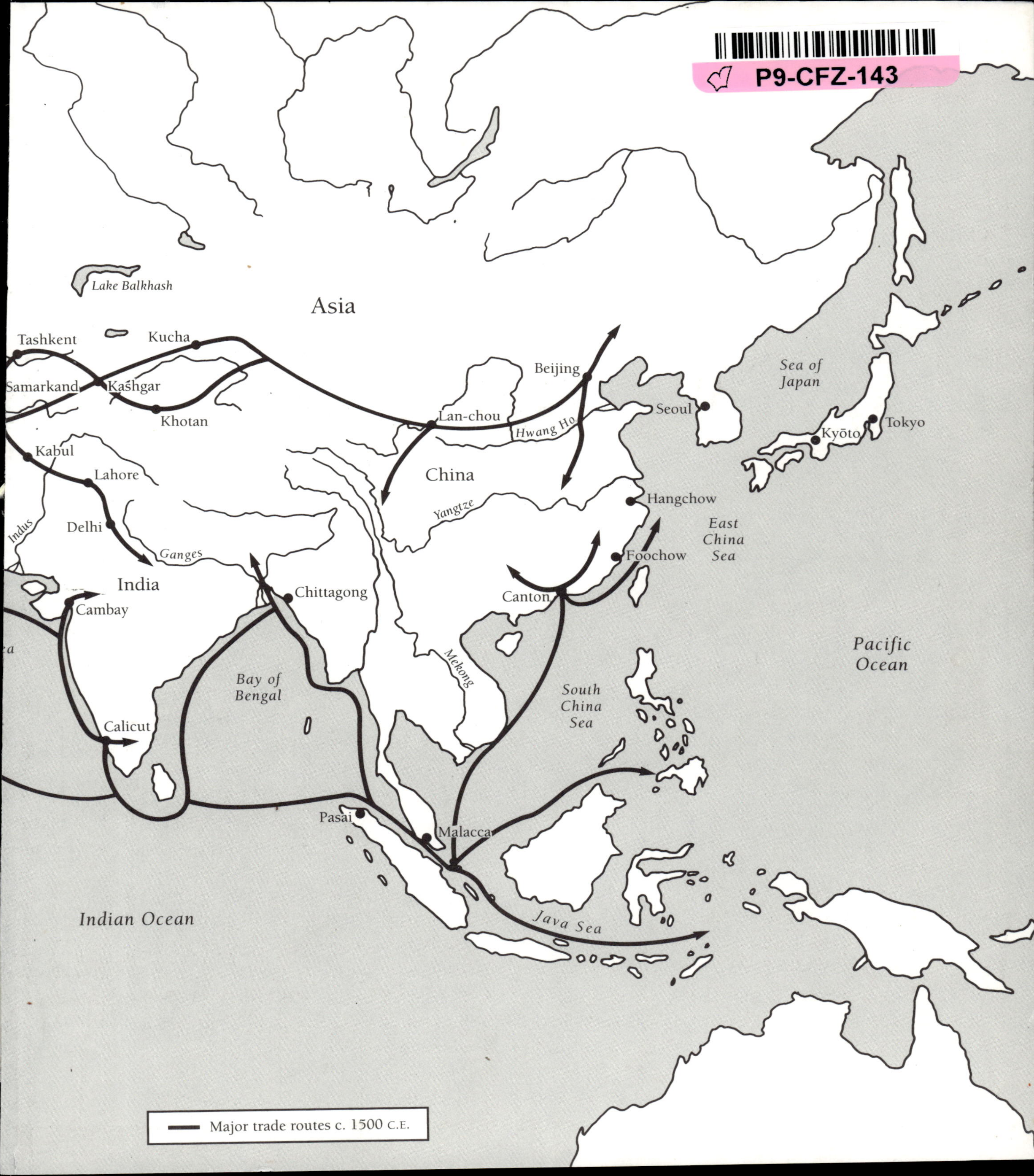
Lake Balkhash
Asia
Tashkent
Kucha
Samarkand
Kashgar
Khotan
Beijing
Sea of Japan
Seoul
Lan-chou
Hwang Ho
Tokyo
Kyōto
Kabul
Lahore
China
Hangchow
Yangtze
Indus
Delhi
East China Sea
Ganges
Foochow
India
Chittagong
Canton
Cambay
Mekong
Pacific Ocean
Bay of Bengal
South China Sea
Calicut
Pasai
Malacca
Indian Ocean
Java Sea
Major trade routes c. 1500 C.E.

Religions of the World

THIRD EDITION

RELIGIONS OF THE WORLD

THIRD EDITION

ST. MARTIN'S PRESS, NEW YORK

Senior editor: Don Reisman
Manager, publishing services: Emily Berleth
Production supervisor: Alan Fischer
Text design: Gene Crofts
Maps: Jeane E. Norton
Photo research: Gene Crofts
Cover design: Ed Butler/Butler Udell

Library of Congress Catalog Card Number: 92-50025

Manufactured in the United States of America.

7 6 5 4 3

f e d c b

For information write:
St. Martin's Press, Inc.
175 Fifth Avenue
New York, NY 10010

ISBN: 0-312-05023-2

PART OPENER PHOTOS

Pages 18–19—*background and panel photo:* Australian Overseas Information

Pages 80–81—*background photo and panel photo:* Reuters/Bettmann

Pages 162–163—*background photo and panel photo:* Shashinka Photo

Pages 220–221—*background and panel photo:* Bruno J. Zehnder/Peter Arnold, Inc.

Pages 280–281—*background and panel photo:* Reuters/Bettmann

Pages 342–343—*background photo:* Peter Southwick/Stock Boston; *panel photo:* Jeff Duhn/Stock Boston

Pages 424–425—*background and panel photo:* Reuters/Bettmann

ACKNOWLEDGMENTS

Excerpt from Henry J. Drewal and Margaret Thompson Drewal, *Gelede: Art and Female Power among the Yoruba* (Bloomington: Indiana University Press, 1983). Reprinted by permission of Indiana University Press.

Excerpt reprinted with the permission of Macmillan Publishing Company and Macmillan Publishers, Ltd. from *Gitanjali* by Rabindranath Tagore. Copyright (New York: Collier Books/Macmillan, 1971).

From Peter Koroche, *Once the Buddha Was a Monkey* (Chicago: University of Chicago Press, 1989). Reprinted by permission of the University of Chicago Press.

Excerpts from J. M. P. Powis Smith and Edgar J. Goodspeed, trans., *The Complete Bible: An American Translation* (Chicago: University of Chicago Press, 1989). Reprinted by permission of the University of Chicago Press.

Scripture quotations are from the New Revised Standard Version of the Bible, copyright 1989 by the Division of Christian Education of the National Council of the Churches of Christ in the USA.

Excerpts from Cyril Richardson, trans. and ed., *Early Christian Fathers.* Reprinted by permission of Westminister Press.

Excerpt reprinted with the permission of Macmillan Publishing Company and SCM Press from *Letters and Papers from Prison,* Revised, Enlarged Edition by Dietrich Bonhoeffer. Copyright © 1971 by SCM Press, Ltd.

Excerpts reprinted with the permission of Macmillan Publishing Company from *The Koran Interpreted* by A. J. Arberry, translator. Copyright © 1955 by George Allen & Unwin, Ltd.

Excerpt from *The Divani Shamsi Tabriz of Rumi,* trans. R. A. Nicholson. Reprinted by permission of Cambridge University Press.

Excerpts from Farid al-Din al'-Attar, *Muslim Saints and Mystics: Episodes from the Tadhkirat al-Awliya,* trans. Arthur J. Arberry (London: Routledge & Kegan Paul, 1966). Reprinted by permission of Routledge & Kegan Paul.

Excerpt from Reynold A. Nicholson, trans., Rumi: *Poet and Mystic* (London: Allen & Unwin, 1950), p. 35. Reprinted with permission of Allen & Unwin.

Preface

The study of the religions of the world is a subject of enormous scope and depth, covering the full range of history and reaching from the most mundane aspects of people's lives to their most sublime thoughts and aspirations. This volume, which is substantially revised from the previous edition, describes in clear terms the principal doctrines, issues, and motifs of each religion and shows how the traditions have responded to their social, cultural, and geographic contexts.

We have been very pleased with the reception students and faculty gave to the first two editions of *Religions of the World*. This third edition retains the authoritative scholarship of its predecessors. In addition, the text has been significantly revised in response to readers' criticisms and to changes in the field. While retaining strong coverage of history and doctrine, this edition contains additional material on significant teachings, rituals, and the lives of believers. Though attention is still given to primary theological doctrines, this is now balanced with more discussions of the effects of beliefs, myths, and rituals on believers' attitudes and daily lives.

As a result, the book has a broader perspective on religious belief and practice. We believe that even though the stories and concerns of the few—the emperors and other rulers—have played an important role in the development of the traditions, far more important for the history of religions have been the broad *cultural* changes affecting adherents' lives—events such as foreign conquests, large-scale emigration from rural to urban settings, or the spread of literacy. This new edition highlights such broad changes and shows how religions have responded to them. Without being reductionistic, we now give more attention to the underlying *social, economic,* and *political* context of the believers and to the ways in which their traditions have adapted. Also, with the introduction of more material on social history as it relates to religion, each chapter now offers more information on the role of women and the conception of gender roles within each tradition.

We believe that the study of religion is an inherently fascinating endeavor. However, to make the content of this new edition more accessible, the presentation has been streamlined. The writing has been given greater unity in style and approach; we hope it is accessible to a wider array of today's college students. We have included more useful maps and time lines. New maps now highlight both cross-cultural developments, such as trade routes and migration routes, and internal links, such as the relationship between sociopolitical factors and religion. More complete time lines show both specific developments and long eras and transformations. A new feature, the comparative box, compares and contrasts features of different religions. These boxes should encourage students to note similarities and differences among traditions in even broader ways. New pictures are more clearly related to the book's content. Pronunciation guides now open the parts. We have added a glossary at the back of the book; each glossary term is boldfaced at its first appearance in the text.

Other changes, we believe, make the experience of teaching and studying from this book even more appealing and more valuable.

A new **introductory chapter** focuses on the relationship between the needs a religion articulates and the means whereby religion addresses those needs.

Part One includes a completely new chapter on primal religions, Chapter 1, which presents an objective but sympathetic model for Australian, Native American, and African traditions. It also discusses earlier models, pointing out how they tended either to scorn or to idealize these religions. Chapter 2 discusses the religions of antiquity.

Part Two presents five chapters on Hinduism, from its origins to the modern period and its role in the developing nationalism. One theme of this part is that Hinduism addresses its believers' changing needs and anxieties. Chapter 8 now places Jainism and Sikhism more logically, adjacent to other Indian religions, and offers a more balanced picture of these traditions.

Part Three, on Buddhism, focuses on the rise and character of early Buddhist doctrine and then shows how Buddhism spread to become a world religion. Its chapters are organized around three concerns that inform the tradition—the varying understandings of the Buddha, the Dharma (teaching), and the Saṅgha (community)—and shows how they changed to reflect historical and cultural circumstances.

Part Four focuses on the religions of China and Japan, showing how the traditions of Confucianism, Daoism, and Chinese Buddhism all respond differently in different contexts to common underlying issues of harmony and balance. Chapter 15 shows how the fundamental nature of Shintō becomes the guiding theme of Japanese religion.

Part Five presents the panorama of Judaism from its beginnings in antiquity to the Holocaust and the rebirth of Israel in the twentieth century.

Part Six follows Christianity from the early church to the pluralism of the modern period. Its chapters reflect the changing views and understandings of Christ, the development of the key ritual (the Eucharist), and the complex relationship between the society and the development of the church.

Part Seven, reorganized to trace historical developments more clearly, offers a detailed presentation of the philosophy, traditions, history, and political context and implications of Islam.

Throughout the text, complex and unfamiliar traditions have been made easier for students to grasp. Though the book remains rich in history, we have tried to ensure that important themes are not lost in a sea of detail. Because much can be learned about religions from their manifestations in everyday life and from the works of art they have inspired, this edition, like its predecessors, offers an abundance of photographs and illustrations. Boxes set off descriptions of special rites and ceremonies, excerpts from primary source materials, and the comparisons mentioned earlier. Annotated bibliographies, updated to reflect the latest scholarship, appear at the end of the volume. These suggest both primary and secondary sources for students who wish to do additional research.

An expanded **Instructor's Manual** is available containing approximately 1,000 test questions, chapter outlines, lists of learning objectives, and suggestions for primary-source readings, films, and videos that can be used in the classroom. For more information, write St. Martin's Press, Inc., College Desk, 175 Fifth Avenue, New York, NY 10010; or contact your local St. Martin's sales representative.

Many people contributed to this third edition of *Religions of the World*. Robert K. C. Forman was the new general editor of the book. John Y. Fenton wrote the introductory chapter. Laura Grillo, also new to this volume, was responsible for the chapter on primal religions. The chapters on Hinduism were written by Norvin Hein. Niels C. Nielsen, Jr., was responsible for the material on Jainism, Sikhism, and Zoroastrianism. Frank E. Reynolds was the principal author of the chapters on Buddhism. Alan L. Miller provided the chapters on the religions of China and Japan in Part Four. Rabbi Samuel E. Karff was the principal author of the chapters on Judaism; Robert Goldenberg contributed significant new portions. Alice C. Cowan wrote the chapters on Christianity; revisions for the third edition were submitted by Elizabeth Leeper. Paul McLean contributed the chapters on Islam. Grace G. Burford provided material on women and religion.

We are deeply indebted to reviewers and users of the second edition, whose criticism, suggestions, and encouragements were indispensable. They include Paul J. Griffiths, University of Chicago; Martin S. Jaffee, University of Washington; Thomas M. Johnson,

Riverside Community College; Walter O. Kaelber, Wagner College; Robert D. Maldonado, California State University—Fresno; R. Blake Michael, Ohio Wesleyan University; Sonya A. Quitslund, George Washington University; Lynda Sexson, Montana State University; Herman Tull, Princeton University; James Waltz, Eastern Michigan University; and Kenneth Zysk, New York University. Scott Lowe of the University of North Dakota reviewed the transliterations of Chinese terms.

Finally, we wish to thank the people at St. Martin's Press. We are especially grateful to Don Reisman, Frances Jones, Bruce Emmer, Richard Steins, Emily Berleth, and Gene Crofts.

Contents

CHAPTER 2

RELIGIONS OF ANTIQUITY 47

PART TWO

Religions of India

CHAPTER 3

THE EARLIEST FORMS OF HINDUISM 83

CHAPTER 4

CLASSICAL HINDUISM: THE WAY OF ACTION 102

CHAPTER 5

CLASSICAL HINDUISM: THE WAY OF KNOWLEDGE 115

CHAPTER 6

CLASSICAL HINDUISM: THE WAY OF DEVOTION 128

CHAPTER 7

MODERN HINDUISM 143

CHAPTER 8

JAINISM AND SIKHISM 151

PART FOUR

RELIGIONS OF CHINA AND JAPAN

CHAPTER 12

ROOTS OF RELIGION IN CHINA 223

CHAPTER 13

THREE VISIONS OF HARMONY: CONFUCIAN, DAOIST, BUDDHIST 238

CHAPTER 14

NEO-CONFUCIANISM: FROM THE CLASSICAL ERA TO MODERN TIMES 246

CHAPTER 15

JAPAN'S RELIGIONS: FROM PREHISTORY TO MODERN TIMES 259

PART FIVE

JUDAISM

CHAPTER 16

GOD, TORAH, AND ISRAEL: THE BEGINNINGS 283

CHAPTER 17

FROM THE HELLENISTIC AGE TO THE DAWN OF MODERNITY: DIASPORA 308

CHAPTER 18

MODERN TIMES:
PERSECUTION, DIVISIONS,
NEW WORLDS 329

PART SIX

CHRISTIANITY

CHAPTER 19

THE FORMATION OF
THE CHURCH 345

CHAPTER 20

THE VISION OF CHRISTENDOM 369

CHAPTER 21

THE SPLINTERING OF THE VISION 389

CHAPTER 22

CHRISTIANITY IN THE MODERN WORLD 407

PART SEVEN

ISLAM

CHAPTER 23

THE BEGINNING: THE WORLD OF MUḤAMMAD 427

CHAPTER 24

ISLAM'S CLASSICAL PERIOD: RELIGIOUS LAW, THEOLOGY, AND MYSTICISM 447

CHAPTER 25

SHĪʿISM, REGIONAL DEVELOPMENTS, AND THE MODERN PERIOD 466

Maps and Time Lines

RELIGIONS OF THE WORLD

THIRD EDITION

Introduction

Religion and Religions of the World

Understanding Religion in the Context of Pluralism

With modern news coverage, international business contacts, and immigration to the United States from many parts of the world, the world's religious traditions have become part of our daily experience. As these cross-cultural contacts have multiplied, the need to understand religions other than our own has also increased.

How can we understand these other traditions? It is not helpful to project from one's own religion to others or to adopt vague simplicities about what religion is or is not. When, for example, someone from another religion insists that my scriptures are corrupted but his or her scriptures are the pure Word of God, it becomes very difficult to carry on any meaningful dialogue. Yet it is equally difficult to carry on dialogue with a person who insists that all religions are the same or that my tradition is just like every other.

What kinds of categories, then, should we use to understand other peoples' religions? During the past two centuries, Europeans and Americans developed categories for understanding other peoples' religions that have—probably unconsciously—served colonialist and racist interests. They suggested that other traditions are primitive, pagan, natural, or premonotheistic. Such categories tended either to provide justification for colonial expansion or to idealize the other as romantic or exotic. But both are misleading. Not only were they demeaning to non-Western cultures, but such categories have also led to profoundly inaccurate pictures of them.

Some scholars have suggested that we sidestep the problem of developing a general characterization of religion by focusing solely on the meaning each religion has for its adherents. This is the so-called insider's meaning of a religion, a description of that tradition by its adherents using indigenous language and categories. Focusing on the insider's view does have the advantage of stopping someone from one culture from projecting that culture's categories onto someone else's religious life. The interpretive concepts would at least be indigenous, not foreign.

However, when we use only this approach, other problems arise. First, there is no unequivocal meaning for *religion,* even within a single religious tradition. Second, if people from different religions use the word *religion* in incompatible ways, interreligious communication breaks down. Finally, if we used only insider approaches, how could we begin to make cross-cultural comparisons?

The insider's point of view should be complemented, then, with cross-cultural approaches. Indeed, the two should correct each other. Many investigators have used cross-cultural interpretive categories from a variety of scholarly disciplines. The insider's view narrows the investigation to fit a particular context, whereas cross-cultural categories broaden the base of the interpretation. Historians of religion, who study religions cross-culturally, use categories like "sacred," "deity," "ritual," "myth," "priest," and "symbol" as organizing principles to describe phenomena that are similar in many religions. Using such cross-cultural categories enables investigators to generalize about the significance of a local study and to use what they discover about one religious tradition to clarify another. Our understanding of religion must be formulated so that its cross-cultural description and its insider's meaning will be complementary. Even persons interested only in their own religious tradition can understand it better when they compare it to other religious traditions. Taken together, we believe, these two perspectives can best illuminate the phenomenon of religion.

We need a cross-cultural definition of *religion,* then, for at least three reasons: we need to use the word unequivocally so that we can apply it to the full array of religious traditions without imposing value judgments; it will allow us to carry out valid cross-cultural comparisons and thus identify underlying common structures; and it will help us to compare the traditions side by side, allowing us to see the uniqueness of each religious tradition more clearly.

Developing a Cross-Cultural Model of Religion: Religious Needs and Satisfactions

There is a relationship between the kinds of needs an endeavor addresses and the ways it satisfies those needs. Medicine, for example, is concerned with a type of need, disease, and addresses it with medical treatment. Psychology grapples with emotional needs and, in many cases, psychotherapeutic solutions. A need like hunger is satisfied with food. Religion, too, involves needs and satisfactions: religions are concerned with basic human needs and the satisfaction of those needs.

What are those needs and their solutions, and what is the relationship between them? There are no simple answers. Each religious tradition, responding to different human situations, articulates life's needs and its solutions differently. Furthermore, the relationship between needs and their satisfaction is different from tradition to tradition. We can say, however, that there is a polar relationship between the need and its satisfaction. They are binary opposites. Just as hot and cold, inside and outside, wet and dry, *define each other* (*dry* is defined as "not wet"), religious needs and their satisfaction also give each other meaning: religious safety is the answer to religious danger, religious pollution is answered by religious purification.

No sharp lines delineate religious needs and solutions from other kinds of problems and solutions. There are no uniquely religious emotions, for example, and religious rituals, forms of social organization, and concepts are not sharply different from nonreligious ones. But unlike the nonreligious, religious people seek satisfaction of their needs in ways that are in some sense extrahuman. Such people feel that our human life is not entirely self-sufficient and that we can reach our fullest development only when we find a proper relationship with some wider and deeper context than ordinary human life offers.

Only that wider context, such people feel, can give human life its fullest significance. People in some religious traditions, for example, regard newborn children as incomplete until their biological nature takes on a transhuman or "sacred" dimension. Through acts such as the giving of the sacred cotton threads *(upanāyana)* to male Hindu youths as a symbolic second birth *(dvija)* or the recitation of sacred words such as "There is no God but God, and Muḥammad is the Messenger of God" in Islam, religious people induct infants into that wider context. This indication also gives them an identity, an acknowledged place in society, and a sanctioned status in a religious community. Seeking satisfaction of human needs from these transhuman dimensions is peculiar to religion, and the relationship to these realities—often called "sacred realities" by scholars—is the unique element that sets religions apart from other relationships.

From the religious viewpoint, the development from child to adult is not merely a natural process of physical maturation but also a symbolic change that relates children positively to the sacred reality. This process transforms children into persons with a new significance and value whom their community recog-

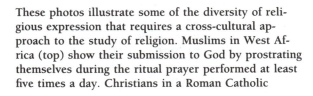

These photos illustrate some of the diversity of religious expression that requires a cross-cultural approach to the study of religion. Muslims in West Africa (top) show their submission to God by prostrating themselves during the ritual prayer performed at least five times a day. Christians in a Roman Catholic church (above left) watch as the priest recites the mass. Aboriginals of Northern Australia (above right) take up their positions for a traditional dance. (United Nations; The Bettmann Archive; Australian Information Service)

nizes and accepts as adults. The transition is a symbolic rebirth that changes the children's social status, patterned after a sacred model of male or female adulthood. Now properly related to this symbolic order, the person is considered to be bound up with the transhuman reality.

The ancient Romans used the Latin word *religio* to refer to the binding quality of the relationship between human beings and the gods. In Roman culture, this relationship usually implied that the humans should perform the gods' rituals dependably. (The popular expression "doing something religiously" derives from this usage.) When the deities accepted gifts, the worshipers in turn expected the deities to return favors such as protection, sanction of the social order, economic or health benefits, or favorable weather. Thus Roman religion, like all religions, bound together needs and their sacred satisfactions.

In sum, religion offers sacred satisfaction of fundamental human needs.

The Structure of Religion

We will describe the cross-cultural structure of religion in a threefold way, exploring each of the following components in turn:

1 Relationships between human beings and sacred realities
2 Processes of transformation
3 Cultural traditions that incorporate systems of symbols

RELATIONSHIPS BETWEEN HUMAN BEINGS AND SACRED REALITIES

Describing Sacred Realities

Describing each religious tradition's views of sacred reality is a major concern of each section of this book. These views spread across a spectrum from an understanding that the sacred is plural (polytheism) to a belief that there is only one sacred reality (monotheism or monism). Some traditions hold that sacred reality cannot be numbered at all (nondualism). Some Native Americans, traditional Africans, and Australian Aborigines, for example, also hold that sacred reality is sometimes best apprehended as personal beings and at other times as nonpersonal forces. Some Hindus understand the many sacred realities or deities to be facets of the one great God or impersonal, eternal Being; other Hindus are monotheists, believing in one God; and still others maintain that personal gods are just preliminary symbols for a nondual, all-encompassing, infinite Being.

Most Christians believe that the one God is triune—that the same God is Father, Son, and Holy Spirit. Jews and Muslims stress the unity of God, excluding any possibility of plurality. Chinese Daoists relate religiously to the Dao (Tao), or Way, which they regard as the source of things while not being separate from things.

We need to find a common denominator among this diversity. Clearly, we cannot assume that the way one tradition uses a concept like "god" or "ultimate reality" will automatically be equivalent to (or better than) the way another tradition uses it. We will use the term *sacred reality* to label this cross-culturally occurring common denominator, the religious source.

Some observers have identified the religious source as transcendence or the Transcendent. This term implies a real being or power that resides in another world beyond the limits of the natural world. But if we use it, we must recognize that religious people also want to be related to the immanent realities in this world and to find significance for human life here and now. Furthermore, though not wrong, the idea that something is beyond nature is a parochial notion that relies on Western ideas of nature and deity. People of other traditions may understand nature and what lies beyond it very differently.

We will also sometimes use the term *ultimate* for this common denominator. Some scholars have applied this to a metaphysical reality or transcendent being beyond the world. But we will intend by this term the point beyond which nothing can go, the last in a series. Or, seen from that end, *ultimate* can mean the first, fundamental, or primordial, the entity that is the basis for all things and for itself as well.

How does the sacred ultimate satisfy religious needs? In medieval Christian scholastic thought, the monotheistic (single) God was said to be *esse, verum,* and *bonum* (being, truth, and goodness). In Hindu Vedāntic thought, sacred ultimacy was *sat, cit,* and

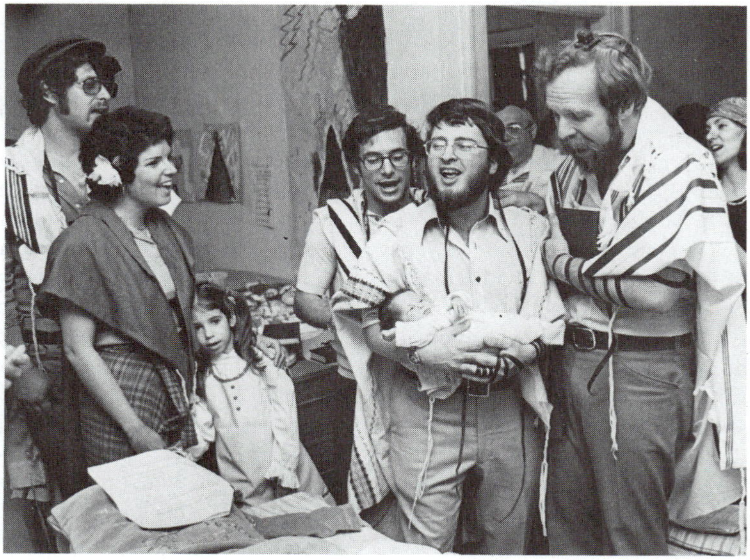

A religious tradition's views of sacred reality are expressed in and reinforced by its personal and calendar rituals. Here a Jewish congregation celebrates the naming of a baby girl. (Bill Aron/ Photo Researchers)

Ānanda (being, consciousness, and bliss). In both traditions, the sacred was seen as the single foundation of all other truth, reality, and goodness.

In polytheistic traditions, sacred ultimacy may be seen as many gods and goddesses, each of which has only a local and limited form. It may be difficult for people reared in Western traditions to grasp the possibility of many ultimates, each of which is limited. Indeed, a limited ultimate may even sound contradictory. But although the idea that the sacred ultimate is universal is common to many traditions, it is only one variation. The sacred ultimate may be seen as universal in some religions but not in others.

Similarly, the sacred realities to which people turn are not always the most important thing in the world for them. For example, an individual might petition a deity for success in a risky business venture, which would in effect be a request for assistance. When he finishes the venture, the business and the petition might be of no further concern. In another example, some Hindus worship deities in hope of relief in times of affliction yet may ignore them when no one is ill.

Religious people often react to sacred realms with awe, fear, homage, and submission. Sacred realities are not under human control, and religious needs may or may not be satisfied. Sacred power can bring punishment and destruction. People typically treat sacred power with meticulous care, and they sometimes surround sacred objects with detailed rules of required or forbidden behavior (taboo).*

Yet these generalities are not universal. Divine beings sometimes have no close relationship with a religion's primary concerns. For example, the gods and goddesses of Theravāda Buddhism have little to do with a person's ultimate fate; in fact, Buddhists believe that these deities are themselves in need of salvation. Nonetheless, they may legitimize a believer's possession of a piece of land, control the weather, or help to heal a disease. Conversely, Theravādan Buddhists teach that the goal of religious striving is not godlike but impersonal. Further, the gods cannot aid humans; only one's own efforts on the prescribed Buddhist path can lead to ultimate liberation.

When individuals give voice to their religious needs, they generally do so in the context of their preexisting religious tradition, which defines for them both the character of the sacred reality and the kinds of prior relationships humans have had with that reality.

**Taboo* or *tabu*, a Melanesian word, refers to the ritual prohibitions that many religious traditions prescribe for occasions when humans come into close contact with sacred powers. Respecting the taboo is believed both to safeguard sacred objects from pollution and to protect people from the sometimes dangerous sacred power.

Myths or sacred stories typically recount how humans and the sacred realities became involved with each other. They often depict an ideal relationship, account for the breakdown of that relationship, and provide ways to restore it. Such myths also provide individuals with models to emulate so that they may form interlocking relationships with sacred realities and with the rest of the world.

Creation stories have a common cross-cultural function: to exhibit the basic structure of the cosmos by giving an account of how the world came to be as it is. In many Hindu creation stories, for example, humans are separated neither from their world nor from the One Reality. They share the being of the One as fragments or parts. The world they inhabit relates to its source as part to whole, outside to inside. In this way, the myths depict the relationship of the individual to the source that may satisfy their needs.

Although our term *sacred reality* conveys a more general notion than a term like *god* in a particular religious tradition, specific religions are not mere accidental variations of a common religious core. Rather, the idea of a sacred reality is something like the fundamental human capacity to speak language that we had as infants, before we learned any particular language. That is, the capacity to speak a language and the basic structure of language appear to be innate and panhuman. This common linguistic structure accounts for the similarities among human languages and our ability to learn the languages of other cultures. Yet the existence of a deep structure does not make one language necessarily similar to any other. Some, like Spanish and Italian, are quite similar; others, like Chinese and German, are quite different. Analogously, Judaism and Islam are relatively similar, whereas Shintō and Christianity are sharply different.

We must emphasize that sacred reality cannot be defined, either by scholars of religion or by religious people themselves; it is mysterious, beyond definition. But religious people do characterize both the sacred realm and the human relationship to that realm. They do so through oral and written utterances, actions, institutional structures, and symbols. The task of religious scholars is to describe and interpret sacred-human relationships in the context of the various religious traditions. As religious scholars and students, we do not have to unravel the mystery of sacred realms. Our task is to describe and interpret how religious people describe their relationship to that mystery.

Sacredness belongs to realms that remain "other," even as they penetrate the human realm. Sacred realities conceal what they reveal, but they reveal enough to tantalize. Religious language referring to the sacred realities conveys more than can be said, and people often use negative language to prevent comparing sacred reality to anything else.

This tension between the mysterious sacred and its overt characterization often makes it extremely difficult to interpret a religious tradition. The opening lines of the Daoist classic Dao De Jing (Tao-te Ching; "The Way and Its Power") articulate this tension: "The Tao [Dao, or Way] that can be told of is not the eternal Tao. . . . Nameless, it is the origin of Heaven and earth; Nameable, it is the mother of all things. . . . That they are the same is the mystery."[1] Sacred reality in itself (the Dao itself) cannot be described directly; what can be described is merely how sacred reality appears to us. That the unnameable is also nameable or that the transcendent reality becomes the origin of all things is the mystery intrinsic to sacred reality.

Most Buddhists deny all eternal realities and consider belief in them to be a prime cause of human suffering. Yet there is, for the Buddhist, something about ordinary experience that can truly satisfy religious needs. To find it, we must become transformed so that we no longer live asleep, unaware, or defensive. Sacred reality is before us in an ordinary way, but we, in our ignorance, cannot see it.

Thus religious language points beyond itself. Religious language reveals a sacred reality that remains a mystery even as it reveals itself. Thus the sacred realm is the source of our definition, but it cannot itself be defined. This is the central impasse, a source of creative tension, for interpreters of any religious tradition, be they insiders or outsiders.

In ordinary English we sometimes refer to books, buildings, or images as "sacred." Such usage is appropriate, but it employs the term *sacred* in a secondary sense as something associated with sacred realities. No one worships a book, a building, or an image. Religious people regard a sacred text, for example, as sacred not because they expect the book to satisfy religious needs but because it puts a sacred reality within reach. Sikhs regard their sacred text, the Guru Granth Sāhib, for example, as the "gateway" to God because its study and recitation lead to God (see Chapter 8). Similarly, Eastern Orthodox Christians and Roman Catholics may use a wooden icon for worship, but it is not the block of wood that matters to them but the God it reveals.

The Relationship between Religious Need and Religious Satisfaction

Each tradition articulates in its own way the relationship between the basic religious need and its satisfaction. For example, Christians regard the fundamental human problem as sin. Correspondingly, they deem the solution as salvation overcoming sin. This pair of opposites is uniquely Christian: sin presupposes a broken relationship with God; its solution comes through salvation in Jesus Christ. This expresses a specifically Christian assessment of what the world is all about. Neither sin nor its solution means the same thing in other religions such as Judaism. Nor does the Christian's "salvation from sin" translate naturally into the Buddhist's "enlightenment that overcomes ignorance." Buddhists see the fundamental problem as ignorance, not sin; its solution is rooting out that ignorance, not faith in a deity. Both the rendering of the need and its solution, as well as the relationship between the two, are very different in the two systems.

Similarly, religions often talk of pollution and purification. Again, these opposites define each other. Yet what constitutes pollution varies from one culture to another. In Hinduism and Shintō, the prime sources of pollution are bodily secretions and human and animal corpses. They are the result of inevitable physiological processes such as urination, sexual intercourse, and death. This sort of pollution is washed away by such efforts as cleansing, ritual purification, and fasting. Again, the needs and their solutions are related like mirror images.

Individuals pick up their understanding of their fundamental need from their religious culture. For example, one will *acquire* the idea that one is fundamentally sinful and hence needs salvation from sin from the Christian tradition. That is why, for example, Christian evangelists spend much of their initial efforts on what they call the "conviction of sin," getting individuals to adopt this notion as a true account of what their need really is. Similarly, Buddhist missionaries must convince people that the problem is ignorance. When one sees the problem in these terms, one may come to see the need as, respectively, salvation from sin or enlightenment from ignorance.

Just as the articulation of the fundamental need differs among religious traditions, so does its answer, religious satisfaction. In one part of the Hindu tradition, liberation involves merging one's individuality into the featureless ocean of the nondual reality called Brahman—the True Self of the self. In the Buddhist tradition, by contrast, there is no self and hence no ultimate reality like Brahman. Because, they believe, craving for eternal realities can cause suffering, Buddhists teach that liberation will occur only when such craving ceases. While the goals of these two traditions are similar, they are also profoundly different—and that difference relates to their accounts of the human problem.

All traditions affirm that they received satisfaction in the past and expect that it can again be gained. Even so, religious people cannot be certain that following their procedures will necessarily provide the solution they seek. Sacred realities are not within human control. Requests may be denied, forgiveness withheld.

How the gap between human need and sacred power can be bridged is the central problem of any religious tradition. But every religion tries to satisfy human needs as it understands them.

PROCESSES OF TRANSFORMATION

Religions satisfy fundamental human needs through a process of transformation. This process can generally be divided into four stages:

1 Diagnosis of disorder
2 Symbolic distancing
3 Liminality
4 Restoration or rebirth

Diagnosis of disorder People must first see themselves as having a religious need. They may remind themselves through ritual; for example, an Episcopal Christian service begins, "O Lord, we confess to you and to one another . . . that we have sinned." People may express this need regularly, following a yearly or monthly liturgical calendar, or irregularly, in crisis situations only. Some attempt to worship constantly, others infrequently. The diagnosis of disorder may make reference to the sacred realities; it may also mention the perceived loss of sacred sanction.

Symbolic distancing The next step is to distance oneself from one's normal status. Dramatically breaking off one's normal relationships expresses the fact that one has a religious need—"I must leave the old way." It announces that one cannot satisfy one's religious needs by oneself.

People distance themselves from normal life in many ways: withdrawing from usual forms of social intercourse, fasting, giving away their possessions. Even the entire community can be symbolically separated from its normal condition: borders may be closed, people may be told to maintain vigils, holidays may be decreed, and usual behavioral patterns may be reversed. At such times, the primary sacred symbols of the society may be concealed; for example, some Christian denominations cover the cross with dark cloths during the last two weeks of Lent as a sign of mourning for Christ's suffering. Symbolic distancing eases the transition into the next phase.

Liminality In the liminal phase (the term comes from the Latin *limen,* meaning "threshold" or "boundary"), symbolic distancing intensifies to the greatest degree possible. One is separated not only from normal cultural categories but also from all possible cultural categories. Symbolically, the whole world disappears; one has gone as far as one can go. One has arrived, so to speak, at (or beyond) the brink of the abyss. The liminal state is without structure.

The nature of liminality varies from one tradition to another. Frequently it is marked by death symbols or regression to a helpless condition. This helplessness seems fraught with danger. Demons may appear and destroy one's most secret forms of self-reliance.

In one of many Christian examples, the liminal phase corresponds to the mourning period between Jesus's death on Good Friday and his resurrection two days later on Easter. Several mystical traditions describe this in-between state as a vacant darkness, a timeless experience of pure consciousness without content. Liminality is thus a state of both "no longer" and "not yet."

Restoration or rebirth At the end of this transformative process, one emerges symbolically new, reborn. One has gained sacred satisfaction, however it is understood. One now has sanction, power, and new significance. Ritually we often see actions symbolizing rebirth, release from bondage, or transfiguration. People who were secluded in the forest or a cave during the liminal phase come forth to a new life or status in society. They may receive new names or new clothes. They may see themselves differently. Others may act differently toward them, ratifying their new status, for example, as peers. Feasting often puts the seal on the transformation.

Certain people may participate in transformation ritually, and the entire community may play a role. Some people—mystics, for example—may have intense encounters with the sacred introspectively, with no ritual markers; the transformation is initially experienced as a private affair.

Puberty Rites among the Bambara of Mali

We may easily discern the four-phase structure of symbolic transformation in certain puberty rites. Among the Bambara people of Mali in western Africa, the traditional rituals for symbolically transforming boys into men begin when a group of boys has reached puberty. The initiation has six phases extending over several years; the last and most climactic ritual is the *Kore.*

Boys undergoing the Kore shed their normal clothes and put on identical white gowns, minimizing their individual identity. Men then lead them out of the village into the forest, thus distancing them.

The boys enter a sacred grove of thorn bushes through a narrow eastern gate in a squatting position with their arms extended forward. They will be "entombed" in this symbolic center of the world for 14 days. The elders whip and flail the boys as they crawl to a central clearing open to the sky, which represents the point of contact between heaven and earth. There they are symbolically "killed" with an iron knife, later "revived" with a wooden knife, and then covered with a blanket of animal hides representing the sky. During this liminal period, elders teach the initiated boys the Bambara symbol system. Finally, they crawl through a dark hole in the earth to emerge into the sunlight at the far end of a tunnel.

On the fifteenth day the boys return to the village as social and religious adults. The structure of Bambara puberty rituals is similar to those described for the initiation of Australian Aborigine boys in Chapter 1.

The Hindu Sacred Thread Ceremony

The Hindu *upanāyana* (investiture with the sacred thread) ritually transforms primarily brāhman (upper-class) boys into young men (Chapter 4). Brāhman boys may be initiated between 8 and 16 years of age, but nowadays the ceremony is sometimes performed just before marriage.

Just before the sacred thread ritual begins, the boy takes his last meal from his mother as a child. Shaving the boy's head and giving him a bath traditionally mark symbolic distancing from childhood. Special clothes (girdle, deerskin, staff, and the sacred thread) then demarcate the liminal state. The teacher's taking the boy's "heart" into his own as symbolic father and mother ushers in a rebirth to student status. The transition from one life stage to the other is a symbolic gestation process in which the teacher becomes "pregnant" with the boy and by virtue of sacred sounds *(mantra)* gives him a second birth *(dvija)*.

The Eightfold Path as Transformation

The four stages in processes of symbolic transformation are clear in most rites of passage. The Buddhist transformative path from suffering to peace—the so-called Noble Eightfold Path—also manifests these four stages.

The Eightfold Path is a process of undoing and discarding false understanding, unrealistic behavior, and unaware and unwholesome attitudes. The movement away from ordinary understanding, behavior, and ignorance eventually results in a complete divorce from the old way of living. Yet it does not translate immediately into a new birth of enlightenment. The in-between period of the Buddhist seeker may last for a very long time, even many lifetimes. Yet if one successfully traverses the path, total nonreliance on all the old defense mechanisms brings about a fundamentally new way of life.

Calendar Rituals

Rituals observed on regular fixed days of the yearly calendar celebrate birthdays of religious founders, set off special days of recognition or remembrance for gods or goddesses or holy men and women, inaugurate the new year, mark seasonal changes, or celebrate central events in the religious history of a community such as the Exodus of the ancient Hebrews from bondage in Egypt or the revelation of the Qur'ān to Muḥammad. People also engage in personal and

Muslim worshipers gather at the Dome of the Rock, a mosque in Jerusalem built around the rock from which Muḥammad is said to have ascended to heaven. Mosques are set aside permanently for worship; they cannot be used for other purposes. (Louis Goldman/Photo Researchers)

communal worship, prayer, and meditation at regular intervals, ranging from several times each day to once weekly. The calendar fixes the time for these rituals (diagnosis). Preparation for the rituals regularly involves suspension of normal business and withdrawal into the special time of commemoration of past events as present experience, the offering of material and spiritual gifts (symbolic distancing), the end of the old period (liminal point), and the new birth of the new (restoration).

Jains celebrate the birth of Mahāvira, the sixth-century B.C.E. founder of their tradition, with a ritual bathing of his image in late summer or early fall. This in part reenacts major events in Mahāvira's development into a Jina, or conqueror of life's problems. Part of the emperor's role in the traditional Chinese Confucian ritual was his conduct of the sacrifice on the Altar of Heaven at the change of seasons. Westerners might be familiar with such calendar rituals as Christianity's Advent in early December and Easter in the spring and the Jewish observance of Rosh Hashanah in the early fall and Passover in the spring.

Sacred Places

Dedication rites transform ordinary places into holy sites. The dedication of a temple puts that territory in a liminal position between ordinary human culture and sacred realms for a considerable period. To enter a sacred place means to leave the world behind and to enter a border area from which concourse with the sacred reality becomes easier. A sacred place is on the edge, in the "twilight zone" between ordinary experience and the sacred realities. Frequent worship in such a place renews its power of access.

Many Hindus believe that the formless God condescends to take on form for the benefit of devotees. God, who is everywhere, appears in particular places and particular forms, being physically present in images and in the houses of God, the temples. In traditional temple architecture, over the site of the divine image, a tower—symbolizing the infinity of Brahman, or ultimate reality—thrusts toward the sky. Beneath the tower is a small rectangular room that is both the seat of the divine image and the womb or egg from which the world was created. This room symbolizes the presence of Brahman in each living being. Thus the worshiper who contains God within comes to worship God in a temple, despite the fact that God is everywhere. The temple thus separates in space what is eternally together so that the worshiper can there bring it together again.

Similarly, although Muslims believe that God is everywhere and closer to us than we are to ourselves, Muslims congregate in special places (mosques or *masjids*) for prayer. Mosques are set aside permanently for worship; they cannot be used for other purposes. Yet permanent places of worship are not themselves sacred. Instead they are separate from the ordinary world so that worshipers can contact sacred realities more easily.

Religious Specialists

Just as a religious site may come permanently to occupy a place between the human and sacred realms, so may some mediating religious roles also become permanent. Initiation rites transform religious mediators to a liminal status, expressed in a distinctive life style. The Buddhist professional monk *(bhikku)* or nun *(bhikkuni)* has a formalized role withdrawn from normal life, even if not yet totally released from human suffering. Buddhist monks and nuns do not marry, nor do they belong to ordinary social groups or possess property. They remain apart from society. They do have restricted, role-determined relationships with lay Buddhists who support them, and their careers serve as inspiration for lay people. The saffron, red, or black robes and shaved heads of monks clearly proclaim that they have a special role on the boundary between those who are enmeshed in social cares and the ideal goal of *nirvāṇa* (liberation). But theirs is not an ordinary social role like tailor or parent.

Priests may temporarily observe similar restrictions in preparation for their roles as mediators between the human and the sacred. To purify themselves in preparation for offering worship to the deities, Japanese Shintō priests take special cleansing precautions and observe temporary restrictions. Many Christian denominations also employ priests as intermediaries; Protestants share with Muslims and Jews the belief that access to God is direct and requires no mediation.

Prophets and shamans (religious healers) often do not undergo formal installation rituals, but accounts of their being called to a spiritual role contain initiation stories that often exhibit the four-phase structure of symbolic transformation. However, since the gift of

Monks, like these Buddhist monks from Beijing, live in a liminal state by separating themselves from their former social roles and personal identity. (Eastfoto)

prophets and shamans is personal rather than institutional, they may eventually lose their power of mediation.

Some religious people, the men and women mystics of many traditions, hope to merge with the ultimate reality continuously. To do so, they remove their psychic attachments to the things and honors of the world to such an extent that they care only about the ultimate reality. They may move into a liminal state by separating themselves from the world temporarily in meditation or into a more permanent liminal state by separating themselves from their earlier identity. They then dwell in an unstructured, will-less state while waiting for a final merging with the ultimate. Some reenter the world as a new, utterly selfless agent, working for the betterment of others.

Followers interpret the founders of some Asian religions—the Buddha (Buddhism), Mahāvira (Jainism), or Nanak (Sikhism)—as intermediaries between the human and the sacred. Whereas according to Theravāda Buddhism, the Buddha based his authority on what he discovered in his mystical experience, the Mahāyāna branch of Buddhism usually views the Buddha much as many Hindus see Kṛishṇa, as an immediate godlike manifestation of sacred reality. The faith that Jesus Christ was and remains the unique mediator for all humanity is the basis of Christianity.

Life after Death

Probably all religious traditions carry out funeral ceremonies, both to transform the deceased into their new status beyond life and to revitalize their survivors. In many cultures, such as those of traditional Africa, people's interest in after-death existence does not extend beyond the interaction of ancestors with the living survivors. Sometimes ancestors provide aid, but more often they bring misfortune if their living descendants do not ritually attend to them properly.

The belief in some form of life after death is widespread. Some people believe that the individual's spirit is reborn. In some traditions (such as certain ones in Africa), the spirits of the dead become part of the life force of their descendants; in other traditions (for example, Hinduism and Buddhism), the dead may be reborn into any form of life, human or nonhuman.

In some religious traditions, such as Christianity, Islam, and the Hindu Śrivaishṇava tradition, people believe in a permanent heaven that offers eternal life. Passage to this realm often depends on the quality of the life the persons lived on earth. Temporary purgatories or eternal hells sometimes complement eternal heavens. Many Buddhists and Hindus seek not heaven but permanent liberation from the cyclical round of birth, death, and rebirth.

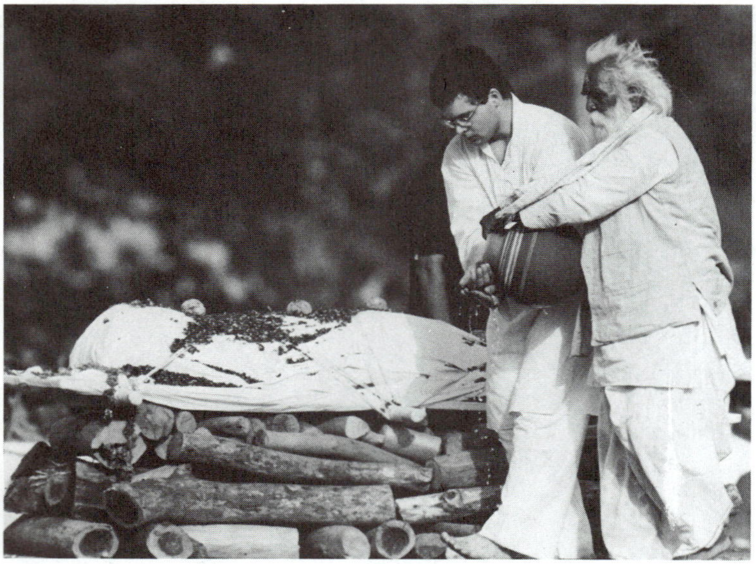

Religious traditions' attitudes toward death and their funeral ceremonies take many forms. An example is the Hindu custom of sprinkling water over the body before cremation. (Reuters/Bettmann)

Life beyond death is not always merely an individual matter. The Western religions—Judaism, Zoroastrianism, Christianity, and Islam—teach that all creation will be fulfilled in a final, permanent transformation at the end of time. The transhistorical purpose of history will be materialized with the inauguration of a new heaven and a new earth. Then either the human world will ascend to the sacred realm, or the sacred world will descend to earth.

The expectation of judgment after death is a powerful sanction for the behavior of the living. Indeed, for some people the central focus of religion is its other-worldly promise. But religious traditions are at least as much this-worldly as they are other-worldly. Although sometimes concern about life after death leads to largely other-worldly attitudes, these attitudes often give shape and significance to life in this world and lead to active involvement in it.

CULTURAL TRADITIONS THAT INCORPORATE SYSTEMS OF SYMBOLS

The certainty that adherents can satisfy their needs by interacting with sacred realities is the foundation for religious traditions. Adherents expect that sacred reality will renew them, justify their existence and their social identity, and provide values and attitudes that orient both themselves and their cultures.

Religions are social by nature. Their forms, ideas, and sanctions have an enormous impact on their societies. They provide a wider symbolic context that people can understand and to which they feel they belong. The relationship between humans and the sacred typically includes a notion of transformation that includes society and reconstitutes it as a religious community.

Most people learn the patterns of their community's religion from the previous generation, much as they learn a language. There are also special communication devices that transmit tradition. Sacred narratives and myths convey a religion's concepts and understandings. So do systematized statements of beliefs such as creeds, stated or unstated behavioral norms, and systematic explanations (theologies). Most traditions are communicated orally, as when a leader explains something or relates a religious myth. But many also have written collections of their central stories and teachings, such as the Buddhist Tripiṭaka and Islam's Qur'ān.

Symbolic transformation is conveyed most directly in communal acts of worship. But in addition, the way members of a community live their lives and interact express and reinforce the religion's structures. Such practices and ways of acting teach norms and values as much as formal instruction, if not more.

A religion, like a language, offers a single overarching structure and vocabulary that makes community-wide communication possible. Yet few societies are completely homogeneous, and each of the many social subgroups—such as educated city dwellers or the peasantry—often have a sense of religious legitimacy that is different from that of the other subgroups or the "official" tradition. Rural people often have religious needs and interests different from those of urban people. A subgroup's religious patterns may reflect that group's special interests. For example, the priestly class may have an interest in enhancing the status of the rituals for which it is responsible.

Religious institutions can be almost any form of cultural association. Family and kinship groups are the most common: children tend to follow the religion of their parents. People in the same neighborhoods incline toward shared religious interests, as do members of a given occupational group or social class. The modern ecumenical movement in American Protestant Christianity is a good example: although it has had some success in merging denominations among churches in approximately the same social classes, it has had much greater difficulty uniting denominations from different social classes. Similarly, in contemporary India, liberalization of relations among different castes has been most successful among castes with roughly the same social standing.

Churches and synagogues, though clearly religious communities, often derive their social forms from nonreligious institutions. The democratic structure of many American churches, for example, is clearly related to the United States' democratic political system. Similarly, the Buddha organized his monasteries according to the principles that his ethnic group, the Śākyas, used to run their government. Architecturally, early Christian basilicas and early Buddhist monasteries were patterned after the secular buildings of their respective lands.

Changes in Religions

Changes in a religion originate partly from the tradition's internal dynamics. Though traditions often view ultimate realities as ancient, eternal, and

A religious tradition is communicated in many ways such as through religious practices, behavioral patterns, artwork, and written and spoken teachings. Here a young Hare Kṛishṇa devotee hears recitations from the Bhagavadgītā. (Religious News Service)

unchanging, their characterizations of sacredness are in history and thus are subject to change. The gap between inherited religious forms and the sacred realities they represent makes possible—even demands—the development of new understandings. Religions thus have a capacity for self-criticism and for new formulations of the transformation processes.

But changes are caused not only by internal dynamics but by other elements as well. One is a religion's interactions with other religious traditions. As we will see in Chapter 14, Chinese Confucianism emerged radically different after centuries of interaction with Buddhism.

Another common cause of change is the interaction of a tradition with nonreligious cultural forces. Major shifts in a society's technology, its food production, its fund of information, or its economic or political structure can set the stage for major alterations in a religious tradition. Conditions in northern Europe percolated for several centuries, for example, before the Protestant Reformation commenced in the sixteenth century. The women's movement for greater independence began under the pressure of a surplus of women in the population of the twelfth and thirteenth centuries. The Black Death killed as much as one-fourth of Europe's population. By way of Spanish Muslims and Jews, Europeans rediscovered Greek mathematics, science, and Aristotelian philosophy. The Crusades, beginning in the twelfth century, drained national treasuries and whetted European appetites for eastern European and Asian goods, both of which stimulated the rise of banking houses and joint-venture businesses. Cities, loci of trade, burgeoned. The invention of the movable-type printing press made all kinds of information, including the text of the Bible, more widely available. These social changes did not cause the Protestant Reformation, but they helped to make it possible and gave it much of its shape.

Both Judaism and Christianity have had to develop new forms to cope with the revolutionary changes accompanying the industrial revolution and modernization. In both traditions, a variety of liberalizing movements developed to recast the religious tradition to fit the new conditions. Conservative countermovements then developed to avoid the dangers of modernization. In twentieth-century Japan, an exodus from the farms to the cities, very rapid industrialization, and defeat in World War II provided the conditions for the so-called New Religions, which combine elements of traditional Buddhism, Shintō, and Confucianism into new forms. These religions have compensated in many ways for the loss of the traditional social structures on which Japanese life and religion once depended.

Among other things, this text will explore the main factors—internal, external, and sociocultural—that have led to the major changes in the world's religions and some of the effects of those changes on society.

Religious Traditions and Their Systems of Symbols

The systems of symbols developed by religious traditions vary dramatically. Meaning is a matter of internal interaction; that is, within each system, ideas or beliefs have meaning only in relation to one another. The parts of the system usually cannot be readily transferred to another system, and indeed, many religious systems are mutually incompatible. For example, both a Jewish bar mitzvah and a Roman Catholic confirmation can be understood as rites of passage, but the two rituals are not interchangeable, nor do they carry the same meaning for their respective communities.

The systemic nature of religious traditions can be conveniently illustrated by the Indian Jain tradition. The routine daily worship patterns of both householders and monastics in the Jain religious traditions include the composition of a design composed of uncooked rice particles in front of the worshiper as he or she meditates. This design represents the cosmos. The bottom figure in the design is a right-handed swastika (from Sanskrit *swa,* "self," and *asti,* "existing") surmounted by three dots in a horizontal row. Above the dots is a crescent opened upward (see Chapter 8). The rotating wheel of the swastika represents the world of birth, change, death, and rebirth into the same or even another life form. At the top of the design the upturned crescent represents release from all suffering and from the round of death and rebirth. Even though the realm above the crescent in the Jain cosmos corresponds structurally to Christianity's heaven, it is by no means the same. Furthermore, no personal god plays any role in securing the release of human beings from the round of rebirth; the whole responsibility falls on the individual. The sacred reality in the Jain

A woman performs the Jain religious ritual of creating a rice design as she meditates. The design represents the cosmos. (Arthur Tress/Photo Researchers)

tradition is systemically unique, as is its means of release or transformation.

Religion and Society

We have said that religions are cultural traditions and that they formulate religious needs and offer sacred satisfactions at the cultural as well as individual level. That means that religions shape and are shaped by their cultural context.

The ways in which religious traditions have influenced their social structures can be readily illustrated. One striking instance is the influence of Islamic faith on the fragmented Arabic culture of the seventh-century C.E. Pre-Islamic culture often engaged in intertribal warfare, had no central government, and was polytheistic. Islam became the unifying force for the new Arab society, enforced peace among Muslims, and reformed the older religious tradition. The newly unified Muslim society then burst out over the borders of Arabia, spreading within a century to Spain in the west and Afghanistan in the east.

The contrary can also be true: social context can shape religious traditions. Take, for example, international missions. Both Buddhist and Roman Catholic missionaries followed a strategy of gradually converting people over the centuries without insisting that all of their indigenous religious and cultural features be immediately replaced by the new faith. The result in the long run was that in both cases the traditions in the various countries combined both indigenous and extraneous elements and ended up with distinctive local flavors.

By contrast, many Protestant Christian missions attempted to transplant Western society's forms of Christianity directly into new cultures while suppressing existing religious and cultural practices. Thus Protestant churches in mission fields such as Africa often have a much more European or American flavor than Roman Catholic churches in the same regions do.

But every religious tradition has to change to fit local conditions. Every religion indigenizes to some degree. Muslims frequently state, for example, that there is only one Islam. Ideally and officially, this is true. But in practice, specific Muslim societies have developed a distinct flavor that resulted from adapting the religion to local conditions and different ethnic groups (see Chapter 25).

Religious traditions clearly have political implications. Many religions have sanctioned existing political structures: Confucianism supported the imperial structures of China for 2,000 years, Protestantism sanctioned nationalism during the Reformation, and religious rhetoric is interjected into political campaigns and warfare even today. Christian missions were initially successful in sixteenth-century Japan because Franciscan and Jesuit missionaries aligned themselves with certain political forces. In another Japanese example, samurai warriors of the fifteenth to nineteenth centuries practiced meditation in the Rinzai Zen Buddhist style because, they felt, it made them better soldiers. Buddhism in many Asian countries endorsed the ruler as the supporter of truth and of Buddhist institutions.

A religion will also relate to other aspects of its context. It may be influenced by economic forces. In Parts Two and Three we will see how Hinduism and Chinese religions were influenced by geographic and climactic factors. We will also see that gender issues are a major latent preoccupation of religion in nearly every culture.

Religious behavior may also be shaped by psychological factors. Some kinds of religious experience and behavior, such as possession by spirits, may appear to a Western psychologist as pathological or evidence of social maladjustment.

The contrast between the official view of a religion from inside (often called the *manifest meaning* by social scientists) and an outsider's view of the religion in concrete contexts that results from the application of social-scientific tools of interpretation (often called the *latent* or *hidden meaning*) sets up a potential conflict in interpretations of religions. Historians of religion tend to interpret religious traditions primarily in terms of the internal dynamics of the religion, whereas social scientists and psychologists tend to develop functional interpretations. The two approaches may result in very different accounts of a religious tradition.

The outsider's preoccupation with the latent functions of religions should be balanced with the insider's manifest meaning. Religions do not serve either latent or manifest functions exclusively. Indeed, both approaches can and should be combined, as we have tried to do in this book, for manifest and latent meanings clarify each other.

How to Read This Book

QUESTIONS TO ASK

The model of religion developed in this chapter will help you to understand the world's religions. As you read about each religious tradition, it will be helpful to keep this model in mind. We suggest that you employ the three parts of this model to ask questions during your reading.

For example, as you read about each tradition, look for the fundamental or characteristic relationship between human beings and the sacred reality around which the religion revolves. What is the sacred reality like to believers? How do their creation stories portray their view of the world? What is the status of human beings? What do they seem to need from sacred realities? How does life obtain its fundamental sanction, value, and significance for practitioners of this religion?

To answer these questions, pay attention to belief systems, cosmologies, myths, and the conceptualization of sacred realities. Ask yourself, what are these people's fears? What is thought to be wrong with human beings that needs to be set right? What provides believers with hope and assurance?

Watch for the enduring elements of themes, issues, and structures. For example, Part Three focuses on three of the key elements of Buddhism—the Buddha, the Dharma (law and doctrine), and the Saṅgha (the monastic community)—and how they have changed over time. Part Six, on Christianity, returns repeatedly to views of Christ and the central ceremony of the Eucharist.

Second, search as you read for the processes of religious transformation. Look for them in rituals, performances, individual and group meditation, development and growth patterns, changes from one life stage to another, and significant changes in the calendar year. How do believers come in contact with sacred power? How do they prepare themselves for this? Do they cleanse themselves? Do they make confessions? Do they seek absolution and forgiveness? Do they give offerings? Do individuals need help from religious specialists? What kind of devotion and prayer or meditation do people practice? Repeated symbolic transformations are typical of the rhythms of religious life.

Then hunt out the cultural patterns of the religious tradition, and map out how the tradition relates to its society. Note its primary social groups and institutions. Who are the religious leaders, and who are the followers? Which group wrote the texts? Are there assigned roles for men and for women? How does the religion shape behavioral patterns? With what economic and social groups are particular religious movements and ideas connected, and why? What meanings are hidden in the symbols people use? (For example, what suppressed meanings might there be in the Christian practice of eating symbolic human flesh and drinking symbolic human blood in the Lord's Supper or Eucharist?)

Finally, what is unique about this religious tradition? What is comparable to other traditions? Throughout this text you will find boxes that highlight certain similarities and differences. Compare other features yourself. Even if some elements of the religious tradition seem similar to elements of others, how do these parts fit together in the religious system to which they belong?

USING MAPS AND TIME LINES

The maps included in the text will help to orient you geographically and, in some cases, historically. Many include information regarding the terrain of a region, often a factor in the development or movement of a religious tradition. Before modern methods of transportation, the ancient trade routes along rivers and through mountain passes were the primary means by which migration and trade took place and by which cultures and religions interacted. On the front endpaper is a map showing the major trade routes c. 1500 C.E., many of which had been active since ancient times.

The time lines provided in the text will help to orient you chronologically. The time lines present both temporally longer and more sweeping periods as well as pinpointing important events and individuals, thus helping you to see key developments in context. A combined time line for all of the religious traditions appears on the endpaper at the back of the book. This can help you to compare developments in different religions during a particular period.

A complete listing of text maps and time lines appears at the end of the contents.

Because the primary time scheme in the West and much of the rest of the world, dated B.C. ("before Christ") and A.D. (*anno Domini,* "in the year of our Lord"), presupposes a specifically Christian theology, we have chosen to employ a more neutral era designation that is in increasing use. B.C.E. ("before the Common Era") replaces B.C., and C.E. ("Common Era") replaces A.D. The numbers for the years are the same in both systems.

We have boldfaced important terms. They are defined in the glossary at the back of the book.

NOTE

1 "Selections from the Lao Tzu (or Tao-te Ching)," in *Sources of Chinese Tradition,* comp. William Theodore de Bary, Wing-tsit Chan, and Burton Watson, vol. 1 (New York: Columbia University Press, 1960), p. 51.

PART ONE

Primal Religions and Religions of Antiquity

PRIMAL RELIGIONS

CHAPTER 1

THE DIVERSITY AND VITALITY OF PRIMAL RELIGIONS

In this chapter we will undertake a tremendous comparative task: to learn and appreciate something of the religious conceptions and expressions of the many peoples of three vast and diverse continents, Australia, North America, and Africa. Our aim is first to gain exposure to at least two different religious realities on each of these continents so that we recognize there is no one "native" religious tradition. Second, since so many religious traditions from different continents are grouped together under one category called "primal," our investigation of them is necessarily comparative. We want to develop a sense of what is comparable and what is distinctive in the ways in which different peoples experience and express religiosity.

Some comparisons we make will be explicit, but others will remain implicit. For example, we will inevitably be comparing the world view of an "other" to our own, even if only by trying to make our vocabulary apply. After all, this is an English-language textbook, and we are heirs to the Western intellectual heritage. The very words we use reflect prevalent perspectives and deeply ingrained patterns of thinking, and we can easily lose sight of their relativity.

One example of this is the notion of religion. As noted in the introduction, one common conception of religion is that it is something external, a set of observable behaviors or an organizational structure. Another considers religion a disembodied system of belief that is separable from other aspects of culture, such as politics or economics. Both make religion into a "thing," separate from its lived context. Such conceptions are relatively modern and primarily Western. It would be misleading to apply such an understanding to the traditions of Australia, Native America, and Africa, for there religion is not a thing apart from culture as a whole. We will study religion not as an entity but as the experience of the sacred in these particular societies and cultures, a part of people's ways of doing and being.

The term *primal* demonstrates how the language we use can influence the portrait of non-Western religious traditions. What does the term actually mean, and can it be applied to the disparate religious traditions of Africa, Australia, and the Americas?

The earliest information about the civilizations that practice "primal religion" came from explorers and missionaries. Their accounts typically projected certain fantasies and fears of an exotic and savage "other." Later nineteenth-century scholarship referred to these societies as "primitive" and claimed that they represented earlier stages of Western culture. This misrepresentation arose from the **evolutionist theory** developed in biology, which, applied to human civilizations, hypothesized that contemporary cultures could be placed on a continuum from simple to complex, primitive to modern. Just as physical scientists were able to understand complex phenomena by extrapolating from simple ones, social scientists tried to draw inferences about the origins of their civilization from observations made about societies that were technologically "less advanced" or less wealthy. However, it is a fundamental mistake to equate material wealth with social, intellectual, or spiritual advancement.

Furthermore, even though primitive societies were characterized as small in scale, having subsistence economies, and isolated from cross-cultural contact, some clearly defied these three criteria. Among them are the militarily and economically powerful African kingdoms of Mali and Ashanti and the ancient Mayan and Aztec empires in Mesoamerica. Nor were they culturally isolated, for through their vast trade routes they contacted foreign ideas and practices. These civilizations were extensive, wealthy, and cosmopolitan.

Most social scientists today recognize that the evolutionist model was both racist and Eurocentric—that is, it took Western culture to be the ultimate of all cultures. This model fell into disfavor, soon to be replaced by a new conception of the "primal." Investigators of primal religions turned their attention to the origins of the religious impulse. They asked, was there evidence of an original primitive monotheism? If so, did it later degenerate into the pantheism and polytheism that they characterized as typical of "primitive" religions? Or is monotheism the apex of a progressive religious sensibility, the product of a theological sophistication that both early societies and contemporary "primitive" traditions supposedly lack? Such questions still assumed that these societies were unevolved vestiges of the European past and that they could therefore shed light on an uncorrupted human condition.

Certainly classifying religions as "primal" seems less pejorative than calling them "primitive," yet in fact the term reflects an equally distorting stereotype of these societies, albeit a positive one. For example, such scholars hold that in primal societies, "man is akin to nature" and that "men live in a sacramental universe where there is no sharp dichotomy between the physical and the spiritual."[1] Primal religions are often portrayed as offering a "spiritual perfection or plenitude," a quality lost in our "corrupt" modern, alienated culture. This romantic view portrays the "noble savage" as being closely identified with nature and looks on him with nostalgia and envy.

Neither the evolutionist nor the romantic approach is truly historical. In each, the hypothetical reconstruction of a primitive and pure religion did not provide an adequate method for approaching non-Western religious systems in their own right.

Other theorists suggest that what distinguishes the "primal" from the "universal" religions is that primal religion is essentially ethnocentric, devoid of the impulse to convert people outside the immediate social context. The primal traditions, like the small-scale societies from which they supposedly emerged, are considered to be too particular to represent the aspirations and attainments of humanity in general. In truth, every religion is meant to be of ultimate significance for *all* humankind. Thus the significance of primal religious traditions is not limited to the tribes from which they sprang. Their insights are intended to have meaning for any human being; they convey something about what it is to be both human and religious.

Our study will be comparative but will not contrast these "primal" religious traditions with those of "universal" religions. Instead, we will emphasize common categories of religious expression. By abandoning the criteria that distinguish between "primal" and "universal," we hope to allow non-Western traditions to be understood on "their own terms," affirming their value for all humanity.

An Approach to Primal Religions

Religion is a total way of life, a vision of reality that provides orientation in the world. The religious traditions that we will investigate here present a view of a dynamic cosmos in which human beings are called to participate fully. They point to an overarching organization of the cosmos that at once binds things together and also allows for constant flux and change within that order. According to this view of the universe, everyday activities—from eating habits to rite-of-passage rituals—reflect a connection to the deepest order within reality. Life is perceived as grounded in the ultimate.

This sense of an overarching order that allows for

change and dynamism is given voice through three critical aspects of religious expression: sacred words (myths), sacred acts (rituals), and sacred places (symbols and sites).[2] Each works in conjunction with the others, and together they weave the fabric of a religious tradition. We will follow this paradigm, exploring sacred speech, sacred acts, and sacred place in some of the religious traditions of Australia, North America, and Africa.

SACRED SPEECH: MYTHS

Myths are one common form of sacred speech. Whether written, spoken, sung, or enacted in dramatic performances, myths are sacred because they provide a vision of what constitutes reality. Myths are more than "just so" stories. They are neither naive explanations nor precursors of scientific thinking. Rather, myths reveal a culture's underlying conceptual framework, its world view. They attempt to express the inexhaustible creativity of the cosmos, to show it to be a web of interdependent activity, and to situate humanity meaningfully in the overall dynamic order.

Myths deal with supernatural events (as fairy tales do), and their protagonists are extraordinary figures (as in legends and epics), but myths differ from these other genres in their perceived sacredness. Fairy tales typically situate their dramatic action "once upon a time," and legends identify the historic time and place in which their drama occurred; in contrast, myths often take place *in illo tempore,* at the beginning of time, and speak of the origins of time itself. These **cosmogonic myths** describe the unique situation of the cosmos as the beginning of time. They trace how the undifferentiated totality that existed before creation became fragmented in time and space to take on the forms of the world as it exists today. However, they do more than just explain the sources of the natural order. They attempt to communicate the preeminently sacred nature of reality. Cosmogonic myths portray the cosmos as saturated with power: "To relate a sacred history is equivalent to revealing a mystery."[3] The sacredness of reality, its power and mystery, is accessible only through symbols that point from the immediate, fragmented world back to the original totality.

Cosmogonic myths have overwhelming significance. They represent all that is real and meaningful. They outline the role played by divinity, ancestors, and cultural heroes in determining the shape and nature of the cosmos. They often tell of **primordial beings**, ambiguous creatures existing only at the beginning of time who are not yet subject to the restrictions of time and space but who help to bring these dimensions into being, thus creating the framework for human existence. The protagonists of myths also set precedents for human action. They provide the charters for social organization, institutions, and practices by showing how its models are grounded in the very nature and structure of the cosmos.

SACRED ACTS: THE RITUAL CONTEXT

Myth and ritual are complementary and in some cultures inextricably interdependent. A cosmogonic myth can provide the model for ritual action. For example, a *mythic* drama of the sacrifice of a primordial being may be reenacted in *ritual* sacrifice. This is not to say that ritual negates time, allowing for a return to the primordial situation. Rather, ritual makes a meaningful connection to that past, thus investing time with continuity and meaning. Moreover, ritual invites participation in the ongoing creative schema of a dynamic physical universe based on transformation and change.

Cosmogonic myths often hold that the human body was created as the microcosm of the physical world. Therefore, the most profound religious notions are expressed in the imagery of the body. Human biological processes reflect the same regulatory rhythms that govern the cosmos. The by-products of the body—blood, milk, semen, feces—are often felt to be charged with sacred power and figure in myth and ritual as basic elements for controlling creation, sustenance, transformation, and renewal. Ritual acts underscore that merely living is itself a religious act. In eating food, for example, humans partake of the sacred vitality of the cosmos. Indeed, the entire progression of birth, growth, decay, and death shows that humans share in the fundamental aspect of the nature of the universe, transformation.

SACRED PLACE: SITUATION IN TIME AND SPACE

The meaning and sacredness of time and space are leitmotifs of cosmogonic myths, which often reveal that the physical world was formed from the resurrected body of the first sacrificial victim, a primordial being. The landscape's changing contours or the regular cycle of the seasons are taken as signs of the dynamism of this resurrected body, which like a human body is in a constant state of transformation. The physical environment is presented as a web of sacred reality linking primordial time to present existence and supernatural beings to human ones. Often this vision of the structure of the cosmos is mirrored in the ordering of cultural space—the architecture of houses and the layout of villages and cities are "maps" of the ordered cosmos. Thus human habitats are sacred places, for they situate people in sacred space.

In sum, primal religions must be understood as offering composite visions of the world and the place of humans in it. Such religions can best be approached through their sacred speech, sacred narrative such as myth, songs, prayers, and invocations; sacred acts, all ritual practices; and sacred places, such as the land, houses, and ritual structures. Although all three aspects of religious expression always work in conjunction with one another, one may dominate in a given context. In Australia, we will see that sacred speech, the myth of the Dreaming, provides the common framework; among North American religions, sacred place will be the predominant concept; and in African traditions, we will see sacred acts as the fundamental dimension of religiosity.

AUSTRALIAN ABORIGINAL RELIGIONS

EARLY INVESTIGATIONS

The word *aborigine* literally means "from the beginning." It refers to characteristics of the earliest inhabitants of a region. The notion that the peoples and religions of Australia reflect primitive beginnings is embedded in the very label "Aboriginal."

Here already we confront the evolutionist theory. Whereas other island cultures of the Pacific—Indonesia, Melanesia, and Polynesia—were influenced by India and Islam, Australian Aboriginal society was thought to be an isolated example of early civilization, existing "from the beginning." As "small, remote communities," the Aborigine societies are still said to represent the "best example of primal communities."[4] Similarly, early investigators considered Aboriginal religion an archaic form, exhibiting a magical mode of thinking. For us, however, Australian religion is best understood as a vision of the nature of reality whose themes point to the overall organization of the cosmos and the significance of human participation in it.

RELIGION BY REGION

There are more than 500 distinct Australian Aboriginal peoples and over 200 Aboriginal languages. There are also many relatively independent religions, grouped regionally according to strong "family resemblances" in beliefs, myths, and rites.[5] Regional differences in terrain and climate have contributed to this diversity. The religions can be organized into four principal groups, divided geographically.

North and northwest The religions of the north and northwest are fertility cults whose ritual complexes are concerned with ensuring the reproduction of life.[6] The Kunapipi myth and its associated ritual cycle originated in the north and spread across the continent. This great religious cycle describes the original travels of the primordial ancestors, who provided the essence of life and created the first people.

Central desert area The religions of central Australia are called "segmentary systems" because the foundational body of religious knowledge is fragmented among the various desert peoples: each of several related groups transmits a particular set of myths and ritual practices, and no group's system is complete in and of itself. The entire religious system is seen only when the various groups cooperate in ritual.

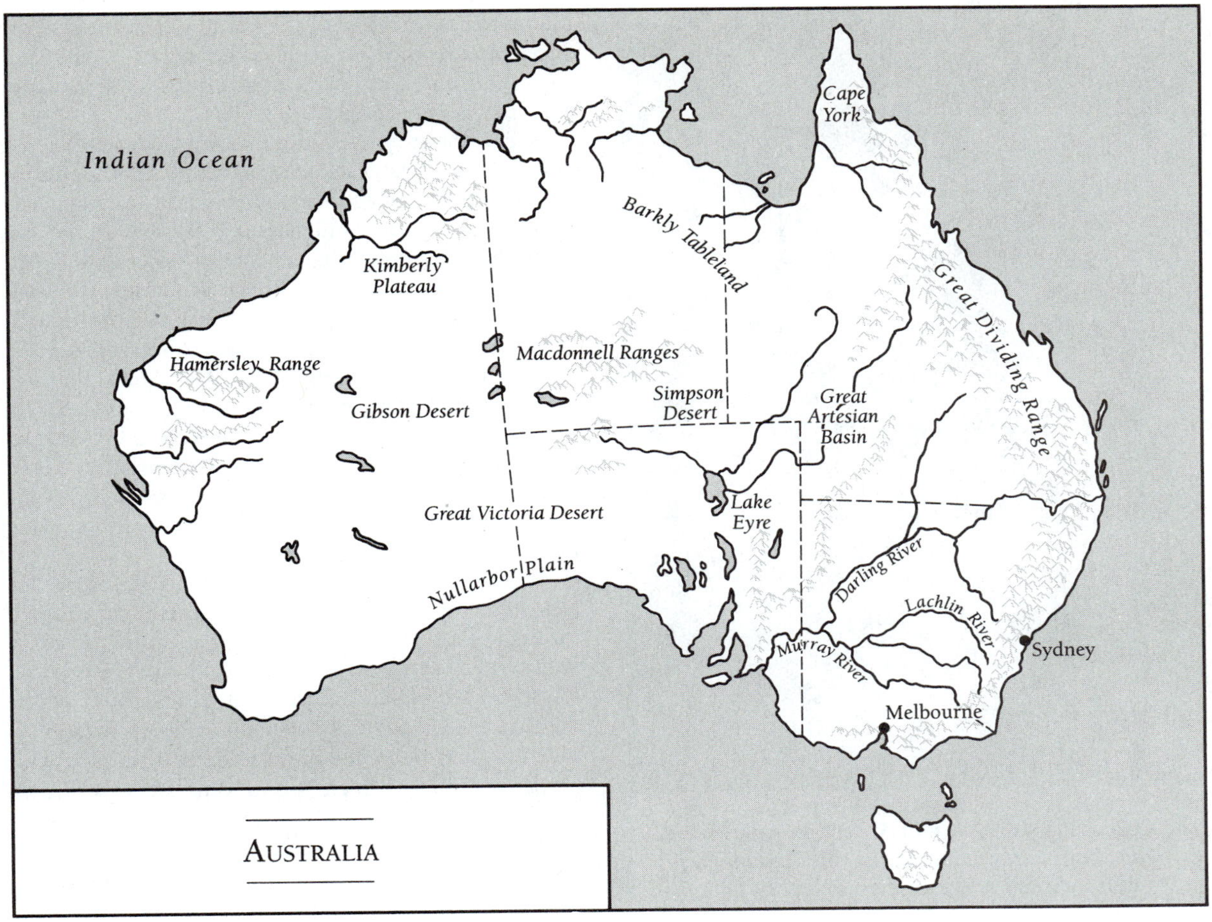

Southwest and southeast In southern Australia, the indigenous religious practice did not remain intact after European conquest, and most information comes from reports of early observers.[7] Here, beliefs in a supernatural sky-world predominated, and the deity, as a "high god," remained aloof from human affairs. Much of southeastern ritual seems to have been preoccupied with magic and the hereafter and with ritually identifying the newly deceased with the primordial mythic beings.

Far northeast Here the spirits of the dead and ancestors are identified with mythic beings. They are invoked through prayer and sacrifice for the protection and renewal of the various totemic species.

SACRED SPEECH: MYTHIC THEMES AND WORLDVIEW

Despite the diversity of the forms of aboriginal religions, a common overarching worldview underlies them all. The order of the cosmos, and the means for human participation in it, is revealed in their many myths. This vision is called the Eternal Dreaming, the Dream Time, or simply the **Dreaming**.

The Dreaming refers to many things simultaneously. First, it is the source and original impulse of creation. According to the myths of the Aranda people of the central desert region, in the beginning the earth was a desolate plane, without distinguishing features.

The underlying worldview of Aboriginal religions is the Dreaming. Representations of the Dreaming appears in Aboriginal art. (Northern Territory Tourist Commission)

The sun, moon, and stars slumbered under the earth. There was no animal or plant life, only shapeless embryonic beings, lying listlessly beneath the earth in an eternal sleep, suspended between life and death. Finally, these supernatural beings awoke. The Aranda word for them is *altjiranga,* which means "having originated out of one's own eternity, immortal, uncreated."[8]

The Dreaming refers most explicitly to the time of the foundation of the world, recounted through myths. During this original creative period, the primordial ancestors wandered the earth as supernatural beings. Their movements and tracks shaped the contours of the physical world. For example, the Warramunga people regard a range of hills as "the path traversed by the mythical Ancestor of the bat totem."[9] Because the ancestors are thought to have bestowed on the land something of their sacred character, particular sites are still considered sacred.

According to myth, the spiritual power of the Dreaming permeates all material reality. It accounts for the profound connections and mystical unity between things and persons and between the living and the dead. For example, the primordial ancestors could change shape, and during their wanderings through the cosmos they took on the forms of the natural world. This is how the material world became suffused with their spiritual energy.[10] For Aborigines, the land is a spiritual resource. Thus human beings can gain access to the sacred at places that were invested with the power and significance of the Dreaming. The land is a living thing; its spiritual power, given it by the ancestors in the time of the Dreaming, may be activated by ritual.

Social reality is also related to the Dreaming. The fundamental bonds of all life forms are affirmed through **totems.** Totems are living creatures or other natural phenomena in the real world that are believed to "share the same life force as the deity with which they are associated."[11] Aboriginal social organization is totemic—based on the identification of groups with particular totems. Each group venerates its totem's sacred power and identifies with its nature. Since each totem embodies some feature of the Dreaming, it also embodies and bears some of the Dreaming's sacred power.

The Dreaming also refers to the moral and social precepts determined in the primordial time. The path the ancestors followed did more than create geography and invest it with meaning; their actions established the way of Aboriginal law and life for all time. By doing the first rituals, they established the patterns for ritual action; similarly, they laid down the patterns of morality. Thus when youths are initiated into the spiritual knowledge of the Dreaming, they are being called simultaneously into fuller participation in the social world. Their spiritual, social, and moral development is an integrated progression.[12]

As we can see, the Dreaming has nothing to do with dreaming as an illusory state of consciousness; rather, it is the most fundamental Aboriginal actuality, the underlying framework of time and space in which Aborigines orient themselves.

SACRED ACTS: RITUAL PRACTICE

The Dreaming is not confined to the primordial past or restricted to the supernatural realm. Its spiritual power also underlies and sustains the present reality. By ritually repeating the paradigmatic acts of primordial beings, the Dreaming and its patterns can be made visible and accessible and thus be tapped to renew or reactivate life.

These rituals are reenacted in ceremonies across Australia. In them, human reality is presented as a microcosm of the primordial cosmos. For example, the life cycle begins with conception and birth and the transfer of sacred power to the living infant. Just as the potential spiritual power of the land had to be activated through ritual, so too every child must receive its spiritual animation from a deity. According to traditional belief, a particular mythic being imparts the essence of life to a fetus so that in a sense every person is a living representative of a primordial being from the Dreaming. The changes one undergoes throughout life are given religious significance in rituals that make explicit the association with the Dreaming.

Rituals also attempt to bring social life and moral order into line with the mythically recounted patterns of the cosmos established in the Dream Time. Mythic beings are not ethical models to be imitated, however. For example, the Walmadjeri of the northwestern desert region tell of the primordial ancestors behaving amorally: the first men trick the women to steal their sacred emblems and their associated powers. They commit acts of treachery including incest, mutilation, and murder. However, their actions always meet with disaster; they are either killed for their transgressions by others or injured by natural disaster. The moral is that the behavior of human beings, like that of their mythic forebears, must be controlled. Everyday behavior that promotes cooperation and reciprocity is modeled by myths and reinforced by ritual action.

Ritual **initiation** is a natural occasion for formal instruction on moral behavior. Initiation into the totemic mysteries and the sacred life of the tribe is an important aspect of Aboriginal ritual practice, and circumcision is the first step. Circumcision rituals enact a ritual killing and the resurrection of the victim to a new and transformed existence, like the mythic ancestors who were swallowed and resurrected in the Dream Time. Each newly circumcised boy undergoes a ritual death and is mourned by the women as if he had died. During a subsequent period of seclusion, the youth "witnesses a number of revelatory rituals associated with his clan's Dreaming."[13] Dances, mime, and songs relate the mythic events of the Wawilak sisters,

Dance is used to relate mythic events during the Australian Aboriginal peoples' religious rituals. (Australian Information Service)

who were swallowed by the Rainbow Snake, only to be regurgitated and revivified to give birth to the first humans.

Blood is also an important mythic and ritual symbol, and blood rites are a prominent feature of rituals throughout Australia. In the Kunapipi initiation ritual, the men sprinkle blood from their opened arm veins over one another and into the trench in which the initiates sit, to represent the creative, primordial blood of the Wawilak sisters.[14] At other times, men drink the blood drawn from the arms of their elders. Blood links these men in an intimate bond with their human ancestors and their community. Blood is sacred, associated with life and the strength of heroes, with the purificatory power of menstruation, generative power, and birth. Perhaps most important, blood connects humans to their mythic ancestors, from whose blood the land and the first humans emerged, and to the world of the Dream Time that sustains all reality.

In sum, the Dreaming is the source of all life; changes in the cosmos result from the activities of the primordial beings. The people's connection to the Dreaming is seen in the human body and in rituals. The order of the cosmos is not static but dynamic and constantly self-renewing, yet it remains grounded in the Dreaming.

North American Religious Traditions

In recent decades, scholars have become increasingly aware that the images of Native Americans sketched by European newcomers are more often projections of their own expectations than accurate portraits. The early documented accounts of Native American traditions came from explorers, conquerors, and immigrant settlers who often did not recognize religion in them at all. After his encounter with "Indians" in 1492, Columbus reported that "they would easily be made Christians, for they appear to me to have no religion."[15] Willful ignorance of the premises of Native American religious traditions has continued to characterize relations between native and immigrant communities. (In fact, it was not until 1978 that the U.S. government passed the American Indian Religious Freedom Act guaranteeing the rights of native peoples to practice their traditions without persecution.)

Just as damaging as ignorance is a perpetuation of the *positive* stereotype of Native American religious traditions, the romantic idea that native ways kept a close attachment to nature and had a wholesome simplicity that modern "civilization" has forfeited. This too is a projection, reflecting a nostalgic longing for a "natural" religion—more a criticism of Western options than an accurate assessment of Native American traditions. Among other things, this romantic view ignores the fact that Native American civilizations are many and varied, each with its own unique identity and history. It is important that the cultural diversity and differences of religious expression among Native Americans be recognized and that they not be reduced to a simplified sameness.

RELIGION BY REGION

It is impossible to speak of a single Native American tradition. Different geographic contours, climatic conditions, and cultural influences (such as the Aztec empire's influence on southwestern tribes) account in part for the striking diversity. The forced migrations and relocations of peoples by immigrant settlers and the U.S. government further complicate the picture. Nevertheless, we can identify a common theme: participation in the flux of a dynamic cosmos. We will focus on how this is visualized in terms of physical place in space. While exploring this broad theme, we must not forget that the geographic subregions and the distinct traditions within them are not the same. Let us look more closely at the peoples of two such subregions, the Great Plains and the Southwestern Pueblo.

Great Plains The native nations of the tallgrass area of the Great Plains in the central United States include the Sioux, Crow, Arapaho, Kiowa, and Cheyenne, each different from the others in language and culture. The Plains peoples were dramatically affected by the influx of immigrant populations that displaced them. Nations such as the Apache that had traditionally occupied territories to the west were forced southward. After horses were introduced by the Spanish in the seventeenth century and the open plains became more accessible, life patterns changed mark-

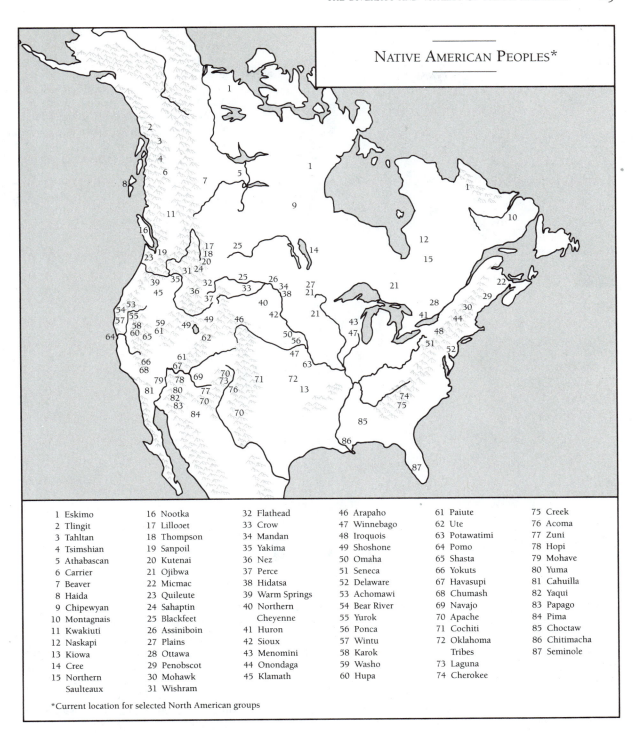

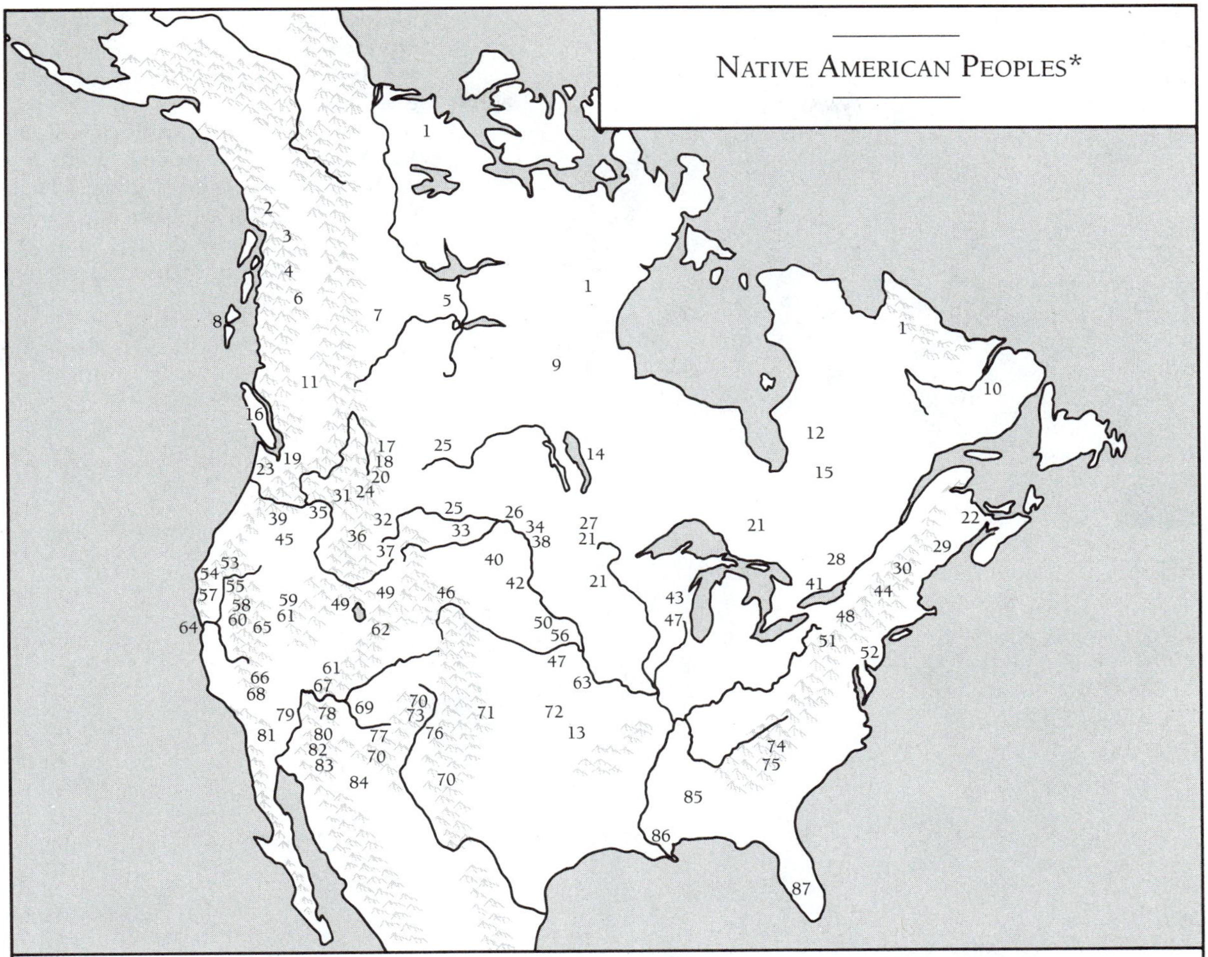

1 Eskimo
2 Tlingit
3 Tahltan
4 Tsimshian
5 Athabascan
6 Carrier
7 Beaver
8 Haida
9 Chipewyan
10 Montagnais
11 Kwakiuti
12 Naskapi
13 Kiowa
14 Cree
15 Northern Saulteaux
16 Nootka
17 Lillooet
18 Thompson
19 Sanpoil
20 Kutenai
21 Ojibwa
22 Micmac
23 Quileute
24 Sahaptin
25 Blackfeet
26 Assiniboin
27 Plains
28 Ottawa
29 Penobscot
30 Mohawk
31 Wishram
32 Flathead
33 Crow
34 Mandan
35 Yakima
36 Nez
37 Perce
38 Hidatsa
39 Warm Springs
40 Northern Cheyenne
41 Huron
42 Sioux
43 Menomini
44 Onondaga
45 Klamath
46 Arapaho
47 Winnebago
48 Iroquois
49 Shoshone
50 Omaha
51 Seneca
52 Delaware
53 Achomawi
54 Bear River
55 Yurok
56 Ponca
57 Wintu
58 Karok
59 Washo
60 Hupa
61 Paiute
62 Ute
63 Potawatimi
64 Pomo
65 Shasta
66 Yokuts
67 Havasupi
68 Chumash
69 Navajo
70 Apache
71 Cochiti
72 Oklahoma Tribes
73 Laguna
74 Cherokee
75 Creek
76 Acoma
77 Zuni
78 Hopi
79 Mohave
80 Yuma
81 Cahuilla
82 Yaqui
83 Papago
84 Pima
85 Choctaw
86 Chitimacha
87 Seminole

*Current location for selected North American groups

The southwestern peoples' dwellings represent their cosmic view. The Navajo hogan was modeled after the first dwelling of the ancestors and is a "map" of the religious worldview. The Pueblo village of flat-roofed, terraced adobe houses, is believed to be at the symbolic center of the cosmos. (Photographs courtesy of National Museum of the American Indian Smithsonian Institution)

edly. The Crow and Cheyenne, for example, quit agriculture altogether and turned to a nomadic way of life as hunting groups following the buffalo in their seasonal migrations. Even sharper changes occurred when white settlers, having conquered the native peoples, restricted them to reservations, where diseases and starvation came close to wiping out entire populations. Such cultural devastation of course affected native religions.

Plains culture is a synthesis of customs, beliefs, and rituals, the result of many groups being forced together on reservations and then relocating, so that "nearly all the basic religious ideas found in other parts of native North America are found on the Plains."[16] To a certain extent, therefore, Plains religion is of relatively recent vintage, evolving in the late nineteenth and early twentieth centuries in reaction to immigrant domination and the misery of the reservations. It reflects a combination of ritual practices. Some, such as the Sweat, a cleansing sauna used for ritual purification, are of precontact origin. Others surfaced in response to postcontact experience. Among these newer practices is the ghost dance, a pervasive Plains practice that originated in the 1860s as a ritual in which participants tried to hasten the removal of whites and the restoration of Indian welfare. Another is the sun dance, which unites its adherents through sacrifice and hardship, a ritual that has now become an important Plains-wide ceremony of community renewal. All these practices and movements have sought unity and spiritual power under conditions of oppression. Although the particular rituals among the peoples still vary, the general religious pattern of the Plains has become a model for today's "pan-Indian" religious movements.

Southwestern Pueblo The many distinct groups of the vast southwestern region have been categorized according to four major language families. The Pueblos might be said to be most representational of the region, as the 31 independent Pueblo communities of New Mexico and Arizona speak languages from all four of these language families.[17] The Pueblos are comprised of the Zuni (east) and Hopi (west), the Navajo and the Western Apaches, although the latter two migrated to the Southwest via the Plains only at the turn of the sixteenth century. In part because they faced less oppression, the Pueblos' complex traditional religious systems have remained largely intact since pre-Columbian times.

SACRED PLACE AND WORLDVIEW

The worldviews of native traditions share a common emphasis on sacred place. A spirit world permeates life and is mirrored by the physical world, especially the land.

The landscape of the Plains region is expansive, experienced as an ever receding horizon. The sacred places of the Plains peoples reflect this dynamic quality. The cardinal directions, for example, are conceived of not as fixed points in the cosmos but as relative ones that, like the horizon, aid orientation but cannot be made permanent. To the Plains peoples, the cosmos is invested with sacred power, called *wakan* by the Sioux and the Lakota. It flows from the creator god, the "most sacred" or Great Spirit *(Wakan Tanka),* through the natural world.

By contrast, the semiarid landscape in the southwestern region has stimulated a different cosmic view. For example, the Tewa people, who live in a river valley surrounded by mountains, see the cosmos as bounded by four great mountains, each representing a cardinal point. Their village, thought to stand at the cosmic center, is surrounded by four permanent rock shrines, representing the cosmic mountains and the cardinal points, where spiritual power converges and the dead can be contacted.

Thus the arrangement of ritual sites and villages corresponds to "maps" of heaven and the underworld. Yet the world order is not static. The natural and the spiritual realms interlock in mutual contact and influence. Sacred places are the sites where the living contact the dead and where the spiritual world comes into contact with the real world.

The peoples' everyday objects and places are infused with signs and symbols of the sacred realm; thus they reflect ultimate values. For example, the Navajo house, the *hogan,* is modeled after the first dwelling of the ancestors, but it is also a "map" of the religious worldview, a microcosm. The following Navajo hogan song to the east is one of four sung to the cardinal directions before and during the building of a house:

Far in the east far below there a house was made;
Delightful house.
God of Dawn there his house was made;
Delightful house.
The Dawn there his house was made;
Delightful house.
White corn there his house was made;
Delightful house. . . .
Water in plenty surrounding for it a house was made;
Delightful house.
Corn pollen for it a house was made;
Delightful house.
The ancients make their presence delightful;
Delightful house.[18]

Notice how the song interweaves the presence of the deities and the ancestors, the natural elements, and food in this house blessing, showing them all to be fundamental sustainers of life. The house is a place where all of these come together.

The Pueblos see the cosmos as a multilayered

structure of superimposed worlds. The first human beings passed through these layers at successive stages until they finally emerged onto the earth's surface through an opening called the "navel of the world." This mythic navel is represented by a hole at the center of every Pueblo village; it represents the connection between the upper and lower strata on the cosmic map and links past and present, the land of the living with the realm of the dead. The Pueblo ancestors emerged from the underworld through the navel of Mother Earth to create this world, dynamic and interwoven. But the superimposed worlds remain intimately connected. Thus, for example, Pueblo people can contact the dead through prayer sticks left at shrines.

The Pueblo world is bounded by the four cardinal directions, north, south, east, and west. At the center lies the pueblo, a village of flat-roofed, terraced adobe houses. Since each cardinal point is a place where power converges, ritual dancers must face them, and songs must have four parts. The cosmic map is also a model for Pueblo social organization. For example, every clan is divided into subgroups, each associated with a cardinal direction. Each pueblo is also situated at what it takes to be the symbolic center of the cosmos. "Thus the Zuni are 'the people of the middle place,' [and] the Hopi . . . live at the universe center."[19]

Sacred and secular, cosmic and human, play their part in the concept of sacred place. For example, the Plains peoples thought of the Milky Way as campfires along the road that the dead travel to the world beyond. This body of stars is more than a place in the cosmos; it is a sacred place linking living and dead, mortal and immortal, secular and sacred. Connections between the cosmic and the human realms are also visible in animals and plants on which sustenance depends. Just as the ingestion of blood in a ritual context in Australia represents the interdependence of all life, this sacred dynamic is acknowledged among Native Americans by the reverence shown for the Buffalo Spirit or Mother Corn.

Most important, perhaps, are the spirits connected with natural places—mountains, waters, deserts, and ultimately Mother Earth herself, all sources of sacred power and life. A human being is a microcosm of this dynamic universe. Thus when the Navajo perform a healing ritual, they identify the patient with the physical universe and its powers. The patient is placed in the center of a sand painting symbolizing the cosmos. A ritual specialist pours the colored sand over the patient, bathing the sufferer with the restorative powers of the earth. To sit at the center of the sand painting is to sit at the symbolic center of the universe and be identified with all its converging elements. As the different-colored sands blend into one, the patient at the center can reintegrate with the power of a harmoniously dynamic and vital cosmos.

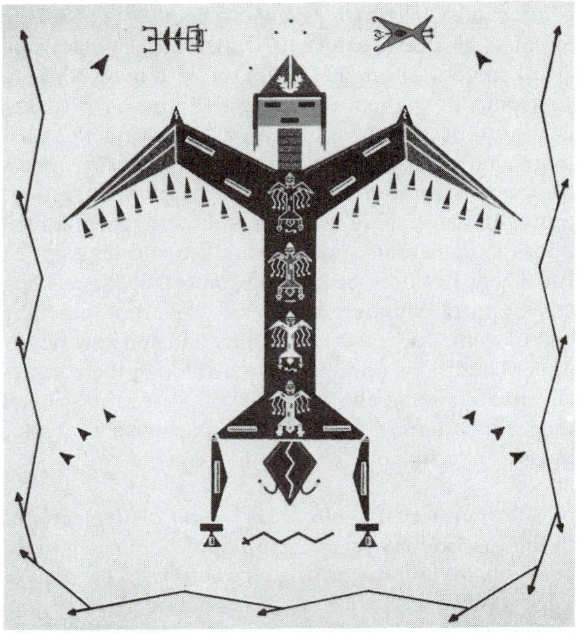

Sand paintings were used as a part of a healing ritual, identifying the patient with the physical universe and its powers. This is a replica of a Navajo medicine man's sand painting. (Photograph courtesy of National Museum of the American Indian Smithsonian Institution)

SACRED ACTS: RITUAL PRACTICE

The human body is also a place where the powers of the world, both physical and spiritual, converge and interact in a creative dynamic. The most prominent rituals in Native American regions are called dances, including the sun dance of the Plains and the Pueblo kachina dances. Dance is a spectacle that celebrates the body as a dynamic, graceful, powerful place where these same characteristics of the sacred are shown and experienced.

Ritual action such as a dance or an initiation gives a human being an orientation in time and space. For example, a ritual reenacting events of the creation myth demonstrates that there is continuity between the beginning and the present moment and shows the elements of the sacred to be constantly manifest wherever human beings live. As Petaga, a medicine man (ritual specialist), prepared himself for a spiritual journey, he said:

> "Life is like a huge design. Each part of the design is made up of the happenings, acts and interactions of people with each other and the world. You must know that this design is completed by the intervention of Wakan Tanka. . . . We were given ceremonies in which we pray with the pipe, ways that we may stand before Wakan Tanka so that he will instruct us about our place in his design."[20]

The **vision quest** is an ordeal undertaken by an individual under the direction of a medicine man as a supplication for guidance from the spirit world regarding a particular problem or crisis. One might seek a vision quest on one's own behalf or on behalf of the community. The supplicant embarks on a physical trial of isolation, fasting, chanting, vigil, and exposure to the elements in order to establish communication with a guardian spirit through a dream or a hallucinatory vision. After much waiting and physical endurance, the spirit appears, usually in the form of an animal, to instruct the seeker. Arthur Amiotte, a seeker who received his vision on the morning of the second day, described it as follows:

> "Upon the beginning of my third round [of prayers to each of the cardinal directions], I noticed a strange appearance in the sky to the south. It was like two parallel rolling clouds that stretched far into the south and far above me. They were not jet streams; they were much larger, and rolling within themselves. It was at this time then that my vision began. I had thought it would be a very mystical experience, or that it would be perhaps more of a dream than a vision, and my first reaction was: 'How strange! This is not at all what I thought a vision was like.' I felt I was perfectly clearheaded. . . . It lasted for what seemed the greater part of that day, gradually revealing a changing series of distinct forms and figures, like a panorama of shifting scenes, whose meaning once again would [later] be revealed to me."[21]

A guardian spirit seen in the vision may also endow the seeker with a supernatural power, such as the gift of healing. The experience of the vision quest is intended to affect the course of a person's life significantly. The seeker is committed to the course of instruction received by the guardian spirit, and this may involve a lifelong path.

The **sun dance** is the central religious ceremony of the Plains tribes. Warriors who vow to perform the dance rite consecrate themselves to the cosmos at the time of the summer solstice, and in their dances they gaze upward at the sun. In preparation, a camp circle is selected for the rite and a cone-shaped tent known as a *tipi* is erected at its center. A feast is held for four days and nights, emphasizing the significance of the four cardinal directions and the four seasons. A tree is then selected for the ceremonial pole, to symbolize the pillar at the center of the world. As the center, it functions as a sort of umbilical cord to the supernatural realm, giving access to the Supreme Being and the powerful forces of life, and thus becomes *wakan,* or sacred. The sun dancers spear their chests with wooden stakes or skewers, attaching themselves to the central pole by long ropes or thongs. They dance and pull in rhythm to the accompanying drumbeat until they tear the flesh of their chests to release themselves or until they collapse from exhaustion. The sun dance is understood as a sacrifice to the Great Spirit and, according to Lakota philosophy, symbolizes the release from ignorance. Through this blood sacrifice, sacred power is tapped and channeled for the benefit of both the individual and the community.

Among the Pueblo there is no vision quest whereby sacred power is made accessible to all. Just as notions of sacred place are more fixed and restricted than in the Plains tradition, in Pueblo practice access to sacred power is limited to ritual societies and their priests. Each society serves particular supernatural beings, and each has a different focus of concern, such as attending to aspects of fertility, war, and healing. Pueblo religious ceremonies follow an annual calendar, climaxing at the summer and winter solstices, when all major religious interests converge.

Kachinas appear in public performances in the guise of masked dancers who impersonate them. This Native American painting depicts the Eagle dancer. (Photograph courtesy of National Museum of the American Indian Smithsonian Institution)

One well-known Pueblo ceremony is the kachina ritual. The term *kachina* has several referents. **Kachinas** are supernatural beings, deities whose powers are manifest in natural phenomena—the sun, stars, and clouds. They are also spirits who take the form of animals, plants, and birds. Sacred narratives refer to kachinas as primordial culture heroes who still dwell in the mountains and who descend to aid and empower humans in their efforts in hunting and agriculture. The kachinas appear in public performances, incarnate in the guise of masked dancers who impersonate them. These sacred performances occur at critical points in the agricultural cycle, making their first appearance at the early phase of crop maturation and withdrawing from the human community at harvest.

The **shaman**, or **medicine man**, is an important religious leader and healer. Found in many cultures, shamans are typically believed to draw their authority and power from their ability to contact the spiritual world and to control mystical experiences. Among the Plains and southwestern peoples, especially the Navajo, access to the spiritual realm is restricted to such religious specialists. Shamanism can also be understood in terms of place, since the shaman is a messenger or intermediary from the spiritual realm to the human one. Shamanism might be considered a type of vision quest in that both are voluntary ordeals that involve encounters with the spiritual realm, undertaken for the purpose of gaining insight into human problems. For the Plains peoples, the supplicant is sometimes granted particular powers by the guardian spirits during the vision quest; similarly, the shaman is granted the knowledge to heal through his encounter with the spirits, who offer him insight into the problems of the human community.

The use of the sacred pipe is found at all Plains ceremonial occasions and has become a symbol of unity among today's Native Americans. The pipe is a medium of prayer; smoke rising carries the supplicant's message to the spirits above. Smoking the pipe is considered a necessary prelude to a ceremony. A symbol of the power to communicate with the spiritual world, the pipe, like tobacco itself, is treated with great respect. By contrast, the dominant and pervasive symbol among the Pueblo is corn or maize, the sustainer of human life. The sprinkling of cornmeal is a fundamental ritual act of sanctification; it is used to mark the spiritual path for the dead as well as the kachinas who mediate between the human and supernatural realms. Both sacred pipe and cornmeal symbolize the common fundamental vision of two interlocking worlds, sacred and secular.

SACRED WORDS: NARRATIVE, SONG, AND PRAYER

As we said at the outset of this chapter, the language we use reflects our conception of reality. Furthermore, speech is essential to the human being as a fundamentally social creature, for it allows for interaction in the community, identified by a shared language. N. Scott Momaday, a Native American scholar, said, "It seems to me that in a certain sense we are all made of words; that our most essential being consists in language. It is the element in which we think and dream and act, in which we live our daily lives."[22] The oral traditions of Native America orient people in the world. The sacred words of the Native Americans are an extension of their rituals because the words are always presented in storytelling, song, or prayer. "In Native American cultures there is a rich array of language acts that are central to religious life. Prayers, songs, and oral performances of stories are the core of many formal religious occasions."[23] Songs are often regarded as given to a person by a guardian spirit through a dream or vision; their performance can offer religious power.

Speech is a creative force. For the Navajo, thought and speech are even personified and figure as protagonists in creation stories. The telling of a story is a creative act. Native American traditions hold that the dynamics of the world recounted in a narrative are perpetuated through their telling. Sacred stories, or myths, are performed, not written, for to write a story would violate the nourishing life of the oral tradition. Stories are kept alive in the vital context in which they are shared. Because of their sacred quality, one tells them only on appropriate occasions. "I cannot tell [my] vision here," insists Arthur Amiotte, "for there is a time and a place reserved for the telling of visions: a sacred setting, the proper songs, the proper preparations."[24] Only qualified performers, sometimes considered the owners of the tales, retain the sole right to recount their sacred stories.

Cosmogonic stories take place in a primal setting and tell how the physical, social, and moral world came to be. To set a story "in the beginning" is a way of establishing the authoritative significance of an event and identifying what is of fundamental value. Native American cosmogonies follow as many as eight different patterns; one prominent southwestern motif is the story of **emergence**. According to this cosmogony, people originally emerged from their subterranean dwellings in search of a new habitable world. Traveling across the universe, they establish the shape and order of the present world. Here we can see a parallel with the Aboriginal Australian myth of the Dreaming.

The **trickster**, another prominent mythic figure, echoes this theme. Known for his humor and his cunning, the trickster, portrayed as an elusive hare, a sly coyote, or some other wily figure, brings about changes in the world through playful disobedience. He is amoral, but his outrageous acts of willful disobedience to the creator god are also comically exaggerated. In overturning every social convention, the trickster ends up in ridiculous predicaments. More serious, his efforts to outwit God and thwart his plans for cosmic order cause the entire shape of the world to change, which the trickster laughs off as a huge joke. Although he usually fails to accomplish his own selfish goals, he is never deterred. He is also the eternal transformer, changing shape at will. Taking exaggerated forms accounts for some of his characteristic buffoonery. In one trickster story, Coyote changes himself into a baby floating on reeds in the river to get close to three bathing sisters he lusts after. When he approaches each of the first two, he transforms himself back and has his way with them. He fails to trick the final sister, however, because when he transforms into a baby, he forgets to change the size of his huge penis.[25]

But the trickster is more than a clown; he is a sacred figure because he reflects the deeper nature of reality and the human condition. Tricksters hold up a mirror to human foibles, but at the same time they make a surprising affirmation that the sacred is revealed in unexpected reversals. They show that the order of the world is not fixed but changing, flawed, and full of contradiction. Life, like a good joke, must be embraced and enjoyed, and the source of creativity lies in overturning the expected. The comedy of the trickster reveals hidden layers of meaning, and this is what gives their clowning religious value.

Half a millennium has passed since Columbus first encountered Native American peoples. The conquest brought devastation. But the religious traditions of North America have persisted and adapted to the new circumstances. Traditions have survived, but not as mere artifacts: they address the situation and satisfy their adherents' needs. They have helped to forge a new identity in continuity with the traditions. Native culture and religion did not die but evolved, and, as the trickster teaches, with change comes creative revitalization.

African Religions

Africa is a larger and even more diverse continent than Australia or North America. Tremendous geographic differences contribute to its cultural diversity. In the west, tropical forests burst with extravagant vegetation. In the east, temperate grasslands spread at the base of magnificent snowcapped peaks. Nor are the cultures of sub-Saharan Africa homogeneous. More than 40 modern nations occupy the continent south of the Sahara, each with its own history and political and economic organization. Each nation is in turn comprised of

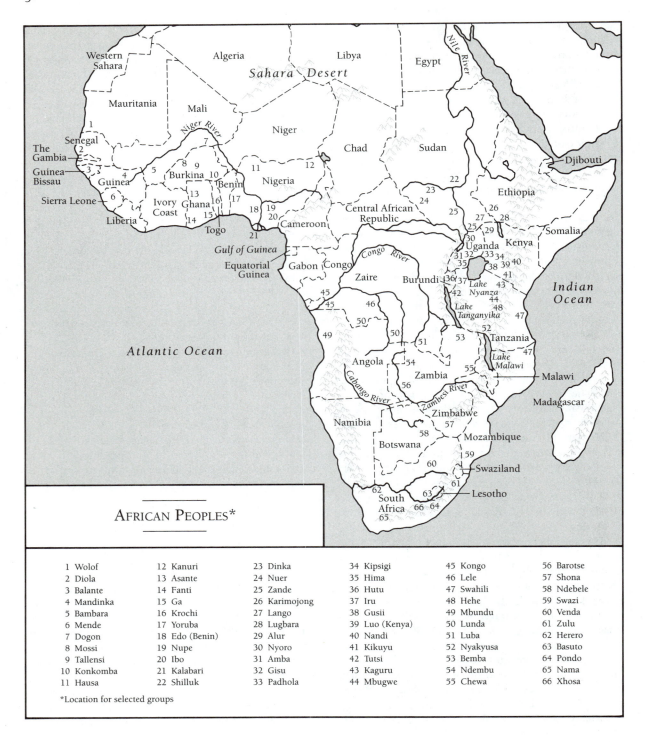

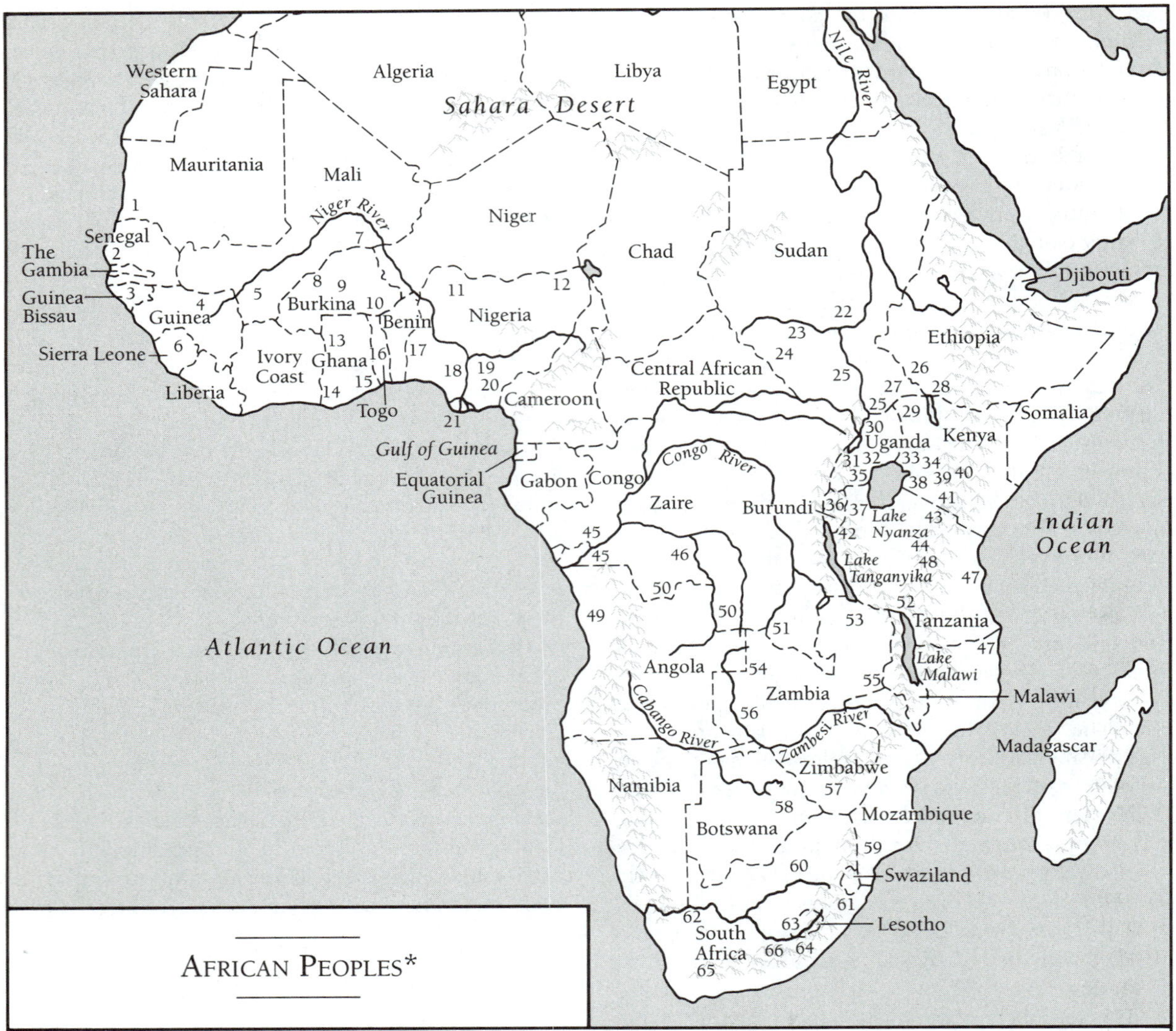

AFRICAN PEOPLES*

1 Wolof
2 Diola
3 Balante
4 Mandinka
5 Bambara
6 Mende
7 Dogon
8 Mossi
9 Tallensi
10 Konkomba
11 Hausa
12 Kanuri
13 Asante
14 Fanti
15 Ga
16 Krochi
17 Yoruba
18 Edo (Benin)
19 Nupe
20 Ibo
21 Kalabari
22 Shilluk
23 Dinka
24 Nuer
25 Zande
26 Karimojong
27 Lango
28 Lugbara
29 Alur
30 Nyoro
31 Amba
32 Gisu
33 Padhola
34 Kipsigi
35 Hima
36 Hutu
37 Iru
38 Gusii
39 Luo (Kenya)
40 Nandi
41 Kikuyu
42 Tutsi
43 Kaguru
44 Mbugwe
45 Kongo
46 Lele
47 Swahili
48 Hehe
49 Mbundu
50 Lunda
51 Luba
52 Nyakyusa
53 Bemba
54 Ndembu
55 Chewa
56 Barotse
57 Shona
58 Ndebele
59 Swazi
60 Venda
61 Zulu
62 Herero
63 Basuto
64 Pondo
65 Nama
66 Xhosa

*Location for selected groups

numerous ethnic groups differing in language and custom. In the West African nation of Ivory Coast alone, approximately 60 distinct groups coexist. Yet some cultural commonalities within subregions can be seen. In West Africa, for example, a long history of migrations, trade patterns, and other contact has lent a certain homogeneity to the region. We will focus on a few traditions from two subregions to underscore the diversity of African religions even as we try to identify common themes and approaches among them.

RELIGION BY REGION

West Africa Although West Africa accounts for only one-fifth of the continent's area, its 120 million people represent about half of Africa's total population. This subregion extends from Senegal, along the Atlantic coast at the farthest western point, to Nigeria, along the Gulf of Guinea.

West Africa has a long history of trade with Europeans and the North African Muslims who established caravan trade routes across the Sahara. As Arabic authors became familiar with the kingdoms of Bilad al-Sudan, the "Land of the Black Men," they recorded encounters with their great civilizations. They wrote of powerful kingdoms such as Ghana, the "Land of Gold," and the Mande kingdom on the upper Niger, now Mali. These empires were rich, peaceful, and well ordered, with effective governments, flourishing markets, and lively trade. Such sophisticated civilizations, with 500-year histories, were a far cry from the self-sufficient village life of so-called tribal society thought to be typical of Africa.

In West Africa, we will focus on the Dogon people of present-day Mali and the Yoruba of Nigeria.

East Africa Eight modern states comprise the subregion of East Africa: Sudan, Ethiopia, Eritrea, Djibouti, Somalia, Kenya, Uganda, and Tanzania. In this region are more than 200 distinct indigenous societies whose languages, cultures, economic systems, and religious beliefs are unique. Although traditionally East Africans were farmers and livestock herders, urban centers were established and sustained by active trade, especially with the Arabs, along the coast. In the thirteenth century, Islam's influence spread, especially at the trading ports and cities along the coast; in the nineteenth century, British power brought Western culture and Christianity. Nevertheless, indigenous religious thought and practices have continued to thrive and to play a significant role in the social and political life of Africa's peoples.

In East Africa, we will focus on two ethnic groups from the dry southern Sudan: the Dinka and the Nuer. When we look at rituals, we will focus on the Ndembu people of the southern region.

EARLY INVESTIGATIONS

Missionaries and colonists portrayed Africa as "savage" and "backward." Its religions were denigrated as unevolved superstition, animism, ancestor worship, and the like. Although scholars no longer defend the view that African religions reflect an inferior "primitive mentality," these prejudices still retain a subtle hold on the popular imagination in the West. Anthropologists conducting more objective, systematic field studies helped to dispel false impressions, but because they often did not set the practices they documented in a historical context, they still presented Africans as passive recipients of unchanging, timeless traditions. This approach wrongly suggested that Africans did not distinguish myth from history or the sacred from the profane. It reinforced the idea that African religion is an endless cycle of ritual repetition, in contrast to Western religions, which emphasize the progress of history. We will emphasize that African religions do differentiate between sacred and profane and that ritual provides the occasion to mediate between the two and thus to participate in the creative flux of the universe.

WORLDVIEW

No single coherent body of beliefs and practices can properly be identified as "African religion." Indeed, African religions are as numerous and diverse as the countless ethnic groups on the continent. Consequently, African religiosity cannot be reduced to an essence, a common creed or orthodoxy.

Nevertheless, we can identify some similarities in ideas and processes across ethnic boundaries. Generally speaking, the creator in African religions is the maker of a dynamic universe, one in constant flux. There are many secondary divinities and ancestors, who along with living people help to sustain and maintain this world of change and motion in proper interdependence and harmony. African ritual practice, such as divination, seeks to orient both the community and the individual within this flux as well as to invite participation in it. Let us consider the main features of these religions' world view.

Supreme Being

The inability of some European observers to identify African practices as religion was due in part to a characteristic absence of a cult to a supreme being, since most rituals are overtly directed to a multiplicity of spirits and localized divinities. Yet a conception of a "high god," a supreme creator, does exist across Africa and probably owes nothing to the influence of Christianity or Islamic monotheism. To the Nuer of the southern Sudan, for example, Kwoth is the spirit "on high." He is associated with all things above—sky, wind, clouds, birds. For the Nuer,

> God is Spirit, which, like wind and air, is invisible and ubiquitous. But though God is not these things he is in them in the sense that he reveals himself through them. . . . Unlike the other spirits God has no prophets or sanctuaries or earthly forms.[26]

The supreme being is concerned with invisible, ultimate reality, not the personal matters of daily life. Many African societies recount a strikingly similar myth to explain why God is withdrawn and remote from human society (see box, "An African Myth."). God complained that woman constantly knocked the heavens with the upward thrust of the pestle as she pounded yams for food. To get away from her, God retreated to the remote skies, becoming inaccessible. Wherever this myth is shared, God is worshiped regularly but is addressed directly in petition only at the most dire of moments. At other times, the lesser divinities serve as intermediaries.

Secondary Divinities

Secondary divinities serve the supreme being as messengers and intermediaries. These local deities and spirits are often identified with sacred places such as important rivers or with natural phenomena such as rain or thunder. Constantly appealed to for both personal welfare and protection of the group, their central place in the community is visible in the many individual shrines and sacrificial altars. Sometimes these gods are portrayed as the children of God, but according to the higher levels of religious teaching, the divinities are understood as refractions of the divine essence.

According to the Yoruba of Nigeria, there are 401 secondary divinities, *orisa,* who "line the road to heaven."[27] The extraordinary number of orisa expresses the omnipresent activity of the divine. These secondary deities and spirits, along with the ancestors, directly control or constrain the living. For example, every Yoruba also has a personal orisa, a guardian who can help the living person to achieve the full potential accorded by the supreme being before birth. (A bad fate is therefore never irrevocable, for divination and sacrificial devotion to the orisa, for example, can alter destiny.) Because the secondary divinities are more immediately involved in everyday human concerns than the supreme being and are more demanding, they can cause those who neglect or defy them to fall ill or to have an accident.

The most dramatic, palpable contact with divinities happens when a divinity or spirit possesses a person. This is not always solicited or desired. Muchona, a Ndembu who was seized by such an affliction, describes the onset of his possession:

> "I was thrown on the mat by violent quivering. I jerked about very much. I did not know how I was doing it. It was on account of the power of *Kayong'u* which attacked me suddenly there. . . . A person in this state [breathes with difficulty]. His ears are completely blocked. His eyes and his whole body are like those of a man who has drunk beer. He slips onto the ground in an epileptic fit. . ."[28]

A diviner may identify the spirit and sacrifice a chicken or a goat to remove the spirit from the possessed victim. In other instances, such possession is actively sought, induced through special techniques to facilitate contact with the realm of divinity. The Ndembu, for example, sometimes provoke possession by inhaling the vapors of a medicinal leaf.[29]

An African Myth

In many African societies, the supreme being is concerned with invisible, ultimate realities but not the personal matters of daily life. This leads to the question, how or why did God become removed from human society? In the following very common African myth (this version is from the Krachi people of the West African country of Togo), an answer to this question—full of humor and good sense—is provided.

In the beginning of days Wulbari [God] and man lived close together and Wulbari lay on top of Mother Earth, Asase Ya. Thus it happened that, as there was so little space to move about in, man annoyed the divinity, who in disgust went away and rose up to the present place where one can admire him but not reach him.

He was annoyed for a number of reasons. An old woman, while making her fufu [pounded yams] outside her hut, kept on knocking Wulbari with her pestle. This hurt him and, as she persisted, he was forced to go higher out of her reach. Besides, the smoke of the cooking fires got into his eyes so that he had to go farther way. According to others, however, Wulbari, being so close to men, made a convenient sort of towel, and the people used to wipe their dirty fingers on him. This naturally annoyed him. Yet this was not so bad a grievance as that which caused We, the Wulbari of the Kassena people, to remove himself out of the reach of man. He did so because an old woman, anxious to make a good soup, used to cut off a bit of him at each mealtime, and We, being pained at this treatment, went higher.

Source: Paul Radin, ed., *African Folktales* (Princeton, N.J.: Princeton University Press, 1970), p. 28.

Ancestors: The Living Dead

In many African religions, death is not the end of human existence but merely a change in form and status. A Yoruba proverb expresses well a prevalent notion of eternal life in death: "The world is a market; the otherworld is home."[30] After death one becomes an **ancestor**, one of the "living dead" who can be important intermediaries in the spiritual realm, with the power to direct human affairs. Not all the dead become ancestors, only those whose conduct in life was exemplary—persons of standing who had lived through a complete life cycle, died at an old age, had an unblemished body, and were moral and dignified. Ancestors are not worshiped but rather venerated for deeds that laid the foundations of culture, set moral precedent, and provided guidance to the living.

The world of the ancestors and the world of the living are mutually enhancing and supportive. The living sustain the ancestors through libation and sacrifice and constantly appeal to them for guidance and support; the dead bless the living, but, like the secondary divinities, they can express displeasure by bringing sickness or other misfortunes. Thus the ancestors awaken descendants to their negligence of duty and reiterate the need to follow the moral precedent.

SACRED ACTS: RITUAL PRACTICE

Ritual is the foundation of religion in Africa, the bearer of society's ultimate values and the transmitter of its most profound insights. There are two interdependent

The Yoruba celebrate female power of the Mothers, both female ancestors and deities, in an annual festival called Gelede. Seen here recreating Orunmila's mythic journey into the realm of the Mothers, the Gelede performer dances with a mask, head ties, and leg rattles. (Henry John Drewal and Margaret Thompson Drewal)

dimensions of ritual: what the ritual hopes to accomplish and what it asserts about reality. Ritual attempts to control and renew the patterns of life, bringing them into conformity with an idealized conception of the universe. "The ritual sphere is the sphere *par excellence* where the world as lived and the world as imaged become fused together, transformed into one reality."[31] Ritual makes visible the invisible and intangible realities of the cosmos. It both identifies the forces that drive and sustain the community and brings human beings to participate in the greater realities.

For example, the Yoruba celebrate the female power of the Mothers, both female ancestors and deities, in an annual festival called Gelede. Gelede ritually asserts that woman possesses the secret of life itself. Her power as transformer is both constructive, evidenced in her ability to bring life into the world, and destructive, demonstrated by the particular force of women's curses and blessings and their celebrated ability in witchcraft. The Gelede masks of the Great Mothers are accompanied by the masqueraders of two secondary divinities: the god of iron, who is also a smith who transforms and shapes the world, and a dreaded trickster and spoiler, who can undo prescribed destiny. Their presence is a visual reminder of the constructive and destructive powers that interact in the cosmos. Some Gelede masks represent the Mothers as bearded women; their sexual ambiguity reflects the double world—natural and supernatural—in which the ancestors, deities, and witches operate. The bird and snake masks they may wear also reflect the motif of the constant tension between heaven and earth.

In Africa, **masks** are more than mere impersonations of the spirits or divinities; they are visual metaphors of the dynamic cosmos. A mask is not just a static object or merely a headpiece hiding the face of the wearer. It is a dynamic composite of the costume, mime, and dance that together communicate meaning. Every element works together to reflect the schema of a cosmos in flux. The mask conceals the identity of the wearer, only to reveal the deeper, invisible reality of the spiritual realm. Like any religious symbol, the mask is a paradox that reveals meaning to all "with eyes to see and ears to hear."

In ritual, whether through the dramatic gyrations of possession or through the physical trials of initiation, the body serves as the microcosm of the cosmos. In it the dynamism of the cosmos—the sacred and the profane, life and death—can be seen. For example, the Dogon people see the joints as the most important aspect of the body, first of all because they permit the differentiation of its parts; differentiation represents the break from the formless totality that existed before creation. The joints also give the body flexibility and strength and so reflect the primary purpose of human existence, work. According to Dogon myth, agricultural labor joins the disparate elements of the universe in working harmony so that the cosmos becomes like a body, every part working in conjunction with every other part.

Because it is only through the body that ultimate reality can be perceived and interpreted, it is a unique template for much religious symbolism. The body and its processes are prominent in ritual symbolism. In Ndembu ritual, a principal symbol is the *mukula* tree, which when cut exudes a red sap that the Ndembu compare to blood. It is used in rituals that are concerned with situations in which the show of blood is prominent: hunting, childbirth, circumcision. The rituals of these events emphasize blood as a life force that must be shed to restore and renew life. Such symbols, and others like them, use bodily processes to express religious meaning.

A **sacrifice** is a ritual death, the purpose of which is to control and renew the forces of life. Sacrifice is a transaction with the divinity that makes use of the reciprocity between the human and spiritual realms. The shedding of blood in ritual sacrifice releases the power or life force from the animal victim. Poured onto objects dedicated to the spirit or deity, the blood is transferred to them so that the deity's power is renewed for the benefit of the devotees. The lyrics of a drummed song in praise of the Mothers at Gelede show sacrifice as a point of contact and reverence:

Mother, Mother, . . . Come and dance
Honored ancestor apake, *come and dance*
Come home immediately. . . .
One who has given birth to many children,
Come home immediately, come home now
I made a sacrifice, I received glory, the day is proper
I sacrificed, I sacrificed, I sacrificed, I sacrificed.[32]

Sacrifice has pride of place in ritual because bloodshed, destruction, and death mark a passage into a new existence. It exemplifies that the forces of life and death, creation and destruction, are in constant tension in a dynamic cosmos. Furthermore, it shows that human participation in this flux is critical to the harmonious working of that dynamic.

Sacrifice is often modeled on a mythic precedent in which a primordial being was sacrificed by God to form the world and distribute the life force throughout creation. For example, one form of Dogon sacrifice draws on a myth of an exemplary sacrificial death, that of Lebe, the first human being. God sacrificed Lebe in order to redistribute *nyama,* the vital force, and to renew life: "Lebe's sacred life-force was infused within the earth so that it could bring forth the fruits of life."[33] Here sacrifice is a transforming and generative act. It is significant that in the language of the Dogon, the word for sacrifice comes from a root meaning "to renew

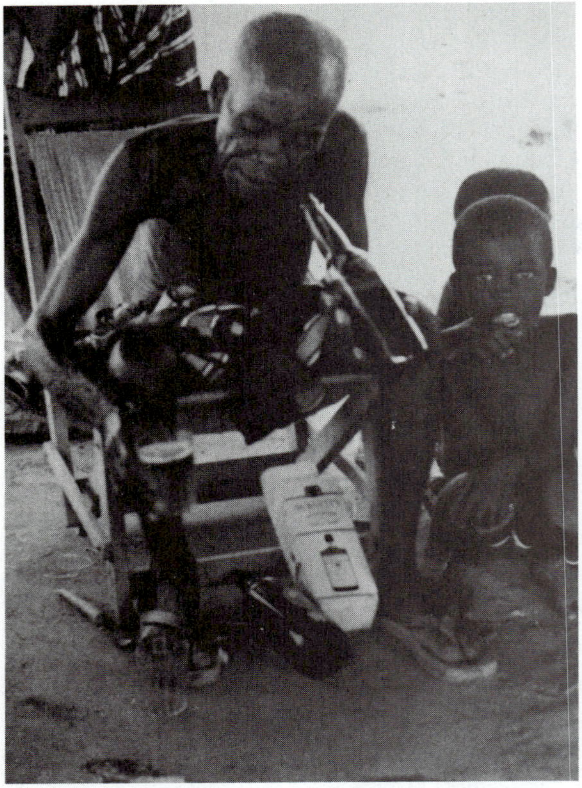

life."[34] Sacrifice acknowledges that human existence is suspended from the interwoven web of life and death.

The sacred acts of ritual in Africa are usually accompanied by sacred words—prayers and invocations. When the Dogon perform animal sacrifices, the officiating priest pronounces sacred words that carry this life force through his own breath as he pours the lifeblood of the victim on the altar. The transaction of sacrifice is effected with sacred words as much as ritual acts. Through the victim's breath and blood, its life force is redistributed for the benefit of the human community.

Among the Dinka of East Africa, for example, words have the power to transform the death of a sacrificial victim into a source of life for the community. According to their myths, the priestly clan wrested its power from a mythical hero, Aiwel Longar, who finally conceded to give them fishing spears with which to pray and the power to invoke, bless, and curse with them. Today Dinka priests are called the Masters of the Fishing Spear, not because of their fishing skills but because their ritual spearing of the victim, when combined with their spoken words—mirroring the spearing and words of Aiwel Longar—can transform a sacrificial death into a source of life for the community. Words here have "instrumental force";[35] not only do they express the intention behind the act of sacrifice, but they also effect the transaction between divinity and the human community.

Just as sacrifice transforms death (of a sacrificial victim) into life (the symbolic resurrection of the community and the renewal of the bond with the sacred), **rites of passage**, such as initiation into adulthood, play on the theme of life issuing from death. A rite of passage marks a transition between physiological stages coupled with a change in social status. More important, such rites reveal the human experience of transformation to be participation in the sacred dynamic of the cosmos.

Sacrifice can take many forms. A young boy watches a ritual being performed in which libation is poured to the ancestors while asking for their blessing. A woman offers a sacrifice of chicken, yams, pineapple, and palm branch to the spirits. The common objects take on symbolic significance within the sacred space. (Laura Grillo)

Diviners play an important role in Dogon society, prophesying the future from natural signs and by age-old rituals. These diviners are from a village in Mali's Sangha area. (United Nations)

Rites of passage proceed in three stages, beginning with *separation* and seclusion from the group. The major portion of the effective ritual action takes place during the second and most critical stage, *transition,* also called the liminal phase. The rite ends with a final *reincorporation* of the initiate into society. The rite aims at the creation of a new being. A child does not become an adult only because of physical transformation at puberty but must be remade into a fully responsible and aware social being. The old self must die, and the person must be reborn as a transformed being, bearing the marks of culture. Sometimes the initiate is cut, the scar becoming a sign of this death and rebirth; it becomes a mark of permanent differentiation and thus the physical expression of social identity.

At the onset of the critical liminal phase, once initiates are separated from society, they are considered dead and may even be handled for a time like corpses. They may be buried, compelled to lie motionless like the dead, or "forced to live for a while in the company of masked and monstrous mummers" representing the "undead," who, like the initiates, occupy an uneasy status that is "betwixt and between."[36] During the liminal period, initiates are stripped of their individual identity, all social stratification among them is abolished, and they are reduced to their barest essence. "They are allowed to go filthy and identified with the earth. . . . Often their very names are taken from them and each is called solely by the generic term for 'neophyte' or 'initiand.' "[37]

Initiates held in ritual seclusion are in a liminal state, and their status between living and dead is represented by the space they occupy, between the village and the bush. They also dress in ambiguous ways:

> They may wear only a strip of clothing, or even go naked, to demonstrate that as liminal beings they have no status, property, insignia . . . indicating rank or role, [or] position in a kinship system. . . . Their behavior is normally passive or humble.[38]

Initiates routinely undergo ordeals and humiliations to destroy further their attachment to their previous status. Having gone through such a limbo, the initiate is made malleable and hence can make a successful passage to a new state.

When the initiates reemerge, they are often symbolically likened to newborn infants; for instance, they are covered with a white chalky substance to resemble the mucous film that covers a baby at birth. Similarly, at the end of a Ndembu rite of male passage, "the novices were carried [like newborns] into the [ritual] camp site for the last time, in new outfits of clothes, oiled, decorated with beads, and shaved around the hairline."[39]

SACRED WORDS: MYTHIC THEMES

The form of African myth does not always fit the genre of Western narrative, for events are not necessarily recounted sequentially with a beginning, a middle, and an end. Instead, during the course of a rite, allusions are made to fragments of events associated with a particular ritual action. Such myths are, in a sense, ritually transmitted, and the meaning is revealed only during initiation. These myths embody profound philosophical reflections. They offer insight into the nature and dynamics of reality and address the most profound questions of the place and purpose of human existence. The themes and motifs we will touch on in this discussion are found throughout Africa and are readily related to ritual.

The primordial smith is one of the chief figures in African mythology, and so earthly smiths often enjoy the status of religious practitioners. The smith manipulates the elements of earth and fire to create tools that are essential to human culture. This hidden transforming process is associated with sexual reproduction. The furnace, often an abandoned termite hill rising some feet from the ground, would be likened to a womb where physical elements merge into new being. Among the Dogon, the primordial being, Nommo, is said to have been a smith. When he fell from the heavens to earth, his amorphous body was broken into joints and given permanent definition; the elbow symbolizes the human capacity to work, to be fashioners of the world, like the divinities. The smith is "the human embodiment of the demiurge."[40] This association of smith and demiurge—a secondary divinity, often evil—shows his powers to be ambiguous. Not only is he the forger of culture, but he is also linked to disorder and wilderness. "The Dogon smith is even thought to wander in the bush, in the form of the 'pale fox' known as Yurugu, or Ogo, the Dogon trickster and patron of divination."[41]

As in North America, the trickster is a mythic character who introduces disorder and confusion into the original divine plan but in so doing paves the way for a new, more dynamic order. "His comic adventures convey a widely recognized African principle: life achieves its wholeness through the balance of opposites."[42] The trickster is

> both agent of social conflict and the peacekeeper of the marketplace, as well as the confuser of humans and the messenger of the gods. His two-sided nature brings together the gods and human beings in cooperative manner through divination and sacrifice, which he supervises.[43]

The myths of Africa reflect the creative dynamic they explore. The tradition of their oral transmission encourages creative revision as they are passed along. A traditional ending to Ashanti tales makes this gentle invitation to reflection and participation: "This, my story which I have related, if it be sweet or if it be not sweet, take some elsewhere and let some come back to me."[44]

In conclusion, while we have seen the tremendous diversity of the wide-ranging African cultures, we have also noted certain common underlying themes. Paradoxically, the cosmos, grounded in a fundamental order given by the supreme being, is characterized by constant change and renewal. Such change may be influenced by the secondary divinities and the ancestors but also by human rituals. The renewal of life through sacrifice, rites of passage, and the use of masks to convey various layers of reality all convey the fundamental dynamism of the cosmos. In myth, too, both culture hero and trickster reflect the complementary nature of good and evil, order and disorder. The religious expressions of the traditions of Africa, like those of Australia and North America, are not static or unchanging. In their forms, they recognize change, and in their content, they celebrate renewal.

NOTES

1 Harold W. Turner, "Primal Religions and Their Study," in *Australian Essays in World Religions,* ed. Victor C. Hayes (Adelaide: Australian Association for the Study of Religions, 1977), p. 32.

2 Kees Bolle, "Myth: An Overview," in *Encyclopedia of Religions,* ed. Mircea Eliade (New York: Macmillan, 1984), vol. 1, p. 261.

3 Mircea Eliade, *The Sacred and the Profane: The Nature of Religion,* trans. Willard R. Trask (Orlando, Fla.: Harcourt Brace Jovanovich, 1959), p. 95.

4 John R. Hinnells, ed., *A Handbook of Living Religions* (Harmondsworth, England: Penguin Books, 1984), p. 414.

5 Max Charlesworth et al., eds., *Religion in Aboriginal Australia* (St. Lucia, Australia: University of Queensland Press, 1984), p. 7.

6 Ibid., p. 8.

7 Eliade, *Encyclopedia of Religions,* vol. 1, p. 529.

8 Charlesworth et al., *Religion in Aboriginal Australia,* p. 9.

9 Mircea Eliade, *Australian Religions: An Introduction* (Ithaca, N.Y.: Cornell University Press, 1983), p. 56.

10 Ronald M. Berndt, "Traditional Morality," in Charlesworth et al., *Religion in Aboriginal Australia,* p. 177.

11 Eliade, *Encyclopedia of Religions,* vol. 1, p. 531.

12 Charlesworth et al., *Religion in Aboriginal Australia,* p. 181.

13 Ibid., p. 241.

14 Eliade, *Australian Religions,* p. 107.

15 Sam D. Gill, *Native American Traditions: Sources and Interpretations* (Belmont, Calif.: Wadsworth, 1983), p. 3.

16 William K. Powers, "North American Indians: Indians of the Plains," in *Encyclopedia of Religions,* vol. 10, p. 491.

17 Peter Whitely, "North American Indians: Indians of the Southwest," in *Encyclopedia of Religions,* vol. 10, p. 514.

18 Cosmos Mindeleff, *Navaho Houses* (Washington, D.C.: Bureau of American Ethnology, 1898).

19 Whitely, "North American Indians," pp. 516–517.

20 Gill, *Native American Traditions,* p. 91.

21 Ibid., pp. 99–100.

22 Ibid., p. 44.

23 Ibid., p. 43.

24 Ibid., p. 100.

25 Ibid., pp. 32–33.

26 Edward Evan Evans-Pritchard, *Nuer Religion* (New York: Oxford University Press, 1956), pp. 2 and 4.

27 John Pemberton III, "Yoruba Religion," in *Encyclopedia of Religions,* vol. 15, p. 536.

28 Victor W. Turner, *Revelation and Divination in Ndembu Ritual* (Ithaca, N.Y.: Cornell University Press, 1975), p. 256.

29 Ibid., pp. 256–257.

30 Henry J. Drewal and Margaret Thompson Drewal, *Gelede: Art and Female Power among the Yoruba* (Bloomington: Indiana University Press, 1983), p. 2.

31 Benjamin C. Ray, *African Religions: Symbol, Ritual, and Community* (Englewood Cliffs, N.J.: Prentice Hall, 1976), p. 17.

32 Drewal and Drewal, *Gelede,* p. 24.

33 Ray, *African Religions,* p. 89.

34 Ibid.

35 Ibid., p. 88.

36 Victor W. Turner, *The Forest of Symbols: Aspects of Ndembu Ritual* (Ithaca, N.Y.: Cornell University Press, 1967), p. 96.

37 Ibid.

38 Victor W. Turner, *The Ritual Process: Structure and Anti-structure* (Ithaca, N.Y.: Cornell University Press, 1969), p. 95.

39 Turner, *Forest of Symbols,* p. 259.

40 Evan M. Zuesse, "African Religions: Mythic Themes," in *Encyclopedia of Religions,* vol. 1, p. 74.

41 Ibid.

42 Ray, "African Religions," p. 64.

43 Ibid.

44 Paul Radin, ed., *African Folktales* (New York: Schocken Books, 1983), p. 19.

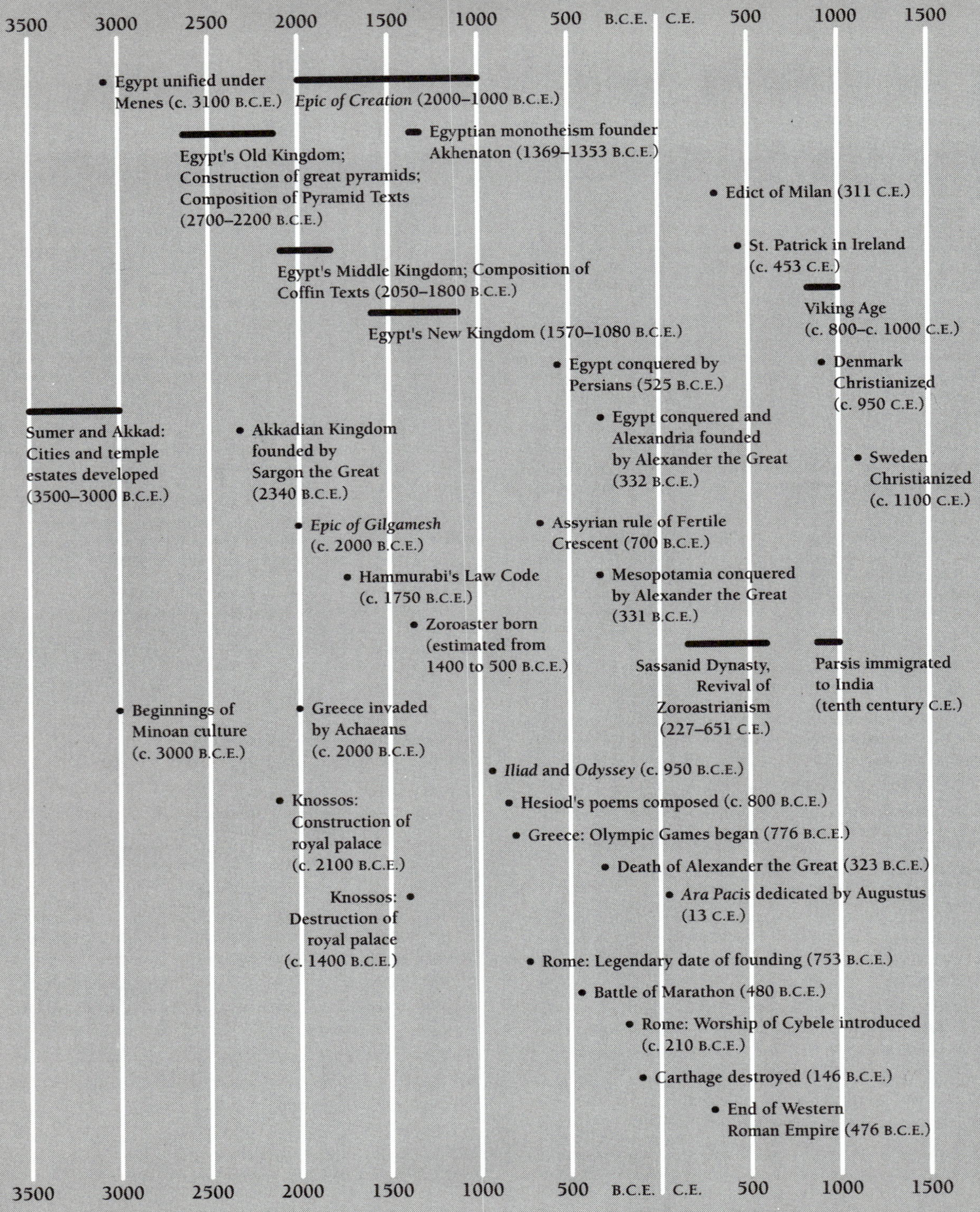

EGYPT, MESOPOTAMIA, GREECE, ROME TIME LINE

CHAPTER 2

RELIGIONS OF ANTIQUITY

RELIGIONS OF ANTIQUITY

EGYPTIAN RELIGION

The Nile is Egypt's lifeline. The annual Nile flood, which usually occurs between late June and October, deposits a rich silt from central Africa and the Ethiopian highlands into the valley and delta. This fertile soil can produce two or even three crops each year, in sharp contrast to the sterile land of the surrounding desert. It is not surprising that for centuries the Egyptians identified the black land with Osiris, the beloved god of immortality, and the red land with Seth, his evil brother. Indeed, the Egyptian creation myth depicts a primal hill rising from the waters, reflecting the close tie between Egypt and the Nile.

Because of the mild climate, good soil, and abundant water, the ancient Egyptians were able to develop a stable, prosperous civilization that lasted for more than 30 centuries. People of all social classes believed in the constancy of nature: like the rhythm of day and night, the annual Nile flood seemed to promise an unchanging universe.

EGYPT IN HISTORY

Egypt's early history was shaped by its geography. Its rich soil is fed by the Nile, which floods annually into irrigation ditches and the many wells built by its inhabitants, making farming effective. It is protected from foreign enemies on the north by the Mediterranean Sea and on the south and east by deserts. Under such circumstances, it is not surprising that as early as the fourth millennium B.C.E. Egypt had become a large and powerful kingdom and was ruled for 25 centuries by a long series of dynasties, headed by the famous pharaohs. Despite periodically suffering under struggles between and demands made by some of these pharaohs, Egypt enjoyed enviable unity and power for many centuries. At the height of its power, between the sixteenth and eleventh centuries B.C.E., it controlled a vast empire stretching from Nubia in central Africa to the Euphrates River in the northeast.

The ancient Egyptians left behind buildings (notably the great pyramids, built as burial tombs for certain pharaohs), inscriptions in pictorial writing called hieroglyphics, scrolls, and other artifacts. What these remains tell us is that many of the pharaohs claimed descent from the gods and that they surrounded themselves with a vast court of administrators, priests, scribes, and artisans who left praises of them in scrolls and on the walls of the great pyramids.[1]

Egypt's days of greatness came to an end in the middle of the first millennium B.C.E., when its armies were pushed out of the conquered territories. It was invaded by the Assyrians in the seventh century, the Persians in the sixth, the Greeks in the fourth, and the

The Nile is Egypt's lifeline and has been important not only for Egypt's economy but for its religion and worldview as well. (The Granger Collection)

Romans in the first century B.C.E. It remained part of the Roman Empire until it was conquered by the Muslims in the seventh century C.E.

RELIGIOUS LIFE IN EGYPT

Religion dominated life in ancient Egypt. So far as can be determined, the Egyptians never prepared an organized, written account of their religious traditions, and as a result, we know much about some of their beliefs and little about others.

Modern scholars have compiled three large collections of Egyptian sacred texts: (1) the **Pyramid Texts**, which are inscriptions on the walls of the pyramids built for the pharaohs of the fifth and sixth dynasties and are concerned with funerary rites and details of the ruler's life in the hereafter; (2) the **Coffin Texts**, which are inscriptions on the inner and outer lids of coffins of individuals who died during the Middle Kingdom and pertain to the cult of the dead, temple rites, and religious myths; and (3) the **Book of the Dead**, which consists of prayers on papyrus scrolls prepared during the New Kingdom and the late period of Egyptian history (the Long Decline).

CREATION MYTHS

Egyptian religion had two main parts: the sacred kingship and the quest for immortality. It was dominated by **polytheism**, the belief in many gods and goddesses, who were often portrayed as natural forces. Although in various parts of Egypt the myths about these gods and goddesses differed in detail, the Egyptians generally perceived the sky as the goddess Nut, whose body was stretched out to form the heavens under which lay the sun, moon, and stars. Nut was supported by Shu, the god of the winds or air. Below Shu was the circular ocean Nun, on which the earth god Geb lay. Part of Geb was red, representing the hostile land of the desert, and part of him was black, representing the Nile delta and valley. According to another account, Nut was supported by the four legs of Hathor, the cow goddess. The sun was perceived as a child who entered the mouth of the sky goddess each evening and was reborn from her lap each dawn. The waters of the Nile were believed to flow down into the land of the dead, the underworld, and the sun took the form of a ship that sailed across the underworld each night.[2]

From these gods and goddesses came the **cosmogonies**, or creation myths. Four were recorded in the Pyramid Texts. Like the other myths, the creation myths also differed in detail, but the basic relationship between sky and earth remained the same, and the significance of the primal hillock, the role of the pharaohs, and the funerary cult changed little for more than 2,000 years. Let us look at the creation myth recorded at Hermopolis.[3]

The Cosmology of Hermopolis

Like many accounts of the origin of the universe, the **cosmology** (account of the universe) of the priests of Hermopolis in Upper Egypt had many deities. Here there were eight: Nun (water) and his wife Naunet, Huh (infinity) and his wife Hauhet, Kuk (darkness) and his wife Kauket, and Amon (air or wind) and his wife Amaunet. Nun was the watery chaos of primeval time stirred by Amon in the act of creation. The four male deities had frogs' heads, and their consorts had serpents' heads, reminiscent of the amphibious creatures that collect in the Nile mud after the annual flood. The city of Hermopolis itself was the primal hillock.

According to one version of this cosmology, the universe hatched from a cosmic egg laid by a heavenly goose known as the "Great Cackler." In another version a lotus flower emerged from the primordial waters. When its petals opened, a divine child was revealed—the sun god Ra. In a third version the lotus opened to reveal a scarab beetle, the symbol of the sun god. The scarab was then transformed into a weeping boy from whose tears humanity was born. Because the lotus opened and closed each day with the sun's rising and setting, it became a symbol of the sun god, who was born from its petals.

Overview of Egyptian Cosmologies

Egyptian cosmologies had the universe originating with a single deity of a primal hillock who created all other things. They typically portrayed Egypt's agricultural cycle as a dependable gift of the gods. They asserted that human life was good and

An enduring symbol of Egypt's Old Kingdom, this great pyramid rises out of the sands of the Sahara with the sphinx in the foreground. This photograph was taken by Francis Frith, c. 1860. (The Metropolitan Museum of Art, gift of Warner Communications, Inc., 1978)

enjoyed divine protection. And they promised the Egyptians a stable existence beyond death.

As we have seen, many of the deities were given animal form. This does not mean that the Egyptians worshiped animals, however. In the ancient world, animal forms were commonly used to characterize and symbolize the sacred. Animal traits conveyed superhuman or transcendent status while symbolically bridging the gap between the human and the divine. The falcon, for example, flew both close to the earth and high in the sky, emphasizing both the distance and the relationship between the human and the divine. Because the falcon was not human, it pointed up the difference between gods and human beings; when it was combined with a human form, it mediated this difference.

The pharaoh was regarded as essential to Egyptian life. Descended from the gods, he was himself a god (though not a "great" god like the higher deities). He was a hero capable of carrying out the age-old ritual of the primal hillock that renewed the power of nature and of government. The pharaoh caused Mayet, the goddess of justice and world order, to continue to exist on earth and served as the ideal mediator between humanity and the gods.

In the tomb of King Horenhab, art on the wall depicts the king talking to the falcon god Horus. (The Bettmann Archive)

POPULAR DEITIES AND BELIEFS

There are countless myths about the deities of Egypt.[4] Horus, the falcon god, was probably the protector of a tribe that entered the Nile valley in predynastic times. Also a warrior god, he was sometimes said to be the son of Ra and at other times the son of Osiris. His main shrine was at Edfu in Upper Egypt, where he had defended Ra's riverboat from hostile crocodiles and hippopotamuses.

Hathor, the great goddess of the sky, was shown as a woman with a cow's face. When Ra's earthly subjects rebelled, the sun god sent his eye against them in the form of Hathor. Turning herself into Sakhmet, the terrible lioness, Hathor tried to devour humanity. To preserve the human species, Ra had his servants set before her great vats of blood-colored beer. After becoming drunk, Hathor gave up the battle and regained her usually friendly disposition. She was generally honored as the goddess of joy and motherhood and as the wife of Horus. Each year their marriage was commemorated when Hathor's image was carried from her main temple at Dendera to that of Horus at Edfu.

Anubis was one of the gods associated with death. Sometimes he was shown as a jackal or a dog and at other times as a man with a jackal's head. His cult was originally confined to Thinis, near Abydos, but it later spread to all of Egypt. At one time Anubis was thought to announce the pharaoh's death by appearing before him with a viper in his hand. He also played an important part in the death of ordinary human beings by supervising the embalming of bodies, receiving mummies in the tomb, and judging the souls of the dead in the underworld.

Bast, a cat goddess of the delta, was the goddess of joy and the fertilizing power of the sun, and her cult was celebrated in processions of barges in the waters of the Nile estuary. Because of her influence the Egyptians regarded cats as sacred animals. A huge cemetery of mummified cats has been found at Bubastis. When the pharaohs of the twenty-second dynasty established their capital near Bubastis, they made Bast into a state deity and restored her temples.

Immortality and the Cult of Osiris

The Egyptians were fascinated by the idea of immortality. During the Old Kingdom period the immortal pharaoh was thought to be able to extend the gift of life beyond the grave to members of his family and high court officials. (Respect for his spirit after death led to the practice of mummification and the building of the elaborate tombs known as pyramids.) The rest of humanity could look forward only to a gloomy existence in the underworld among the ghosts of the dead. All this changed, however, toward the end of the Old Kingdom period when a new religious devotion became popular with Egyptians of all social classes, the cult of Osiris.

Osiris has been described as the most vivid and complex achievement of the Egyptian imagination and is similar to other Near Eastern agricultural fertility deities (for example, the Canaanite Baal). He was especially loved by the common people. To villagers anxiously awaiting the annual floodwaters, Osiris offered hope of both fertility for the land and survival after death.

The Osiris myth, which first appears in the Pyramid Texts, has been told in its entirety only by Plutarch, a Greek writer of the second century C.E. According to his version, the sky god Geb and the earth goddess Nut had two sons, Osiris and Seth, and two daughters, Isis and Nephthys. Isis became the bride of Osiris, and Nephthys was married to Seth. Ruling as Egypt's divine king, Osiris civilized his subjects, teaching them to raise grains and to worship the high gods. His reign was a golden age. One day, however, Osiris's envious brother Seth invited the king to a banquet at which Osiris was persuaded to get into a coffinlike box. Seth and his helpers quickly shut the lid and threw the box into the Nile, where it floated down to the Mediterranean and eventually washed up on the Syrian shore near Byblos. Osiris's dead body inside was found by his faithful wife, Isis, who carried it back to Egypt.

Seth then appeared and cut Osiris's body into many parts, which he scattered all over Egypt. But with the help of Nephthys, Isis found the parts, and the two of them constructed the first mummy from his body. Although unable to bring Osiris back to life, Isis was still able to conceive by him a son, Horus. The places in Egypt where the parts of the god's body were found became shrines, and Osiris was mourned as a handsome young god slain in his prime.

Horus led his father's supporters in a fierce war against Seth and his forces. Ultimately the victor, Horus reigned over Egypt, and Osiris ruled the underworld.

The respect that Horus showed his dead father was symbolized by the devotion that the living pharaoh (who was identified with Horus) showed his dead predecessor (identified with Osiris). Osiris was beloved for 3,000 years because of his gifts of immortality and the fertility of the soil, and Isis was honored as the model of womanly dignity and marital fidelity.

Journey to the Underworld

Devotion to Osiris increased during the Middle and New Kingdom periods. Even though another god, Amon-Ra, was declared the supreme deity by the pharaohs and the priestly elite, Osiris's popularity grew until he was worshiped in the late period of Egyptian history as the lord of the whole universe.

The common people believed that their love of Osiris would offer them a better afterlife than their ancestors had known. They conceived of the underworld as a region parallel to and partly beneath the Nile valley, into which the souls of the dead entered by going through a series of gates that opened only in response to secret passwords. Here the spirits were led into the hall of judgment, where Mayet, the goddess of order and justice, presided over a great set of scales. On one side was placed the heart of the dead person and on the other a feather, Mayet's symbol. During the weighing ceremony, conducted by Anubis, the deceased urged his or her heart not to reveal transgressions committed on earth, such as lying, pride, or treason. If the heart and the feather were in balance, the dead person was pronounced "justified."

The emphasis was on how the dead had carried out their civic obligations rather than ethical concerns. Guilty spirits were torn to bits by a fierce monster that was part crocodile, part lion, and part hippopotamus. Righteous spirits were led by Thoth before the throne of Osiris, who allowed them to enter the kingdom of the blessed. Here the Egyptians expected to be united with their families and friends and looked forward to a pleasant existence much like, though inferior to, the one they had known in Egypt.

The tombs of the pharaohs of the archaic period contain some evidence of human sacrifice. This practice, traces of which have also been found in Mesopo-

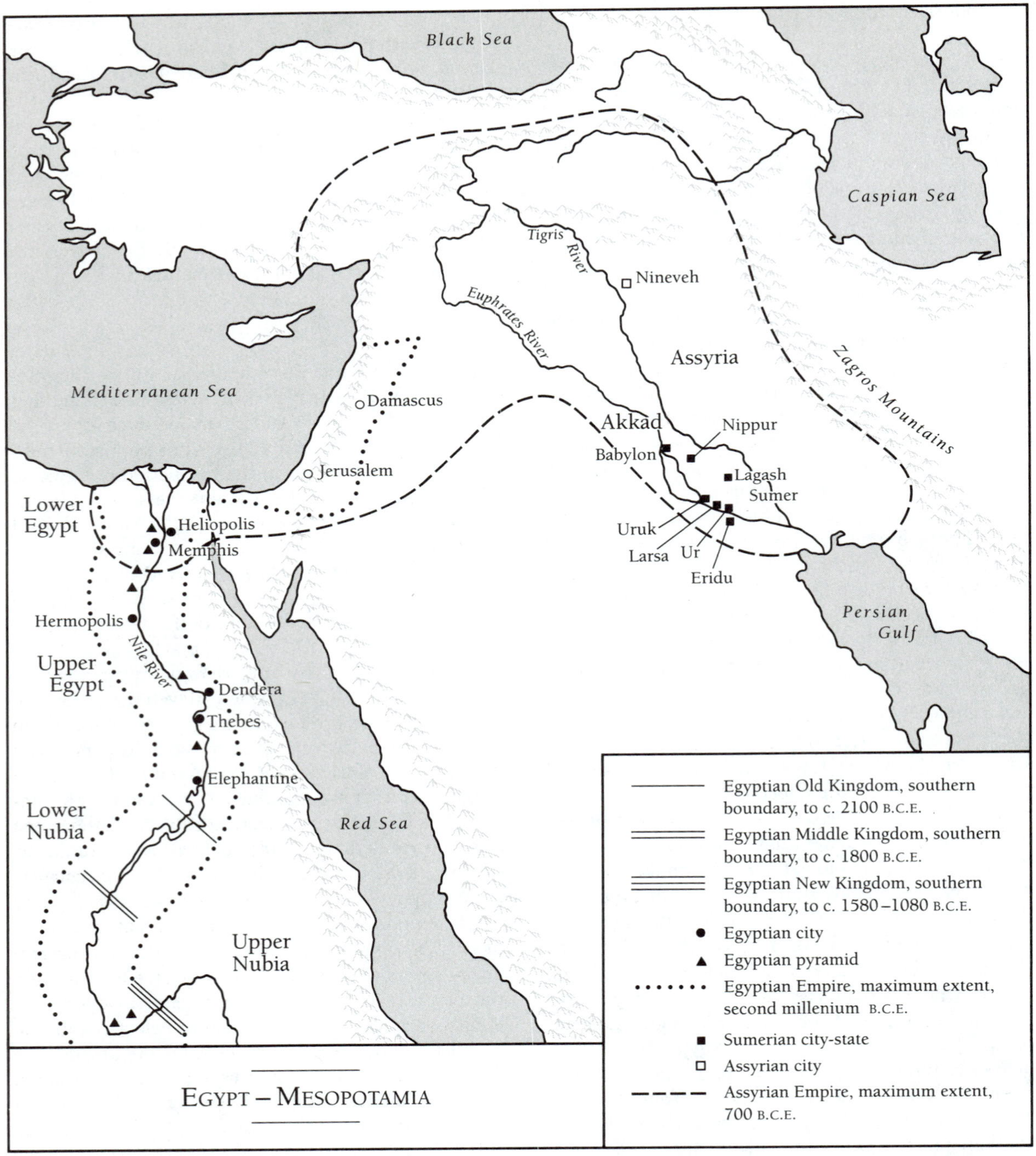

EGYPT – MESOPOTAMIA

tamia and in China, disappeared during Egypt's Old Kingdom period. Like other peoples, the Egyptians substituted small figurines *(ushabtis)* of wood, stone, or pottery, which were placed in the tombs to perform all the services required by their masters and mistresses in eternity.

Survivors regularly visited the family graves, bringing offerings of food and drink and conducting elaborate rites to ensure the deceased's immortality. The soul was believed to consist of three elements: (1) the *Ka,* a twin separated at birth and reunited at death that lived on in the tomb and required food offerings to survive; (2) the *Ba,* the spiritual aspect of a person, depicted as a bird that at death was thought to fly off to heaven; and (3) the *Akh,* the dead person's ghost, which wandered through the kingdom of the blessed reflecting the person's deeds on earth.

Akhenaton, the Religious Innovator

During the New Kingdom period a revolutionary ruler, Akhenaton (ruled c. 1369–1353 B.C.E.), briefly challenged Egypt's ingrained conservatism and polytheism. He ascended the throne as Amenhotep IV, which means "Aton is satisfied," but changed his name to "Glory to Aton" to announce his faith in Aton, the creative principle of the sun, as Egypt's sole god.

Attacking the power of the priests of Amon-Ra at Thebes, Akhenaton defaced the monuments of their god and inaugurated a cultural revolution. But despite the existing unifying and monotheistic trends in the Egyptian religion, Akhenaton's beliefs contradicted Egypt's tradition of tolerance, and his excessive zeal, combined with administrative and military failures, doomed his reforms. After Akhenaton's death his name and symbols were removed from the monuments, and the priests quickly recovered their old authority. The cult of Osiris gradually surpassed in importance that of Amon-Ra, and Osiris himself gradually took on some of the characteristics of the sun god.

THE LEGACY OF EGYPTIAN RELIGION

During the second millennium B.C.E., respect for Egyptian achievements in the arts, sciences, and religion spread throughout the Mediterranean world. The Hebrew Bible refers to the "wisdom of Egypt," and early Greek philosophers like Thales and Pythagoras reportedly studied geometry in Egypt. Osiris and Isis were numbered among the official gods of the Roman Empire, and the promise of immortality in the Osiris myth may have influenced the Orphic mysteries of ancient Greece and prepared the way for Christianity. Furthermore, the Egyptian concept of Mayet, or world order, may have influenced the philosophy of the Stoics, as well as the Logos of Saint John's gospel.

Egyptian influences have survived to the present. Statues of Isis with the infant Horus in her arms are thought to have inspired the Madonna and child motif of the Christian tradition. Masonic ritual still keeps alive the memory of Egypt, as does the popular belief in spells, oracles, and astrological lore. In addition, the idea that divine wisdom or revelation should be written down and collected and that written books (scrolls) have greater prestige than oral traditions does seem to be largely an Egyptian invention. It was a popular assumption among the Greeks and Romans that books of revelation came from Egypt.

MESOPOTAMIA: POWER CONFLICTS AND ORDER

About 3500 B.C.E. a great civilization began to develop in Mesopotamia on the hot, dry plain through which the Tigris and Euphrates rivers flow into the Persian Gulf. Bounded on the northeast by the Zagros Mountains and on the southwest by the Arabian Desert, the region corresponds roughly to present-day Iraq. The surviving monuments of this ancient culture are few: its mud brick temples and palaces have crumbled into heaps of rubble, and the remnants of its once flourishing cities are negligible compared with what remains of ancient Egypt's structures. Archaeologists have succeeded in uncovering the outlines of vanished cities and canals.

Amid ruins of temples and palaces they have unearthed vast libraries of religious, commercial, and political records. Hundreds of thousands of clay tablets with cuneiform (wedge-shaped) inscriptions provide valuable insights into the history and beliefs of the early Mesopotamians. Thorkild Jacobsen, an authority on ancient Mesopotamia, pinpointed the great differ-

Cuneiform writing was an invention of the Sumerians. These tablets record business transactions in Babylonia during the sixth century B.C.E. (The Metropolitan Museum of Art, gift of Matilda W. Bruce, 1907)

ence between Egypt's geographic security and the exposed location of the Tigris-Euphrates valley:

> Mesopotamian civilization grew up in an environment which was signally different. We find there, of course, the same great cosmic rhythms—the change of the seasons, the unwavering sweep of sun, moon and stars—but we also find an element of force and violence which was lacking in Egypt. The Tigris and Euphrates are not like the Nile; they may rise unpredictably and fitfully, breaking man's dykes and submerging his crops. There are scorching winds which smother man in the dust, threaten to suffocate him; there are torrential rains which turn all firm ground into a sea of mud and rob man of his freedom and movement; all travel bogs down. Here in Mesopotamia, nature stays not her hand; in her full might she cuts across and overrides man's will, makes him feel to the full how slightly he matters.[5]

By 6000 B.C.E. there were villages on the Mesopotamian plain and adjacent hills. Some of these communities were pastoral, others were agricultural, and still others were a mix of the two. After 4000 B.C.E., farmers began to build irrigation canals close to the riverbanks in order to control the floodwaters. Later, as the advantages of a continuous artificial water supply became obvious, the canals and ditches increased in complexity.

The population expanded, and by the time the first written records were compiled, between 3500 and 3000 B.C.E., an elaborate social system had developed. People of different backgrounds and languages lived side by side. But unlike Egypt, Mesopotamia was politically unstable, and despite cultural exchanges, there was much rivalry between the Sumerians of the south and the Akkadians of the north.[6]

SUMER AND AKKAD

No one knows exactly where the Sumerians' original homeland was in the southernmost area of Mesopotamia. Their language was not an Indo-European dialect, nor was it related to the Semitic speech of the Akkadians. The Sumerians were a highly creative and innovative people who perfected the potter's wheel, designed ox-drawn plows, and invented cuneiform writing. Cuneiform was written with a reed stylus on a wet clay tablet, which when fired became a durable record. The Sumerians were also busy traders, and their sailboats and rafts crisscrossed the bayous and lagoons of Sumer and visited points along the Persian Gulf; their pack trains followed overland routes into Asia Minor. From distant lands the traders brought back stone, metal ores, and timber—materials in short supply in their own land.[7]

The flat landscape was dominated by ziggurats—tall, pyramidal temple towers with stairways leading to a shrine at the top. Surrounded by farms and orchards, the temples were an important part of the social and religious life of Sumer's urban centers—communities like Eridu, Uruk (or Erech), Lagash, Larsa, Nippur, and Ur, which were history's first city-states.

At first the city-state was regarded, at least in theory, as the property of its chief god. In practice, however, much of the territory was privately owned by great landlords or small farmers and was controlled by an assembly of free male citizens who elected a governor *(ensi)* with limited powers. As the struggle for power among the city-states and the external threat from the barbarians of nearby deserts and mountains grew, the assembly sometimes chose a king, the *lugal,* to be their military leader in times of danger. This king was empowered to raise and train an army of infantrymen and charioteers. Eventually the king's position was made hereditary, and the royal palace became a center of influence equal to that of the temples.[8]

At Lagash, and possibly in other communities, there was a power struggle between the palace and the temple, which was won by the king. To justify his assumption of supreme authority, the king claimed to be able to protect the ordinary citizens from the priests'

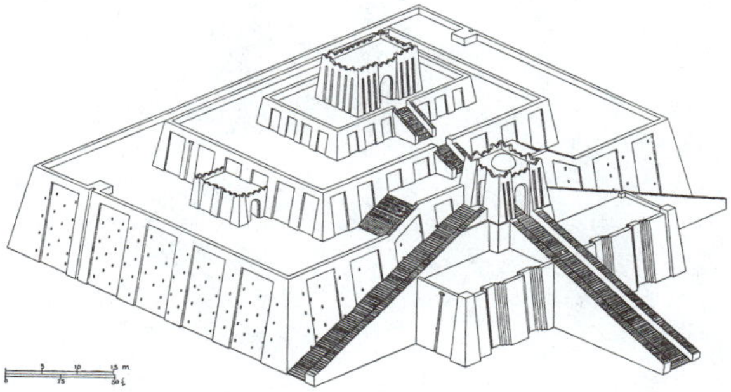

The flat landscape of Mesopotamia was dominated by ziggurats. This photo is of the remains of the great ziggurat of Ur-Nammu. The drawing illustrates how the complete ziggurat probably appeared. (The Granger Collection)

oppression and bolstered his assertion with religious ritual.[9]

Around 2060 B.C.E., Ur Nammu, the king of the old Sumerian city of Ur, established the Neo-Sumerian Empire, which lasted for a century. He issued the first known law code, which proclaimed him a divinely appointed ruler called to bring justice to the whole realm.

Religion in Sumer and Akkad

Both archaeological and textual data on the religious beliefs of the early Sumerian civilization survive.[10] A typical temple was constructed of mud bricks and adorned with buttresses and many small cones of different colors. Inside was a niche for the image of the deity, in front of which was an offering table. The early sanctuaries were simple in style, but the later temples contained spacious courts, rooms for attendant priests, and a ziggurat.

Three types of textual materials have been discovered: prayers, descriptions of the rituals conducted by the priests, and mythological literature. The prayers were always associated with specific rites to be performed by the person offering the prayers or by a priest attached to the sanctuary. The prayers consisted of invocations to the gods, requests for assistance, and expressions of gratitude for past favors or for dangers averted. As a rule, the worshipers did not emphasize such spiritual or moral topics as death, survival, and contact with the divine.

The mythological literature is difficult for present-day readers to understand, and we do not know the extent to which such myths reflect early religious beliefs.

At its beginning, Mesopotamian religion expressed harmony between humanity and the natural powers on which it depended for survival. The Sumerians recognized thousands of deities, many of whom were associated with the earth and the sky, plants and grains, and herds and flocks. Some of the deities had human forms, and others had plant or animal forms. As time went on, the gods and goddesses were increasingly shown as having human forms. According to Jacobsen, the plant and animal forms represented powers of nature that were gradually transformed into anthropomorphic images. Later the older nonhuman forms were regarded as the divine emblems that accompanied a deity. For example, the sun disk came to symbolize the sun god Uto, who had a human form.[11]

Pluralism and Polytheism

The deities were accepted as a pluralistic power fragmented and distributed in various places. They were associated with the natural forces and various livelihoods and reflected the political pluralism of the city-states. As the rulers of the cities, the deities were believed responsible for the welfare of the whole community. The Sumerians and Akkadians saw their gods and goddesses as living in a kind of democracy, and at a gathering similar to the early city assembly all the deities met under the leadership of An, the god of the sky, and Enlil, the god of the wind and air, to decide the fate of the city-states and their rulers.[12]

The cosmos, or nature, was viewed as a multitude of divergent and conflicting wills in which order could be maintained only if these forces were kept in harmony.[13] Many of the cosmos's powers were associated with four major deities. At first the Sumerians considered An, the god of the sky, leader of the heavenly assembly. His authority was represented by his scepter, crown, and shepherd's staff, and his symbols were a star and the number 60, the basis of the Sumerian system of calculation. (We still divide the hour into 60 minutes.) An's center was at Uruk, but because he was such a remote figure, he eventually lost his influence.

Enlil, the god of the air and storms, gradually took over the paramount position. Known as the "father of the gods" and the "king of heaven and earth," Enlil carried out the decrees of all the other deities. Although feared because of his power to unleash destructive storms, he was also loved as the guardian of Sumer.

Another of the leading Sumerian deities was the goddess Ninhursag, or Ninmah ("exalted lady"), revered as the mother of all creatures and associated with the stony and rock regions of the earth. Among her children were the wild asses of the desert. Her main centers were Adab and Kish.

Another well-known goddess was Ashtar, the goddess of the morning and evening star. Ashtar had a long history as the goddess of love and fertility. She was Ishtar to the Babylonians, Astarte to the Phoenicians, Aphrodite to the Greeks, and Venus to the Romans.

BABYLONIA AND ASSYRIA

The Neo-Sumerian Empire came to an end about 1950 B.C.E. with an invasion by the Elamite people of the Zagros Mountains. Later Hammurabi, the king of the Amorites in the west, conquered Mesopotamia and built his capital at Babylon on the Euphrates River. Hammurabi (ruled c. 1792–1750 B.C.E.) was an energetic ruler who drew up a code of law aimed at achieving a just society, based on the concept of fair punishment.

But Hammurabi's prosperous society did not last long, and at this point the history of this area becomes one of repeated conquests by alien peoples. In the sixteenth century B.C.E. the empire was taken over by the Hittites (possibly an Indo-European people) and later the Kassites, from the northwest. Finally it was dominated by the Assyrians, who ultimately assembled a great empire extending as far west as Egypt. But they were in turn overthrown by the Medes and the Chaldeans.

King Hammurabi ruled Mesopotamia in the eighteenth century B.C.E. and is remembered for his code of law aimed at achieving a just society based on fair punishment. Hammurabi is shown receiving the law from the hand of the Sun God in this ancient relief. (The Bettmann Archive)

This decline of 1,000 years ended, and Mesopotamia's fortunes turned more favorable, when Nebuchadnezzar (ruled 605–562 B.C.E.), the king of the Chaldeans, rebuilt Babylon as the capital of the Chaldean, or Neo-Babylonian, Empire. Babylon again became the center of a mighty realm. Nebuchadnezzar continued the Assyrian custom of removing the inhabitants of newly conquered provinces, and in 586 B.C.E. the king of Judea and many inhabitants of Jerusalem were taken captive to Babylon. At this time Babylon was transformed into a city of great splendor, surrounded by walls and terraced gardens, the famous "hanging gardens" counted among the wonders of the ancient world. Nebuchadnezzar erected a seven-story ziggurat 300 feet high that is believed to have inspired the Hebrew Bible story of the Tower of Babel.

Religion in Babylonia and Assyria

The Babylonians and Assyrians retained the deities and rites of the Sumerians and Akkadians, and Sumerian continued as the ritual language long after it had been replaced in everyday affairs by the Semitic tongues of the new conquerors. An and Enlil, the old high gods, were treated with respect, but after the Babylonian conquest their position of leadership in the assembly of the gods was assumed by Marduk, the chief god of Babylonia. Marduk was the absolute lord of heaven, just as the Babylonian king was the absolute ruler of the earth. Later Marduk was replaced by Ashur, the supreme and absolute deity of Assyria.

The king was still considered the servant of the high god and a vessel of sacred power, but sometimes he was thought of as only semidivine. As the distance between the people and their imperial leader grew, so also did the distance between humans and the gods. "Personal" deities—sacred beings of limited power who took a personal interest in their worshipers and conveyed their concerns to the higher divinities—began to appear in contemporary writings.

The Epic of Creation

A Mesopotamian poem known as the *Epic of Creation*, written in the second millennium B.C.E., tells how the young god Marduk and his companions succeeded in vanquishing the forces of chaos led by the sea goddess Ti'amat and the demon Kingu. It also describes the early watery chaos before the formation of the world.

Three intermingled elements were personified as water deities: Apsu represented the sweet waters; Ti'amat, the sea; and Mummy, most likely the cloud banks and mists. The world began in conflict, alluding to the formation of new lands in an alluvial region. Apsu married Ti'amat to symbolize the coming together of the sweet waters of the rivers and the salt waters of the sea. The cloud banks hung low, and the primeval silt built up. As the waters separated, the gods danced on Ti'amat's belly.

The conflict surrounding the beginning of the world was between an earlier inertia and the new deities who advanced the process of creation. Disturbed by the noise of the younger gods, Apsu wanted to kill them. But the water god Enki put him into a deep sleep, tied him up, and killed him.

Ti'amat, Apsu's now angry widow, created monsters, snakes, and demons. Giving the tablets of destiny to her second husband, Kingu, she started a war. The sky god An, the old Sumerian chief deity, tried to subdue her, but only Marduk, the champion of the Babylonians, was powerful enough to overcome her. As his price he demanded absolute authority over the assembly of the gods, which they granted him.

The struggle was fearful: Marduk split the goddess's skull and cut her corpse in two, one half becoming the sky, the other the earth. The Tigris and Euphrates rivers flowed from her eyes. Next Marduk snatched the tablets of destiny from Kingu and tied him up. Kingu died when his veins were cut, and from his blood, mixed with clay, humanity was created. After Marduk had reorganized the world, the gods swore "benefits and obedience" to him, a permanent fealty that was the mythological counterpart of absolute human monarchy as well as its justification.

The Temple Cult

The temple was an important part of Mesopotamian life. The temple lands with their farms and orchards were proof of the presence of the god or goddess. Priests were organized into corporations to serve the deity, and schools were organized to teach future priests the skills they would need, such as writing and arithmetic. Apprentices were trained to copy the old myths over and over.

Just as servants were bound to their masters, the Mesopotamians felt bound to their gods and offered them food and drink, recited hymns of praise, and requested divine attention and favor. To discern the will of the deities in regard to the specific concerns of the worshipers, several methods of divination were devised, including examination of the livers of sacrificial animals and interpretation of dreams and omens. Rites were designed to thwart evil omens. The flight of birds and the movements of heavenly bodies were observed. In addition, the deities were believed to predict, through prophets, the future of human beings. (Divination techniques in most religions had a common structure: after invoking the attention of the deity, a chance or random device—for example, casting lots—was used in the expectation that the deity would intervene to determine the outcome.)

Stories were also told about Dumuzi, the god of fertility, and Inanna, the goddess of storehouses and the queen of heaven.

Gilgamesh

Perhaps the best-known Babylonian legend is the *Epic of Gilgamesh,* a poem written in its present form in about 2000 B.C.E. It is a morality tale about Gilgamesh, the haughty king of Uruk, who ruled so harshly that his subjects begged the gods to send them a savior. In response, the gods fashioned a wild man named Enkidu who was full of vitality and enjoyed chasing panthers for sport.

At first Gilgamesh and Enkidu fought each other fiercely, but they became fast friends and heroic adventurers. Among their exploits was the killing of a fearful monster who guarded the forest of the wind god Enlil.

The themes of destiny and immortality were struck when Enlil condemned Enkidu to die. Gilgamesh lamented his friend's death in words of great affection.

For seven days and seven nights Gilgamesh mourned his friend, and then he set out on a journey to look for immortality. On his way he met a woman who ran a tavern, who proclaimed the futility of his quest:

Gilgamesh, wither are you wandering?
Life, which you look for, you will never find.
For when the gods created man, they let
death be his share, and life
withheld in their own hands.[14]

Traveling beyond the waters of death, Gilgamesh encountered one of his ancestors, Utnapishtim (a prototype of Noah in the Old Testament), who told him the story of the flood (a myth present in many religious traditions). Warned that the gods were planning to destroy all life on earth by means of a deluge, Utnapishtim built a big boat and, before the rains fell, took refuge on it with his wife and two of all the animals. The ark kept them safe, and as the waters receded, it came to rest on a mountaintop. Emerging unharmed, Utnapishtim offered a sacrifice to the gods. The wind god Enlil, who had encouraged the gods to send the flood, thereupon regretted his harsh treatment of humans and animals, and to make amends he sent Utnapishtim and his wife to a distant land and conferred on them the gift of immortality.

After this interlude about the flood, the epic returns to the adventures of Gilgamesh, who remained for six days and six nights in Utnapishtim's house. His relatives offered him magical food and told him about the plant of immortality that grew at the bottom of the sea. This plant was so tough that it could tear human hands, but it gave eternal life to those who ate from it. Gilgamesh left in the boat of Utnapishtim's ferryman. Pausing midway on his journey back to the mortal shore, Gilgamesh dived into the water and brought up the plant of immortality.

Gilgamesh made the mistake of pausing to bathe and refresh himself. While his attention was diverted, a snake stole the plant, ate from it, and obtained immortality (symbolized in its shedding its skin and being "reborn"). Gilgamesh had lost the means to restore his friend to life.

The *Epic of Gilgamesh* is an entertaining story that is deliberately unresolved. It represents the futile struggle against evil and death, the loss of which is seen as mainly an accident of fate. According to the Mesopotamian view, human beings are helpless, their sufferings beyond understanding, and like the Dumuzi myth, the story of Gilgamesh is appropriately a lament, a literary form first used in Mesopotamia.

THE LEGACY OF MESOPOTAMIAN RELIGION

The myths of Mesopotamia had an extensive influence on the Greek, Judeo-Christian, and other traditions, including the biblical accounts of the creation of the universe and humanity, the Flood, and the Tower of Babel. Traces of the birth account of Sargon the Great may be found in the stories of the births of Moses and Jesus, as well as of Kṛishṇa in India. The Sumerian literary lament also appears in the penitential Psalms and the complaints of Job and Jeremiah. The Mesopotamian techniques of divination and astrology passed into the common legacy, as reflected in the Gospel of Matthew's tale of the Magi, wise men from the east who followed a star that led them to Jesus, the newborn king of the Jews.

ZOROASTRIANISM: THE BATTLE BETWEEN GOOD AND EVIL

In the sixth century B.C.E., **Zarathustra** (in Greek, **Zoroaster**), the great prophet of Persia, brought the message of a supreme God, **Ahura Mazda**, who commanded all human beings to join the forces of good in the struggle against the forces of evil.

Zarathustra's genius was in symbolizing clearly and powerfully the duality between truth and lie, good and evil, light and dark, investing it with new moral meaning. The world has witnessed many variations on the theme of dualism, among them the cosmic yin-yang, positive-negative dualism in China and the more ascetic matter-spirit dualism in India. Unlike these religions, Zarathustra's approach was primarily ethical. From his perception developed a paradigm that profoundly influenced a number of later religions.

HISTORICAL ROOTS

By the sixth century B.C.E., religion in ancient Persia, like that of the ancient Vedic people in India, had been influenced by the traditions that the Indo-European invaders brought with them around 1500 B.C.E. The Indo-Persians recognized two kinds of gods: the *daevas* (*dei* in Latin), or heavenly beings, and the *asura* or *ahuras,* or beings with occult powers. Later in India the Sanskrit term *asura* came to mean a kind of demon. In Persia, however, the *ahuras* were raised to the heavenly sphere, whereas the *daevas* were reduced to the status of evil spirits.

ZARATHUSTRA'S CAREER

Of all the founders of the world's leading faiths, Zarathustra is probably the most difficult to date chronologically. He is commonly reported to have lived in the sixth century B.C.E., but some scholars have placed him as much as half a century earlier. His career is known to us mainly from the ***gāthās,*** hymns ascribed to Zarathustra himself that make up the oldest part of his followers' sacred book, the Avesta. Persia was then

Zarathustra (or Zoroaster) brought the message of a supreme God, Ahura Mazda, to the people of Persia in the sixth century B.C.E. This reconstruction by D. F. Karaka is recognized by experts as the most authentic image of Zarathustra. (The Bettmann Archive)

largely a society of cattle raisers and farmers who were frequently attacked by marauding nomads. Zarathustra's message was one of protest against the abuse of authority and the dominant cult. Throughout his lifetime he fought a priesthood that he saw as oppressive. Thus he was from the start the prophet for a powerless and disenfranchised people. But even after he converted members of the royal court, he retained his connections with herdsmen and rural society. His beliefs were not compromised when he joined the power elite who served the monarchy.

According to legend, Zarathustra was born at Rhages, a town near present-day Tehran. The third of five sons in a family of poor warriors, he showed a religious bent and was trained to conduct sacrifices and intone sacred chants. At the age of 20 he left his parents' home to meditate in the mountains. When he was 30 years old—a significant age for many spiritual leaders—he had his first vision.

Zarathustra was freed from his material body and raised up to the court of heaven. There Ahura Mazda revealed that he was opposed by **Aura Mainyu**, the spirit and promoter of evil, and charged Zarathustra with the task of calling all human beings to choose between him (good) and Aura Mainyu (evil). The prophet continued to receive revelations from six archangels whom he regarded as aspects of Ahura Mazda. Zarathustra's God remained a mighty, somewhat abstract being:

> He that in the beginning thus thought, "Let the blessed realms be filled with lights," he it is that by his wisdom created Right. . . . I conceived of thee, O Mazdah, in my thought that thou, the First, art [also] the Last, that thou art father of Good Thought . . . and art the Lord to judge the actions of life.[15]

Partly as a result of this vision, the prophet enjoined his listeners to lead ethical lives under the direction of Good Thought. Those who joined the worldwide struggle on behalf of the good would gain prosperity in this world and immortality in the next. After the day of judgment and the final victory of Ahura Mazda's forces, the earth would be purified and the forces of evil destroyed.

In organizing the new religion, Zarathustra forbade sacrifices in honor of Aura Mainyu and his associates, who were identified as daevas, and animal sacrifices combined with drinking the intoxicating ***haoma*** because this practice often led to drunkenness and sexual excesses. But the prophet did not abolish all sacrifices, only those that honored evil spirits or involved haoma. He also retained the ancient cult of fire, which he identified with purity, and its associated fire temples. Despite the support of the king, Zarathustra encountered resistance among the *magi* (priests) of the old gods and their adherents. According to some authorities, he died while defending a fire temple from an attack by his enemies.

EARLY ZOROASTRIANISM

Our main source for Zoroastrianism is the **Avesta**, or **Book of the Law**, a fragmentary and obscure collection of sacred writings divided into four parts: (1) the *Yasna,* liturgical works written in old Persian that include the gāthās; (2) the *Visperad,* invocations and rituals to be used at festivals honoring the ahuras; (3) the *Yashts,* hymns of praise; and (4) the *Videvdat* or *Vendidat,* spells against demons and prescriptions for purification.

Compiled over many centuries, the Avesta was not completed until the second period of the Persian Empire under the Sassanid dynasty (established in 226 C.E.). Only about one-fourth of the Avesta has survived. In the ninth century C.E., after the Muslim conquest, the *Bundahishn,* an account of the creation and structure of the world, and the *Denkart,* a compendium of religious lore that includes a summary of the Avesta, were prepared.

BELIEFS OF EARLY ZOROASTRIANISM

The Avesta framed Zarathustra's dualistic message in terms of Ahura Mazda and his attendant ahuras (divine beings) who opposed the daevas (evil forces) and stressed the moral difference between truth *(asha)* and falsehood *(druj)*. Particularly noteworthy in early Zoroastrianism were the emphasis on people's freedom to choose between good and evil, which is affirmed with uncompromising single-mindedness, and the introduction of a dynamic and linear view of time.

Zarathustra departed from the old Indo-Persian polytheism through his elevation of the worship of Ahura Mazda to virtual monotheism. As we shall see, however, monotheism in Zoroastrianism never took on the absoluteness that it assumed in Judaism and Islam. But Zoroastrianism held that only Ahura Mazda, the highest god, was worthy of worship. The gāthās portrayed him as the creator of heaven and earth, the source of the moral order, and the judge of all humanity. The followers of Aura Mainyu were by definition evil because they chose him, and hence darkness, the lie, and evil, of their own free will.

Zoroastrian ethical dualism is also reflected in its cosmology. According to Zarathustra, at the beginning there was a meeting of two spirits, Spenta Mainyu (the holy spirit) and Aura Mainyu (the destructive spirit), who were, like humans, free to choose "life" or "not life." From this choice arose the principle of good that corresponded to the Kingdom of the Truth and the contrary spirit of evil that corresponded to the Kingdom of the Lie, which was populated by the daevas. This dualism is subsumed under monotheism—a single all-powerful God—because, according to the gāthās, Ahura Mazda was the father of both spirits and allowed them to split into opposing principles.

The Zoroastrian struggle between good and evil involved neither determinism (the belief that all acts are under divine control) nor predestination (the belief that all events, including one's destiny, are divinely determined in advance). Zarathustra emphasized that human beings remain free to choose the rule of the Wise Lord or that of Aura Mainyu and the Lie. Through good deeds the righteous could earn an everlasting reward of integrity and immortality, but those who chose the Lie were condemned by their own conscience and by the judgment of the Wise Lord to a state of punishment similar to the Christian hell. A decision made could not be reversed.

A person's every act, word, and thought affected his or her life after death. In Zarathustra's vision, there will come a day of judgment at the end of time when the world will be destroyed by fire and molten metal and then renewed, with the virtuous receiving an eternal reward and the evil condemned to everlasting torment.

After death the individual soul is judged by Ahura Mazda. Each has to step onto the Bridge of the Separator, but only the righteous can cross in safety to enter a kingdom of eternal joy and light. Evil souls tumble from the bridge into a realm of darkness, where they will remain until the visible world comes to an end during the final conflict between good and evil. After the destruction of Aura Mainyu and the forces of evil, the universe is to be renewed in splendor, and the righteous will live forever in paradise.

This doctrine implies a linear concept of time, progressing from creation (past) to our decision (present) to the day of judgment (future), that influenced the Jewish, Christian, and Muslim notions. It is a sharp departure from the cyclical pattern seen in older religions. It emphasizes the future consequences of every present act. Indeed, Zarathustra's own concerns seem always to have centered on the ultimate rewards for actions. Ahura Mazda will reward ethical behavior even if the consequences are not immediately apparent.

LATER ZOROASTRIANISM

It is not clear how or precisely when Zoroastrianism became the religion of the Persian Empire. We do know that it developed into a state religion under the rulers of the Achaemenid dynasty.

Alexander the Great (ruled 336–323 B.C.E.) invaded the Persian Empire, and in 331 B.C.E. the Greek army defeated the forces of Darius III (ruled 336–330 B.C.E.), the last of the Achaemenid rulers. During the ensuing 500 years of Greek rule and Hellenism, Zoroastrianism virtually disappeared.

But in the third century C.E. arose a new Persian dynasty, the Sassanid, whose rulers were committed to reestablishing the Persian Empire. During the Sassanid period there were substantial religious changes and innovations, many of which Zarathustra doubtless would have opposed. The principal ones were these:

1 *The revival of dualism.* The new religion still focused on the contest between good and evil for the control of the universe, but Ahura Mazda, now known as Ormazd, was placed on relatively equal terms with Ahriman, the name by which Aura Mainyu was henceforth known. Some theologians even tried to explain the existence of evil by attributing all power to Zurvan (Time), a supreme God who had sired both Ormazd and Ahriman.

2 *The revival of the old Indo-Persian deities.* In the Achaemenid period, Mithra, the god of light, and Anahita, the goddess of water and the moon, were worshiped, and their cults and those of other deities were acknowledged in the fire temples.
3 *New religious emphases.* The cosmos was still viewed as a battleground between the forces of good led by Ormazd and those of evil led by Ahriman. It was Ormazd who in the course of the struggle created the earth. Finally, humanity was regarded as participating in immortality. But Zoroastrianism now conceived of a dualism between body and soul in addition to the dualism between good and evil. They were not parallel. In the religion, there was no suggestion that the soul was associated with good and the body with evil.

The Sassanids retained the linear concept of time, which became divided into four periods of history, each lasting 3,000 years. The first three periods were construed as an era of struggle between the forces of good and evil, but in the last period a savior would come to lead the forces of good to victory. According to some authorities this savior would be Zarathustra himself. According to others his three sons—born miraculously at intervals of 1,000 years—would come down to earth. On judgment day the bodies of the dead were to arise and share in the eternal bliss or sorrow of the souls.

Manichaeism

Shortly after the establishment of the Sassanid dynasty, Mani (c. 216–276 C.E.), a wandering preacher from Mesopotamia, began to teach an extreme form of dualism that combined elements of Zoroastrianism and other Persian religions with concepts of Buddhist and Christian origin. To Mani the world was divided between the forces of light (God's kingdom) and the forces of darkness (Satan's kingdom). For a time Mani was allowed to make converts in the Persian Empire, but later the magi denounced him and his followers as heretics. Around 276 C.E. he reportedly became a martyr.

The religion Mani established, **Manichaeism**, became an important spiritual force in the West: Augustine spent his early years as a Manichean (later turning against his former religion). In medieval Europe, Manichaeism became popular for a time among the Albigenses of southern France.

ZOROASTRIANISM TODAY

The old religion survives today only among some 10,000 Gabors—their name means "infidel" to the dominant Muslims—in Iran. About 120,000 **Parsis** live in India and still revere the Avesta and Zoroastrianism's other sacred writings. In 637 C.E. an army of Muslim invaders destroyed the Sassanid Empire. After the empire was incorporated into the new world of Islam, most Persians adopted the religion of their conquerors through either persuasion or persecution, and Zoroastrianism declined in vitality. Today, successful in trade and industry, the Parsis are a close-knit community and live primarily in the Bombay area. Thanks to well-supported schools, they are among the best-educated groups in India.

Priests hold ceremonies of worship and purification in fire temples, which are generally inconspicuous buildings. Officiating priests are members of a hereditary body descended from the magi priesthood. A special group of priests care for the sacred fire, which is kept in an urn on a four-legged stone pedestal inside the temple. At least five times each day the sacred flame must be fed to keep it from going out.

The main ceremony, the *Yasna,* consists of a sacrifice before the sacred flame. Offerings of bread and milk are made while portions of the Avesta are recited. Lay worshipers come by themselves to the sanctuary. After washing, they remove their shoes, give offerings of money and sandalwood to the priests, and recite prayers. They then leave the sanctuary without turning their backs to the sacred flame. Despite the reverence shown to fire, Parsis are not fire worshipers. They regard it, like water and air, as a purifying element.

Parsi funeral practices, one of the world's most unusual, are hauntingly beautiful. Any contact with dead bodies or other impure objects is thought to contaminate; thus burial in the earth or cremation could contaminate air, fire, water, or earth. After a brief mourning period at the family home, the body is then placed on a bier and carried to a ***dakhma*** "tower of silence", a stone column with a circular well in the center and separate sections for the bodies of men, women, and children. The bier is taken to the top of the tower, where the body is stripped of its clothing and left to be eaten by vultures. After the vultures have done their work—it takes only a few hours—the dried bones are deposited in the well.

This method of disposing of the dead, though unlike the funeral practices of the West, should not convey the impression that the Parsis are gloomy or eccentric. On the contrary, they accept death courageously and, in accord with the positive nature of their faith, await with confidence the reward of all their good deeds on earth in the paradise of Ormazd, Mithra, and the other heavenly beings.

THE GREEK HERITAGE

The ruins of the Acropolis in Athens are vivid reminders of the debt the Western world owes Greek civilization. Built in the fifth century B.C.E., the temples and statues of the Acropolis have a symmetry, proportion, and freshness of beauty that are typical of the best aspects of Greek culture. These and other masterpieces of Greek art, literature, and philosophy have made a lasting contribution to the Western way of life.

But even though there are many surviving texts, it has been difficult to draw a clear picture of Greek religion. First, Greek religion changed greatly over the centuries from its emergence in late Neolithic times until its replacement by Christianity in the fourth century C.E. Second, the available data on Greek religion have been supplied by diverse disciplines—anthropology, archaeology, ethnology, comparative religion, and the history of religions—which often give seemingly conflicting interpretations. And finally, the writers of ancient Greece were curiously reticent about explaining what their rites meant to them and what they thought about their gods and goddesses.

AEGEAN CIVILIZATION: CRETE AND MYCENAE

In prehistoric times Greece was inhabited by a people of obscure origin who probably did not speak Greek or any other Indo-European language. In the third millennium B.C.E. the remarkable Minoan culture of Crete took root on the islands of the Aegean Sea. The Cretans, who used bronze tools and weapons, were skillful shipbuilders and traders. Fleets carried exports

The Acropolis in Athens is crowned by the Parthenon, the Doric temple of Athena built in the fifth century B.C.E. (The Bettmann Archive)

Agamemnon might have passed through this portal, the Lion Gate in the wall of Mycenae, the center of the second great flowering of Aegean civilization. (The Bettmann Archive)

of olive oil, pottery, and metal jewelry to the markets of Egypt, Asia Minor, Syria, and Sicily.

The kings of Crete were also priests, and their religion was based largely on the religious practices of Mesopotamia. Goddesses were important, and the main deity was the Great Mother, whose symbol was a double ax. She was worshiped in a way similar to that of the Mesopotamian fertility goddesses and the Babylonian Ishtar. Surviving images of the Great Mother show her as the mistress of animals, standing between two lions with an arm around their necks. Small statues have also been found of a snake goddess wearing a long skirt around which snakes are coiled, but no public temples or large statues have been discovered. Perhaps the ceremonial dances and processions were held outside or in the throne room of the palace.

Shortly after 2000 B.C.E. the Greek-speaking Achaeans, an Indo-European people from the north, conquered Greece and built walled cities at Mycenae, Pylos, and Thebes on the mainland. Mycenae became the center of the second great flowering of Aegean civilization, known as the Mycenaean culture. This culture was destroyed shortly after 1200 B.C.E. by a new group of Indo-European invaders, the Dorians. There are practically no records of what happened in Greece during the next 400 years, but it was apparently a time of confusion and cultural decline.

THE HOMERIC AGE

Around the middle of the ninth century B.C.E. two of the earliest and greatest works of Greek literature, the *Iliad* and the *Odyssey,* were composed. These magnificent epic poems about the gods and heroes of Greece are attributed to a blind poet named Homer, who is said to have lived in the Greek settlement of Ionia and to have composed his verses for aristocratic audiences. But most scholars now consider the Homeric poems not the work of a single writer but rather collections of the oral recitations of wandering bards.

The *Iliad* tells the story of a Greek military expedition against Troy (in Greek, Ilion), a city in Asia Minor. Paris, one of the sons of King Priam of Troy, seduced Helen, the wife of King Menelaus of Sparta. Because Helen's abduction violated the sacred rules of Greek hospitality, the country began a ten-year struggle against Troy. The leader of the Greeks was Agamemnon, the king of Mycenae, and their great champion was the brave and headstrong Achilles. A quarrel broke out among the Greeks when Agamemnon took from Achilles a slave girl won in battle. After the angry Achilles withdrew to sulk in his tent, the Trojans, under the leadership of their champion Hector, almost defeated the Greek forces. Achilles was persuaded, however, to return to the aid of the Greeks, and the epic ends with the destruction of Troy.

The *Odyssey,* a sequel to the *Iliad,* celebrates the return to Greece of the victors in the Trojan War. Its protagonist is Odysseus, a hero admired as much for his cleverness as for his fighting ability. For ten years he wandered about the Mediterranean, aided by Athena, the goddess of wisdom, and threatened by Poseidon, the god of the sea. Upon Odysseus's return to his home at Ithaca, he discovered that interlopers had taken possession of his kingdom and were wooing his faithful wife Penelope. With the aid of his young son Telemachus, Odysseus slew them and regained possession of his kingdom and his spouse.

The Twelve Gods of Olympus

The *Iliad* and the *Odyssey* are our major sources of information about the public or state religion of the Homeric age. According to them, all important acts were determined by the gods, and to gain their favor, sacrificial rites were carried out: libations of wine were poured on the earth; cows, goats, and sheep were slaughtered; parts of the sacrificial animals were burned; and feasts were held to placate the gods and obtain their goodwill.

Although the Greeks revered many divine spirits in the sky, on earth, and beneath the earth, they all worshiped the 12 major gods who formed a divine family on Mount Olympus.[16] Homer described the mountain in these words:

> [It is] the seat of the gods established for ever. It is not shaken by winds nor ever wet with rain, and the snow comes not nigh; but the clear air spreads without a cloud, and the white light floats over it. There the blessed gods take their pleasure for all their days.[17]

The Greek gods all had human forms, although the animals or birds often associated with them may have been drawn from earlier nonhuman forms. From their thrones on Olympus, the divine spirits were interested spectators of the Trojan War, some favoring the Greeks and others supporting the Trojans. They even participated in the battles, fought with one another, and often came down to the Trojan plain to rescue one of their favorites in time of danger or to guide his arrows and spears to an intended target. The very human conduct of these gods and goddesses was probably intended to portray that of the early Greek aristocrats.

Besides these allusions to the Greeks themselves, the Homeric poems also borrowed from older myths. Some of the Greek gods were Indo-European sky deities, and others were based on other traditions.

Zeus (Jupiter)* was known as the father of the gods and the ruler of the universe. Associated with the sky and its power, Zeus brought storms and lightning bolts. As the bringer of rain and the lover of mortal women, Zeus was the progenitor of many semidivine heroes and various forms of subhuman life. For example, in several of the myths he would pursue a goddess, who assumed an animal form to escape him. But Zeus would then take on a similar animal shape, mate with the goddess, and help to create a new animal species. His sacred symbol was the eagle, and he often received a sacrifice of bulls, which was seen as the return of a divine gift to him.

Hera (Juno), the jealous wife of Zeus, was the goddess of women, marriage, and childbirth. Her main center was Argos, her favorite flower was the lily, and flocks and herds were sacred to her. Her marriage to Zeus, a kind of sacred marriage, may have represented the union of the invading Achaeans with the earlier inhabitants of the Greek mainland.

Apollo, the son of Zeus and Leto (Latona)—a mortal woman—was the god of archery, prophecy, and music. Apollo was associated with the sun and was the prototype of youthful male beauty. Although typifying the Greek spirit of the Homeric age, Apollo had a foreign origin and was a comparative newcomer to mainland Greece. According to some authorities, his cult began in northern Europe; others think that his earliest home was Asia Minor. Oracles were dedicated to Apollo in Ionia, on the island of Delos, and in Delphi.

Artemis (Diana), the goddess of the moon and hunting, was Apollo's twin sister, whom Homer called the "mistress of wild animals." Artemis was respected for her virginity and punished any of her attendant nymphs who were unchaste.

Other members of the divine family were Demeter (Ceres), the goddess of vegetation and grain; Ares (Mars), the god of war; Athena (Minerva), the goddess of wisdom; Hermes (Mercury), the messenger of Zeus

*The Latin name of the Greek deity is shown in parentheses if it differs from the Greek.

and the god of the highways; Poseidon (Neptune), the god of the sea; Aphrodite (Venus), the goddess of love and beauty, who was born from the sea near the island of Cyprus; Hephaestus (Vulcan), the god of fire and the husband of Aphrodite; and Hestia (Vesta), the goddess of the hearth.

Moira: The Influence of Fate

Although the Greeks of the Homeric age respected the superior beauty, power, and wisdom of the gods, they also acknowledged the influence of another power, *moira,* a person's fate or lot in life. Before going into battle, the Trojan hero Hector told his wife Andromache, "But I tell you that no one, brave man or coward, escapes *moira* when once he is born."[18] Indeed, Hector was slain by Achilles because it was Hector's time to die. Although Zeus could have reversed his fate and saved Hector, it would have been unseemly for the father of the gods to do so. Nonetheless, this belief did not totally prevent freedom of action, though death and other misfortunes could not be avoided, since they were an inevitable part of the human experience.

For the Homeric heroes, death was a disaster. Odysseus, at one point in his long voyage, descended to the land of the dead. Encountering there the spirit of Achilles, Odysseus told him of the high honor he enjoyed among the living. Achilles replied: "Seek not to console me for death, glorious Odysseus. I would rather be on earth as the hired man of another, in the house of a landless man with little to live upon, than be king over all the dead."[19]

Hesiod and the Creation Myths

The works of Homer are not particularly concerned with the origins of the gods and the universe; speculations regarding these topics were collected by Hesiod, a poet who lived around 800 B.C.E. In his *Theogony* ("Birth of the Gods") Hesiod stated that the world had been created from four primary spirits: Chaos (Space), Gaea (Earth), Tartarus (Abyss), and Eros (Love). Hesiod's account combined Greek and earlier ideas, including many from Mesopotamia. Chaos produced Night and Erebus, a dark region where death was found, and Gaea created Uranus (Heaven), the mountains, and the sea. Taking Uranus as her husband, Gaea gave birth to monsters, giants, and powerful creatures known as the Titans. When Uranus and his offspring Cronus (Time) became enemies, one of the Titans castrated his father, with Gaea's help. Cronus (in Latin, Saturn) and Rhea, his wife and sister, then became the rulers of the universe.

Like Uranus, Cronus was a cruel father who swallowed his offspring as soon as they were born. Only Zeus, the sixth child, escaped because Rhea hid him in a cave. When Zeus became an adult, he forced Cronus to disgorge all the children he had eaten. With the help of his brothers and sisters, Zeus then overcame him and the Titans and threw them from the earth into Tartarus, the underworld. Afterward, Zeus and his brothers, Poseidon and Hades (Pluto), cast lots for control of the universe. Zeus received sovereignty over the sky, Poseidon over the sea, and Hades over the realm of the dead.

Like Homer, Hesiod used many of the earlier stories about the gods, though both written accounts of the old oral myths were selective and rather artificial. Yet several centuries later, when more sophisticated thinkers in Greece began to speculate about the nature of the universe and the gods, the poems were the best sources, as the tradition of the bards had long died out.

GREECE IN HISTORY

After the Homeric age Greek society underwent many changes. The confusion caused by the Dorian invasion gradually came to an end, and in mainland Greece and the Greek colonies of Ionia, independent city-states were created. The city-state, or *polis,* had two parts: a fortified high city *(acropolis)* that served as a religious center and a place of refuge in time of war and a marketplace *(agora)* and residential district below it.

Among the many Greek city-states, two—Athens in the region of Attica and Sparta in the region of Laconia—became particularly powerful. Athens became, late in the sixth century B.C.E., a prosperous democracy. Sparta remained essentially an oligarchy.

In the second half of the sixth century B.C.E., Athens fought and won a drawn-out war with the Persian Empire, the dominant power in western Asia. Athens was then free to embark on an ambitious program of

Germania
Po River
Arno
Tiber
Rome
Adriatic Sea
Italian Peninsula
Black Sea
Thrace
Macedonia
Troy
Aegean Sea
Tyrrhenian Sea
Ionian Sea
Delphi
Thebes
Athens
Eleusis
Mycenae
Argos
Peloponnesus
Pylos
Sparta
Sicily
Carthage
Knossos
Crete
Mediterranean Sea
Cyrene
Africa
GREECE – ROME

Dionysus as Michelangelo imagined him, crowned with a garland of grapes and lifting a cup of wine. (The Bettmann Archive)

political and commercial expansion. The Athenians rebuilt the Acropolis, which the Persians had burned, and it became the best example of this now classical period of Greek culture. At the same time writers and philosophers began to explore seriously the great moral and scientific themes of human existence, particularly the concept of free inquiry.

Despite their cultural achievements, the Greeks were unable to maintain peace among themselves. Athens and Sparta became embroiled in a long and bitter struggle, the Peloponnesian War (431–404 B.C.E.), which weakened the entire country. In 338 B.C.E. Philip II, the king of Macedonia, a state on the northern border of Greece, put an end to the political independence of the Greek city-states.

When Philip died, his son, Alexander the Great (ruled 336–323 B.C.E.), began an extraordinary career of military conquests. He created an empire stretching from Europe to India, including Greece, Egypt, the Middle East, and Persia. After Alexander's death this vast territory was divided among his generals, and soon Greek culture, in a new international form known as Hellenism, began to sweep across the lands of the eastern Mediterranean and the Near East.

During the second century B.C.E. more civil wars among the Greeks lowered their resistance to the rising power of Rome, and in 146 B.C.E. Greece was incorporated into the Roman Empire. Nonetheless, Greek culture remained a vital force for many centuries.

Civic Religion and Festivals

Like people of nearly every culture, the Greeks of the classical period did not always know why a particular sacred place was revered or why a specific custom or ritual was observed. Earlier traditions might be overlaid with new concepts and their original meaning forgotten, but nonetheless a city-state depended on its gods for protection and prosperity. Although there was no official clergy to intercede with the deities, there were local holy persons who gave professional assistance at sacrifices, and individuals might come to a temple for worship or visit an oracle to obtain advice or healing.

The state protected its temple property and expected its citizens, particularly officials, to show respect for public religious ceremonies, which were also important civic celebrations. The Greater Panathenaea festival, held at Athens every four years in midsummer, was a solemn procession symbolizing the union of the city and its surrounding territory of Attica. An ancient image of Athena was carried from the temple on the Acropolis, bathed in a purification rite, and then returned by torchlight after being given a new robe woven by the women of the city. Its purpose was to renew the city's alliance with the protecting goddess and thus to ensure its continued wealth.

Many festivals were also held in honor of Dionysus (Bacchus), the god of wine. At a festival in the spring, both the power of fertility and the memory of the dead were celebrated. At other festivals an image of Dionysus would preside over drama contests. Since attendance at these performances was both a civic and a religious duty, every effort was made to help the poorer citizens attend at public expense.

The first Olympic Games also had religious overtones. Held at Delphi every four years, they were conducted under the auspices of Zeus. The games began in 776 B.C.E. and continued for more than 1,200 years. The victors were crowned with olive wreaths, and their fame and prowess were celebrated by poets and sculptors.

Folk Religion

In addition to the religion described in the works of Homer and Hesiod, there was also a folk religion, observed by the family and based in the home. Besides worshiping Zeus, king of the gods and protector of households, each family also honored its own gods, both in daily rites and in times of crisis and transition. Such rites varied from region to region and from household to household and included obeisance to one's ancestors.

The Greeks saw all their spirits as both helpful and threatening. Besides the gods, there were other supernatural forces, who could be ignored only at great risk. Chthonic forces (gods of the earth) were an important part of death and fertility ceremonies, and deceased heroes and great nobles were often deified, inspiring both fear and awe as mighty beings who could influence the fate of the living. In addition to these there were ghosts, demons, and the Furies, nebulous spirits who punished mortals for their offenses against the gods.

The Growth of Humanism

Aside from its complex and fascinating mythology, Greece's principal contribution to Western thought—and the main features of what came to be known as Hellenism—was its **humanism**, its high esteem for the individual and an emphasis on human possibilities, achievements, and reasoning. Western rational philosophy was born here; rationally and consistently, Greek philosophers emphasized humans' capacity to understand the universe and the origin of life. The earliest dramas were also written here; they emphasized that humans can determine their own destiny.

The earliest playwrights, Aeschylus (c. 525–455 B.C.E.), Sophocles (c. 495–406 B.C.E.), and Euripides (c. 480–406 B.C.E.), highlighted human choice, the Fates, and justice. Zeus, for example, was often shown as the supreme administrator of divine justice who issued orders to the other gods and sent the Furies down to earth to punish impious human beings. Although Sophocles believed Zeus to be merciful, Euripides, an unbeliever, was sympathetic to human suffering and questioned the unjust actions of Apollo.

THE MYSTERY RELIGIONS

The Greeks were also devoted to so-called **mystery religions**. Unlike the official cult, the secret rites of the mysteries associated with Demeter, Dionysus, and Orpheus offered ecstasy to ordinary humans. (These cults gave rise to the later phenomenon of *mysticism.*) Eating, drinking, dancing, music, and sex were all thought at one time or another to be means of communicating with these deities.

Demeter and Dionysus were both mentioned by Homer, and they were included among the earth deities. In the secret rites held in their honor, human actors reenacted the stories of the gods in rituals that promised life after death.

The Eleusinian Mysteries

The religion of Eleusis centered on the legend of Demeter, the goddess of grain, who was once in love with Zeus, by whom she had a daughter, Persephone

(Proserpine), the spirit of spring.[20] One day as Persephone was gathering flowers in a meadow, Hades, the god of the underworld, carried her off to his land of the dead. This implied that neither spring nor fertility would again be found on earth. Demeter wandered the earth, seeking her daughter, going ultimately to Zeus. He insisted to Hades that she be returned to earth. Hades agreed to let her go, but she had eaten six pomegranate seeds, perhaps the symbol of marriage. As a result, henceforth she had to spend six months with him each year as the queen of the underworld—accounting for winter. Each spring Persephone returned to earth, bringing flowers as a symbol of nature's rebirth. The Eleusinian mysteries celebrated this myth of the sorrowing mother and the spirit of loveliness that must die.

Many details of the central rite at Eleusis—the act of initiation in which candidates were brought to a supreme vision—are unknown, but entrance into the new faith was thought to take two steps. The Lesser Mysteries, held each spring in an Athens suburb, included ritual fasting, purification, and sacrifices. The Great Mysteries, which took place in the fall, lasted for eight days. On the fifth day the celebrants moved in procession from Athens to Eleusis. The sanctuary was illuminated by torches, and the night was spent singing, dancing, and reenacting the wanderings of Demeter in search of her daughter. After the Eleusinian divinities adopted the candidates, a secret was revealed to them, assuring them of life after death. As one hymn puts it, "Happy is he who goes beneath the earth having seen these things. He knows the end of life, and knows its god-given beginning."[21]

Other Cults

The myth of Dionysus tells that he was born as the divine son of Zeus and Semele, a woman of Thebes. At the suggestion of Hera, who hated all the women with whom Zeus was in love, Semele asked a favor of Zeus. Without finding out what she wanted, Zeus swore by the Styx, the river leading to the underworld, that he would give her whatever she asked. Her request was to see her lover in majesty as the king of the gods. When Zeus appeared before her, Semele was melted away by his splendor. As she died, Zeus carried off her baby, which was almost ready to be born. Sewing the infant into his thigh, Zeus protected him from Hera.*

When he was full-grown, this baby, Dionysus, wandered about the earth, teaching human beings to grow grapes and to worship him in secret rites. But in Dionysus's native city of Thebes, the local king prevented the god from introducing this new form of worship. Although Dionysus succeeded in overpowering the ruler, Zeus became angry at the insult to his son and made the king blind. Later Dionysus descended to the underworld to rescue his mother. He carried Semele up to Olympus, where the gods agreed that even though she was a mortal, she could live among them, since her son was divine.

Dionysus's cult manifested both the joyful and the dangerous aspects of drinking wine. The god himself was identified with the vital force in wine and in all reproduction, and his excess of vitality was linked with water, blood, and semen. Dionysus's initiation ceremonies, which included the use of intoxicants, were known for their orgiastic dances, loud cries, and wild ecstasies. His adherents attempted to surpass the human condition: "I have escaped from evil and found something better," the initiate would exclaim. At times, a kid or a bull was torn apart by the raging devotees, who would eat the flesh of the animal in the belief that it embodied their god. By consuming this flesh, his followers hoped to attain union with the god on earth and immortality in the next world.

Another sect of some reknown was the Orphic cult, far less violent than the Dionysian mystery cult and far more reflective. Its practices include rites of catharsis (purgation from sin) and asceticism. Wearing white garments, the initiates refrained from having sex and eating meat except the sacrificial meat representing the flesh of the martyred Dionysus Zagreus, which they ate in their rituals. They sought to achieve self-realization through knowledge rather than rapture. Members of the Orphic cult studied astronomy, music, medicine, and mathematics and appear to have influenced the

*This is a depiction of androgenous birth, the birth of a child from the father. The birth of Athena (who sprang from Zeus's brain) is another example. Abnormal or nonsexual conception and birth are in many religions symbolically associated with deities and sacred knowledge. All these accounts share the concept that sacred beings and sacred knowledge are fundamentally different from human beings and human knowledge.

philosophy of Pythagoras (c. 582–507 B.C.E.). (The followers of Pythagoras, who also believed in the transmigration of souls, considered numbers the basic element of the universe.) In addition, the Orphic cult is thought to have been the religious foundation of at least part of Plato's interpretation of the universe.

ROMAN SOCIETY AND RELIGION

Just as Athens was dominated by the Acropolis with its temples and statues of the protecting goddess Athena, Rome also had a central symbol in the Roman Forum. Originally a modest marketplace at a crossing of the Tiber River, the Forum developed gradually into a crowded cluster of temples, government buildings, and triumphal arches. Whereas Athens remained a relatively compact political and intellectual center, Rome became the cosmopolitan seat of a mighty empire. Because the early Romans subordinated everything in life, including the worship of their gods, to the service of the state, Roman religion became a patriotic duty expected of every citizen.

THE EMERGENCE OF ROME

Ancient Roman history begins about 2000 B.C.E., when a western band of **Indo-Europeans**— the same peoples that invaded Greece, Iran, India, and other areas around that time—began to settle in the Po valley of northern Italy, where they mingled with the original populations. Out of this mixture came a people called the Latins, who eventually took possession of the Tiber valley and the surrounding plains. Between the twelfth and ninth centuries B.C.E. the Etruscans—a people of unknown origin who may have reached Italy by sea from Asia Minor—began to found city-states along the west coast of the Italian peninsula. These talented shipbuilders and ironworkers slowly subjugated the Italic peoples, forming a loose confederation of city-states. Though not of Indo-European origin, the Etruscans adopted many features of Greek culture, including the Greek alphabet, the use of statues of their gods, and burial rituals. Thus the peninsula's culture and civilization came to be similar to the Greeks'.

This Etruscan sculpture of wood and bronze dates from the sixth century B.C.E. (The Metropolitan Museum of Art)

Rome emerged as the greatest of the peninsula's cities by about 850 B.C.E. It was ruled by a series of kings, but in about 500 B.C.E. Rome's people expelled the last of them and set up a republic in which power was held by an elite class, the patricians, or nobles. During the fifth and fourth centuries B.C.E. Rome began to conquer the neighboring city-states and by 270 B.C.E. controlled all of Italy south of the Po valley. Next the Roman legions waged three wars against Carthage, a maritime empire in North Africa. After many battles, the Romans destroyed Carthage in 146 B.C.E. and annexed its territories. Soon Rome also dominated vast portions of Europe, Africa, and Asia.

As Rome became a world power, its republican system of government proved inadequate. Dissent among the people finally led to the rise of military dictators like Julius Caesar (c. 102–44 B.C.E.) and Octavian (c. 66 B.C.E.–14 C.E.), who was given the title

Augustus and founded the imperial system of government that endured for hundreds of years. The western portion of the Roman Empire eventually collapsed late in the fifth century C.E. as a result of internal weaknesses and invasions by Germanic tribes, but the eastern half, the Byzantine Empire, continued the Greco-Roman tradition for another 1,000 years.

ROMAN RELIGION

The Romans attributed their success in warfare to their religious devotion.[22] (The term *religion* comes from the Latin *religio,* which means either "scrupulous observance" or "a way of binding oneself with respect to the gods.") Through rituals and sacrifices the people sought to strengthen the tie between heaven and earth and to obtain divine favor.

Basic Concepts

The Roman attitude toward religion can be summarized as follows.

1 The Romans expressed their reverent fear of the gods through a "contractual" or juridical approach: *do ut des* (I give so that you[the god] may give to me). The early Romans were a practical people who did not invent beautiful and imaginative myths like those of the Greeks. They had little interest in stories about divine couples or semidivine heroes and made a clear distinction between the human and the divine, in contrast to the Greeks.
2 The Romans perceived the deities as functional. They assigned the many different agricultural tasks to specific minor gods, such as Insitor (the god of plowing), Imporcitor (the god of cross-plowing), and Terminus (the god of the property boundary between farms).
3 To the Romans, the interests of the state were paramount. Through their worship of the major gods of the state and the gods of various occupations, the Romans strengthened their feeling of belonging to a community.
4 The Romans' conservatism, which included respect for the old Roman gods, was combined with a spirit of open-mindedness, which allowed equal respect for foreign deities. Gods and goddesses of foreign origin were adapted to or blended with the Roman deities and admired for their foreign characteristics.

According to legend, Numa, the second of Rome's early kings, established the state religion. He organized colleges for the priests, appointed the *rex sacrorum* (leader of rites) and the *flamines* (priests), and drew up a calendar of festivals. The three high gods were Jupiter, the god of thunder and the sky; Mars, the god of war; and Quirinus, the deified form of Romulus, the legendary founder of Rome. Janus, originally the god of the home's doorway, became identified with the power of the state: the portal of his temple was closed when Rome was at peace and kept open in time of war. Similarly, Vesta, the goddess of the hearth, became a symbol of Rome's divine protection. In her round temple in the Forum, six carefully chosen daughters of patrician families, the Vestal Virgins, tended an eternal flame.

The state religion began as a form of family worship when Rome was a small farming community. Early Italic farmers were accustomed to acting as priests in their own homes, and each *paterfamilias* (head of family) led his wife and children in worshiping the family spirits. Janus, as the protector of the doorway, was often invoked first. In the center of the house was the *atrium* containing the hearth, which was sacred to Vesta. The family remained silent during the first and second courses of a meal and placed a portion of the food on the fire as an offering to the gods. They also honored their family ancestors.

The early king acted as the paterfamilias of the extended family of the Roman city-state. He was assisted by "family members," priests, and priestesses. The various priesthoods were united in a college over which the king presided as *pontifex maximus* (high priest). (This title was later used by the Roman emperors and is still used by the Roman popes.)

Tradition and Innovation

Toward the end of the monarchy new deities were introduced, and their identifying characteristics were adapted to those of the Greek gods and goddesses. Juno, an Etruscan goddess, became, like the Greek Hera, the goddess of women and the wife of Jupiter. Diana, originally a goddess of the forest, was respected as the Roman version of Artemis and was especially revered by women wishing to bear children. Minerva, a goddess of artisans, was elevated to the

The Roman Forum, once the center of a mighty empire, as it appears today. (Italian State Tourist Office)

position of Athena, the goddess of wisdom. In about 500 B.C.E. on the Capitoline Hill in Rome, a great temple was dedicated to the triad of Jupiter, Juno, and Minerva.

The Romans respected the deities of their former enemies; in fact, they designed a special ceremony, the *evocatio* (summoning), that called on the foreign deities to take up residence in Rome.

During their republican period the Romans adopted the Etruscan legend of Aeneas and his Trojan followers, and in particular they associated their devotion to Apollo, the Greek sun god, with the Sibyl of Cumae. The books of prophecies kept in the Sibyl's cave (the Sibylline Oracles) were brought to Rome and deposited in the temple of Jupiter, Juno, and Minerva, where they were consulted in time of crisis. According to legend, at the suggestion of the Sibyl of Cumae, the Romans began worshiping Bacchus, Ceres, and Proserpine (in Greek, Dionysus, Demeter, and Persephone, respectively).

During the Second Punic War between Rome and Carthage (c. 218–201 B.C.E.), when a Carthaginian army was threatening Rome with destruction, the keepers of the Sibylline Books urged that a stone sacred to Cybele, the Great Mother of the Gods, be imported from a shrine in Asia Minor. The introduction of the worship of Cybele at Rome marked the beginning of the slow ascendancy of religious practices from the Middle East. Much later Augustus had the Sibylline Books recopied and installed in a new temple of Apollo that he had built on the Palatine Hill in Rome.[23]

The Indo-European Heritage

Georges Dumézil, a specialist on ancient religions, has argued that the religions of all the Indo-European peoples had a common heritage. They all featured three social classes—warrior-rulers, priests, and farmer-herders—each having different functions, mirrored in the high deities' functions. For example, in the Roman religion, Jupiter stood for both magical and juridical sovereignty, Mars represented physical and military strength, and Quirinus was associated with the pastoral and agricultural forms of fertility and prosperity.[24]

Priesthoods and Festivals

The college of priests, headed by the pontifex maximus, regulated the priesthoods of the various deities, established the calendar of festivals, supervised sacrifices, dedicated new temples, and authorized the introduction of new gods into the Roman pantheon. The priests also presided over ceremonies of lustration (ritual purification), prayers, and sacrifices, but they did not interpret omens. This was done by a separate college of augurs who attempted to discern the future by observing the weather, flights of birds, and entrails of dead animals. Roman military and naval units regularly carried into battle flocks of sacred chickens. If the birds refused to eat before an engagement with the enemy, it was taken as an evil portent.

About 100 days of the year were devoted to festivals honoring the gods. Members of the *Salii* (dancing priests)—a patrician priesthood dedicated to the worship of Mars—danced each year on the feast of the Tubilustrium (March 23), which marked the opening of the season of military campaigns and spring plowing. Clashing their shields and shaking their spears, the priests performed a ceremony designed to purify the cavalry horses. At the end of the season, a new purification ceremony was held on the feast of Armilustrium (October 19) when the sacred shields and spears were placed in storage until the following year.

February, the last month of the ancient Roman calendar, had nine purification days. The feast of Feralia (February 21) promoted harmony between the living and the dead, and commemorative ceremonies were held on behalf of the whole community. In mid-May the festival of Lemuria paid obeisance to the ghosts of ancestors who had died in war or in a distant land. It was felt that if their *manes* (shades) were not properly honored, they might return to their former homes and cause harm to the living. This festival did not express a sophisticated theory of life after death but rather reflected a strong feeling of family loyalty and piety. The Saturnalia, which began on December 17 and lasted for several days, was a time of rejoicing. Military activities were suspended, government and private offices were closed, presents were exchanged, and all members of a family, including the slaves, ate together.

Later Developments

The civil wars and military dictatorships of the first century B.C.E. marked a turning point in religious attitudes. With Rome's increasing political and military power, the simple ceremonies of the old family and early state religion no longer satisfied the people's needs, nor did the ceremonies honoring the Greek deities correlate with the older Roman gods and goddesses. Augustus attempted to restore the old state religion. Temples that had fallen into disrepair were refurbished, opulent new buildings of marble were constructed, and the great *Ara Pacis* (altar of peace) was erected in 13 C.E. as a symbol of the *Pax Romana,* the Roman peace.

Despite these efforts to restore the old order, the lower classes in Rome and all over the empire were increasingly drawn to the Greek mystery religions and to the worship of the Egyptian Isis and Osiris. Soldiers serving in the Middle East brought back the Persian religion of Mithraism, which was particularly appealing because of its theory of struggle between good and evil and its promise of immortality. Members of the legions erected altars to Mithra at their military camps in far-off Britain and Germany. A Mesopotamian sun god revered as Sol Invictus (the unvanquished sun) was the focus of a mystery religion favored by certain emperors. The Jews living in Rome introduced Judaism, and during the first century C.E. Christian missionaries preached the new religion of Jesus.

As doubts about the state religion spread, members of the upper classes embraced the teachings of the Greek philosophers. Epicurianism, Stoicism, and the philosophies of Plato and Aristotle were popular in intellectual circles. In addition, beginning with Augustus, the Roman emperors were regularly deified as soon as they died, and some received divine honors while still alive. In time the spirits of the emperor and of Roma, a goddess who personified the state, were also worshiped, particularly in the provinces. Imperial officials insisted that as a patriotic duty, all citizens pay homage to the state. For this reason the Roman Empire, which had earlier been tolerant of foreign religions, proscribed Christianity until the fourth century C.E., when it became the official religion.

NORTHERN EUROPEAN MYTHOLOGIES

THE CELTS

Early in the second millennium B.C.E. the Celts, a branch of the Indo-European family of peoples, lived in what is now western Germany and eastern France. Carrying iron weapons and riding horses, they spread across much of Europe, from Spain and the British Isles in the west to Galatia in Asia Minor in the east. In 390 B.C.E. an army from northern Italy moved south to threaten Rome, and in 270 B.C.E. a band of marauding Celts plundered the Greek sanctuary at Delphi.

By the dawn of the Common Era, however, most of the Celts had been either subjugated or displaced by the Germanic tribes or the Romans advancing into northern Europe. The Celtic culture collapsed as quickly as it had arisen, and the Celtic languages survive today only in Wales, Scotland, Ireland, and Brittany. We have no written records of the Celts, as they were forbidden to commit their oral traditions to writing. Our best sources of information about the early Celtic religion are the writings of Julius Caesar and the folk literature of Ireland, where the Celtic culture survived for a long time.

During the first century B.C.E. Caesar led his legions against the Celts of Gaul, whom he conquered for Rome. Caesar's account of this encounter, the *Commentaries on the Gallic Wars,* speaks of the Celts' devotion: they believed that all things in life happened according to the will of the gods, they accepted their fate as inevitable, and they faithfully performed all the ceremonies their gods required. It is not clear how well Caesar understood the beliefs of his enemies, and it is possible that he reinterpreted their practices in terms familiar to him. But we have been able to supplement Caesar's descriptions of the Celtic religious ceremonies with archaeological evidence from excavations of altars and other artifacts.

According to Caesar, the Celtic tribes worshiped gods and goddesses similar to Jupiter, Mars, Apollo, Minerva, and Pluto. An important deity was a god known as Llow in Gaul (France) and Lug in Ireland, whom the Romans associated with Mercury, the messenger of the gods. (At least 27 places in Europe today are associated with the name of this god, including Lyons in France.) Many of the Celtic deities were unique, however, and were believed to be magicians. Caesar reported that the Celtic priests, the druids, performed animal and human sacrifices. (His accusation regarding human sacrifices has not been confirmed by other sources.) Thus in accordance with Roman law, Caesar forbade the taking of human life for religious reasons in all territories occupied by his legions.

The Druids

The role of the **druids** has often been misunderstood or misrepresented. One reason for this is that the druids themselves, though probably literate, forbade the preparation of written records or scriptures. They were members of an organized priesthood dedicated to a religion of elaborate ceremonies honoring many gods, and they enjoyed an exalted status in Celtic society comparable only to that of the brāhmans in Hindu society. Unlike India's brāhmans, however, they were not a hereditary caste: membership in their ranks was open to both men and women of all social classes. As a result, they were supported by both the lower classes and the nobles. The term *druid* means "very wise," and in fact the druids were in charge of educating the young.

According to legend, the druids conducted their services in groves of trees. They taught the mysteries of the Celtic religion, offered sacrifices, and practiced magic. They are reported also to have speculated about the origin of the earth and the movement of the stars. Further, it is thought that the druids believed that humans could aspire to immortality, possibly through successive rebirths. But the druids were more than just religious arbiters: they also advised the Celtic kings about military matters and influenced the selection of future kings. Too, the druids were empowered to exclude both unbelievers and transgressors from religious sacrifices.

THE GERMANIC AND SCANDINAVIAN TRIBES

The religion of the tribes living in Germany and on the northern coast of Europe emerged out of a common

Burial mounds of the Druid kings at Old Uppsala in Sweden. (Swedish Information Service)

Indo-European heritage. Yet this Germanic and Scandinavian heritage was very different from the beliefs of the other Indo-Europeans, owing perhaps to the fact that their life was filled with a sense of continual danger and a spirit of belligerence.

The Twilight of the Gods

The major Scandinavian and Germanic gods were Odin (Woden), Thor (Donar), and Ty (Tiw).* The relative importance of each of these gods shifted according to place and time, but each was regarded, under certain circumstances, as the sovereign god of the universe.

The triad of Odin, Thor, and Ty is reminiscent of the sets of three gods found among other Indo-European peoples, in which the first god was a magician (Odin or the Roman Mercury), the second a war god (Thor or Mars), and the third a worker-producer god (Ty or Quirinus).

The Germanic pantheon consisted of two groups of gods, the Vanir and the Aesir. At first there were only the Vanir, but as soon as the Aesir, a younger group of deities, appeared, the two groups fought a battle in which the Aesir were victorious. Afterward a peace was concluded, and at least three of the Vanir joined the Aesir or were admitted to their company as hostages. All the gods lived in splendor in Asgard, their home high above the sky. Here Odin had a great hall, Valhalla, with many doors through which he surveyed the cosmos with his single, piercing eye. Valhalla was separated from the earth by a shimmering bridge, the rainbow Bifröst. The earth was perceived as a great disk surrounded by the ocean where the Midgard serpent lived. Beyond the ocean lay Jötunheim, the mountains of the giants, whose city was called Utgard. And beneath the earth was Hel, the realm of the dead.

This shining vision of the universe lay under the constant threat of destruction, an event known as Ragnarök (*Götterdämmerung* in German—the so-called **twilight of the gods**). When, at the end of time, the gods had fulfilled their purpose, the destruction of the world would be foreshadowed by horrible events: civil wars, struggles to the death of brothers against brothers, and outbreaks of incest. Monsters would be let loose. The hound of Hel, Garm, would begin to howl, and Fenri, the wolf, would escape from his chains and open wide his massive jaws. The Midgard serpent would thrash about in the ocean. The gigantic ash tree, Yggdrasil, whose top scraped the sky, whose branches extended over the whole earth, and whose

*The names of the northern deities sometimes varied in different regions. The first form is the one used by the Scandinavians, and the second, in parentheses, is that used by the Germanic tribes.

roots stretched down into Hel, would be shaken to its very foundations. The mountains of the giants would begin to groan.

As the bridge of Bifröst crumbled, a giant named Surt would breathe forth fire, and the final struggle between the gods and the giants would begin. Fenri would swallow up Odin, but then the world would be crushed by the massive boot of Odin's son Vidar. Thor would slay the Midgard serpent, but he himself would die from the serpent's bite. Garm would attack Ty, and both would perish. Flames would shoot into the sky, the stars would fall, and the earth would sink into the ocean. Although the universe would be destroyed, there was still hope of a new beginning, and in the end a new heaven and a new earth would appear.

Historical Sources

There is little historical information about Germanic religion prior to the first century B.C.E. In the earliest period there were few temples, since worship was held outdoors in forests or on the shores of lakes and streams. Archaeological remains are very few. The major documentary sources are Caesar's *Commentaries on the Gallic Wars* and a work titled *Germania* ("Germany") by the Roman historian Tacitus (c. 55–117 C.E.). Though Tacitus supplied useful information about the beliefs and social practices of the Germanic tribes, he tended to exaggerate the virtues of these tribes while condemning the decadence of his fellow Romans. But after the Germanic armies overran the western half of the Roman Empire, many of the invaders converted to Christianity. In general, the new converts viewed their old faith with scorn and hatred. Hence their discussions of it, like Tacitus's, were also biased and not always accurate.

Scandinavian Religions

During the age of the Vikings (c. 800–1000 C.E.), pirates from Scandinavia attacked the British Isles, France, the Low Countries, and other parts of Europe. Some remnants of the Viking religion have been gleaned from the accounts of their victims—the inhabitants of Christian Europe—as well as from the Christian missionaries who eventually succeeded in converting the Scandinavians. This task of conversion was long and difficult: the Danes were converted in about 950, the Norwegians and Icelanders in about 1000. The Swedes clung to their old fertility rites and to the Nordic concepts of valor in battle, honor, and family pride until shortly after 1100.

As early as 870 C.E. Norwegian chieftains and their followers began to settle permanently in Iceland, bringing with them a body of oral literature. Many of these poems were written down after the Icelanders'

This picture-stone (c. 700 C.E.) shows Thor riding his famous eight-legged horse. (The American-Swedish News Exchange)

conversion to Christianity. One of them, the *Elder Edda,* is a thirteenth-century collection of alliterative verse about the formation of the world, the fate of the gods, and the dialogues among the gods and heroes. In addition, the skalds, or bards, of Iceland and Norway wrote poems on such themes as victory in battle, love, and sorrow. In about 1221 Snorri Sturluson (1178–1241), an Icelandic historian and teller of sagas (heroic tales), prepared the *Heimskringla,* a history of Norway; the *Younger Edda,* a prose work advising skalds how to write heroic poems; and a collection of Norse myths.

Historians are not sure whether the religious traditions of Norway and Iceland were the same as those of Denmark and Sweden. Although the concepts and the general background of their myths were similar, they did differ in detail.

The basic myths can be outlined as follows. Odin, the chief god of the pantheon, was a mysterious, powerful, and sinister figure who also had some shamanistic traits. He was passionately attracted to wisdom, and for its sake he sacrificed one eye. Odin was also the god of aristocrats, warriors, and skalds, and he owned a magic spear, a self-renewing golden ring, and a swift horse.

Odin helped humans by giving them the runes (an early form of Nordic writing and a symbol of knowledge and magic power), and he defended their crops using magic. Yet his moral character was often in question, as he was also a deceiver, a breaker of oaths, and an inspirer of lawless fury.

Odin—Woden to the Anglo-Saxons—is named in the day of the week that the Romans dedicated to Mercury, which is our Wednesday. Frigg, Odin's wife, has been compared with the Roman Venus, and her day, Friday, is the same as Venus's day.

Thor, a strong, red-bearded god who rode an eight-legged horse, was the most beloved of all the Scandinavian gods. His favorite animals were the wolf and the raven, and his weapon was a hammer, which he hurled at his enemies. He was the protector of the Viking peasants, a tireless fighter whose thunderbolt personified great strength. He was the favorite god of farmers, blacksmiths, fishermen, and sailors. Thor's day, our Thursday, is the day the Romans dedicated to Jupiter.

All the gods were members of the divine group known as the Aesir. In Scandinavia three older gods, members of the Vanir, also were popular. They included Njörd, the god of the winds and wealth, who liked to live along the seashore; his son Frey, the god of fertility; and Freyja, the daughter of Njörd and the sister of Frey, who was also considered a symbol of fertility and was sometimes portrayed in a carriage drawn by large cats.

Baldr (Balder), the son of Odin and Frigg, was the god of light and male beauty. His mother forced all the plants and animals to swear they would never harm him, and he seems to have been invincible until Loki, who was half god and half devil, learned from Frigg that this protective oath had not been required of the mistletoe, as it seemed too weak to harm the glorious sun god. The malicious Loki then gave a sprig of mistletoe to Hoder, a blind god, and helped him throw it at Baldr. Changing himself into the mistletoe, Loki guided it to Baldr's heart. Baldr was killed, and Loki persuaded the queen of the dead, Hel, not to release him from the underworld. Thus Baldr became a symbol of suffering and martyrdom. According to legend, he would rise again after the twilight of the gods (Ragnorök) and ascend into the new heaven.

Such Norse myths were meant in part to persuade both gods and humans to accept their fates—which were determined by the Norns, the goddesses who controlled the past, present, and future—and to meet the challenges of their world with courage.

NOTES

1 William H. McNeill, *The Rise of the West: A History of the Human Community* (Chicago: University of Chicago Press, 1963), pp. 80–82.

2 Veronica Ions, *Egyptian Mythology* (London: Hamlyn, 1968), p. 24.

3 R. T. Rundle Clark, *Myth and Symbol in Ancient Egypt* (New York: Grove Press, 1960); Ions, *Egyptian Mythology*.

4 Ions, *Egyptian Mythology,* pp. 67–103 passim.

5 Thorkild Jacobsen, *The Intellectual Adventure of Ancient Man* (Chicago: University of Chicago Press, 1946), pp. 126–127.

6 McNeill, *Rise of the West,* p. 31.

7 Ibid.

8 Samuel Noah Kramer, *The Sumerians: Their History, Culture, and Character* (Chicago: University of Chicago Press, 1963), p. 74.

9 McNeill, *Rise of the West,* p. 43.

10 A. Leo Oppenheim, *Ancient Mesopotamia: Portrait of a Dead Civilization* (Chicago: University of Chicago Press, 1964), pp. 172–183.

11 Thorkild Jacobsen, *Toward the Image of Tammuz and Other Essays on Mesopotamian Religion and Culture,* ed. William L. Moran (Cambridge, Mass.: Harvard University Press, 1970), pp. 16–17.

12 Ibid., p. 18.

13 Ibid., pp. 16–38; Kramer, *The Sumerians,* pp. 112–164.

14 Henri Frankfort et al., *Before Philosophy: The Intellectual Adventure of Ancient Man* (Baltimore: Penguin Books, 1949), p. 226.

15 Yasna 45:5–7, in J. H. Moulton, *Early Zoroastrianism* (London: Williams & Norgate, 1913), pp. 344 ff.

16 William K. C. Guthrie, *The Greeks and Their Gods* (Boston: Beacon Press, 1955), pp. 27–112.

17 F. M. Cornford, *Greek Religious Thought from Homer to the Age of Alexander* (Boston: Beacon Press, 1950), p. 1.

18 *Iliad* 6:487.

19 Cornford, *Greek Religious Thought,* p. 18.

20 Based on Edith Hamilton, *Mythology: Timeless Tales of Gods and Heroes* (New York: New American Library, 1940), p. 16.

21 Guthrie, *Greeks and Their Gods,* p. 294.

22 Based on R. Schilling, "The Roman Religion," in *Historia Religionum: Handbook for the History of Religion,* ed. C. Jonco Bleeker and Geo Widengren (New York: Scribner, 1969), vol. 1, pp. 442–494.

23 Michael Grant, *Roman Myths* (New York: Scribner, 1971), pp. 62–63; *Encyclopaedia Britannica,* 15th ed., s.v. "Roman Religion."

24 Georges Dumézil, *Archaic Roman Religion,* trans. Philip Krapp (Chicago: University of Chicago Press, 1971), first published in France as *Le réligion romaine archaïque* in 1966.

PART TWO

RELIGIONS OF INDIA

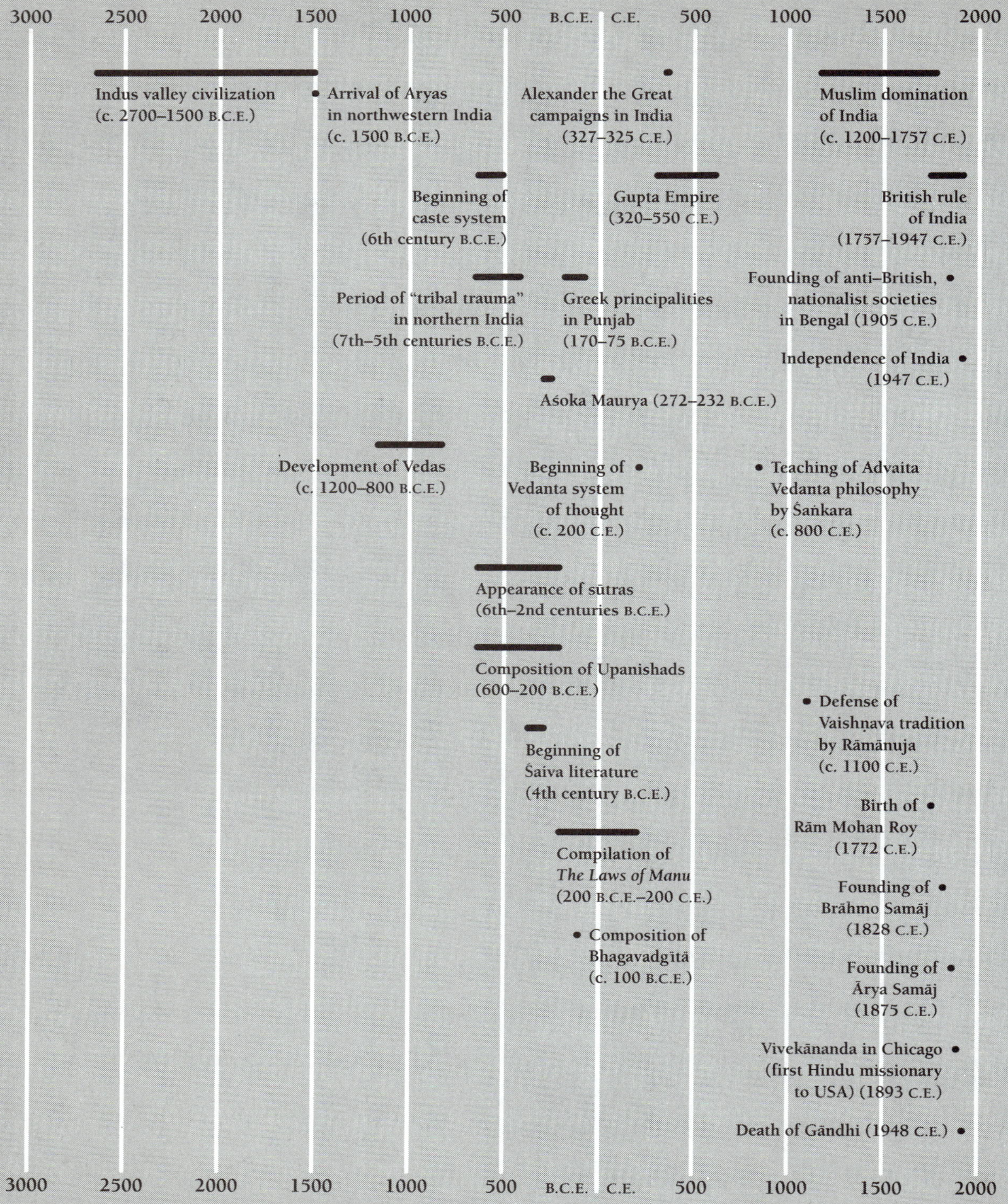
3000
2500
2000
1500
1000
500
B.C.E.
C.E.
500
1000
1500
2000
Indus valley civilization (c. 2700–1500 B.C.E.)
Arrival of Aryas in northwestern India (c. 1500 B.C.E.)
Alexander the Great campaigns in India (327–325 C.E.)
Muslim domination of India (c. 1200–1757 C.E.)
Beginning of caste system (6th century B.C.E.)
Gupta Empire (320–550 C.E.)
British rule of India (1757–1947 C.E.)
Period of "tribal trauma" in northern India (7th–5th centuries B.C.E.)
Greek principalities in Punjab (170–75 B.C.E.)
Founding of anti-British, nationalist societies in Bengal (1905 C.E.)
Independence of India (1947 C.E.)
Aśoka Maurya (272–232 B.C.E.)
Development of Vedas (c. 1200–800 B.C.E.)
Beginning of Vedanta system of thought (c. 200 C.E.)
Teaching of Advaita Vedanta philosophy by Śaṅkara (c. 800 C.E.)
Appearance of sūtras (6th–2nd centuries B.C.E.)
Composition of Upanishads (600–200 B.C.E.)
Defense of Vaishṇava tradition by Rāmānuja (c. 1100 C.E.)
Beginning of Śaiva literature (4th century B.C.E.)
Birth of Rām Mohan Roy (1772 C.E.)
Compilation of *The Laws of Manu* (200 B.C.E.–200 C.E.)
Founding of Brāhmo Samāj (1828 C.E.)
Composition of Bhagavadgītā (c. 100 B.C.E.)
Founding of Ārya Samāj (1875 C.E.)
Vivekānanda in Chicago (first Hindu missionary to USA) (1893 C.E.)
Death of Gāndhi (1948 C.E.)
3000
2500
2000
1500
1000
500
B.C.E.
C.E.
500
1000
1500
2000

HINDUISM TIME LINE

Religions of India

CHAPTER 3

The Earliest Forms of Hinduism

Hinduism, literally "the belief of the people of India," is the predominant faith of India and of no other nation. About 85 percent of all Indians declare themselves to be Hindu, along with a substantial minority in neighboring Bangladesh. In addition, conversions and migrations have given rise to small groups of Hindus in Sri Lanka, Indonesia, Africa, and Great Britain. There are half a million Hindus in the United States, as well. But like Confucianism in China and Shintō in Japan, Hinduism belongs primarily to the people of one country and has exceptionally strong ties to the national culture.

The term *Hindu* is of Persian origin. Muslims who conquered northern India in the twelfth century C.E. used it to describe persons belonging to the original population of Hind (India) and their religion. But India is also the birthplace of Jainism, Buddhism, and Sikhism; to distinguish Hinduism from these faiths we sometimes call it Brahmanism because it was taught by the ancient priestly class called **brāhmans**.* The authority of the brāhmans is one of the factors that sets Hinduism apart from these other beliefs.

Hinduism arose among a people who had no significant contact with the biblical religions. Hindu teaching does not consist of answers to the questions asked by Western faiths. For instance, Hinduism does not insist on any particular belief about God or gods. People reared in religions holding firmly to certain beliefs regarding God are often baffled by Hinduism's relaxed attitude in theology.

We must recognize that the special emphases of Hindu religion arose out of the problems that are especially acute in India and that Hindus' hopes are shaped by what seems desirable and possible under the special conditions of Indian life. Hindus, like others, seek superhuman resources to help to preserve life and to achieve its highest blessedness, but they perceive life's threats and promises as those posed by the Indian land and climate.

*This Hindu term can be confusing, for several related terms have developed over the centuries. *Brāhman* is the class or caste of priests. The brāhmans chanted the ancient scriptures (Vedas), and their sacred words came to be called *brahman*. The same term became associated with the world soul or divine absolute, the capitalized *Brahman* (not to be confused with a later creator deity, Brahmā). Certain religious texts were referred to as the *brāhmaṇas;* each of those texts has a name, for example, the *Aitareya Brāhmaṇa*.

Pronouncing Sanskrit

In transliterated Sanskrit, consonants and vowels, including those with accent marks on them, may generally be pronounced as in English—the differences are subtle and not readily apparent to people untrained in Indian languages. Observe the following: *ś* is pronounced "sh" as in *sure; c* is pronounced "ch" as in *chew;* and *th* and *ṭh* are pronounced not as in *the* or too*th* but as separate sounds, as in nu*th*atch or an*th*ill. Long vowels, with a bar over them, are held a little longer than their short counterparts: *a* is as in *maternal, ā* as in f*a*ther. We have used standard Monier Williams transliterations, with one exception, replacing that system's *ṡ* with *ś* (*Journal of the American Oriental Society* style).

GEOGRAPHIC SETTING

Two geographic factors have shaped many of Hinduism's themes and emphases: India is an agricultural land, and India is an isolated land.

India: A Land of Farmers

India was famed throughout the ancient world as a vast and fertile land of fabulous wealth. The rich soil of the northern river valleys, which extend about 2,000 miles from west to east, has supported a very large population for millennia. To a greater extent than any other major modern culture, India has been agrarian. And despite the recent growth of industrial cities, it remains overwhelmingly a land of farming villages.

The Hindu cosmology (view of the universe) is the creation of minds constantly aware of the natural cycles of plants and animals. Nature itself is seen as feminine, and female deities have a prominent place in classical Hindu mythology.

The persistent anxieties of India's farmers have had a dramatic impact on Hindu religion. India has always been both blessed and cursed by natural conditions, the most frightening of which is the matter of adequate water. As a rule, rainfall is plentiful, but several times each century the monsoon clouds fail to develop, rain does not fall, and crops do not grow. This persistent threat may account for the great attention paid to water in Hinduism's rituals. Scarcely any ritual is performed without preliminary bathings, sprinklings, sippings, libations, or other ceremonial uses of water. In Hindu mythology, Indra, the god of rain, is called king of the gods, and the mythology of many goddesses reflects an ever present concern with water.

Many goddess myths are also connected with the earth's fertility. The personalities of these deities reflect some of the forces controlling the agricultural world. In their worship of these goddesses, Hindus attempt to establish better relations with a generative force conceived as a mother who is usually generous but also moody and capable of violent anger. The ambivalence of this power is reflected in the goddess's different forms and dispositions; the divine mother may be the affectionate Ṣītā or Pārvatī or the dangerous Kālī, an irritable parent who sometimes destroys her children in inexplicable rages. The dual focus of worship symbolized the capricious pattern of abundant harvests and catastrophic droughts. And persistent anxiety about the food supply explains Hinduism's great tolerance for the pursuit of practical goals in worship.

India's Isolation and Stability

The second important geographic influence on Hinduism is the barrier of mountains and seas that has protected the subcontinent from invasions. On India's southern flanks the seas are wide, and powerful empires were far distant. India's north is shielded by the Himalayan mountains: no army approaching from China or Tibet has ever conquered India. Invaders have often used passes in the northwestern mountains, but to reach these they had to traverse wide deserts that limited the size of their armies. Only one early incursion—by the Aryas—has ever penetrated India so effectively as to transform Indian society.

In historical times Persians, Greeks, Scythians, Huns, Mongols, and others have invaded India in modest numbers and set up kingdoms on the northern plains. But they were always few in relation to the rest of the population, and they were able to rule successfully only by using local assistants, administrative institutions, and languages. The invaders soon intermarried with Indians and were given a traditional Indian social status. In the thirteenth century C.E. Muslims invaded and ruled most of India for 500 years, but the tide receded without leaving it an Islamic land. Even the British domination of the past two centuries did not radically transform the age-old Hindu social order. India's agricultural villages, the basic units of Hindu civilization, have always been too numerous and too remote to be forced into change.

THE QUEST FOR INNER PEACE AND HARMONY

India's cultural security has helped to determine Hinduism's prominent concerns. The Hindu scriptures are not preoccupied with the survival of a threatened tradition, nor is the Hindus' memory haunted, like the Jews', by recollections of past cultural traumas. India's natural defenses made the established order of Hinduism a secure cultural possession.

Yet the very cultural security that minimized one great problem created another: living with changeless-

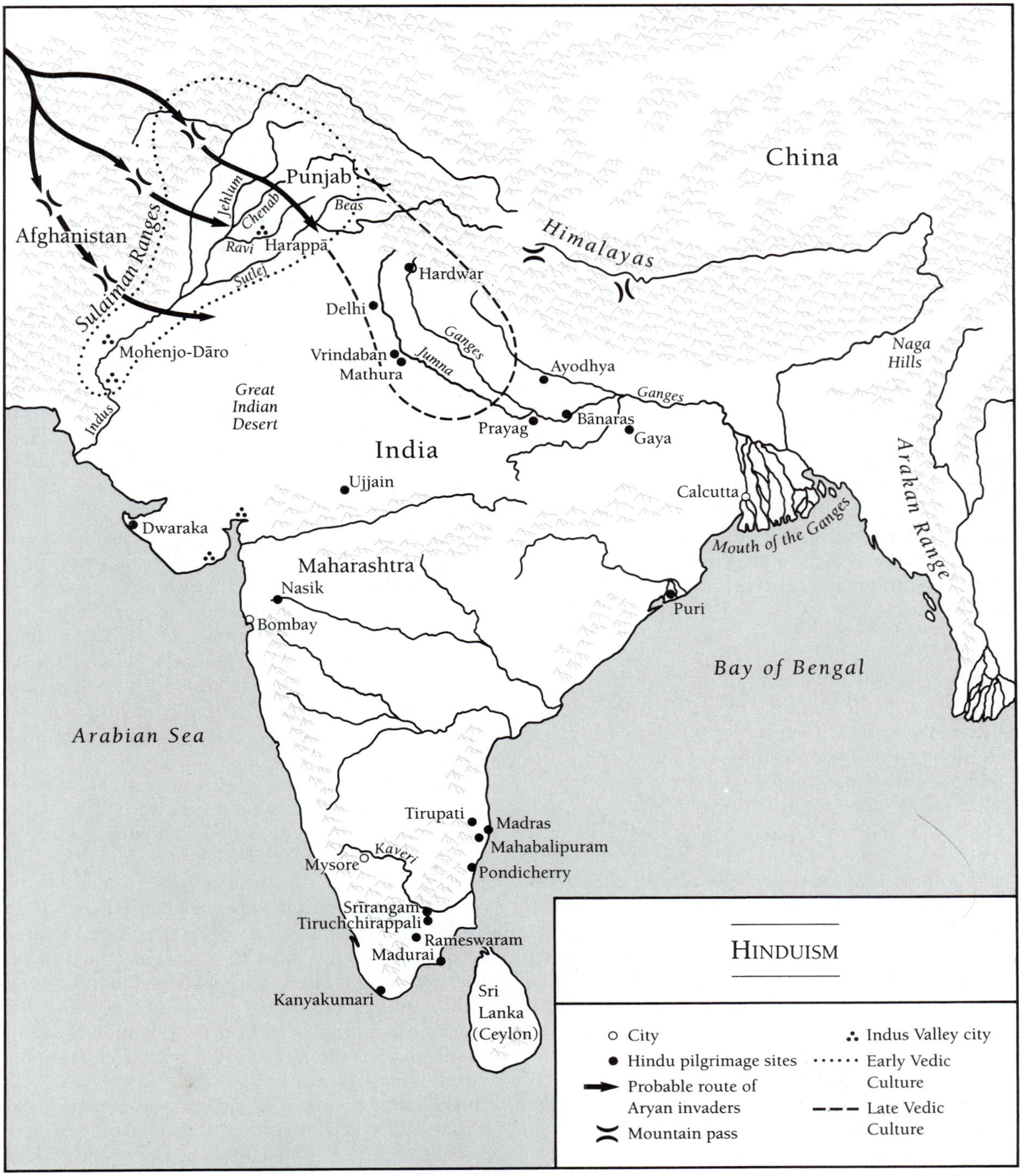
China
Himalayas
Afghanistan
Sulaiman Ranges
Punjab
Jehlum
Chenab
Beas
Ravi
Harappā
Sutlej
Hardwar
Delhi
Ganges
Jumna
Mohenjo-Dāro
Vrindaban
Mathura
Ayodhya
Naga Hills
Great Indian Desert
Indus
Prayag
Bānaras
Gaya
India
Ujjain
Calcutta
Arakan Range
Dwaraka
Mouth of the Ganges
Maharashtra
Nasik
Puri
Bombay
Bay of Bengal
Arabian Sea
Tirupati
Madras
Mahabalipuram
Kaveri
Mysore
Pondicherry
Srīrangam
Tiruchchirappali
Rameswaram
Madurai
Kanyakumari
Sri Lanka (Ceylon)
HINDUISM
City
Hindu pilgrimage sites
Probable route of Aryan invaders
Mountain pass
Indus Valley city
Early Vedic Culture
Late Vedic Culture

ness. India's traditional villages preserve even today a pattern of social relations that has not changed significantly for more than 2,000 years. Most Hindus have labored in an inherited occupation and died in the rank into which they were born. Hindu society's restraints on its members are severe and deeply felt, even if not resisted or even resented. The frustration of individual Hindus is experienced as a general sense of living in a bondage involving no external object of blame. Hindus rarely blame their problems on society or demand that their discontents be remedied by social changes. In Hinduism the responsibility for resolving tensions with the world lies squarely with the discontented person. One is to change oneself, not change the world. Inner adjustment is the way to tranquillity.

One distinguishing mark of Hinduism is its deep interest in techniques of self-examination and self-control that can enable individuals to attain peace of mind. At the most ordinary level these methods of inducing tranquillity take the form of moral teaching. The Hindu literature praises the saintly person who preserves emotional stability by mastery of impulses. In the Hindu classic, the Bhagavadgītā (Song of the Lord), the truly holy man is described in these terms:

When he sets aside desires
All that have entered his mind, O Pārtha,
And is contented in himself and through himself,
He is called a man of steady wisdom.

He whose mind stirs not in sorrows,
Who in joys longs not for joys,
He whose passion, fear, and wrath are gone,
That steady-minded man is called a sage.[1]

(Bhagavadgītā 2.55–56)

Beyond such moral encouragement, Hinduism has deeply introspective techniques for calming troubled minds. In meditational disciplines called **yoga**, Hindu teachers offer guidance in subjective processes that can still passions and replace the tedium of life with feelings of joyful release that are believed to be a foretaste of a blessed immortality. As a final resort, the seeker is urged to enter the separated life of the world-abandoning *sannyāsī*.

If a religion can be defined by what it holds to be the most blessed condition that humanity can know, Hinduism is the religion of tranquillity of self and society. Since it regards tranquillity as its highest goal, Hinduism subordinates other values, such as social progress, material well-being, and justice as we understand it in the West. In responding to this (or any other) religion, we must of course note the attainments that it holds in highest esteem and recognize that no faith will be effective in reaching goals that it does not seek.

The Indus Civilization

Until the twentieth century, scholars believed that the much-revered scriptures called the **Vedas** contained the oldest materials of the Hindu tradition. The Vedas were the hymns of a people called the **Aryas** who migrated into India from Iran in the middle of the second millennium B.C.E. Recent archaeological excavations have revealed, however, that 1,000 or more years before the Aryas arrived, an agricultural people had already settled in the Indus River valley. This **Indus civilization**, also referred to as the Harappans after the modern name of one of their cities, built carefully planned cities and developed a system of writing. Scholars now recognize a dual origin for Hinduism: the religious heritage of the Vedas, long studied and moderately well known, and the culture of the Indus civilization, which, because its writings have not yet been deciphered, is still poorly known. Yet much that is distinctive in Hinduism clearly came from this Indus source.

The Indus civilization dates back nearly as far as the cultures of Mesopotamia and Egypt. In 2700 B.C.E. the Indus valley was already dotted with farming villages. Shortly thereafter, the people began building cities. By about 2400 B.C.E. the culture was in full bloom, manifesting the distinctive style of life that was to characterize it for almost 1,000 years. Two hundred towns and five large cities have been identified so far. The two biggest cities, Harappā and Mohenjo-Dāro, both in present-day Pakistan, were true metropolises. Reaching as far east as Delhi and south into Maharashtra, the Indus civilization was the most extensive of the world's very early cultures.

The Indus people made simple tools of copper and bronze. They grew wheat and other grains and kept cows, sheep, pigs, and chickens. Their still undeciphered writing is found mainly in short inscriptions

The Indus people made tools of copper and bronze, as well as art. This bronze figure of a dancing girl from Mohenjo-Dāro dates from c. 2000 B.C.E. (The Granger Collection)

carved on soapstone seals that were used to mark trade shipments. On the face of the seals, plants and animals are carved with remarkable skill in a style that is one of the distinguishing marks of this civilization.

The crowning achievement of the Indus people was their city planning and sanitary engineering. In these aspects the Indus civilization had no rivals. Towns were laid out in a grid of wide, straight, intersecting thoroughfares. The houses, grouped into residential districts, were of a type still prevalent in India today, with plain walls facing the street and small rooms clustered around a central open-air courtyard. Carefully sleeved wells topped with broad masonry curbs were the source of household water. Each house had a bathroom with a latrine and large water pots from which the toilet could be flushed. Waste water ran into sewers buried under the street outside.

Many features suggest the presence of an effective ruling elite. A uniform measure of length used by builders and a precise system of merchants' weights suggest a system of official oversight, as does the regularity of the towns' layout. On a mound just beyond the western boundary of every Indus town we find a complex of facilities thought to be the administrative center. The mound at Mohenjo-Dāro features an assembly hall and a unique bathing pool, and both Mohenjo-Dāro and Harappā had large granaries. Archaeologists at first took these raised terraces to be citadels, but further excavations showed few barracks, weapons, or fortifications. From this we infer that methods of social control were most probably nonviolent—the presence of large granaries suggests that the early rulers were already using India's characteristic nonviolent method of controlling populations through the collective distribution of food. Another perennial method for ensuring conformity and order was also employed: the inculcation of reverence for established ways.

RELIGION IN THE INDUS CULTURE

Even the best scholarship cannot outline a religious system whose language is not understood. Our information on Indus religion is based only on what the spades of archaeologists have laid bare. Inferences from those findings continue to stir debate, but we shall present a few tentative conclusions.

Our first generalization is that the Indus people probably looked back on their ancestors with exceptional reverence. As archaeologists studied the development of city life from the earliest strata to the latest, they saw a scrupulous adherence to original patterns. For example, the city limits did not expand or contract, nor did the street layout change. When houses collapsed, they were rebuilt on the precise lines of the old foundations. For 1,000 years there was no change in the artistic style of the seals, tools, or weapons or in the alphabetic characters engraved on them. The Indus people probably looked on the ways of their ancestors as sacred and inviolable. Already, here in India's first civilization, something existed of the historic Hindu view that the hope of humanity lies not in the new but in the past, the sole source of holy truth.

Another aspect of Indus religion was an almost reverent regard for water. In the Indus cities water was carefully channeled in cleverly designed wells, drains, and toilets. The Mohenjo-Dāro bathing pool, elevated above the level of the city and surrounded by imposing arcades, suggests that bathing rites had a place in the solemn processes of government. Alas, archaeology cannot tell us the ideology behind these official lustrations. Their importance may rest on the fact that, especially in the area's arid climate, successful agriculture required much attention—and thus ritual attention—to water. Or we can speculate that here, as in later Hinduism, bathing was an essential preliminary to worship because it was believed to make "unclean" mortals fit to deal with the sacred realities. Or we can note that even today in rural India, wells, pools, and streams are held to be the residing places of superhuman beings and are often destinations of sacred pilgrimage. There may be a historical relationship here, for water has had a prominent place in both Indus and modern Hindu practice.

Goddess worship was widespread in Indus religion. In almost every house archaeologists have found small figurines, the most common of which was a broad-hipped and elaborately dressed female figure; some scholars hold that these figurines personified the earth. Near one such image, oil or incense had been burned in a cup, evidently in a home ritual. One well-preserved seal shows a female figure upside down, a bushy plant springing from her womb. Another shows what seems to be an animal sacrifice being offered to a goddess who is standing next to a large tree. This farming culture probably—and understandably—revered the earth, its source of plenty.

Seals like the ones mentioned earlier, hundreds of which bear inscriptions, will someday be a rich source of information on Harappan religious life. Though we cannot yet read the words, we can interpret the pictures. Some seals show interactions between beings with human characteristics but also superhuman traits. Tales about superhuman heroes and deities are no doubt being portrayed; some of the roots of Indian mythology probably lie here. Though we do not see the familiar divine forms of later Hinduism, some scholars feel that we are looking at their early representations. For instance, the male figure shown in lotus position on four of the seals is plausibly thought to prefigure the later god Śiva. Other observers point to his seated posture as evidence that yoga was already being practiced 4,000 years ago.

Goddess worship was widespread in the religion of the Indus civilization. This clay figurine was found in the ruins of the ancient Indus metropolis of Mohenjo-Dāro. (Borromeo/Art Resource)

In addition to such early god and goddess figures, impressive male powers are also often represented on the seals: great bulls, rhinoceroses, tigers, and elephants are carved with mighty horns and splendid musculature. Myths and perhaps even philosophical ideas probably circulated about interactions between these various male and female forces.

According to the scholar Marija Gimbutas and others, goddess worship and additional factors suggest that governance and organizational power in the Indus civilization may have been to a significant degree in the hands of women. At the very least, the social and religious values of this culture seem to reflect a very different orientation from the patriarchal and patrilinear Aryan civilization that was to follow it.

END OF THE INDUS CIVILIZATION

By 1900 B.C.E. Harappā and Mohenjo-Dāro were falling into disarray. Decay was staved off for a few centuries more in daughter cities of the Indus type that had been established far to the south. But by 1600 B.C.E. no Indus cities remained inhabited. The cause of their abandonment remains a mystery. A likely immediate cause was failure of the grain supply to the granaries of the cities. The deeper cause, some have proposed, was misuse of the soil, climatic change, or catastrophic floods. Other scholars believe that the cities ended bloodily—in massive attacks by the Indo-European people called the Aryas, who are known to have been on the move in Iran in the eighteenth century B.C.E. and to have occupied northern India by force by about 1600 B.C.E. The Aryas were indeed the next known people to have dominance in the Indus valley, and they could have seized control directly from the Indus rulers. But there was no wholesale slaughter of the Indus people or even of the population of their cities. Rather the cities and towns were abandoned one by one over several centuries through processes that left few signs of violence. The Aryas did not drive the population from the land as even some Vedic texts suggest, nor did they drastically change the agricultural life of the indigenous people.

What came to an end was city life, along with the high culture and skills that were distinctly urban. With the cities went urban planning, the sewers, the seals, the alphabet, and in time the pre-Aryan languages. The Aryan conquest caused the most radical linguistic displacement India has ever known. When 1,000 years later inscriptions were again written in India, they used entirely new alphabets expressing new languages belonging to the Indo-European family, and the dominant religion became that of the Aryan elite.

But quietly, among laborers and farmers, much of the pre-Aryan heritage in religion and custom would continue, to reappear centuries later in different form. After 500 B.C.E. many of the social and economic aspects of the old Indus life returned: intensive agriculture, great cities, and rulers exercising strict control. Elements of the old Indus religion, which had served populations under such conditions, became popular again. Mingling occurred, and the dominant religion became the blend that we now know as Hinduism.

THE RELIGION OF THE VEDAS

The Aryas are first noted in Mesopotamian records of 1800 to 1400 B.C.E., when they were probably migrating also into northwestern India. Those who settled in India first revealed themselves in a great body of oral literature composed and compiled by their priestly class between 1200 and 800 B.C.E. Whereas the religion of the Indus culture is known only from the discoveries of archaeologists, the outlook of the Aryas has been recovered from the Vedas, the oldest of the Hindu scriptures.

THE CULTURE OF THE EARLY ARYAS

In the Vedas we discern a people with a life style quite different from the Indus people's. These early Aryas built no cities, and they were less advanced than their predecessors in most of the sciences and arts. But they had developed superior metallurgy and weaponry, and they were skilled in riding horses and using war chariots. They grew grains on land near their villages but also kept large herds of grazing animals. The Aryas were divided into five tribes, each led by an independent chieftain who was responsible for defense and internal order. Though they shared a common ethnic identity, the tribes were not united politically. Three social ranks were recognized: priests (brāhmans), the warrior class, and the general population. Membership in these classes was not hereditary.

THE VEDAS

Though the Aryas had no system of writing when they entered India and remained without one for a long time, they brought with them from Iran a tradition of oral poetry and took exceptional delight in their language. By about 1200 B.C.E. certain groups of Aryan priests had begun to memorize with exceptional care the poetry then in liturgical use. By about 800 B.C.E. their religious poetry had been gathered into four collections (saṃhitās) that are known as the four Vedas. Even though preserved in memory only, the texts of these poems were as firmly fixed as if they had been printed. We may thus speak of these recited Vedas as "books."

The Sanskrit of these Vedas belongs to the Indo-European language family. *Veda,* a cognate of the English words *wit* and *wisdom,* means "wisdom"—the sacred wisdom of the Aryas. The Vedic age, when a single cult was dominant in literature, lasted from about 1200 to 600 B.C.E. We shall focus on the religion around 800 B.C.E., when the cult had its greatest following. By this time three collections already had the status of Veda: the Ṛigveda, the Sāmaveda, and the Yajurveda. An independent fourth collection, later called the Atharvaveda, was already in existence but not fully formalized. Each of these Vedas was preserved by a separate guild of priests.

The Ṛigveda

The **Ṛigveda** was the liturgical book of the *hotars,* an ancient order of Aryan priests who originally performed the sacrifices alone. Soon the hotar was given assistants who took over the manual and musical aspects of the ritual, and the hotar became a specialist in hymns of praise. The hotar's lasting role was to recite, at certain key moments in the ritual, one or more hymns in honor of a god or several gods. Each verse of these hymns of the hotars was called a *ṛic,* or praise stanza. This term gave the collection its name, the Ṛigveda, the sacred wisdom consisting of stanzas of praise. The Ṛigveda, most of which is the oldest Veda, is made up of 1,028 hymns organized in ten divisions or books. The preserved names of the poets of these and other hymns indicate that both men and women contributed to them.

The Sāmaveda and the Yajurveda

The **Sāmaveda** is the anthology of the enlarged priestly troupe's specialists—both male and female—in the songs *(sāmans).* The Sāmaveda is a compilation of verses selected almost entirely from the earlier books of the Ṛigveda, arranged in the order in which the singer needed them when performing ceremonial duties.

The **Yajurveda** was compiled for the use of another new participant in the ritual, the **adhvaryu**, whose duty it was to make the physical preparations for the rite and to handle the offerings during the ceremony, at the same time muttering short incantations *(yajuses)* declaring the purpose and meaning of each ritual act. About half of these are fragments extracted from the Ṛigveda; the remainder are new prose compositions.

The weaving together of the individual performances of the specialists became a complicated and worrisome matter. Great powers were believed to be set in play by the priestly utterances, and slips in performance were dreaded, so a fourth priest was added to listen, detect errors, and remedy all mistakes. At first any knowledgeable priest could become such a silent supervisor; soon, however, the position became the monopoly of a group of experts in medicine called **Atharvans**.

The Fourth Veda

The original work of the Atharvans had nothing to do with the great public rituals for which the other three Vedas were composed. The Atharvans had been personal medical practitioners and counselors. In crises they had served both ordinary individuals and kings, warding off battle wounds and threats to the prosperity of their realms. Atharvans often became royal chaplains and as such the supervisors of court rituals. In a natural step they became the silent supervisory priests on the staff of the dignified Vedic sacrifices. Through this elevation of the Atharvans to the status of fourth priests at the great fire altars, the Atharvans' professional lore rose in status also, eventually coming to be regarded as the fourth Veda, the **Atharvaveda**. Incorporating many popular hymns and incantations that had been in use for centuries, the Atharvaveda differs significantly in content and purpose from the other three Vedas. These spells were not suitable for introduction into the Vedic rituals around the sacred fire, but some Atharvans continued to use them therapeutically.

THE VEDIC WORLDVIEW

In the Vedic age people were only beginning to reflect seriously on philosophical problems; the great Hindu systems of thought did not yet exist. Although some metaphysical questions about humanity and the universe were beginning to be asked, the answers were diverse and underdeveloped, as seen in opinions of the time on major topics of concern.

Humanity What is the essence of the human being? The Vedic age was content with commonsense answers. Perceiving that when breath goes, life goes, discussion of the life essence centered on the breath or a similar airy substance believed to permeate the living body. **Prāṇa**, an internal air current of the body, is often spoken of as the basic animating principle. But the favorite term was **ātman**, which is atmospheric in its connotations but less concrete in its reference. Ātman was conceived as a subtle substance existing within the human body yet separable from it.

At death this subtle life-breath leaves the body and rises in the updraft of the funeral pyre to a luminous heaven above the atmosphere. Vedic people expected to reach that lofty place of song and to dwell there with their ancestors indefinitely. All who acted correctly and performed the rituals faithfully could be confident of enjoying in heaven all that was best in earthly life. They did not, however, dislike their earthly bodies or long to leave the earth. On the contrary, worshipers often petitioned the gods for life spans of 100 years. The Vedic religious practices were meant to maximize the earthly life, not to replace it with existence on a different level of being.

The universe The substance, structure, and origin of the universe did not yet receive systematic discussion. Understanding the essence of the universe was not as important to the practical-minded people of this age as being able to control it. But several basic cosmological ideas were well developed and generally accepted. One of the commonest was the understanding of the universe as composed of the **three realms**. These realms were conceived as three horizontal strata, one above the other. The lowest was the earthly realm, the disk on which humanity lived and walked. The second was the realm of the atmosphere, in which birds flew and the chariots of the gods were sometimes seen. Its upper boundary was the vault of the sky, through which birds cannot fly and vision cannot penetrate. Above this vault was the mysterious heavenly realm, the home of the deities and the refuge of the blessed dead. When Yama, the first human, died, he discovered the path to heaven for all who followed him; there he presides over the departed ancestors. It was the god **Vishṇu** who established these great divisions when he marked off the entire universe in three of his giant strides.

Ṛita, the basis of order All natural actions in this three-layered universe are governed by an impersonal principle called **ṛita**. Ṛita enables natural bodies to move rhythmically and in balance, without undergoing the disorganizing effect otherwise implicit in motion. Because of ṛita we have an ordered universe that undergoes change without becoming chaos: the sun follows its daily rhythm of setting and rising; the stars fade at dawn but twinkle again at dusk. Ṛita is a dynamic principle of order, manifesting itself in change, not rigidity.

In human affairs ṛita is the propriety that makes social harmony possible. In speech ṛita is truth, and in interpersonal dealings it is justice. When humans observe ṛita, order prevails and there is peace. In worship ṛita is the pattern of correct ritual performance. Right ritual maintains harmony between humanity and nature, humanity and the gods, and one person and another.

Ṛita is not the command of any deity. The great Vedic god **Varuṇa**, the upholder of order, is the special guardian of ṛita. He punished those who do not speak the truth or who commit improper actions. Not even Varuṇa, however, created ṛita. All the gods are subject to it. Ṛita is a philosophical principle, an ancient Indo-European abstraction that from the beginning was independent of theology. In India the word *ṛita* was eventually replaced by the term *dharma,* "duty," referring to what is right as an unchanging standard. The major Indian orthodoxies still retain the original impersonality of Indian ethical theory. In no other aspect of thought is India more different from the Semitic religions than in this.

The ultimate source of things Vedic composers addressed themselves only casually to the problem of the world's origin and final substance. Their tentative stories about cosmic beginnings varied greatly, though most of their speculations included two original entities: the divine beings and some material with which they worked. As to the nature of the deities' materials, they had no settled answer. Ṛigveda 10.90 traces the main features of the world back to a great primeval sacrifice performed by the gods in which the body of a victim called Purusha ("primal man") was dismembered, his limbs and organs being used to form the parts of the human and natural world. Whence this Purusha may have come and what he was are not explained.

Other speculators considered the possibility of a sexual origin of the world, saying that all things had been generated through intercourse between the Sky Father and the Earth Mother or by a single potent procreator. Such efforts to explain the origin of the world in terms of divine sexuality produced no generally acceptable cosmogony.

They gave rise, rather, to a realization that the **devas** (gods) could provide no answer. Each of the deities was conceived to have a spatial location, and many, even most, were defined by their association with some natural power. Conceptualized as a part of the natural world, a deva could not reasonably be understood to be the creator of that world. This was not monotheism. When at last in the late Vedic passages we find intense consideration of the origin of things, we find seers who perceive, as the primal source, a divine essence rather than a divine person—an impersonal essence from which the divine beings themselves arose. One of the earliest and finest expressions of this dominant view occurs in the last book of the Ṛigveda, in hymn 10.129.

Ṛigveda 10.129: A Hymn of Creation

This hymn reminds us of the first chapter of Genesis. Here, too, there is mention of primeval waters and a sense of the tantalizing mystery of an event so distant in time that it is inaccessible to all the usual means of human knowing. As this daring thought proceeds, however, the thinker's mind reveals its own distinctive tendency as it asks, "What moved on the face of that mysterious deep?" Whereas the Hebrew would reply, "In the beginning God . . . ," the Vedic poet considered the potentialities of all the gods and sought elsewhere for the aboriginal reality:

1. *Nonbeing then was not, nor was there being;*
   there was no realm of air, no sky above it.
   What covered them? And where? In whose protection?
   And was there deep unfathomable water?
2. *Death then existed not, nor the immortal;*
   sheen was there none of night and day.
   Breathless, That One *breathed of its own nature;*
   aside from that was nothing whatsoever.
3. *There was darkness hid in darkness at the outset;*
   an unillumined flood, indeed, was all this.
   That Creative Force covered by the void,
   That One, was born by the power of brooding.

Contemplating the condition that must have prevailed before the world took form, the seer stresses its otherness from all that is now familiar. Even the three realms (1b)* had not yet been marked out. Neither mortals nor the gods were yet there (2a), nor had day and night made their appearance (2b). Where were these things then hidden, and by what (1c)? That they were sunk away in a formless watery abyss is first suggested tentatively (1d) and then asserted positively (3b). Life and being were represented in that primeval waste by a solitary creative force, vital inasmuch as it breathed and yet breathing as no living thing breathes now (2c). This single source of what has breath was not a personal God but a neuter It (2c). It was not even eternal but arose in the oceanic void through a natural incubating warmth or perhaps through the intense mental activity of unidentified mediators (3d).

4. *Desire came into it at the beginning—*
   desire that was of thought the primal offspring.
   The tie of being in nonbeing found they,
   the wise ones, searching in the heart with wisdom.
5. *Transversely was their severing line extended—*
   what was there down below, and what was over?
   There were begetters—mighty beings!—
   fertile power below, and potency up yonder.

Out of this pool of undeveloped life the actuality of living beings proceeded to appear, through the rise of erotic desire (4a) and then of male and female procreators (5d). The initiating factor again (3d) was power generated by the introspection of meditators whose identity and origin are not explained (4d). In the hearts of these sages, thought gave rise to desire (4b), and this erotic urge became the cord, so to speak (4c), by which creatures were drawn up out of the formless abyss in which they had been hidden. This primal desire was the cord also by which the line of sexual differentiation was drawn across the universe (5a), distinguishing creatures into interacting males and females of great creative power (5c, d).

6. *Who really knows? Who can here proclaim it?*
   Whence is it born? Whence is this creation?

*The number refers to the stanza of the hymn, the letter to the line, in the order *a, b, c, d*. Thus "1b" is the second line of the first stanza.

The gods are later than this world's creation
so who can know from what it came to being?
7. *That from which this creation came to being,*
whether created 'twas, or not created,
He who is its Overseer in highest heaven,
He only knows—or He may know not!

Here the author confesses that his picture of these remote events is not based on the knowledge of witnesses (6a); the gods, the most ancient of all knowing beings, are themselves the products of these processes and cannot testify about the beginning of things (6c). But the author is not sure that even a supreme god, the present ruler of creation, is old enough to be able to bear witness to that time (7d). His only confidence is that all life proceeded from a single divine source, which must have been of a nonphenomenal nature. Though persons were derived from it, it in itself was so different from everything known that it cannot be given a personal name. It can be called only "That One."

The Devas or Vedic Gods

Each hymn of the Ṛigveda is designated for use in the worship of one or more of the superhuman devas. The word *deva* is derived from the noun *div*, meaning "radiant sky." Thus these beings abide primarily in the heavenly realm. But some dwell in the other two realms as well. The gods of rain and wind, for instance (Parjanya and Vāyu or Vāta, respectively), live in the atmosphere; Ṣoma is a god of the earthly realm; and Agni, divinized fire, has seats in all three spheres—earth, atmosphere, and heaven. All members of the pantheon are formally classified by the realm that is their normal residence. This classification makes it clear that the devas are thought of as existing somewhere in nature as parts of the natural order.

Most of the Vedic deities can be understood as half-personalized conceptions of powers controlling nature. The god Vāyu is the power of the wind. Depicted as a bearded figure in a running pose, Vāyu's loose hair flies backward in wild strands, and his cloak billows. Likewise, the Vedic poet who speaks of Agni, the fire god, has visible fire in mind, whether in the heavenly sun, atmospheric lightning, or the earthly fire ritual. Parjanya is addressed in language applicable to rain and is taken to *be* rain. Sūrya is the sun as seen when the actual solar disk traverses the sky. When the

The image on this North Indian coin from early in the Common Era represents the Vedic god Indra, a great battle god shaped by the migrating Aryas' military experiences. Note the war god's pike at left, the pommel of his sword at right, and his crested helmet with eagle emblem. (Norvin Hein)

priest in the morning sacrifice faces Ushas, the goddess of the dawn, it is the dawn itself that he faces as he sings:

We see her there, the child of heaven, apparent,
the young maid, flushing in her shining raiment.
Thou mistress of all earthly riches,
flush on us here, auspicious Dawn, this morning.

(Ṛigveda 1.113.7)

Even **Indra**, a great battle god shaped by the migrating Aryas' military experiences, acquired in India a connection with rain. Assuming that all deities operate or can operate in some sphere of nature, India asked this great Aryan warrior god to fight also against the land's most threatening enemy, **Vṛitra**, the evil demon that withholds the waters or the monsoon.

The extent to which the devas are understood to control aspects of nature can be seen in the petitions that we find in the hymns addressed to them. The deities are revered but at the same time are asked to apply their powers to the worshipers' needs. In hymns to the dawn goddess Ushas, for example, the composer

The Pattern of the Śrauta Sacrifice

Here we shall be content to bring together the most common elements of a śrauta sacrifice in a simple imaginary performance. Let the time be shortly after 800 B.C.E. Already the priestly staff required had reached four. The place is the Panjab. A cattleman has herds numbering in the hundreds, but he is ill at ease. For reasons that are not quite clear, his animals are not increasing and are not in good health. Is it the condition of the pasturelands? His reputation for good husbandry is also at stake. Perhaps, the rancher believes, his fortunes may be suffering by reason of poor relations with the superhuman powers that affect his profession. He has heard of a priest of good reputation who is just now moving from ranch to ranch in the next district. He has invited the brāhman and his staff, and a day has been set.

On the day before the scheduled sacrifice, the adhvaryu of the famous troupe had arrived to prepare a site for the performance, bringing in his cart all the necessary materials and implements: a goat to be sacrificed, a hand drill for kindling a fire, cooking pots, barley meal for making offering cakes, bowls and strainers for preparing **soma**, a sacred inebriating drink, and some sacred grass for seating gods and humans.

In the open air, between the ranch house and the cattle pens, the adhvaryu selected an area for the rite and dug in it three shallow fire pits, one square, one round, one semicircular. With the excavated soil he raised an earthen altar of irregular shape to hold the offerings. Setting slim poles in the ground, he raised a light open shed over the fire pits. On the floor of this booth he strewed the sacred grass. At sundown on this day of preparation, the sponsoring rancher entered the booth to begin a night of purifying seclusion. His hair and nails were trimmed, and after bathing, he put on a new garment. Thereafter he consumed nothing but warm milk, kept his fingers doubled up like those of a baby, and spoke only with a stammer. He conceived himself to be undergoing rebirth into a state of purity fitting him for relations with the gods. (In short, using the model presented in the introductory chapter, he went though the ritual stages of distancing, liminality, and rebirth.)

The next morning, the adhvaryu's first duty was to kindle the sacrificial fires. The house fire could not be used. With much sweat he accomplished this task with a fire drill. As the time of sacrifice approached, a few neighbors assembled to observe the performance. Any Arya might attend such proceedings with merit, but the rite was understood to be the rancher's personal ceremony, and he alone was expected to receive its special benefits.

At the appointed hour the three other priests came: the hotar, the singer, and the supervisor. All took their seats on the grass along with the rancher's wife and the rancher himself, who was now allowed to open his fists and speak clearly. The adhvaryu poured on the fire a libation of melted butter. As the flames shot up, the hotar began the rite by reciting an invocatory hymn:

Agni I praise, the household
priest,
the god and priest of sacrifice,
chief priest and bestower of
great gifts.
May Agni, worthy to be praised
by sages ancient and of now,
may he bring hitherward the
gods.
Through Agni may we treasure
gain
and welfare get from day to
day
and honor and most manly
sons.
(Ṛigveda 1.1.1–3)

The fire god, Agni, who can move in all three spheres of the universe, was now presumed to rise from the fire and carry an invitation to the appropriate gods in their heavenly abodes. The divine guests were believed to descend unseen to seats reserved for them on the fragrant grass. There they were entertained with lofty and flattering poetry, such as the following hymn to Indra in honor of his great victory over Vṛitra:

I will proclaim the manly deeds
of Indra,
The first that he performed,
the lightning-wielder.
He slew the serpent, then
discharged the waters
And cleft the caverns of the
lofty mountains.[6]
(Ṛigveda 1.32.1)

(Usually sacrificers praised the god for deeds they wanted the gods to repeat, such as the release of rain by Indra.)

The singing priest then intoned his distinctive and religiously powerful songs, the *sāmans*, while the adhvaryu moved around and offered food and drink as refreshments to the gods. As he did so, he muttered short prose formulas (*yajuses*) that explained his actions. The supervisor did not recite at all but listened carefully, correcting any errors made by the other priests.

To quench the deities' thirst, the adhvaryu periodically poured into the fire libations of milk or the heavenly soma. (The soma plant is said to have been transplanted from heaven to certain high mountains. Its gathered stems were pounded, and the juice was then strained to make a golden inebriating drink.) Cups of soma were given to the priests also, who then sensed a divine presence within themselves:

We have drunk Soma and
become immortal;
We have attained the light the
gods discovered.
What can hostility now do
against us?
And what, immortal god, the
spite of mortals?[7]
(Ṛigveda 8.48.3)

The adhvaryu offered food to the gods by dropping it into the fire. Butter, curds, and cakes were among these offerings. Portions were handed to the patron and the performing priests. At a high moment, the sacrificial goat was untied from its painted post, strangled, and cut up. Portions of its flesh were offered in the fire, but most of it was boiled or roasted and eaten by the participants. Every part had to be consumed, either by the sacrificers or by the fire. As the gods were being praised and entertained in these ways, they were often reminded, pointedly, of the needs and hopes of the rancher.

The ritual completed, the satisfied gods returned to their abodes. The fee for priestly service was now presented. The priests' expected reward was high—the gift of a cow, perhaps. The rancher paid, then bathed and put on his usual clothing. The adhvaryu gathered up the implements of the sacrifice, throwing some into the fire and others into water. He picked up the strewn grass, tossing it into the fire. The sacrifice was over.

first observes that as the initiator of each day's work, she controls its success; then the humans pray for material boons:

> *Mete out to us, O Dawn, largesses: offspring,*
> *Brave men, conspicuous wealth in cows and horses.*[2]
>
> (Ṛigveda 1.92.7)

Likewise, a prayer to Pūshan, the sun's light, is well aware of his functions as a guide and a revealer of paths and asks for practical guidance:

> *Lead us to pastures rich in grass,*
> *Send on the road no early heat.*
> *Thus, Pūshan, show in us thy might.*[3]
>
> (Ṛigveda 1.42.8)

To a degree, the worship of these gods and goddesses can be seen as an effort to live successfully amid the awesome forces of the natural world.

This insight does not elucidate the entire Vedic pantheon, however. Particularly, the naturalistic explanations help very little in understanding Indra and Varuṇa, two of the most important deities. These two gods are mentioned mainly in connection with activities that are human and social rather than natural.

Indra is called the chief of the gods. The fact that fully one-fourth of the Ṛigveda's hymns are dedicated to him confirms his preeminence. But Varuṇa is called the foremost of the gods in almost the same terms. Together the two constitute a cooperating pair of rulers whose authority is somehow complementary. They are a committee of two, so to speak, whose authority is the Vedas' nearest approach to that of a monotheistic God.

But neither god's importance rests on control of any vital aspect of the natural world. A seat in nature has been allotted to each of them, it is true. Though Varuṇa's place is the vault of the sky and he is conceived as being present also in bodies of water, he does not *personify* the sky or the ocean. The sky is the vantage point from which Varuṇa surveys human deeds, and he is a water god only to the extent that he inflicts disorders of the bodily fluids on human beings as punishments for violations of ṛita. These marginal connections with nature are not the basis for his vast importance, as will become clear.

Indra has a dramatic connection with the rain clouds, but only in the single myth of his combat with Vṛitra, the demon of drought. But like Varuṇa, Indra in no way personifies rain or clouds, nor is his connection with rain his primary feature. That was visualized 1,000 years later when the emperor Kanishka issued a gold coin bearing Indra's likeness. It shows Indra's fundamental character: the Aryan battle god. In full armor, eagle-crested, armed with both sword and spear, he is a personification of the ideal powers and virtues of the males of the Aryan warrior class.

Unlike Varuṇa, the Indra of the Ṛigveda has nothing to do with morality, either in function or in character. In Vedic mythology he was a ruffian from birth—a lecherous youth and a drunken, boastful adult. After consuming offerings of thousands of buffalo and drinking lakes of intoxicants, Indra lurches off to the wars and there assists his people. He protects them from the power of alien peoples and from terrifying demons. His domain, then, is the hazardous area where his worshipers must cope with hostile outside forces. Immensely strong, Indra promises the warrior class confidence and mastery of battles with foreigners.

Varuṇa is equal to Indra in rank, but there the similarity ends. Whereas Indra protects from dangers lurking at the community's outer boundaries, Varuṇa, his co-ruler, guarantees order by defending the right, guarding the harmony of internal social life. His omnipresent spies examine the truthfulness of what people say and the justice in what they do. Guardian against anarchy, Varuṇa is also the celestial patron of earthly kings, the legitimizer of their authority, and the chief deity addressed in the Aryan coronation ceremony.

Natural danger is not the focal problem in the worship of either Indra or Varuṇa. These two deal, each in his own area, with interpersonal, social dangers—threats to the community from outside or from within. Vedic religion, like other religions, addresses its adherents' most acute insecurities, whatever they be.

In sum, the worship of the Vedic gods is directed toward three types of insecurity. The first is natural: the danger of injury, disease, and want. In this area Vedic worshipers supplemented normal human efforts by invoking the many nature deities and by resorting to the Atharvans' magical rituals. The second insecurity is moral, caused by destructive individualism within the community itself. In the face of such danger, Varuṇa is worshiped as the guardian of ṛita; he punishes antisocial behavior and supports the authority of kings. The third insecurity is military, arising in warfare with alien civilizations. Here Vedic worshipers call to a god of unbounded force, seeking strength and a rallying point in war. In this area they worshiped Indra, just as in economic need they worshiped the nature gods and for social stability they worshiped Varuṇa.

The gods of the Veda have varying moral natures. Varuṇa is a highly moral deity. Nature gods like the solar Savitṛi are amoral, and Indra as a personification of Aryan might is not moral at all. Because Western religions are now highly specialized in dealing with the moral crises of modern societies, many Western students may find it difficult to understand how Vedic worshipers could revere any of these deities save Varuṇa. They should remember that science has only recently become humanity's defense against natural ills. Most religions, past and present, address the whole range of human insecurities. Vedic religion was as broad in its scope as the anxieties of its people.

RITUALS OF THE VEDIC AGE

In rituals we see a religion in action and can often discern a people's deepest concerns and hopes. Life in the Vedic era was rich in rituals of many kinds. About some of them—Aryan ploughing festivals, marriages, funeral rites—we know very little. We know only a little more about the daily fireside rites in each Aryan home, performed for the well-being of the family. In them the husband's role was dominant, but the presence of both the husband and the wife was necessary if the deities were to regard this as a family home and look after it as such. The husband—or presumably the wife in his absence—kept the domestic fire going and offered milk with bits of food in it, accompanied by simple prayers. This tradition of family rituals was to continue, grow in recognition, and at last be described in scripture.

Of another popular ritual we know a good deal because its poetry had the good fortune of being preserved in the Atharvaveda. Most of that Veda consists of incantations that the ancient Atharvan order of priests used at the family hearth when called into the home in a medical or emotional emergency to bring supernatural aid to the suffering family or afflicted family member. Here is an Atharvan's spell for a child with a severe cough:

As the sun's rays fly quickly away,
So also you, O cough, fly forth
In conformity with the ocean's ebb.[4]

(Atharvaveda 6.105.2)

Though gods of the recognized Vedic pantheon are sometimes named in this Veda's verses, they are not approached seriously as personal beings. The divine names are chanted with imperious determination among other awesome words that are thought to empower the ritual. The Atharvan often uses herbs in his treatment also. (The Atharvaveda, also called the Ayurveda, is considered the foundation of the still-used Ayurvedic system of Indian medicine.) In another verse the Atharvan is directing his therapy—herbal as well as verbal—against leprosy:

Born in the night art thou, O herb,
Dark-colored, sable, black of hue:
Rich-tinted, tinge this leprosy,
And stain away its spots of gray.[5]

(Atharvaveda 1.23.1)

The Atharvans had spells also for gaining the affection of a beloved person and for countering a sorcerer's curse. They had charms to control dice in gambling, to cancel the effect of wrongful acts, and to void the disastrous consequences of blunders in performing rituals. This last ability, as we have seen, raised the social status of these magicians immensely.

The Śrauta Rites

Śrauta is the name for the most formal and dignified Aryan sacrifice. The word comes from the noun *śruti,* a synonym for *Veda.* The śrauta rites are those in which the first three collections of Vedic hymns were used. Patronized for many centuries by the Aryas' political and economic elite and served by their most learned priesthood, this type of ritual was handled with such care as no other religious practice of the Vedic age received. Many complicated śrauta ceremonies were developed for use in special situations. There was a royal coronation ritual, a horse sacrifice by which a king could assert and confirm the boundaries of his realm, and an Agnishṭoma rite for times of drought, involving much dripping and splashing and pouring of the ambrosial libation to suggest and induce a downpour of rain. Many śrauta rituals went on for days, and book-length treatment would be required to describe them in full (see "The Pattern of the Śrauta Sacrifice").

LATER LITERATURE OF THE PRIESTLY SCHOOLS

In the early Vedic period, the memorized Ṛigveda was handed down in priestly families. But by 800 B.C.E. a second stage began when professional guilds took over teaching both the literature and the skills of the sacrifice. Recruiting young brāhman boys for the priesthood, the organizations trained their apprentices in their own schools. When the place for education shifted away from the home, brāhman daughters usually remained with the family, and only the boys received the priest's training. In part as a result, a great educational chasm developed between high-caste men and women. This helped to foster a differentiation of **gender roles**: girls were trained in domestic skills in preparation for marriage, and boys were educated in Vedic studies. With different roles came different ideals: women gradually came to value and be valued for characteristics such as fertility and humble devotion to the husband, whereas men were respected for their ritual and literary knowledge.

Preparing for their order's ritual role, the boys memorized the Ṛigveda and learned how to use the text in actual performances. They also heard lectures about the myths and commentaries explaining the Vedic passages, and they were warned about the missteps that are often made by badly trained priests. They heard for the first time that knowledgeable priests were really more important than the gods in producing the boons of the sacrifices. These collateral lectures became traditional in content and form, and the young priests began to memorize them as they memorized the hymns. The lectures too became scriptures, a second stratum of the Vedic religion's holy "books," called **brāhmaṇas**.

The guilds' practical training in ritual performance next underwent a similar codification into a form that could be learned by heart. By about 600 B.C.E. manuals called **śrauta sūtras** were being created that laid down instruction in every act and utterance of the sacrifice. To minimize the effort needed in memorization, these manuals were cast into a very compact new form of literary expression, the **sūtra**, or "thread" of discourse on a particular topic. Composed of a series of succinct and carefully worded prose sentences, a sūtra is easy to memorize. The Śrauta Sūtras of the various guilds became the third stratum of Vedic scripture. Having memorized his Śrauta Sūtra, his guild's brāhmaṇa, and its body of hymns, a young priest was equipped to take his seat at the sacred fire.

THE UNITY OF VEDIC RELIGION

Despite changes in practice and in thinking, the ritualistic religion we have been studying has been held in unity by the unchanging character of its goals. From beginning to end, worshipers at the fire pits strove to maximize the values of this world. They sought to live a healthy, long life amid plenty with a good reputation. When life was done, they both hoped and expected to be accepted into a celestial realm that was not radically different from this world but rather its perfection. Though petitioners at the rites asked generally for personal benefits to themselves, they were not utterly indifferent to the general welfare. The prayer of a king at a royal sacrifice assumes that he and his subjects will benefit together:

> May the cow be rich in milk, strong the draught ox, swift the steed, fruitful the woman, eloquent the youth. May a hero be born to the sacrificer. May Parjanya give rain at all times according to our desire. May the corn ripen.[8]
>
> (White Yajurveda 22.22)

Vedic hearts were not pessimistic about the attainability of such hopes. The gods were thought to be favorably inclined, on the whole, toward dwellers on the earth. Approached through wise priests, they would confer all necessary favor on their worshipers, who even after death would enjoy a blessed life in a place of endless light. Though happy in this assurance, people of the Vedic age were not preoccupied with thoughts of the afterlife, nor did they long either to depart to or to replace this world with a heaven. Rather, Vedic religion showed a firm attachment to earthly values and a persistent confidence in their realizability.

COMPARISON

Vedic and Hebrew Ultimates Compared

Whereas in the earlier Vedic hymns the gods were semipersonalized natural phenomena, in the later Vedas the ultimate source of creation is typically conceived of impersonally. As we saw, in Ṛigveda 10.90 creation derived from the operations of a great cosmic sacrifice. In the Hymn of Creation reality is again brought about by an impersonal process, the breathing of "That One." It is no accident that later Hinduism comes to represent the ultimate reality as an impersonal "essence," Brahman, which is to be found immanently within the world and within each individual.

Throughout the Hebrew scriptures, by contrast, the ultimate is typically conceived of as analogous to a person. Like a person, this God has intentions: through a great act of will, he "created heaven and earth," he "watches over" Israel, and so on. He is thought of as having humanlike intelligence, providing creation with a direction. He is a ruler and a giver and enforcer of law; Brahman is not. Like a person, he has emotions: he can be jealous, angry, loving. And just as two people are separate from each other, this ultimate is conceived not as immanently within but as transcendent to or separate from people: Adam "heard the sound of God walking in the garden" (Gen. 3:8); God "called to [Moses] out of the bush" (Exod. 3:4). In later tradition, naturally, he is not typically searched for within, as Brahman is, but, like a respected person, is to be honored, obeyed, and loved.

THE RISE OF THE CONCEPT OF BRAHMAN

Over the centuries, as witnessed by the texts, the understandings of how the sacrifice could accomplish its goals changed. As priests reflected on that problem, they arrived at the conception of **Brahman**, the single source of all that is. Brahman was destined to become a key concept in later Hindu thought about final salvation, but when the term first appears, it occurs as a late answer to the question, how do the sacrifices exert their power?

That the sacrifices do produce their promised boons, no Vedic spokesman had any doubt. In early centuries of the Vedic age the explanation was simply that worship is a relationship between persons, human and divine. Just as earthly rulers can be mollified and influenced by praise and presents, gods too can be induced, by ingratiating speech, gifts, and fine entertainment, to exercise their powers for worshipers. But in later literature, beginning with the Yajurveda, authors are found who can no longer conceive of the gods in such personal terms or believe that the fruits of sacrifice are produced by such a personalistic process (see "Vedic and Hebrew Ultimates Compared"). It seems likely that the close identification of many gods with natural forces had worked against a deep belief in the gods as persons. Under intense contemplation the gods of wind and rain seemed to some believers to be personal beings by metaphor only or dubious impositions on a broad, ineffable reality. The separateness of their powers, too, was questionable. In thinking of the solar deities—Sūrya as the solar disk, Ushas as the dawn, Pūshan as the illuminator of paths—the separateness of these powers is not self-evident. The deities merge, plausibly becoming a single dynamic force operating in the whole of nature. The gods who exerted their powers for worshipers became mere names to many priests, many of whom now believed that their own insights and powers were more potent than those of the gods in producing the benefits of the rituals. Even the dynamic of the sacrifice came to be viewed impersonally: acts or words of the sacrifice have hidden ties with cosmic realities, and the priest, by manipulating these tokens, can bring about desired effects in the outer world. The symbols in the ritual become handles on the great realities that they symbolize. The masterful priest who knows these secret correspondences can activate the cosmic powers to which the symbols refer and bring about the development for which his client hopes. "This fire is yonder moon," a priest mutters as he casts a libation into the flaming semicircular fire pit. The strained identification seemed nonsense to scholars until they understood that to the priest the fire is a potent moon symbol, by reason of its yellow glow and half-moon shape. The priest's power over the fire gives him mastery over the moon, the cosmic metronome, for instance, that marks off the passage of time. Measuring off the months, the moon consumes the remaining life span of his ailing client. By knowing and using the power hidden in the symbols of his ritual, the priest is undertaking to extend the life of his patron. By such thinking, priests remained assured of the power of their rituals even when they could no longer believe them to be effective through the intervention of personal gods.

In their search for power through the connections to their ritual, the priests became fascinated with what they might be able to do through the outreach of their rituals' words. All people perceive that their words correspond to external realities and sometimes cause things to come into existence or to disappear. Thus it came to be believed that the awesome words of the Vedic hymns could have marvelous effects on aspects of the outer world. An obsession arose in the minds of the ritualists that there might be a word of all-embracing reference that would give access to power over *all* things.

Thus there arose in the late Vedic age a fascination with the term *brahman*. It meant at first a Vedic prayer or a holy spell, but in time it came to mean all liturgical utterances and the Vedas themselves as the collection of sacred sounds. Since *brahman* referred to the entirety of scriptural words, it was believed to have ties with the entire natural world. By the end of the Vedic age, *Brahman* had become a favorite term for the source and moving essence of the whole universe. "That One" of the creation hymn had found a name.

There was as yet no stress on the identity of self with Brahman, no notion of finding eternal peace in Brahman. Success in earthly life remained the end in view. Only the means had changed because there was little faith in the intervention of personal gods. Mastery of the forces that could satisfy one's needs was being sought not by manipulating deities but by manipulating in ritual the microcosmic extension of those forces. Brahman provided a verbal handle on the universe, by which the whole world could be moved and the fundamental needs addressed.

THE VEDAS IN LATER HINDUISM

In the eight and seventh centuries B.C.E. Vedic religion attained its highest development; its acceptance declined after 600 B.C.E as suppressed social classes rose in status and introduced non-Aryan elements into the mainstream. In direct challenge to the brāhman priesthood, Jainism and Buddhism arose as independent religions. The followers of these new religions rejected the materialistic goals and the bloody sacrifices of the Vedic rituals. Even those who remained attached to the Vedas criticized the animal sacrifices. Though few brāhmans questioned the effectiveness of the sacrifices, even among the priests many began to question the value of the boons that were promised. The interest of many members of the priestly guilds turned from the performance of ritual to a fascination with the mystical contemplation of Brahman. A new Hinduism was emerging (discussed in the following chapter).

Nonetheless, some aspects of the Vedic tradition have survived to the present day. The ability to recite the Vedas and to perform the ancient sacrifices has never completely disappeared. Study of the Vedas has remained the most prestigious form of Hindu scholarship. Periodically, Hindu political leaders have revived the rites to legitimize their rule or as a symbol of their loyalty to indigenous custom.

Although today almost all Hindus follow religious practices that originated after the Vedic period, they continue to count on the ancient priesthood. As the old guilds died out, new organizations were formed of brāhmans who were willing to serve as the priests and scribes of new religious movements and who presented themselves as extenders of the Vedic tradition rather than rebels against it. Although the upanishads (later scriptures discussed in Chapters 5 and 6) reflect a new religious faith and a new approach to the problems of life, Hindus understand them to be a continuation and clarification of the Vedic tradition. For this reason the upanishads are referred to as the Vedānta ("end of the Vedas"), extending recognition to the upanishads as the last literary installation of the Vedas.

In time Hinduism produced new religious literature, strikingly different in content from the Vedas, including lawbooks, epics, and Purāṇas (mythological works), with known human authors. The Veda specialists granted such **smṛiti** (human tradition) works great authority nevertheless, considering them necessary and nearly error-free restatements of the meaning of the *śruti* (divine revelation). Indeed, few movements within the broad and diversified river of Hinduism have been openly hostile toward the Vedas. In intention Hinduism is still Vedic, and "the Vedic religion" remains one of the most widely used identifications that modern Hindus apply to their faith.

NOTES

1 All translations in Part Two are by Norvin Hein, except where noted.

2 Arthur Anthony Macdonell, trans., *Hymns from the Ṛigveda* (Calcutta: Association Press, n.d.), p. 37.

3 Ibid., p. 32.

4 K. G. Zysk, *Religious Healing in the Veda* (Philadelphia: American Philosophical Society, 1985), p. 45.

5 Arthur Anthony Macdonell, *A History of Sanskrit Literature* (Delhi: Munshi Ram Manoharlal, 1958), p. 197.

6 Macdonell, *Hymns,* p. 47.

7 Ibid., p. 80. With the advantage of modern experience we recognize that soma may have had psychedelic properties. S. Gordon Wasson, in *Soma, Divine Mushroom of Immortality* (New York: Harcourt Brace Jovanovich, 1968), identified the plant with some plausibility as the mushroom *Amanita muscaria* (fly agaric).

8 Arthur Berriedale Keith, *The Religion and Philosophy of the Vedas and Upanishads* (Cambridge, Mass.: Harvard University Press, 1925), vol. 1, p. 290.

Religions of India

Chapter 4

Classical Hinduism: The Way of Action

In the sixth century B.C.E., Indian society entered a period of great transformation. The Aryas, who now dominated the entire Ganges valley, had cleared away the thickets and plowed the fertile plains. Tribal chieftains ruling loosely over groups of herders were replaced by kings governing from fortified cities. By the third century B.C.E., these regional kingdoms had given way to vast empires.

In this more settled world the stresses of life also changed. As the people became dependent on tilled fields, rulers could exercise tighter military and social control over them, and economic and political relationships hardened into rigid patterns. India's geographic isolation exacerbated the culture's tendency toward stasis, and its social rigidity generated new stresses and brought alterations in religious life.

The old sacrifices of the Vedic age were all but swept away. Curiously, the brāhmans did not disappear; in fact, they emerged from the centuries of transition more honored and more influential than ever before. Originally the experts only of ritual, the brāhmans came to influence wider and wider aspects of social life, formulating society's ideals and articulating its moral teachings. These ideals and values have provided a pattern for the lives of many Indians even to this day. Indeed, because of their influence, the new religious orthodoxy that emerged by the second century B.C.E., here called "classical Hinduism," has often been called Brahmanism.

SOCIAL CODES OF THE NEW SOCIETY

The brāhmans' abilities to read and memorize gave them a leading role in creating and recording the standards for this new age. Using their compact literary invention, the sūtra, to state these standards, they slowly expanded the range of their authority. In works called **gṛihyasūtras** ("discourses on domestic rites"), which prescribed how householders should perform their home rituals, the priests began to lay down rules for performers other than themselves. In a dramatic new development, between 600 B.C.E. and 200 C.E., works called **dharmasūtras** ("prescriptions on social duty") appeared, in which the brāhmans began to lay down rules for social behavior not related to the rituals. For the next 1,000 years, more expanded verse texts, called **dharmaśāstras**, elaborated on these rules. The most famous, *The Laws of Manu,* attributed to the sage Manu, articulates the etiquette and duties of each class (*varṇa*) and of each age group (*āśrama*) in the new brāhman-dominated society.

These new texts, which accompanied this era's social revolution, centered on a new term, **dharma**, which inherited much of the meaning of the Vedic conception of ṛita (discussed in Chapter 3). Both words refer to a principle of justice or right that is rooted in the universe, to which humans' actions should conform. But there the similarities between the two terms end, for their respective conceptions of the universe and the patterns of life they envision are profoundly different. *Ṛita* comes from a verbal root that means "to run, go rightly, fit in." To follow ṛita is to run with the harmonious flow of things in a world that forever changes. *Dharma* is formed from a verb meaning "to hold steady, make firm, restrain, preserve." The duties to which it refers are components of a sacred world that is imagined to be firm, stable, steady, and unwavering. Like all else that is good in such a world, the path of dharma does not change over time. Indeed, one's sacred duty (dharma) is an eternal duty (*sanātanadharma*), and sanātanadharma has become a favorite name for this orthodox religion itself. Adherents believe that the world and their lives are based on a blessed pattern that is eternal. The virtuous person is restrained and never allows passion to sway him or her from that path. By remaining in traditional duties one supports the firmness of the universe. This notion that social duties are unchanging reinforced the fixity of the new social patterns. Henceforth, classical Hinduism would view change as destructive and would resist open innovation.

This cobbler follows one of the most visible of the outcaste occupations. His usefulness is great, but his social standing is low for he handles leather. Because of this sanitary scruple, high-caste Hindus avoid touching shoes with their hands. (Allan L. Price/Photo Researchers)

THE CASTE SYSTEM

For over 2,000 years the caste system has provided the pattern for Hindu society. Castes (in Sanskrit, **jātis**, or "births") are hereditary occupational groups hierarchically ranked by popular estimation of the purity and dignity of each group's traditional work.

Firm hereditary occupational distinctions did not exist among the Aryas. During most of the Vedic age, class distinctions were few and flexible. The Vedic poems, however, did mention three social classes: the brāhmans, or priests; the **rājanyas** or **kshatriyas**, rulers and warriors; and the **vaiśyas**, or common people. Although the sons of warriors and priests generally adopted their fathers' occupations, they were not forced to do so. For example, sons of commoners could become priests, and a priest's child could become a potter.

Origin of the Social Classes

The earliest indication of a turn toward caste occurs in a late hymn of the Ṛigveda. Ṛigveda 10.90 tells of a sacrifice in which the giant Purusha, a cosmic man, was the victim. From Purusha's limbs and organs all the prominent features of the world were formed, including the social classes:

The brāhman was his mouth;
His two arms became the rājanya;
His thighs are what the vaiśya is;
From his feet the śūdra [menial class] was produced.

We should note in this verse the appearance of a new, distinctly Indian order of class precedence. In Aryan societies of the Middle East and Europe, the warrior class always occupied the highest level of leadership, but in India the priesthood has from this time onward been supreme and has served as the model for much that is distinctive in Hindu civilization.

In this verse, a new depth of class consciousness is shown: the moderate social differences of earlier Vedic times have been sharpened. In addition to the original three classes, we now see a class of menials, the **śūdras**, who ranked lower than ordinary citizens and were to perform the humblest tasks. There are now four social divisions or **varṇas** (literally, "colors"), each with a characteristic occupation.

Scholars have still not determined the reason for this development. It may have been a way to justify the Aryas' control of an indigenous serf population, or the four-class theory of Ṛigveda 10.90 may be a hint of the rising influence of discriminations that survived from a pre-Aryan culture.

Duties of the Social Classes

The author of *The Laws of Manu* cited Ṛigveda 10.90, making its scheme of the four varṇas the theoretical framework for the new Hindu society. The classical social order that Manu describes goes far beyond the Vedic idea, however. The varṇas are now hereditary, and their inequality in dignity is proclaimed with a new emphasis. There is special stress on the exceptional rights of the brāhmans, whose duty is to perform sacrifices, to study and teach the Vedas, and to guard the rules of dharma (*Manu* 1.88–101). Because their work is sacred, the brāhmans are supreme in purity and rank, and injuries committed against them are punished more severely than offenses against members of other castes. Personal service by śūdras is their right at any time. If brāhmans are in economic difficulty, they are permitted to take up livelihoods proper to the kshatriya and vaiśya classes (*Manu* 10.81 ff.).

The kshatriyas are warriors, the protectors of society—kings were typically of this varṇa. They were to rule according to the dharma codes, heeding the counsel of brāhmans. Warriors must never do the work of brāhmans, but in times of misfortune they may enter the occupations of vaiśyas and śūdras.

Members of the vaiśya caste, according to Manu, were to be traders, herders, and farmers. In later times they turned over their farming and herding roles to the lower groups; trading became their distinctive occupation. In distress, they may resort to the work of śūdras. Vaiśyas are considered to be full citizens of Hindu society and are allowed to study the Vedas.

In the Vedas the śūdras were a beggarly group, the lowest of the varṇas; Manu's description accords in part with that picture. In dignity there is a great gulf between them and the elite classes above them, whom they were to serve meekly. Śūdras were not to study the Vedas or attend any Vedic ceremony. It was not proper for them to be wealthy, though they were to be protected from outright starvation. Over time they have traditionally been herders and farmers as well as artisans and manual workers. Manu described their many groups of artisans as jātis, or hereditary occupational groups, and suggested that they arose from ill-behaved members of the higher varṇas who were punished by demotion to the śūdra rank. But to suppose that a major portion of the population of a vast country was created by such a process is very hard to believe.

Manu completes his social picture by sketching the life of a group even lower than the śūdras. These are the corpse handlers, executioners, hunters, leather workers, and fishermen. Because their occupations are associated with dead bodies and filth, which are considered contaminating, they cannot be dignified with the name of any Aryan class. Their houses must be built outside the village limits. They may not enter the village at night. No one may teach them the sacred texts. Their personal morality is of little concern. Manu calls them "no-class people"; they are today called **outcastes**. Again unconvincingly, Manu traces these groups—essential to the economy and significant in number—to forebears of the Vedic varṇas who were punished for offenses by being stripped of all Vedic rank.

Clearly, the Aryas had incorporated into their social system a subjected people who had a ranking system of their own based on hereditary occupations. Out of the two stratifications, a single social hierarchy developed, the three original classes of the Aryas becoming the aristocracy. But probably as a remnant of the indigenous system, all the varṇas in time became subdivided into specific hereditary occupational groups.

Manu on the Stages of Life

The tendency of classical Hinduism to identify people in terms of social rank expresses itself further in a conception that each individual's personal career is divided into four stages of increasing dignity. These are the **āśramas**, or stages of spiritual effort. One must honor as superior, the law books say, those who have attained a higher āśrama than one's own. Even within the familiar circle of one's own caste or family, age, gender, and effort bring elevation and differences in status. Thus the law codes strive, using many devices, to remove all ambiguities about the social position of any person and to eliminate controversies about rank. Thus when two orthodox Hindus meet, one almost certainly owes deference to the other—if not by reason of caste, then by reason of seniority. The person in the inferior position will greet the other using an appropriately respectful salutation. The languages of India are rich in words by which one can honor those to whom respect is due.

The Student Stage Between the ages of 8 and 12 a boy of any of the three upper varṇas is expected to apply to a teacher and begin formal study of the Vedas. The teacher is to instruct the boy in the recitation of the sacred texts. In return, the pupil must obey, serve, and show respect for his teacher.

The Householder Stage When the young man concludes his studies, he should marry. In doing so, he enters the second āśrama, that of the householder. He must beget sons and earn a living for his family through work appropriate to members of his caste. In addition, he must give alms to those who have passed into the higher āśramas.

Since the Hindu woman was not taught the Vedas and hence could not enter the student stage, the householder stage was the only one in which men and women, as husband and wife, shared a common purpose of life. Even so, the respective roles of the husband and wife were different and socially unequal. Manu stipulates that the husband must protect the wife, as did her father and as would her sons later in life. Her husband is to provide her with adornments and to "approach her" in due season. The woman is described by Manu as a subject: "In childhood a female must be subject to her father, in youth, to her husband, and when [he] is dead, to her sons; a woman must never be independent" (*Manu* 5.148).[1] Even if he was an unscrupulous libertine, "a husband must be constantly worshipped as a god by a faithful wife" (*Manu* 5.154).

The Stages of the Forest Dweller and the Sannyāsī When a man is a grandfather and his hair is white, ideally he should leave his home and thereafter devote his life to spiritual practices in the forest (*Manu* 6.2). In actuality, many people deferred this departure from society until a future life, but it remained a cherished ideal. We describe these two āśramas together because in both the literature and modern practice, the former runs into the latter.

The stage of the forest dweller designates an early phase of the full-time monkish life. Here one may still perform one's old habitual rituals and live in forest settlements but must attempt to quell passions and to generate spiritual power. A man's wife may accompany him at this stage, though he is to begin to detach from her even as she serves him.

When the forest dweller has overcome all spiritual impediments, he may cease all ritual and ascetic practices, sever all remaining social ties, and enter the final stage of life. This is the stage of the **sannyāsī**, the total renouncer of the world, when final liberation itself is his goal. Homeless and not careful about bodily comforts, he is to devote himself to study of the upanishads and to meditation on the soul within himself and all beings. His goal is a serene liberation that will continue eternally, even beyond death.

Men who live in either of these stages have left caste, social status, and family behind. It is nonetheless a highly revered life style. For women, the stage that follows the householder stage is more ambiguous. Since her reason for living was to keep her husband alive and well, if he dies or leaves her for the spiritual path, she is seen by the tradition as living without a purpose. In widowhood, a position held in low esteem, a woman was to shave her head, dress plainly, and serve her sons.

KṚISHṆAPUR: A TWENTIETH-CENTURY CASTE COMMUNITY

Hindu communities of the age of the dharmaśāstras were characterized, as we have seen, by a systematic stratification of society, firm assignment of hereditary social roles, and conceptions of justice that included unequal privileges. Society restricted one's choice of occupation and of marital partner, and it extended freedoms unequally according to social rank. The dignity and wealth of any person depended heavily on his or her caste; the unequal service that was required of the various classes was rationalized as a requirement of the divine law.

Evidence shows that the picture we have just seen accurately portrays Hindu social life even into the present century. The ranked caste system and the āśramas have remained the persistent background of Hinduism's beliefs and practices and indeed have been the framework in terms of which those beliefs and practices often get their meaning. Modern sociologists' fieldwork in village India has shown the continuing reality and importance of the social ideals proclaimed by Manu.

Based on those sociologists' reports, let us construct a picture of an imaginary village that typifies traditional caste life, both to show its continuities with the ancient ideals and to show realities of its life not recorded in the ancient texts. We will call our village Kṛishṇapur.

Located in the plains of northern India, Kṛishṇapur has about 1,500 inhabitants belonging to some 30 castes. Varṇas exist in Kṛishṇapur not as organized social groups but as collections of jātis (castes). Public opinion assigns each caste to one of the four varṇas or to none. The members of some castes believe that their caste deserves a higher varṇa classification by reason of its unappreciated virtues and secret noble origins, but the general opinion of their neighbors compels them to be silent. At certain public events in the village, caste representatives participate in the order of their precedence, thus publicly acknowledging their rank.

Most of the inhabitants have heard of the dharmaśāstras, but almost none have read (or could read) those ancient books. They do not turn constantly to the texts for guidance; rather they assume that the requirements of those respected texts were long ago incorporated into the local rules governing village behavior. The ancient pattern of the four varṇas provides the community's broad theoretical framework, but the active organizations of the village are the jātis, whose members earn their livelihood by one or another of the village's several dozen occupations. When the dharmaśāstras were written, only the lowest varṇas were thus subdivided, but the model was infectious, and now even the high varṇas are subdivided into occupational castes.

Among the brāhmans we find different castes of priests who perform the rituals of childhood, adulthood, and death, respectively. In addition, a village may have among its brāhmans an astrologer and a physician practicing traditional Indian medicine. Most of the kshatriyas are landowners engaged in farming; a few brāhmans, exercising their special privilege, also own land. The third varṇa, the vaiśyas, includes the local groups who keep official records, as well as moneylenders, goldsmiths, and dealers in grain. The śūdra castes contain the groups that perform manual tasks not regarded as impure or morally tainted, such as florist, truck gardener, carpenter, herder, barber, and tailor. Finally, there are the outcastes, those who have no varṇa, whose jobs are deemed grossly unclean. They include washermen, sellers of liquor, fishermen, tanners, toilet cleaners, and handlers of dead bodies.

Each caste is represented by a small group of families, and each governs its internal life by its own traditional caste law. This is an unwritten code that lays down rules for personal habits and for relationships within and between families. Intimate matters that in many societies are left to personal taste, custom, or etiquette are firmly regulated in Kṛishṇapur. Each caste has its own rules regarding foods that may not be eaten and persons who may not join caste members at dinner. Restrictions on the company in which orthodox Hindus may dine are so severe that few ever eat with any but members of their own caste. Bodily contact with persons of a lower caste communicates contamination to any individual of higher rank, and from such a tainted person some degree of impurity could be spread to other members of the caste.

A member who has undergone serious contamination must promptly remove the taint by bathing or undergoing more drastic rites. Members must select mates for their sons and daughters from certain families of the same caste. Caste rules are enforced by a council of caste elders, who punish offenders with fines and social boycotts.

Another important unwritten code is the traditional village law. It prescribes all villager's duties to castes other than their own. It covers economic relations, professional services that each caste is expected to render, and the services or goods that are to be provided in return.

Economically, the castes fall into two broad groups: food producers and providers of services. The former group consists primarily of farmers. The latter contains the many artisans and laborers who offer the goods and services needed to maintain farms and to equip homes. An ingenious exchange of food, goods, and services is the basis of economic life, rather than money payments. The village code outlines the duties of each worker and his share in the farmer's harvests.

Representatives of the town's most prominent castes make up the village council. Workers who fail to make the traditional contributions of food or services are brought before the council. After hearing the complaint, the council can bring a rule breaker into line by ordering all castes to shun the offender, cutting off all services.

Kṛishṇapur is a restrictive society that limits personal freedom—for example, in the choice of mates and occupations—even more severely than the ancient dharmaśāstras did. The caste and village codes establish an order of precedence so precise that no one in the community has an exact equal. Another person is always either superior or inferior. Talent, wealth, and seniority ordinarily bring leadership in one's own caste, but they do not necessarily give eminence in the village as a whole. Formal precedence belongs to those who are born to it, and economic advantages are distributed unequally. The freedom to enter alternative occupations, just as in the teaching of Manu, belongs to the castes of the upper varṇas alone. The brāhmans and kshatriyas of Kṛishṇapur have used this freedom to acquire and farm the land, a freedom that has helped them in the struggle to survive.

In the present century industrialization has introduced a money economy into rural India and affected the livelihoods of many of the castes. For at least 2,000 years, however, Hindus have accepted the life of communities structured in the traditional pattern, which has been the persistent social background of Indian religious thought. This distinctive society has greatly influenced the content of Hindu religion. Sometimes its presence is reflected in the categories in which Hindus think. Sometimes its influence is seen in the provision of religious remedies for the special tensions of this society or rational justifications for its social lots. The explanations of Hindu religious doctrine have allowed this unusual social order to survive and have enabled Hindus to live happily, generation after generation, in one of the most unequal and yet enduring societies the world has ever known.

Karma and Rebirth

The intimate connection between Hindu doctrine and Hindu society is illustrated dramatically in the belief that human beings are born again and again to lives of varied fortune in a course controlled by the moral quality of their accumulated deeds. It is an idea central to Hinduism. With slight variations, it is accepted by Buddhists and Jains. The belief in reward and punishment through rebirth appeared in the very age in which the classical Hindu caste system was being organized. Several upanishads that describe the concept as a new teaching belong to the period when the dharmasūtras were outlining the new social system.[2] From that time onward, **karma**, rebirth, and the caste system developed in a combination that became the central pillar of classical Indian culture. To understand the doctrine of karma and rebirth solely as a philosophical concept would be to understand only a fraction of its function and power.

In its most rudimentary sense, *karma* means "an action." In ethical discussions it means an action that is morally important because it is required or prohibited by the codes of dharma. Karma means, next, an unseen energy believed to be generated by the performance of such a dutiful or undutiful act. Long after the act has been completed, its energy continues to exist. At an appropriate time, it discharges itself on the doer, causing the person to receive the consequences of the original act. Accumulated karma gives to some meritorious persons sharp minds, good looks, and long and healthy lives. It brings the opposite to others, for equally valid reasons.

Karma is believed to exert itself with particular force at the times in our individual careers when we are about to be reborn. At the moment of our conception in the womb, the accumulated moral force of our past deeds is believed to move us into a family of an appropriate caste. All persons born into one of the castes of Kṛishṇapur are believed to have been brought to that special lot by karma, of their own making, and that alone justifies their social rank.

Some Hindu writers conceive of karma as an energy that emerges from the doer of an act; it hangs overhead like a thundercloud. Without warning, like a thunderbolt out of the blue, that karma descends on the doer at the proper time to effect its perfect retribution. Other Hindu thinkers describe karma as a force within the doer that operates by conditioning personal disposition and drives that then cause those who are on wrong paths to persist on them until they are ruined by natural processes. Monotheistic Hindus hold that God oversees the retributions of karma. The only inevitability is that we shall bear the consequences of our good and evil deeds.

Whatever their understanding of how karma operates, Hindus believe that human beings are not totally helpless before it. To continue in wrongdoing is easy but not inevitable. By persistence—over many lives, if necessary—we can master our evil tendencies.

The Hindu belief in rebirth according to karma has convinced the people of Kṛishṇapur that their places in society are appropriate and advantageous. Each villager is understood to have a long personal history of good and evil deeds done in former lives, and each one's present situation is seen not only as just but also as that person's best opportunity for betterment. Because they are limited in their capacity by their past karma, people are fit only for the particular opportunities offered by their present caste and sex. To attempt to take on the duties of another social station would be not only unjust but also dangerous, since it would lead to poor performance and then to even more restricted future rebirths.

About the afterlife the inhabitants of Kṛishṇapur accept for the most part the beliefs set forth by Manu: offenders against the dharma rules will, when reborn, be punished. Some may be reborn as lesser animals—tortoises, fishes, snakes, lizards, spiders. Some may come back as grasses or shrubs. Very great offenders will be condemned by Yama, the judge of the dead, to dreadful hells where they will be scorched in hot sand, boiled in jars, or devoured by ravens. A person who has performed his or her dharma well may be reborn as a noble animal or into another human life. The very virtuous may be born into pleasant celestial realms. Manu describes several, the highest of which is the marvelous heaven of Brahmā the creator. Though ideas about the afterworlds vary greatly, most Hindus believe that the processes of retribution are highly developed and extremely thorough.

The idea of karmic retribution, the promises and dangers of a life lived virtuously or otherwise, and the justification of one's present status based on past deeds have undergirded the caste system's structures and controls and have helped to make Hinduism's culture a lasting one.

THE RITUALS OF CLASSICAL HINDUISM

A natural sequel to our study of the social institutions of the post-Vedic culture would be a survey of the religious ceremonies that are common in communities like our hypothetical Kṛishṇapur.

The social transformation that occurred at the end of the Vedic age was accompanied by equally radical changes in worship practices. The Vedic sacrifices fell from vogue and became rarities. Dozens of the Vedic gods were quietly retired from active worship. Rituals of unprecedented types emerged into literary notice—rituals that have endured even to the present. Some words and phrases of the Vedic hymns persisted in these new rites as linguistic ornaments, but the warp and woof of post-Vedic liturgies seem to have come from other sources, perhaps from the subjected non-Aryan classes. Whatever their source, they have been handed down for centuries by the brāhman caste, who either teach the rituals to the householders or perform them on the householders' behalf. We shall learn what we can about rituals that are prevalent in traditional Hindu homes and go on to speak of activities in special houses of worship.

The Sandhyās ("Meditations of the Twilight")

The **sandhyās** are personal meditations to be performed at the important transitional hours in the sun's daily passage—dawn, noon, and evening. The dawn meditation still survives among devout high-caste Hindus, who rise very early for this purpose. First they spend a few moments in formal breathing exercises (*prāṇayāma*). Just as the rim of the sun appears on the horizon, the worshiper stands and recites the lines of Ṛigveda 3.62.10, called the Gāyatrī mantra:

> *Let us meditate on that excellent glory*
> *Of the divine vivifying sun;*
> *May he enlighten*
> *Our understanding.*

In the final moment of the rite the worshiper pours out from joined palms an offering of water to the sun.

The Sandhyās are personal meditations to be performed at dawn, noon, and evening. The dawn meditation survives as seen here as the worshiper pours out an offering of water to the sun. (Kit Kittle)

The Saṃskāras ("Rites of the Rounds of Life") The **saṃskāras** mark the important transitions in the lives of Hindus of the three highest castes, from the moment of conception to death. They enable families to surround their members with affection and to try to protect them from harm at times of change. These rituals are performed in the home, usually near the family hearth. Even funeral observances, which culminate at a cremation ground, begin and end at the home. The father and the mother are the primary actors in many of these performances, and the father himself may officiate at them if he knows how. Apart from funerals, almost all such observances are happy occasions involving a joyous gathering of relatives.

Today many of the ancient rites have dropped out of use. But the traditional marriage and funeral ceremonies are part of every Hindu's career, and other saṃskāras are still practiced by a minority of high-caste families. (The initiation, wedding, and funeral ceremonies are described in the accompanying box, "Rites of the Rounds of Life.")

Pūjā, the Ritual of Image Worship The most frequently performed of all Hindu ceremonies is a form of worship called **pūjā**, which is addressed to an image of a deity. The use of idols—pūjā's main innovation—is of uncertain origin. It arose in connection with a belief that the celestial deities, if properly approached, could be induced to adopt earthly residences and thus become more permanently available to their worshipers.

To enable a particular celestial being to descend and remain on earth, first a sculptor has to create a form displaying the known features of the deity. Next, a rite of installation induces the divinity to descend into the image and become available to worshipers, to remain as long as the god is cared for and honored. It cannot be neglected: it must be given personal attention and offerings of food and drink. The provision of these necessities through a daily routine of rituals is the basic activity in pūjā. If requisite ritual care is not given, the deity will abandon the image.

In pūjā, as in the Vedic sacrifice, the object of worship is a single deity or at most a pair, and the worship is not done as a congregation but as an individual worshiping for personal reasons or for the benefit of a household. The types of gain sought in the earliest pūjā that we know about were the same as those pursued in the older sacrifices: health, wealth, safety, and blessed afterlives in heavenly places. But in accordance with the new cosmology, the desire to accumulate good karma was soon added.

One of the most common sites of pūjā is a home shrine where at least once a day the image, kept in a niche or a cabinet, must be accorded the proper rites, usually by a family member. Near the deity certain utensils are stored: a vessel for water with a ladle for purifying the area with sprinklings, a bell, an oil lamp to be circulated before the image, and trays on which flowers, fruit, or cooked meals may be offered. The deity's image is cared for throughout the day. It may be roused from sleep, bathed, fed at mealtimes, wreathed with flowers. Often an evening song is sung while the god enjoys the spiritual essence of the food it is served; then a courteous goodnight wish is expressed, and the ceremony ends with a circulation of lamps.

Rites of the Rounds of Life

From birth to death, the primary transitions in the Hindu's life are signified by the saṃskāras, the rites of the rounds of life. Here are three common ones.

THE INITIATION CEREMONY

The initiation ceremony, or *upanāyana,* is one of the great events of upper-caste Hindu boyhood. Performed between the ages of 8 and 12, it is the ritual occasion at which the boy is presented to his religious teacher to begin instruction in the Vedas. The ritual begins when the boy spends the night before the ceremony in complete silence (symbolic distancing). At breakfast he eats with his mother for the last time; henceforth he will eat with the men. He then bathes and is led to a canopy under which he formally accepts his **guru**, or teacher (thus entering the liminal phase). The guru drapes over the boy's shoulder and chest a sacred thread to be worn thereafter as a mark of a twice-born Hindu man. After this ceremony, the boy may begin to study the Vedas, through which he will be spiritually born again into the heritage of Vedic learning. After his period of studentship, he is no longer considered a boy but rather an adult.

THE HINDU WEDDING

The Hindu wedding is a group of social customs focusing on a central uniting sacrament. The first action is the parent's settling on a suitable match for the child. Because chastity is so highly valued in wives, this is often done when the girl is just reaching puberty or even earlier. The groom may be of any age. A sizable dowry must be negotiated, to accompany the bride from her father's family to her husband's.

On the wedding day the groom travels in procession with friends and relatives to the bride's house, where he is received with formal honors. In the rites that follow, conducted by a brāhman, the prominent elements are intended to unite

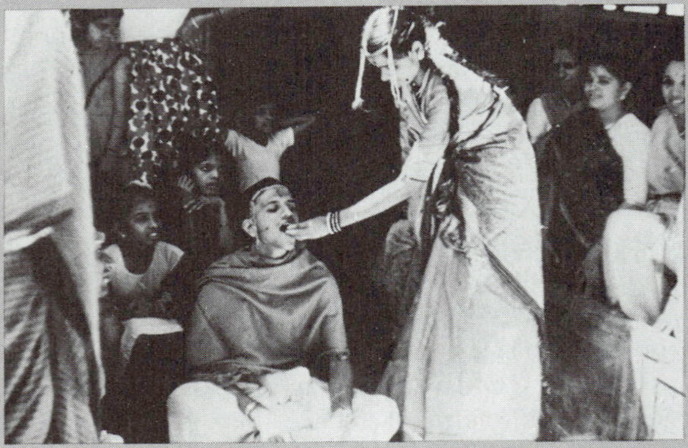

The Hindu wedding ceremony involves many symbols of undertaking new obligations. One of the wife's duties is to feed her husband and family; this is represented in the episode shown here. (James Martin)

In the Hindu "rite of the translated body," the body is placed on the carefully constructed funeral pyre and the eldest son sets the pyre aflame while reciting the traditional prayer. (Reuters/Bettmann)

the new couple visibly, to sanctify their union with a commingling of divine energies, and to ensure that their life together will be long, fertile, prosperous, and undisturbed by harmful superhuman forces.

Standing before the fire that is the visual focus of the ceremony, the groom clasps the bride's hand and says, "I seize thy hand . . . that thou mayest live to old age with me, thy husband." The bride places her foot on a stone to symbolize the firmness of her resolve. The ends of their flowing garments are knotted together, and they then enter into the ceremony's climactic and binding act: walking arm in arm three times around the sacred fire, each time in seven steps. The groom then touches the bride over the heart, saying, "Into my heart will I take thy heart; thy mind shall dwell in my mind." He paints on her forehead the vermilion cosmetic mark of a married Hindu woman. To symbolize their union, they eat a common meal while sitting together, though such commensal eating will not be their general practice as husband and wife. On the evening of their wedding day the two go out under the sky and look up together at the unchanging Pole Star, their model in a marriage that is indissoluble.

FUNERAL RITES

In any home, when a mature person has died, an observance follows that is called *aurdhvadaihika,* the "rite of the translated body." Within a few hours a procession of hurriedly summoned relatives and friends starts to move toward the local cremation site, led by the eldest son of the deceased as the chief mourner. The body is carried on a litter. The grieving marchers cry out the name of the god Rāma or sometimes the name Hari (Vishṇu). At the cremation ground the body is laid on a pyre of wood constructed according to strict rules. The son then performs the difficult duty of setting the pyre aflame with a firebrand that has usually been carried from home. He prays, "O Fire, when the body has been burnt, convey the spirit to its ancestors." The mourners return in a group toward their homes, without looking back, and they bathe in their clothing before entering any dwelling. Following this rite, ritual offerings are made every month for a year and once yearly thereafter.

THE HINDU TEMPLE AND ITS RITUALS

Another common site of pūjā, and a much more exalted one, is the Hindu temple. For 2,000 years the creation of temples and their images has been Hindu artists' principal outlet. In the outer walls of a temple, dozens or even hundreds of images may be set. But temple worship focuses on its main image, which is housed in a windowless cubic sanctuary at the temple's center. This cell is almost always topped by a spire, sometimes of soaring dignity.

In the tiny sanctuary there is neither room nor provision for assemblies of communal worshipers, as is found in churches, mosques, and synagogues. Hindus come as individuals, bringing personal salutations, petitions, and gifts and hoping to enjoy the benefits of viewing a deity. A priest enters the sanctuary and presents the offerings on the worshiper's behalf.

Temples are public institutions in the sense that Hindus of any varṇa may enter and worship. (Temple ceremonies, unlike the Vedic sacrifices, have always been open to the participation of śūdras, though only since India's independence have outcastes been welcome inside.) But in other respects the temples do not express the collective Hindu life. As a rule they are built by individuals, and worship there is the worship of individuals.

Pūjā is understood in many ways, and it is performed for many purposes, both self-interested and self-sacrificing. Some worshipers seek earthly favors through the deities' goodwill, to be won through human gifts. Others seek, by the merit of their worship, to attain after death a more fortunate rebirth on earth or in blessed realms above. Pūjā also serves as a form of expression for salvation seekers who dare to hope for liberation through the power of a personal God. Even Hindu monists (see Chapter 5) often participate in temple worship as a useful discipline.

All Hindu temples, both old (top) and new (right), possess the porch for shelter of worshipers and the spire rising above the cell where the icon of the deity is kept. (James McKinsey; Religious News Service)

RITES OF THE VILLAGE GODLINGS

In rural India another type of pūjā survives. The deities involved are minor beings unknown to Sanskrit literature. Our information about them comes from observations of Hindu life. Travelers approaching a typical Hindu village may see beside a well a pile of stones daubed with red paint or a conical mound of earth into which a red pennant has been thrust. Some such structures are earthen cells containing mud figurines. All are shrines of local godlings who must be worshiped in their own humble abodes.

These godlings are thought of by many people as destructive forces that from time to time disrupt the security of their villages. Human afflictions of unknown cause are believed to be the work of such local spirits who have been offended. When a calamity occurs—an epidemic, a drought—someone with shamanistic gifts must be found who can learn the identity of the irritated spirit and the cause of its anger and then prescribe the rites and offerings that will appease the vengeful deity.

Many of these spirits are believed to be female. The most powerful fall into two major classes: goddesses who protect particular villages and those who inflict particular diseases and other kinds of harm. The rites addressed to the village godlings are pūjās in general outline, but they differ from the pūjā rituals described so far. The officiating priest is not a brāhman but a person of low caste. The liturgical language is not Sanskrit but the local dialect. Animals are often sacrificed, and deliberate cruelties are sometimes inflicted on them in an apparent effort to satisfy the fury of the godlings through sufferings less grave than the loss of human life. The sole aim of such rites is to avert dangers; no notion of salvation or even of generating merit is involved.

It may be tempting to identify these rituals with magic rather than with religion, but the rites are religious in that superhuman beings are addressed by ritual. Another factor that is often considered characteristic of religion is social concern. In the worship of these deities, the usual individualism of Hindu religious activity is set aside for collective action to meet a common crisis, and local populations are drawn together in rare unity. During the short span of these gory performances, the fragmented Hindu village becomes a community in the fullest sense of the term. Thus, although these cults are often called forms of "lower Hinduism," in this one respect their achievement is high. Today, however, such practices are on the wane, giving way to the more effective remedies of modern science.

THE PLACE OF RELIGIOUS PRACTICE IN HINDUISM

In the eyes of outsiders, Hindu religious duties fall into two classes: ritual obligations and social obligations. Hindus do not regard this distinction as important; their aim is simply to fulfill the requirements of dharma, which applies to all the acts required by tradition. All the duties described in this chapter, whether ritual or social, are alike in that they are viewed as the requirements of dharma. The householder's offerings of water at the domestic shrine, a king's defense of his realm, and the work of a potter are all sacred duties; all produce merit or demerit, and all determine the future of the doer, for good or ill.

In Vedic times Hindus believed that through the pleasure of the gods, the observance of the traditional duties would surely lead to immortal life in heaven. But later Hindus conceived of the process of reward more mechanically, in terms of the accumulation of karma, and concluded that everlasting blessedness could not be earned by good deeds, whatever their number. The good karma produced by one's deeds will remain finite in quantity, no matter how long the life of virtue continues. Final liberation is infinite in length and in worth, and in a just universe one's merit, which is always finite, cannot deserve or attain this infinite reward. Good actions alone cannot bring final salvation from the round of births and deaths. At most, good actions can lead to blessings in this life and in future lives. Thus Hindus joined thinkers of other religions who have held that salvation cannot be obtained by good works alone.

Desolated by this loss of hope, Hindus groped for new paths to a life beyond all deaths. In time they established their classic plans of salvation: the Way of Knowledge (*jñānamārga*) and the Way of Devotion (*bhaktimārga*). Those seeking eternal beatitude shifted their hope from the life of religious duty to one of these new paths. After the Way of Knowledge and the Way of Devotion were recognized as divisions of Hindu life, the older discipline of the customary duties came also to be thought of as a way— the *karmamārga,* or Way of Action. It is the Hinduism of the Way of Action that we have been examining until now.

The conception of the three mārgas is one of the favorite Hindu formulas for identifying the distinctive forms of Hindu religious life. We shall use its categories to outline the subject matter of the next two chapters. In using the idea of the three mārgas we should not suppose, however, that all three ways begin at the same point or lead to the same destination. All Hindus are born into the pattern of customary living that makes up the karmamārga, and all travel on this way in their early years. Ideally, they become aware in time that the Way of Action does not end in salvation but in rebirth, and they consider taking up one of the two paths that do promise salvation.

It is not possible to divide all Hindus clearly into three definite groups according to mārga. Most Hindus, moreover, participate in two of them: millions continue to perform faithfully all the duties of the Way of Action, yet they have made a strong commitment also to one of the two ways of salvation. And in the understanding of the Way of Devotion, the requirements for liberation can be met while remaining completely faithful to all the duties of the Way of Action. The concept of the three mārgas is more useful in distinguishing types of Hinduism than in separating individual Hindus into types.

NOTES

1 All translations of *The Laws of Manu* in Part Two are from G. Bühler, trans., *Sacred Books of the East, Vol. 25: The Laws of Manu* (Oxford: Oxford University Press, 1886).

2 Chāndogya Upanishad 5.10.7 and Bṛihadāraṇyaka Upanishad 3.2.13, 4.4.5, 6.2.1–16. Unless specified otherwise, extracts from the upanishads have been translated by Norvin Hein from the Sanskrit texts published in S. Radhakrishnan, *The Principal Upanishads* (New York: Harper, 1953).

RELIGIONS OF INDIA

CHAPTER 5

CLASSICAL HINDUISM: THE WAY OF KNOWLEDGE

The distinctive form of Hinduism known as *jñāna-mārga,* the Way of Knowledge, first appears in the **upanishads**, a series of texts that began about 600 B.C.E. They arose after the Vedic period (Chapter 3) and were roughly contemporaneous with the development of the caste system (Chapter 4). The doctrines of this discipline have been respected in all segments of India's highly structured society ever since. The followers of the Way of Knowledge have typically been persons, like those born in Kṛishṇapur, who grew up in the Way of Action. In studying the religion of the upanishads, we are thus not looking at a different religion but are rather exploring another aspect of the religious life of the same society. The religious life of Kṛishṇapur and the mystical practices we shall now observe are complementary, two parts of the religious whole of classical India.

In contrast to the Way of Action, the Way of Knowledge implies a new kind of religious life that does not center on ritual and social duties but rather on mental disciplines involving *jñāna,* knowledge. This does not imply a stress on training in doctrines or putting one's trust in philosophical methods. The word *jñāna* is rendered most accurately by the Greek word *gnōsis,* as conceived of by the ancient Gnostics; both terms imply a religion based on secret wisdom, taught by sages and drawn from mystical experiences and esoteric sources not available to ordinary people.

The spirit of this path has been described well by the author of the Mārkaṇḍeya Purāṇa:

> He who thirsts after knowledge thinking "This should be known!" "This should be known!" does not attain to knowledge within a thousand *kalpas* [cosmic ages]. . . . He should seek to acquire that knowledge which is the essence of all, and the instrument for the accomplishment of all objects.[1]

THE UPANISHADS

The word *upanishad* means "a secret teaching" and has come to apply to scripture that contains such confidential teaching. The upanishads offer secrets in the sense that they tell of realities that are not perceived by ordinary persons, and their teaching can be understood only by persons who have entered into the life of meditation. They are the particular scriptures of the followers of the Way of Knowledge. More than 100 mystical writings of many ages are called upanishads, but the status of revealed scripture *(śruti)* has been given only to a canon of 13 of the earliest of these, composed in the four centuries ending about 200 B.C.E. These principal upanishads are believed to have been revealed in the same superhuman manner as all the Vedas and thus to be part of the Vedic corpus.

In part because their Sanskrit is now standard, the upanishads are the oldest literature that today's educated Hindus can comprehend readily. Hindus therefore tend to derive their impression of the substance of Vedic teaching from the upanishads. Deemed to contain the culmination of Vedic teaching, these works are called the **Vedānta** ("Vedas' End").

The 13 original upanishads have been used as authoritative sources to justify the doctrines of many later forms of Hindu metaphysical thought. We do not have space to give attention to one of them, the fascinating Sāṃkhya system, which now has little direct following and had only slight support in the upanishads. As our example of a system of the Way of Knowledge, we will focus instead on the Vedānta system, which evolved from the upanishads, and has long been the predominant form of this path.

The upanishads came into being in a post-Vedic social world and deal with problems that arose during that period. This is the era during which the dharmasūtras were composed; the stratified caste system had taken form as well, supported by belief in rebirth governed by karma. The sacrifices, though still well remembered, attracted very few people, in part because they did not address the anxieties that then prevailed. To meet these new concerns, daring new lines of thought were being proposed in upper-class Aryan circles. Priestly lessons were being interrupted by persons who insisted on asking new questions. Fathers and sons were exploring new issues. Kings were sponsoring metaphysical debates at their courts. The most noted spokespersons of the new thinking, however, were not courtiers but forest wanderers, who made only brief and rare appearances in the assembly halls. People who were inspired by their message also left their homes, dwelling henceforth in secluded places, living on alms, and spending their hours in meditation. Unlike their Vedic predecessors, their strivings were internal. They sought control of their destiny by the power of *jñāna,* knowledge.

Scholars for a century have tried to discern the nature of this storm against tradition. Some saw in it a parallel to the Christian Reformation—a drive to compel the leaders of an old religion to give up their monopoly on religious leadership. Religious leaders of the kshatriya caste, according to this theory, were the prime instigators of this revolt. The rituals of the brāhmans were being swept away to make room for new, more vital religious movements. These scholars who saw a class struggle in the upanishads pointed to some kshatriya names among the leaders of the new movement and to some bitter words against arrogant brāhmans.

But this theory has not earned general acceptance. Recent studies show that most of the leaders of the new faith were in fact brāhmans and that the texts of the upanishads were preserved in the brāhmans' priestly schools. Criticism of the priests of Vedic sacrifice is seldom vehemently hostile. Nor are brāhmans accused of fraud: sacrificers do obtain the promised benefits. The upanishadic charge is rather that the fruits of sacrifice are of no lasting worth. They do bear sacrificers to heaven, as the priests promise, but the rituals' merit will eventually waste away. Heaven will end, and we will return to earth to have to endure again the wretched process of aging and dying (Muṇḍaka Upanishad 1.2.7–10).

The explosive factor in the upanishads is not the rise of a new class of leaders but the rise of a new class of problems. The old way of dealing with death has broken down. The new doctrine of karma, so useful for its justification of the discriminations of the new stratified society, has had the unintended effect of destroying the Vedic faith in a permanent refuge from death. For the person of the Vedic tradition, all that is visible on the horizon now is an eternal return to deaths (*punarmṛitu,* literally "again-death") and, as bad, to circumscribed lives of little freedom and minimal satisfaction.

Death is of course considered unpleasant in most cultures. But in India the doctrine of rebirth gave the problem special distressing dimensions. Vedic salvation came to be seen as transient, and old age, suffering, and death came to seem unpleasantness without end. The assurance that one will return from death to new lives brought no consolation to people of this new age. They knew life's weariness too well. No compensation lay ahead—in this life or the next ones—for the misery of multiple deaths. When one asks, "What is these people's greatest distress?" the upanishads' answer is clear: "May the evil of death not get me!" (Bṛihadāraṇyaka Upanishad 1.5.23); "To hoary and toothless and drooling old age may I not go" (Chāndogya Upanishad 8.14). These people longed for freedom in a stable, unchanging existence of another nature. The upanishads offered a solution for that problem, a gospel of liberation (**moksha**) from the endless round of worldly life. We must see what that salvation was and how it was attained.

Discussions of Brahman

The hope for eternal life rested on the discovery of a secret bridge between the human soul and an immortal spirit in the outer universe. On the one hand, the seers searched the outer universe for the fundamental principle of the cosmos; on the other, they conducted internal probes for the essential self. They thus employed an already ancient Indian method of searching for hidden correspondences between the worshiper and the cosmos.

The search for the fundamental outer principle centered on the term *Brahman*. Already much discussed in the Vedic era, the term was first used to refer to a mysterious power that was felt when one heard the sonorous sounds of the recited Vedic hymns. These awesome words were thought, like all words, to have ties with realities in the outer universe and to have power over them. As time went on, Vedic thinkers conceived of the totality of the sacred words of the Veda as a single power suffusing the outer universe. They called this all-pervasive unseen power *Brahman*. Imagined at first by priests interested in giving unlimited power to the sacrifice, Brahman came to be seen also as an energy that was the essence of the entire world and, as such, a powerful resource for the solution of the age's new anxieties.

Famous passages of the upanishads elaborate further on the concept of Brahman. It becomes the usual name for the mysterious "That One" who in Ṛigveda 10.129 lay originally on the waters of nonbeing and became the single source of all that breathes. One upanishad makes the point that Brahman is the whole of the power that resides in gods. Even the greatest of the Vedic deities appear and confess that they have no power aside from their share in the power of the mysterious Brahman dwelling in them (Kena 3). Asked how many gods there are, the sage Yājñavalkya reduces the traditional high number first to 33, then to three, and finally simply to one: Brahman (Bṛihadāraṇyaka Upanishad 3.9.1–9). The Brahman of the upanishads is the successor to the Vedic gods as the object of religious aspirations. It is more than a sacred power, however. It is the universal essence, the ultimate source of souls, the being from which all things spring, yet it remains one and makes the universe one. Chāndogya Upanishad 6.2.1 calls it "One only without a second."

The upanishads go on to stress that Brahman is not a material thing. We might say that Brahman is pure spirit. As the unifier of material things, Brahman cannot itself be material but must be a reality of a different, invisible, superior order. In one passage the boy Śvetaketu, who has never before heard of a "world soul," doubts his father Uddālaka's constant talk about a universal presence that cannot be seen. The father then demonstrates by example that realities that elude the senses do exist. He gives his son a lump of salt, asking him to drop it into a cup of water. After some time, Uddālaka asks Śvetaketu to return the salt to him. The boy gropes in the cup but cannot find the salt; he declares it gone. The father then asks Śvetaketu to sip from one side of the cup and then the other, and he complies. Then the boy admits that the salt is indeed there, in every part of the water, though nonexistent to touch or sight. Like that, says the father, Brahman can be present throughout the universe, though nowhere seen. Through the vision of the mystic only can its presence be directly known.

A second great affirmation is that Brahman is generative: itself a seeming nothing, it gives being to everything. It is the source of the whole phenomenal world. Uddālaka again offers his son a demonstration. Standing under a huge spreading banyan tree, Uddālaka asks his son to pluck one of its seed pods from a branch, then to crush the pod and extract a seed, then to split the seed open. "What do you see there?" the father asks. Seeing no seed kernel inside, Śvetaketu says, "Nothing at all, sir!" Just as from this "hollow" shell sprouts this mighty banyan tree, says the father, such is the case with great "world tree." It arose from an empirical nothing that no one can see and that some deny. The invisible Brahman has brought forth endless worldly forms—yourself included—and now sustains them (Chāndogya Upanishad 6.12).

Many passages in the upanishads dwell on the failure of all human language to describe Brahman. Those who search through the material world can report their discoveries in familiar terms, but spiritual realities are a different matter, for they lie beyond the competence of our descriptive words. Adjectives that speak of form, color, sound, smell, and so on can only misrepresent Brahman, for it cannot be described in sensory language. The truest words about Brahman are that it is indescribable. One can know the bliss of Brahman, but from Brahman itself both words and the mind fall back in defeat (Tattirīya Upanishad 2.4.1). Even those happy persons who have actually known Brahman can only point and say in ecstasy, "This is it!" (Kaṭha Upanishad 5.14).

Thus the searchers who sought the final cosmic principle reported that all being rests in Brahman, a spirit that is one throughout the universe, the life-giving principle, the source of all, a reality that can be experienced but not described in the words of any lexicon.

The Search for an Undying Soul

The spiritual seekers on the Way of Knowledge probed the inner world as ardently as the outer in hope of discovering a basis for immortality. After asking, "What is the universe?" they asked, "What, ultimately, is my very *self?*" The word is *ātman,* the reality that is the lasting and indispensable basis of one's being. *Self* is a possible translation of the word, but *self* does not suggest the religious nature of the quest for ātman. Let us speak of the drive to know the *soul,* though *soul,* too, is not a perfect rendering, for it misses psychological dimensions of the Sanskrit word. In using *soul* we should stand ready to attach new meanings to it.

The upanishads searched within for the basis for permanence in the individual. Asking, "What is the real person?" the authors first scrutinized the processes of birth, growth, decline, and death, seeking some enduring physical factor. Some said that there is a tiny inner person, the size of a thumb, that is the soul from which we are reconstituted again and again after death. Others found the essence in the old Vedic thinking about *prāṇa,* life-breath. Of course, in such physical constituents, real or imaginary, no basis for immortality was ever shown to exist. Hence the search for something deathless turned inward, to realities reported by persons given to introspective meditation. Indian thought has always accepted observations made in introspection as just as valid as observations of the outer world.

For lack of experience in meditation, outsiders often find the upanishads' descriptions of subjective explorations difficult to understand. Yet even outsiders can see a certain conceptual pattern occurring again and again: the soul is a core reality concealed from ordinary observation by multiple obscuring sheaths. These sheaths are impediments that must be overcome in order to apprehend the existence of the soul. Something akin to concentric rings are involved, in the midst of which the soul stands like the bull's-eye of a target. Three very different but complementary traditional sketches of the soul behind triple barriers have their beginnings in the upanishads.

The soul veiled by material stuff Three concentric shells of progressively coarser material are understood to be gathered around the soul. First and finest is the *causal body,* consisting of one's accumulated karma, in the form of deposits of very fine matter. This karma stuff clings to the soul throughout rebirths and even through dissolutions of the cosmos, causing one to be born again and again according to one's just desserts. Only when one enters final liberation will that innermost sheath be dissolved so that only one's soul, one's true self, will continue.

Just outside the causal body lies the sheath called the *subtle body,* made up of irreducible atoms, so to speak, of five kinds. Each kind of atom, when present in a compound thing, is detectable to a specific sense—sight, taste, touch, and so on. When not combined—as when making up the subtle body—these atoms elude all senses. So subtle bodies are not seen by the eye. They are the ghostly bodies of deceased persons. After death, in one's conjoined causal and subtle body, one goes to retribution in heavens or hells.

When reborn into the world according to one's remaining karma, one takes on again the third kind of body, the *gross body,* the outermost of the rings. That course sheath is the only self that ordinary persons see. The gross body is made up of five kinds of molecules, so to speak, each compounded from the atoms of which the subtle body is made.

This picture of three concentric bodies has influenced Hindu mysticism and shows how different the soul is conceived to be from any material substance. It also suggests how inaccessible the soul is to all of our ordinary means of knowing.

The soul as pure consciousness Chāndogya Upanishad 8.7–12 describes four levels of consciousness. In the *waking consciousness* we experience everyday life. The material world dominates, and the soul is utterly unknown. At night we sometimes dream, thus entering the *dreaming state,* in which we continue to perceive subtle material forms. Even in the dreaming state, however, material entities may still give us nightmares and thus distress us. Third is the *dreamless sleep* state of consciousness. In it the whole panorama of worldly things, both subtle and gross, vanishes. A blissful state, it is a premonition of the blessedness that will be known in the ultimate unity. Yet we remain residually aware that it is we who are in this blissful condition; we retain a remnant of self-consciousness.

Something lies beyond this state of deep, dreamless sleep—an ultimate state of consciousness. That highest state of awareness has no descriptive name. The upanishads simply call it *turīya,* "the fourth." In this state, blissful consciousness exists alone, without awareness of any object or concept. There is no awareness of material objects, gross or subtle, or of the individual who is conscious. There is neither longing for nor loathing of material objects. Only consciousness itself exists, the consciousness that is the very nature of the soul. Omnipresent, a reality without a second, its unity is like that ascribed to the cosmic Brahman.

The soul seated in a web of psychic organs Individuals make their appearance in the world by an evolutionary extension of consciousness from the soul into psychic faculties. They remain imbued with consciousness by reason of continuing contact with the soul from which they have emerged. The course of the evolution of the individual brought into existence first the conscious intellect called the **buddhi**, by which a person ponders information, decides, and initiates action. Then, by extension from the buddhi emerged the **manas**, or lower mind, which receives stimuli from the senses and identifies sense objects. Finally, the senses themselves—the faculties that have eye, ear, nose, tongue, and skin as their physical organs—emerged and began their work of apprehending the realities of the physical world.

But none of these faculties have any power to give one reflexive knowledge of the soul itself. They were so formed and so directed that they point outward only, making contact solely with the phenomenal world. The soul lies at the inward, not the outward, end of the line that is the sense process. To seek the soul through the operation of the senses is as foolish, to use modern terms, as to try to catch the operator of a powerful searchlight in the beam of the searchlight itself.

A searcher for the soul who looks outward to the phenomenal world only misdirects the power of knowing by which the soul itself could be revealed. How then *could* the soul be revealed? The pattern just outlined suggests that only introspection could be of any use—the tactic of retroversion to which the mystic must and does resort in the discipline called yoga. If consciousness can be withdrawn from things and turned back toward the center of our being, our power of knowing might be intensified and focused intensely on the soul. By such introspection we might merge our consciousness in that central pool of radiant consciousness from which the consciousness animating all of our psychic organs once emerged. As the Kaṭha Upanishad suggests:

The Creator pierced the sense-holes outward,
So one looks out, not toward the soul within.
Some wise man seeking deathlessness
With eyes inverted saw the soul direct.

No verse of the upanishads reveals the self-understanding of its mystics more effectively. Not the casual report of an explorer, it is the proclamation of a discoverer, testifying to a culminating inner experience. In the upanishads there are many such attestations to the experience of the oceanic trance. To post-Vedic India this experience brought relief from great distresses—particularly to a burning question about the afterlife. The obscuring sheaths have been penetrated and the true self has been found in an interior ocean of light that has no islands and no shores; immune to the changes wrought by time, that universal consciousness is all that one has ever been or ever will be. Hope for a stable afterlife, lost at the end of the Vedic age, is regained on a different basis, and the world's sufferings and oppressions can now be seen as fantasies of no importance. Peace is suggested in Chāndogya Upanishad 7.35.2:

Not death does the seer see
Nor illness nor any sorrow.
The seer sees just the All,
Attains the All entirely.

The reference to the All indicates that searches for the final reality within and the final reality without had led to a single conclusion: a reality that is immaterial, indescribable, generative, and yet eternally one. "Thou art That" was Uddālaka's final word to his son. Your soul is the world soul, Brahman, and shares its eternity and bliss. The discovery opened the way for a new kind of religious effort that became a way of salvation, the Way of Knowledge. (See the accompanying box, "The Way of Knowledge in a Upanishad Text.")

Of course, the trance that dissolves the mystic's fears appears to dissolve the mystic himself. The sage replies that nothing that ever truly was will vanish through this discovery. All that disappears—and rightly—is the ignorant supposition of individuality

The Way of Knowledge in a Upanishad Text

If you have become interested in this mystical religion, you should undertake, early, some direct reading in the upanishads. If you have little background in the meditative life, the ideas and references in these texts may be puzzling, but the struggle to understand may be fascinating. The following passages are from the sixth chapter of the Maitrī Upanishad, a scripture that expresses some of the teaching we have presented in this textbook—on Brahman, on the practices and processes of yogic meditation, on the final vision, and on the benefits that spring from the attainment of long-hidden knowledge of Brahman (here spelled, in stem form, *Brahma*).

3. There are, assuredly, two forms of Brahma [Brahman]: the formed and the formless. Now, that which is the formed is unreal; that which is the formless is real, is Brahma, is light.

17. Verily, in the beginning this world was Brahma, the limitless One—limitless to the east, limitless to the south, limitless to the west, limitless to the north, and above and below, limitless in every direction. Truly, for him east and the other directions exist not, nor across, nor below, nor above.

Incomprehensible is that supreme Soul (Ātman), unlimited, unborn, not to be reasoned about, unthinkable—He whose soul is space! In the dissolution of the world He alone remains awake. From that space He, assuredly, awakes this world, which is a mass of thought. It is thought by Him, and in Him it disappears. . . .

To the unity of the One goes he who knows this.

18. The precept for effecting this [unity] is this: restraint of the breath (prāṇāyāma), *withdrawal of the senses* (pratyāhāra), *meditation* (dhyāna), *concentration* (dhāraṇā), *contemplation* (tarka), *absorption* (samādhi). *Such is said to be the sixfold Yoga. By this means*

When a seer sees the brilliant
Maker, Lord, Person, the
Brahma-source,
Then, being a knower, shaking
off good and evil,
He reduces everything to unity
in the supreme
Imperishable.

19. Now, it has elsewhere been said: "Verily, when a knower has restrained his mind from the external, and the breathing spirit (prāṇa) *has put to rest objects of sense, thereupon let him continue void of conceptions. Since the living individual who is named "breathing spirit" has arisen here from what is not breathing spirit, therefore, verily, let the breathing spirit restrain his breathing spirit in what is called the fourth condition* (turīya)*." For thus it has been said:*

That which is non-thought, [yet]
which stands in the midst of
thought,
The unthinkable, supreme
mystery!
Thereon let one concentrate his
thought
And the subtle body, too,
without support.

20. Now, it has elsewhere been said: "One may have a higher concentration than this. By pressing the tip of his tongue against the palate, by restraining voice, mind, and breath, one sees Brahma through contemplation." When through self, by the suppressing of the mind, one sees the brilliant Self which is more subtle than the subtle, then having seen the Self through one's self, one becomes self-less. Because of being self-less, he is to be regarded as incalculable, without origin—the mark of liberation (moksha). *This is the supreme secret doctrine. For thus has it been said:*

For by tranquillity of thought
Deeds (karma), *good and evil,*
one destroys!
With soul (ātman) *serene,*
stayed on the Soul (Ātman),
Delight eternal one enjoys!

24. Now, it has elsewhere been said: "The body is a bow. The arrow is [the sacred sound] Om. *The mind is its point. Darkness is the mark. Having pierced through the darkness, one goes to what is not enveloped in darkness. Then, having pierced through what is thus enveloped, one sees Him who sparkles like a wheel of fire, of the color of the sun, mightful, the Brahma that is beyond darkness, that shines in yonder sun, also in the moon, in fire, in lightning. Now, assuredly, when one has seen Him, one goes to immortality." . . .*

28. Now, it has elsewhere been said: "Having passed beyond the elements, the senses, and objects of sense; thereupon having seized the bow whose string is the life of a religious mendicant and whose stick is steadfastness; and with the arrow which consists of freedom from self-conceit having struck down the first warder of the door to Brahma [egoism]—he who has confusion as his crown, covetousness and envy as his ear-rings, lassitude, drunkenness, and impurity as his staff, lord of self-conceit, who seizes the bow whose string is anger and whose stick is lust, and who slays beings here with the arrow of desire—having slain him, having crossed over with the raft of the syllable Om *to the other side of the space in the heart, in the inner space which gradually becomes manifest one should enter the hall of Brahma, as the miner seeking minerals enters into the mine. Then let him disperse the four-fold sheath of Brahma by the instruction of a spiritual teacher* (guru).

"Henceforth being pure, clean, void, tranquil, breathless, self-less, endless, undecaying, steadfast, eternal, unborn, independent, he abides in his own greatness.

"Henceforth, having seen [the soul] which abides in his own greatness, he looks down upon the wheel of transmigrating existence (saṃsāra) *as upon a rolling chariot-wheel."*

For thus has it been said:

If a man practices Yoga for six
months,
And is constantly freed [from
the senses],
The infinite, supreme,
mysterious
Yoga is perfectly produced.

But if a man is afflicted with
Passion and Darkness,
Enlightened as he may be—
If to son and wife and family
He is attached—for such a one,
no, never at all!

Source: Robert Ernest Hume, *The Thirteen Principal Upanishads* (New York: Oxford University Press, 1931), pp. 424–443.

and personhood. Over millennia that experience and that reasoning about the true self have been accepted gladly by millions of persons who found little satisfaction in the careers available to them in their place and age.

Millions of other Hindus, it will be noted, hesitated to make that drastic sacrifice. Lovers of the world or lovers of persons human or divine, they turned away from such disappearance of persons and raised up other understandings of salvation.

THE VEDĀNTA TRADITION

When the canon of the great upanishads was completed, the new and powerful religion called the Vedānta began its long history. The Vedānta is based on a distinctive kind of mystical experience and on belief in the underlying unity of all reality. This belief in an all-inclusive oneness left thinkers with a paradox. The upanishads often speak, on the one hand, of the complex world as an actuality. On the other hand, the undivided and all-inclusive Brahman they declare to exist alone. But how can the universe be divided and not divided at the same time? If Brahman, the sole reality, is one, must not the multiform world of experience be ruled out as nonexistent? And if the many things of the world are real, then must not the universal Brahman be a fiction?

The Vedānta tradition quietly grew for 1,000 years, recording its thinking on these disturbing questions in aphoristic texts on Brahman known as the **brahmasūtras**, the earliest of which is the Brahmasūtra of Bādarāyana (c. 200 C.E.). The first full presentation of the Vedānta system is a commentary on this work by the founder of the important Advaita (nondualistic) Vedānta School, Śaṅkara, writing around the year 800. Śaṅkara mediated between the two sides of the paradox, on the one hand the claim that plurality is real and Brahman is unreal versus the claim made by some Mahāyāna Buddhists (see Chapter 10) that the world is an unreal phantasm. He taught a *monistic* system: all things *do* have a substantive ground (Brahman), and that substance is one.

"What am I?" That is a basic question in any Indian outlook. Śaṅkara saw that we take ourselves to be separate individuals, each with a separate body that is a real and lasting part of ourselves. Therefore, we associate ourselves with the history of our changing bodies, thinking that our real selves undergo disease or death. Because our bodies are separate, we see ourselves as separate from others, and we are filled with thoughts of "I" and "mine." We think we can make ourselves happy with physical comforts, pleasure, or wealth. If we fail to attain these goals, we become dejected; if we succeed, we are elated, though only for a moment. We are, in short, never satisfied. We are constantly miserable but unaware of the reasons for our misery. We want liberation from rebirth but do not know how to attain it.

What the revealed upanishads assure us, says Śaṅkara, is that we are not separate individuals, winning or losing life's competitive struggles. In fact we are eternally one with the universal and immortal Brahman, the only reality. That perfect being is always characterized by consciousness, existence, and bliss. Since Brahman is the self in all of us, its blessed characteristics are ours also. In our daily life, however, we do not perceive the blessed unitary Brahman, and we do not know its bliss. How, then, can we believe the upanishads' statements about Brahman to be true?

Levels of Knowledge

In reply, Śaṅkara pointed out that even in everyday experience our senses can deceive us. There are several levels of what we call knowledge, and they are of unequal value in revealing truth. Even as unenlightened persons we are aware of one grade of experience that yields only *deluded knowledge*. For example, when we look out over a hot shimmering plain and see in the distance a lake that is only a mirage, our knowledge of the lake is deluded knowledge. Or we may mistake a shell on a beach for a shiny coin. Such perceptions are based on apprehension, but the object of experience is misperceived. Perceptual mistakes like these are corrected by comparison with later experiences and with the experiences of others. Śaṅkara's point is that experience can be deceptive and that seeing is not necessarily believing.

Empirical knowledge is the kind of knowledge that we get when we see real lakes or real coins. Their reality stands the test of repeated observations or other people's descriptions. It is this empirical knowledge that convinces us that we are all separate persons. It convinces us, too, that in our real selves, we are bodies—bodies that suffer injuries, grow old, and die. Therefore, Śaṅkara asserted, empirical knowledge is open to correction. Fortunately, empirical knowledge too can be superseded when we rise to the insight of a still higher grade.

Supreme (pāramārthika) knowledge is the final and highest form of experience open to us. It yields knowledge that is absolute truth. Unlike empirical knowledge, pāramārthika knowledge is not obtained through the senses, the mind, or the intellect but directly through consciousness, ātman. This supreme experience comes when our fallible senses are made to cease their operation and the conceptualizing activities of the intellect are stopped. When our psychic organs are put to rest and all our power of consciousness is concentrated in our innermost self, a unique state of consciousness called **samādhi** is reached. In this introverted state, a distorting film is removed from consciousness, and we can apprehend reality as it actually is. The understanding of what is real and what is unreal undergoes a remarkable reversal:

In what all beings call night
the disciplined sage awakes;
That wherein beings awaken
that the silent one sees as night.

(Bhagavadgītā 2.69)

Direct perception, then, convinces the mystic that the separateness of persons is false and that the oneness of all is the truth. Just as the upanishads teach, reality is a single ocean of consciousness without any real division. Utterly homogeneous, it is beyond any effect of time and change. This one immortal being is not only pure consciousness but also pure bliss. In it one is immune to all ills. The defects of our bodies and our bodies themselves are delusions comparable to a mirage. There is liberation from all distress for those who have attained this knowledge, for once gained, it is never lost. Those mystics are at peace now and forever who realize their oneness with the blissful Brahman.

Śaṅkara's Doctrine of Māyā

If universal oneness is the reality, why do we so persistently misconceive of ourselves as separate individuals? Because the effect exists (because there is delusion), it must be inferred that a cause exists, a factor that makes us project onto the unitive Brahman the many figments that make up our everyday world. Analogous to the factor that makes us see lakes and coins when the reality is something else, a cosmic factor causes our social delusions of plurality. Śaṅkara calls it **māyā**, "illusion," which he uses in several different senses. First, māyā is the factor creating cosmic delusion. It is māyā that is operative when our consciousness misinforms us that the universe is composed of many things. It is māyā also that causes us to apprehend ourselves wrongly as separate individuals, each composed of a separate body and soul. To māyā as a factor distorting our subjective understanding Śaṅkara also applies the term *avidyā,* or ignorance.

Even though its metaphysical status is a mystery, this factor cannot be conceived of as real (that is, included within Brahman) because Brahman includes no second thing. Nor is it unreal (apart from Brahman), for no thing—except nothing—is apart from Brahman. Clearly, māyā is not nothing: it acts, with catastrophic consequences. Neither real nor unreal, māyā is a unique entity that is the cause of all human sin and misery; it is the supreme impediment to our salvation. It causes individuals to appear separate, to believe in their separateness, and to act selfishly. It causes a material world to distract souls into love and hate for its figments. It binds illusionary individuals to illusionary bodies and illusionary worlds and to illusionary responsibility for their illusionary acts. Our one noble desire is the desire to end the ignorance that makes us desire individual material gain. We can hope to attain liberation only if we are willing to renounce the world and adopt the arduous life of seekers of salvation through the Way of Knowledge.

The Sannyāsī, Renouncer of the World

It was recognized from the start that seekers of the extraordinary knowledge of the hidden oneness of things must use extraordinary means. Old values were to be purged; new sensitivities were to be developed; the mind was to be retrained with full-time dedication. In the upanishads the original proponents of the new mystical religion are presented as men who abandoned house and property and wandered off into the forest. Residence in secluded places is described as advantageous to the practice of meditation, and as time went on the mystical literature became more and more insistent on a clean break with the workaday world. At first the leaders of the mystical movement are spoken of in general terms as wanderers or ascetics, but the later dharmaśāstras give them the specific and standard name *sannyāsī,* "renouncer." The caste society since its first creation has generated, through its heavy restrictions and its imposed tasks, a massive secession from strictly ordered life. The renunciation **(sannyāsa)** that sannyāsīs have undergone is understood to have been a severe and permanent renunciation—not merely of desires or of one's profession but of the world. The term *sannyāsī* to this day, when applied to a religious mendicant, credits that person with serious study of Vedānta teaching and a sincere desire for final liberation. That is the kind of monk we shall be discussing. (Female renunciants have always been rare.)

For 2,000 years most Hindus have believed that some day, in some rebirth or other, they should abandon the life of the householder for the life of the wandering monk. And throughout those millennia, mendicants in saffron robes, carrying a staff and a begging bowl, have been conspicuous on the Indian scene and have had the respect and support of Hindus.

Becoming a sannyāsī is therefore a much-honored act, but it is an act of free personal choice. At what age, or even in what life, the move must be made, the scriptures do not say. As the upanishads grew more influential, a massive number of young persons on the very verge of adulthood began to adopt the forest life. By the second century C.E., as expressed in the Bhagavadgītā, many in Hindu society were dismayed at the loss of the services of the young renunciants. The dharmaśāstras drew up a defensive rule that world renunciation should be delayed until the declining years of life, when one's skin is wrinkled and one's hair is white (*Manu* 6.2). This delaying of the turn to the monastic life has remained the ideal, but in practice insistent young persons have always been allowed to make the move. The one essential qualification is an inner one: disillusion with worldly pleasures and a deep longing for liberation from further births.

Even while still living the life of a householder, Hindus committed to the Way of Knowledge are able to make preparations that should hasten the time of their salvation. They should curb the ego, calm their minds by selfless performance of their duties, and avoid bad conduct, which destroys serenity (Kaṭha Upanishad 2.24). The same need of mental calm before even attempting advanced meditation underlies a requirement that one must perfect in oneself five moral virtues: nonviolence, truthfulness, honesty, chastity, and freedom from greed. These five virtues, together, are always identified as the first of the traditional eight-limbed yoga. They may be perfected while one is still living in the world. The same is true of five further essential virtues, of mental nature, that comprise the second step: cleanliness in body and in diet, the practice of being contented, austerity (developing powers of self-denial and endurance), study of religious texts and doctrines, and meditation on the Lord. This last, meditation on a personal deity, is thought to be useful for beginners on the Way of Knowledge, even though they will eventually surrender the personal concept for an impersonal conception of the divine.

Instructions for the life of laypersons are often given in terms that are less formal than these lists. Śaṅkara simply says that spiritual seekers should meditate on Vedānta truths constantly, study the upanishads, and ponder such scriptural statements as "I am Brahman."

After years or lifetimes of such preparation, it is believed, a householder will suddenly perceive that it is time to renounce the world. The precipitating factor is often some dramatic manifestation of the transience of life—there is a death in the family, or a king looks in the mirror and finds the first gray in his beard. At root there may be some catastrophic reversal of fortune—great financial loss or the collapse of a reputation. The event may be a domestic quarrel or even a single chiding word. The routine duties of a person's life suddenly become suffocating and meaningless, and the tools of his trade are dropped, never to be picked up again. Or a drive for great wealth succeeds, and success brings a realization of the vanity of possessions and the need for something eternal. The lives of famous saints often tell the story of these spectacular turning points in spiritual careers.

The actual departure of the would-be sannyāsī from his family and village is a solemn ritual. In a round of farewell calls, the departing one gives away his prized possessions. He performs his last ritual as a householder. In a formal separation, he leaves his village on foot, and his son escorts him for a stated distance on his way. Finally, at a certain spot father and son take a back-to-back position, the son facing toward the village, the father toward the unknown. Both stride off resolutely in their respective directions without looking back. The father must walk straight ahead until the end of the day without stopping. Theoretically, he should never again mention the name of his village or even think of it.

For him a completely new life begins. He becomes a wandering beggar, building no fire and cooking no food. Appearing at a house door just after the time of dinner, he eats whatever scraps he may be given. He sleeps wherever night overtakes him—ideally under a tree, but perhaps at a temple or a charitable shelter for monks. Rarely, such seekers reside for extended periods in a monastic establishment, but in contrast to Buddhist and Christian monasticism, no special value is attached to cloistered living. Mendicants rove at will, visiting temples, attending religious fairs, or lingering on mountains noted as places of meditation. The monk has no family obligations, no ritual duties, and no work to do. He has faith that he will attain in his own time, alone, the liberation he is seeking.

In this spontaneous new life, the irritations of a restrictive society are eased. The former caste of the holy man is forgotten, and its restrictions no longer oppress him. If gifted, the holy man may become an eminent teacher or spiritual guide. He is now his own master, free to roam and to live on alms, on the sole condition that he forever separate himself from society's concerns. Sannyāsa has been the outlet for millions of sensitive Hindu men who could not endure the confinements of caste life. It has also been the safety valve of the caste community, siphoning off the discontent of people who might otherwise have destroyed it. Sannyāsa, like the doctrine of karma, has been a strong supporting pillar of the classical Hindu culture.

Since the skills developed in the worldly life do not help in the inner explorations now to be carried out, the renouncer quickly seeks out the expertise of a teacher who has made the mystical journey and reached the other shore. It is believed that destiny provides each seeker with his own true teacher and that this guru and his disciple will recognize each other when they ultimately meet face-to-face.

The guru now administers the rite of initiation into the final stage of life. It is irreversible, a ritual death to the world and a rebirth into the realm of transcendence. The teacher rips off the disciple's sacred thread and cuts off his queue, the signs of honorable status as

This Hindu ascetic sits in the characteristic meditation position. He remains motionless and seemingly oblivious to the world. (Religious News Service)

a conforming Hindu. Henceforth the disciple will no longer belong to any caste. The names by which he has been known are uttered for the last time, and the teacher confers on him a new name devoid of caste significance but evocative of some religious truth. The guru should instruct his disciple in doctrine and in proper monkish living. When the disciple is deemed ready, he is guided in the advanced meditational discipline that is called yoga.

Yoga

The term *yoga,* like its English cognate *yoke,* means "to join, unite" and also "to harness up, set seriously to work." Followers of the monistic Vedānta tradition understand yoga as training that can bring about conscious union of one's own soul with the universal soul. There are several systems of yoga.

Haṭhayoga is a physical discipline used to tone the body; it may or may not be followed by deeper meditations. The Tāntric schools, whose position is marginal in Hinduism, practice a *kundalinī* yoga that has its own unusual imagery. Some modern mystical movements have developed their own unusual yogic practices. But for most Hindus yoga refers to a version of the eight-stage meditational discipline attributed to the ancient sage Patañjali. An early variation on the formula was seen in the box "The Way of Knowledge in a Upanishad Text," in Maitrī Upanishad 6.18. Patañjali's *Yoga Sūtra* outlines the "limbs" or stages of the yogic path more fully: moral restraint, mental discipline, posture *(āsana),* breath control *(prāṇāyama),* withdrawal from sense objects *(pratyāhāra),* steadying of attention *(dhāraṇā),* meditation on religious insights *(dhyāna),* and concentration on or mystical merging with the ultimate *(samādhi).*

The first two, discussed earlier, are preliminary stages, consisting of moral and meditational preparation. The third stage prescribes physical postures that are thought to be conducive to serenity. The meditator is to take a bodily posture such as the lotus position (legs crossed, hands cupped with palms upward in the lap), which is designed not to strain the body but to make it possible to forget the body so that a higher identity may be known. Next comes the control of breath, which is related to a common belief that breath is at the root of life and that breath control can therefore bring one nearer to the basis of one's being. More obviously, breath regulation brings one's attention into sharp focus and creates calmness.

Mental calmness is also the goal of the fifth step, the withdrawal of the senses from attention to all objects of sense. The process is compared to a turtle's retraction of its limbs into its shell. Immunity from the upsetting effect of outside circumstances is the end in view, and freedom to concentrate one's attention on inward matters. The sixth step, the steadying of attention, assumes that freedom from distractions has been achieved and involves development of the ability to hold one's attention firmly on one focal point as long as desired. The seventh stage provides for positive meditation on chosen religious themes such as the thought "Thou art That" or "I am Brahman"—great words of the upanishads—or the sacred syllable *Om,* the sound symbol of Brahman. Such meditations, long continued, are designed to bring the nation of individual selfhood near to extinction. If the meditator is bold enough to accept that extinction and press on, he is said to enter into the culminating experience of monistic meditation that is called samādhi. This last stage of yoga begins when the yogi's awareness, long focused on a single point, swells explosively to encompass a limitless reality. A sense of all-reaching participation in a living cosmos sweeps over him, and his individuality appears

Two modern advocates of the doctrine of monism: left, the Shankaracharya of Dwarka Peeth, the abbot of one of the monasteries founded by Śankara; right, Sarvepalli Rādhākrishnan, creative modern philosopher. The abbot's accoutrements indicate that, despite his commitment to the impersonal Brahman, he allows or practices the worship of the personal god Śiva. Note the forehead lines, the large beads, and the trident held by his attendant. (Religious News Service)

to be dissolved in the light of a luminous ocean. The sense of infinite oneness is understood by the mystic to be a revelation taking precedence over all earlier insights: it is the final truth about the nature of things. Plural things and plural souls are no longer seen as real. But the disappearance of individuality does not bring nothingness. The real person is found in a universal consciousness in which there are no distinctions, no possibility of change, and no sense of time. Births become phantasmal events that do not really occur, and deaths become appearances without reality. Meditators who know this experience understand themselves to be forever free. Life beyond death will be a continuation of this experience, which is a revelation to the living of the nature of moksha, final salvation.

In the assurance of immortality implicit in the unitive mystical experience, seekers of the age of the upanishads recovered, substantially, the paradise that had been lost at the end of the Vedic age. Attained by different means, it was a different paradise that could be enjoyed only by renouncing all earthly values and even personal existence itself.

People who undergo this experience are called *jīvanmuktas* (the liberated while still living) or simply "enlightened." Irreversibly stripped of all sense of self and incapable of any self-serving act, they will acquire no new karma. When their old karma is expended, their bodies will die for the last time. They will then enter into final liberation in Brahman, never to be born again.

Some of the most famous Hindu saints have been natural mystics who had no need to practice yoga but achieved the unitive experience spontaneously and without conscious effort. There are some teachers today who deny the necessity of yoga and urge their disciples to await such a natural revelation.

Will all who take up the search for mystical enlightenment achieve it? Hindus have usually held that the chance of success is small for those who remain in society as householders (Maitrī Upanishad 6.28). It is admitted that even renunciation of the world and a lifetime of meditational effort are often insufficient. Although meditation practices may help, the outcome of yoga ultimately lies beyond human control. If realization is not achieved in the present life, however, all agree that the efforts of strivers are not lost. Reborn to more favorable situations, these people will eventually attain illumination and the liberation that is their goal.

NOTE

1 Manmatha Nath Dutt, *A Prose English Translation of Mārkaṇḍeya Purāṇam* (Calcutta, 1896), p. 181.

Religions of India

CHAPTER 6

Classical Hinduism: The Way of Devotion

The third of the Hindu mārgas, the Way of Devotion or *bhaktimārga,* places its hope for liberation in the power of a personal God of the universe. Two great theistic movements in Hinduism—one centered on Śiva, the other centered on Vishṇu—have been exceedingly popular for 2,000 years. Together they probably hold the allegiance of a majority of Hindus today. These two forms of Indian religion are the most similar to the faiths of the West.

Like the Way of Knowledge, the Way of Devotion was a product of the stressful period when followers of the Vedic religion for the first time experienced a regimented social order and when even the heavens no longer offered hope of lasting freedom. The Way of Knowledge and Buddhism offered release from karma and the unwanted round of lives, but at the cost of continuing existence as a person. Many Hindus cherished their own individuality too highly to find satisfaction in such liberations. In intellectual struggles they gradually worked out a different plan of salvation through a personal God of new stature. This development was difficult for people reared in the Vedic tradition because the comprehensive forces that control human life—ṛita, or dharma, and karma—were conceived of as impersonal principles. The personal gods of the Veda, by contrast, were thought to reside in some specific region of the natural world, exercising only limited powers and functions. Even the greatest gods were believed to control only a portion of the universe.

Speculation about a cosmic god with universal jurisdiction is evident in the late Vedic hymns, but the notion of such a deity developed into monotheism only slowly. The rise of the concept of a universal "world essence" helped greatly in the emergence of monotheism when, in the Śvetāśvatara Upanishad (around the fifth century B.C.E.), the Vedic god Rudra (now known as Śiva) is described as Brahman, the totality of all being and all power. As such, the Lord Śiva rules over all. He pervades persons, is present in their hearts, and thus may be perceived by meditators who practice yoga. When we see him in ourselves as Śiva the Kindly, we respond with devotion (**bhakti**); God in turn responds with gracious help. It was he who created karma, and what he created he can break. When the fetters of karma are broken, there begins a life of freedom, including freedom from death. A century or two later, the writings known as the Bhagavadgītā expanded this idea about Brahman into a monotheistic theology: Brahman became the universal power of God. This doctrine soon entered all branches of the bhaktimārga.

The term *bhakti* derives from a verb meaning "to divide and share," as when food is divided and shared at family and caste gatherings. The noun *bhakti* recalls the loyalty and trust that prevail at such meetings—the generous portions of food, the junior members' willingness to serve, and the protectiveness of the elders. *Bhaktas,* devotees who follow the Way of Devotion, have discovered such affection at the center of the universe in "the great Lord of all the worlds, a friend of all creatures" (Bhagavadgītā 5.29). While sharing this common attitude toward God, the Way of Devotion has from the beginning consisted of two separate streams: the worshipers of Śiva, known as **Śaivas**, and the worshipers of Vishṇu, called **Vaishṇavas.** Let us begin with the Śaivite tradition.

THE WORSHIP OF ŚIVA

Śiva is known in the Vedas as Rudra, the Howler, a power operating in destructive rainstorms. His face is red, and his neck is blue. He dwells isolated in the mountains, and his retainers include robbers and ghosts. His weapons include sharp arrows and the dreaded thunderbolt, and in the Vedic hymns none who worship him assume that they are safe from him. He attacks with fever, coughs, and poisons, yet he is also a physician who possesses 1,000 remedies.

Persons impressed by life's harshness and brevity have been drawn to the worship of Śiva. For his worshipers, safety can be found—if at all—only by dealing with the one who presides over such dangers. They see Śiva as the special divine force behind all natural processes of destruction; consequently, Śaivism attracted small groups of Hindu society's alienated, morbid, and misanthropic members, drawn by the religion's stark realism. Yet there are many more optimistic souls who are also part of the Śaivite circle who worship him as the supreme monotheistic deity.

The Liṅgam and Yoni Emblem

Shrines dedicated to Śiva began to appear in the first century B.C.E. In some shrines the object of worship was a stone pillar resembling the male generative organ: Śiva had come to be regarded as a source of procreation as well as destruction! Images of Śiva in human form were also common. Worship of the phallic emblem did not become dominant until it had evolved into an only vaguely phallic upright cylinder rounded at the top, called a **liṅgam**, which is clearly a symbol rather than a representation of the sex organ. Four faces often look out from the sides of the shaft. These indicate the omniscience of the god, who faces in all directions.

Within a few centuries it became customary to seat the cylinder in a shallow, spouted dish that was at once a basin for catching liquid oblations poured over the liṅgam and a symbolic **yoni**, or female organ, representing Śiva's **śākti**, or female reproductive power. A combined liṅgam and yoni icon usually stands at the center of shrines to Śiva. Modern Hindu scholars insist that this emblem refers to metaphysical truths only, even though it uses symbols of the human genitals. Indeed, the rites of liṅgam worship have never been orgiastic or erotic. The icon makes a statement about the cosmos: Śiva's potent generative power is eternally at work, and it is feminine as well as masculine, a force for life as well as for destruction.

Because the people of the Indus valley civilization used similar phalluses in their cult, many scholars speculate that the liṅgam and perhaps other aspects of Śiva worship entered Hinduism from this old source.

A more dramatic but less common recognition of femininity in Śiva's nature is the icon of the half-woman Lord (Ardhānārīśvara) in which the image's left half is full-breasted and wears the ornaments and clothing of a woman while the right half is presented as male. The same tendency manifests itself in the development of many new myths about Śiva's powerful wife, called, Umā, Pārvatī, or Durgā.

Śiva's feminine side was conveyed also in the growing body of Śiva mythology produced between the first and fifth centuries C.E. In the epics and Purāṇas, Śiva develops a dual nature, showing a kindlier side while maintaining his destructiveness. He haunts the cremation grounds and smears his body with the ashes of the dead. (One still prepares for the worship of Śiva by rubbing ashes over one's body and marking one's forehead with three horizontal stripes of white ash.) Śiva wears a necklace made of the skulls of past deities, whom he has outlived and whose creations he has brought to an end. Stories of his wildly destructive acts continue to be told, and he is given new names that stress his ferocious and unpredictable nature. Some orders of ancient Śiva devotees shocked their contemporaries by dwelling in creation grounds, practicing bloody sacrifices, or using skulls as alms bowls.

As Śiva became a universal God, however, new myths showed him using his dreadful powers in

Though Śaiva artists sometimes give Śiva a human form, this simpler representation appears in the usual shrine. Śiva is seen here as the universal male power in everlasting union with his female energy. By their combined force, the world comes into being and evolves. (The Metropolitan Museum of Art, gift of Samuel Eilenberg, 1987)

constructive ways. One favorite myth tells how Śiva saved the world from danger: when the sacred River Ganges fell in a destructive torrent, Śiva caught it in his heavy hair. Thus Śiva's role as the protector is often symbolized by a gentle river spouting from his matted locks.

Śiva as the One God

After 400 C.E. several new groups arose that worshiped Śiva as the supreme God. Some sects composed Sanskrit manuals called *āgamas* that articulated their beliefs and guided their members in rituals, image making, and temple building. Another sect, the South Indian Śaivasiddhānta theological tradition, developed in the seventh century; it still thrives. But the most significant development in Śaivite religion was the appearance of a series of remarkable religious poets who wrote in the South Indian Tamil tongue. Beginning in the seventh century with Appar and Sambandar, their beautiful hymns are still sung. As recently as the seventeenth century, there were new surges of devotion in Tamil literature, and a poet named Śivavākkiyar praised the uniqueness of Śiva in these lines:

Not Vishnu, Brahmā, Śiva,
In the Beyond is He,
Not black, nor white, nor ruddy,
This Source of things that be;
Not great is he, not little,
Not female and not male—
But stands far, far, and far beyond
All being's utmost pale![1]

The early Tamil poets' belief in a personal God was challenged, however, by the philosopher Śaṅkara's arguments for an impersonal Brahman (see Chapter 5). Śaivite theologians like the South Indian Meykandār and his disciple Aruḷnandi in the thirteenth century defended Śaivite beliefs: by calling Śiva *Paśupati,* the Lord of Cattle, the Śaivasiddhānta theologians wished to emphasize the protective aspect of Śiva's nature. Like Western religions' notion of a "good shepherd," it stresses Śiva's concern for human souls; like a shepherd, Śiva seeks to free them from the tethers that prevent them from attaining liberation.

Souls, according to the Śaiva theologians, are deluded about their nature, imagining themselves to be physical beings only and thus separated from others. They are not aware that God dwells in and guides them all. Ignorant of Śiva's helping powers, they are bound by the three tethers of ignorance (believing they are isolated beings), the karma of past actions, and māyā (the physical world and its pleasures, which dominate human attention).

Śiva, as *pati,* or Lord, offers many kinds of spiritual assistance to help humans liberate themselves from these bonds. In many shrines in southern India, the principal Śaiva beliefs are expressed in images of Śiva as the supreme dancer. Śiva is worshiped there as the creator, preserver, and destroyer of life and as a gracious guide. As he dances, Śiva continually creates, preserves, and destroys all things physical so that souls may live and learn.

The union with God of which these Śaivas speak is not like the mystical union with Brahman of the Advaita (Chapter 5) because it entails neither a loss of individuality nor any sense that the worshiper has become divine. Śaiva teachers agree with Muslims and Christians in saying that it would be blasphemous for human beings to identify themselves with God.

THE ŚĀKTAS

We take up Śāktism at this point because much of its thought was contributed by the Śaivas, with whom the Śāktas have interacted for 2,000 years. The **Śāktas** accept and use Śaivite myths and symbols and share their apprehension of the world as filled with both natural and supernatural menace. The Śāktas also acknowledge Śiva as the supreme deity; yet they worship not his masculine aspect, which they understand to be passive, but rather Śiva's active feminine reproductive power, śākti. That śākti is often identified with the great goddess **Durgā**, the active power that actually determines the course of the natural universe.

Our earliest evidence of the Śākta movement is from Sanskrit literature of the early first century C.E., which mentions that fearsome goddesses were being worshiped in rural villages. The **Mahābhārata** epic (c. third century epic narrative that became a compendium of legends and literature) takes more serious note of them, even naming some of these non-Vedic deities, including the wild-haired **Kālī**, who roams battlefields devouring human flesh and drinking the blood of the fallen; the gaunt Cāmuṇḍā, enemy of all life, who kills especially by famine; and Durgā, whom wild tribes worship with offerings of meat and liquor. Though sometimes the goddesses look down on people with motherly tenderness, they are ordinarily depicted as full-breasted, fanged, and dangerous. Fundamental to Śāktism is a starkly realistic approach to the grimmer aspects of the world.

Early Śāktism conceived of many śāktis and consorts of Śiva, but Śaivism's quite early effort to unify the universe as the realm of a single deity influenced Śāktism also, in time. The appearance, in about the sixth century, of the *Devī Māhātmya,* a Sanskrit poetical work on the heroic deeds of Durgā, marked the emergence of Śāktism into Brahmanic culture and the appearance of a monotheism focused on the goddess Durgā. Durgā thenceforth became the one cosmic Śākti, and other goddesses, though still named and worshiped, were regarded as various forms that Durgā assumed from time to time to cope with various demonic forces. Kālī in particular continues to be worshiped very widely as one of Durgā's most dreadful and powerful manifestations.

In late September and October, the entire Hindu population of Bengal celebrates the annual Durgā Pūjā, a festival in which Durgā's deliverance of the world from the attack of the buffalo demon Mahisha is celebrated. Local enthusiasts in each neighborhood erect clay images of Durgā brandishing many weapons in her many hands and retell night after night the story of her combats. On the last night of the recitations, the festival is concluded by sacrificing a goat or a buffalo as an offering to Durgā. In this rite survives the sole remnant of animal sacrifice in modern Brahmanic Hinduism.

Here Śiva emerges from the world pillar as the world's central power. Infinite in outreach, he is beyond the comprehension of the greatest of the gods. Brahmā is represented in the upper left as a śwan and Visṇu is represented by a boar at the bottom. (Reunion des Musees Nationaux, Paris)

Śiva as the Dancer who activates the rhythms of the universe. His sending forth of the cosmos is suggested by the drum in his right hand. In his left, a flame indicates his power of destruction. At center, one hand makes the sign of reassurance, while the other points to his feet, at which worshipers may fall and receive his help. (Cleveland Art Museum)

In Śākta worship two quite different moods are found. Sometimes the furious goddess is seen as taking the field as the champion of life. At other times Śākta believers perceive her rage as directed against themselves, and they pray that her wrathful visitations may be averted.

The assurance given by Śākta teaching enables believers to accept harsh experiences with equanimity. Such calm acceptance of the tragedies of life is found in the Bengali poetry of Rāmaprasād Sen (1718–1775), the greatest modern poet of Kālī devotion, who expressed his view of his own sufferings in these words:

Though the mother beat him,
the child cries, "Mother, O Mother!"
and clings still tighter to her garment.
True, I cannot see thee,
yet I am not a lost child.
I still cry, "Mother, Mother." . . .
All the miseries that I have suffered
and am suffering, I know, O Mother,
to be your mercy alone.[2]

Although the Hindu conceptions of Durgā and Kālī are shocking, reflection will show us that the needs at the center of Śākta worship have been deep concerns in other religious traditions as well.

Śāktism is of particular interest as the modern world's most highly developed worship of a supreme female deity. The worship of Durgā has most of the characteristics of monotheism. Her power alone is understood to create, control, and destroy all phenomenal things, and thus no Śākta worship is directed to any being who is not one of her forms or appearances. But Durgā is not understood to be the whole of the divine nature; the realm of the transcendent and changeless is Śiva's, and those who seek liberation from the world (moksha) must seek it by meditation on Śiva in yoga. Śāktas, however, express little desire for moksha. As people concerned about the world, they seek from the goddess health, wealth, and general well-being.

Tāntrism

A closely related form of religion called **Tāntrism** arose in ancient times out of the same popular goddess worship from which Śāktism was born. Tāntrists often follow Śākta patterns in their public life. They are equally feminist in their theology. But Tāntrism has moksha, or liberation, as its goal, and it is set off from Śāktism by erotic ritual practices and by an elaborate yoga that is sexual in its concepts. Although it had an important parallel in Vajrayāna Buddhism (see Chapter 10), Tāntrism was disdained by most Hindus and was never more than a marginal development with a small following.

THE WORSHIP OF VISHṆU

Vishṇu in the Vedic Age

The second of the two great bhakti traditions has long honored the name of the Vedic Vishnu and has absorbed much of the lore of that kindly deity. The Vishṇu of the Vedas is associated with the sun and is seen as promoting growth. He is present in plants and trees, provides food, and protects unborn babies in the womb. Although he rides a sun-eagle and is armed with a discus that represents the orb of the sun, he is not the sun itself. His jurisdiction is not limited to a single part of the natural world.

Although not a great god in the Vedic pantheon, Vishṇu appealed to many in post-Vedic times because of the stories of his deeds on behalf of humanity. For example, Vishṇu assumed the form of a dwarf and went as a beggar before Bali, the king of the demons, and asked as alms the gift of as much space as he could mark out in three steps. The demon granted him this seemingly small favor. Vishṇu then resumed his cosmic stature and paced off in the first giant step the whole earth, as an abode for living persons. Then he marked off the atmosphere, and in the third step he established the high heavenly world as a pleasant refuge for the deceased. Vishṇu was the one god of the Vedic pantheon who was known to care about the happiness of the dead.

The cult of Vishṇu attracted persons concerned about the problem of immortality and also those who had at heart the welfare of society. Vishṇu worship appealed to those who saw the universe as friendly and good. Salvation seekers of the post-Vedic age who could not conceive of the violent Śiva as their savior found an alternative in one or another of Vishṇu's forms. Vaishṇava religion attracted the more settled citizens and civic leaders of the Hindu world.

Origins of the Vaishṇava Tradition

The Vaishṇava religion did not arise directly out of Vedic circles that worshiped Vishṇu, however. Its institutional history began with the Sātvatas, a tribal people who from the fifth century B.C.E. worshiped the non-Vedic deity **Kṛishṇa Vāsudeva.** In its early phases, this religion was often called the Sātvata faith or sometimes the Bhāgavata faith because its great god was given the title *Bhagavat,* "Bounteous One."

Due to its military prowess, this non-Aryan Sātvata tribe eventually attained kshatriya (warrior) status, and with that came participation in life around the courts and contact with brāhmans. Some brāhmans became active adherents and even teachers of the Sātvata faith, assisting the sect in establishing its simple monotheism on the basis of the upanishads' doctrine of the oneness of the world in Brahman. The **Bhagavadgītā**, a work of the second or first century B.C.E., was the literary legacy of this creative encounter between the monotheistic and monistic religious traditions. It was received with such favor that it was incorporated immediately into the great epic, the Mahābhārata, that brāhman editors were beginning to enlarge at that time.

THE BHAGAVADGĪTĀ

The Bhagavadgītā consists of 18 short chapters of Sanskrit verse. Often printed separately from the Mahābhārata, it has become the most widely used of all Hindu scriptures. One reason is its anonymous author's ability to find positive value in the teachings of other Hindu forms of religion; this text's pluralistic spirit has allowed it to be appreciated and used by millions of Hindus who are not devotees of Kṛishṇa at all. But the main reason for the wide acclaim that the work received at the time of its writing was the solution that it offered to a critical social problem: many young men and women, inspired by the message of the late upanishads and other religions, had renounced their social station and had become forest hermits in order to seek liberation. The Bhagavadgītā discusses this practice in detail.

The author knew the major upanishads well and believed that Kṛishṇa himself had revealed them (15.15). He was inspired by their message that the universe had a metaphysical unity in Brahman, but he did not regard all teachings as equally true and effective. Politely but firmly, he subordinated the impersonal Brahman of the upanishads to the control of a personal Lord (14.27; 13.12). With great emphasis he corrected the view that seekers of liberation must abandon the world and cease performing their duties. His method is an ingenious analysis of how doing our duty can damage us and how we can perform our duty without harm.

The Bhagavadgītā opens with a scene that exemplifies this great problem. Arjuna, a sensitive warrior, is contemplating the grim duty that Hindu society requires of his military caste, and he recoils at the thought of the injuries and guilt that will follow his fighting. Arjuna is the hope of the army of the Pāṇḍavas and is bound by duty to fight the forces of the Kaurava prince, Duryodhana, who has committed great wrongs. But as Arjuna looks down the ranks of opponents he is expected to slay, he is paralyzed by the thought of the dreadful harm that he is likely to inflict on the relatives and respected teachers that he sees among them. Dropping his weapons, Arjuna throws himself down, saying it would be better to live by begging as monks do than to commit such deeds (2.5). Confused about what is right, he asks for the advice of Kṛishṇa, who is serving as his chariot driver.

Though it is the duty of a warrior that is discussed in this story, the case of Arjuna epitomizes the moral problem of the members of every occupation. Must we, as the upanishads taught, abandon our worldly work with its imperfections and endless retribution if we aspire to liberation?

Cāmuṇḍā, one of the Seven Mothers, with her weapons (note the sword above her head) and the bowl from which she drinks blood. Śāktas understand her to be a manifestation of Durgā, the universal mother, and try to accept natural destruction at her hands with trustful worship, like the figure at the bottom. (Trustees of the British Museum)

Kṛishṇa responds first with conventional arguments: disgrace descends on all who flee their duties; in using arms no real harm is done, since the soul cannot be slain. Kṛishṇa then begins to reveal the real reason why the duties of life need not be abandoned: because they can be performed in a new spirit that prevents the acquisition of karma and makes them a means of liberation rather than of bondage. It is the selfish desire with which we act, not the action itself, that binds acts to us and makes their impurity our own. If we can perform our duties simply because the scriptures require us to perform them or simply as a service to God, with no desire to make any personal gains, then those acts will have no real connection with us in the operation of the processes of retribution. No karma will be created by those acts, no ties with the world will be deepened by them, and no future births will ensue. After a life lived in the selfless performance of one's social role, the dispassionate soul, unfettered still despite a fully active life, is forever freed.

Kṛishṇa explains that he himself as the Lord of the Universe creates and maintains the world in that desireless spirit: it is only to secure the welfare of the world that he carries on his eternal cosmic activity (3.20–25), and it is only to save the world from evil that he descends to mundane births in age after age (4.5–15), and thus his work entails no bondage.

Human workers in the world can emulate that selflessness and share in that freedom. The author explains how meditation can be used to achieve mastery of desires. The necessary discipline involves turning one's attention away from sense objects and redirecting it toward the soul, Brahman, or, best of all, the personal Lord. Even simple devotees can make a beginning in such refocusing by contemplating Kṛishṇa's deeds and singing his praises and then moving on to deeper exercises. The author knows and teaches progressive introspections much like the eight-stage yoga of the Way of Knowledge. He insists on modifications. He omits the tactics that lead to preternatural luminous visions and seeks rather an experience of utter tranquillity into which one enters through complete elimination of desire. That supreme serenity is the experience of Brahman, the very state of consciousness that *is* Brahman. Created by desirelessness, it is a moral state and a basis for desireless action in a continuing life of devotion to duty.

Brahman entered by the serene meditator is not

merely a psychological state, however; it is also a metaphysical one. It is the stuff of the universe, divine in nature, and one's state in final liberation. But it is not autonomous, nor is it the highest reality; it is God's stuff contained in him, the stuff with which God creates the world. The divine stands above it and uses it, and even the human being does not vanish as an individual upon attaining it (6.30). All who consciously participate in this universal Brahman discover also their tie with all other living beings and feel empathy with them:

O Arjuna, he who sees in all
Sameness with himself
Whether in happiness or sorrow,
His is the highest yogī.

(Bhagavadgītā 6.32)

We compare with this the understanding of the Brahman seeker of the upanishads, who found in Brahman only assurance of his own immortality.

In realizing Brahman, the successful meditator also discovers a tie with God, for Brahman is God's "world essence." A passage at the end of the text (18.54) shares the general Vedānta view that the experience of Brahman is the state of eternal liberation but at the same time teaches a special understanding of how that liberation comes about. When the mystic discovers the reality of his relationship with God, devotion to God arises, and one enters final liberation, which is life in and with the Lord.

Arjuna does not respond very quickly to his charioteer's arguments, but when he is granted a vision of Kṛishṇa not in his worldly form but in all his cosmic greatness as the be-all and end-all of existence even greater than Brahman (11.37), he is awed. Arjuna at last understands Kṛishṇa to be the very source of the duty (14.27) that he is resisting. Arjuna is moved, and in verse 18.37 he vows to Kṛishṇa, "I shall do your word."

Like Arjuna, many generations of Hindus have been moved by the charm and reasoning of the Bhagavadgītā to remain faithful to their duty. With great creativity the unknown author of this small scripture adapted the metaphysics and the mysticism of the upanishads to the religious needs of a civil society. In doing so he transformed his small sect into a major support of the Brahmanic order.

THE LATER VAISHṆAVA TRADITION

The subsequent history of the Vaishṇava religion centered on two kinds of developments: (1) a gathering of congenial groups around the original users of the Bhagavadgītā and (2) special responses to pressures and needs that arose later. During a history of 2,000 years, the Vaishṇava tradition grew into a great family of religions bound together by common acceptance of the Bhagavadgītā and several other scriptures and by allegiance to Vishṇu.

The Identification of Kṛishṇa with Vishṇu

The author of the Bhagavadgītā, in a few subtle statements, indicated that to him Kṛishṇa in his heavenly form was the Vedic deity Vishṇu (11.24, 11.30, 11.46). At stake in this and other efforts to establish a tie between Kṛishṇa and the Vedic god was the orthodoxy of Kṛishṇa's sect in the eyes of other Hindus. The deciders of such claims were neither the Sātvatas nor the general population but learned brāhmans, for the brāhmans, by arriving at a consensus, could authenticate a religion. If Kṛishṇa (even under another name) or some other deity was understood to have been mentioned in the Vedas, then worship of that deity could be deemed a form of Vedic religion and hence orthodox. Brāhmans could then serve the sect as priests, and the religion and its texts could be considered part of the revealed Vedas.

After five centuries of negotiation with brāhmans, the worshipers of Kṛishṇa won full recognition of their tie with Vishṇu and thus won the right to be called Vaishṇavas ("Vishṇuites"). In that final settlement, not only the brāhmans made concessions. The Vaishṇavas stopped exalting kshatriyas as religious leaders, and they restrained their earlier tendency to minimize the importance of caste rank. Through such compromises brāhmans and Vaishṇavas together became the mainstays of the caste civilization.

The Avatars

One of the most distinctive and most important of the Vaishṇava ideas is that the deity descends to earth and is born there in many different forms or incarnations (**avatars**). This belief first appears in the

Bhagavadgītā, where Kṛishṇa speaks of his alternation between two realms:

Though I am an eternal unborn Soul,
the Lord of Beings,
relying on my own materiality
I enter into phenomenal being
by my own mysterious power [māyā].
Whenever righteousness declines
and wickedness erupts
I send myself forth, O Bharata [Arjuna].
To protect the good and destroy evildoers
and establish the right, I come into being
age after age.

(Bhagavadgītā 4.6–8)

In the Bhagavadgītā, Kṛishṇa is addressed as an avatar ("descent") of Vishṇu (11.24, 11.30). Most Hindus believe that Vishṇu is the heavenly source of all avatars.

This idea of an avatar is clearly post-Vedic. Even the ideas that were necessary for its creation are post-Vedic—the conception of a supreme deity, of repeated births, and of a metaphysical link between the divine and human states.

The number of the avatars has never been settled. Most Hindus today recognize ten, named in this order: Matsya, the fish; Kurma, the tortoise; Varāha, the boar; Narasiṃha, the man-lion; Vāmana, the dwarf; Paraśurāma, an ax-wielding man; Kṛishṇa, whom we have already met; Rāma, a folk hero; Gautama Buddha, the founder of Buddhism (a desire to include Buddhists in the Vaishṇava faith is apparent here); and Kalki, the avatar yet to come. The myth of Kalki is particularly interesting. Pictured as a swordsman on a white horse (or a horse-headed figure), Kalki is to appear at the end of the present evil age to unseat from their thrones the wicked barbarian rulers of the earth and to restore the righteous Brahmanic order. This hope in Kalki expresses Hindu India's revulsion in the first three centuries C.E. to the long and often hostile rule of foreign dynasties and faith in a deity concerned with the world.

Although the ten figures are recognized as divine by all traditional Hindus, only the Vaishṇavas feel obliged to worship any of them, and among Vaishṇavas it is customary to select one favorite avatar for personal or family worship. Currently, the worship of only Rāma and Kṛishṇa is widespread; they are the most popular of the Hindu divinities. The Bengal Vaishṇavas and some others deny that Kṛishṇa is an avatar of Vishṇu but, pointing to the Bhagavadgītā, believe that Kṛishṇa Vāsudeva himself is the supreme deity and the source of all avatars.

Defenders of Vaishṇava Belief

The sect that produced the Bhagavadgītā continued to grow for 1,000 years. Its identification of Kṛishṇa with the Vedic deity Vishṇu—rapidly ac-

Kalki, the tenth avatar, is envisioned as a swordsman on a white horse. Kalki is to appear at the end of the present evil age to unseat the wicked barbarian rulers.

cepted—placed Vaishṇava religion within the pale of Vedic faith in the eyes of most Indians. The incorporation of the upanishadic notion of Brahman into the Bhagavadgītā created another tie with Vedic literature.

Yet even though the Bhagavadgītā made Brahman out to be a secondary aspect of a supreme being who is personal, the great monistic teacher Śaṅkara, writing around 800, thought otherwise. He maintained that the ultimate was the impersonal Brahman and that plural things and persons—even the divine person—are miragelike appearances imposed falsely on Brahman. To Śaṅkara, worship of a personal God was useful only to persons of weak intelligence and should not be persisted in, for it focused on an illusion. The respectability of the Vaishṇava worship of a personal God was again in danger.

Stung by this belittling of their faith in a personal God, leaders of Vaishṇava movements for centuries wrote responses in the form of new commentaries on the Vedāntasūtra. These became fundamental documents in the theologies of great sects. We shall explore the first and most famous of these commentaries, written about 1100 by Rāmānuja for the use of his Śrīvaishṇava community of South India.

Rāmānuja's examination of Śaṅkara's monist argument might run as follows: Where does this māyā you speak of—this creator of all plurality and persons—exist? Does it exist in Brahman? That is impossible: Brahman is homogeneous and can have within it no separate thing. Brahman is perfection and can have within it no evil thing. Brahman is knowledge and could accommodate ignorance within itself only by destroying itself. Brahman is the real and contains nothing that is not real; if māyā exists in Brahman, it is real, and its alleged products—personal beings, the personal God, and the plural world—are also real, as we Vaishṇavas hold. Is māyā then located outside Brahman? Outside of Brahman, the sole reality, there is only nothing. If māyā is nothing, it has produced nothing—not even the illusion that you hold our world to be.

By these and many other arguments, Rāmānuja exposed weaknesses in the logic of Śaṅkara's teaching and defended the Vaishṇava belief in the reality of persons, both human and divine. Rāmānuja declared the divine, all-inclusive reality that the upanishads call Brahman to be no neuter reality but rather the personal Lord. Brahman was simply one of the many names of Kṛishṇa Vāsudeva, the basis of all being.

Rāmānuja's understanding of the nature of mystical experience and its place in the religious life is a representative Vaishṇava view. Vaishṇavas aspire to *darśana,* a physical or spiritual "seeing" of the beautiful form of the Lord. In its lower grades, darśana can be merely a reverential viewing of an image in a shrine. At a higher stage of contemplation, darśana can become a powerful inner meditative vision of a deity. Rāmānuja's comment on this higher darśana is that it is not a direct perception of the deity but a subjective vision shaped out of recollections of one's previous experiences. It is not a direct means to liberation; rather, its importance is that it is a powerful generator of devotion (bhakti), which is the last human step toward liberation. Not all Vaishṇavas state as clearly as Rāmānuja did that such visions of deity are subjective, but all followers of the Way of Devotion agree that final liberation does not arise from the power of such visions but from the power of God, who responds to the devotion that such visions can generate.

The Cult of Gopāla

Our account of Vaishṇava history has so far followed a tradition that flowed for centuries from the Bhagavadgītā and promoted its values. We confront the real complexity of the Vaishṇava movement, however, when we encounter a powerful new development in Kṛishṇaism: the worship of Kṛishṇa as **Gopāla**, the cowherd boy.

The *Harivaṃśa Purāṇa,* written around 300 C.E. began the new tradition. The author says in his introduction that he is filling in the omissions of the Mahābhārata, which had failed to tell the whole story of Kṛishṇa. The author then proceeds to relate dozens of new stories about the early exploits and antics of Kṛishṇa, from his birth to his unseating of his wicked uncle Kaṃsa from the throne of Mathurā. All are retold more fully in the *Vishṇu Purāṇa* and again in the *Bhāgavata Purāṇa* (eighth or ninth century). Distinctively lighthearted, these tales recount the child Kṛishṇa's impudence in stealing butter from his mother's pantry and evading punishment through alibis and of his wheedling tasty curds from the cowherd women. In the accounts of Kṛishṇa's adolescence, his naughtiness takes a flirtatious turn. He teases the *gopīs* (cowherd girls) shamelessly and does audacious things to excite their romantic feelings (see the accompanying box, "Krishna and the Gopīs").

COMPARISON

Kṛishṇa and the Gopīs

The story of Kṛishṇa's dance with the gopīs (girls of the cowherd caste) is the most sacred of the Gopāla cult's myths and the source of much of its symbolic language. The favorite version, found in *Bhāgavata Purāṇa* 10.29–33, is retold in popular poetic recitations, songs, and operatic performances.

On a certain full-moon night in autumn, Kṛishṇa stood at the edge of a forest near the settlements of the cowherds. With a mischievous smile he put his flute to his lips. The flute's enchanting notes carried afar until they reached the houses of the cowherds, where the dutiful wives of the herdsmen were preparing food and faithfully attending to the needs of their families. But when they heard the bewitching notes, they were helpless. They dropped their wifely tasks and hurried into the dusk. At the forest's edge they came upon Kṛishṇa. He feigned astonishment and addressed the gopīs thus:

KṚISHṆA: O ladies, you surprise me. What service can I do you?
GOPĪS: You have called us, and we have come.
KṚISHṆA: I was playing the flute merely for my own pleasure. Why have you come here?
GOPĪS: Why do you ask why we have come? You have called us. It is to see *you* that we have come!
KṚISHṆA: Now you have seen me. It is a dark night, this is a dangerous forest, and it is not a time for ladies to be roaming. Go home now to your husbands.

The gopīs protest that Kṛishṇa is a rogue for enticing them and then rebuffing them. They hang their heads, falter in their speech, and finally are able to stammer out the real justification for their presence in the forest: "You are our real husband, our only husband, the only husband of the whole human race, and it is only you that we wish to serve!"

Kṛishṇa is pleased by this declaration and agrees to sport with the gopīs. Rādhā, their leader, joins him in organizing them for dancing. They form a revolving circle. Pleasure and excitement grow as the dance whirls on. The gopīs begin to be proud that they are in the company of the Lord of the Universe. Not content to think of themselves as the luckiest women in the world, they begin to think of themselves as the best and most beautiful women in the world. They demand services of Kṛishṇa, saying, "Fasten my earring!," "Comb my hair!," "Carry me!" Suddenly leaving their midst, Kṛishṇa disappears into the forest. Forlorn and humbled, the

For many centuries after this first blossoming, it was this child Krishna and not the Kṛishṇa of the Bhagavadgītā who captured the attention and creative talents of the Vaishṇavas. No Vaishṇava flatly rejected the Bhagavadgītā, of course, but it was now the naughty little prankster, not the lecturer about duty, whom Vaishṇavas worshiped with delight. Scholars have been puzzled by this radical change in the moral content of Kṛishṇa worship. Why did the civic-minded Vaishṇava community turn from the morally inspiring divine teacher of the Bhagavadgītā toward worship of an uninhibited young prankster Kṛishṇa?

We must consider how, in 400 years, the distresses of the average Hindu of Vaishṇava faith had changed. The second century B.C.E., which gave rise to the Bhagavadgītā, was a time when many Hindu youths

gopīs search for him in the gloom, calling out his name as they wander through the dark glades and asking the trees and vines for hints of where he may have gone. Unable to find him, they gather in a clearing in the forest and begin to console themselves by telling each other about Kṛishṇa's deeds. Peering through the trees, Kṛishṇa observes the gopīs' new humility and devotion; he relents and returns to their circle. Then he begins the magnificent Mahārāsa, the rāsā dance in its most splendid form. Moving into the circle of the dance, Kṛishṇa multiplies his own form until there is a Kṛishṇa at every gopī's side. As the partners whirl on, romantic feeling rises to a crescendo with the music. Every gopī's longing for Kṛishṇa is satisfied by his special presence beside her.

This tale of Kṛishṇa's meeting with the cowherd women uses the language of romantic love, but it refers to nonsexual aspects of the religious life.

(Photo: Cleveland Museum of Art, Mr. and Mrs. William H. Marlatt Fund, 60.45.)

were alienated from their world and fleeing their caste duties. Politically, Greek and Buddhist rulers of India were indifferent to brāhman social ideas and were threats to brāhman social leadership. Responding to this situation, the Bhagavadgītā had rallied Hindus behind the brāhmans' leadership and called for acceptance of the caste patterns. The Vaishṇavas helped reverse the retreat from the Brahmanic social order.

The whole situation changed following the second century C.E.: the last foreign dynasty crumbled, and the Gupta emperors — who were Hindus — came to power. Henceforth caste rules regarding occupations were enforced by the state, and brāhmans became the judges of law and social mores. At this point the Bhagavadgītā's social hopes had become the rule of the land. Its moral ideals, far from repudiated, were in fact realized.

India now enjoyed the rule of religion in both professional and family life, as well as in relations between the sexes.

But what Hindus now lacked was personal freedom. Caught in the grip of Brahmanic rectitude, Vaisṇavas did not respond with the old enthusiasm for the Bhagavadgītā's divine moralist. Their hearts were uplifted, rather, by the new lore of a roguish young god who used his divine prerogative to live in unbounded freedom. In new myths about this libertine god, they created a refreshing and wishful picture of their own ultimate liberation, and in the meantime they could enjoy a certain freedom of mental fantasies. The transformation of Kṛishṇa reminds us of the transformation of the battle god of the Aryas of ancient Iran, who in India became Indra, the god of rain. Gods often change as the needs of a people change: they change, or they cease to be worshiped.

Especially during the Muslim domination in India (c. 1200–1700), large sects of worshipers of the child Kṛishṇa were founded. They continue to have a great following today. The adherents of one sect are well known in the West for chanting the name of Kṛishṇa in public places and are therefore often called the Hare Kṛishṇa people.

The religious practices of the Gopāla faith center on contemplation of Kṛishṇa's *līlās,* or frolics. Sometimes in Sanskrit but more often in vernacular versions, the narratives of the tenth book of the *Bhāgavata Purāṇa* are read, sung, or performed in operetta style with dance preludes in an unusual kind of miracle play called the *Rāslīlā.* To rehearse Kṛishṇa's līlās mentally and to envision them before the inner eye are the Gopāla cult's equivalent of yoga. Kṛishṇa devotees seek to obtain visions of their God in the course of private meditations or at climactic moments of these emotional religious assemblies. Sometimes religious ecstasies overwhelm some spectators; these are cherished as tokens of divine favor. Mathurā and Vrindāban, cities sacred to Kṛishṇa, have become great centers of pilgrimage and retirement for those who wish to pursue the spiritual life in these ways.

THE WORSHIP OF RĀMA

The story of Rāma occurs for the first time in a Sanskrit epic poem called the *Rāmāyaṇa,* written by Vālmiki around the fourth century B.C.E. It may be based on memories of an actual prince Rāma of the North Indian

During the Muslim domination of India, large sects were founded that worship the child Kṛishṇa. Hare Kṛishṇa people are well known in the West for chanting the name of Kṛishṇa in public places. (UPI/Bettmann)

kingdom of Ayodhyā. In the spirit of heroic legend rather than myth, Vālmiki tells of Rāma's great southern expedition to defeat a demon, Rāvaṇa, who had abducted his wife, Sītā. After many heroic trials, Rāma returns to his kingdom of Ayodhyā in the north and rules with model righteousness in a golden age of prosperity and justice.

The characters in the epic include numerous members of an illustrious royal family who almost without exception exemplify the Hindu ideals of good behavior. This is especially true of Rāma's wife, Sītā, whose virtue and unhesitating willingness to serve her husband have served as a model for millions of Hindu women. Functionally, the *Rāmāyaṇa* serves as a supplement to *The Laws of Manu,* reinforcing the codal prescriptions with word pictures of ideal lives.

The first and last books of the epic, added about the time of Christ, show the beginnings of a worship of Rāma as a god, deemed the eighth avatar of Vishṇu. In North India in particular, Rāma worship has become a major form of religion through the impact of an extremely popular version of the *Rāmāyaṇa* called the *Rāmcaritmānas* by Tulsī Das (c. 1575). It is the most widely read of all Hindi books. Yet even the illiterate learn Rāma's story at a great autumn festival called the Rāmlīlā, in which the entire *Rāmcaritmānas* is recited and enacted annually. The great popularity of this *Rāmāyaṇa* has broken the hold of Śāktism in North India and made this heartland of India predominantly Vaishṇava.

The relation between the cults of Rāma and Kṛishṇa is one of mutual support. In heavily Vaishṇava communities today, the people participate in the festivals of both deities, and the worship of Rāma and Kṛishṇa has become loosely joined in a composite religion. With theological consistency, Vaishṇavas can include both Kṛishṇa and Rāma in their devotions, explaining that as different avatars of one and the same deity, they are identifiable with each other and are not different objects of worship. It is the difference between these two deities, however, that makes it easy to combine their worship. As moral beings seeking self-control and social order, Hindus worship Rāma. As intellectual beings seeking reasoned understanding, they turn to the thoughtful Bhagavadgītā and to the systematic theologies of the Kṛishṇa cult. As emotional beings oppressed by the heavy restraints of Hindu social life, they worship Gopāla Kṛishṇa, the carefree divine prankster.

ACTION, DEVOTION, KNOWLEDGE: A RETROSPECT ON THE THREE WAYS

In Chapters 4 through 6 we have seen among followers of Hinduism's three ways some dramatic similarities and differences. Longing for liberation from the world has remained an acute distress among followers of the Way of Knowledge and a persistent concern of followers of the Way of Devotion as well. Only those who live their lives in the routines of the Way of Action say little or nothing about liberation. Even so, one cannot say that pangs of such longing are entirely absent in them. It is a matter of degree, and it is not wrong to say that transcendence of the world is the goal of traditional Hinduism.

Those who do strive for liberation differ on the means that will bring about that happy event. The knowledge seekers rely on the power of rare insights generated in the course of difficult introspective meditations. Devotees, by contrast, seek, through worship, to establish intimacy with a God of cosmic power who can release them from the bondage of retribution for past acts.

Whether one elects to seek liberation through knowledge or through devotion entails differences in the form and content of one's practical religious life. The Way of Knowledge requires deep and long-continued meditations, usually in seclusion. Knowledge seekers have thus characteristically been sannyāsīs, renouncers of the world. Devotees also sometimes renounce the world if their feeling of alienation is intense, but isolation in the forest is not really helpful to the development of emotion in worship. Devotees more typically seek out what they call *satsang,* the company of the good; they are most often found not in forest solitude but in these emotional gatherings for worship in story and song.

Also in their conceptions of the ultimate life of the liberated there is a difference between devotees and followers of the Way of Knowledge. For the latter, final beatitude is a merging in Brahman, where no second being is known. Devotees also seek transmutation to a transcendent realm and status, but for them the ultimate blessedness is a life of fellowship in which the love between the deity and the worshipers can be sustained. Some speak only generally of attaining God's realm or presence. Others elaborate on that simple faith, often describing in vivid details the eternal life of the liberated in the special heaven of their deity, be it Śiva, Śākti, or Kṛishṇa Gopāla.

However traditional Hindus conceived of their goal—as a personal or an impersonal state—none imagined that this workaday world itself could ever be the site of life's final blessedness. Even for the world-concerned author of the Bhagavadgītā, the hope of humanity lay elsewhere, in the transcendent:

Transient and troubled is this world;
On reaching it, venerate Me.

(Bhagavadgītā 9.33)

NOTES

1 Robert Charles Caldwell, trans., "Tamil Popular Poetry," *Indian Antiquary,* April 5, 1872, p. 100.

2 Quoted in Dinesh Chandra Sen, *History of Bengali Language and Literature* (Calcutta: University of Calcutta, 1911), pp. 714 ff.

Religions of India

CHAPTER 7

Modern Hinduism

We have completed a study of a remarkable cultural tradition that shaped the lives of millions of human beings for several thousand years. Hinduism's cosmologies are among humanity's most sophisticated intellectual constructions; ingeniously integrated with a highly organized society, they laid the basis for a tranquil civilization of long endurance. If our only aim were to become acquainted with the world's great alternatives to Western religion and culture, our purpose would be accomplished at this point.

But we hope also that our study will prepare us to meet Hindus as they are today; for that we need to supplement our study. India during the past 800 years has undergone an almost unprecedented breaching of its natural defenses and has suffered powerful incursions of foreign peoples. These events have brought it new problems and great changes.

The first of these great invasions was that of the Muslims, who conquered most of India from the northwest and ruled for five centuries. They zealously promoted their faith, and by 1700 several parts of India had become predominantly Muslim. Yet the subcontinent as a whole remained loyal to Hinduism.

After the death in 1707 of Aurangzeb, the last great Mughul emperor, the Mughul Empire declined rapidly. For the next 50 years, India lay in a state of anarchy. European merchants, protected by a few soldiers, had long operated trading posts along the Indian coastline. Now, raising mercenary armies, the Europeans began to move into the political vacuum left by the Mughul Empire's disintegration. By 1757 the British East India Company had gained control of India's most prosperous provinces, and by 1818 the British had eliminated all serious rivals for the control of the entire land.

THE BRITISH PRESENCE

Two centuries of British rule (1757–1947) were much more disturbing to the old Hindu civilization than the previous 500 years of aggressive Muslim control. There were two reasons for this. First, the British, unlike the Muslims, brought to India powerful new economic institutions. Their ships and trains drew India into a worldwide commercial network, and soon Calcutta, Bombay, Madras, and inland cities as well became huge trading centers.

This development brought with it a great increase in the proportion of the population engaged in trade and making a living outside the tightly knit economy of the villages. Large numbers of people in the new cities became immune to the traditional penalty for nonconformity, termination of livelihood. Family and caste assemblies could still bring heavy pressure on their individual members, but once the industrial revolution reached India and factories became a major employer in the towns, millions of Hindus became freer to exercise personal choice in employment—and in religious matters as well.

The second reason for the strong impact of British culture was the British government's promotion of education. Although by today's standards the schools of British India were not extensive, they far exceeded the public education available under earlier Hindu and Muslim rulers. As early as 1817, the Hindu College was established in Calcutta to instruct young Indian men in the English language and literature. The local response was positive, and Christian missionaries soon opened similar schools and colleges.

In 1835 a momentous decision was made to conduct government-supported education mainly in English and to make the Western arts and sciences a main part of the curriculum. In the same period European printing presses made the literature of Europe easily available to the increasing numbers of Indians who could read English.

To appreciate the collision of ideas that then occurred, we need to examine the Hinduism prevailing around 1800 and note the shocking contrasts it had to confront. Many of the popular Hindu practices sought protection against the dangers of the natural world. The central Hindu ideas had the function of supporting the caste system. Belief in karma and rebirth rationalized the assignment of hereditary work and unequal distribution of opportunities and honors and justified the subjection of women and the harsh treatment of widows. The deprivations that old Hinduism imposed on many were made tolerable by reflections on the evil of material desires, by thought about loftier satisfactions in transcendent realms, and by denying the significance—or even the reality—of the whole physical world. Hinduism provided no rational justification for attempting to change the world. The way to happiness did not lie in transforming the world but in liberating oneself from it. It was the soul, not the world, that was capable of salvation.

The idea of one's *nation* traditionally had little importance—in fact, the major Indian languages had no precise word for that idea. In the traditional Hindu conception of identity, the notion of one's nation scarcely figured. One understood oneself to be submerged in the collectivity of family, clan, and caste; nationality was not a central aspect. With the coming of the British there arrived in India a conception of one's nation as a prime aspect of personal identity, as an entity to which one owed heavy moral responsibility, and as an essential unit to be involved in struggles for a better life.

The British brought with them also an optimism, unusual even in the West, about the possibility of social improvement—of freedom from disease through medical science, of freedom from poverty through industrialization, and of freedom from injustice through reform.

The Europeans of that time not only proclaimed faith in the world's regeneration but also took actions toward that end, with impressive results. The power of Western learning was as obvious to Hindu observers as the power of the new steamboats that could transport huge cargoes upstream on Indian rivers. Vaccination was clearly more effective than offerings to the smallpox goddess. Young Hindus did not take long to decide that they wanted to absorb Western knowledge and to participate in its power.

This clear decision among the early generations of Western-educated Indians soon began to give rise to new movements within Hinduism. Between 1800 and 1947 there were few Hindu champions of innovation who were not also reformers of religion. The first Hindu movement that reflected the Western impact was the **Brāhmo Samāj** (Society of Believers in Brahman), founded in 1828 by a Bengali brāhman named Rām Mohan Roy (1772–1833).

THE BRĀHMO SAMĀJ

Rām Mohan Roy's family had for generations served Muslim rulers, so they of course sent their son to Muslim schools, where he learned Persian and Arabic and absorbed Muslim attitudes, including hostility toward the British. In 1803, however, their son took employment with the British East India Company, and under the guidance of a friendly British official, he studied English and Western literature and thought. Reversing his prior opinion of Western culture, Roy became an advocate of Western education and eventually founded many schools that taught the Western arts and sciences.

In 1814 he retired from his post to focus more intensively on religion and morality. He studied the Bible and, though he did not accept Christian theology, developed an admiration for the example and teachings of Jesus. The Brāhmo Samāj, which he founded in 1828, used in its worship the upanishads—which he regarded as Vedic scriptures, of course—and he and

Rām Mohan Roy founded the Brāhmo Samāj (Society of Believers in Brahman) in 1928. This was the first Hindu movement to reflect the impact of Western influence on India. This detail is from a painting by Rolinda Sharples (City Art Gallery, Bristol, England)

his circle of educated people were convinced that the Vedas were not polytheistic but, like the Bible, monotheistic. Their new religious association, like a church, met weekly for congregational worship—a novel pattern in Hindu religious life. The new association denounced idols and idolatry, gave up all claims to privilege on the basis of high caste rank, and undertook to provide education for men and also for women.

After the death of Rām Mohan Roy, the members of the society undertook a more thorough study of the entire Veda and concluded that its outlook was in fact polytheistic after all. They thereupon relinquished their use of Vedic scripture—and their claim to be orthodox Hindus—and resorted to reason and conscience as their final authorities in religion. Their social teachings became more radical: they asked their members to drop their caste identities completely, they developed new nonpolytheistic family rituals, they pressed for laws forbidding the marriage of children, and they supported a British edict forbidding **satī**, the burning of widows. Through the nineteenth century the Brāhmo Samāj kept the Hindu upper classes in an uproar of argument for and against their daring demands. The views of the Brāhmo Samāj on the gods and the scriptures were in the end seldom adopted, but the association won its battle for social reform.

THE ĀRYA SAMĀJ

While the reformist commotion of the Brāhmo Samāj was at its height in Bengal, Svāmī Dayānanda (1824–1883) launched a very different kind of reform movement in northwestern India. (*Svāmī* is a respectful title for a religious teacher.) Even as a child in Gujarat, Dayānanda spurned the devout Śiva worship of his family. Soon he became an ascetic and wandered about in search of a teacher. He found his guru finally in a fiery eccentric teacher named Virajānanda who allowed his disciples to study only the oldest Vedic scriptures and taught them to loathe the Purāṇas and dharmaśāstras and all the gods of popular Hinduism. In 1863 Dayānanda began his own reformist campaigns, lecturing in Sanskrit against idolatry, polytheism, *pūjā,* and pilgrimages and denying the divinity of Rāma and Kṛishṇa. In 1874 Dayānanda wrote *The Light of Truth* in Hindi, and in 1875 he founded the **Ārya Samāj** (Aryan Society), a religious society that spread rapidly throughout northern India proclaiming the doctrines of his book. Let us summarize the main teachings of the society:

The Vedas alone are the Word of God and the only basis of Hinduism. By Vedas Dayānanda meant only the saṃhitās, the four early books of hymns. Only when they are in complete agreement with the four Vedas do the brāhmaṇas and the upanishads have any force. Later scriptures—even the Bhagavadgītā—have no place at all in Hinduism. The Vedas teach the worship of one personal God only. They do not mention or justify the *jātis* or professional castes, and even brāhmans have no right to any inherited privilege. The varṇas are mentioned in the Vedas as social classes, but admission to them is by merit, not heredity.

The Vedas are the source of all truth, scientific as well as religious. Employing unusual translation methods, Dayānanda maintained that the sages who wrote the Vedas already knew the steam engine, telegraph, and other inventions. The Vedic sciences were later forgotten, but Indians who study them now are not taking up Western ideas but merely recovering lost Vedic knowledge.

The ancient Vedas record the undefiled original religion of humanity. This religion, diffused throughout the world, was distorted as it spread. But the Vedas remain the ultimate source of all the fragmentary and corrupted truths that non-Hindu faiths teach. Adherents of those faiths should return now to the uncontaminated source of all truth, the Vedic religion of the Ārya Samāj.

Dayānanda vilified Kṛishṇaism, Islam, and Christianity. He was particularly incensed at efforts to spread these two latter faiths and indeed at all foreign influences in India. The society has persistently opposed child marriage, polygamy, and the suppression of women and has justified widow remarriage and intercaste eating and marrying.

The Brāhmo Samāj and the Ārya Samāj are small organizations now—the former with a few thousand members, the latter with half a million. But they are small because they were so successful. Their social demands were so widely accepted that liberal Hindus are no longer driven from their families and castes and compelled to seek refuge in radical brotherhoods like these. Thanks to a century of reformist agitation (and industrialization), the old rules regarding occupation and social mingling are relatively ineffective in the cities and resistible in the countryside. Caste continues to be important in marriage matches, however, and often provides the competing units in political struggles.

The Ārya Samāj is now a nonpolitical religious association, but it has revived in Hinduism a long-lost understanding that political concerns are religious concerns, and it has produced important political leaders. It also began an important modern Hindu tendency to glorify the Hindu past and to seek ancient models for political action. As India faced the prospect and then the actuality of self-government, reformed Hinduism led in the effort to bring the resources of religion to bear on the truly critical problem of organizing a harmonious Indian nation and led in the tendency to abandon to science Hindu religion's former obsession with matters of health and economic well-being.

HINDU RELIGIOUS NATIONALISM

Dayānanda's resentment of Western influence was a light squall preceding a hurricane. In the late nineteenth century the sons of upper-class Indian families began to graduate from Indian universities with a new ambivalence toward Western culture. Western studies, like flowers transplanted from another climate, did not root easily in Indian soil. Even students who acquired a deep knowledge of the West were often offended by the aloofness of Europeans, who did not grant them the dignity of full social acceptance.

About this time, Western orientalists' search for India's forgotten past was uncovering records of a happier and greater India of pre-Islamic times, when enlightened Hindu rulers had patronized brilliant systems of thought and great works of literature and art. Hindu religious leaders now called on the young men of India to identify themselves with that brighter ancient heritage. Beginning about 1890, a passionate nationalism with religious overtones began to grow in the minds of many literate young Hindus. They viewed the West as a crass and worldly civilization, advanced only in the natural sciences, and saw the East as a spiritual culture destined to teach the world the art of lofty living. All the emotional devices of the Way of Devotion were brought into the service of a new object of devotion, the Indian nation. Seeing foreign rule as a moral outrage, the liberation of India became the goal of this semireligious nationalism.

India was sometimes conceived of as a divine mother in the form of the goddess Kālī. Beginning in 1905, secret societies dedicated to violent revolutionary action were organized. At altars of Kālī bearing heaps of revolvers, recruits vowed to bring bloody offerings to the Mother. A training manual titled *Bhavānī Mandir* (The Temple of Kālī) assured future assassins that their acts would attract the world to the light of Hinduism. Those less accustomed to making blood offerings cultivated a reverence for a milder figure called Bharat Mātā (Mother India).

The first great leader of Hindu ultranationalism was a brāhman of western India named Bāl Gangādhar Tilak (1856–1920). It was he who first made Hindu festivals occasions for political agitation, and he revived understanding of the Bhagavadgītā as an inspiration to military action (as in "Fight, O son of Bharata!" 2.18). Tilak's militant Hindu spirit all but dominated the Indian independence movement between 1908 and 1917. During those years, more than 100 officials of the British government were killed or wounded by assassins of this outlook. The resort to bloodshed was put down, but the spirit lived on through the next decade in political movements that were more circumspect, notably the ardently Hindu society for the promotion of nationalism called the Hindu Mahāsabhā—formed in the 1920s but still a powerful nationalist organization—and its paramilitary auxiliary, the Rāshṭriya Svayamsevak Saṅgha. These twin organizations have been a hotbed of revisionist thinking about the re-creation of India as an exclusively Hindu nation. They insist that India must be one undivided nation geographically and racially, with one language, one culture, and one religion—Hinduism. Religious minorities are to be treated as foreigners, without civil status or automatic rights. Since the advent of self-government in India in 1947, Hindus of this chauvinistic outlook have formed political parties with similar agendas. Opposing the more religiously neutral parties founded by Mahātma Gāndhi and Jawaharlal Nehru, some of these Hindu nationalism parties have become powerful.

MAHĀTMA GĀNDHI

Fortunately for the outside world, India's independence was not won by such ultranationalists but by forces led by Mohandās Gāndhi (1869–1948), a religious leader of a radically new type. Born in Gujarat into a family of the vaiśya (merchant) class, Gāndhi was first a lawyer and later a social reformer and political leader. Neither a brāhman nor a scholar in Hindu literature nor even a systematic religious thinker, Gāndhi's religious leadership has nevertheless touched to some degree all present-day Hindus, who everywhere speak of him reverentially as Mahātma (the "Great-souled One"). After studying law in England, Gāndhi moved his practice to South Africa, where for many years he led a nonviolent movement to protect the rights of Indians there. Returning to India, he became in 1920 a leader of the Indian National Congress. Thanks to his skillful direction, India at last became a free republic in 1947. The following year, while conducting a prayer meeting in New Delhi, he was assassinated by a fanatical Hindu nationalist of the outlook just described, who resented Gāndhi's kindness toward Muslims.

The scriptures that Gāndhi loved most were the *Rāmcaritmānas* of Tulsī Das, the Sermon on the Mount in the New Testament, and, especially, the Bhagavadgītā. His choice of scriptures reflects the centrality of moral and social concerns in his religious life. Yet Gāndhi was not bound by the authority of any of these scriptures but held rather that one should check their teachings against the inner voice of conscience, for it could reveal the way of right action. Though Gāndhi's assumptions about the nature of God and the universe were generally those of the Vaishṇava monotheists, he was not interested in theoretical discussions and preferred the simple statement "God is truth." By this he meant that God is the basis for order and law and the force that supports moral righteousness in the world. Yet God for him was not an abstract principle but a spirit filled with purpose who hears prayers and supports and guides people who struggle in the cause of right in all areas of life, including politics.

To Gāndhi, all religions originate in the inner voice, which is universal. They differ only externally, in their linguistic and cultural expressions. Yet those different expressions make each religion uniquely effective for its followers: the religion of one's own culture cannot effectively replace the religion of some other culture.

Gāndhi's courageous tactic for social reform was called **satyāgraha** ("holding on to truth"). It was based on his confidence that God, in the form of truth *(satya)* and the inner voice that utters it, is present also in the hearts of wrongdoers. Gāndhi taught that believers in satyāgraha must seek to awaken the inner voice in the oppressors so that they will themselves perceive their wrongdoing and voluntarily stop it. One should not seek personal victories over opponents but the victory of truth, which belongs as much to one's opponent as to oneself. Such victories cannot be attained by violent means. Gāndhi's great campaigns for national independence were often launched under the guidance of his own inner voice; in essence, they were demands that the British rulers consult the voice within themselves with regard to what was right. Gāndhi's faith so impressed the world that in the 1960s, Martin Luther King, Jr., made effective use of satyāgraha techniques to advance the goals of the American civil rights movement.

RECENT RELIGIOUS LEADERS

In the modern period, the religious life of most Hindus has followed traditional patterns under the guidance of old-style leaders. Let us look at several key leaders.

Rāmakṛishṇa Paramahaṃsa

This many-faceted holy man has had great impact on modern Indian cultural history. Little concerned with Western ideas, Rāmakṛishṇa Paramahaṃsa (1836–1886) was a man of visions who experienced many kinds of trances and apparitions. He was born of poor brāhman parents in rural Bengal and lived for most of his adult life in a temple of the goddess Kālī near Calcutta. As a young man, he fell into a despair approaching madness following the death of his father. He appealed to Kālī to give him some token of her regard, and on one dark day he snatched a sword from the temple wall, intending to commit suicide by offering the goddess his life's blood. At that moment, Rāmakṛishṇa reported, the goddess emerged from her image in an ocean of light and enveloped him in wave after wave of her love. This experience ended his fears; he became a composed and effective teacher.[1]

Although Rāmakṛishṇa was a devotee of Kālī, he had visions of many other deities and types. He experienced, for example, mystical trances of the Advaita type, in which personal deities played no role. He also had visions of Christ and of Muḥammad, which led him to believe that he fully understood Christianity and Islam. Thinking them to be mystical religions of Hindu type, he concluded that they were valid faiths; he therefore taught the unconditional equality of all religions, a position from which his followers later withdrew. Rāmakṛishṇa's vivid testimony to direct religious experiences drew back into traditional Hinduism many of his contemporaries who had been drawn to the Westernized cults.

Svāmī Vivekānanda

Foremost among Rāmakṛishṇa's disciples was Vivekānanda (1863–1902), who organized an order of monks, the Rāmakṛishṇa Order, to carry on the master's teaching. Vivekānanda had a university education and shared the patriotic feeling and social concern of India's English-educated elite.

In dedicating itself in India to works of social service, the Rāmakṛishṇa Order has proposed by its example a new activist ideal for the life of the sannyāsī. The monks carry out relief work at times of famine and flood and operate excellent hospitals and clinics. Rather than focusing on Rāmakṛishṇa's worship of the personalistic Kālī, they emphasize his Advaita form of mystical experiences of absolute oneness and teach a modified Advaita Vedānta doctrine: unlike Śaṅkara's, their account of māyā permits an acceptance of the world as real.

For many educated Hindus, their neo-Vedāntic outlook has served as a new rallying point. In this view, other religions may be valid as far as they go, but they are incomplete; in the end they must be completed in the Advaita experience of absolute oneness. This perception that monism is the ultimate religion that completes other faiths has become the basis for a Hindu mission to the world. In 1893 Vivekānanda represented Hinduism at the World Parliament of Religions in Chicago and remained to become the first great Hindu missionary to the West. In the United States at present there are 11 centers of the Rāmakṛishṇa a Mission, where meditation and Advaita Vedānta philosophy are taught.

Maharishi Mahesh Yogi

A recent and very aggressive promoter of the Advaita outlook is Maharishi Mahesh Yogi, who at the time of this writing is still alive. His organization, the Transcendental Meditation Program, has trained thousands of westerners in a simple form of Hindu meditation. Maharishi has removed the aura of exoticism that formerly surrounded yoga. His extraordinary impact on Europe and America is based on the simplicity and effectiveness of his meditation techniques, his organizing ability in establishing meditation centers, and his willingness to allow yoga to be used not only for spiritual rewards but also for the attainment of emotional equilibrium and physical health.

Rabindranāth Tagore

A very different kind of influential Hindu has been Rabindranāth Tagore (1861–1961), who received the Nobel Prize in literature for his *Gitāñjali* ("A Handful of Song-Offerings"), a booklet of devotional poetry in English. A prolific poet in Bengali and in English, Tagore poured forth his personal faith, using many of the images of the Gopāla cult but using language with universal intelligibility and appeal. He was born into a leading family of the Brāhmo Samāj and remained true to the family's belief in a personal

Rabindranāth Tagore, a noted Hindu poet, wrote in both Bengali and English. The poetry makes use of the images of the Gopāla cult but has worldwide appeal. Rejecting the notion of the world as illusion, Tagore celebrated a unifying divine presence in nature and in humanity. (Wide World)

God. In time he moved quietly away from the rationalism of the Brāhmo Samāj, however, toward a mystical substantiation of his faith. Yet his mysticism was not that of yogic introspection. Awareness of the divine presence came to him in open-eyed moments of loving contemplation of the beauty of nature and of living beings:

> *When I go from hence, let this be my parting word, that what I have seen is unsurpassable.*
> *I have tasted of the hidden honey of this lotus that expands on the ocean of light, and thus I am blessed—let this be my parting word.*
>
> *In this playhouse of infinite forms I have had my play, and here have I caught sight of him that is formless.*[2]

A person of cosmopolitan spirit, Tagore had a distaste for religious and cultural jealousies and stood aside from nationalistic forms of Hinduism.

THE MORALE OF CONTEMPORARY HINDUISM

There was a time, a century ago, when the population that was nominally Hindu was filled with restlessness and resentment. It was by no means clear that the coming generations would continue to call themselves Hindu or that Hinduism would be an important shaping factor in their lives. It is clear now that Hinduism has passed through a century of severe testing and survived. The once-restrictive social orthodoxies that generated disaffection have been broken by reformers, and idealists have found ways whereby the force of religion can be directed to problems that have disturbed modern people. No Hindu is now compelled to subscribe to medieval cosmologies, prescientific approaches to nature, or the privileges of an ancient aristocracy.

Hindu despisers of their tradition are now rare. It is true that a vehement hostility toward brāhmans is sweeping the Tamil area in the south, but brāhmanism is not the whole of Hinduism, and the hatred has not spread beyond the Tamil area. Significant numbers of people of low social rank continue to become Muslims or Buddhists—but these are groups who had never, in fact, had membership in the Hindu community. It could also be said, of Hinduism as of other religions, that a great central mass of its people knows little and cares little about the religious tradition, but the rank and file that formerly ran from the indifferent to the disaffected now runs from the indifferent to the ardent. Young persons are willing to identify themselves as Hindu without hesitation.[3] With their participation, the ritual life of families and villages goes on, with some simplification. Attendance at temples is high, and new temples and monasteries are being built at an unprecedented rate. Hordes of astounding size throng the pilgrimage trails and attend religious fairs. With a new freedom, charismatic religious leaders rise up and become gurus, instructing thousands not merely in meditation but also in the moral life, thus helping to fill the vacuum left by the decreasing relevance of the dharmaśāstras. The India of the foreseeable future will be predominantly a Hindu India.

Just what the word *Hindu* will come to mean, however, is not clear. It is idle to suppose that Hinduism will not be a national, and even a nationalistic, religion because the problem of uniting and preserving the nation is an acute one, and religions deal with acute problems. But it is also hard to believe that India, which in religion has entered into dialogue with the world, will spurn the world concern of such great figures as Rāmakṛishṇa, Maharishi, Tagore, and Mahātma Gāndhī. The moderation of these leaders of international mind will surely moderate the spirit of a national Hinduism. All depends on choices yet to be made by millions of people, who will make Hinduism what they wish it to be.

NOTES

1 *Life of Śrī Rāmakṛishṇa* (Calcutta: Advaita Ashram, 1964), pp. 69–72.

2 Rabindranāth Tagore, *Gitāñjali* (New York: Macmillan Publishing, 1971), pp. 108–109, verse 96.

3 Philip H. Ashby, *Modern Trends in Hinduism* (New York: Columbia University Press, 1974), ch. 3.

Religions of India

CHAPTER 8

Jainism and Sikhism

Jainism

THE FOLLOWERS OF THE VICTOR

Jainism is a religion of asceticism par excellence. It exemplifies, in the extreme, what in India is called *karmamārga,* the Way of Works. In this religion of approximately 2 million principally Indian adherents, a model of liberation through rigorous personal discipline and denial of the body is taken to the extreme and made a key part of the faith. Jain asceticism is closely linked to a second principle, the doctrine of **ahimsā**: noninjury of any living being.

Scholars believe that the religion appeared more or less in its present form in northeastern India about 2,500 years ago in reaction to changing conditions of Indian life and religious systems. It was a time of ferment, the era of the Buddha, the upanishads, and new religions emerging to satisfy new religious needs. In the panorama of Hindu thought, Jainism was constituted from non-Brahmanic, lay, and unorthodox themes. The hereditary priesthood, along with its sacrifices and other rituals, was rejected. Moreover, it included very early religious traditions, probably dating back to pre-Aryan, Dravidian times.

As compared with the vast diversity of Hindu mythology and reflection, Jainism has been more carefully disciplined and systematic. An ethical religion, it has been properly described as a philosophy but not a theology—there is no God. Instead experience is controlled by an all-inclusive and morally determined chain of cause and effect.

The Jains unify what we in the West usually split into two: matter and emotion. For them, the physical world is a nonliving realm consisting of matter, space, time, and the agents of motion and rest. The key, though subtlest, form of this is **karmic matter**, which is a side effect of each person's desires, passions, and attachments. Greed, for example, is considered the result of binding attachment. Thus if one is moved by a greedy desire, one takes on the subtle material form of such negativity and carries it like baggage. This shapes one's future in this life and succeeding lives, for, like Hindus and Buddhists, Jains believe in transmigration of the soul (rebirth after this life into another earthly life). The goal of the religion is to be liberated from all passions and desires and hence to be freed from the subtle bonds of matter. When truly freed, one gains a permanent state of moksha ("release" or "enlightenment").

According to Jains, the transformative path of self-mortification was originally laid out by the "ford finders," **Tīrthaṃkaras**, who crossed over—transcended—the river of life and found release from matter's clutches. According to Jain theory, there were 24 Tīrthaṃkaras in all, beginning with Ṛisabha, who lived for 8.4 million years. The nineteenth

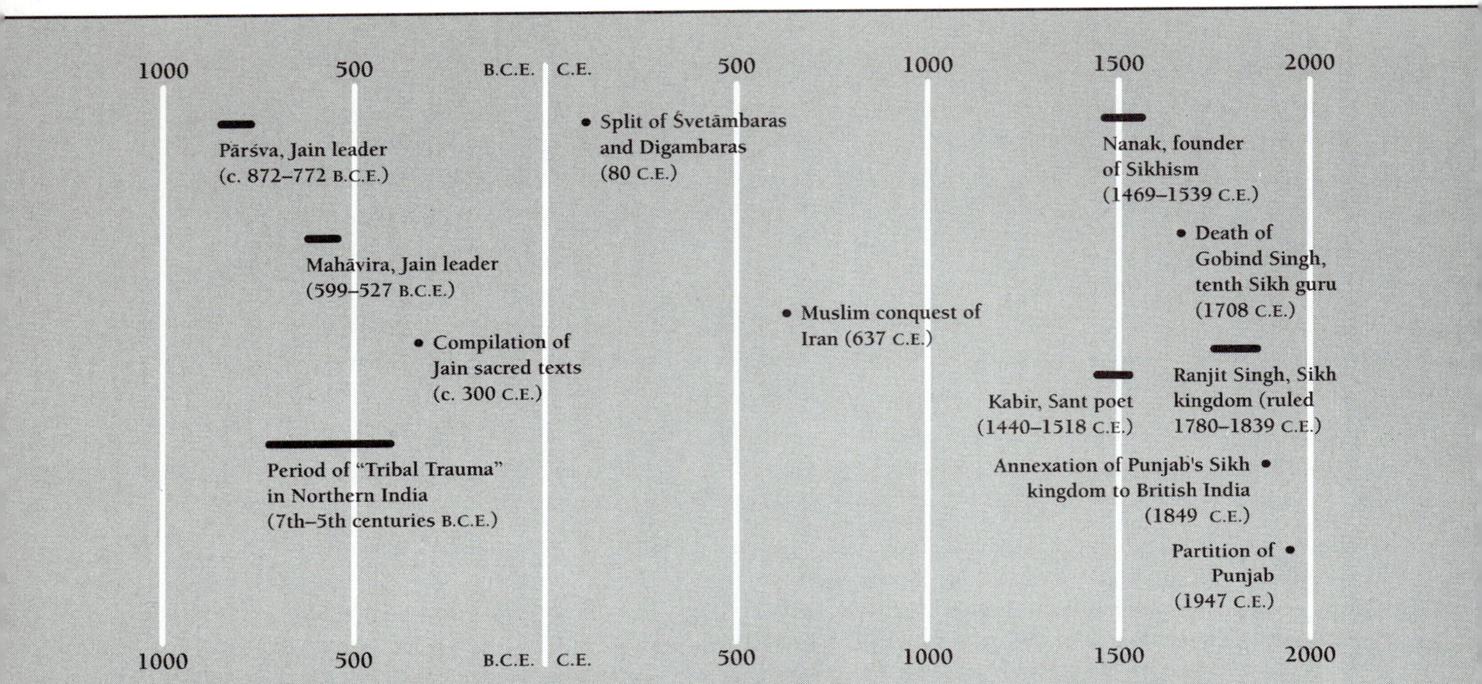

JAINISM AND SIKHISM TIME LINE

Tīrthaṃkara, Mallinātha, is said to have been a woman. Modern scholars believe that the first 22 Tīrthaṃkaras are mythic figures, but they do accept Pārśva (born about 872 B.C.E.) and Mahāvira as historical.

But neither evoking the ancestral ford finders nor following their path can rid a person of passions. Since the gods are themselves regarded as finite beings subject to rebirth, they cannot help others on the solitary crossing toward freedom. One must do it oneself: "Man, thou art thine own friend. Why wishest thou for a friend beyond thyself?"

Rather than relying on anyone else, the Jains practice austerity: meditation, long periods of fasting, control of the emotions, and other ascetic techniques. Such efforts help to purify the self, thereby aiding release from one's passions, matter, and one's karmic accumulations.

Like Buddhism, Jainism first grew up as a monastic and an ascetic religion and only later developed a lay following. Connected to their desire to accumulate no bad karma is the Jains' emphasis on ahimsā, "non-injury." Jains are famous for their attempts to avoid injuring any living creature, since they believe that every living thing has a soul. A Jain monk covers his face with a gauze mask or handkerchief to guard against breathing in (and thus killing) insects. He carries a broom to sweep the path ahead of him to avoid stepping on any living beings. At night Jains refrain from drinking water for fear of unintentionally swallowing a gnat. Jains are strict vegetarians; they refuse not only to eat meat but also to use leather. They were also the first advocates of "animal rights," so popular in the West in recent years.

MAKERS OF THE RIVER CROSSING

Scholars believe that Jainism was given its present form by Nataputta Vardhamana, known as **Mahāvira** ("Great Hero") and as **Jina** ("Victor"). Tradition establishes his life from 599 to 527 B.C.E., although some modern historians place him about 60 years later. Either way, he was roughly a contemporary of the Buddha. The era in which these great religious leaders lived was characterized by rapidly changing conditions of Indian and religious systems, the growth of cities and their merchant class, and a decline in Vedic ritualism.

Mahāvira was preceded as a ford finder by **Pārśva**, often referred to as Pārśvanātha (the Lord Pārśva), who was born in about 872 B.C.E. in what is now the city of Banāras. Tradition has it that Pārśva was married to the daughter of a king but was not interested in the luxuries of the court. At the age of 30 he renounced worldly pleasures and began a life of austerity. Pārśva wandered throughout India, gathering disciples and teaching them to observe the four vows: not to take life, not to lie, not to steal, and not to own property. At last he finally purified himself of his karma and achieved liberation (moksha) on Mount Sammeda in Bengal, which is revered by Jains today as the Hill of Pārśvanātha.

It was some three centuries after Pārśva that Mahāvira gave Jainism its present shape. As noted, he was born in the sixth century B.C.E. near Vaisali (in present-day Bihar), in northeastern India, into a Jain family of the warrior caste. After tearing out his hair by the roots, Mahāvira donned a monk's robe. Stripping off his robe 13 months later, he began to go about naked. Such nudity, long regarded as an ideal, was interpreted as a sign of renunciation of all worldly possessions. (Such public nudity is no longer practiced.)

For the next 12 years Mahāvira led an austere and disciplined life of meditation and asceticism. His reward was moksha, when he finally became a victor over his body and his passions (the name *Jain* means "follower of the victor"). After this enlightenment, Mahāvira began to preach and teach, converting many to the Jain way of life.

After Mahāvira's death, the sacred texts of Jainism, said to have been composed by him, were at first preserved in oral form and written down only two centuries later. At about that time, around 300 B.C.E., the Jain monks began to quarrel, ultimately splitting into the **Śvetāmbaras** ("white-clothed") and the **Digambaras** ("sky-clothed"), who took the vow of nudity. About 80 C.E. the split between the two became irreversible; indeed, it persists today. The Digambaras'

Nataputta Vardhamana, known as Mahāvīra ("Great Hero") and as Jina ("Victor"), is credited with giving Jainism its present form. Here he is represented surrounded by the other Tīrthaṅkaras. (Seattle Art Museum. Eugene Fuller Memorial Collection)

center is in Mysore in the Deccan region of southern India. Śvetāmbaras are found mainly in India's western cities. Both sects have their own sacred books and commentaries.

Each Jain monastic community is governed by an *acarya*, or superior, who decides disciplinary and doctrinal matters. The details of the Jain monastic life pattern are carefully defined with rules for truthfulness, study, wandering, and begging as well as confession and penance. The monks do not travel around the countryside during the season of the monsoon rains. At that time, because the wet soil is swarming with small creatures, monks take refuge in a fixed place and, along with members of the laity, receive religious instruction. Their days and nights are divided into periods of requesting alms, eating, studying, meditating, teaching, mortifying the body, and confessing faults. Monastics are easily identified by their shaved heads. Many Jain sects have communities of nuns who follow many of the same practices, despite the Jains' typically ascetic condemnation of women as the greatest temptation and the cause of most sinful acts.

JAIN PHILOSOPHY AND COSMOLOGY

Jain monks in their reflection developed a wide variety of philosophical subtleties. The Hindu idea of māyā, the world as illusion, was rejected. Instead, in their realism, Jains affirm that mind and matter are and will remain eternally separate. The visible universe—made up of souls, matter, space, and the principles of motion and rest, as well as time, which is eternal and formless—is continually in the process of change but indestructible. It operates on its own internal principles. Beyond it, unperceived by the senses, is the indestructible and eternal realm of limitless knowledge and infinite power, the pure state of endless release.

Jain philosophy is described by westerners as a pluralistic substantialism that emphasizes particularity and refuses to give up the continuing reality of change. It is especially interesting because of its both/and rather than either/or orientation. The key principle, *syādvāda,* indicates that all judgments are made from a certain angle and hence are relative. Reflection is led to a yes-and-no position that allows no absolute judgments. Everything has an infinite number of qualities, it is premised. Hence reality must be viewed from many different perspectives. Any attempted definitive statement will inevitably be one-sided, excluding important aspects. At the same time, the Jain emphasis on intuitive religious knowledge has led to definite conviction.

For example, Jains view the universe as eternal and uncreated, rejecting the concept of a supreme being or a creative spirit. Temporal spans are vast. Jains understand the present era as a degenerating and descending one, but they believe that it will be followed by a more ascending, expansive period. They use the figure of a wheel with 12 spokes to symbolize different world ages. The growth of happiness and knowledge during the positive part of the cycle is represented by the first six spokes; as the wheel turns, however, it is followed by retrogression until the cycle begins again. Jains even speculate that 24 new Tīrthaṃkaras will live on earth in the new augmenting period.

The cosmos, immense and enduring through eons, is envisaged as a colossal standing human figure. At the base are the hells, populated by overwhelmingly wicked beings. The middle world in which humans live is represented by a thin disk. It is only at this level that the conquest of karma can be accomplished. Deities (no one absolute) come and go as they visit it. Where perfected souls dwell, the top of the world, is represented by the figure of a crescent moon or an inverted umbrella.

As noted, all actions in people's present and previous existences produce particles of karma that weigh them down and bind their jīvas to an endless cycle of existence. When at last freed from karma, the person's soul rises up to the zenith of the universe, where it remains forever, motionless and free of suffering. Actually, Jains believe that many souls will never achieve final release; instead they will migrate and wander forever.

JAIN ETHICS

In principle, Jains are forbidden to have any occupation that involves the destruction of living beings. They may not eat meat or eggs. Even farming is taboo, since operations like tilling the soil and weeding the crops may harm living creatures.

Whereas monastics take only five vows, laymen affirm a longer list of 12 oaths, expanding those of the monastics: (1) never intentionally take a life or destroy a **jīva** (soul or unit of life); (2) never lie or exaggerate; (3) never steal; (4) never be unfaithful to one's spouse or think unchaste thoughts; (5) limit oneself in the accumulation of wealth and give away all extra possessions—for example, contribute to the maintenance of temples or animal hospitals; (6) limit chances of committing transgressions, for example—impose limits on travel; (7) limit the number of personal possessions; (8) guard against unnecessary evils; (9) observe periods of sinless meditation; (10) observe special periods of personal (ascetic) limitation;

This statue, carved from a single piece of stone, represents Jain saint Gommata. (Religious News Service)

(11) spend some time living as a monastic; and (12) give alms to a monastic community.

When they feel death approaching, Jains are obligated to take a vow of nonattachment and dispose of their earthly goods. They are even encouraged to starve themselves, for as one might expect in a religion with such an ascetic orientation, starving oneself to death is an ideal.

JAIN LAITY

Jainism evolved from an ascetic's path into a religion of the urban merchant class, of affluent city dwellers. In part this was because Jain lay practitioners chose to become merchants for largely religious reasons. Supported by sympathetic monarchs, the Jain communities built many temples and shrines, some quite magnificent. During the twelfth century, however, a resurgence of Hinduism led to the persecution of Jains, and in the thirteenth century the Muslim conquest of India was followed by persecutions of all faiths other than Islam. Unlike Buddhism, which has all but disappeared from India, Jainism managed to survive in the land of its origin. It even enjoyed a revival under the tolerant Mughal emperor Akbar. Today, the largest

Many Jain laypersons make pilgrimages to their temples, sacred places that express the distinctive orientation of the religion. (Government of India Tourist Office)

number of Jainism's 2 million adherents live in the Bombay area.

JAIN TEMPLES

Since Jainism denies that its saints can help adherents on the path, it offers no cult of relics. Many Jain laypersons do, however, make pilgrimages to the temples, for their temples are sacred places that express the distinctive orientation of the religion. The temples are adorned with the Jain symbol, a swastika surmounted by three dots and a half-moon. The dots

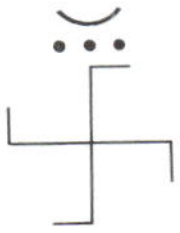

represent the three jewels of Jainism: right faith, right knowledge, and right conduct. The half-moon symbolizes moksha. The arms of the swastika stand for four types of beings: those born in hell; those born as insects, plants, or animals; those born as humans; and those born as spirits of gods or demons.

In the Śvetāmbara temples the images are shown in the meditative seated position with crossed legs; many statues wear loincloths and have glass eyes. In the Digambara temples the ceremonies can be conducted only by a Jain, but the Śvetāmbaras often permit non-Jains to officiate on religious occasions. Though it runs counter to official Jain doctrine, the laity do manage to offer sweetmeats, flowers, and fruits and burn incense lamps and lamps before the images in hopes that the saints might help them traverse the crossing.

SIKHISM

THE WAY OF THE DISCIPLES

Sikhism's primary emphasis is not on prophecy or ritual but on the consciousness of God in human persons. It seeks not an escape from the world but rather spiritual insight during earthly life. The name derives from the Pāli *sikkha,* meaning "disciple." Each disciple is expected to lead a life of prayer and recite or read a prescribed number of hymns each day as well as to serve the religious community. Sikhs define themselves as people who believe in one God, accept the teachings of the first ten guru leaders of the community, and believe in its scripture, the **Adi Granth** ("Original Book").

Today there are more than 17 million Sikhs, about 85 percent of whom live in the Indian state of Punjab. Sikh communities also exist in Malaysia, Singapore, East Africa, England, Canada, and the United States. India's youngest religion, Sikhism underwent two principal developmental stages, the first pacific and the second more militant.

EARLY SIKHISM

Begun in northern India in the fifteenth century C.E. by Guru Nanak, Sikhism sought to harmonize Hinduism and Islam. Reacting to conflicts between Hindus and Muslims, Nanak tried to go beyond contending doctrines and viewpoints to the subject of faith itself. For him the different religious institutions did not matter, only God's word, and he urged his followers to turn away from the outward forms by which humans identify the deity.

His path stresses meditating on the divine name, which is to cleanse humans of impurities and enable them to ascend higher and higher until they achieve union with the eternal One. The path also features worship, which emphasizes adoration without rites of sacrifice or propitiation. In addition, since the path cannot be separated from morality, he encouraged his followers to be courageous and to overcome lust, anger, greed, and egotism. By these means a Sikh can hope to escape from the cycle of birth and rebirth.

THE SANT BACKGROUND AND THE POET KABIR

As stated, Sikhism sought to integrate Hinduism and Islam. To Islam it owes its monotheism: God is held to be the one and true divine being and, as Islam emphasizes, must not be represented in any human form. Despite these debts, the religion is more an offshoot of Hinduism than a true syncretism with Islam.

Sikhism's principle heritage is the Hindu **Sant** devotional movement. Dating from the early thirteenth century, the Sant movement continued even after the founding of Sikhism. The Sant emphasis was on unity rather than duality: human beings would continue to encounter suffering until they attained union with God. The Sants did not identify God with the world; to them he was manifest in creation, especially through his immanence (indwelling) in the human soul.

Sikhism is especially indebted to the Sant poet **Kabir** (1440–1518). This beloved bard rejected the authority of the Hindu Vedas and upanishads and of the Islamic Qur'ān. He was convinced that all human beings were brothers and sisters before the mystery of the divine and that religion without love was empty and powerless. The path of salvation required the invocation of God's name: "Utter the name of God: He extinguishes birth and death. I utter His Name, and whatever I see reminds me of Him; whatever I do becomes His worship."[1]

Visitors approach the Golden Temple at Amritsar. Unlike Hindu shrines, it is open on all four sides, signaling that members of all four principal castes have equal status as disciples. (United Nations)

Kabir had his own telling metaphor for describing the release that is possible through the love of God: God, the true guru, discharged the arrow of his word into the world. The man or woman slain by this word finds true life in a mystical union with God the ineffable.

NANAK'S CAREER

Few details are known for certain about the life of **Nanak** (1469–1539), the founder of Sikhism; critical historical research is only now beginning. His writings are preserved in the Adi Granth. Tradition recounts that he was born to a Hindu family of the warrior caste in Taluandi, a village on the Ravi River about 30 miles from Lahore. He attended a Muslim school, where he was taught elementary Arabic and Persian and learned about Islam. Thus from early in his career the need to integrate the two religions was important.

He married at 19, eventually fathering two sons. During this time he befriended Mardana, a Muslim servant and musician in the home of an important local official. Soon Nanak gathered about him a group of followers who bathed together in a river every day before dawn and met in his home in the evening to sing religious songs he had composed. Mardana accompanied the group on the rebec, a stringed instrument. Thus from the first his constituency was both Muslim and Hindu.

When Nanak was 30 years old, he received what he took to be a divine call. One day he failed to return from his morning bath in the river. His friends, finding his clothes on the riverbank, dragged the waters in a vain attempt to find his body. Three days later Nanak reappeared. At first he gave no explanation for his absence but made only the following cryptic statement: "There is neither Hindu nor Mussulman [Muslim], so whose path shall I choose? I shall follow God's path. God is neither Hindu nor Mussulman and the path which I follow is God's."[2] Later Nanak told them that in a vision he had been carried up to God's presence. God gave Nanak a cup of nectar and then the following message:

> I am with thee. I have given thee happiness, and I shall make happy all who take thy name. Go thou and repeat my Name; cause others to repeat it. Abide unspoiled by the world. Practice charity, perform ablutions, worship and meditate. My name is God, the primal Brahma. Thou art the Holy Guru.[3]

Inspired by his vision and the promise of happiness as well as his special mission to honor the name of God, Nanak began his career as a guru. He expressed his faith in the following statement, which begins the part of the Adi Granth prayed silently each day by all observant Sikhs:

> There is but one God whose name is True, the Creator, devoid of fear and enmity, immortal, unborn, self-existent, great and bountiful. The True One was in the beginning, the True One was in the primal age. The True One is, was, O Nanak, and the True One also shall be.
>
> (Japji 1.1[4])

Nanak's teaching remained in the Hindu Sant tradition. Rejecting the magic spells and divine images of popular religion, he urged his followers that

COMPARISON

SIKHISM AND ṢŪFISM

As a religion, Sikhism integrated many Muslim and Hindu tenets. Partly as a result, Sikhism became in many ways like Islam's mystical wing, Ṣūfism (Chapter 24).

Both Sikhism and Ṣūfism describe the ultimate in theistic terms, using language about God, as opposed to an impersonal term like *Brahman*. Both employ monotheistic language, agreeing that God is one. Both emphasize God's unity. Both religions, like many others, employ metaphors of light; both suggest that some aspects of the human perceptual or psychological system obscure that light. In fact, both invoke the figure of a veil that hides the ultimate light. Yet both religions are also optimistic in the sense that each promises a direct experience of God. Both suggest that it is by removing the veil or certain impurities that this experience may be brought about and that meditation practice may be helpful in doing so.

Yet in many ways these two religions differ: Sikhism, in alignment with other Indian religions, accepts the idea of karma and the rebirth of the human soul; Ṣūfism, in accord with Islam and other Western religions, rejects this idea. Sikhism, like many religions, regards itself as the true faith and thus rejects Islam and Hinduism as incomplete and wrong. As the Adi Granth states, "Neither the Veda nor the Kateb (Qur'ān) knows the mystery!" (Maru Solaha 2.6).

meditation, worshiping God, and singing hymns (especially in the soft light of the morning) would bring about consciousness of the deity.

It is not certain how widely Nanak traveled in India and other lands. Often accompanied by Mardana, Nanak moved from place to place singing and spreading his religious message. During his later career, life in northern India became unsettled. The invasions of central Asian Muslim warriors, led by Babur (1483–1530), plunged India into a prolonged period of violence and bloodshed.

Nanak did not regard his own sons as suited to guide the community, so before his death he appointed Lehna (or Lahina), a member of the warrior caste, as the second guru of the faith. Calling Lehna to him at a public gathering, the old guru placed before his successor a coconut, the symbol of the universe, and five coins, representing air, earth, fire, water, and ether. He then handed over a book of hymns, which represented the message of the new faith, and a woolen string, a symbol of renunciation.

When Nanak died, his body was claimed by both Hindus and Muslims. He had lived in both the Hindu and Muslim worlds, seeking to overcome their respective limitations through a fresh understanding of the deity. (See the accompanying box, "Sikhism and Ṣūfism Compared.")

THE FOUNDER'S TEACHING

By meditating on the divine name, human beings are cleansed of impurities and enabled to ascend higher and higher until they achieve union with the eternal One. The process, Nanak said, is comparable to the experience of persons blinded by self-centeredness: awakened from such perversity, they begin to "see" or recognize the presence of God in the surrounding world; they begin to "hear" the voice of God speaking mystically in their souls and thus gain union with God. Having gained such union, human beings become freed from the cycle of birth and rebirth and ultimately pass beyond death into a realm of infinite and eternal bliss.

Nanak used the Hindu word *māyā* to describe the world, but not in its original sense of "illusion." The world is unreal for Nanak only insofar as it is mistaken for something it is not: "delusion" is thus a better translation, which again stresses the role of human error. We are deluded because we misinterpret nature and the purpose of the world, thinking it and the world to be separate from God. Seeing the world delusionally in this way is referred to as *anjan,* a black salve for the eyes and a traditional North Indian symbol of darkness and untruth.

The Concept of God

Besides God there is no other—this is the essence of Nanak's approach to the supreme being. The affirmation is similar to Muḥammad's affirmation "There is no God but Allāh" and Judaism's Shema. In fact, the religion is monotheistic, but not in the same way as Judaism, for it lacks the Jewish sense of history. God's essence can be known only through a personal experience of mystical union, not through the working out of historical events. Nanak was not a prophet but a guru. Moreover, Sikhism does not identify God as immanent within the world in the same way as Hindu monism did in its concept of Brahman. God is beyond all human categories yet is in them. Nanak used the names of other deities as conventional figures to speak of God. "God is Hari, Rām, and Gopāl, and He is also Allāh, Khuda, and Sāhib" (Rāmakali Ast 1.7). Despite his many manifestations, God alone exists; there is no other like him. He is eternal, omniscient, and omnipotent. Yet Nanak did not teach that God had become incarnate, in the same way as Christians speak of Jesus as an incarnation. Such a concept, in the Sikh perspective, would involve God with death, the supreme enemy, as well as with an unstable world.

LATER SIKHISM

From the death of Guru Nanak in 1539 until the death of Guru Gobind Singh in 1708, the teaching of the founder was continued and fostered by his nine successors. Under Ar jan (ruled 1581–1606), the fifth guru, the Sikh community constructed large water reservoirs, began to build the Golden Temple of Amritsar, and enlarged its small pool into an artificial lake. The temple had four doors, signaling that unlike Hindu shrines, it was open on all sides and that members of all four principal castes had equal status as disciples. Guru Ar jan also gathered the hymns of the first four gurus, put them into the Adi Granth, and enshrined the Sikh scripture in the Golden Temple. When he refused to remove from the Adi Granth passages that contradicted Islamic and Hindu orthodoxy, the Mughul emperor had him tortured and executed.

The Sikh struggle against the Mughul empire was intense and protracted. The tenth guru, Gobind Singh (1675–1708), known as "the Lion," reunited the Sikhs in a fellowship of suffering and triumphant devotion. To fend off the Mughals, Gobind Singh founded the **Khalsa**, a militaristic community of the pure. Calling together a gathering of Sikh warriors and reminding them of the dangers of their situation, the guru called for five volunteers to die for the Sikh cause. Claiming that God demanded a blood sacrifice, the leader led five warriors one by one into his tent and emerged four times with a bloody sword. After the fifth man had gone into the tent, Gobind brought out all his warriors alive. A goat had been substituted for the sacrifice of the five men.

Gobind Singh then administered to the five heroes the rite of *pahul,* an initiation by the sword into a new kind of brotherhood of soldier-saints. He gave each man a two-edged dagger and declared that they were henceforth to be known as *singh* ("lion"). A member of the Khalsa was identified by special symbols (the "five *K*'s"): he was not to cut the hair of his head or his beard *(kes);* he was to carry a comb *(kangha);* and he was to wear a steel bracelet *(kara),* a sword *(kirpan),* and short pants *(kacch).* The uncut hair was to be kept in a topknot under a turban, giving Sikh men a distinctive look they retain to this day. Women too could join the Khalsa. They received a single-edged dagger and took the title of *kaur* ("princess"). When the guru opened the Sikh religion to members of all castes, substituting the Khalsa for caste affiliation, naturally many individuals from the lower classes eagerly embraced the faith.

Gobind Singh's rule was also a watershed with respect to the role of the guru. After all four of his sons were assassinated, he proclaimed that the line of gurus would end with himself. In the future there would be only the Khalsa, the community of Sikhs, and their holy book, the Adi Granth.

Though the militaristic Khalsa is theoretically open to men and women of all castes, its members have come to form an elite within the Sikh community. They are admitted only after an initiation ceremony at which they pledge themselves to an austere code of conduct. They are to bathe daily at dawn and then spend some time in meditation. They are to avoid liquor, tobacco, and narcotics. They pledge loyalty to the teaching of the gurus and the Adi Granth and swear to join the crusade for righteousness in the world. During the initiation ceremony each candidate comes before the assembly and proclaims: "The Khalsa is of God, the victory is to God." The candidate then is given a drink of nectar, and nectar is also sprinkled on the hair and eyes.

SIKHISM IN THE MODERN ERA

After the death of the last guru, the Sikhs became increasingly rebellious. Members of the Khalsa took refuge in the hill country, coming out at opportune times to challenge Mughul power. In 1799 the Sikhs captured Lahore and made it the capital of a Sikh kingdom ruled by Ranjit Singh (1780–1839). Ranjit Singh's administration also granted religious freedom to Hindus and Muslims.

During the nineteenth century the Sikhs fought valiantly against the British invaders. When the Khalsa was finally crushed in 1849, the Sikh realm was annexed to British India. The British proved to be fair administrators, and the Sikhs remained loyal to them during the Great Mutiny of 1857 and were welcomed into the British army. Sikhs became highly respected soldiers and policemen in Burma, Hong Kong, and other parts of the British Empire.

When independence came to the Indian subcontinent in 1947, the Sikhs were bitterly disappointed at England's decision to partition the Punjab. West Punjab was given to Pakistan, East Punjab to India. Sikhs and Hindus subsequently joined in a bloody war against the Muslims in Pakistan that resulted in over a million deaths. Eventually 2.5 million Sikhs were forced to migrate to East Punjab.

The Sikh demand for a separate state has continued into the late twentieth century. Indian government policy in reply has encouraged division in the Sikh community, at times even supporting a fundamentalist political party. Sikh fundamentalists turned to violence and occupied the Golden Temple in Amritsar. There was bloodshed when it was stormed in 1984 by national troops on orders from India's prime minister, Indira Gāndhi; in reprisal, one of her guards, a Sikh, assassinated her. Violence against the Sikhs became nationwide, and hundreds of innocent persons were killed. The unrest in the Punjab, where the majority of Sikhs still live, has become a threat to secular democracy in India. The conflicts between Hindus and Sikhs have proved difficult if not impossible to control by military force alone. Religious intolerance, protest against which had led to the founding of the religion, continued.

A Sikh pilgrim is seen washing his feet before entering the Golden Temple, the most sacred shrine of the Sikhs. (United Nations)

Although Sikhism has been opposed to the caste system since the time of Nanak, caste distinctions still exist among believers to some degree. The largest Sikh caste today is that of the *jats* (farmers). Next come the skilled workers, followed by members of the upper classes.

Sikhs also differ on the matter of eating meat. Some eat beef, and others eat all meat except beef. Still others are vegetarians who do not eat meat, fish, or eggs. At community meals *(langars),* no meat is served.

Since Sikhs regard marriage as a binding contract, it is taken very seriously: there is no child marriage, divorce is discouraged, and adultery is a serious breach. Sikhs are monogamous, and in accordance with the teachings of their founder, men show respect to women. Widows may remarry.

Funerals are usually held on the day after death. Although burial at sea or in the earth is allowed, the Sikhs' accepted method of disposing of the dead, like the Hindus', is cremation.

Sikhs are supposed to visit their local **gudwaras** (sanctuaries) often. The gudwaras vary greatly in size and appearance; some are magnificent temples in the elaborate Mughal style; others are simple buildings. All must have a copy of the Adi Granth inside, and all must fly the ***nishan sāhib,*** the yellow flag of Sikhism.

In the central room, the Adi Granth is displayed on cushions, usually beneath a canopy. Men and women remove their shoes before entering this area and, out of respect, cover their heads. Any man or woman may read from the holy book. Offerings are made and hymns are sung. As they leave, worshipers walk backward out of the room, never turning their backs on the scripture. There is no priesthood per se. The congregation of each gudwara elects its own officers and votes on all important matters. Women can be present at meetings, but they do not usually participate in the discussion. In recent years some Sikhs have adopted secular habits, though any man who discards the turban and cuts his hair is considered an apostate. Readmission to the community is allowed only after a period of penance.

NOTES

1 John Clark Archer, *Faiths Men Live By* (New York: Ronald Press, 1934), p. 314.

2 W. Owen Cole and Piara Singh Sambhi, *The Sikhs: Their Religious Beliefs and Practices* (London: Routledge & Kegan Paul, 1978), p. 9.

3 Archer, *Faiths Men Live By,* p. 315.

4 M.A. MacAuliff, *The Sikh Religion: Its Gurus, Sacred Writings and Anthems I* (Oxford: Clarendon Press, 1909), p. 35.

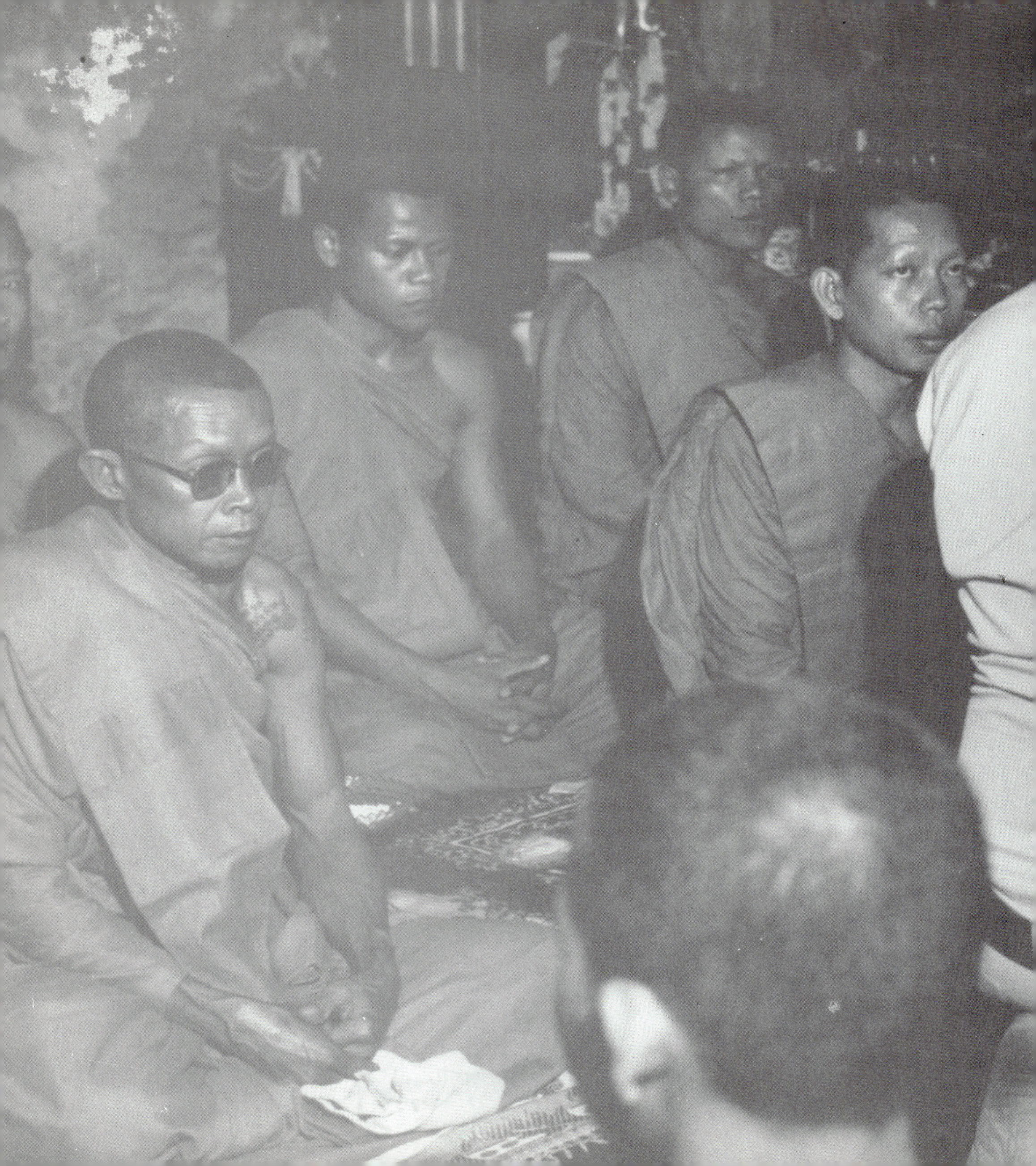

PART THREE

BUDDHISM

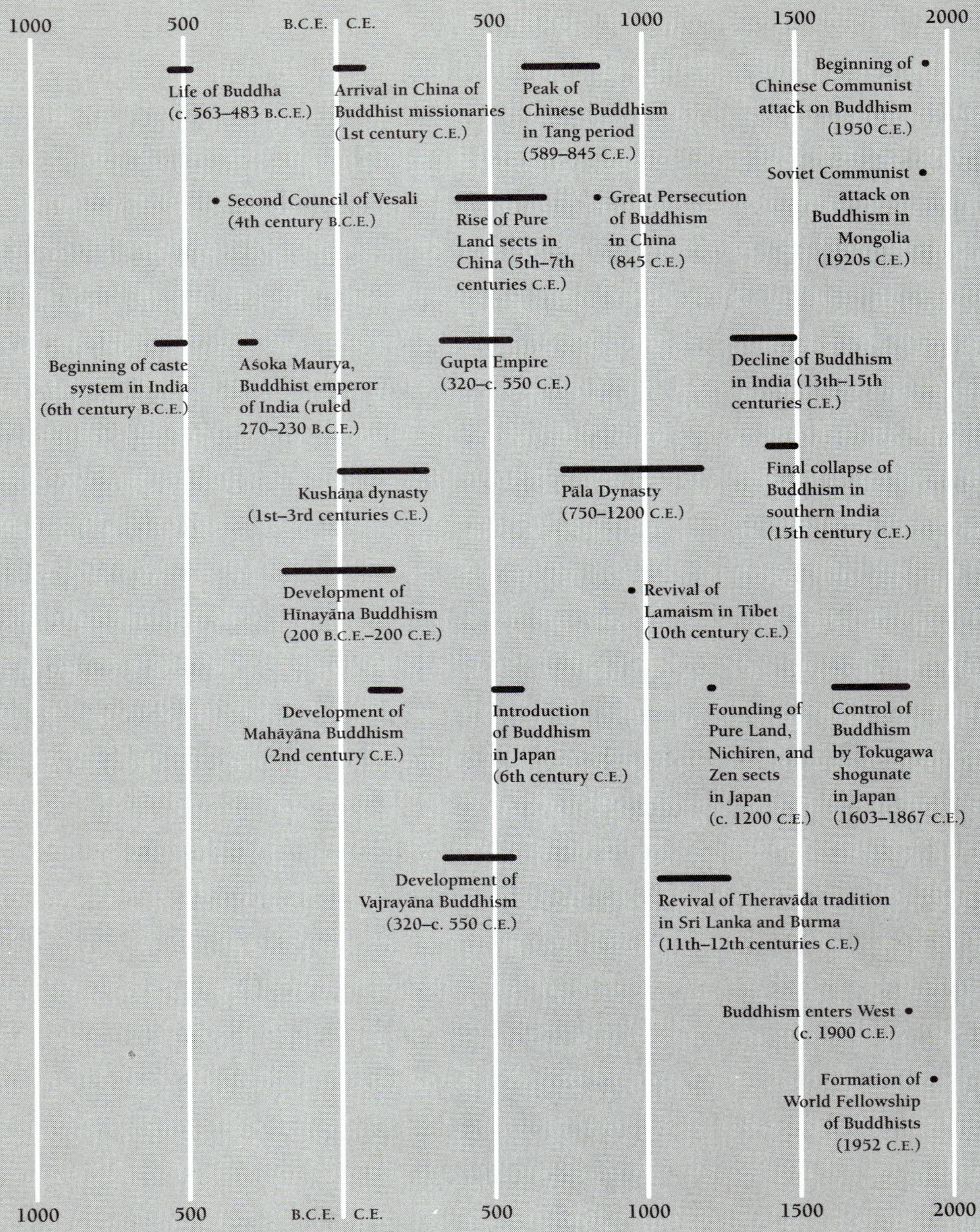
1000
500
B.C.E. C.E.
500
1000
1500
2000
Life of Buddha (c. 563–483 B.C.E.)
Arrival in China of Buddhist missionaries (1st century C.E.)
Peak of Chinese Buddhism in Tang period (589–845 C.E.)
Beginning of Chinese Communist attack on Buddhism (1950 C.E.)
Second Council of Vesali (4th century B.C.E.)
Rise of Pure Land sects in China (5th–7th centuries C.E.)
Great Persecution of Buddhism in China (845 C.E.)
Soviet Communist attack on Buddhism in Mongolia (1920s C.E.)
Beginning of caste system in India (6th century B.C.E.)
Aśoka Maurya, Buddhist emperor of India (ruled 270–230 B.C.E.)
Gupta Empire (320–c. 550 C.E.)
Decline of Buddhism in India (13th–15th centuries C.E.)
Kushāṇa dynasty (1st–3rd centuries C.E.)
Pāla Dynasty (750–1200 C.E.)
Final collapse of Buddhism in southern India (15th century C.E.)
Development of Hīnayāna Buddhism (200 B.C.E.–200 C.E.)
Revival of Lamaism in Tibet (10th century C.E.)
Development of Mahāyāna Buddhism (2nd century C.E.)
Introduction of Buddhism in Japan (6th century C.E.)
Founding of Pure Land, Nichiren, and Zen sects in Japan (c. 1200 C.E.)
Control of Buddhism by Tokugawa shogunate in Japan (1603–1867 C.E.)
Development of Vajrayāna Buddhism (320–c. 550 C.E.)
Revival of Theravāda tradition in Sri Lanka and Burma (11th–12th centuries C.E.)
Buddhism enters West (c. 1900 C.E.)
Formation of World Fellowship of Buddhists (1952 C.E.)
1000
500
B.C.E. C.E.
500
1000
1500
2000

BUDDHISM TIME LINE

Buddhism

CHAPTER 9

The Rise of Buddhism

Buddhism is based on the life and teachings of Śākyamuni Buddha,* a spiritual master who lived in the fifth century B.C.E. in what is today Nepal and northeastern India. Although the roots of Buddhism are in the Indian subcontinent, so that it shares many of the concerns of the complex of religions known collectively as Hinduism, it seeks to transcend all cultures and traditions and to lead all beings—humans, deities, animals—up to perfect enlightenment and complete liberation from all suffering. Buddhism regards itself as the **Dharma**, the "eternal truth about reality," and it teaches that the Dharma is, over immensely long periods of time, forgotten and then rediscovered by beings who have fully awakened to reality as it is and are therefore called **Buddhas** ("awakened ones"). From this perspective, the so-called historical Buddha, Śākyamuni, is only the latest in a series of Buddhas.

Consistent with its transcultural view, Buddhism is a missionary religion. It has spread throughout Asia and divided into two main forms—Theravāda in Southeast Asia and Mahāyāna in central and eastern Asia. Today it is adapting to life in many countries outside of Asia, especially in Europe and North America.

Buddhism has so many different teachings that it is impossible to fit them into a single, coherent, logical system. They do, however, fit together as therapies or medicine. (In fact, Buddhism is often seen in North America as being closer to psychotherapy than to what is commonly regarded as religion.) Buddhism teaches that beings are sick, and the Buddhas are the physicians. Just as a wise physician has a different cure for each disease, so the Buddhas have different teachings for different beings. And just as medicines do not relate to each other but all lead to health when properly used, so the teachings of the Buddhas are sometimes contradictory, but for the right being at the right time, each can be effective for liberation.

The heart of Buddhism is the Triple Treasure *(triratna)* of the Buddha, the Dharma, and the **Saṅgha.** The Buddha is the teacher, the Dharma is the teaching, and the Saṅgha is the community of those who follow, preserve, and transmit the teaching. We will use the Triple Treasure as the focus of our study of Buddhism.

*In full, Śākyamuni Gautama Siddhārtha, which consists of a title attached to his clan name ("sage of the Śākyas"), followed by his family name or surname ("of the lineage of Gotama") and his given name ("success").

The Life of the Buddha

Scholars have tried for years to reconstruct the life of Śākyamuni Buddha and his teachings but have not reached a consensus. Even his dates are still debated:

some experts place him around 563–483 B.C.E., others between 448 and 368 B.C.E. However, all agree that the Buddha lived in the northeastern Indian subcontinent during a period of religious and social turmoil. Scholar Charles Drekmeier has coined the expression *tribal trauma* to describe the situation. The older "tribally" oriented social structures were breaking down, and a new, more cosmopolitan society was beginning to develop. From a predominantly pastoral and agricultural society, cities and merchants were beginning to emerge and together were growing increasingly wealthy and powerful. Politically, monarchy was developing, and certain northeastern Indian kings were expanding their domains into other parts of the subcontinent.

In this situation of rapid social and economic change, the older Vedic way of religious life, which had been well suited to an agrarian peasant world, was losing its hold on the loyalties of the people, including the new political and economic elites. This was particularly true in the dynamic northeast, where Vedic influence had never been thoroughly incorporated into the local culture. The result was great anxiety and insecurity, accompanied by exploration into new, more relevant religious patterns.

This is the era of Hinduism's upanishads and the emergence of the Jains and other schools. Many people were leaving their place in ordinary society to take up life in alternative communities made up of wandering ascetics called **śramaṇas**. By the time of the Buddha, there were many such communities, often advocating new kinds of religious beliefs, practices, and patterns of community life. Many were organized around a charismatic leader who taught a doctrine that promised a final salvation through which the problems of life in this world could be totally transcended. The Buddha—who, it is generally agreed, was a member of the nobility (the kshatriya caste)—was one of those persons who gave up worldly life to seek new ways of addressing such problems. After many years of religious experimentation and exploration, he achieved and later taught about a final salvation, the solution to human problems.

Either during his lifetime or very shortly thereafter, the Buddha's followers began to tell stories about his life. In recounting these tales, no effort was made to distinguish between accurate reporting of historical events and mythic elements that expressed the tradition's teachings.

According to the stories, the Buddha was the son of the ruler of the Śākya kingdom in the northeast of the subcontinent. His birth is described as a "descent" from the Tushita heaven, where he had been residing as a result of his good deeds in his previous lives. The birth itself was miraculous and painless and was followed by predictions from the court brāhmans that he would become either a **Cakravartin** (universal monarch) or a Buddha (supremely enlightened sage). Fearful of the prophecy that he might renounce the throne, his father did his best to keep his son happy and contented, surrounded by beauty and insulated from sickness, decay, and death. The young Siddhārtha was given the best possible education and was married to the most beautiful princess, Yaśodharā ("she who radiates brightness or fame"), by whom he had a son. However, he named his son Rāhula, "the fetter"—possibly indicating his or the tradition's ambivalence about the value of married life.

Restless, Siddhārtha wanted to go out of the palace. Wary of earlier predictions that he might become a Buddha, his father ordered all sick and aged persons, all monks, and all funerals banished from the streets of the city while his son passed by. But somehow an old man slipped through the security guards. Siddhārtha was deeply shocked and asked his driver:

> "Good charioteer, who is this man with white hair, supporting himself on the staff in his hand, with his eyes veiled by the brows, and limbs relaxed and bent? Is this some transformation in him, or his original state, or mere chance?"

His driver replied:

> "Old age it is called, that which has broken him down—the murderer of beauty, the ruin of vigour, the birthplace of sorrow, the grave of pleasure, the destroyer of memory, the enemy of the senses.
>
> "For he too sucked milk in his infancy, and later in course of time he crawled on the ground; in the natural order he became a handsome youth and in the same natural order he has now reached old age."

Hearing these words and learning that old age was the fate of everyone who is born, the prince

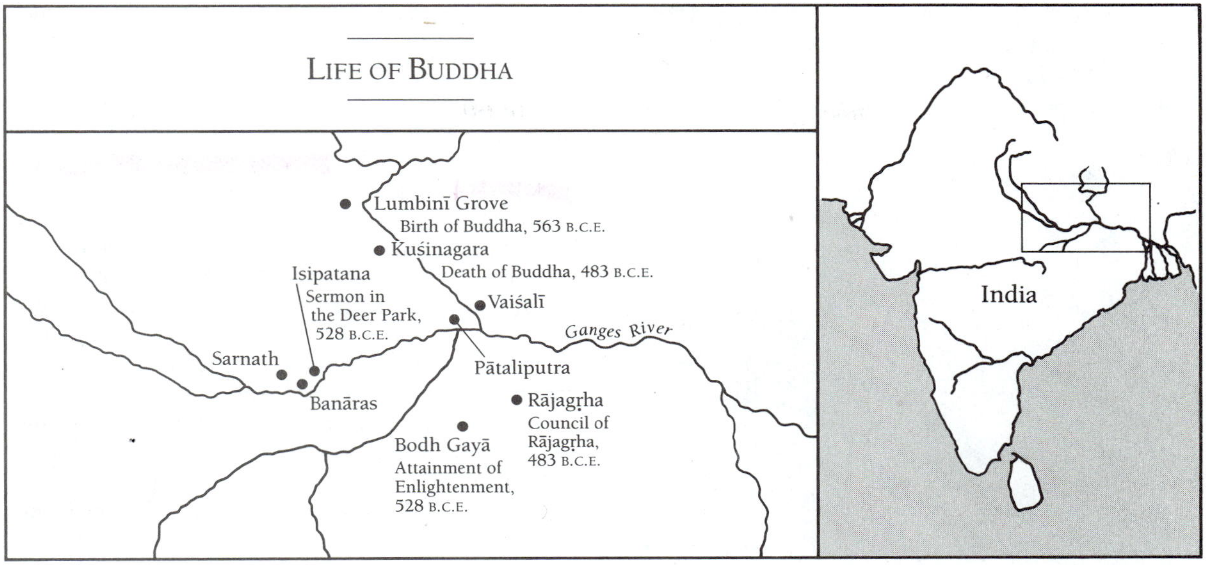

> sighed deeply and shook his head; and looking on the festive multitude he uttered these words in his perturbation:
>
> "Thus old age strikes down indiscriminately memory and beauty and valour, and yet with such a sight before its eyes the world is not perturbed.
>
> "This being so, turn back the horses, charioteer; go quickly home again. For how can I take my pleasure in the garden, when the fear of old age rules in my mind?"[1]

So despite all the precautions, Siddhārtha had seen the first of the four things that would cause him to turn away from a life as a worldly ruler. In two further excursions from the palace, he saw a sick man and a corpse. In these three sights the Buddha—and the tradition—recognized the problem of existence, transiency: everything that comes to be ceases to be, whatever we are now we will not be later, and whatever we have we will lose. The situation seemed hopeless. But then Siddhārtha saw the fourth and last sight, a homeless wanderer (sannyāsī) or monk. This man was calm and peaceful; he radiated a serenity that said, wordlessly, "I have found it!" In him the Buddha and the tradition saw the possibility of a life other than that devoted to getting things that are then lost, a life that sought the cause of death.

So one night, leaving Yaśodharā and Rāhula asleep, Siddhārtha left the palace and fled to the forest. There, much as later monks would do, he took off his jewelry, exchanged his robes for simple clothes, dismissed his horse (which, it is said, died of a broken heart and was reborn as a god), and began to live as a sannyāsī, a forest-dwelling ascetic.

In those days the forests of the Indian subcontinent were full of sannyāsīs, and Siddhārtha sought a teacher among them. He found, however, that although there were many who knew how to attain exalted states of consciousness and deeply peaceful ones, none had found the secret of liberation from **saṃsāra**, the cycle of birth, death, and rebirth. Therefore, he abandoned all teachers and sought the truth for himself. He thought that he might be able to free his mind or soul from his body by denying his body—according to the most extreme accounts, he ate only one grain of rice a day, becoming so thin that he could grasp his backbone through his abdomen, and he lost so much weight that if he stood up on a windy day, he would be blown over! At any rate, he seems to have practiced forms of asceticism that despite their severity are not

This temple in Bodh Gayā, India, is said to be erected on the site of the bodhi tree where Siddhārtha withstood the temptations of Māra. (Religious News Service)

unusual among sannyāsīs in the Indian subcontinent even today.

However, the experiment failed, and he was in a quandary. When he had been in the palace, eating, drinking, and sleeping all he wanted, he would become drowsy and confused. Now, hardly eating, drinking, or sleeping at all, he also became drowsy and confused. The only difference was that when he ate he was strong and when he didn't eat he was weak. In neither case was he any nearer to ending the birth-and-death cycle.

Then he remembered a time when as a child he had sat under a tree and allowed his mind to calm down. As his mind calmed, it became clear, and as it became clear it became manageable. He tried to repeat this experience. First he ate something, just enough to build up his strength. Thus he began the tradition's "middle way" between the hedonism of worldly life and the self-denying asceticism of the forest dwellers. He then sat under a tree that would become known as the Bodhi, or "Enlightenment Tree,"* focused and stabilized his mind in meditation, and vowed that he would not move until he had attained perfect and complete enlightenment. Meditation would henceforth be a part of nearly every lineage's path.

At first he was beset by hallucinations of greed and hate and by demons, led by Māra, the god of illusion. Finally, seeing through Māra's trickery, his mind cleared, and as the morning star rose, he proclaimed:

> Through many a birth I wandered in saṃsāra,
> seeking, but not finding, the builder of the house.
> Sorrowful is it to be born again and again.
> House-builder! You are seen. You shall build
> no house again. All your rafters are broken. Your
> ridge-pole is shattered.
> My mind has attained the unconditioned.
> Achieved is the end of craving.
>
> (Dhammapada 153–154)

So saying, he decided to vanish from the phenomenal world, convinced that it would be useless to teach what he had seen. However, one of the deities (who also, according to Buddhism, are trapped in saṃsāra, and therefore wish to know how to end the cycle), told him that if he would but look, he would see that there were many beings "with little dust on their eyes" who would understand him and be helped by what he knew.

Thus began 45 years of traveling in the Ganges basin area, teaching whoever would listen. Many who heard him were so attracted to his words and his way of life that they wished to follow him, and he received them as *bhikshus,* or Buddhist sannyāsīs.

*A descendant of this tree still exists, in the village of Bodh Gayā, Bihar, India, on the spot where the Buddha is supposed to have sat.

During the early years, according to the stories, many ascetics—chief disciples Ānanda and Devadatta among them—became Siddhārtha's followers. But wealthy merchants and powerful administrators too were converted, and by the end of his life even kings and princes were making pilgrimages to his doors. Such stories emphasize the variety of converts to his Saṅgha and the vast range of his appeal, which cut through long-established social and economic barriers.

The Buddha taught into old age. He died after eating some rancid food and, passing into **nirvāṇa** (final release), disappeared from the phenomenal universe. His remains were cremated and memorial mounds, called **stūpas**, were built over portions of his relics, which were distributed throughout the neighboring kingdoms. Although the Buddha had disappeared in person, he could still be contacted through the Triple Treasure he established.

THE TEACHINGS OF THE BUDDHA: THE DHARMA

THE FOUR NOBLE TRUTHS

As it has proved impossible to recover the life of the Buddha with historical accuracy, so it is difficult to say precisely how much of the Dharma comes from the Buddha and how much from his followers. But once again there is agreement among almost all Buddhist lineages. The heart of the Dharma is traditionally contained in the Four Noble Truths set forth in the so-called first sermon of the Buddha at Banāras. They are (1) suffering *(duḥkha),* (2) the arising of suffering *(samudaya),* (3) the cessation of suffering *(nirodha),* and (4) the path leading to the cessation of suffering *(mārga).*

Suffering

The Four Noble Truths begin with a formulation of the problem that from the Buddha's perspective was the basic human problem, the one that encompassed all of our more specific difficulties and anxieties: suffering. All sentient beings, he contended, live lives in which suffering is an inevitable and ultimately dominant component. Some persons, because of the law of karma, which ensures that good deeds will be rewarded and bad deeds will be punished, have more enjoyment and less suffering than others. Given the law of karma, it is both possible and advisable to perform good deeds in the present in order to maximize future enjoyment and to minimize future suffering. But despite the Buddha's emphasis on the doctrine of karma and the consequent advantages of moral activity, he was steadfast in this: so long as life continues, suffering cannot be avoided.

This emphasis on the pervasiveness of suffering clearly struck a responsive chord among people who had lost their tribal affiliations. All sentient beings are caught up in an ongoing process of continuing birth, suffering, death, and rebirth. Because of the morally structured workings of karma, those who do good deeds in one life can assure themselves of a better condition in their future lives. Every action has a consequence that affects future rebirths. Acts of charity and compassion, for instance, result in a better rebirth; harmful acts and immoral acts lead to a rebirth that involves greater suffering. But even the best kind of life

The great stupa in the Deer Park near Banāras (Varanasi), marking the spot where Buddha delivered his first sermon. (Stephen Borst)

is impermanent and is tinged with the suffering that impermanence brings.

The Cause of Suffering

The analysis of the problem of suffering that constitutes the second of the Four Noble Truths asserts that the cause of suffering is desire and craving (*taṇhā*). Why does the cycle of rebirth, suffering, death, and rebirth continue? Why is the impermanence of life experienced as suffering? Because craving is an ever present force that drives the life process forward, and in this life process every object of desire that is gained is, because of its inherent impermanence, ultimately lost.

The Cessation of Suffering

The third Noble Truth affirms that a solution to the problem is available—that release from suffering is possible. Though the term *nirvāṇa* is not used in the classical formulations of the Four Noble Truths, later Buddhists recognized that what they had come to call nirvāṇa is the goal to which the Buddha was pointing. Nirvāṇa means literally "blowing out" or "extinguishing," as of the flame of a candle. Here it suggests the extinguishing of all craving and desire and hence all suffering. When the mind no longer grasps and craves what is by nature impermanent, suffering ends. The early texts present this nirvāṇic experience as very positive, analogous to (but more desirable than) the experiences of bliss, joy, heaven, and the like.

The Path out of Suffering

The fourth and culminating truth affirms that there is a path that releases those who follow it from the realm of suffering, the so-called Noble Eightfold Path—as expressed by the Buddha in his first sermon: right view, right thought, right speech, right action, right livelihood, right effort, right mindfulness, right concentration. As we saw earlier, this path presents a middle way between the overly rigorous asceticism the Buddha first tried and the slothful self-indulgence he saw in most people. The stories about the Buddha himself show that he followed such a middle way in his own quest for enlightenment and throughout his ministry.

CORRELATED BUDDHIST DOCTRINES

If the Four Noble Truths constitute the most famous and most dependable summary of the Buddha's message, the two doctrines that most clearly distinguish his teaching are the closely correlated claims concerning interdependent arising **(pratītya samutpāda)** and no self **(anātman)**. Both of these teachings are sufficiently distinctive and pervasive in the early Buddhist tradition that it is highly probable that they originated in the experience and reflection of the founder himself.

Pratītya Samutpāda: Interdependent Arising

The doctrine of interdependent arising was the Buddha's most sophisticated way of accounting for the existence of the world and individuals, in a way that permitted transcending life's inevitable suffering. Unlike many other religious teachers, the Buddha did not believe in a creator God who creates and continues to sustain individuals and the world. In fact, there is considerable evidence that the Buddha did not reject the belief in gods, demons, and the like. But from his perspective, any gods that might exist were, just like humans, caught up in the suffering-filled round of saṃsāra.

Through the doctrine of interdependent arising, the Buddha sought to describe the entire process in which all beings originate and participate and in so doing suggest how individuals might bring the process to a felicitous end. Though we do not know the exact form in which the doctrine of interdependent arising was originally taught, the early texts set forth both a short formula and a classical summary of the teaching. The short formula is this:

> *When this is, that is.*
> *This arising, that arises.*
> *When this is not, that is not.*
> *This ceasing, that ceases.*

The classical summary explains this obscure formula: all phenomenal reality, both cosmic and personal, comes into being through a process in which 12 constituent elements are continually arising interdependently (that is, dependent on and in conjunction with one another). These 12 constituents are ignorance, karmic predispositions, consciousness, name and form, the five sense organs and the mind, contact, feeling-response, craving, grasping for an object, action toward life, birth, and old age and death.

All reality can be seen as a kind of circular chain, the links of which are these 12 constituent elements. Each one of these elements, and the suffering it involves, therefore depends on each other link, in the same way that each link in the circular chain must remain connected to another link. Therefore, it becomes possible for any individual person at any time to stop his or her involvement in the process by eliminating one or more of the links in the circular chain. Clearly, for the Buddha, the two weak links that are the most susceptible to minimization or elimination—through meditation, behavior changes, or learning the Dharma —are ignorance (which, since it is listed first, seems to be given special importance) and desire or craving.

Anātman: No Self

The other very distinctive doctrine of the Buddha is anātman, the belief that there is no inherently existing self. It meshes neatly with the notion of interdependent arising. At one level the doctrine of anātman serves the same purpose of liberation by denying the existence of any kind of permanent reality behind or within the psychophysical elements that constitute phenomenal reality. But it adds that there is also nothing behind or within our feeling of a sense of self or ātman. Rather, one is really a series of processes that together perceive, categorize, and act. The individual is made up of five psychophysical elements, or *skandhas:* corporeality or physical form (which includes physical objects, the body, and the sense organs); feelings or sensations; ideations, with which we label and understand those feelings; mental formations or dispositions— the likes, dislikes, and impulses we have about those ideas; and consciousness, the awareness of any or all of these elements. By analyzing the person into such constituent elements, the tradition makes more explicit its claim that there is no substantial or inherently existing ātman. And if there is no ātman, there is no essential "I" to protect and fight for. Thus egoistic striving is seen to be delusory, and one's own suffering is reduced. One is also more available to others, for one is freed from one's own agenda. (For a comparison of Buddhist beliefs on salvation with those of other religions of the same region, see the accompanying box.)

EARLY COLLECTED TEACHINGS

During the early centuries of Buddhist history, these and many other teachings attributed to the Buddha were passed down orally; they were supplemented by teachings formulated by members of the community that were often attributed to him, and they were molded into more or less integrated systems of thought and practice. The oral collection of the Buddha's teachings, called *sūtras,* and the collection of monastic regulations **(Vinaya)** were formalized soon after his death. The process of gathering collections of teachings continued for several centuries. Finally, as doctrinal systems started to develop, new types of summaries were gathered into the Abhidharma collections preserved by particular Buddhist traditions. Collectively, the sūtras, Vinaya, and Abhidharma are known as the **Tripiṭaka**, the "Triple Basket," which came to form the core of Buddhist scriptures. Several schools developed, each of which had its own authoritative Tripiṭaka and thus its own rendition of the Buddha's Dharma, or doctrine. Ironically, Buddhism, which began as a rejection of the received traditions of its day, developed a well-defined, though always contested, tradition of its own. In so doing it established its position as one of the several full-fledged religions that were actively competing for the loyalty of the peoples of ancient India.

THE EARLY BUDDHIST COMMUNITY: THE SAṄGHA

The historical Buddha, in addition to being a great teacher, was an extremely effective community organizer. He gathered around him a large number of wandering mendicant followers and lay supporters. He organized a community *(Saṅgha)* of monks and developed a discipline designed to guide their behavior and to regulate the functioning of the community as a whole. At the urging of Ānanda, a leading disciple, he

COMPARISON

Buddhism, Upanishadic Hinduism, and Jainism on Salvation

Roughly simultaneously with early Buddhism and arising out of the same social and religious context, two other religious traditions developed. Like Buddhism, both Jainism and the upanishads of Hinduism both embodied ancient Indian concepts such as saṃsāra (transmigration), karma (law of action), and moksha (enlightenment). And like Buddhism, these two traditions rethought and reworked these ideas, particularly with regard to the goal of the religious life and the most effective means of achieving this goal. The upanishads moved away from the sacrifice-centered Vedic tradition toward a more ascetic, meditational form of religious behavior. The Jains also emphasized ascetic renunciation and self-discipline as the effective method for salvation.

The upanishads were similar to the early Buddhist texts in their criticism of Vedic rituals, which they regarded as superfluous and a hindrance. Emphasizing renunciation and asceticism, both traditions stressed the need for insight and knowledge rather than the "proper" performance of the sacrifice. The upanishads were, however, quite unlike Buddhism in their conception of the ultimate goal of the religious quest. Whereas among Buddhism's central tenets were the doctrine of anātman, which denies the existence of a substantial self, and the doctrine of impermanence, the upanishads maintained that there is an ātman, an essential self that transcends all individuality, limitation, decay, and death.

Furthermore, the upanishads taught that by realizing, through meditation, the funda-

somewhat reluctantly organized a community of nuns along similar lines.

In addition, he took great pains to develop a positive and mutually beneficial relationship between himself and the monks and nuns of the Saṅgha, on the one hand, and his lay supporters on the other. The monastics were expected to provide the lay supporters with models of ideal Buddhist behavior and to offer guidance in the knowledge and practice of the Dharma. For their part, the members of the laity were expected to know and practice the Dharma as best they could, given the constraints of ordinary social life, and to provide the food and other requirements that the monastics needed.

Monasteries began to be established very early, perhaps during the Buddha's own lifetime. They probably started with the mendicant practice of settling in one particular place during the three-month rainy season that inhibited travel. During this three-month period of settled life, close ties between individual monastics and particular lay people could be forged. Soon the Buddhist laity in particular localities began to donate land and buildings to the monastics they knew and respected, so that they could take up permanent residence. Once these lands and buildings were available, many of the mendicants gave up their wandering ways and taught and received support from their local lay communities.

BUDDHIST LIFE STYLES

Scholars of Buddhism have often noted the persistence of two different life styles within the Buddhist community, that of the monastics and that of the laity. But as we will see, once the monasteries appeared on the mental identity between the ultimate Brahman and the individual ātman, liberation from saṃsāra could be obtained. Buddhism rejected such ideas, claiming that all reality was impermanent, and therefore all notions of an essential ātman or an ultimate Brahman were false.

Buddhism is even more similar to Jainism than to the upanishads. Jainism, like Buddhism, had a human founder, Mahāvira, who like the Buddha lived in northeastern India in the sixth and fifth centuries B.C.E. Like Buddhism and the upanishads, the Jains emphasized saṃsāra and the importance of karma. To transcend saṃsāra, the Jains held, one must renounce this world and become an ascetic. Like Buddhism, Jainism stressed meditation and the perfection of acts as techniques leading to insight and liberation.

The early Jain community stressed a severe and often extreme form of renunciation and asceticism, whereas early Buddhism stressed the middle path between extreme asceticism and worldly life. Buddhism also stressed the absolute impermanence of this world and characterized liberation from this world as nirvāṇa, the extinguishing of all sensation. The Jains, in contrast, formulated a system in which the individual soul, or *jīva,* eventually achieves release from saṃsāra, recovers its essential nature, and is reunited with other *siddhas* (perfected beings) at the pinnacle of the universe.

All three traditions—Buddhism, Jainism, and the upanishads—grew out of a common religious and social situation in northern India, borrowing, reformulating, and critiquing many of the same key doctrines. Each at the same time developed new doctrines and practices to meet the needs of its particular community. Over time, as the differences between the various new ideas, practices, and religious ideals deepened, the common core of the three traditions became more and more obscure.

scene, three distinct but nonexclusive life styles developed within the early tradition and are found today throughout much of Theravāda Buddhism. The third we will call forest monks, men who retained the wandering mode of life.

Forest Monks

In the earliest years of the tradition, the forest monks were renunciants who refused to be subjected to the highly regulated and, from their point of view, overly domesticated existence that became increasingly characteristic of life in the monasteries. Unfortunately for scholars, these mendicants were not greatly concerned with the collection and codification of texts from which we might be able to reconstruct the details of their life patterns. We may, however, deduce certain characteristics of their life styles from the texts that we do have and from archaeological and inscriptional materials.

These renunciants lived for the most part in forests and caves and clearly spent a great deal of their time in isolation from other members of the Saṅgha. They were stricter (and often more idiosyncratic) in their asceticism than Buddhists associated with established monasteries. But at the same time they seem to have been less concerned with strict adherence to the Vinaya behavioral rules that were operative in the communal setting. They emphasized the practice of various forms of yoga and tended to value the authority of yogic masters and yogic experience more highly than texts. Some reports reveal among them a special fondness for frequenting the sacred places where stūpas had been established, thus adding to the importance of these sites as pilgrimage destinations.

Exactly how numerous or influential these forest

monks were in the early community we cannot say with certainty, but there are clear traces of their presence. For example, evidence suggests that the Buddha's cousin Devadatta was a rather extreme example of such a monk. Indeed, according to some sources, he may have had sufficient support to challenge the Buddha's leadership and to threaten a schism in the Saṅgha. In many cases the legitimacy of the forest dwellers' style of life was recognized by the Buddha himself. Thus despite the rise of the established monasteries throughout India, forest monks continued to play an important role throughout Buddhism's early years.

Settled Monastics

The second style of life that was evident in the early Buddhist community was that pursued by the more settled monks and nuns who lived in Buddhist monasteries. These monastics tended to place a much stronger emphasis than the forest monks on the detailed rules that the Buddha and his successors had developed to regulate the Saṅgha. They continued to supplement these orally transmitted rules until they were finally written as the Vinaya. These texts spell out in great detail the rules that the Buddha envisioned as the middle way between extreme asceticism and self-indulgence.

For the members of the Saṅgha, the Vinaya prohibits killing, stealing, lying, sexual misconduct, and drunkenness; it also requires celibacy and the renunciation of all material goods except for the four requisites of food, clothing, shelter, and medicine. The Vinaya also requires great decorum in such matters as dress, social behavior, and bodily functions. In good Buddhist fashion, it focuses on intentions as a part of action and relates its rules and interpretations to the goal of rooting out the preeminent Buddhist vices of lust, hatred, and confusion.

The Vinaya also codifies procedures for the Saṅgha's ceremonies and rituals. For example, it establishes procedures for the ordination of new members, offers guidelines for the regular practice of confession and expiation for offenders, regulates the management of communal property, and formulates a quasi-legal framework for the resolution of internal disputes.

The Vinaya code, though relevant to all Buddhist life styles, was clearly oriented toward life in the monasteries. Yet there its rules and procedures were not always strictly followed, though it did foster a more formal, more restrained mode of existence as well as less idiosyncratic forms of behavior and meditational practice. Perhaps most important, great emphasis was placed on mastery of the Buddha's teaching in the form of the transmission and study of textual traditions. It is these texts, first oral and then written, that came to define "standard" Buddhism.

Lay Supporters: Householders

The third life style practiced in the early Buddhist community was developed for and by nonmonastic lay supporters. The Buddha himself was very concerned to attract lay followers and to instruct them in modes of activity that would enable them to practice the Noble Eightfold Path at the same time that they lived and worked as **householders** (people who lead domestic, nonascetic lives). Among his most famous sermons is one addressed to a young householder named Sigala. In this sermon, which some later Buddhists have called a Vinaya for the laity, the Buddha enumerates six preeminent vices, describes the motives that lead to evil actions, warns against six ways of dissipating wealth, and differentiates among kinds of friends. Having noticed that Sigala was in the habit of each day performing a series of rituals honoring the six cosmic regions, the Buddha informs him that he should instead show proper honor and respect to his parents (the east), his teachers (the south), his wife and children (the west), his friends and companions (the north), servants and workmen (the nadir), and religious teachers and brāhmans (the zenith). The Buddha became renowned for such reinterpretations of established religious practices.

Though the Buddha encouraged his followers to show respect to all authentic "religious teachers and brāhmans," from a very early date Buddhist laypersons were especially drawn to venerate the Buddha himself. It is difficult to determine the exact nature or expressions of this veneration during the Buddha's own lifetime. But it is certain that following his death, he was reverently honored by both monastics and lay followers at the pilgrimage sites that marked key events in his life. It is also clear that both monastics and lay supporters performed rituals of veneration at stūpas where his relics were deposited. By the beginning of the Common Era, images of the Buddha were becoming a primary focus for the expression of devotion. Such developments demonstrate that Buddhism was adapting to the needs of a wide social constituency.

Buddhist laypersons also venerated the monastics and gave them gifts to provide for their material support. Some gifts were given to the forest monks (who were often thought to possess special powers that could be tapped to meet lay needs), enabling them to maintain their mendicant life style. Other gifts were given to the settled monastics, permitting them to adhere to their discipline, pursue their studies, and provide local spiritual guidance. Like gifts given symbolically to the Buddha (at stūpas, images, and elsewhere), gifts given to members of the Saṅgha were understood to be prime sources of merit *(puṇya)* that created beneficial karma. Through these gifts, given with a pure heart and without thought of self, the giver could gain a better life in this world and the next and could also advance along a path that would ultimately lead to final release (nirvāṇa).

Early Buddhism and the "New Society"

As noted earlier, Buddhism originated in the northeastern subcontinent during a period when momentous changes were taking place in all areas of life. The Buddha's claim to be the proper focus of religious authority was convincing to many of his contemporaries because his message was relevant to the prevailing social, political, and economic situations of his day. The Buddha's message satisfied the religious needs of many people, and the evidence suggests that large numbers were attracted to his community.

Significantly, most early Buddhists were members of the social, political, and economic elite. The earliest texts depict many very successful encounters between the Buddha and kings and members of their royal courts and between the Buddha and representatives of a rapidly rising class of rich and powerful merchants. There is strong evidence to suggest that although the renunciant orders were open to persons of all castes, a preponderance of those who were actually ordained were either brāhmans (priests) or kshatriyas (rulers, warriors, and administrators). It is also apparent that much of the lay support came from members of the new society who wielded great power and commanded considerable wealth.

These groups had recently lost the moorings of their tribal roots and the associated religious rituals and structures. Like so many city dwellers even today, they faced new questions about the meaning of their lives and the new challenges of a more cosmopolitan life. They experienced a freedom from the personal and emotional controls of the small, tightly knit social groups associated with tribal communities, and at the same time they faced the loss of the sense of participation and place, the security of belonging to such a community.

In contrast to the Vedic tradition, the questions that Buddhists asked and answered were no longer centered primarily on the needs of the group, nor did Buddhism offer a legitimizing rationale for a particular social structure, such as caste. Rather, the Buddha and his early followers addressed the problems of both the individual and society in the new cosmopolitan circumstances.

The Buddha's recommended Eightfold Path emphasized the role of individual responsibility, effort, and intention, each of which found resonance among the self-reliant merchant classes and other city dwellers. His message also responded to the social needs of the time, emphasizing the moral responsibilities of kingship and an ethic of compassion and harmony among competing individuals and groups. His message was universal in that it addressed all men and women regardless of affiliations, it was social in that it set forth new ideals of political and social leadership, and it was individual in that it made each person responsible for his or her own destiny.

Buddhism in the Mauryan Empire

So it is not surprising that the expansion of Buddhism and the spread of the new political and social order occurred in tandem. During the century or two following the Buddha's death, Buddhism became established in many other parts of the subcontinent.

Within this same time span, the area where the Buddha had carried on much of his ministry became the center of a new imperial order, the Mauryan dynasty. This lineage soon came to control and influence the entire subcontinent.

The exact connections between the expansion of Buddhism and the establishment of the Mauryan regime are impossible to trace. However, it is clear that these processes began in the same region at the same time and were linked in a major event in Buddhist history. In the early decades of the third century B.C.E. Aśoka Maurya, the king who completed the Mauryan conquest of the subcontinent, became a supporter of Buddhism. Aśoka's vast empire incorporated virtually all of what is now modern India, and he ruled it for approximately 40 years (c. 270–230 B.C.E.). After his death, he became idealized as a model of Buddhist kingship.

The edicts of this Indian emperor are our oldest Buddhist documents. Inscribed on rocks and pillars, they record that Aśoka honored the Buddha and made pilgrimages to Buddhist shrines; that he espoused and sought to spread a Dharma that, from his point of view at least, was consistent with the Buddha's teachings; that he recommended that certain Buddhist texts be given special attention by his subjects; that he supported the Saṅgha and tried to ensure its unity; and that he dispatched Buddhist missionaries far and wide.

Some analysts have argued that Aśoka was a truly devout Buddhist trying his best to spread Buddhism throughout his empire. Others have argued that, having extended the Mauryan Empire to its natural geographic limits, he adopted a watered-down, quasi-Buddhist version of the Dharma to pacify and unite his empire's many regions and peoples. Either way, his reign marked a major turning point for Buddhism; it became a great religion of Pan-Indian and ultimately Pan-Asian significance.

NOTE

1 E. H. Johnson, *Aśvaghoṣa's Buddhacarita, or Acts of the Buddha* (Delhi: Banarsidass, 1936, 1984), pp. 36–38.

BUDDHISM

CHAPTER 10

THE DEVELOPMENT OF BUDDHISM IN INDIA

During the seven centuries following King Aśoka's death, the so-called post-Aśokan period (c. 200 B.C.E.–500 C.E.), large parts of the subcontinent were ruled by a succession of emperors. Under these empires India enjoyed relative political stability, economic prosperity, and some degree of religious and cultural unity. Hindus during this period developed the religious culture that eventually dominated the land. Simultaneously, Indian Buddhists developed their distinctive religious culture, which also played a significant role in Indian life. They also began in earnest the missionary activities whereby Buddhism came to influence virtually all of Asia.

During the long post-Aśokan period, Buddhism's fortunes rose and fell according to the favor of the reigning sovereign. When the Saṅgha was at peace, due to royal protection and even sponsorship, the monastics had the leisure to reflect on and develop the Dharma. The words of the Buddha, as preserved in the tradition, were memorized, ritually chanted, meditated on in private, debated in public, and made the subject of many commentaries. Although details of this process and its causes have been recovered only in part and remain a topic of scholarly debate, Buddhism emerged during this period as two streams, Theravāda and Mahāyāna, each claiming to be the authentic Dharma.

Theravāda (tradition of the *theras,* or senior monks), or Conservative Buddhism, is best understood as a single lineage based on a comparatively small body of texts preserved in Pāli, a language similar to Sanskrit. It passed into most of South and Southeast Asia, taking on distinctive but clearly related forms in each country, frequently being a major factor in the growth of national identities. Its most characteristic feature is the social visibility of the monastics in their orange or yellow robes and the close symbiotic relationship between the monastics and the lay people. This arrangement was probably very similar to that of the Buddha's own time. Emphasizing rationality, individual effort, and self-discipline, Theravāda promised salvation for a religious elite.

Mahāyāna appears to have begun as a reform movement in the subcontinent around the beginning of the Common Era. In calling itself Mahāyāna, the "Greater Vehicle," it self-consciously distinguished itself from the rest of Buddhism, which it stigmatized as **Hīnayāna**, or the "Inferior Vehicle."* Claiming that Conservative Buddhism had become an elitist profession for monastics, Mahāyāna preached that everyone, whether monastic or lay, had an equal chance of

*When Mahāyāna arose, it branded traditional Buddhism as Hīnayāna, the "Lesser Vehicle," a pejorative term. A significant wing of traditional Buddhism called itself Theravāda, the tradition of the senior monks or elders, but not all of its schools were so named. The scholar Hajime Nakamura refers to this wing by the more neutral term Conservative Buddhism. All names refer broadly to the same traditional wing.

The Young Quail Jātaka

Jātakas, stories of acts the Buddha supposedly performed in his previous lifetimes, have been told from Buddhism's earliest days; some may even have been told by the Buddha himself. While in some of these stories the future Buddha was born as a human being or occasionally as a god, in most of the Jātakas—like "The Young Quail Jātaka" recounted here—he appears as an animal. The stories often illustrate a particular point of Buddhist doctrine; in this one both the difficulties in following the Dharma and the power of the adept's discipline are illustrated.

Even fire is powerless against words redolent of truth. One should therefore make a practice of speaking truth.

According to tradition, the Bodhisattva [the future Buddha] was once born as a young quail in the jungle. Some nights after hatching, his tender wings had still to develop, and he was so puny that all the separate parts of his body were clearly discernible. His parents had taken pains to build a nest in a bush well hidden by deep grass. Here he lived together with his numerous siblings. But even in this state he had not lost his sense of what is right, and he was unwilling to eat the living creatures that his parents offered him. Instead he kept himself alive on millet, banyan figs, and other such food as they brought. As a result of this coarse and inadequate diet, his body did not fill out and his wings did not develop properly, while the other little quails, who ate whatever they were given, grew strong and fully fledged. For it is a fact that he who eats anything, without worrying about right or wrong, is happy and prospers, while he who wants to live in harmony with nature and is therefore careful about what he eats has a hard time in this world. (Moreover, the Lord said: "For the shameless crow who is aggressive, bold, and not fastidious, life is easy, though tainted. But for the man who has a sense of shame, who desires only what is pure, who is retiring, diffident, and honest, life on earth is beset with difficulties.)

While they were living like this, a huge forest fire broke out not very far away. The noise it

attaining liberation. It taught that the Buddha had not (as the Theravāda said) disappeared into nirvāṇa but that he could still be contacted in prayer, meditation, and visions. As it developed, Mahāyāna divided into many lineages that can be broadly grouped into two: central Asian forms based on Tibetan texts and East Asian forms based on Chinese texts. Different Mahāyāna schools emphasized mysticism, faith in Buddhas and bodhisattvas, and devotion.

THE BUDDHA

One of the keys to Buddhism's great success during this period was the appeal of the mythology and rituals associated with the Buddha. The Buddha came to seem bigger than life, a man who had both discovered and established the true religion, the great being ***(mahāpurusha)*** who had both attained and transcended the *made was terrifying and incessant; smoke spread in thick clouds, and the advancing line of flames showered sparks. It caused havoc in the depths of the forest and terrified the animals who lived there. Tossed by the wind, its flames outspread like arms, leaping and roaring, with smoky hair wildly disheveled, it seemed to be performing some intricate dance. The animals panicked, and the grass, swaying under the impact of the violent wind, seemed to be fleeing in terror. But the fire pounced on it in fury and scorched it with a shower of glittering sparks. Whole flocks of birds took alarm and flew away in terror. Wild beasts ran around in circles, stricken with panic. Thick smoke enveloped everything, and with the hoarse crackle of flames the forest seemed to be roaring aloud in pain.*

Goaded on by the sharp wind, the fire gradually penetrated the jungle and reached close to the nest. Immediately the young quails, with shrill, discordant shrieks of terror, flew up, without a thought for each other. But the Bodhisattva made no attempt to follow them: his body was too frail, and he was not fully fledged. Yet the Great Being, sure of his own powers, remained unruffled. As the fire approached impetuously, he politely addressed it as follows: "My feet hardly deserve the name of feet, and my wings have not grown. Also, my parents, in awe of you, have taken flight. I have nothing suitable to offer you as a guest. So, Fire, it would be best if you turned back from this spot." This, the plainest truth, was what the Great Being said. And the fire, though fanned by the wind and raging amid deadwood and thickets of parched grass, immediately died down: faced with these words of his, it was as though it had come to a swollen river. To this day, a forest fire, however much its blaze is stirred up by the wind, shrinks back—like a many-headed snake charmed by a spell—smothers its darting flames, and dies down altogether when it reaches that famous spot in the Himalayas.

What, then, does this story illustrate? The saying goes that just as the billowy ocean, with its waves like the hoods of serpents, cannot break its bounds, just as the seeker of the spirit cannot disregard the discipline prescribed by a great sage—so even fire cannot neglect the command of those for whom truth lies at the core of existence. Therefore one should never desert truth.

So, then—even fire is powerless against words redolent of truth. One should therefore make a practice of speaking truth.

Source: Peter Khoroche, *Once the Buddha Was a Monkey* (Chicago: University of Chicago Press, 1989).

qualities associated with universal kingship on the one hand and those of a great **yogī** on the other. What is more, he was perceived as a preeminent exemplar of compassion: merely remembering him or making a pilgrimage to some place associated with him—a stūpa, a reliquary, a site where his footprints were carved in stone—could inspire his devotees and speed them along the path to a better life and ultimately to nirvāṇa.

The stories that were told about the Buddha included not only accounts of his final life as Gautama but also stories, called **Jātakas**, or birth stories of acts he supposedly performed in his previous lives (see the accompanying box, "The Young Quail Jātaka"). Some of the Jātakas are presented as sermons attributed to the Buddha in which he illustrates a point about the effects of karma. Most are folkloric tales in which the future Buddha appears as an animal, a human being, or—very occasionally—a god. Many stories recount how the Buddha cultivated certain virtues, though in many cases the doctrinal points are difficult to discern.

Already by the second century B.C.E., certain Jātakas were being iconographically represented on the great stūpas that were being constructed at the time. By the beginning of the Common Era, collections of Jātaka stories had begun to appear. In one, the *Cariya Pitaka,* a set of relatively short Jātakas are associated with the cultivation of the ten virtues or perfections, held to be characteristic of the Buddha in his final life as Gautama. In certain areas, particularly in northwestern India, individual Jātakas were associated with particular geographic sites where the events that they recount were supposedly performed. Thus the land itself was transformed into a collection of the future Buddha's "traces" and virtues.

As their mythology expanded, Buddhists developed new kinds of visual symbols. For the first five centuries Buddhists did not sculpt images of the Buddha. He was sometimes represented by a relic, an empty throne, a footprint, a stūpa, or some other aniconic symbol. Figurative images, as far as we know, were never used.

Around the beginning of the Common Era, however, for reasons that are not yet clear, images of the Buddha began to appear. These sculptures and paintings portrayed the Buddha as a *mahāpurusha.* He is often depicted as possessing the 32 bodily signs that the Indian tradition identified with the attainment of universal sovereignty. He is shown in a variety of poses and situations, but most often in the midst of his enlightenment experience.

Once the practice of making images and representations began, it very quickly spread throughout the Buddhist world in India and beyond. Even before these iconic representations appeared, Buddhist sculpture and art had begun to play an important role in the life of the Buddhist community, for example, at the sites of the great stūpas that were built during the second and first centuries B.C.E. However, the iconic representations of the Buddha added a new dimension that became central to all later Buddhist traditions. These images taught the often illiterate Buddhists about events in the life of the Buddha. They also came to play a central role in the rituals (pūjā) in and through which the Buddha was venerated. Buddha images were not merely seen as his representations but were believed to make him spiritually present for members of the community.

Ritually, these images came to be used in meditational practices that involved the remembrance and visualization of the Buddha and in devotional practices of veneration of the Buddha. Thus with these sculptures and icons as aids, Buddhism developed its own forms of meditation and worship that enabled it to compete with Hinduism's newly developed theistic forms of meditation and devotion.

Theravāda and Mahāyāna Attitudes toward the Buddha

As Buddhism developed into the two streams that would become Theravāda and Mahāyāna, rival teachings evolved concerning the number of the Buddhas and whether or not they could be contacted in worship and meditation.

Broadly, Theravādins maintained that although there have been many Buddhas in the past and there will be many in the future, only one Buddha appears at a time, and he appears only in the human realm. Having restored and communicated the Dharma, he then disappears into nirvāṇa. Although he can subsequently be *imagined* as present, he can only be contacted through the Dharma and the Saṅgha. Thus, while not worshiping him as actually present, Theravādins concentrated on Gautama, the historical Buddha, whom they remembered in meditation.

Mahāyāna teachers maintained that the departure of the Buddha into nirvāṇa was an expedient means *(upāya)* to assist those who would be paralyzed with fear if they thought that it was necessary to remain in saṃsāra until all beings had been liberated. In fact, said the third-century Lotus Sūtra, not only do Buddhas continue to exist after their apparent deaths, but they have always existed and have always been enlightened. Their becoming Buddhas is a show, an expedient means to inspire unenlightened beings to effort. Many Mahāyāna sūtras also spoke of countless numbers of Buddhas in other worlds and even in the specks of dust of this world. As a consequence, Mahāyānists taught that all Buddhas could be contacted in meditative visualization and in the worship of their properly consecrated images.

One striking result of these new thoughts was that

Around the beginning of the Common Era, Buddhist sculpture and art began to play an important role in the life of the Buddhist community. As sculpture, paintings, and stained glass have been used in many religions and many cultures, reliefs at the great stupas were used to teach people about events in the life of Buddha. Dating from the eighth century C.E., the Borobodur temple in Java includes miles of temple carvings such as those shown here depicting the life history of Buddha. (The Bettmann Archive)

Śākyamuni Buddha, although he always remained important, ceased being central to Mahāyānists. Replacing him, a whole pantheon of Buddhas and bodhisattvas gradually developed. In some contexts these Buddhas and bodhisattvas (some of which seem to have been deities absorbed from other traditions) were organized in a systematic pattern. For example, many Mahāyānists recognized a group of five particular Buddhas, called Dhyāni Buddhas. In this particular formulation—which appears in many sculptures and paintings—one Buddha occupies the cosmic center (Vairocana), one the eastern quarter (Akśobhya), one the southern quarter (Ratnasambhava), one the western quarter (Amitābha), and the fifth the northern quarter (Amoghasiddhi).

In other contexts, particular Buddhas or bodhisattvas emerged as central, becoming quasi-divine figures who were the focal point for particular forms of devotion. One of the earliest examples of this sort was the Buddha Amitābha, who became the focal point of a cult of meditative devotion and visualization. Amitābha, whose name means "immeasurable radiance" or "unlimited light," first appeared around 100 C.E. Faith in Amitābha promised rebirth in a "pure land" that could lead directly to the attainment of release. The bodhisattva Avalokiteśvara ("one who looks down"), who first appeared in the third century, became the embodiment of the Buddhist virtue of compassion and as such a source of comfort and support for many Mahāyāna devotees.

DHARMA

During the post-Aśokan period the earlier collections of sūtras and the Vinaya were extended, more systematic texts were developed, and new items were incorporated. By the beginning of the Common Era the older "texts" that had been transmitted orally and the new texts that were being composed were written down, usually in Sanskrit. Very soon writing came to play a central role in the preservation and dissemination of Buddhist teaching.

Conservative Doctrines: Abhidharma

Conservative Buddhism developed the earliest explanatory or philosophical school, called **Abhidharma** ("advanced Dharma"). This seems to have begun with the attempt to classify the elements of the personality as observed in meditation.

What we perceive as a person initially seems a unity, an inherently existing being. Closer inspection reveals that a person is composed of at least two very different elements—one that is directly evident to the senses and one that can only be inferred on the basis of the sensory data. That which is directly evident is called *rūpa* by Abhidharma; it is broadly similar to what English refers to by the word *matter* or, better, *materiality*. But as a living being a person is clearly more than mere matter. The intangible element, the existence of which can only be inferred, the Abhidharma calls *nāma,* literally "name"; *nāma* is similar to what is called the *mind* or *mentality* in English. On even closer inspection, *nāma* can itself be divided into four groups: sensory input, perceptual categories, habitual reactions, and self-awareness. Together with *nāma,* these four are identified as the five "clusters" *(skandha)* mentioned in Chapter 9. By a similar meditational analysis, Abhidharma identifies 12 bases of sense *(āyatana)*—including the eye and things seen, the body surface and tangible objects, and the mind and cognizable items or *dharmas*—and 18 fields of operation of sense *(dhātu)*—such as the visual, olfactory, and mental fields. The groups of *skandhas, āyatanas,* and *dhātus,* known as *lists,* first suggested around the time of Aśoka, formed the basis of all later schools of Abhidharma, which proposed longer and more detailed lists of elements. Two main schools of Abhidharma survive: the Theravāda school, still employed as a living system; and the Sarvāstivāda school, whose texts, extant only in Tibetan and Chinese, are used by the Mahāyāna for preliminary training in what it calls Hīnayāna.

The intent of the Abhidharma is to provide a kind of owner's manual for the body-mind. Like all such manuals, it is boring and irrelevant when read as literature, but it comes into its own when put to practical meditative use. By understanding and clearly identifying the elements that create and sustain saṃsāra, saṃsāra can be deconstructed and escaped.

Mahāyāna Doctrines: Mādhyamika and Yogācāra

Mahāyāna developed its own sūtras and, based on them, two main explanatory schools, Mādhyamika and Yogācāra. The Mādhyamika school is based on a group of sūtras called *The Perfection of Wisdom.* The oldest text, "The Perfection of Wisdom in Eight Thousand Lines" (c. 100 B.C.E.–100 C.E.), was first subjected to considerable expansion between 100 and 300 C.E. and then, over the next two centuries, to reduction into summaries or "epitomes." The sūtras are sometimes explicitly said to have been spoken by disciples rather than by the Buddha, but adherents regarded them as reliable because the disciples have realized the true nature of the Dharma, so that what the Buddha's disciples teach can be considered as the work of Tathagata, the Buddha himself.

The two best-known sūtras of the *Perfection of Wisdom* group are the Diamond Sūtra and the Heart Sūtra. The Diamond Sūtra, "The Sūtra on the Perfection of Wisdom That Cuts [Ignorance] like a Diamond or Thunderbolt," is a dialogue between Śākyamuni Buddha and his disciple Subhuti that initially sounds more like a dialogue between schizophrenics, for example:

> The Lord [Buddha] continued: "What do you think, Subhuti, can the Tathagata be seen by the possession of his marks?"—Subhuti replied: "No indeed, O Lord. And why? What has been taught by the Tathagata as the possession of marks, that is truly the possession of no-marks." The Lord said: "Wherever there is possession of marks, there is fraud, wherever there is no-possession of no-marks, there is no fraud. Hence the Tathagata is to be seen from no-marks as marks."[1]

The Heart Sūtra, literally "The Sūtra on the Heart of the Perfection of Wisdom," is even more curious. It says that reality is emptiness and that

> in emptiness there is no form, nor feeling, nor perception, nor impulse, nor consciousness; No eye, ear, nose, tongue, body, mind; No forms, sounds, smells, tastes, touchables or objects of mind; No sight-organ element, and so forth, until we come to: No mind-consciousness element.[2]

That is, everything in the Abhidharma lists is nonexistent—rather, it exists, but it does not *ultimately* exist.

These curious *Perfection of Wisdom* texts, which began the movement that became known as the Mahāyāna, were explicitly a protest against what the Mahāyānists regarded as the mistakes of Conservative Buddhism. While accepting the same basic doctrines such as the Four Noble Truths and the doctrines of *pratītya samutpāda* (interdependent arising) and anātman (no self), the *Perfection of Wisdom* writers felt that the Abhidharmists had taken themselves too seriously. Instead of regarding their dharma lists as operational and therapeutic, the Abhidharmists had taken them as absolutes and had hardened them into dogma. Thus, the Mahāyānists claimed, complete liberation was no longer possible through the Abhidharma.* *The Perfection of Wisdom* articulated what the Mahāyānists regarded as the Buddha's original teaching: all entities, whether whole beings or single dharmas, are empty of inherent existence.

This emptiness *(śūnyata),* which can also be called openness or transparency, is stated in *The Perfection of Wisdom* and is argued for in the Mādhyamika school, whose foundation is attributed to Nāgārjuna, a teacher who probably lived in South India in the first century C.E. Nāgārjuna's most frequently employed argument is from absurdity: followed through to its logical conclusion, any view of reality that is taken as absolute, as the one and only view of reality, has absurd consequences and must therefore be abandoned. Only emptiness, he claimed, which was not itself a view but the "purgative" of views, did not result in absurd conclusions. It followed, then, that even the distinction between saṃsāra and nirvāṇa was empty and could not be held to absolutely. Hence reality as it is, the here and now, opened up to liberation, and dogma evaporated.

Whereas the Mādhyamika school focused on logic, dialectic, and debate, the Yogācāra school was more concerned with the nature of perception, which it examined in meditation. Begun in the fourth century C.E. by the brothers Asaṅga and Vasubandhu, Yogācāra was based on the Saṃdhinirmocana Sūtra, "The Sūtra That Unties the Knots." Although it seized on different issues than the Mādhyamika, Yogācāra came to a similar conclusion: reality is empty of inherent existence. Its proof, however, was not logical but experiential: when subject and object are examined closely, with meditative insight, they are seen to have no *absolute* distinction.

While accepting the operational existence of things, Mādhyamika and Yogācāra thinkers both denied the absolute existence of things. The denial of an absolute distinction is called *nonduality*. However, this denial is only a denial: it is not an implied affirmation of the opposite proposition, monism, or "all is one." But it is nothing more than a denial of duality—it is not the denial of everything; it is not nihilism.

SAṄGHA AND COMMUNITY

Taking advantage of the sponsorship of various imperial dynasties during the seven to eight centuries of the post-Aśokan period, Buddhism expanded enormously, both geographically and socially: it established itself not only throughout India but also through much of Asia, not just among the elite but at all strata of the populace.

Forest monks (and perhaps nuns, about whom there is virtually no information) continued to play an important role in the structure and dynamics of Indian Buddhism. Their presence and influence are attested in a variety of texts, as is the awe in which they were often held by other Buddhists. Many of these forest monks were charismatic figures who were believed to have reached high levels of meditational and mystical attainment and to be able to exercise various magical powers. Some monks seem to have operated quite independently of any organized group; others were more closely associated with particular segments of the monastic community. Another group seems to have

*Defenders of Theravādin Abhidharma have responded that it remained operational and did not exhibit the hardening that the Mahāyānists pejoratively attributed to it.

played an important role in the loosely organized communities known as **bodhisattva-gaṇas** ("congregations of future Buddhas") that grew up around certain stūpas.

There were also more settled monastic orders. Both textual and archaeological data indicate that during the post-Aśokan period, monasteries all across the subcontinent proliferated in both towns and countryside, especially along the principal trade routes, where they also served as hostels. Endowing a monastery was one way in which a king or a wealthy person could show devotion and generosity. Some of these monasteries were large, well-endowed establishments that housed substantial monastic populations. Most monasteries were constructed in spacious aboveground compounds. But there were also large monastic complexes—for example, the well-preserved one at Ajantā in central India—located in extensive networks of natural caves. In addition to the major monasteries, there were other smaller monastic complexes of various types.

All Buddhist monasteries of this period provided living quarters for monks and, in a few cases at least, nuns. They usually had a central hall in which the most sacred ceremonies were performed, often in front of some symbol—typically one or more images—of the Buddha or bodhisattvas. Many monasteries were decorated with sophisticated artworks expressing Buddhist devotion. Monasteries often also featured, in a more or less dominant position, a stūpa containing a relic or other "trace" of the Buddha that served as another center for veneration and for making offerings.

The life style in the various monasteries differed greatly. Some establishments possessed great wealth; others were quite modest. Some of the great houses were centers of interactions with monks from all of the Indian subcontinent and other parts of Asia; in others the focus was much more local. Some monasteries strongly emphasized study, meditation, and devotion, whereas in others the monks were more deeply involved in practical affairs. In some the rules of the Vinaya were rigorously followed; in others the regimen was much more lax. But in spite of (or perhaps because of) this diversity, the Buddhist monastic tradition throughout this entire period displayed a remarkable vitality and exerted an extraordinary influence on people of all social levels.

During the post-Aśokan period, settled monastic orders began to appear. In at least some cases, living quarters for nuns existed as well, though little information exists today regarding them. Here modern Chinese nuns are seen at the Nizhong Buddhist Theological Institute in the Sichuan Province. (Eastfoto)

The monasteries that concentrated on study were somewhat like universities, in which one of the main occupations was public debate in order to establish what the Buddha really said and what he really meant. It was this activity that first led to the compilations of authoritative texts and later served as the seedbed of the Mahāyāna as it split off from Conservative Buddhism.

The great flourishing of Buddhist monasticism during the post-Aśokan era was necessarily both the cause and the effect of a rapid expansion of the lay community as well. Buddhism became a favored religion among the Indian rulers and royal courts of the period. Following their Aśokan experience, Buddhists developed their early notions of Buddhist kingship, and a great many Indian monarchs of the time—especially those who had imperial aspirations—identified with one or more of Buddhism's idealized images of royalty. These included the king as Dharmarājan (one who ruled in accordance with Dharma), the king as Cakravartin (a universal sovereign who is a kind of secular counterpart of the Buddha), and the king as the successor of Aśoka, who was taken to have ruled a great Indian empire in accord with dharmic principles. Some kings were even celebrated as mahāpurushas, identified by means of symbolic images and ritual actions as bodhisattvas or even Buddhas.

In addition to kings, queens, and courtiers, many other members of the Indian elite supported the Buddhist cause. These included rich and powerful merchants who, in addition to whatever religious piety they may have had, maintained close business connections with the network of monasteries that extended along the great national and international trade routes. At the same time, other segments of the population also became increasingly involved. In the cities and the villages, many ordinary citizens became members of the Buddhist laity, who supported Buddhist monks and took part in other forms of Buddhist practice. These ordinary people adopted (and adapted) various Buddhist activities, including calendric celebrations, pilgrimages, simple devotional practices, merit rituals for themselves and their ancestors, and exorcistic rites.

Conservative and Mahāyāna Communities

The story of the development of the Buddhist community in the post-Aśokan era is a story of its rapid expansion at various levels. But it is also a story of the development of the community's diverging religious ideals and diverging opinions about the distinctions between the monks and nuns of the Saṅgha and the lay community. These are some of the key issues over which the Theravāda and Mahāyāna traditions split.

The origins of this split are obscure and controversial. From one point of view, the division probably had at least some roots in the differences between two groups that can be identified in earlier Buddhism. Hīnayāna developed in the community centered around the earliest Buddhist monasteries. Mahāyāna evolved from diverse other sources, one of which was the communities of bodhisattva-gaṇas that had grown up around the stūpas. These bodhisattva-gaṇas, which included both forest monks and lay supporters, eventually became organized into monasteries in a process much like the one that had taken place in the very earliest phase of Buddhist history. As this process gained momentum, the Mahāyāna tradition emerged as a serious competitor to the Conservative path.

Conservative Buddhist communities In Conservative Buddhism, as still today in Theravāda, the lay people materially supported the monastics by donating the so-called Four Requisites—food, clothing, shelter, and medicine. In return the monastics, now freed from the need to provide for the present life, concentrated on what pertained to future lives and eventual liberation: study and meditation. Because only the monks and nuns had the time and discipline to meditate and study in earnest, they came to be regarded as spiritually preeminent. As a result, a sharp distinction was made between the monks and nuns of the Saṅgha and the laity.

The possibility of a layperson's gaining nirvāṇa, of course, was not completely denied. Indeed, many members of the Buddhist laity (including Buddhist kings) were considered to hold high positions in the soteriological hierarchy. But the presumption was that although lay people might be able to reach final enlightenment, it was extremely unlikely. Indeed, if they did, one text said, they would die within the week unless they entered the monastic order.

Mahāyāna communities Against the Theravādins' espousal of the privileged status of the monastics, Mahāyānists proposed that the true practice of Buddhism was not a matter of one's ordination into the Saṅgha but of one's attitude. If the heart of Buddhism was compassion, as the Conservatives said, then, the Mahāyānists claimed, whoever had the greatest compassion was the greatest practitioner. And, they went on, compassion can be practiced in any state of life whatever: one had only to repeat a vow that whatever one is about to do is being done with the motive of liberating all beings from all suffering.

A person who takes such a vow the Mahāyānists called a bodhisattva. This was a term used by the Conservatives for Śākyamuni Buddha in his previous lives and for the newly developed objects of devotion such as Amitābha. The Mahāyānists broadened it to

THE MAHĀYĀNIST "THOUGHT OF ENLIGHTENMENT"

Like all the great religions of the world, Buddhism has produced a variety of inspirational works. Śāntideva, a Mādhyamika philosopher of the early eighth century, extolled the religious life of the Mahāyāna in a famous devotional poem called *Entering the Path of Enlightenment.* After praising the thought of enlightenment *(bodhicitta),* Śāntideva confesses the transgressions that have, in the past, kept him in bondage to the phenomenal world of impermanence and suffering. He then launches into a great affirmation of compassion and of the central element in life for all Mahāyāna followers, the act of *bodhicitta-parigraha,* or grasping the thought of enlightenment.

I rejoice in exultation at the goodness, and at the cessation and destruction of sorrow, wrought by all beings. May those who sorrow achieve joy!

I rejoice at the release of embodied beings from the sorrowful wheel of rebirth. I rejoice at the Bodhisattvahood and at the Buddhahood of those who have attained salvation.

I rejoice at the Oceans of Determination (cittotpāda), *the Bearers of Happiness to all beings, the Vehicles of Advantage for all beings, and those who teach.*

With folded hands, I beseech the perfect Buddhas in all places: May they cause the light of the Dharma to shine upon those who, because of confusion, have fallen into sorrow. . . .

Having done all this, let me also be a cause of abatement, by means of whatever good I have achieved, for all of the sorrow of all creatures.

I am medicine for the sick. May I be their physician and their servant, until sickness does not arise again.

With rains of food and drink may I dispel the anguish of hunger and thirst. In the famine of the intermediary aeons between the world cycles (antarakalpa) *may I be food and drink; and may I be an imperishable treasury for needy beings. May I stand in their presence in order to do what is beneficial in every possible way. . . .*

The abandonment of all is Nirvāṇa, and my mind (manas) *seeks Nirvāṇa. If all is to be sacrificed by me, it is best that it be given to beings.*

I deliver this body to the pleasure of all creatures. May they strike! May they revile! May they cover it constantly with refuse!

May they play with my body! May they laugh! And may they be amused! I have given my body to them. What do I care about its misfortune?

May they do whatever deeds bring pleasure to them, but let there never be any misfortune because of having relied on me.

include anyone—monastic or layperson—who was earnestly seeking enlightenment *for the sake of others.* They accused the Conservatives, especially the monastics, of seeking enlightenment for themselves alone.

Connected to this new attitude, the bodhisattva path was made more accessible to the ordinary layperson as well as to the monk and nun (see the accompanying box). New forms of meditation and visualization were developed that allowed practitioners to achieve a special kind of communion with the great Buddhas and bodhisattvas. New rituals were developed in which a man or woman would enter the Mahāyāna path by taking the bodhisattva vows. New devotional practices arose, including praising the Buddha, offering

If their opinion regarding me should be either irritable or pleasant, let it nonetheless be their perpetual means to the complete fulfillment of every aim.

Those who wrong me, and those who accuse me falsely, and those who mock, and others: May they all be sharers in Enlightenment.

I would be a protector for those without protection, a leader for those who journey, and a boat, a bridge, a passage for those desiring the further shore.

For all creatures, I would be a lantern for those desiring a lantern, I would be a bed for those desiring a bed, I would be a slave for those desiring a slave. . . .

So may I be, in various ways, the means of sustenance for the living beings occupying space, for as long a time as all are not satisfied.

As the ancient Buddhas seized the Thought of Enlightenment, and in like manner they followed regularly on the path of Bodhisattva instruction;

Thus also do I cause the Thought of Enlightenment to arise for the welfare of the world, and thus shall I practice these instructions in proper order.

The wise man, having considered serenely the Thought of Enlightenment, should rejoice, for the sake of its growth and its well-being, in the thought:

Today my birth is completed, my human nature is most appropriate; today I have been born into the Buddha-family and I am now a Buddha-son.

It is now for me to behave according to the customary behavior of one's own family, in order that there may be no stain put upon that spotless family.

As a blind man may obtain a jewel in a heap of dust, so, somehow, this Thought of Enlightenment has arisen even within me.

This elixir has originated for the destruction of death in the world. It is the imperishable treasure which alleviates the world's poverty.

It is the uttermost medicine, the abatement of the world's disease. It is a tree of rest for the wearied world journeying on the road of being.

When crossing over hard places, it is the universal bridge for all travelers. It is the risen moon of mind (citta), *the soothing of the world's hot passion* (kleśa).

It is a great sun dispelling the darkness of the world's ignorance. It is fresh butter, surging up from the churning of the milk of the true Dharma.

For the caravan of humanity, moving along the road of being, hungering for the enjoyment of happiness, this happiness banquet is prepared for the complete refreshening of every being who comes to it.

Now I invite the world to Buddhahood, and, incidentally, to happiness. May gods, anti-gods (asuras), *and others, truly rejoice in the presence of all the Protectors.*

Source: Quoted in Marion Matics, *Entering the Path of Enlightenment* (New York: Macmillan, 1970), pp. 153–156.

flowers, confessing transgressions, and cultivating sympathetic delight in the merits of the Buddhas and bodhisattvas. These practices paralleled the Hindu devotional pūjās to their deities.

The new emphasis on the availability of the bodhisattva path to anyone was closely correlated with a new notion of the community: Mahāyānists affirmed a greater parity between the lives of the monk and nun and the layperson. Yet Mahāyānists did not abandon monasticism, and monasteries and temples continued to be the center around which the layperson's life revolved. Indeed, in practice there was often very little difference between Mahāyānists and Conservatives in regard to the relationship between monastics and laity.

High attainment and final liberation, however, were attributed more often to nonmonastic Mahāyāna practitioners.

BUDDHISM AND SOCIETY IN CLASSICAL INDIA

By the end of the post-Aśokan period (c. 550 C.E.), Buddhism had become a major force in Indian life. From one vantage point it was an integral component in the thriving Sanskritic civilization that included other religious components, such as post-Vedic Hinduism. But Buddhism had also developed its own distinctive character.

A number of the large, well-endowed monasteries became cultural institutions of the highest order. They maintained the basic orientation and practices of traditional Buddhist monasticism, but as time went on they became major centers of Indian learning and culture. In many cases these large complexes took on the form of monastic universities, and as such they assumed a primary responsibility for the preservation and transmission of not only the Buddhist tradition but also other aspects of Indian culture: brāhmanic and Hindu approaches and materials as well as the various arts and sciences dealing with such matters as logic, literary studies, astronomy, astrology, and medicine.

Also at the level of the elite, many Indian rulers, both at major centers of imperial power and in more distant parts of the country, performed Buddhist rituals that impressed their subjects and involved many of them. The rituals that these rulers sponsored often included the donation of expensive gifts to Buddhist monasteries and individual monks. By making these gifts, the rulers were able to confirm the legitimacy of their claim to authority; to gain Buddhist-style merit, which enhanced their social prestige; and—what is sometimes forgotten—to support Buddhist institutions and individuals who played an essential role in maintaining and advancing the great Sanskritic traditions of knowledge and culture.

By the end of this period, Buddhists had also established their tradition as a major religiocultural force in the Indian countryside. Many stories were told in which the Buddha chastens or converts local deities such as *yaksas* (often associated with sacred groves) and *nāgas* (serpentlike deities who served as guardian spirits protecting local regions). Other Buddhist stories, including Jātakas, were told in ways that reflected common folkloric themes and often merged with local traditions.

Once Buddhism was established, the village monks, many of whom had been trained in the larger monasteries and monastic universities, became both the spiritual guides for their followers and a primary channel of mediation between Buddhist-oriented Pan-Indian culture and the traditions of local, largely agrarian villages. The Buddha (often represented by an image or a relic that was the focus of a local myth), along with deities supposedly converted to his cause, were venerated at village shrines. The Dharma was reinterpreted by recasting it in terms of the mythology and folklore of this new rural constituency. Similarly, Buddhist rituals involving both monastics and the laity were adapted to suit the traditions and rhythms of the peasantry.

THE APOGEE AND DECLINE OF INDIAN BUDDHISM

As we have seen, Buddhism in the post-Aśokan period expanded in adherents, doctrine, and influence. In the next era, the so-called medieval period in India (c. sixth to eleventh centuries), this pattern changes: Buddhism deteriorates in India yet, paradoxically, achieves some of its most sophisticated and important doctrines, rituals, and techniques, notably in Mahāyāna and in a newly developed "vehicle," Vajrayāna Buddhism. Although these developments were to have great significance for the rest of Asia, they could not staunch the ebbing of Buddhism's lifeblood in India, and after around 1300 Buddhism survived there no longer.

We can see early evidence of Buddhism's decline in the sixth-century destruction of northwestern Buddhist monasteries by Hun invaders. We can also see signs of decline in southern India, where as early as the seventh century a militant and often explicitly anti-Buddhist Hindu Śaivism began to surge to the fore and to gain the support of various southern dynasties. In the centuries that followed, Buddhism's decline continued in these areas and spread to other parts of India as well.

However, in the northeast, the region where Buddhism had originated and where the imperial centers of the Mauryan and Gupta dynasties had been located, the faith continued to flourish for another 500 years. It received strong royal support, first from Harsha Vardhana (c. 605–647), who was able to extend his rule over much of northern India, and then from successive members of the Pāla dynasty, who ruled over most of Bihar and Bengal from 750 until about 1200. With this protection and support, Buddhism displayed a remarkable degree of vitality and creativity. It was here, in the northeast, that Buddhism in India experienced its greatest achievements between the sixth and eleventh centuries.

CONSERVATIVE, MAHĀYĀNA, AND VAJRAYĀNA BUDDHISM

During the medieval period the Conservative tradition continued to hold the loyalty of many Buddhists. Although Theravāda probably remained the majority group, there is little evidence that its leaders offered particularly creative adaptations to the changing circumstances.

From the sixth century on, the dynamism had shifted to other segments of the Indian Saṅgha. The Mahāyānists, for example, continued to develop their understanding of the Buddha, their interpretations of the Dharma, and their structures of communal life. Their pantheon of Buddhas and bodhisattvas was continually extended through both internal developments and an ongoing interaction with classical Hinduism and local traditions. Kings during this period sponsored many debates between Hindus and Buddhists, which further encouraged the development of doctrines and practices. Out of such a dynamic cauldron, Mahāyāna teachings were continually refined and extended. For example, the Mahāyānists expanded their notions of the bodhisattva path to an increasing variety of meditational levels. Śāntideva (early eighth century), for example, described some 15 stages of meditational attainment; in other formulations there were even more. Monasteries also developed new structures and meditation procedures to bolster these new levels of attainment.

The most dynamic and creative developments within Indian Buddhism, however, first emerged not in Mahāyāna monasteries but among the nonmonastic male and female ascetics on the fringes of the Buddhist community. They—or their idealized adepts—came to be known as **siddhas** and began to appear in the north and east of India around the eighth century. From their teachings emerged the third major strand, **Vajrayāna** Buddhism. Its distinctive new character can be seen in the following story.

Sometime during the late eighth century there lived in Orissa, in the east of the subcontinent, a rich brāhman named Saraha. By day he observed the commandments of orthodox Hinduism, but by night he was a Buddhist. And contrary to the rules of both religions, he drank alcohol. Brought to task for this, he plunged his hand into a vat of boiling oil, swearing, "If I am guilty, may my hand burn," and took it out unharmed. But his accusers did not believe him. So in one gulp, Saraha drank a bowl of molten copper. Still, people said, "He *does* drink alcohol!" So Saraha challenged someone to jump into a large tank of water with him, saying, "Whoever sinks is guilty." Saraha floated, and the accuser sank. "Even so," said the people, "he *does* drink alcohol!" However, the king, who had been watching this contest, said "If he has this kind of power, let him drink!"[3]

There are several features to be noted in the story, which is typical of accounts of siddhas.[4] First, by drinking alcohol, he breaks the fifth grave precept of Conservative Buddhism. Second, he breaks the fourth grave precept by lying about it. And third, he is unaffected not only by alcohol but also by boiling oil and molten copper. Consequently, he is recognized as having an unusual kind of power. This power is known as *siddhi,* "achievement," because of which he is called a *siddha.* Siddhis are recorded in many Hindu and Buddhist texts as an occasional by-product of high attainment, but in this case the siddha's consciousness was believed to have "penetrated the seeds of karmic manifestation and altered the usual process of illusory emanation at will."[5]

Vajrayāna Developments of Dharma

This feature of altering the illusion is the most important characteristic of the new form of Buddhism that the siddhas were developing, the vehicle that became known as the Mantrayāna ("mantra vehicle"),

Vajrayāna ("diamond vehicle"), or Tāntric Buddhism.

Because the practices of Vajrayāna are so distinctive, many people have thought of it as a third vehicle in addition to Theravāda and Mahāyāna, but because it differs only in its practices from the latter, it is more properly regarded as a variant of Mahāyāna. For example, Vajrayāna author Saraha wrote:

To a fool who squints
One lamp is as two;
Where seen and seer are not two, ah! the mind
Works on the thingness of them both.[6]

That is, a deluded mind perceives reality as absolutely divided into subject and object. Though subject and object are in fact nondual, a deluded mind reifies their inherent existence. Such a statement might be found in many Mahāyāna texts. The distinctiveness of Vajrayāna is that it advocates living in nonduality in the here and now, in this very body. Vajrayānists called other forms of Buddhism "Path Buddhism" and called their own teachings "Fruit Buddhism." In Path Buddhism one strives to become a Buddha. In Fruit Buddhism one *already is* a Buddha and so acts like one, with all the powers that a Buddha has, such as being unaffected by boiling oil and molten copper.

The teaching that one already is a Buddha might also be found in Mahāyāna writings. But according to Vajrayānists, Mahāyāna generally did not take this teaching seriously: it stated that one was *intrinsically* a Buddha but not *actually* a Buddha. Vajrayānists, however, tried to take seriously the teaching that one already is a Buddha, and maintained a nonduality between their intrinsic and actualized Buddha mind. Vajrayānists said that they worked from a "pure" perspective; that is, they saw reality purely, as the Buddhas see it. Since the rest of us do not see reality like this but live in the illusion of saṃsāra, the Vajrayānists described their path as the vehicle that stops, destroys, or cuts off the illusion we call ordinary reality.

Living Buddhas of Vajrayāna

Vajrayānists' avowals that one already is a Buddha and their emphasis on their siddhas led to a new ideal of religious attainment. In the Theravāda tradition the great models were the arhants, or fully perfected saints; to the Mahāyānists the great heroes were the bodhisattvas, who had postponed their own attainment of nirvāṇa in order to work for the salvation of all beings. In Vajrayāna a third kind of hero emerges, the siddha or guru (master), who had attained both freedom from bondage and magical domination over it. Unlike many Mahāyānists, who held that it would take many lifetimes to become a bodhisattva, Vajrayānists maintained that one could and should become a Buddha much faster. Practitioners with less spiritual maturity might require several additional rebirths—as many as 17, according to some texts. But for those who were more spiritually advanced, the possibility of attaining Buddhahood in this very life was real indeed.

This new affirmation of their religious adepts is also evident in the art of Vajrayāna, which is rich, even voluptuous. Myriads of saints in lush and complex realms were celebrated in vibrantly colorful art. This is seen especially in the Tibetan Vajrayānists' style of painting called *thangka* (Tibetan for "painted picture") in which the Buddhas and other realized beings appear in radiant bodies.

New Vajrayāna Practices

From the Vajrayānists' new perspective, nothing is seen as intrinsically bad, evil, or impure. This means that the passions themselves, which earlier Buddhism had vilified, were now seen as the manifestation of pure mind. In order to work with this new teaching, Vajrayānists developed new practices centering on visualization. First, drawing on general Mahāyāna meditative customs, the practitioner might be asked to visualize the compassionate energy of the Buddha mind as the bodhisattva Avalokiteśvara, seen as a calm, smiling youth. Then, if the teacher judges that the practitioner is ready, he or she is instructed in the visualization of Avalokiteśvara as a fierce, black, scowling, stamping, and roaring man-beast called Mahākāla, the "Great Dark One." If the meditation has been done correctly, the anger of Mahākāla will be found to have eradicated whatever was hindering the compassionate activity of the mind. Other passions may be tapped by visualizing other so-called wrathful deities.

It is at this level, of visualizing passions, that the famous "sexual yoga" was practiced. This is undoubtedly the most misunderstood part of Vajrayāna. It has nothing to do with sex for its own sake, which is, quite simply, saṃsāric involvement in the passions. And it usually has nothing to do with actual copulation. Most commonly, it is a meditation, done while sitting alone, in which compassion, visualized as male energy, and wisdom, visualized as female energy, are imaginatively perceived as uniting sexually. Their union is understood to represent their nonduality. Buddhist sexual yoga is substantially a manipulation of symbols in meditation, and in this respect it is similar to the sexual mysticism found, for example, in Vishṇavite Hinduism and in the bride mysticism of medieval Catholicism.

Two of the most distinctive features of Vajrayāna practice are the maṇḍala and the mantra.

Maṇḍala is a Sanskrit word that means "circle." In Vajrayāna, a **maṇḍala** is the dwelling, or palace, of a pure being such as a Buddha or a bodhisattva. When represented on a flat surface, a maṇḍala looks like a circle inside a square, divided diagonally into four segments. Such a representation, however, is only a plan or blueprint used as a teaching aid in the initiation into the liturgy of the maṇḍala. When visualized properly, it becomes a three-dimensional palace, a cube or sphere of such gigantic proportions that it overwhelms the calculating mind and is seen as the structure of the entire universe.

The **mantra** is understood in the Vajrayāna as a way of bringing out pure mind through speech. Most Buddhas and bodhisattvas have, according to Vajrayāna, their own *bīja-mantras* ("seed sounds"). For example, the bodhisattva Avalokiteśvara's bīja-mantra is *"Oṃ maṇi padme hūṃ."* These syllables are the manifestation in sound of the compassionate mind that manifests visually as the bodhisattva Avalokiteśvara. By repeating this expression over and over, Vajrayāna claims, the compassionate energy of one's Buddha mind is nourished.

Vajrayānists extended this understanding of the importance of sacred sounds. In certain circumstances the entire universe was seen—or better, heard—as a vast concatenation of sacred sounds and syllables. Furthermore, just as each of the various deities in the pantheon was believed to have its bīja-mantra, each of the psychic components within an individual was also associated with a particular bīja-mantra. Thus to know and manipulate the appropriate sounds makes it possible to bring the psychic as well as cosmic forces under control and to achieve the various levels of attainment.

The Vajrayāna Saṅgha

The various Vajrayāna masters, together with their disciplines, constituted the core of the fully developed Vajrayāna community. Some of these masters were forest monks who followed, in somewhat modified form, the rather unorthodox life style that had been characteristic of the early siddhas. Some combined more traditional monastic behavior patterns (including adherence to the Vinaya and the study of texts) with more specifically Vajrayāna patterns. These life styles were not mutually exclusive, and many Vajrayāna practitioners moved back and forth between the two.

Considerable evidence suggests that certain Vajrayāna masters were closely associated with the Pāla court in northeastern India (eighth to twelfth centuries), and these masters probably took the lead in developing Buddhist Tāntric liturgies that were specially designed for the use of kings. These included rituals performed in part for the purpose of enhancing the Buddhist status of the kings, perhaps even to consecrate them as bodhisattvas or living Buddhas. They also included rituals designed to protect the ruler and his kingdom against the intrusion of evil forces that might threaten their well-being.

There are also good reasons to suspect that Vajrayānists helped in maintaining the loyalty of the lay community. Both the religious and the intellectual attainments of the siddhas were well known, and their magical powers were widely respected. Many Western scholars have maintained that the Buddhist appropriation of Tāntric elements was a cause of the Buddhist loss of popular support in India. In fact, the new vitality that the Vajrayāna practitioners introduced into Indian Buddhism probably enabled it to retain popular support much longer than it would otherwise have done.

THE DECLINE OF BUDDHISM IN INDIA

We have observed that despite the great medieval efflorescence of Buddhism in the northeast, Indian Buddhism as a whole suffered a long series of devastating setbacks. By the eleventh century the decline of Buddhism that had already occurred elsewhere in India began to be seriously felt in the northeast as well. By the middle of the thirteenth century, Buddhism as a living religious and cultural force in India had ceased to exist.

Though scholars have debated the causes for this decline for many years, no adequate explanation has been put forward. However, it is possible to identify four factors that help to account for Buddhism's fate. These four factors were interrelated, though their relative importance varied from time to time and from region to region.

Socioeconomic considerations The first factor was associated with Buddhism's social stature. In its early years, Buddhism had the greatest appeal to people in the upper echelons of the social, political, and economic hierarchy. Even during its heyday, it was very much a high-culture tradition that received strong support from the political and economic elite. This does not mean that Buddhism cut itself off from the lower classes or failed to establish itself in the villages where the great majority of Indians lived. It does mean, however, that the penetration into the grassroots of society was not as extensive or as deep as the penetration achieved by Hinduism. Thus Buddhism was especially vulnerable to the forces of political and economic change.

Monks versus laity A second closely related factor in the decline of Buddhism in India was the development of a widening gap between the monastic communities and the lay populations with which they were supposedly associated. According to the Buddhist ideal, they were interdependent: the monks were to provide the religious ideal and dharmic teaching, and the lay community was to provide material support such as food, robes, and housing. However, as the monasteries became well-endowed, landowning institutions, the monks stopped needing to cultivate lay support; as a result, their day-to-day interactions with the people diminished.

Hinduism's vitality These internal characteristics and developments made the Buddhist communities vulnerable to challenges from without. The third important factor in the decline of Indian Buddhism was the increasing vitality (and in some cases the increasing militancy) of new and dynamic forms of post-Vedic Hinduism. The new theistic traditions of Vaishṇavism and Śaivism that began to take form during the centuries approaching the year 1000 shared, from that time forward, the support of Indian kings and the rest of the Indian elite. They took very deep root among virtually all other segments of the population as well.

With the passage of time, the Hindu traditions gained in strength, appropriating many aspects of Buddhist teaching and institutional life. For example, Śaṅkara, the great Hindu leader who lived in the ninth century, developed a Hindu philosophy that incorporated many Buddhist insights; he also played a major role in establishing a network of Hindu monasteries that followed the Buddhist model. In South India, Hindu traditions gained the upper hand before the millennium—well before any major incursions from outside forces.

Foreign invasions A fourth factor that played a crucial role in the demise of Buddhism in the north was invasion by foreign forces. Over a period of seven centuries, invasions into northern India gradually destroyed the political regimes and monastic institutions on which Buddhism had come to depend.

Already toward the end of the Gupta period, the invasions had begun with a first wave of Huns coming into the northwest from their earlier homelands in central Asia. Chinese pilgrims who subsequently visited the area reported widespread destruction of Buddhist monasteries. In the eighth century, Muslim Arabs arrived at the mouth of the Indus River and established a relatively benign Muslim regime in the northwest. Later, however, Muslim Turks arrived on the scene, and the process of destruction gained momentum. Gradually, the Turks extended their raids farther and farther to the east. By the end of the twelfth century, the famed Buddhist monastic university at Nālandā had been sacked and largely destroyed, and early in the thirteenth century, the great sister institution of Vikramaśīlā suffered a similar fate.

By the middle of the thirteenth century, Buddhism

in India was, except for a few pockets in eastern Bengal and South India, a thing of the past. In the very subcontinent where Buddhism had originated and come into its own as a great religion, the descendants of the Buddhist population were absorbed into the ranks of Hinduism and Islam. Only the monuments remained, and many of them were abandoned or transformed. For the Buddhist world that now extended across virtually all of Asia, the ancient center had collapsed.

NOTES

1 Edward Conze, trans., *Buddhist Wisdom Books* (London: Allen & Unwin, 1958–), p. 28.

2 Ibid., p. 89.

3 After Keith Dowman, *Masters of Mahāmudrā* (Albany: State University of New York Press, 1985), pp. 66–68.

4 See Herbert V. Gunther, trans., *The Royal Song of Saraha* (Berkeley, Calif.: Shambala, 1973).

5 Dowman, *Masters of Mahāmudrā,* p. 69.

6 Gunther, *Royal Song,* p. 63.

Buddhism

CHAPTER 11

Buddhism as a World Religion

BUDDHIST EXPANSION

The same missionary outreach that led to Buddhism's original growth and expansion within India carried the tradition into many other parts of Asia as well. The earliest known effort to introduce the Dharma beyond the Indian subcontinent took place during the reign of Emperor Aśoka in the third century B.C.E. According to the edicts and later chronicles, Aśoka sent Buddhist emissaries to the Himalayan regions in the north and northwest, to Suvannabhumi (the "Land of Gold") in the southeast, and to Sri Lanka in the far south. Buddhism soon took root both in the northwest and in Sri Lanka.

During the following centuries, Buddhism spread from northwestern India all along the central Asian trade routes that led to the cities of northwestern China. By the early centuries of the Common Era, Buddhist communities in central Asia and northern China were well established. By the sixth century, several Buddhist kingdoms were thriving in Southeast Asia along major trade routes, and Buddhism was spreading rapidly through China and entering Korea and Vietnam. Around that time Buddhism was also introduced into Japan, where it quickly put down roots and assumed an important role in Japanese life. It was established in Tibet by the year 800. Thus by the time that Buddhism died out in India in the thirteenth century, it had spread throughout virtually all of southeastern, central, and eastern Asia, where it has maintained a continuous presence ever since.

Patterns in the Spread of Buddhism

Without making absolute generalizations, we can note a definite pattern in Buddhism's spread. First, the central beliefs and modes of practice stayed close to what they were in India. Emphasis remained on the historical Buddha and a glorification of his life, and both the practice of relic veneration and the building and worshiping of stūpas continued. Monastic institutions were established in the new areas, modeled on their Indian counterparts.

Second, there was a close correlation between the Buddhist vehicle that was on the rise in India at the time of each phase of expansion and the tradition that ultimately became dominant in each new area. Thus when Buddhism was introduced into Sri Lanka and Southeast Asia, Indian Buddhism was basically Conservative, and the Theravāda form came to be dominant there. When Buddhism entered East Asia, Mahāyāna had come to the fore, and it continues to attract the greatest number of adherents in China, Korea, Vietnam, and Japan. Vajrayāna was beginning to emerge in India when Buddhism entered Tibet, and so that is the vehicle that became dominant there.

BUDDHISM IN "GREATER INDIA"

The history of Buddhism in Sri Lanka and Southeast Asia falls rather clearly into three periods. The first began with the introduction of Buddhism into Sri Lanka (and probably Southeast Asia as well) during or close to the reign of Emperor Aśoka. The Theravāda reform that took shape in the eleventh and twelfth centuries began the second period. The third phase occurred when British and French colonialism entered the picture in the nineteenth century.

During the first period, Sri Lanka and Southeast Asia were part of an area that some scholars have called "Greater India." Though this designation is not completely accurate, it does make it clear that many of the religious and political developments that took place in Sri Lanka and Southeast Asia were intimately linked with occurrences in India itself, especially specifically Buddhist developments.

Literary and archaeological evidence indicates that from the time of the Aśokan mission, Buddhism has had a more or less continuous history in Sri Lanka. According to much later Sinhalese (Sri Lankan) chronicles, the Sinhalese king was converted by Aśoka's son, and the famous Mahāvihāra monastery was established in the capital city of Anuradhapura. By the first century B.C.E., Buddhism had become an integral part of Sri Lankan life. A Sinhalese mythology soon developed that claimed that the Buddha and the Sinhalese kings shared a common lineage, that the Buddha had visited Sri Lanka and prepared the country for the reception of his religion, and that important relics of the Buddha (including the famous Tooth Relic) had miraculously come of their own volition from India to Sri Lanka. By the fourth or fifth century of the Common Era, Sinhalese texts were claiming that Sri Lanka was singled out to become the *Dhammadipa* ("island where the Dharma prevails").

Mythology developed claiming that the Buddha had visited Sri Lanka and that important relics of the Buddha had miraculously come of their own volition from India to Sri Lanka. Here, drummers parade before the temple housing the famous Buddha tooth relic in Kandy, Sri Lanka. (Ceylon [Sri Lanka] Tourist Board)

During the early centuries of the first millennium C.E., Conservative Buddhism was dominant in Sri Lanka, and it probably also retained more influence there than in most areas of the subcontinent itself. Mahāyāna traditions, however, became firmly established in the largest and most influential Buddhist monastery (Abhayagiri), and from at least the eighth century onward, Sri Lanka was a major center of Vajrayāna learning and practice.

In contrast to those in Sri Lanka, Buddhist kingdoms in lower Burma, in central Thailand, and at the tip of the Indochina peninsula were set up only in the Common Era. Archaeological evidence and reports by Chinese travelers suggest that Conservative traditions were the first to be established and that they persisted most strongly in Burma and Thailand. After about 500 C.E., the Mahāyāna and Vajrayāna traditions gained vigor in these areas and completely dominated Buddhist life between 500 and 1000 in Malaysia, Indonesia, and Cambodia.

GROWTH AND CONSOLIDATION OF THERAVĀDA TRADITIONS

Though the history of Buddhism in Greater India closely parallels the history of Buddhism in the subcontinent, distinctive new developments did take place. The most important occurrence was the growth and expansion, within the Conservative tradition, of a Theravāda

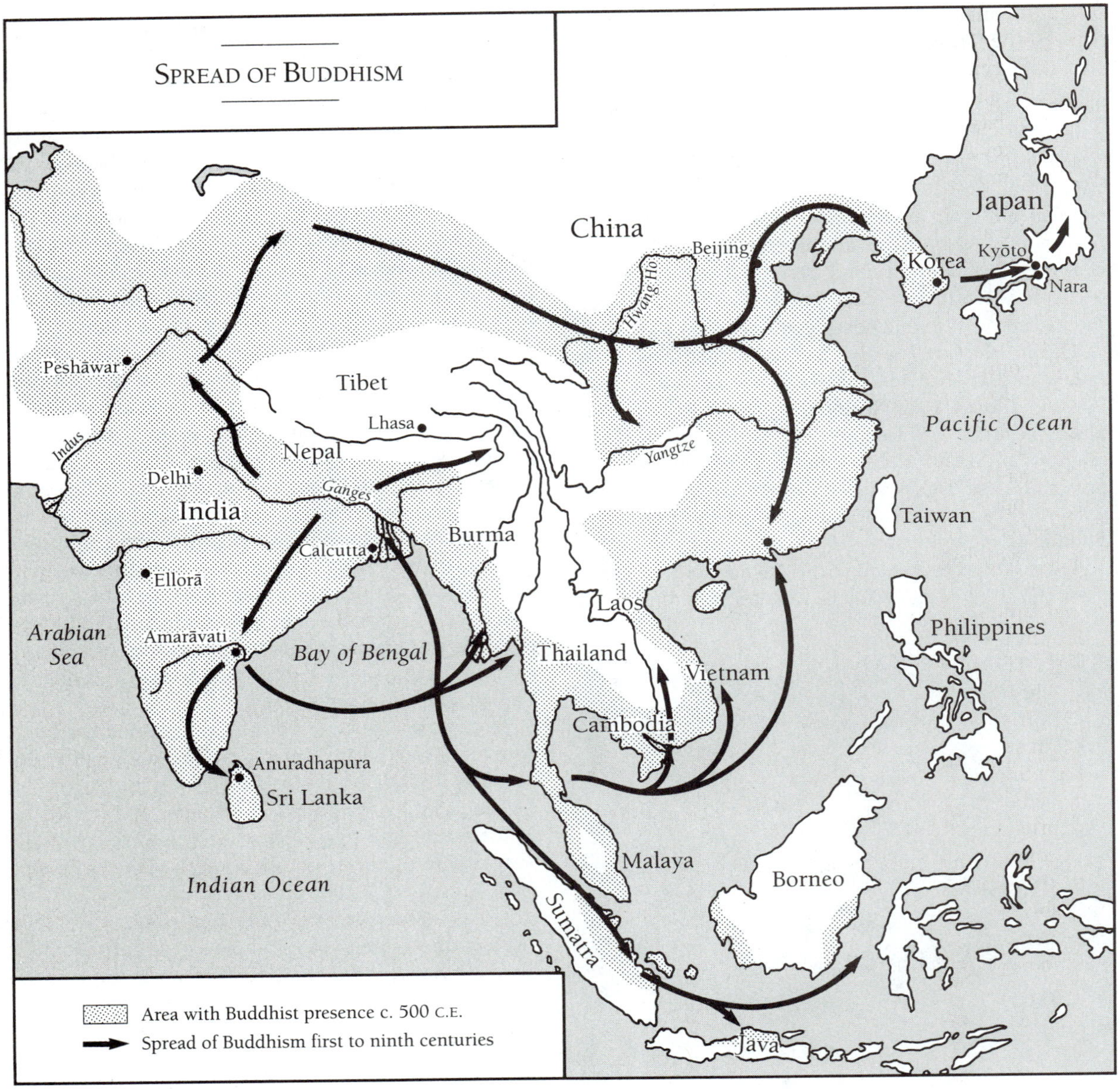

school that used Pāli rather than Sanskrit as its sacred language. These Theravādins tended to emphasize the central importance of the historical Gautama and to represent him as a mahāpurusha (great person) who had in the course of his many lives achieved liberation through his own efforts. They recognized the existence of other Buddhas, but among these only the future Buddha Maitreya played a significant role.

At the level of the Dhamma (the Pāli name for the Sanskrit *Dharma*), the Theravādins had their own version of the Tipiṭaka (Sanskrit, *Tripiṭaka*), written in Pāli, which they considered the language of the

Buddha himself. A major turning point in the evolution of the Theravāda tradition occurred in the fifth and sixth centuries C.E. when a series of great scholars generated a large body of commentary texts in Pāli that became a basic resource for later Theravāda practitioners. The key figure in this process was Buddhaghoṣa, a monk from India or lower Burma who translated many commentaries on the Tipiṭaka from Sinhalese into Pāli and wrote an extremely influential summary of Theravāda doctrine, *The Path of Purification.*

In Sri Lanka and Southeast Asia, some Theravāda Buddhists produced an esoteric interpretation of the Pāli texts and adopted various forms of Vajrayāna ritual. Some of these practices were associated with extreme forms of asceticism; others were oriented toward the laity. In many cases, these practices were designed to generate a permanent *dhammakāya* ("Dharma body") symbolized by a "crystal globe" that would appear in the center of the body near the navel. In other cases, rituals that involved a symbolic return to the womb were presented as a means to the immediate attainment of nirvāṇa. The significance of these Vajrayāna expressions of the Theravāda tradition has been recognized only recently.

The Theravāda community involved forest monks and other practitioners of yogic meditation who lived on the fringes of society. It also included monks who lived in settled monasteries such as the great Mahāvihāra in Sri Lanka, heavily endowed institutions deeply involved in local intellectual and economic life. Its lay supporters and practitioners included kings, nobles, and commoners. However, prior to the Theravāda-oriented reforms that took place in the twelfth century, probably the majority of the laypersons who supported the Theravādins also supported other Buddhist schools and in some cases Hindu shrines and practitioners as well.

ROYAL TRADITIONS IN SOUTHEAST ASIA

A second Buddhist development that occurred in Greater India was the extension of the Indian tradition of Buddhist kingship. This development—carried to its furthest extent in Southeast Asia—involved an evolution of Indian patterns whereby notions of the Buddha, the Dharma, and the Saṅgha were closely correlated with notions of kingship, the principles of social order, and the state. Unfortunately, no Southeast Asian texts from this period have survived, but it does seem that there was an intimate link between the king and the Saṅgha: the king was generally the official sponsor and protector of the Saṅgha; he was its most important patron and was responsible for the building of many large monasteries and Buddhist monuments, some of which are the most impressive religious monuments ever constructed.

Buddhist Religious Monuments

One of the most interesting examples of Buddhist royal architecture in Southeast Asia has been unearthed at sites associated with Dvaravati, a kingdom in central and northeastern Thailand during the late first millennium. Heavily influenced by Conservative traditions that used both Sanskrit and Pāli, the Dvaravati kingdom encompassed numerous cities and villages. Many such places had, at their center, Buddhist stūpas constructed of brick.

At about the same time, a powerful king who reigned in central Java was sponsoring the construction of what many Buddhologists and art historians consider the most magnificent Buddhist monument ever built. Constructed over a natural hill, Barabuḍur is a massive stūpa. Its extensive and sophisticated sculptured surface is decorated with complex Mahāyāna and Vajrayāna imagery.

Although the details are unclear, it is generally agreed that Dvaravati and Barabuḍur were designed to integrate three kinds of reality: (1) the great cosmic Buddha and the dharmically ordered cosmos he ruled, (2) the traditional ancestral spirit of the mountain and the spirit realm he ruled, and (3) the king who sponsored the construction and the great dharmic order of the kingdom he ruled.

A variation on this theme was seen in the thirteenth-century Cambodian temple-city of Angkor Thom, constructed by King Jayavarman VII. Jayavarman consolidated and helped to legitimize his rule by building a magnificent new city that would be an architectural embodiment of the cosmos. In contrast to most of his predecessors at Angkor, who were Hindus, Jayavarman VII was a Mahāyāna Buddhist; thus he built his city as an embodiment of a dharmically ordered cosmos conceived in Mahāyāna terms.

Jayavarman's city included a great central temple constructed in the form of a sacred mountain, the Bayon. The impressive tower that rose above the center of the temple had four sides on each of which an identical royal face was engraved. This face—presented as that of the bodhisattva Avalokiteśvara, the guardian spirit of the Angkor kingdom, and Jayavarman VII—looks out over the four quarters of the temple, the city, and the kingdom in the four cosmic directions. Below the great central tower, the main mass of the Bayon is decorated with extensive sculptures that depict, as an integral part of the dharmically ordered kingdom, elements and activities associated with the various provinces over which Jayavarman VII ruled.

Our evidence does not tell us how deeply Buddhism penetrated the lower echelons of Southeast Asian Buddhist societies. The great effort and expense that were invested in building Buddhist monuments and their high level of sophistication demonstrate that Buddhism was at certain times and places a major religious, political, and cultural force. Clearly, rulers and commoners alike were followers of Buddhism. Yet equally clearly, almost everywhere that Buddhism flourished, it coexisted with forms of Hinduism and with indigenous beliefs and practices.

THERAVĀDA CULTURE IN SRI LANKA AND SOUTHEAST ASIA

The decline of Buddhism that was in full swing on the Indian subcontinent by the early second millennium extended to much of Greater India as well. In some areas, especially in Malaysia and Indonesia, Buddhism lost its hold, while Hindu theism and Tāntrism gained strength. In later centuries successful Muslim traders gradually converted local rulers and their subjects to Islam. Well before the intrusion of European colonialism, Islam had spread throughout the previously Indianized areas in Malaysia, Sumatra, and Java. Buddhist institutions (and Hindu ones) were almost completely supplanted by Islamic successors.

In Sri Lanka and in mainland Southeast Asia, the collapse of Buddhism in the Indian subcontinent had a very different effect. In these areas, the cessation of Indian influences coincided with the emergence of a series of powerful reform movements that succeeded in establishing Theravāda Buddhism as the dominant local religious force.

The first of these movements occurred in the eleventh century, when kings in northern Burma and Sri Lanka both instituted Theravāda patterns that had been preserved among the Mon peoples in lower Burma. The most important Theravāda reform occurred in twelfth-century Sri Lanka. It was organized by a very successful Sinhalese king, Parakkamabahu (1153–1186), who worked with a group of reform-minded forest monks associated with the Mahāvihāra monastery. They were able to create a unified structure for the Sri Lankan Saṅgha and raise the Theravāda tradition to preeminence.

These reforms also stimulated a burst of literary creativity and promoted Theravāda Buddhism as a popular religion. The Theravāda monks composed new commentaries and other texts in Pāli and Sinhalese, some highlighting Buddhist devotion and others teaching meditational techniques. This new flurry of vernacular writing was part of a general movement whereby Theravāda Buddhism penetrated into virtually every area of Sinhalese life and culture. Just as pilgrimage had become an important Buddhist practice in India, Sri Lankan Buddhists developed their own pilgrimage sites. Places that had long been considered sacred by the indigenous traditions, such as mountain peaks, were incorporated into Buddhist practice. The Buddhists developed their own calendar rites, their own festivals honoring various Buddhas and bodhisattvas, and their own funeral rights.

The Sri Lankan Theravāda reforms quickly spread to Southeast Asia, where they melded with reforms that had already begun in Burma. By the end of the fifteenth century, the reformed Sri Lankan Theravāda tradition was firmly established at the various Burmese royal courts. Farther to the east, the Theravāda tradition was adopted by the Thai kings and peoples. In Cambodia, the Theravāda tradition became preeminent at Angkor, which had once been a Hindu-Mahāyāna empire.

Like the reform-oriented Sri Lankans, the Theravādins of Southeast Asia carried their teaching and practice far beyond the boundaries of the political and cultural elite, reaching out to most of the local ethnic groups. Though earlier Buddhist and Hindu traditions that had been established in various regions remained at least partly intact, the Theravāda reformers gradually extended their own influence.

The thirteenth-century C.E. Cambodian temple-city of Angkor Thom, constructed by King Jayavarman VII, was built as an architectural embodiment of the cosmos. The city includes a great central temple constructed in the form of a sacred mountain, the Bayon. The temple city is often called the "eighth wonder of the world." (Tass from Sovfoto)

By the time the first Europeans arrived in the area in the sixteenth and seventeenth centuries, Theravāda had become the dominant and pervasive religious force in the central rice-growing areas of Burma, Thailand, Laos, and Cambodia. Buddhist beliefs and stories had merged with regional and local traditions; Theravāda rituals had become embedded in the cycle of agricultural rites performed at the royal courts and in the villages. Theravāda ideals of community life, both monastic and lay, had become firmly established among both the elite and the populace as a whole.

RELIGIOUS TRENDS IN THERAVĀDA CULTURE

Theravāda Buddhism served as an international religious culture throughout Sri Lanka and Southeast Asia. Theravāda Buddhists shared a common sacred language, Pāli, a sense of common religious identity, common ideals of religious salvation and sainthood, and common norms of monastic and lay behavior, all of which continuously interacted.

Developments of Buddhology

Gautama Buddha (along with the future Buddha Maitreya) was always the primary focus in Theravāda. However, in each area, the veneration of Gautama Buddha was closely correlated with local traditions. Legends were told of his visits to the local area, and relics and images came to be associated with local sites and practices. Among the famous regional symbols of the Buddha's presence were his footprint, venerated on a sacred mountain in Sri Lanka; the Tooth Relic, the center of an important royal cult in the Sinhalese capital of Kandy; the Mahāmuni ("great sage") image in Burma; and the Prabang image, which gave its name to the Laotian capital, Luang Prabang.

Wherever Theravāda prevailed, alongside or below Gautama Buddha came Hindu-related or indigenous deities, venerated or propitiated in accordance with local practices. In Sri Lanka, the Buddha himself headed a pantheon of deities, each associated with certain sacred sites. In Burma, the old Vedic god Indra, who came to occupy one of the important heavens in the traditional Theravāda cosmology, was identified with a powerful *nat* (local guardian deity) who headed a pantheon of lesser nats that resided on a famous mountain. In Laos, Theravāda rituals performed at the great stūpa in the old capital of Luang Prabang included the reenactment of the process whereby the Laotian ancestral deities had purportedly created the natural and social order within which the Laotian peoples lived.

Extensions of Dharma

In all the various Theravāda countries, the primary source of Dharma was a common tradition of Pāli texts that included the Tripiṭaka and its corpus of commentaries. There were, however, many other Pāli texts of more limited distribution that took a very distinctive form in each of the major Theravāda kingdoms in Southeast Asia. Some Pāli texts contained Vajrayāna ideas and practices.

A corpus of vernacular texts that played a very important role in forming and expressing the local tradition was written in the regional languages of Burma, Thailand, Cambodia, and Laos. One classic example is *The Three Worlds of King Ruang,* a fourteenth-century Thai-language cosmology that exerted a major influence in central Thailand's religion, culture, and society.

Saṅgha and Community Life

Similar patterns of commonality and difference can be observed across the premodern Theravāda world. The ancient forest monk tradition continued in all Theravāda countries. This tradition was particularly influential in the areas along the northern and northeastern perimeters of Theravāda religious culture—northern Burma, northern and northeastern Thailand, Laos, and Cambodia. The forest monks were most active in promoting the Vajrayāna in these peripheral areas.

As a part of the unifying reforms that were initiated in twelfth-century Sri Lanka, the Theravādins developed a new kind of relationship between the religio-social hierarchy and the monastic community. The king, who was now recognized as a bodhisattva, headed a hierarchically structured social order that acknowledged the spiritual authority of the monks. The monastic order was set up as a parallel hierarchy; it was headed by a *saṅgharājā* ("Saṅgha king") who was usually appointed or confirmed by the king. These two hierarchically structured orders, each headed by its respective king, worked in tandem to constitute Theravāda Buddhist society.

This Sri Lankan pattern was adopted as an ideal by the religious and political elite in many Southeast Asian kingdoms. However, it was implemented much more effectively in some countries than in others. It was most successful in kingdoms, such as the Ayudhia kingdom in central Thailand, where there were a strong centralized power and long periods of relative political stability. It was least effective in places and times of political and social disruption, such as Sri Lanka in the seventeenth and early eighteenth centuries.

Relationships between Theravāda monks and their lay supporters were often close, particularly in small towns and villages with local monasteries. The monks provided religious services, spiritual guidance, and educational training to the local lay community, and the laity contributed moral and material support, supplying food and robes, building shelters, and contributing to the upkeep of the monasteries. The closeness of the relationships that actually developed between the monks and the laity was, however, deeply affected by differences in local customs. In Sri Lanka, the degree of mutual involvement was somewhat limited by the fact that entrance into the Saṅgha generally implied a lifetime commitment to the monastic way. In many areas of Burma, in contrast, every young boy was expected to spend a certain time as a novice within the monastic community. In central Thailand, temporary ordination was regularly practiced; every young Thai man would spend at least one three-month rainy season as a fully ordained monk. Thai men of all social classes, from peasants to kings, were also commonly reordained for periods lasting from days to years. Such practices inevitably strengthened the bonds between lay people and monks by partly integrating the two very different life styles.

BUDDHISM IN CENTRAL ASIA, CHINA, AND JAPAN

The spread of Buddhism from India to central Asia and on into the very different civilizations of East Asia is a stunning testimony to the universality and vitality of its message and institutions. In contrast to the Buddhist expansion into Sri Lanka and Southeast Asia, which continued Indian Buddhism's central motifs and ideals, expansion into central Asia, China, and Japan took the faith far beyond its original Indian context and implanted it in a radically different religious and cultural milieu.

The history of Buddhism in central and eastern Asia can be divided into two overlapping periods: a first during which Indian influences were strong and a second in which China (later supplemented by Japan) replaced India as Buddhism's main center. The first period began with the expansion of Buddhism into central Asia and China around the beginning of the Common Era and drew to a close toward the early decades of the ninth century. The second period began in the fifth and sixth centuries and continued until the massive intrusions of European power in the nineteenth century.

NORTHWESTERN INDIA AND CENTRAL ASIA

The Buddhist missions dispatched from the Aśokan court included one that was sent to the area that is now Pakistan, and by the first century B.C.E. Buddhism was well established there. During the first and second centuries C.E., three important developments occurred. First, the Kushāṇa dynasty, of central Asian origin, with its capital in northwestern India, came to rule an empire that extended from deep in central Asia far into the Indian subcontinent. Second, major trade routes expanded; these—the famous Silk Roads—extended from northwestern India through the now-pacified Kushāṇa domains in central Asia on into China. Third, Kushāṇa kings and many of their subjects were converted to Buddhism.

Buddhism spread to China along the Silk Roads through the deserts of central Asia. Many of the merchants who organized the caravans were Buddhist supporters, and Buddhist monks who joined the caravans settled in various localities to help to establish monasteries that served as hostels for weary traders and travelers. Many of the local rulers became supporters of the Buddhist cause, and significant numbers of their subjects followed their lead.

During the early centuries of the first millennium, the dominant Buddhist traditions in northwestern India and central Asia were Conservative. Over time, however, Mahāyāna Buddhism gained strength. Some scholars believe that many Mahāyāna developments originated in this area. For example, it is often claimed that Buddhists in northwestern India or western central Asia modeled the mythology of Amitābha Buddha on the Iranian god Mithra. This Buddha became the focus of Pure Land Buddhism, which grew into the most popular form of East Asian Buddhism. Some scholars have even suggested that certain important Mahāyāna texts, such as the famous Lotus Sūtra, were composed in central Asia.

Although during the middle centuries of the first millennium travel along the Silk Roads sometimes

This Chinese translation of a Buddhist work was found at Tun-huang and dates from 868 C.E. Buddha is shown addressing Subhuti, an aged disciple. (The Granger Collection)

became difficult, it never ceased. Many different religious traditions spread along these routes, including Zoroastrianism, Manichaeism, Christianity, and Islam. In this multireligious environment, Buddhism—both Conservative and Mahāyāna—maintained an important presence at many points along the way.

The southern caravan route entered China at Dunhuang (Tun-huang), at the western end of the Great Wall. Dunhuang is an extraordinary city of elaborately carved and painted cave temples. In one of these temples, around 1035 C.E., an unknown person concealed thousands of manuscripts on Buddhism and other subjects written in Chinese, Tibetan, and Uighur. These remained hidden until an itinerant monk rediscovered them in the early twentieth century. Still incompletely studied, the Dunhuang material is one of the richest sources of Mahāyāna texts and iconography.[1]

After the sixth century, traveling the Silk Roads became increasingly precarious. Marauders often made the routes virtually impassable. The prosperous oasis kingdoms were devastated, and Islam became dominant in many areas. By the 900s, the central Asian links that had for centuries connected the Buddhists of India and China had been severed, and the once-thriving centers of Buddhist learning and practices, so crucial in the development of Buddhism, had become virtually extinct.

CHINA

The Golden Age from Han to Tang

The establishment and spread of Buddhism in China marks a remarkable breakthrough. To this point, we have been discussing Buddhism as it developed in its homeland and in other areas where it was one of the first religions with a tradition based on written texts and institutional ideals correlated with large-scale patterns of political and social organization. In China, by contrast, Buddhism interacted with a culture that had its own highly sophisticated texts and political and social patterns.

China had developed two interrelated and complementary systems, generally known in the West as Confucianism and Daoism (Chapter 12). Confucianism was primarily concerned with personal relationships, politics, and society, and secondarily with more cosmic matters such as the place of humans in the universe. Daoism focused on cosmic matters and only secondarily on politics and society. Buddhism supported and criticized both systems.

Confucianism, centered on the family and the state, regards the stability of both as of supreme importance. Buddhism allied itself with Confucianism by stressing kindness and generosity, especially to one's parents, and its elaborate funeral services appealed to the Confucian reverence for the ancestors. However, it struck at the heart of the Confucian system with its notion of rebirth, according to which one's sacred ancestor might have been reborn as a dog. In addition, a son or a daughter who became a Buddhist monk or nun had to take a vow of celibacy, going against Confucianism by imperiling the continuity of the family line. And since initiation into the Buddhist monastic order involves the shaving of the head, Confucians could claim that, for all its talk of kindness to parents, Buddhism was in fact insultingly unfilial, for the *Book of Filial Piety (Xiao Jing)* says: "Seeing that our body, with hair and skin, is derived from our parents, we should not allow it to be injured in any way. This is the beginning of filiality."[2] Further, Buddhist monastics followed the Indian custom of regarding themselves as superior to the sovereign and refused—until a compromise was worked out—to follow the Chinese convention of kowtowing to the emperor, whom Confucianism regarded as the Son of Heaven.

In general, Buddhism attempted to nurture the Confucian emphasis on kindness and then extend it to nonhuman forms of life and to offer sons and daughters an alternative to marriage and the continuation of the family.

Buddhism sided with Daoism against Confucianism in regarding matters of state as subsidiary to cosmic harmony and immortality. Indeed, the Chinese at first mistook Buddhism for a variety of Daoism and supposed that the Buddha had been a student of Lao-zi, Daoism's legendary founder. It seemed that perhaps Buddhism had a recipe for immortality that might be superior to that of Daoism in that it did not require the ingestion of a somewhat toxic elixir, that the Daoists recommended. But Buddhism wished to go beyond Daoism as much as beyond Confucianism. When the

Indian Buddhist missionary Bodhiruci was asked if Buddhism had any recipes for immortality that compared to those of Daoism, he spat on the ground and replied:

> What do you mean? How can you compare the two? Where in this land [of China] could you find the formula for immortality? Even if you should remain young and live forever, you would still be within the realm of saṃsāra![3]

The point here is that Daoism seeks to prolong life and prevent death, whereas Buddhism seeks to end what it regards as an indefinitely long cycle of lives and deaths.[4]

The beginning of Buddhism in China is ascribed to a dream in which Emperor Ming (58–75 C.E.) of the Han dynasty saw a golden, flying deity. His advisers interpreted this as a vision of the Buddha who, they said, was an Indian who had attained the Dao, the Way, and could fly. Impressed, the emperor dispatched envoys to the Indian subcontinent to gain more information. They brought back the *Sūtra in Forty-two Sections,* a collection of sayings of Śākyamuni Buddha modeled on the *Analects* of Confucius. Whatever the truth of this legend, it is certain that Buddhism penetrated China from the top down.

After the collapse of the Han dynasty and therefore of Confucian control, Buddhism was able to make some headway. Its progress was quite different in the north and the south of the Chinese subcontinent. The north was ruled by the leaders of nomadic tribes, mostly Huns and Turks, who had broken through the Great Wall and established a series of kingdoms. Many of these rulers and their followers became supporters of the Buddhist cause and ardent practitioners of Buddhist rituals that promised worldly benefits.

The old Han aristocracy had fled south to escape the invaders who had taken over the north. Buddhists took advantage of the fact that the recent defeats had lowered the prestige of the ancient Confucian and Daoist traditions. Many members of the old elite were converted to Buddhism, and they soon developed a distinctive "gentry Buddhism" that placed a strong emphasis on philosophical reflection and refinement. Sophisticated Indian philosophical texts were translated into Chinese, thus laying the foundations for the development of distinctively Chinese versions of Buddhist doctrine that became established among the elite.

During the golden age of Buddhist influence in China, rulers sponsored temples and monasteries, giving them great wealth. Here a gilded roof ornament in the shape of a dragon head is part of the decoration of one monastery. (Eastfoto)

During the fourth through sixth centuries, however, both in the north and in the south, Buddhism spread far beyond the ruling elite. Buddhist monks, acting both as teachers of the Dharma and as experts in magical practices, converted large numbers of people in town and countryside. Monasteries were established, pagodas (Chinese stūpas) were constructed, and devotional cults spread broadly among the people.

When the Sui and Tang dynasties (sixth through

tenth centuries) unified China, they turned to Buddhism as a religion that could help them engender geographic and social unity. For more than 250 years (589–845), its golden age, Buddhism enjoyed substantial support from the imperial power, the aristocracy, and the common folk. Buddhist texts were translated from Indian and central Asian languages, producing a Chinese Buddhist Tripiṭaka, a compendium of Conservative, Mahāyāna, and Vajrayāna texts. Many Buddhist schools flourished, including several distinctively Chinese schools that influenced all of East Asia. Buddhist influences were felt in every aspect of Chinese culture and art, from architecture and sculpture to painting and literature.

Throughout this golden age, Buddhist institutions and ritual practices flourished. Temples were sponsored by the rulers; others were privately endowed, and many received lavish donations that gave them great wealth and control over vast estates. The chanting of Buddhist sūtras, or spells, and the performance of all sorts of merit-making acts became ubiquitous, both at the royal court and among ordinary people. Festivals such as the celebration of the birthday of Śākyamuni Buddha and pilgrimages to sacred mountains associated with Buddhas and bodhisattvas were participated in by large numbers of people from most segments of society.

Notwithstanding its great success in its first eight centuries, Buddhism was never able to overcome completely the sense that it was a foreign religion, nor was it able to neutralize completely the accusation that its monastic order (which became increasingly wealthy and therefore increasingly vulnerable to criticism) was a threat to family life and a drag on the economy. Thus anti-Buddhist movements were able periodically to challenge Buddhism's favorable position in the Chinese court and in Chinese life.

Finally, in the middle of the ninth century, these anti-Buddhist feelings became the catalyst for a violent attack that brought the golden age of Buddhism in China to an end. In 845, Emperor Wuzong mounted a massive anti-Buddhist persecution that resulted in the destruction of thousands of Buddhist temples, the appropriation of their lands, and the defrocking of more than 200,000 monks and nuns. Even though this persecution was short-lived, the monasteries suffered a serious economic and cultural blow from which they never completely recovered.

From Tang to the Present

The persecution of 845 C.E. took away much of the institutional independence of Chinese Buddhism. Subsequently, Buddhism became more a part of than an exotic addition to Chinese culture.

Pure Land Buddhism, with its emphasis on recitation of the name of Amitābha Buddha, a practice that could be carried out in the midst of one's daily work, became popular with the laity. In the monasteries, recitation of the name of Amitābha Buddha was combined with formal periods of Chan (Zen) sitting. Between 1280 and 1368, the Mongols brought in a Tibetan form of Vajrayāna. Chinese Buddhism as we find it today is a combination of Pure Land and Chan practice on a theoretical base of the more technical schools that flourished until the Tang, with occasional Vajrayāna elements.

Philosophically, Buddhist doctrines and practices were incorporated into Neo-Confucianism. Practically, the Chinese tended to turn to the Buddhists for funeral ceremonies.

During the Communist revolution of Mao Zedong, Buddhism, along with Confucianism and Daoism, underwent a further major persecution, but there is evidence that it is again recovering (Chapter 14).

KOREA AND VIETNAM

East Asian studies in the Western academic establishment have concentrated on China and Japan and have neglected Korea and Vietnam. Some Western scholars are now working with Korean materials, and we are beginning to glimpse the rich contributions of Koreans to the history of Buddhism. Vietnamese Buddhism still remains largely unstudied.

It is traditionally held that Buddhism was introduced to Korea by the Chinese monk Shun-dao in 372 C.E. On the basis of Chinese forms, Koreans developed five native lineages, of which the most important was the Dharma Essence *(Popsong)*, founded by Wonhyo (617–686). This was the first attempt to unify all teachings in one lineage, a characteristic feature of Korean Buddhism. Chinul (1158–1210), whose work has just become available in English, showed how the wordlessness of *Sŏn* (Zen) could be seen as compatible with the wordiness of intensive study.[5] In 1916, Venerable Sotaesan founded Won Buddhism, which, under the slogan "Develop our spiritual morality while the material civilization is being developed," preaches a universalist message uniting all religions, and all Buddhist lineages, in the naturally enlightened mind, symbolized by an empty circle.

Vietnam received Theravāda, apparently via the sea route, about the first century C.E. and various forms of Mahāyāna by land from China between the sixth and seventeenth centuries. It produced its own version of Zen (called *Thiền*) and, as in China and Korea, blended it with Pure Land practice. All lineages were combined into the Unified Buddhist Church of Vietnam in 1963. Buddhism has played an important part in various Vietnamese patriotic uprisings, and, during the so-called Vietnam War, was highlighted by the international press for its resistance to the United States.

JAPAN

The first known introduction of Buddhism into Japan took place in the mid-sixth century, when Buddhist images and scriptures were brought by a diplomatic mission from Korea. The new religion quickly gained support, and within a few decades the prince regent, Shōtoku Taishi (574–622), became a Buddhist and chose to model his ideal centralized government after the pattern of China's Buddhist-oriented Sui and Tang dynasties. Seeing China as the source of both high civilization and true Buddhism, Japanese monks made pilgrimages to the continent and, on their return, established Japanese lineages. Two of the most famous of these pilgrims were Saichō (762–822) and Kūkai (774–835).

Saichō established the Tendai lineage on Mount Hiei, just to the northeast of Kyōto. The temples on Mount Hiei multiplied and grew in strength to become a kind of monastic fortress overlooking what was then the capital of Japan. The government, feeling threatened, sent forces against it in 1570 and reduced its approximately 3,000 temples to 125. From the religious standpoint, Tendai, as a compendious lineage encompassing, as it claimed, all of the teachings of the Buddha, both Hīnayāna and Mahāyāna, became the seedbed for later lineages. During the Kamakura period, as imperial power waned in favor of the military junta, it began to break up. The most important progeny of Tendai were Japanese forms of Chan (Zen) and Pure Land Buddhism and a native lineage called the Lotus Lineage *(Hokke-shū)*.

Japan, unlike China, Korea, and Vietnam, made, as much as it could, a firm institutional distinction not only between Zen and Pure Land Buddhism but also among the many sublineages that developed on the archipelago.[6] It counts at least two major forms of Zen and two of Pure Land. Rinzai Zen, established by Eisai (1141–1215), is a vigorous form emphasizing alarming techniques such as shouting and beating and the posing of apparently impossible riddles *(kōan)* to awaken the student's innate Buddha mind. Sōtō Zen, which is more popular with the common people, is a quieter form relying on "just sitting" *(shikandaza)* until the student's Buddha mind manifests itself. The Pure Land Buddhism of Hōnen (1133–1212), known as Jōdo-shū ("Pure Land Lineage"), recommends the recitation of the name of Amitābha Buddha as often as possible in order to draw his wisdom and compassion into the defiled mind of the believer. The reform of his disciple Shinran (1173–1262), known as Jōdo Shinshū ("True Pure Land Lineage"), became the dominant form of Buddhism in Japan. Jōdo Shinshū simply surrenders to the power of Amitābha, which it finds already present and operative in the believer's mind.

The Lotus Lineage was founded by Nichiren (1222–1282), an extraordinarily outspoken Tendai monk who claimed that only his form of Buddhism was the true one. Indeed, followers held, it alone could save Japan from the invasion that the Mongols were then planning. Nichiren was condemned to die, but, it is said, just as the executioner raised his sword, there was a bolt of lightning, and his sentence was commuted to exile.

Kūkai returned from China with the plans of two great maṇḍalas from two different streams of Chinese Vajrayāna, from which he innovatively formed the distinctively Japanese Vajrayāna lineage known as Shingon-shū ("Mantra Lineage"). The mysterious rituals of Shingon, known as *mikkyō*, "esoteric teaching," appealed to the heart of Japan in a way that Tendai did not, for they resonated with the indigenous cult of the mountain shaman or *hijiri*, with which Kūkai became identified.* Kūkai attempted to unify the Sinified city

*Elements of *mikkyō* are also found in Tendai, but they are not so prominent.

culture with the native Japanese rural culture by establishing both Tōji, a city temple near Kyōto, and Kongōbuji, a somewhat inaccessible country temple on Mount Kōya. He also used his two maṇḍalas to develop a synthesis of Shintō and Buddhism and is traditionally credited with developing the Japanese syllabic writing system *(kana)* to ensure the proper pronunciation of the Shingon mantras. Mount Kōya became an important national cemetery, with the graves of Japanese notables lining the path leading to Kūkai's resting place, where, legend says, he is not dead but resting in deep samādhi from which, at the proper time, he will arise to lead the people.

During the Tokugawa period (1603–1867) the government kept all religions under tight control, and Buddhism was largely reduced to the status of a funerary cult, from which it has had difficulty recovering. Much of the religious power in present-day Japan is in the hands of the newer sects, primarily reformed versions of Shintō.

BUDDHIST TRENDS IN EAST ASIA

Throughout its long and eventful history in East Asia, Buddhism remained remarkably faithful to its Indian and central Asian origins. At the same time, however, Chinese, Vietnamese, Korean, and Japanese Buddhists made important selections, adaptations, and additions. When compared to other Buddhists, such as in Sri Lanka, the Buddhists of East Asia tended to emphasize the unity between the ultimate and the relative. Affirming the sacredness of this-worldly phenomena, their religious practices were designed to lead to a realization of this unity of the religious and the secular and to a positive view of the religious value of the natural world. At the level of community life, they tended to develop patterns of organization that reduced the differentiation between the Saṅgha and the laity.

New Roles for Buddhas and Bodhisattvas

The full range of Buddhas and bodhisattvas of India and central Asia was gradually introduced into East Asia, although inevitable changes gave the pantheon an East Asian cast. For example, in China, where bureaucratic modes of thought were pervasive, it took on a rather bureaucratic form. The various Buddhas and bodhisattvas were given East Asian mythologies and iconographies, and many indigenous deities were incorporated.

In China, the historical Śākyamuni Buddha's life story came to resemble the biographies of the traditional Chinese sages, and social virtues such as filial piety were emphasized. Popular stories connected many of the great Buddhas and bodhisattvas with life in China. In addition, various Buddhas and bodhisattvas were associated with Chinese pilgrimage sites and were endowed with many attributes and functions borrowed from native deities.

In Japan, the process of adaptation was carried on by identifying the Buddhas and bodhisattvas with indigenous deities and spirits known as *kami.* For example, the Shingon sect identified the Buddha Vairocana with the greatest of the Shintō kami, the sun goddess. Other Buddhas and bodhisattvas were identified with kami associated with various sacred locales.

In East Asia, Śākyamuni retained an important and often central position and continued to be a major focus of interest and veneration in many of the indigenous schools such as Tiantai (Tendai), Chan (Zen), and Nichiren. But in other East Asian traditions, Śākyamuni was almost totally eclipsed. In the Pure Land sects, Amitābha Buddha was the principal figure, and in the East Asian Vajrayāna tradition, Vairocana—though a far less compelling and less popular figure than Amitābha—was recognized as the primal manifestation of the enlightened mind.

There were also changes in the character of the great bodhisattvas. During the early period of Buddhist development in East Asia, Maitreya, for example, was the central figure in one of the major traditions. Over time he gradually lost his role as a focus of Buddhist practice, but he assumed two other quite different identities. In one strand of the tradition, he retained his identification as the future Buddha and became a central figure in a series of revolutionary peasant rebellions.

The second transformation of Maitreya was less important but more surprising. At a certain point in the history of Chinese Buddhism, Maitreya was in certain circles identified with an eccentric tenth-century Chinese monk named Budai and subsequently came to be represented as a potbellied, innocuous figure known as the "laughing Buddha." In this form he became one of the most ubiquitous figures in the popular pantheon of East Asian Buddhas and bodhisattvas. His image, situated at the entrance of Chinese monasteries, is revered primarily by laypersons seeking health, wealth, and happiness.

Another example of the process of adaptation is the transformation of the bodhisattva Avalokiteśvara. In India and central Asia, this great exemplar of compassion had typically been a male bodhisattva and remained so during the early phases of Chinese Buddhist history. But by the second millennium, Avalokiteśvara was commonly portrayed as a female figure resembling an ancient Daoist deity known as the Queen of Heaven. In this new form, Avalokiteśvara (in China, Guanyin, and in Japan, Kannon) became an extremely popular deity who was especially revered as the patroness of women and of childbirth.

Dharma: The Great Synthetic Schools

During the centuries when East Asians were first appropriating Buddhism, they established direct counterparts of various Indian schools. Thus the Conservative tradition was represented by several Chinese and Japanese schools that were the direct descendants of their Indian and central Asian predecessors. The Mādhyamika tradition was also represented by Chinese and Japanese schools, as was (at a much later date) the Yogācāra tradition. The Buddhists in East Asia, however, soon began to create different and more influential Mahāyāna and Vajrayāna schools that were distinctively their own. These new schools can be divided into two groups: the first consisted of those with more universalist or "catholic" orientations, namely, Tiantai (in Japan, Tendai), Huayan (Kegon), and the esoteric school known as Chenyan in China and Shingon in Japan. The second group, Mahāyāna schools with a more elitist or focused perspective, included the Chan (in Japan, Zen) school, various Pure Land groups, and the uniquely Japanese Nichiren sect. Each of the three universalist schools of Buddhism in East Asia had its own way of classifying the vast corpus of Buddhist texts and doctrines, as well as its own way of interpreting the Dharma.

Tiantai/Tendai The Tiantai system, formulated during the sixth century, classified the various strands of the tradition according to five different phases in Śākyamuni Buddha's ministry. During the first, it said, the Buddha preached the Avataṃsaka Sūtra, a long text presenting a variety of sophisticated Mahāyāna stories and doctrines. When the Buddha realized that this sūtra was too profound and complex for his uninitiated hearers to understand, he devoted the next three phases of his ministry to preaching sermons with a simpler, more straightforward content. These included such collections as the Conservatives' *Piṭakas* and the Mahāyānists' *Great Perfection of Wisdom.* Finally, they said, the Buddha revealed the ultimate truth by preaching the Lotus Sūtra. Evaluating the phenomenal world highly, the Tiantai taught that all beings have an inherent Buddha nature that could be brought out through Buddhist practices. Tiantai exerted a major influence on most later East Asian Buddhist schools.

Huayan/Kegon The Huayan school, which remained a philosophy and never developed into a practiced lineage, originated in the sixth century. According to the Huayan teachers, the Huayan (Avataṃsaka) Sūtra rather than the Lotus Sūtra provided the fullest and most complete expression of the Buddhist Dharma. In regard to doctrine, the Huayan teachers extended the Tiantai teaching on the identity of the absolute Buddha nature with each phenomenon by emphasizing the complete harmony and interpenetration among the phenomena themselves. Thus they also affirmed a positive understanding of reality that had a great appeal to the this-worldly sensibilities of the Chinese. This emphasis on the interconnectedness of all aspects of reality was also used by rulers as a way of reaffirming the need to maintain a stable, unified, and harmonious state.

Chenyan/Shingon The Vajrayāna (*Chenyan* in China, *Shingon* in Japan) was brought to China in the eighth century by a series of famous Indian missionaries. Initially a failure in Japan, it succeeded there when reintroduced by Kūkai. Shingon is most distinctive for its modes of iconographic representation, visualization, and ritual practices. The East Asian Vajrayāna schools shared with their Indian and Tibetan counterparts a strong emphasis on symbolic representation both to express the nature of reality and to aid in religious practices. Shingon used two maṇḍalas, one to represent the indestructible, immutable aspect of the enlightened mind and the other to reflect its dynamic manifestation in and through all phenomena. By properly meditating on these two maṇḍalas, the practitioner can realize nonduality.

Dharma: Other East Asian Schools

Despite the great contributions of the comprehensive Tiantai, Huayan, and Chenyan schools, they did not remain the dominant Buddhist traditions in East Asia. The most popular schools to develop were those of Chan (Zen) and Pure Land, both of which had a more focused perspective.

Chan/Zen According to legend, the **Chan** school was established in China by a famous Indian missionary named Bodhidharma (c. 500) who popularized the practice of formless—neither visualizing nor intellectualizing—meditation. The Chinese Chan masters concentrated on evoking a direct insight into the **Buddha nature**. This Buddha nature was identified with the true self, cleansed of all attachments and distortions, and with the natural world, which was thought to exhibit the Buddha nature in a pure and unspoiled way. This is stated in the Sūtra of Hui Neng:

> Within our Essence of Mind these Trikaya [three bodies] of the Buddha are to be found, and they are common to everybody. Because the mind [of an ordinary man] labours under delusions, he knows not his own inner nature. . . . But should we be fortunate enough to find learned and pious teachers to make known to us the Orthodox Dharma, then we may with our own efforts do away with ignorance and delusion, so that we are enlightened both within and without, and the [true nature] of all things manifests itself within our Essence of Mind.[7]

Many Chan masters went so far as to challenge the usefulness of scriptures, images, and other elements traditionally associated with Buddhist belief and practice.

The "sudden enlightenment" school, known as Linji in China and Rinzai in Japan, emphasized the discipline of grappling with enigmatic riddles (in Chinese, *gongan;* in Japanese, *kōan*). The more popular "gradual enlightenment" school, known as Caodong in China and Sōtō in Japan, emphasized the practice of meditational sitting devoid of any object or goal. One simply recognized that since one was already Buddha, there was nothing else to be done.

The Chan/Zen tradition also placed a positive value on manual work, the cultivation of the arts (for example, gardening, painting, and the tea ceremony), and the practice of military skills.

Pure Land The other focused perspective, the Pure Land schools that developed in China, traced their lineage to patriarchs of the fifth and sixth centuries. According to the Pure Land tradition, the process began when Huiyuan (334–416) introduced a visualization and devotional practice centering on the Buddha Amitābha and promising rebirth in his realm, the Pure Land. Then, during the first half of the sixth century, Tanluan (476–542)—who had reportedly received the Pure Land Sūtras directly from an Indian missionary—succeeded in establishing a full-fledged Pure Land school. In Japan, in the twelfth and thirteenth centuries, related but distinctively new Pure Land sects were formed out of the Tendai and Shingon schools that had for several centuries dominated the Japanese Buddhist scene.

Proponents of the Pure Land tradition maintained that the world was in a state of decline and that the epoch in which they lived was thoroughly degenerate. In this situation, easier methods of salvation were needed. These easier methods involved a dependence on the "other power" of the Buddha Amitābha (in Japan, Amida) together with the very simplest form of practice, the repetition of Amitābha's name, a practice called *nienfo* in Chinese and *nembutsu* in Japanese. In the Japanese Jōdo Shinshū (True Pure Land) school founded by Shinran, the emphasis on faith in Amida and his grace became so exclusive that even the usefulness of such recitation was called into question. In many East Asian Pure Land traditions, the older Buddhist goal of attaining nirvāṇa was completely replaced: Pure Land adherents now sought rebirth in a heavenly paradise.

Nichiren Although the Nichiren school had much in common with the Japanese Pure Land groups, it displayed a character all its own. Nichiren adherents shared much of Nichiren's own militantly prophetic spirit and followed his lead in accepting the authority of the Lotus Sūtra. Along with religious devotion, they advocated the recitation of a sacred formula, *Namu myō hō renge kyō* ("Hail to the Sūtra of the Lotus of the True Dharma"), which was believed to be more reliable than the repetition of Amida's name. Their goal, however, was not limited to rebirth in a heavenly paradise; it included the purification of the Japanese nation and the establishment of Japan itself as a "land of the Buddha."

Saṅgha: Patterns of Communal Life

Like Buddhism in southern, southeastern, and central Asia, Buddhism in East Asia maintained the ancient forest monk traditions associated with itinerant wandering and radical forms of asceticism. In China, for example, an imported notion of the great saints, which had been developed in some Indian Buddhist contexts, soon became associated with indigenous traditions of the hermit's life and ascetic discipline. Thus there developed in Chinese Buddhism an ideal of Buddhist *lohans* or saints, who were similar in many respects to the important *xian* (immortals) of popular Daoism.

In Japan, there were two different types of Buddhist forest monks. The first type were sophisticated monastics who gave up settled Saṅgha life to wander the countryside. Many of these highly cultured wanderers quite self-consciously practiced a distinctively Japanese "way of poetry," composing marvelous poems that expressed a distinctively Japanese Buddhist view of the beauty and sacredness of the natural world. The second type is represented by the *yamabushi* (mountain ascetics) and other miracle workers who were associated with the more shamanic aspects of the indigenous kami tradition.

Early patterns of East Asian mainstream monastic life remained similar to the Indian model. But as Buddhist monasticism interacted with its new environment, several changes were made. The community soon began to revise its heritage in a way more in line with the historical and biographical modes of thinking characteristic of East Asia. During the fourth and fifth centuries, Indian and central Asian sources were used to reconstruct the history of the transmission of the Dharma in India to the first Chinese patriarch. During the Song period in China, Tiantai monks produced a treatise listing nine of its early patriarchs, and the Chan community produced its own genealogical literature, including the famous *Records of the Transmission of the Lamp*.

The Saṅgha gradually adapted itself to China's emphasis on the primacy of family and state. Buddhists justified the monks' and nuns' vocations primarily in terms of their contribution to the moral and social order, as well as the merit they accumulated for their parents and ancestors. Institutionally, the Saṅgha was made subordinate to state authority, both symbolically and in fact. Generally speaking, the monks accepted state control over such matters as the ordination, registration, and unfrocking of members of the Saṅgha. In Japan, the Chinese tradition of state control was quickly adopted by the authorities. By Tokugawa times, the Japanese shōguns had thoroughly subordinated the ecclesiastical structure to the purposes of state.

A different kind of East Asian Saṅgha adaptation involved relaxing the prohibitions against "mundane" activities. In the Chan/Zen tradition, for example, the rule against performing manual or agricultural work was rejected, and Zen monastics were required to earn their living by tilling the soil (hence the Zen maxim, "One day no work, one day no food"). Certain proponents of this requirement went even further by maintaining that such work, if performed with proper intent, could help one to attain enlightenment.

The Vinaya rule of celibacy for monks was also relaxed in Japan. A major turning point came in the thirteenth century when Shinran, founder of the Jōdo Shinshū sect, popularized the practice of clerical marriage. Along with the customs concerning inheritance that it fostered, a married clergy soon came to be accepted not only in Shinran's lineage but in other groups as well. Thus many Japanese Buddhist temples became family-dominated institutions that were passed on from one generation to the next.

Saṅgha: The Laity

In East Asia, as elsewhere in the Buddhist world, the laity has always played a significant role in the Buddhist community. As early as the fifth century, many East Asian rulers assumed the roles of the great Buddhas and bodhisattvas. At about the same time, lay members of the Chinese aristocracy in southern China developed a lay-oriented form of "gentry Buddhism" that placed a special emphasis on the Vimalakirti Sūtra, in which the protagonist is a lay bodhisattva. In Japan, the samurai (warrior) caste generated its own forms of lay practice associated with intense self-discipline and cultivation of the martial arts. In each particular East Asian area, laypersons of social rank from king to peasant provided support for the monastic community and adapted traditional Buddhist teachings and practices to their own local needs and concerns.

Later, the increasingly worldly orientation of the

Part of a mural painting in the 1,300-year-old Potala Palace in Lhasa, Tibet, is seen here. The palace was the residence of the Dalai Lama until his exile under the Communist Chinese conquest of Tibet. (Eastfoto)

Saṅgha (along with its submission to state control) was countered by the appearance of new, predominantly lay organizations and movements. In China in the seventeenth and eighteenth centuries, many Buddhist lay people formed organizations that were committed to the serious practice of basic Buddhist morality and meditation. In Japan, a number of laypersons formed anticlerical groups and assumed responsibility for their own initiations, communal rites, and programs of religious instruction. During the final centuries of the premodern period in East Asia, these lay movements enlivened Buddhist traditions that were otherwise rather stagnant and uncreative.

BUDDHISM IN TIBET

Though Buddhism had been established from the early centuries of the Common Era in various areas around the high and remote Himalayan region of Tibet, it did not actually penetrate into the Tibetan plateau until the seventh or eighth century. Once Buddhism was entrenched in this harsh and rather desolate environment, it was adapted to its new context, and a distinctive form gradually took shape. Tibetan Buddhism was the direct successor of the Vajrayāna tradition that developed in the Indian subcontinent during the Pāla period (750–c. 1200). But Tibetan Buddhism has also, throughout its history, been profoundly influenced by the particularities and dynamics of Tibetan culture, politics, and religion.

This Tibetan tradition, with its esoteric teachings, its rich iconography, its complex and colorful liturgies, its shamanic and exorcistic practices, and its highly accomplished and venerated leaders called **lamas** (gurus), has held great fascination for westerners, both scholars and spiritual seekers. Other Western observers, however, particularly those better acquainted with Theravāda Buddhism, have sometimes been shocked by the strong emphasis that the tradition has placed on esoteric rituals that are reputed to employ sexual techniques, seemingly mechanistic ritual performances, and magic. Still others have been put off by the extensive political and economic involvement of the lamas in a theocratically organized feudalistic society. The distinctiveness of Tibetan Buddhism, however, is due mainly to the pervasive presence of

Vajrayāna elements, with which these observers were unfamiliar.

THE ESTABLISHMENT OF BUDDHISM IN TIBET

The history of Buddhism in Tibet is sometimes divided into three periods—the establishment of Buddhism in Tibet, its reestablishment after persecution, and the period of the dominance of the Dalai Lamas.

In the first period, King Songtsengempo (c. 620–649) established a central government and is credited with introducing Buddhism through two wives, one from Nepal and the other from China. This report, whose historicity is in doubt, symbolizes that Tibetan Buddhism, like Tibetan culture, is at the meeting point of Indian and Chinese influences, although at the so-called Lhasa Debate (c. 792—its historicity is also disputed), Tibetans decided to emphasize Indian forms of Buddhism over Chinese. During the reign of Songtsengempo a Tibetan script, adapted from an Indian model, was invented, and a form of literary Tibetan was developed specifically for the translation of Buddhist texts.

The first effective missionary was Padmasambhava, who arrived around 779. His life is surrounded by mystery and enlivened by miracles. He is said to have converted Tibet by first converting the local deities: arriving in a village, he would challenge the deity to a contest in magic. The deity would do its best, but Padmasambhava would do better. The deity would submit to Padmasambhava and be appointed a "protector of Buddhism." The human inhabitants of the village would then follow their deity's example and take refuge in the Three Jewels. Padmasambhava's school of Buddhism is known as Nyingmapa ("Ancient Ones") and has a heavy emphasis on Vajrayāna, which it sees as divided into three outer and three inner Tāntras.

About 836, King Langdarma succeeded to the throne and began a vigorous suppression of Buddhism. He was assassinated in 842 by a man wearing a black cloak and riding a black horse. His black cloak, however, had a white lining, and the horse was actually white but painted with a dye that washed off in water. Riding his horse through a river and then reversing his cloak, the assassin made good his escape.

THE REESTABLISHMENT OF BUDDHISM

For some time there was no central authority in Tibet, but Buddhism made a slow comeback. Rinchen Zangbo (958–1055) began a retranslation of the Buddhist texts, initiating what came to be known collectively as the Sarma ("New") translation schools, in contrast to the Nyingma ("Old") translation schools.

Atīśa (982–1054) came to Tibet from India in 1042 and founded the Kadampa, a school that is respected by all the Sarma lineages, especially for its practical advice,[8] as in the Seven Points of Mind Training, teaching how the ups and downs of everyday life can be regarded as aids on the path to enlightenment.

Marpa (1012–1096), a married man known as the Translator, is credited with the founding of the Kagyupa school. His most famous pupil was Milarepa (1040–1123), who gave his teaching in songs that are known and loved by Tibetans of all lineages.

The Sakyapa school was founded by Könchog Gyelbo (1034–1102). It has a distinctive teaching on the unity of the sūtra (exoteric) and Tāntra (esoteric) practices, which it calls Path and Fruit, respectively. In the thirteenth century, after Tibet submitted to Chingiz Khan but had managed to convert Kublai Khan to Buddhism, Sakyapa lamas became advisers to the court of the Great Khan and were established as rulers of Tibet.

THE GELUKPA REFORM

Dzongaba (1357–1419) was deeply concerned at what he regarded as the corruption of Buddhism in Tibet in his day. A man of prodigious learning, he fearlessly challenged the greatest teachers to public debates and soundly defeated them. His reform, known as the Gelukpa ("Virtuous Ones") school,* restored the tradition of monastic celibacy and attempted a comprehensive presentation of all the Sarma schools. In the spirit of their founder, the Gelukpa emphasize learning and debate as means to enlightenment. Monastic

*During certain rituals, Gelukpa monks wear large, gold-colored headgear. This so impressed early Western observers that they dubbed the monks "Yellow Hats." This unhelpful term is still occasionally used.

debate sometimes lasts far into the night and is cheered and jeered like a sport.

In 1578, Altan Khan bestowed the title of Dalai Lama (Mongolian for "Great Ocean" and understood to imply great wisdom) on the Gelukpa teacher Sönam Gyatso. He was subsequently identified as the *third* Dalai Lama, and, until the Chinese invasion in 1950, the Dalai Lamas, regarded as rebirths of themselves, were the effective political rulers of Tibet; their Gelukpa order became the dominant, and sometimes the only authorized, Buddhist teaching.

RELIGIOUS TRENDS

From Tibetan Buddhism's earliest stages, the Vajrayāna tradition was the most distinctive formative influence. However, the Tibetans—and later the Mongols—gradually created their own version of this tradition, their own way of understanding and expressing the Dharma, and their own patterns of religious authority and social organization.

Buddhas and Bodhisattvas

Tibetan Buddhism shares with Theravāda a reverence for the importance of Śākyamuni as the historical Buddha, but as a Mahāyāna tradition it expands its focus to include other Buddhas and bodhisattvas in other world systems.

Dividing the Dharma into three levels of teaching, it recognizes three different manifestations of Buddhas and bodhisattvas—human forms for the elementary or Hīnayāna teaching, divine forms for the intermediate or Mahāyāna teaching, and transdivine or ultimate forms for the Vajrayāna teaching. The Buddhas and bodhisattvas manifest themselves at the lower levels as peaceful entities and at the higher levels as fierce entities whose pure, egoless energy compassionately destroys all obstacles to enlightenment.

In addition, at the Vajrayāna level, refuge is taken in many nonhuman, spiritual guides such as the protectors and female ministers. The most popular objects of worship are Jenrayzee, the Tibetan form of Avalokiteśvara (who, in contrast to the Far East, appears in Tibet only as a male), and Tārā, a motherly manifestation of the compassionate mind, who is said to have taken a vow to become a Buddha without (as is the rule) being reborn as a male.

The Dharma

Tibetan Buddhism divides the Dharma into three levels or "vehicles" *(yāna)*.* The Hīnayāna is the path of negation (no harm) and self-improvement, the Mahāyāna is the positive path of compassion and assistance extended to all sentient beings, and the Vajrayāna cuts off ordinary appearance (the delusion of saṃsāra).

These vehicles are to be practiced in order, and it is a distinctive feature of the Tibetan Dharma that it has a "graded path" of a set sequence of courses, inherited from the great Indian Buddhist universities. Only after having attained some internal peace (through the practice of Hīnayāna) can we help others (through the practice of Mahāyāna) without projecting our problems onto them. But only when altruistic action has become second nature are we ready to practice the Vajrayāna, in which we live no longer in saṃsāra but in the reality of Buddha consciousness.

Tibetans translated and assembled their own collection of scriptures, dividing the hundreds of volumes broadly into two groups—the Kanjur, or "Translation of the Buddha Word," and the Tenjur, or "Translation of the Teachings," or commentaries.

The Saṅgha and Society: Continuity and Enrichment

The Vajrayāna tradition in Tibet was characterized by a tension between its more restrained and more uninhibited forms. The more restrained practice was represented by the Kadampa and the later Gelukpa schools, which recognized the importance of the Vinaya and the sūtras as well as the Tāntras. Schools advocating the more uninhibited approach focused on oral traditions and the Tāntric manuals. These schools tended to be more lax in their enforcement of the monastic rules, particularly those prohibiting marriage and the consumption of alcoholic beverages, and also to be more skeptical of the value of intellectual pursuits. In some cases they encouraged extreme forms of ascetic activity.

Despite the schools' differing degrees of conservatism, the various segments of Tibetan Buddhism all drew on native traditions to acquire both worldly and

*The Nyingmapa teaches nine vehicles, by subdividing the Hīnayāna into two and the Vajrayāna into six.

mundane powers. These contributed to the advancement of beliefs concerning human consciousness and of rituals designed to promote healing in this life or a better rebirth in the next.

Although not a Buddhist text per se, the Tibetan *Book of the Dead,* which claimed to be a guide through the various states and opportunities encountered between death and rebirth, was probably recited in this kind of ritual context. In addition, dramatic and colorful rituals accompanied both traditional monastic practices and community liturgies and festivals.

One form of indigenous belief recognized the existence of demons who were capable of invading individuals. To expel these demons, the monks performed elaborate rituals, involving the chanting of Buddhist mantras and texts, the performance of often comic dramas, and the ritual feeding and expulsion of the invading demons. These were public events for an entire village. The demons can be regarded as having either an objective or a subjective existence, depending on the level of the Buddhist teaching. Thus their ritual exorcism can be considered a form of meditation.

AUTHORITY IN THE TIBETAN TRADITION

The affinity between Indian and Tibetan Buddhism is apparent in matters of community life. The forest monk tradition was continued by wanderers and hermits who maintained and extended the typically Vajrayāna emphasis on extreme and often idiosyncratic forms of religious asceticism. These wanderers and hermits were in many cases renowned practitioners of various forms of black and white magic; as a result, they were both highly respected and greatly feared.

Tibetan Buddhist monasteries often operated as universities, like their Indian counterparts, maintaining high standards of intellectual life and carrying on the great traditions of study and debate. Within their massive walls, the Indian arts and sciences were cultivated and transmitted. In addition, small monasteries dotted the country, many functioning as local temples.

Over time, Tibetans generated their own distinctive patterns of leadership. The most obvious example was the emergence of the lama as a primary locus of religious prestige and authority. *Lama* is a translation of the Sanskrit word *guru* and is used in Tibet to refer to one's spiritual teacher. Only certain teachers are called lamas, and they may be lay people or monastics of either sex.* The new emphasis on the lama can be seen in the Tibetan formula of refuge:

I take refuge in the lama.
I take refuge in the Buddhas.
I take refuge in the Dharma.
I take refuge in the Saṅgha.

Although the lama is added as a fourth *phrase* to the Triple Refuge, he or she is not a fourth *refuge* but rather the human being who is believed to manifest the Triple Jewel most clearly. A lama is chosen with great care. Only after extensive testing of a person whom one thinks might possibly be one's lama is the commitment made.

As the office of lama became the typically Tibetan institution concerned with personal guidance, so the *tulku* became associated with public authority. *Tulku* is Tibetan for *Nirmāṇa-kāya,* the human manifestation of a Buddha, within the system of the three bodies of a Buddha or bodhisattva. Although belief in rebirth is common to all Buddhist traditions, Tibetan Buddhism is the only form that regularly identifies particular persons as tulkus of particular Buddhas or bodhisattvas.

The institution of the tulku was emphasized by the Gelukpas after they rose to power. Since they maintained celibacy, they could not follow the custom of passing on high office from parent to child. So they developed the teaching that certain important persons succeed themselves, so to speak. After a tulku dies, his or her rebirth is sought according to strict and elaborate rules, and after thorough testing, the rebirth is recognized and reinstated.[9] Many tulkus, such as the Dalai Lama (regarded as a manifestation of Jenrayzee), the tulku who is most widely known, have held and continue to hold considerable political power.

BUDDHISM IN THE MODERN ERA

During the nineteenth and twentieth centuries, Buddhists of every tradition and geographic region have

*Early Western observers incorrectly coined the misleading word *Lamaism* to refer to Tibetan Buddhism.

faced unprecedented challenges and opportunities. At the ideological level, they have confronted powerful intrusive forces, such as Christianity, Western rationalism, scientific and industrial technology, democracy, and communism. At the institutional level, they have had to deal with political and economic domination by Western powers that had little understanding of or sympathy for Buddhism. They have had to endure the disruption of the traditional social and economic patterns in which Buddhism had played a role. In addition, Asian Buddhists have had to cope with local movements committed to limiting or even eliminating Buddhist influence.

The Buddhist response has varied from conservative resistance to reform to bold new initiatives, and the results have varied. In some areas the tradition has been severely disrupted; in others it has been maintained with differing degrees of vitality; and in some parts of the world new Buddhist communities have become established.

REFORM MOVEMENTS

Attempts to maintain and revitalize Buddhism in this age of rapid change have brought important innovations. Buddhists who were influenced by modern modes of thought and social forces began to devise new ways of appropriating and presenting the tradition. They introduced new interpretations of the Buddha, new ways of understanding his teachings, and new approaches to the life and organization of the Buddhist community.

Buddha

Modern reformers' interpretations of the Buddha have underscored his humanity and the rationality of his approach to the problem of human suffering. They have written new biographies removing the most problematic features of the traditional accounts. Some of these biographies have presented him as a social reformer carrying on a crusade against the Hindu caste system; others have emphasized his achievements as a master of meditation and his role as spiritual therapist; still others responded to modern needs by presenting him as the teacher of a rationally grounded ethic.

Dharma

New interpretations of Buddhist teaching have been made in sophisticated philosophical terms and in a more popular vein as well. Many Buddhists have related Buddhist thought to Christianity, to Western philosophical perspectives, and to scientific modes of thinking. In Japan, this has been done for two centuries by sophisticated scholars, especially those of the so-called Kyoto School of philosophy. Strong Buddhist apologists have begun to appear in the past century in the Theravāda countries as well: in Sri Lanka, for example, Gunapala Dhammasiri has mounted a very sharp and pointed Buddhist polemic against Christianity, and in Thailand, Bhikkhu Buddhadasa has formulated an equally sophisticated but more conciliatory approach.

At the same time, many have stressed the relevance of Buddhist teachings for social and ethical issues, highlighting distinctively Buddhist traditions of social responsibility. Some Buddhist apologists have maintained that Buddhism can be the basis for a truly democratic society; some have contended that Buddhism and Marxism can be creatively synthesized; and some have insisted that Buddhism, as a nontheistic religion, can provide a foundation for world peace. In the 1930s, a Buddhist message of social activism was strongly set forth by a famous Chinese Buddhist reformer, Abbott Taixu. In more recent times, a similar message has been dramatically promulgated by Thich Nhat Hanh, a Vietnamese monk who emerged as an internationally known Buddhist leader during the Vietnam War.

Saṅgha

On the community level, Buddhist reformers have tried to "purify" the monastic order and to redirect its activities to make them more relevant to modern conditions. They have tried to discourage monastic activities that have little immediate practical value while requiring an extensive investment of resources. They have introduced new kinds of education designed to train monks for nontraditional religious and social roles that they consider more relevant in the modern world. They have encouraged monks to assist in providing secular education at the popular level and to perform such social services as aiding the poor and caring for orphans. In some countries, including Thailand and Myanmar (Burma), monks have been trained to carry on missionary activities among non-Buddhists (particularly among minority ethnic groups) and to participate in government-sponsored programs of national development.

Laypersons have been encouraged to study the Buddhist scriptures and to practice forms of meditation particularly suited to their distinctive needs and situations. Lay associations have become influential in virtually every Buddhist country; they sponsor a variety of Buddhist programs, defend the cause of Buddhism in national affairs, and provide the leadership for Buddhist ecumenical movements.

The laity in various Asian countries has also supported the Mahābodhi Society, organized in the late nineteenth century to reclaim and restore the sacred sites and monuments of Buddhist India. Lay leaders took the initiative in organizing the celebrations of the 2,500-year anniversary of Buddhism held in the 1950s in various parts of the Buddhist world. Lay activity was especially prominent in Burma, where a major Buddhist council (the sixth according to the Burmese reckoning) was convened. Lay leadership was also essential to the formation, in 1952, of the World Fellowship of Buddhists, which has met every four years since then.

THE COMMUNIST CHALLENGE

Despite the remarkable continuity in Buddhist reformist trends during the modern era, the fates of various Buddhist communities have been very different. In the Communist-dominated regions of the Asian mainland, including Inner and Outer Mongolia, North Korea, China, Tibet, and Indochina, where for centuries the majority of the world's Buddhist population has been concentrated, the vitality of Buddhism has been seriously undermined. In some of the non-Communist areas, such as Sri Lanka, Southeast Asia, Taiwan, South Korea, and Japan, Buddhist communities have been able to maintain their basic integrity and continue their activity. In addition, distinctively new Buddhist communities have been established in both Asia and the Western world.

The basic pattern of Communist dealings with Buddhism has been evident since the Bolshevik takeover in Russia and the establishment of the Soviet-inspired Mongolian People's Republic in the early 1920s. The Communist governments moved as quickly as possible to replace Buddhist teachings with Communist ideology, to weaken and then eliminate the economic privileges and powers of the monasteries, and to isolate and discredit the monastic leadership. In this way they were able, within a few decades, to divest the Mongolian monastics and their followers of any real power or influence. However, with the recent breakup of the Soviet Union, Mongolian Buddhism has experienced a significant revival.

In China, the Communist rise to power came much later. It was preceded by a long period of Buddhist adjustment to Western and modern influences during which many intellectual and social reforms were attempted. However, these reforms did not succeed in breaking the close and long-standing ties between Buddhism and traditional Chinese society. When the Communists took over, Buddhism—like many other aspects of Chinese life—suffered severe setbacks. The traditional rights and privileges of the monasteries were rescinded. Large numbers of monks were defrocked and forced into materially productive occupations. The buildings were taken over and made into museums or used for government purposes, and the Buddhist associations that had been organized by the earlier reformers were unified and brought under strict government supervision.

The state-dominated Chinese Buddhist Association was founded to foster Chinese relations with Buddhist countries but was given little opportunity to advance the Buddhist cause within China itself. During the late 1950s and the early 1960s, the already weakened tradition was further undermined by the antitraditionalist campaigns mounted during the Cultural Revolution. Since the death of Mao Zedong in 1976, however, there have been increasing indications that the government is adopting a more moderate policy toward all religions, including Buddhism.

After the Chinese conquest of Tibet in 1959, Tibetan Buddhism came under an even stronger attack than the Maoist regime had mounted against Buddhism in China itself. Tibet's traditional isolation left it unprepared for the new situation. The Dalai Lama was forced to flee, along with thousands of others.

The Chinese unleashed a brutal repression, including the persecution of the monks who had remained. This policy has continued to the present time. Yet

Rare pieces of art, such as this seventeenth-century spiral silk wall decoration, have been smuggled out of Tibet by fleeing monks. The refugees have presented the pieces to the Dalai Lama in India, where they join him in exile. (UPI/Bettmann)

much evidence exists that the policies of the Chinese invaders have failed to break the Buddhist hold on the loyalty of the Tibetan people. The exiled Dalai Lama continues to command the respect of large segments of the Tibetan population and the world; he was awarded the Nobel Peace Prize in 1989 for his efforts to free his nation.

The Communist takeover in Indochina is so recent that its long-range effects are difficult to predict. At first, government policies in Vietnam, Laos, and Kampuchea (Cambodia) were similar to those employed by Communist regimes elsewhere in Asia. Buddhist teachings were disparaged, Buddhist practices were discouraged or prohibited, the privileges enjoyed by Buddhist monasteries were eliminated, and the influence of Buddhist institutions was eroded. In Kampuchea, when the Pol Pot government was in control (1975–1979), Buddhist leaders and institutions were the special objects of a persecution pursued with unprecedented violence and intensity.

In recent years, however, there has been a significant change. In Vietnam, there are signs of a small-scale Buddhist revival that is not being repressed by the government. In Kampuchea, Buddhism has made a significant comeback and is once again playing a role in many aspects of national life. And in Laos, where the repression of Buddhism was never as severe as it was in other areas of Indochina, Buddhism seems to have retained the loyalty of much of the populace and to be slowly regaining at least grudging recognition from the government.

BUDDHISM IN NON-COMMUNIST ASIA

Outside the Communist orbit, Buddhism has fared better. For example, in Sri Lanka, Myanmar (Burma), and Thailand, Theravāda Buddhists have been able to retain both a dominant religious position and a strong political and social influence. The groundwork for the continued preeminence of Buddhism in these three countries was laid during the colonial period in the late nineteenth and early twentieth centuries. At that time, an intimate bond was forged between the local Theravāda traditions and an emerging sense of national identity and destiny. In Sri Lanka and Myanmar, this bond was established in the context of resistance to British rule. In Thailand, it was cultivated by an indigenous elite engaged in a successful struggle to maintain Thai independence.

In Sri Lanka and Myanmar, the strong association between Buddhism and a militant, ethnically oriented nationalism has led to Buddhist involvement in intense and bitter conflicts with non-Buddhist minority groups. In Sri Lanka, Buddhism has become associated with the Sinhalese side in the brutal struggle between the Sinhalese majority and the Hindu (Tamil) minority. In Myanmar, Buddhism has become associated with the government side in the seemingly endless struggle between the government and the minority groups that live in the hills. In Thailand, where

Buddhism's position as a state religion has never been seriously threatened, the government and the various ethnic groups have avoided major conflicts.

The most interesting and dynamic developments have occurred in Japan. The modern period in Japan began with the Meiji Restoration (1868), which brought with it the elimination of the special privileges Buddhism had enjoyed under the Tokugawa shōgunate. State Shintō became the national religion until the Japanese defeat in World War II, when Japan became a secular state. Nevertheless, despite the loss of the special position it once held, Buddhism has remained a significant part of Japanese life. Japanese Buddhists have retained many of their ancient beliefs, practices, and patterns of communal organization; at the same time, they have adapted to the changing conditions.

During the modern period, several important Buddhist-oriented "new religions" have appeared. The most dynamic of these—for example, Reiyūkai (Association of the Friends of the Spirit), Risshō Kōsei Kai (Society for the Establishment of Righteousness and Friendly Relations), and Sōka Gakkai (Value Creation Society)—have their roots in Nichiren Buddhism and popular folk traditions. They are lay movements that focus on attaining practical goals such as health and material well-being. Appealing originally to the lower and middle classes, they have made many millions of converts and currently exert a significant influence, not only on the religious life of the country but also on its economic and political life.

EXPANSION IN INDONESIA AND INDIA

Buddhism's survival and activity in the modern world can also be seen in the distinctively new Buddhist communities that have been established in other areas of Asia, especially in Indonesia and India. In Indonesia, the Buddhist revival has been rather limited. But the revival in India represents a major development in contemporary Buddhist history.

The first stirrings of new Buddhist life in India began in the early decades of the twentieth century, when several Buddhist societies were formed by small groups of intellectuals. The members of these societies discovered in Buddhism a form of spirituality that they could reconcile with both their newly acquired rationalistic attitudes and their reformist ideals of social equality. Since the late 1950s, several communities of Tibetan refugees, including one headed by the Dalai Lama, have established an additional Buddhist presence in India.

By far the most interesting and important aspect of the Buddhist resurgence in India has been the mass conversion of members of the lowly "scheduled" castes. This has taken place primarily in Maharashtra state, of which Bombay is the capital. The conversion process was initiated in 1956 by Dr. B. K. Ambedkar, the leader of the Mahar people. Ambedkar publicly adopted Buddhism on the grounds that it was the religion best suited to the spiritual, social, and economic well-being of his followers. Initially, some 800,000 persons were involved in the new Buddhist movement, and the number of adherents has more than doubled during the past 35 years.

EXPANSION IN THE WEST

Buddhism had never seriously penetrated into the West prior to the modern period. But since the late nineteenth century, Buddhists have established a religious and social presence in practically all parts of the Western world, particularly the United States. The primary impetus for the spread of Buddhism to the West was the establishment of immigrant communities from China and Japan. These communities have continued to grow and to develop new forms of Buddhist life suitable for the Western environment. Currently, Buddhist communities composed of Asian-Americans are firmly implanted in Hawaii, California, and many other states. Some are identified with traditional schools such as Pure Land and Zen; others represent new Buddhist movements such as Risshō Kōsei Kai and Sōka Gakkai. More recently, the population of Asian-American Buddhists has been significantly expanded by the arrival of Theravāda Buddhists from Southeast Asia and of Tibetan Buddhists.

The penetration of Buddhism into the West has not been limited to immigrant communities. Beginning in the 1890s, Buddhist societies have been founded in various European countries, Australia, and the United States. The leaders of these societies have included

Buddhism in the West has not been limited to immigrant communities, but has been the object of widespread popular interest. Here worshipers gather at a Buddhist monastery in Woodstock, New York. (Maggie Hopp)

scholars of Buddhism as well as spiritual seekers drawn to the religions and philosophies of the East. More recently, Buddhism has also become the object of widespread popular interest, particularly in the so-called counterculture that flourished in the 1960s and 1970s. This interest has been stimulated and nurtured through the writings and activities of Asian missionaries such as the great Japanese scholar D. T. Suzuki, Tibetan exiles such as Tarthang Tulku, and native enthusiasts such as Philip Kapleau. Buddhist influences also appeared in the works of avant-garde literary figures of the 1950s and 1960s such as Jack Kerouac and Gary Snyder. The surge of interest in Buddhism during the 1960s and early 1970s encouraged the establishment of a network of Buddhist organizations and meditation centers across the United States, from Honolulu and San Francisco to Vermont.

BUDDHISM AND THE FUTURE

Will the Buddhist communities that stretch from southern Russia through China to Southeast Asia be able to regain their strength despite the effects of devastating attacks by Communist rulers? Will the Buddhist communities in the fringe areas of southern and eastern Asia continue to enjoy the kind of government support or toleration that they now receive? If so, will they be able to achieve the delicate balance between conservatism and reform that will be needed if they are to maintain their vigor and relevance? Will the fledgling Buddhist groups in Indonesia, India, and the West be able to sustain their dynamism and become permanently established in their new environments? Only time will tell.

NOTES

1 The mystery and romance of Dunhuang is well captured in the novel *Tun-huang* by Yasushi Inoue, translated by Jean Oda Moy (Tokyo and New York: Kodansha International, 1978), and the album *Tunhuang* by Kitaro on Canyon Records (© 1981).

2 Mary Lelia Makra, *The Hsiao Ching* (New York: St. John's University Press, 1961), p. 3.

3 *Taishō Shinshū Daizōkyō,* vol. 50, p. 470.

4 For a selection of texts defending Buddhism against Confucian

and Daoist criticisms, see Chapter 5 in William Theodore de Bary, ed., *The Buddhist Tradition in India, China, and Japan* (New York: Modern Library, 1969).

5 Robert E. Buswell, Jr., *The Korean Approach to Zen: The Collected Works of Chinul* (Honolulu: University of Hawaii Press, 1983); Robert E. Buswell, Jr., *Tracing Back the Radiance: Chinul's Korean Way of Zen* (Honolulu: University of Hawaii Press, 1992).

6 *Japanese Religion: A Survey by the Agency for Cultural Affairs* (Tokyo: Kodansha International, 1972) lists many hundreds of lineages.

7 A. F. Price and Wong Mou-Lam, trans., *The Diamond Sutra and the Sutra of Hui Neng* (Boulder, Colo.: Shambhala, 1969), pp. 54–55.

8 For a selection of this advice, along with a representative anthology of texts from the other major Tibetan Buddhist schools, see Stephen Batchelor, ed., *The Jewel in the Lotus: A Guide to the Buddhist Traditions of Tibet* (London: Wisdom Publications, 1987).

9 In accordance with the Buddhist teaching of the lack of an inherently existing self (anātman), the rebirth is neither identical with nor entirely different from the former incarnation. An intriguing account of a Spanish child who has been identified as the rebirth of a famous Tibetan tulku is Vicki MacKenzie, *The Boy Lama* (San Francisco: HarperCollins, 1988).

PART FOUR

RELIGIONS OF CHINA AND JAPAN

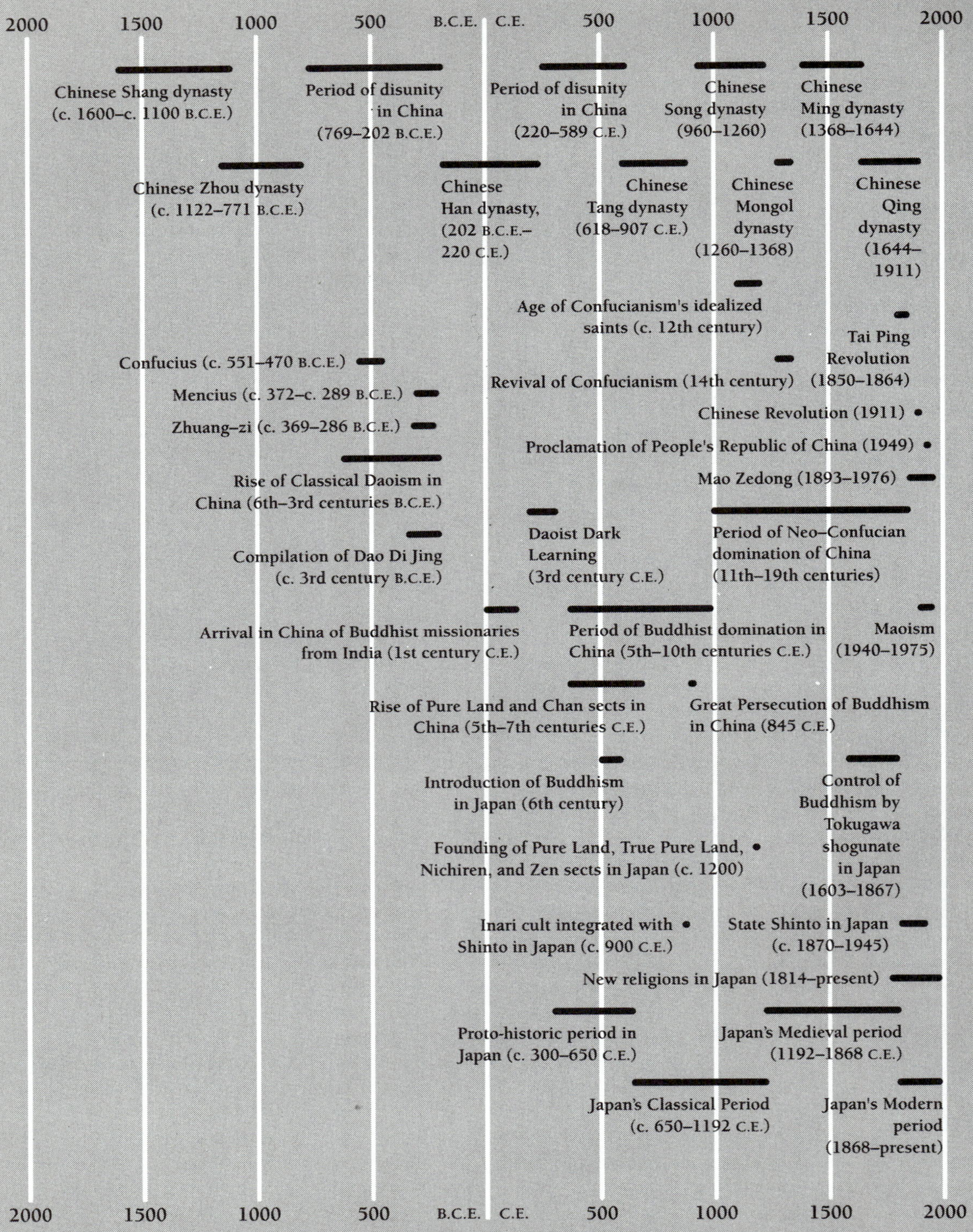
2000 1500 1000 500 B.C.E. C.E. 500 1000 1500 2000
Chinese Shang dynasty (c. 1600–c. 1100 B.C.E.)
Period of disunity in China (769–202 B.C.E.)
Period of disunity in China (220–589 C.E.)
Chinese Song dynasty (960–1260)
Chinese Ming dynasty (1368–1644)
Chinese Zhou dynasty (c. 1122–771 B.C.E.)
Chinese Han dynasty, (202 B.C.E.–220 C.E.)
Chinese Tang dynasty (618–907 C.E.)
Chinese Mongol dynasty (1260–1368)
Chinese Qing dynasty (1644–1911)
Age of Confucianism's idealized saints (c. 12th century)
Tai Ping Revolution (1850–1864)
Confucius (c. 551–470 B.C.E.)
Revival of Confucianism (14th century)
Mencius (c. 372–c. 289 B.C.E.)
Chinese Revolution (1911)
Zhuang-zi (c. 369–286 B.C.E.)
Proclamation of People's Republic of China (1949)
Rise of Classical Daoism in China (6th–3rd centuries B.C.E.)
Mao Zedong (1893–1976)
Compilation of Dao Di Jing (c. 3rd century B.C.E.)
Daoist Dark Learning (3rd century C.E.)
Period of Neo-Confucian domination of China (11th–19th centuries)
Arrival in China of Buddhist missionaries from India (1st century C.E.)
Period of Buddhist domination in China (5th–10th centuries C.E.)
Maoism (1940–1975)
Rise of Pure Land and Chan sects in China (5th–7th centuries C.E.)
Great Persecution of Buddhism in China (845 C.E.)
Introduction of Buddhism in Japan (6th century)
Control of Buddhism by Tokugawa shogunate in Japan (1603–1867)
Founding of Pure Land, True Pure Land, Nichiren, and Zen sects in Japan (c. 1200)
Inari cult integrated with Shinto in Japan (c. 900 C.E.)
State Shinto in Japan (c. 1870–1945)
New religions in Japan (1814–present)
Proto-historic period in Japan (c. 300–650 C.E.)
Japan's Medieval period (1192–1868 C.E.)
Japan's Classical Period (c. 650–1192 C.E.)
Japan's Modern period (1868–present)
2000 1500 1000 500 B.C.E. C.E. 500 1000 1500 2000

CHINA AND JAPAN TIME LINE

CHAPTER 12

ROOTS OF RELIGION IN CHINA

Chinese religions share not a common founding figure but a common geographic home. Even so, we will see a leitmotif running through all of them, for the faiths of China, perhaps more than those of any other region, have shown a profound continuity in worldview, goals, and patterns of behavior. Despite their 4,000 years of history, Chinese religions remain, at heart, one.

The leitmotiv we will see is an emphasis on harmony. In this traditional view, what is most important is not an individual person, thing, or power but rather the nature and quality of their interrelationships. These interconnections are between nature and human society. Commitment to this ideal of universal harmony has led many religious leaders to formulate methods and programs by which it can be brought about and preserved.

This is not to say that the evolution of China's religions has been without drama. On the contrary, these religions have a long and complex history, centering on the rise of two contending ways of life, Confucianism and Daoism, and interactions between them. Both had appeared by the beginning of the fourth century B.C.E. By roughly 200 B.C.E., Confucianism had become an organized entity, serving the religious needs of China's elite ruling class: adopted as the state orthodoxy, it remained so for some 400 years. At about the beginning of the Common Era, Daoism rose to the fore, appealing especially to the disenfranchised peasants and the common people; it continued to offer them hope, meaning, and solace for 2,000 years. In the second century B.C.E. Buddhism entered as a third player on the field, brought by missionaries from India by way of central Asia. A century later, when Confucianism became discredited following the collapse of its patron, the Han dynasty, both Daoism and Buddhism grew rapidly at all levels of society. After reaching their zenith of influence in the Tang dynasty (600s–800s C.E.), both Buddhism and Daoism gradually gave way to a rejuvenated Confucianism, now called Neo-Confucianism, which dominated the religious and cultural life of China until the start of the twentieth century.

But we must never forget that this drama unfolded over a background of values, attitudes, and expectations that have, over the ages, changed little. One

On Transcribing and Pronouncing Chinese
Chinese names can be rendered in English according to two systems of transliteration, pinyin and the older Wade-Giles. Because it is easier to sound out accurately, pinyin is becoming the preferred system and the one that we use in this text, but where a name is commonly known in its Wade-Giles transliteration, that spelling is given in parentheses.

Pinyin is pronounced as it looks, with the following exceptions: *ong* at the end of a word is pronounced "ung"; thus *Song*, a dynasty, rhymes with *hung*. The letter *x* is pronounced like "sh," but with the tongue placed against the front teeth. And *q* is pronounced "ch"; hence *Qin*, the dynasty from which the country's English name derives, is pronounced "chin."

metaphor used to describe China's religious tradition is that of a great tree with common roots and trunk but many branches. The root attitudes, which emphasize the harmonious interrelatedness of all things, have remained largely intact, changing slowly if at all over time; the three isms constitute the main branches, each of which has produced many twigs and flowers. We will first explore the substratum of belief that is common to Chinese religions, discerning its earliest manifestations and connections, and then explore some of the blossoming branches.

THE UNITY OF CHINESE RELIGIONS

The goal of life, according to most Chinese religions, is the establishment, maintenance, and enjoyment of harmony in this world. This means that this world has at least the potential to fulfill the deepest needs and highest ideals of human life. It also means that orderliness is vital to the good life: all things, natural as well as human, must have a proper place and function within the whole.

This need for an overriding order may ultimately derive from the ancient Chinese people's long struggle to survive along the middle reaches of the Yellow River. The inland climate was harsh: its summers were hot and its winters cold. Although the silt the river deposited renewed the fertility of the soil, periodic floods presented a constant danger. To the north lay vast steppes inhabited by tribes of seminomadic herders and hunters, the feared northern barbarians, whose way of life was alien and whose propensity to wage war was feared. As a defense, the earliest Chinese built fortified towns that grew eventually into cities. The same threat led a millennium later to the construction of the Great Wall. Such large projects demanded that power be centralized in the hands of a strong aristocracy that was then able to organize the people for military defense and large-scale irrigation and agricultural projects. Thus the need for an overarching order and a harmonious society was probably felt in China from its very earliest days—indeed, long before the first written records (dating from around 1500 B.C.E.) found on bones and bronze castings. By that time, the first historical dynasty, the Shang, was well established, along with an entrenched hierarchical structure and a corresponding emphasis on order and harmony.

Even though life was to be fulfilled in this world rather than in an other-worldly heaven, the Chinese, like many other peoples, nevertheless believed in an afterlife. At physical death people were thought to enter a shadowy, nonphysical mode of existence that permitted them, now as "ancestors," a limited interaction with the world of ordinary life. The Chinese neither held out the promise of heavenly bliss nor feared hellish punishment but rather sought a this-worldly salvation.

The quest for harmony in this world takes several directions. One is the pursuit of social, political, and intellectual control. Rules of behavior—what we might think of as etiquette or formal behavior—became especially important as the primary means of regulating both human-to-human and human-to-nature interactions. If everyone knows how one is expected to act in every situation, no one will disrupt the order of life. This leads to a highly formalized, even ritualized pattern of living—the emphasis especially of Confucianism. In a related way, harmony will be enhanced if the individual is submerged in the group. Traditionally, the Chinese boy or girl is socialized through an elaborate set of decorum rules that regulate behavior in part by insisting on adherence to a strict social hierarchy. This emphasis on conformity to social norms leads to another key Chinese notion: in any given situation, everything and everyone has a single proper place ("a place for everything, and everything in its place"). This attitude gives Chinese society a distinctively personal character in that all things, both natural and human, are viewed through this model of interpersonal relations. For example, one conducts government, business, or family affairs based not on objective laws or rules applicable to all equally but on the exchange of gifts or personal favors: one seeks to establish a personal relationship with the people or powers on whom success depends. Thus various rites of hospitality, such as gift giving and sharing of meals, characterize not just more intimate family interactions but all of life, including religious activities.

The quest for harmony goes beyond family and government to encompass the physical, natural realm. The architecture of ancient China reflected this interest in order, harmony, and proper place. For example, the

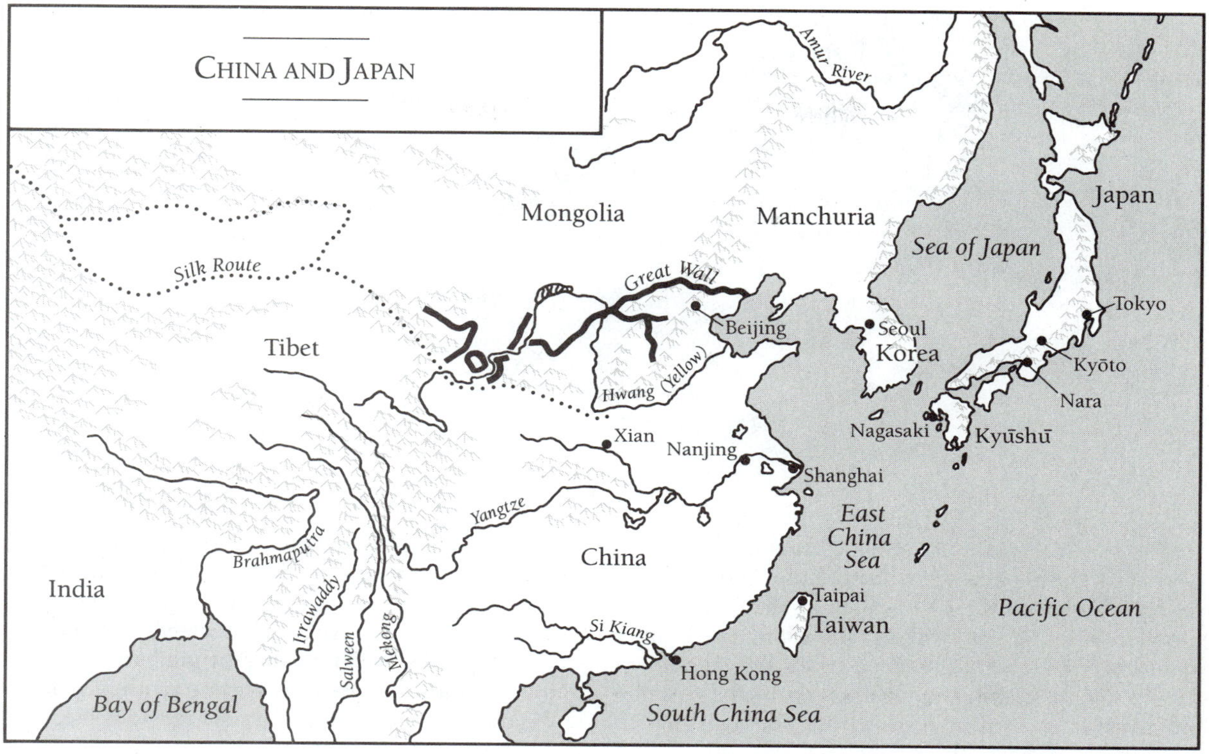

walled compound of a local feudal lord was commonly rectangular; the gates that pierced each of the four sides were aligned with the four cardinal directions. Inside, the lord's residence and ancestral hall were placed at the center; the mound of earth sacred to the "god of the soil," the chief agricultural deity, was always to the south, its "proper" direction. When large cities were built, their architects employed the same precise pattern. This arrangement both symbolized the hierarchical order of the human world and reflected a more fundamental harmony with the powers of earth and sky. Such architecture, in turn, helped to reinforce the emphasis on place and order. When the feudal lords—and later princes, kings, and emperors—performed rituals, they sought to ensure, through gifts (sacrifices) and praise (prayers), a cosmic harmony. They felt that the survival of human life depended on harmony and order. We can get a clearer sense of this substratum of common belief if we look at China's earliest religions, for they exhibit these patterns clearly.

CHINA'S EARLY RELIGIOUS HISTORY

THE SHANG DYNASTY

China's most ancient artifacts date from the Shang dynasty (1500s–1100s B.C.E.). Settled around the Yellow River in north central China, the Shang were an agricultural people who built large fortified towns, probably to protect themselves from invaders from the north. Although our data are incomplete, we can say that their society was highly stratified. It was probably dominated by a ruling class of warriors, perhaps descendants of a once-distinct group that had conquered an agricultural people. Their main source of wealth was grain crops like wheat and millet. The male aristocrats probably spent most of their time making war, hunting, and cultivating the arts. We know little of women's activities.

The Hall of Supreme Harmony was the location of the emperor's dragon throne. The quest for harmony was central to Chinese religion and life, going beyond family and government to encompass the physical, natural realm. (Shashinka Photo Library)

The two most important Shang religious practices were apparently concerned with bountiful harvests and devotion to ancestors. As is common among agricultural peoples, animal symbolism predominated, and animal sacrifices were the chief means by which the people sought to influence the powers of the cosmic order that in turn ensured the earth's bounty. Dragon and serpent designs, the symbols of life-giving rain, clouds, and mist—and thus also of abundant harvests and of the mysterious life-giving power of the earth—were also frequent and have been found even on pre-Shang pottery from the region.

Shang rites showed that human beings, animals, and plants were seen as participating in the great cosmic processes of planting, growth, and harvest. The rituals suggest that survival was acknowledged as being dependent on a smooth relationship with this cosmic process.

The hidden world of the ancestors played a part in this cosmic scheme. The Shang believed that at death, a person joined the ancestors. More powerful than in life, an ancestor could influence his or her descendants' future and the natural world. Shang-di ("Supreme Ruler"), the most important deity, was the divine ancestor of the ruling family; his envoy, the wind, was the ruler of the spirit powers. An ancestor would reward or punish the behavior of the living just as the various gods and goddesses could. To ensure that the ancestors would be well disposed, survivors who could afford to do so provided elaborate grave furnishings and made offerings of food and clothing.

In addition to lessening the sense of loss felt by the surviving family members, the rites of ancestor reverence clearly reinforced the notion of place. These rites also tended to associate the society's established customs with the ancestors, thereby inhibiting innovation. Ancestor reverence thus became another element in the traditional pattern of Chinese religious life, one that persists even to this day.

The quest for order and harmony apparently also encouraged the important Shang practice of divination. In divination one consults with spirit beings to interpret natural phenomena and predict future events. The Shang's favorite method was to inscribe a yes-or-no question on a tortoise shell or a piece of animal bone. Then they would scratch the words *yes* and *no* randomly on the object, which was then roasted over the fire. Cracks that appeared near a *yes* or a *no* were taken to be answers from the spirits. Typical questions were "Will the harvest be good?" "Will I live a long life?" and "Will we be successful in war?"

THE ZHOU DYNASTY

The patterns of traditional Chinese religion can also be seen in the next major period, that of the Zhou (Chou) dynasty (1122–771 B.C.E.). The Zhou, who overthrew the Shang rulers, had been a farming people living about 300 miles southwest of the Shang kingdom. Once they wrested power from the Shang, they ruled through a pyramidal feudal system in which each lower member owed allegiance to the higher members. But the prestige of the Shang remained so awesome that the Zhou preserved much of their previous culture, even adopting many of the Shang's religious practices and laws. In fact, they even saw to it that sacrifices to the ancestors of the deposed Shang rulers were continued.

The most important continuity was that, though they expressed it in their own way, the Zhou embraced the Shang concern for order and harmony. This can be seen in the Zhou ancestral cult, as we have it from their *Book of Songs,* from which comes most of our knowledge of this early period. The main celebrations renewing ties to the ancestors occurred in conjunction with their spring and autumn rituals. The activities centered around a rite of hospitality. The ancestors were invited as honored guests to the house, where they were treated to an elaborate ceremonial meal. The ancestral souls were called forth by pouring libations on the ground and by burning food. Prior to this summoning, the eldest son of the family entered a period of mourning and purification. Usually, a grandson or another kinsman of the most recently deceased male was selected to be "possessed" by the dead during the banquet. Thus as the ancestors were experienced as actually present, enjoying the food and gifts, the assembled family gained access to them and their blessings. When, at the end of the ritual, they asked the ancestors if they were pleased with the gifts, the people could be assured that they could look forward to continued harmony and blessings.

Like so much of Chinese popular religion, Zhou rites were directed toward the goals of abundant life, good harvests, and avoidance of calamities. A more subtle function of these rites undoubtedly was to heighten the sense of the meaningful order of all life by ritually showing that each family member belonged to a biologically and socially enduring stream of life. The living must have seen themselves as part of a larger community that included the dead and must have felt an increased obligation to live up to their forbears' idealized behavior.

Zhou Deities and the Dao

Among the ancestral figures that came to assume a more distinct identity as a deity was **Hou Ji**, the god of millet and first ancestor of the ruling Zhou family, who was thought to have discovered agriculture. He gave his descendants the first millet and other seeds and taught them the secrets of cultivation. According to the myth preserved in the *Book of Songs,* a goddess became pregnant as the result of "stepping on the footprints" of the high god Shang-di. After giving birth to Hou Ji, she performed the ceremony of placing the child upon the earth, thus acquainting him with the site of his future labor. Hou Ji's divine parentage thus provided everyday agricultural activities with divine significance. In addition, planting and harvest rites in his honor served to ensure that these activities remained in harmony with the larger cosmic order.

Another important deity unique to the Zhou was **Tian** (T'ien), usually translated as Heaven. It may seem odd to call heaven a deity, but the Zhou people thought of the vault of the sky not as a place but as a force, for it was the original source of natural and moral order. Indeed, Tian was originally the supreme Zhou deity; though eventually identified with Shang-di, Tian was always more vaguely defined and less personal. The Zhou rulers never claimed Tian as their ancestor. When the ruler came to be called the Son of Heaven, this was understood to signify a status relationship, not descent. In later times, emperors were thought to continue as rulers only because their behavior accorded with the norms of morality and ritual correctness and not because of hereditary right; this was known as the Mandate of Heaven (Tian-ming).

Just as the lands occupied by the Zhou people were thought of as the center of the world, so the king's palace in the capital city was its focus, the center of the entire heavenly realm. The king himself was identified with the stationary North Star, around which the heavenly canopy revolved—one more display of a cosmic harmony integrated with humanity.

The ordering principle that made such cosmic harmony possible was called **Dao** *(Tao),* a key concept in Chinese religions. The most basic meaning of the word *Dao* is "road" or "path," especially with reference to the stars' celestial paths and by extension the whole orderly procession of heavenly bodies. Other regular patterns were also associated with this term, especially the seasonal cycles of cold and hot, wet and dry, and dormancy, growth, and harvest. Early calendars were essentially descriptions of Dao in that they integrated all these elements.

In the concept of Dao the Chinese emphasized that order and harmony were matters not only of space but

COMPARISON

Social Order and Natural Order

Many cultures understand their social patterns to be on a continuum with natural and supernatural phenomena. For example, the Vedic people conceived of their societal obligations in terms of *ṛita,* a term that they also applied to the order followed by natural phenomena. To act according to ṛita was, for them, like going with the harmonious flow of a world that is forever changing. Later Hindus conceived of their social roles and duties in terms of *dharma,* a principle of right that was rooted also in the universe, but a universe that was firm, steady, and unchanging. Thus society's rules, too, would be unlikely to change; indeed, once texts like Manu's had laid out the particulars of dharma, they remained nearly unchanged for centuries.

The Chinese conceived of their world in terms of the *Dao,* a term originally signifying the stars' celestial paths and hence the whole procession of stars, planets, and other heavenly bodies. Humans, spirit beings, weather patterns, and other natural phenomena all followed the same Dao. Because they conceived of it temporally, from very early days the Chinese were driven to write careful histories, trying to detail how natural patterns correlated with human ones.

In detail these notions differ, but they share a sense that human processes are associated with the natural order and that there is a close relationship between human obligation and natural forces.

also of time. Just as there is but one proper time to plant or harvest, so there was but one Dao for all activities; there was but one proper pattern for human life. The natural and the social—both were manifestations of this ultimate Dao (see the accompanying box).

The assumption that the natural and human realms reflect each other led to the practice at the king's court of appointing a so-called grand recorder. It is thanks to such officials—part astronomer, part historian, and part astrologer—that we have early records. These men and their aides were charged with carefully observing and recording any unusual events, celestial or terrestrial, in the natural or human realm, so that their meanings might be read. Histories came to be kept so as to record patterns in the past; similar patterns in the present might then be used to predict the future. All these unusual events were indicators of the Dao; to discern them was to know the Dao. Then, too, some events were disruptive of the cosmic and human order: they were against the Dao and were sometimes accompanied by terrible consequences. The worst of these, from the point of view of the king and his court, was the withdrawal of the Mandate of Heaven, which meant the destruction of the dynasty.

Yin and Yang

Closely related to the idea of the cosmic Way were the twin notions of **yin** and **yang**. These were the names given to the two opposite but complementary forces or tendencies inherent in all things by which it was possible to understand the nature of the dynamism or changeableness of things. After all, the cosmic order, Dao, was not a changeless, timeless reality; rather it pointed to a pattern of orderly and to some extent predictable change. Probably *yin* originally meant "covered as by clouds," hence dark, secret, and cool;

yang meant something bright and shiny, hence light, open, and warm. Each thing's nature and its changes resulted from the mixture of these two principles.

Scholars have proposed that these twin notions arose in early China as a reflection of seasonal rhythms, climate, growing seasons, and the division of labor between the sexes. The summer, when it was warm and the rains would fall, was the time to plant, harvest, and fatten the herds. This work fell to men, often at some distance from the family hearth. During the cold winter season, indoor work became dominant, especially the weaving of cloth. These labors fell to women. Thus human activities, and maleness and femaleness, were correlated with the rhythms of nature. Summer eventually came to be correlated with male work, maleness itself, and thus yang; winter meant women's work, femaleness, and finally yin. Neither yang nor yin was considered inherently good or bad. Both were necessary components in the world's proper operation. Good was the proper mixture of both; bad was an excess of either.

Ultimacy

Our recognition of a sense of ultimacy in this common substratum of Chinese religion leads us to several conclusions. First, ultimacy was encountered in ordinary things and events of this world. Human life was not in conflict with ultimacy in part because the ultimate was perceived not as transcendent but as immanent, found in everyday life and within the individual. Second, certain things and certain persons were thought to be more sacred than others. Especially sacred were the forces of nature, the gods and goddesses thought to control these forces, the revered ancestors, and living persons of high status, such as kings and emperors. Third, ultimacy was experienced not so much as a personal, direct relationship to a deity or an ancestor (on a vertical or transcendent axis) but rather in the net of relationships that included all things (horizontal or immanent within the pattern of life). The great sage Confucius articulated this well in teaching that participation in the rituals that establish and reinforce the lived web of interrelationships is at least as important as the individual elements within them.

THE AGE OF THE HUNDRED PHILOSOPHERS

During most of the Zhou dynasty, the feudal political structure remained relatively stable. This began to change dramatically in the eighth century B.C.E. As the old feudal structure of Zhou society slowly disintegrated, barbarous tribes invaded from the west. In 769

As this set of bronze sacrificial vessels shows, both the Shang and their successors, the Zhou, were expert metalworkers. (The Metropolitan Museum of Art, Munsey Bequest, 1924)

B.C.E. an army of dissidents sacked the capital, killing the Zhou emperor. China was soon carved into a number of independent states, each headed by a ruler who hoped to unify China under a new dynasty. The period became one of constant warfare.

Such warfare brought in its wake serious political and economic disruption. This was especially troubling to the Chinese people, for whom harmony and order held such importance. Not surprisingly, many thoughtful individuals attempted to discern the causes of the disharmony and the meaning of human existence and to find new solutions to the problems ravaging people's lives—so many, in fact, that the sixth century B.C.E. became known as the age of the hundred philosophers. It was during this unsettled time that the two main players in the drama of Chinese religion, Confucianism and Daoism, emerged. Both came to address the needs of this period for a new way to understand and bring about harmony, and both tapped the roots of Chinese beliefs to do so. Far from rejecting custom, they sought to articulate and clarify the wisdom hidden within it.

CONFUCIUS: THE RITUALIZATION OF LIFE

During this period of strife and philosophical speculation, the great moral philosopher and teacher Kong zi (formerly known as Kung Fu-tzu, romanized as Confucius; 551–470 B.C.E.) was born. According to tradition, Confucius came from an impoverished family of the lower nobility. He became a petty government bureaucrat, but possibly because of his reputation for speaking his mind, he never rose to a position of high responsibility. He continued to criticize government policies and made a modest living as a teacher. In his later years he is said to have devoted himself to editing the classical books of history now known as the *Wu Jing* ("Five Classics"). Teachings attributed to him were collected as the *Analects (Lun Yu)*.

For the past 2,000 years the teachings of Confucius have had a great influence on the thought, government institutions, literature, arts, and social customs of China. Confucianism has also been influential in Japan, Korea, and Vietnam. Many people consider it primarily a social and moral philosophy, yet as practiced by the educated upper classes, Confucianism had definite religious dimensions.

Li *and Social Order*

Confucius saw the answer to his era's problems in the ritualization of life, which was found in the practice of **li**. *Li* was the most important term in Confucius's thought. It encompassed a number of ideas conveyed in English by separate words, such as *ritual, custom, propriety,* and *manners*. That li was applied to so many human activities is itself significant because li was thought to be the means by which life should be ordered and the proper harmony established. A person of li was thus good and virtuous; a state ordered by li was harmonious and peaceful.

The oldest meaning of *li* referred to the sacred rites of hospitality, particularly the important ancestral rituals. Indeed, for the early Chinese the term *li* was nearly synonymous with religion. Confucius took this core idea—of activity specifically pertaining to ultimate things—and enlarged it so that all activities could be viewed as ultimate. On the one hand, this meant that every act took on an aura of mystery and seriousness hitherto reserved for ancestral rites and solemn sacrifices to the gods. On the other hand, it also meant that specifically religious rites themselves were judged by Confucian society as relatively less important. As Confucius himself put it, "Devote yourself earnestly to the duties due to men, and respect spiritual beings, but keep them at a distance" (*Analects* 6.20). This distancing of spiritual beings, which included the ancestors, was both a sign of respect for their power and a refocusing of religious concern onto human affairs. Confucius and his followers continued to perform the ancient rites, but their main goal was to make the attitudes and sense of order appropriate to these rites pervade all the affairs of life. For this, li was essential.

The first step in the Confucian program to establish the proper order of things (Dao) among human beings was to reform government. Confucius himself briefly held a position in the administration of his native state of Lu (modern Shandong). His pupils, however, were much more successful as office seekers, and much of the discussion between master and pupil recorded in the *Analects* pertained to the proper conduct of state affairs. By the time China was reunified in the late third century B.C.E., Confucian scholars dominated the bureaucracy that ran the imperial government.

Far from favoring an egalitarian and democratic ideal, the assumed direction of influence in the

Confucian view of the state was from the top down. Confucius believed that if the leaders could be changed, the people would also "rectify" themselves by correcting their behavior. The *Analects* put it this way:

> Lead the people with legal measures and regulate them by punishment, and they will avoid wrong-doing but will have no sense of honor and shame. Lead them with the power of virtuous example *(de)* and regulate them by the rules of *li,* and they will have a sense of shame and will thus rectify themselves. (2.3)

In the phrase "regulate them by the rules of *li,*" the term translated rather abstractly as "to regulate" had the very revealing concrete and primitive meaning of kernels of wheat filling the ear evenly. This simple yet powerful image conveyed the Confucian emphasis on order in a single and concise image: kernels regularly and predictably filling their assigned space in an assigned pattern, over and over. The image conveyed regularity, predictability, and continuity—all the cornerstones of order—as well as a sense of each thing fitting in its proper place. The goodness and abundance of this order was also found in the image of a good harvest.

To act according to li was thus to do what was right in the proper manner at the proper time—that is, to follow the Dao. This exemplification of the Dao could not help but be imitated by the people. Coercion, therefore, would not only be unnecessary but would also indicate a falling away from the Dao. The ideal was neither to coerce people nor to give them anarchic freedom but rather to lead them to participate voluntarily in the rhythm of li and, in effect, the social structure.

The use to which Confucius sought to put li might be called a form of social engineering, although such an idea would have been alien to him because it implies *arbitrary* manipulation. He sought to create an environment in which people would naturally be harmonious and thus virtuous, but he believed that there was only one right way, the Way, to do it. Harmony was an unavoidable consequence of the shaping power of li because li was the perfect reflection of cosmic order, Dao, as applied to human society. A land whose people acted according to li was a civilized country; one whose people did not follow li was not civilized, and its people were not fully human in the sense that they had no means of realizing their potential as human beings.

This etching represents Kong zi (romanized as Confucius). Confucius was a great moral philosopher and teacher and redirected Chinese religion to a concern about human affairs. (The Granger Collection)

As Confucius said in the *Analects:* "Respectfulness without li becomes laborious bustle; carefulness without li becomes timidity; boldness without li becomes insubordination; straightforwardness without li becomes rudeness" (8.2).

Ren *and Humaneness*

We all have the potential to become people of **ren**, of humanity or humaneness. To embody this quality of humaneness was the goal of Confucius's followers. But ren was more than humanity in the external sense; it was the measure of individual character and, as such, the goal of self-cultivation. Self-cultivation could be attained just by conforming to li; ren is the human quality that results from acting according to li. Li and ren are thus two sides of the same coin. But when Confucius spoke of ren, he emphasized in the following question the individual effort required in the proper performance of li: "If a man is not humane [*ren*], what has he to do with ceremonies [*li*]?" (3.3). This individual effort was thought of as self-control or self-mastery. As Confucius said, "To master or control the self and return to li, that is ren" (12.1).

The psychological aspects of this doctrine, which later became important in China when psychologically sensitive Buddhism came to the fore, were never fully clarified by the Confucians themselves. Some thought of the road to ren as the control of individual impulses and desires, an effort of the will aided by social pressure. This tended to make Confucianism a rather rigid set of uniform social rules. But others, notably the Neo-Confucian schools of thought that developed much later, saw ren as a quality of an individual's inner being: the self had been mastered in the sense that it had been transformed under the impact of li. A famous autobiographical statement by Confucius in the *Analects* supports this later view:

> At fifteen, my mind sought learning. At thirty, my character was firmly set. At forty, my doubts were at an end. At fifty, I knew the will of Heaven. At sixty, I could hear the truth with equanimity. At seventy, I unerringly desired what was right. (2.4)

Thus Confucianism contained within it a degree of differentiation from the Chinese substratum described earlier. Individualism, though still very much in the service of the whole, has crept in to this hierarchical system.

The Confucian Sage and the Glorification of the Past

Confucius did not see himself as an innovator, though in some respects his doctrines were quite new. As we have seen, he made li, the ancient ritual pattern, into an all-encompassing style of life, a significant reinterpretation. Yet he claimed and probably himself believed that he was only trying to return to the original and proper way of the ancient **sages.** Confucius idealized these figures as holy men who embodied perfect wisdom. Their very presence in the world was enough to bring about a golden age. They were perfect beings, possessing powers of knowledge, insight, and virtue far beyond those of ordinary people. Four sages are mentioned in the *Analects:* Yao and Shun were legendary kings of remotest antiquity and models of the perfect ruler; Yu the Great was part divine protector of agriculture and part irrigation engineer who tamed the floods of the Yellow River; and the duke of Zhou was the brother of the dynasty's founder. Confucius especially revered the duke of Zhou as the ideal scholar-administrator that Confucius himself aspired to become and into which he sought to turn his students.

The most important quality such sages exhibited was **de** (*te,* virtue), best understood as a sacred personal force, something akin to charisma, inherent in a sage's very presence. De had the power to change the course of history by bringing about a harmonious order during the sage's lifetime. The virtue of the ancient sage-kings and hence their connection with the Dao was so great that they could rule by "inactivity." As Confucius put it in the *Analects,* "He who exercises government by means of his virtue [*de*] may be compared to the north pole star, which keeps its place and all the stars turn toward it" (2.1), a reference to an ancient Zhou image. Later Confucian masters taught that all humans could and should aspire to a sage's de.

Confucius used the image of the ancient sages and their de as the inspiration for proper conduct. To emulate the great sages of antiquity, one first had to study the ancient books to learn their Way. Thus study and imitation of the sages became part of the Confucian way. "Most exalted is [the sage] who is born with knowledge; but next is the man who learns through study" (16.9). It was this more modest goal to which Confucius aspired and to which he urged his disciples. Not daring to rank himself among the sages, Confucius said of himself: "I strive to become such without satiety, and teach others without weariness" (7.3).

The Ideal Man and the Ideal Woman

Confucius struggled against the entrenched privileges of the feudal hereditary aristocracy of his day. Its members used political power to indulge their own pleasures and protect their own wealth and status. To him this was a gross distortion of the proper order as embodied in the Way of the ancients. The ideal that Confucius taught was called **zhunzi** *(chün-tzu),* usually translated now as "superior man" or "true gentleman." Confucius altered the meaning of the term from a person born to a position of wealth and privilege to one honored for individual merit. What mattered was character, not background. To build character meant to study and learn the Way of the ancients and scrupulously to follow li.

Confucius's superior man was similar in many ways to the gentleman of Victorian England. He was cultured and reserved. He was expected to exhibit a thorough knowledge of manners (li) and to care more for his own integrity and inner development than for wealth. Specifically, the superior man had the following qualities:

1. *He was above egoism.* He looked at the humane impulses within himself, and if all were well there, he did not worry about his relations with others. He served the common good, which was the reason he sought public office. Even in his official duties as adviser or administrator, he did not argue or contend; he simply stated the truth without concern for the consequences to himself.

2. *He was not narrow.* The superior man's function, his role in the world, was not to carry out any technical occupations or specific arts or crafts. As Confucius explained, "The superior man is not an implement" (*Analects* 2.12). His usefulness lay in the transforming power of his character. When his disciple Fan Ch'ih asked to be taught husbandry, Confucius answered:

> "I am not so good for that as an old husbandman." . . . Fan Ch'ih having gone out, the master said, "A small man, indeed, is Fan. If a superior man love li, the people will not dare not to be reverent. If he love good faith, the people will not dare not to submit to his example. If he love good faith, people will not dare not to be sincere. Now, when these things obtain, the people from all quarters will come to him, bearing their children on their backs—what need has he of a knowledge of husbandry?" (13.4)

3. *Above all, he was a man of ren.* In the context of the zhunzi, ren is best rendered as "altruism," since it included empathy for all and concern for their well-being. But such altruism should not be expressed indiscriminately; the goal was not an egalitarian society but an orderly, harmonious hierarchy of persons and things. Through the structure imposed by li, one was concerned with justice—that is, with seeing to it that all persons were treated as befitting their station in life. Confucius advised his students to requite good with good and evil with justice and to love what is good and hate what is evil. His was not a universal ethic of love but an ethic ordered by li.

Although the Confucian ideals were defined primarily in terms of male standards, the tradition also defined a parallel set of standards for its women. In the cosmic principles of yin and yang, Confucians found the model for both male and female gender roles. As yang was seen as active and strong, men were supposed to initiate strong actions. Yin, in contrast, was identified with earth: inferior to heaven, yielding, passive, and weak. Women's proper behavior was understood as upholding and reflecting this necessary complement to the dominant role of heaven/yang/man. In her roles—defined as a daughter, wife, and mother—she was to be obedient to the appropriate dominant male, namely, her father, husband, and son or sons, in that order.

This ideal of passive servitude, however, required more of women than helpless inactivity. At marriage a woman joined her husband's family; since her life was dedicated exclusively to maintaining order and contentment in that family, the ideal Confucian woman exhibited a great deal of courage and personal strength. In later thought she was held responsible not only for her own "wifely way" virtue but for the moral character of her husband as well.

MENCIUS, DISCIPLE OF CONFUCIUS

For more than two centuries after Confucius died, progress toward the peaceful and harmonious way of life he advocated was slow. Contending states still made war on one another. The government still remained in the hands of military men and the old aristocracy. Yet increasingly, Confucianism made its mark on China, especially on its intellectuals. Indeed, by the fourth century B.C.E., most of the kings had gathered communities of scholars or philosophers to adorn their capital cities with a glow of high culture.

Among these was a brilliant Confucian scholar called Meng-zi (romanized as Mencius, c. 372–289 B.C.E.). True to his master's teaching, Mencius urged the rulers of the various states to adopt Confucian principles. He taught that rulers were given the Mandate of Heaven on the basis of the Confucian ideal of virtue; the ruler who was himself without virtue and was unconcerned for the welfare of his people would lose the Mandate. Mencius even taught that if a ruler is unjust and lacking in virtue, and thus without the Mandate, his subjects have the right to revolt. In doing so, they become the instrument of heaven, exercising its natural tendency toward return to the proper world order.

Mencius venerated Confucius, and at one point he is said to have exclaimed, "There never has been another Confucius since man first appeared on earth."[1] Mencius not only accepted his master's teachings but, being a creative thinker himself, also amplified them and added to them. While he accepted Confucius's vision of a cosmic order regulated by li, Mencius sought to develop a more systematic ethical system for the zhunzi. He grounded ethics in human nature: humans were essentially and originally good, and all else followed naturally from this inborn tendency. The basis of this goodness was the quality of ren, which needed only to be nurtured and channeled into appropriate paths as described by li. Thus not only was the order of harmony of the world visible in the regular patterns of nature and the perfect society, but it could also be experienced in the depths of human instinctual goodness. "Can it be that any man's mind naturally lacks Humanity [*ren*] and Justice? If he loses his sense of the good, then he loses it as [a] mountain [loses] its trees."[2] Just as trees grow naturally on a mountain, so does goodness flow naturally from the human heart. Human actions not in accord with the Way and those that result from the inevitable bustle of daily activities obscure this inner correctness. Yet one's true nature always remains; it can be known "in the still air of the early hours."

Mencius never lived to see a ruler institute his principles. But some 1,500 years later his thought became central to Neo-Confucianism. Two of his ideas came to be especially appreciated: his belief that sagehood was inherent in all human beings so that, if properly nurtured, it could grow in this world and his efforts to discover the inner life of the human mind.

LAO-ZI AND THE BEGINNINGS OF DAOISM

The disruption and anxieties of the period of warring states produced another body of thought, Daoism. Although this new religion had its roots in the common substratum of Chinese thought, it viewed the world very differently from Confucianism. More important, it proposed very different solutions to the problems of disharmony raised during the era of constant warfare.

Daoism earned its name from the central importance it gave to the concept of Dao, the Way. Its founder is traditionally said to have been Lao-zi (Lao-tzu), supposedly an elder contemporary of Confucius. Although today few scholars believe that any such person lived, it is still convenient to speak of Lao-zi as the author of the obscure but fascinating *Dao De Jing* (*Tao Te Ching,* "Classic of the Way and Its Power"). This text—combining religion, philosophy, poetry, and mysticism—dates from the beginning of the third century B.C.E. It has exerted a great influence on Chinese thought and attitudes and was eventually adopted by the popular Dao sects as their most important scripture.

Like Confucius, Lao-zi sought harmony in this world, but he located ultimacy not in social life but in nature itself. This he symbolized with the term *Dao*. If one could achieve a direct experience of the Dao, he said, its power would transform the individual, who would come to embody the Dao. Since it is ultimate reality and by nature harmonious and orderly, contact with it will transform a person, melting away problems and anxieties. No Confucian-style preaching of virtue, no reverent imitation of the ancients, no scrupulous attention to ritual, is necessary. Indeed, these things are quite dangerous—part of the problem, not of the solution. Because they are human rather than natural products, they derive from selfish human ambitions and not from the Dao, which is purely natural and spontaneous.

For Lao-zi, the Dao—and, indeed, human existence—was far more mysterious than it was for Confucius. Again and again, the *Dao De Jing* sounds the theme of the unknowableness of ultimate reality:

The Dao that can be told of is not the real Dao;
The name that can be named is not the real name.

This bronze piece, dating from the Song dynasty, depicts Lao-zi riding a water buffalo. Today few scholars believe that any such person lived, but it is still convenient to speak of him as the author of the *Dao De Jing*. (Worcester Art Museum)

This nameless thing is the origin of heaven and earth;
One may call it the Mother of all things.

(*Dao De Jing* 1)[3]

The mysteriousness of the Dao meant that one cannot adequately describe or conceptualize it. It exceeds human grasp both intellectually and practically. Beyond human possession or control, no words or thoughts can capture it:

One who knows does not speak;
One who speaks does not know.

(*Dao De Jing* 56)[4]

Nonetheless, this Dao is not a transcendent ultimate, removed from the world, but is immanent, found in the world. It is in fact active and present in all things, including human beings. One can for this reason encounter the Dao directly as ultimate power and mystery, in a mystical experience beyond concepts and reason. Through such experiences one can learn to yield to the Dao and live within its peace and harmony, for it is harmony itself. Thus Daoism recasts the common Chinese emphasis on harmony and the Way by focusing on the mystical experience of it.

To experience the Dao requires no Confucian ritualistic guidance. The Daoist sage was thought to be truly free to act without forethought or ritual plan. The sage could act spontaneously and do so without anxiety because the basis of his or her actions was the experience of the Dao itself.

One result of the *Dao De Jing*'s mystical emphasis is that, like many mystical texts around the world, its language and imagery are deeply paradoxical: one learns to be without learning; one acts without action. The truth, like the Dao, is hidden and unexpected. What is weakness to ordinary people is seen as strength; the apparently weak will eventually triumph over the seemingly strong. Only fools try to impose their will through force. Real strength is not like stone but like water:

There is nothing softer and weaker than water,
And yet there is nothing better for attacking hard and strong things.

(*Dao De Jing* 78)[5]

Other paradoxical images abound: to be active, one must be passive, like the traditional Chinese woman, who was able to accomplish her ends by attracting a willing man. The wise should be like an uncarved block of wood: pure, unpretentious, and without ego or artifice.

Naturalness

Just as the most obvious and accessible aspect of the Dao is the reality of nature that one can see, smell, and touch, so the most important characteristic of the Dao is **naturalness** *(ziran),* the quality of a thing's just being itself, spontaneously and without deception or calculation. A tree that has been shaped by wind and climate is natural; one that has been pruned into the shape of a swan is not. A person who is in tune with the Dao is spontaneous; one who is concerned to act a part or impose his or her will on others is not.

Daoism thus seeks a goal similar to that of Confucianism, harmony, but conceives of it and pursues it differently. Unlike Confucius, who emphasized trying to act in conformity with ritualized li, Lao-zi emphasized acting naturally. Only then will one be in perfect harmony; no ritualized behavior patterns are needed.

Daoism would also object to other societies, not just Confucian ones: compared to the natural world, almost any human society would be unnatural. When humans begin to think, they also begin to scheme and calculate for selfish ends. Not knowing the truly good—the Dao—we make false distinctions between good and evil that merely serve our own petty ends. Indeed, every doctrine of virtue is itself a sign that the proclaimer has lost the Dao, for the true sage would have no need for doctrines, concepts, or self-conscious concerns for virtue. This leads Lao-zi to a vision of a utopian society (*Dao De Jing* 80). Disdaining all artificiality, people in the utopian land will forgo the use of eating utensils; needing only natural simplicity, they may even give up writing. Content in themselves, they will not be curious to gossip about their neighbors.

The natural person forgets the self. To show how, Lao-zi distinguishes between action *(wei)* and nonaction **(wu-wei)**. Wei is willful, selfish action; it is always harmful because it is not in harmony with the Dao. Proper action is thus paradoxically called *nonaction;* since the sage's actions merely reflect the Dao, he does not act; the Dao acts through him.* We might say that the Daoist sage seeks harmony within himself and in the process loses himself to the Dao, whereas the ideal Confucian zhunzi seeks it outside himself and in the process loses himself to ritual. Virtue for Lao-zi became a mysterious internal power of the Dao itself, not a social program flowing out of the cultivation of character. For Lao-zi, the wise are to turn inward, not outward, to find the ultimate. Only when this way of life became general would the world achieve harmony.

ZHUANG-ZI AND THE DAOIST LIFE

The book that tradition ascribes to Zhuang-zi (Chuang-tzu; c. 369–286 B.C.E.) and bears his name is often paired with the *Dao De Jing* as the other of the two basic books of classical Daoism. It dates from the same era as its more famous companion and articulates a very similar view of the Dao. Whereas Lao-zi wrote as a poet, delighting in ambiguity and multiple meanings, Zhuang-zi wrote as a philosopher who turned the analytical and logical tools of philosophy against thinkers who describe reality in words. While Lao-zi played with paradoxical images, Zhuang-zi played with paradoxical arguments. He made fun of the Confucian conceptual framework, and Confucius himself often appears here as an ironic figure, uttering outrageously un-Confucian statements.

Unlike Lao-zi, Zhuang-zi sought to describe the practical procedures and consequences of a Daoist life. He often used parables, harnessing everyday events to illustrate his points. A famous example titled "Mastering Life" tells the story of a woodworker named Qing who won praise for making a bell stand so perfect that it seemed fashioned by supernatural powers. Qing modestly denied any real artistry and apologized for his technique:

> When I am going to make a bell stand, I never let it wear out my energy. I always fast in order to still my mind. When I have fasted for three days, I no longer have any thought of congratulations

*Although a sage could be male or female, Lao-zi, like many Chinese, employed the male pronoun when referring to sages. But to reach the ultimate stage, a sage would have to transcend social and gender limitations.

> or rewards, of titles or stipends. When I have fasted for five days, I no longer have any thought of praise or blame, of skill or clumsiness. And when I have fasted for seven days, I am so still that I forget I have four limbs and a form and body. By that time, the ruler and his court no longer exist for me. My skill is concentrated and all outside distractions fade away. After that, I go into the mountain forest and examine the Heavenly nature of the trees. If I find one of superlative form, and I can see a bell stand there, I put my hand to the job of carving; if not, I let it go. This way I am simply matching up "Heaven" with "Heaven."
>
> (*Zhuang-zi* 19)[6]

Here we see the practice of fasting used as a meditative technique for calming the mind and turning the attention away from external, egoistic things and toward the inner, immanent Dao. Other techniques such as breath control and physical exercises, Zhuang-zi suggests elsewhere, may also help to open one to the experience of the Dao. When it comes, quite unexpectedly, its power flows into the person to accomplish great things, spontaneously and effortlessly.

Zhuang-zi also echoes Lao-zi's austere view of the Dao: not only is the Dao, like the sage, without compassion, without humaneness, but the true sage should joyously embrace this impersonal pattern of change. All things are a part of the Dao and thus subject to endless transformation. While we live, we should playfully "ride upon the Dao." When it comes time for us to die and face the great transformation, we should not foolishly cling to what we have been:

> Suddenly Master Lai grew ill. Gasping and wheezing, he lay at the point of death. His wife and children gathered round in a circle and began to cry. Master Li, who had come to ask how he was, said, "Shoo! Get back! Don't disturb the process of change!"
>
> Then he leaned against the doorway and talked to Master Lai. "How marvelous the Creator is! What is [it] going to make out of you next? Where is [it] going to send you? Will [it] make you into a rat's liver? Will [it] make you into a bug's arm?"
>
> (*Zhuang-zi* 6)[7]

If one is properly attuned to the Dao, one has no anxiety. The sage had learned to forget knowledge, to forget the distinctions of life and death, good and evil, on which the value systems of the ordinary world are based. He could see things as they really are—all part of a single organic whole, the ultimate harmony of the Dao.

Zhuang-zi's name for this exalted state of mind was *wu-nian,* literally "no thought" or "no mind," a term later appropriated by the Chan (Zen) Buddhists to describe the state of enlightenment within the world. The sage's state of "no thought" was a state of self-forgetfulness, a state of tranquil acceptance of all things, a state of mind beyond the feelings of sorrow and joy that accompany ordinary life. Paradoxically, this state is described as accompanied by a higher kind of joy that takes delight in all things equally. This transcendent, mystical state makes ultimacy available in this world as a lived experience of the profound harmony of the Dao. No adversity can touch such a person; no anxiety can disturb such a mind.

NOTES

1 W. A. C. H. Dobson, *Mencius* (Toronto: University of Toronto Press, 1963), p. 88.

2 Ibid., p. 141.

3 Wing-tsit Chan, trans. and comp., *A Source Book in Chinese Philosophy* (Princeton, N.J.: Princeton University Press, 1963), p. 139.

4 Ibid., p. 166.

5 Ibid., p. 174.

6 Burton Watson, trans., *Chuang Tzu; Basic Writings* (New York: Columbia University Press, 1964), p. 127.

7 Ibid., p. 81.

RELIGIONS OF CHINA

CHAPTER 13

THREE VISIONS OF HARMONY: CONFUCIAN, DAOIST, BUDDHIST

Toward the end of the third century B.C.E., the armies of the northern Chinese state of Qin conquered the last rival state and established the first truly centralized government for the whole of China (221–207 B.C.E.). The victorious prince proclaimed himself emperor with the grand title Shi Huang-di ("first sovereign ruler-god") and declared the founding of the new Qin dynasty. To eliminate opposition to his new regime, the emperor ordered the destruction of all nonpractical and nontechnical books, including Confucius's sayings. Fortunately, scholars—especially Confucians—hid many of the texts and were able later to reconstruct much of the traditional classical literature. For our purposes, the most important legacy of the Qin dynasty was the establishment of the pattern of imperial rule that was to last for more than 2,000 years. Thus we enter the period known as classical China. Not only was the imperial structure permeated with religious values and practices, but the rulers also saw themselves as the regulators of the religious lives of their subjects.

THE HAN DYNASTY (202 B.C.E.–220 C.E.)

The ruthless and inhumane methods of control and exploitation of the Qin dynasty led to its overthrow after only a few years. Its successor, the Han dynasty, brought several centuries of political stability, economic prosperity, and cultural flowering. With it the stimulating but dangerous period of the hundred philosophers was over. Instead, the Han Chinese sought not innovation but consolidation of past gains. For example, editions of the Confucian literary classics were prepared, and a national library and university were founded.

Religious events and trends, as always, were tied to the cultural and social patterns of the period. For example, a new social class arose during this period: the literati, or scholar-officials. These highly trained civil servants took an increasingly larger responsibility for the operations of the government. The literati were drawn from a new kind of landowning gentry, the so-called *hundred families*. Their wealth made it possible for their sons to pursue the lengthy process of education (daughters were permitted no schooling). And in an attempt to institutionalize the Confucian rule of merit, education at this time became the gateway to government service and social prestige.

The practical goal of education was to prepare a young man for the difficult **civil service examinations,** which were required for a government career. The content of the exams was overwhelmingly Confucian, consisting of the Five Classics and their Confucian commentaries: the *Chun Jiu* (Spring and Autumn Annals), attributed, probably erroneously, to Confucius; the *Yi Jing* (Book of Changes); and the *Shu Jing*

(Book of History). The members of the ruling class, the cultured elite, were therefore steeped in Confucian learning, values, and attitudes.

Because the zhunzi, or true gentleman, was expected to exercise authority and to bring harmony to the people in his care by moral example and by ritual observance more than by enforcement of law or by coercion, the Confucian bureaucrats were not prepared by their education to be experts in any technical area. As Confucius had hoped, they were schooled in the "arts of living," what we would call the arts and the humanities; anything else could be learned in the process of administration or delegated to underlings. Moreover, the official duties of the government officeholder included many ceremonial activities such as participating in local or imperial rituals of the state cult. There was no independent priesthood; hence, inevitably, officeholders' duties took on religious overtones.

Confucianism triumphed as the imperial ideology in part because it offered a religious way of ensuring cultural harmony and unity without requiring the harsh methods seen in the Qin period. By reviving court ceremonies and emphasizing the role of the emperor as a mediator between heaven and earth, Confucianism supported the throne and its rule with an air of ultimacy and legitimacy. In addition, since the literati largely controlled the government, they were often able to thwart the ambitions of aristocratic or military adventurers and to blunt the arbitrariness and self-indulgence that often accompany imperial rule.

The Confucian interest in ritual as a means of promoting wider social harmony often coincided with the imperial concern to solidify its temporal and spiritual power. This can be seen in the phenomenon of the Ming Tang, or calendar house. Confucians had long admired the western Zhou period for the purity of its ritual observances. Based on their reading of the ancient texts, the Han scholars reconstructed an idealized building in which the Son of Heaven would imitate the path of the sun through the zodiac and perform many of the rites intended to ensure the abundance of crops and the peace and harmony of the empire. This graphically shows that the Confucians used ritual to ensure that the harmony inherent in the natural world would be transferred to the human world and also to establish that the emperor is the representative of all humanity in these rituals.

Such an understanding—that the natural world and social harmony are related and are centered in the rule of the emperor and the other authorities—is expressed by Dong Zhonshu (second century B.C.E.), the Han period's greatest Confucian thinker. By combining the Confucian concern for ritual and the virtue of the zhunzi with the ancient notion of yin and yang, Dong sought to relate the recurring patterns of natural and social order to the pattern of historical events. Yin and yang, he taught, give rise to five "elements" or agents: wood, fire, earth, metal, and water. All phenomena (for example, colors, tones, directions, seasons) result from the combination of these elements, and they succeed each other with regularity and predictability. Just like natural phenomena, historical events and eras are dominated by these various agents. Furthermore, all historical events flow naturally from previous events in a historical pattern that is the mirror of the cosmic pattern. Thus just as the five agents have a natural sequence, so do the various dynasties naturally succeed one another in a predictable fashion.

These correspondences were designed to explain everything and therefore to provide a framework of meaning in which all events could be seen as part of a cosmic pattern and process. To people of the Han period—at least the Confucian elite—this cosmic and historical harmony was a necessary part of a meaningful world. Even disasters like the fall of dynasties or earthquakes made sense as parts of a well-functioning system that was, in the long run, benevolently disposed toward humanity. Such a view also gave new significance to the old idea of the Mandate of Heaven, which was made known through the harmony and prosperity of a reign; the removal of the Mandate would be recognized by the absence of these indicators. Thus the old folk wisdom was reinforced that the government take note of any usual occurrences that might signal the will of Heaven. This theory also supported the widespread belief in omens and divination, for the natural and human worlds are interconnected.

POPULAR RELIGION DURING THE HAN

The Confucian attitude toward the religious yearnings and practices of the common people was one of either limited affirmation or hostility. The government affirmed the family cult of ancestor reverence and filial piety by building it into its own system of ritual and hierarchical social relationships. It also supported some of the many popular cults of local mountain and agricultural deities and others by awarding their temples and shrines imperial grants and titles. In this way the Confucian government not only enlisted these deities in the promotion of the prosperity and harmony of the state but also increased the loyalty of these cults' followers.

Among the popular beliefs and practices of the Han period were various techniques aimed at producing a long life or, sometimes, magical powers, such as the ability to levitate. Loosely connected to such beliefs was devotion to the **immortals** *(xian)*, mysterious and capricious figures who were thought to have achieved immortality and great magical power through a combination of alchemy, asceticism, meditation, and good deeds. This belief in the immortals was sometimes embraced also by the elite: one of the great military leaders of China, Emperor Wu Di (141–87 B.C.E.), sent a group of explorers into the East China Sea with instructions to find the home of the immortals and bring back the elixir of eternal life.

Beyond this, the Confucian elite largely ignored the beliefs of the people except when they threatened the power of that elite. For example, Daoism was becoming an important influence among the common people, and in recognition of this in 164 C.E. the emperor had a temple to Lao-zi built in the capital, using in it rituals based on the official sacrifices to Heaven. However, when, in the second half of the Han period, Daoism became powerful enough to threaten the Confucian elite, the government forcibly suppressed it.

Popular Daoism

The new religion that became such a threat to the authorities, called popular Daoism, must be viewed against the social, economic, and religious frustrations of the common people. As the Han elite appropriated more and more of the wealth and shielded it from taxation, the burden of financing the government was shifted more and more onto the small landholders and tenant farmers. These people had the least stake in the status quo and were not drawn to the lofty idealism of the zhunzi or interested in the great rituals of cosmic harmony. Nor did they have the leisure or the education necessary to study the classics. Thwarted of any realistic hope of sharing social or economic power, the powerless and poor came to seek remedies through armed uprisings and religious fervor.

The popular religion was centered first in rituals asking the gods and goddesses for a share in the good life and second in an ultimate Dao that was mysterious yet also accessible to human appeal through powerful magical rituals. Popular tales of immortals and other adepts with amazing powers to overcome the limitations of ordinary human life gave credence to the hopes of the people, especially when charismatic leaders arose who claimed to know the secrets of these powers.

Two major Daoist sects were active during the second half of the Han dynasty, and although their political ambitions were eventually crushed, they continued to exist throughout the period of disunity after the fall of the Han (third through sixth centuries). The first was the Celestial Masters group, which was formed in about the middle of the second century in western China, where it carved out an autonomous theocratic state. The second was the Yellow Turbans group, which began in the northeastern peninsula (Shandong province) and eventually controlled eight provinces before it was put down in bloody battles at the end of the second century. Both sects emphasized the art of healing, the confession of sins, and magical rituals, and both were led by charismatic leaders who functioned as magical healers as well as military leaders.

They also shared an essentially utopian vision of life, which held that once the Confucian state had been overthrown, there would be a time of peace, prosperity, and harmony. This hope was held most fervently by the Yellow Turbans, who called themselves the followers of the *Tai Ping Dao* (Way of the Grand Peace). They believed that they could achieve this blessed state through purification rites and rituals expressing the harmony inherent in the nature of things.

These two Daoist sects focused on healing, both of the individual and of the group. The individual sought to be healed of physical and mental disease. According to the Chinese popular worldview, disease was closely tied to the various divine powers—some malevolent, others benevolent—that were thought to control the phenomena of the world. Individuals seeking to be healed or protected had to bring about a state of harmony between themselves and these largely unseen powers. This would in turn help to make their relationships with both spirits and other humans function smoothly. Thus a healthy individual required a healthy group. To enhance the health of the group, parishes were organized around a priesthood and a regular set of congregational (group performance) rituals. Daoist priests healed both by serving as ritual intermediaries to the spirits and by administering magic potions and formulas.

The concern for healing also bound together other elements of organized Daoism. For example, morality was cast in its light. In addition to traditional values such as honesty, filial piety, and respect to various deities and spirits, now moral prohibitions against injury to living beings were added, probably under the influence of Buddhism. To fail to live up to the moral code was regarded as a major cause of suffering and disease. Confession of one's transgressions and asking for forgiveness thus became a new feature of Daoist ritual life. It was often seen as a prerequisite to healing. In the Celestial Masters sect, for example, misdeeds and repentances were written on three pieces of paper; the first paper was buried, the second was placed on a mountaintop, and the third was thrown into a river. The purpose of this ritual was to inform all the cosmic powers of one's repentance and thus encourage them to restore one's health.

During this period the ancient quest for a long life and even for immortality also became associated with the popular Daoist sects. The cult of the immortals and the practice of alchemy were now incorporated into organized Daoism. Individuals themselves could become adept at such practices or use the powers of experts. They might also seek the elixir of immortality or some other means of prolonging their lives.

There were many techniques for achieving a long life. Some used **alchemy**, which combined ritual and meditative preparations in a rite of purification. Daoists also elaborated rituals of purification into a meditative, even ecstatic discipline, thus taking a major step beyond what was hinted at by Lao-zi and Zhuang-zi. Henceforth a direct and ecstatic experience of the Dao not only was a result of disciplined withdrawal from a hostile social and economic environment but was seen as a method by which one could overcome the limitations of ordinary life while still immersed in it.

Daoist meditation techniques were just as much based on the popular notions of healing as they were on Lao-zi's ideas of the Dao. Lao-zi had formulated the belief that the microcosm (an individual human being) and the macrocosm (the world of nature and the Dao that lay behind it) could be brought into harmony. Popular Daoism's meditation techniques took this idea much further by assuming a very detailed set of correspondences between what might be called the inner and the outer worlds.

The deeper the Daoist mystics probed, however, the more preoccupied they became with appropriating the sacred powers of the many popular deities. While meditating, people could apprehend these divine powers inside themselves and experience themselves as internally identical with the divine powers of the cosmos. Purification rites and meditation became viewed as a way to live in perfect harmony with these powers, which were regarded as the manifestation of the Dao in the inner world.

This popular form of Daoism represented a departure from Chinese religious tradition. Heretofore the people of China had participated in religious activity according to their membership in different kinds of groups, such as the family, the village, or the scholarly profession. These new Daoist sects were voluntary organizations that cut across earlier organizational lines and forged a new kind of group loyalty.

RELIGION IN THE PERIOD OF DISUNITY (220–589)

Early in the third century, the Han dynasty collapsed, and China was plunged into a long period of political disunity and instability, marked by wars and social upheaval. As often happens in such periods of dramatic social turmoil, the religions also changed. First of all, the failure of the dynasty served to destroy the Confucian government and generally to discredit Confucianism both as a philosophy of government and as a way of life for the cultured and educated elite. Many among this group turned instead to the Daoist tradition of Lao-zi and Zhuang-zi. They did not simply embrace this old religion, however, but adapted it to suit their new outlook. The result was a form of Daoism known as the **Dark Learning**, which combined elements of both elite Daoism and Confucianism. At the same time, among the common people, the popular forms of Daoism already developed in the late Han times continued to flourish. In addition, Buddhism, brought at this time by missionaries, began to take root in Chinese soil, particularly among certain intellectuals.

The Retired Intellectuals

Daoism as a way of life was explored by disappointed scholars and court officials who fled the corrupt petty states of the fragmented empire in search of a simple life far from the political world. Daoism provided not only a basis for rigorous philosophizing but also a justification for casual gatherings of "retired" intellectuals, referred to as the Pure Conversation movement. Scholars, poets, and painters who disdained official positions would meet to discuss their respective pursuits and to enjoy one another's company. Daoism provided them with a sense of participation in the mysterious and dark life of the cosmos, and no doubt it helped to compensate them for the loss of their influence in the political world. At the same time, these intellectuals were unconsciously forming a pattern of behavior and a life style that would henceforth become available to educated persons who went into retirement either voluntarily or involuntarily. As time went on, Buddhism—especially the Chan sect, known as Zen in Japan—would adopt this pattern.

THE BUDDHIST CONTRIBUTION TO CHINESE LIFE AND CULTURE

Buddhism began to enter China around the beginning of the Common Era when it was still a strong, vital religion in India. Missionaries followed the trade routes across central Asia during the Han dynasty and soon founded centers of Buddhist learning in northern China. After the fall of the Han, Buddhism flourished under the patronage of some of the various petty states established by the non-Chinese conquerors of northern China. But the common people knew little of this exotic foreign religion; even Chinese intellectual circles had at first only a distorted picture. Many saw Buddhism, with its elaborate rituals, meditation, complex philosophies, and withdrawal from the world, as a variant of Daoism. The tendency to identify Daoism with Buddhism during this period eventually led to considerable borrowing between the two groups. Buddhism thereby lost much of its foreign flavor, and Daoism was enriched by assimilating foreign ideas.

The first Buddhist enclaves in China were centers of learning whose primary function was to translate into Chinese the vast and abstruse Buddhist literature of India. But soon the most exotic feature of the new religion became known: the organization of its adherents into monasteries and convents. The monastic institution was not only the heart of early Chinese Buddhism, but in many ways this presented the greatest obstacle to its acceptance. As we have seen, devotion to family values and filial piety were deeply ingrained at all levels of Chinese society. Yet here was an institution that, symbolically at least, required its members to turn their backs on the world, abstaining from not only its pleasures but also its family responsibilities. Buddhist monks and nuns, because they were celibate, could not carry on the family line. In the monasteries and convents they lived in new "families," and their duty was no longer to their parents or to human society.

Despite this handicap, Buddhism did gain adherents, especially among the young educated gentry, many of whom found in the monastery's quiet, contemplative atmosphere a haven from the uncertainties of official life. There both women and men were freed from their strictly defined Confucian social and religious roles and could cultivate scholarly, meditative, and aesthetic pursuits while moving always toward the experience of nirvāṇa (enlightenment). For the Buddhists, the final goal of nirvāṇa required the experience in meditation of the truth of oneself—or, as they often put it, detachment from the false notion of self.

Buddhism, with its monastic system, seems to have struck a chord among many Daoists of that day, as it reinforced the Daoist aversion to the artificiality of the ritualized and hierarchical Confucian life. Consequently, the Daoists began to build their own monasteries and convents. The already well established Daoist tendency to produce hermits adapted readily to the Buddhist example: Daoists seeking individual religious experiences and enlightenment came to live together as "communal hermits."

CULTURAL FLOWERING IN THE TANG DYNASTY (618–907)

After the more than three centuries of internal weakness and foreign domination, China again achieved political unity and stability. The Tang dynasty was an especially prosperous period marked by creativity in literature and the arts and an unusual degree of cosmopolitanism. Caravans crossing central Asia linked the markets of India and the Mediterranean ports with the Chinese capital of Changan (modern Xian), which became a center of foreign ideas as well as foreign goods. An increasingly international China became home to Christian missionaries, Jewish communities, and Tibetan monks of the Vajrayāna Buddhist lineage.

With Confucianism still weak, Daoism flourished during this time, although it was overshadowed by Buddhism, which dominated Tang intellectual and artistic life. For some time Buddhism received the enthusiastic official support of the emperors. Its adherents were from all classes of Chinese society, and thousands of Chinese men and women retired to monasteries and convents to meditate and learn the Buddhist Dharma.

The Buddhism of the Tang dynasty was divided into a number of schools or denominations, each with its own teacher lineage, monasteries, and even preferred script. The most important division was between **universalist ("catholic") schools**, which tried to be inclusive of all Buddhist scriptures and practices (most notably the Huayan and Tiantai schools), and **exclusivist sects**, which gave exclusive attention to a single strand of the tradition (the Pure Land schools) or put nearly exclusive emphasis on a single practice (the Chan schools). The universalist schools were by far the more politically active and the wealthier of the two and were much more involved in the high culture of art and literature. Thus they largely assumed the functions of the old Confucian literati in Tang society. They emphasized elaborate and costly ritual performances—a kind of Buddhist li—and made effective use of the arts of painting, sculpture, and architecture to enhance the impact of these rituals and to reinforce their role as culture bearers. They expanded and

These sketches were drawn by an anonymous artist on the back of a sutra fragment, a hand scroll dating from the ninth or tenth century C.E. By the end of the Tang dynasty, religion powerfully influenced all aspects of Chinese cultural life, including artistic creation. (William Rockhill Nelson Gallery of Art—Atkins Museum of Fine Arts)

mastered the increasingly Buddhist philosophy, which gave them a claim to intellectual leadership.

Among the exclusivist sects, by far the largest were the Pure Land sects. Though based on three texts translated from Sanskrit, the Chinese transformed Pure Land practice from the elite, monastic meditation technique it had been in India to a simple devotional practice suitable to the poorest and least educated layperson. Anyone could chant the **nienfo** (*nembutsu* in Japan), the words "Namo Omito Fo." To chant it was to invoke the name of the Buddha Amitābha, who, it was believed, would enable the chanter to be reborn in his other-worldly paradise, the Pure Land. One could therefore live in this life, enjoying its pleasures and enduring its pain, while at the same time working toward a more pleasant life after death.

The other influential exclusivist school was Chan. The word *chan* means "meditation" (derived from Sanskrit *dhyāna,* "meditation"), and as its name implies, the Chan school emphasized meditation as its central practice. It claimed with some justification that this was true to the original intention of the Buddha himself. Also, Chan remained strongly dedicated to monasticism as providing the best environment for meditation. But its meditative practices developed in a manner unique to China. For example, the enigmatic riddles used as meditation objects *(kōan)* seem to owe more to the classical Daoist love of paradox and mystery than to the more coldly logical Prajñāpāramitā literature of India. And whereas Indian Buddhists clearly knew of a realm of mind beyond the rational, the Chan rejection of any philosophical system appears to owe more to Lao-zi's poetic declaration, "The Dao that can be told of is not the real Dao / The Name that can be named is not the real Name." The austere simplicity of Chan monastic life also echoes Lao-zi's admonition to live naturally and without desire or ceremony. Finally, it is significant that Chan poetry and painting show a love of nature not characteristic of Indian Buddhism but markedly shared with the Daoists, who saw in nature the manifestation of the Dao's simplicity and naturalness as an outward reflection of the inward harmony of enlightenment.

The worldly success of Chinese Buddhism also led to its downfall. The more dominant Buddhism became, the more it came to be resented by many Confucians and Daoists at the court, who increasingly spoke out against what they regarded as its foreign values and way of life. Its monasteries, they noted, had become wealthy, and its communities represented an organized

This seated Buddha dates from the eighth century C.E., the Tang dynasty, during which time Buddhism dominated intellectual and artistic life. (The Metropolitan Museum of Art, Rogers Fund, 1943)

body independent of state control. By imperial order in 845, thousands of monasteries were forcibly closed, and tens of thousands of monks and nuns were compelled to resume their lay lives.

The purge was successful. Never again would Buddhism exercise significant political or economic power in China. Moreover, the intellectual and cultural ascendancy of Buddhism was also seriously undercut, making possible the reemergence of Confucianism in the following Song period. An important, if unintended, result of the persecution of the ninth century was that from the Song dynasty onward, the Pure Land schools dominated Chinese Buddhism at all levels. These schools were less affected than the universalist schools in part because their religious practices were simpler and required much less economic and political involvement with the world. In addition, these schools represented a far greater degree of accommodation to Chinese values, being largely the product of the Chinese mind acting on the received Buddhist tradition.

After the persecution, Chinese Buddhism increasingly merged with folk religion. By the fourteenth-century Ming period and continuing into modern times, many Chinese had come to believe in karmic retribution, reincarnation, multiple hells and heavens, and a number of Buddhas and bodhisattvas—all derived from Buddhism. Yet they had little sense of themselves as Buddhists. Instead, they practiced their unorganized folk religion within the family or at the local temple without concern for the quest for enlightenment that preoccupied Buddhist monks. Further, Pure Land Buddhism largely lost its independent existence; most of its monasteries became places where both Chan and Pure Land practices were carried out. At the same time, temples that were not monastic centers usually used Pure Land devotional practices. Of these, devotion to the bodhisattva Guan Yin became especially popular. Evolving from the remote male Avalokiteśvara of Indian conception, who "looks down" with compassion on suffering beings, the female Guan Yin intercedes in the ordinary problems of faithful men and women.

Beginning in the Tang and completing the process in the Song dynasty, Confucianism slowly regained its old position of prominence. Yet Chinese Buddhism had made such a lasting contribution to Chinese religious life that even Confucianism was significantly influenced by the long centuries of Buddhist domination.

CHAPTER 14

NEO-CONFUCIANISM: FROM THE CLASSICAL ERA TO MODERN TIMES

THE REVIVAL OF CONFUCIANISM

The dominant religious, philosophical, and political force in China from the Song dynasty of the tenth century until the end of the imperial system in the early twentieth was Neo-Confucianism. After the fall of the Tang, the first Song ruler called on the reemerging Confucian literati to help him bring stability to the administration. On their recommendations, the conservative emperor dropped the Daoist and Buddhist texts from the school curriculum and reinstated the Confucian classics. Although most Chinese continued to follow popular religious cults that included elements of Daoism and Buddhism, members of the official and scholarly classes turned back to the Confucian classics; writing new commentaries, they developed workable new theories of government, insight into the human condition, and a satisfying and meaningful way of life. Neo-Confucianism thus became the religion of the ruling elite.

Although Neo-Confucianism had been launched in official circles somewhat earlier, its cause was greatly advanced by highly respected commentaries on the Confucian classics written by two philosopher brothers, Cheng Hao (1032–1085) and Cheng Yi (1033–1107). Some time later two other philosophers gained prominence: Ju Xi (1130–1200) consolidated the earlier writings, prepared a standard commentary on the classics, and drew up a compendium of Confucian philosophy, and Wang Yangming (1472–1529) was greatly influenced by Buddhist thought.

Neo-Confucianism blended the old Confucian way with Buddhism. From old Confucianism it derived an emphasis on moral principles: Neo-Confucians sought properly ordered, harmonious human relationships, reflected in rule-governed behavior. But they recast this orientation in a very Buddhist light, teaching that all thought, ordinary experience, and performance of ritual are based on a single absolute, ultimate reality. Just like the Buddha nature, this absolute was thought to be the one principle essential to both gaining and organizing knowledge, and it could be directly encountered in an experience that would be ultimately transforming. It was the goal of a properly ordered life. The Neo-Confucians called this absolute **Li**. Though pronounced the same, this a different word from the *li* (ritual) discussed earlier. This *Li* means "reason, principle, order." The Confucian classics had used this idea merely to refer to the orderliness of things that li (ritual) had established. But to the Neo-Confucians, Li became a metaphysical entity, reality itself.

Cheng Yi spoke of this Li with the same tone of awe and celebration with which the Buddhists had spoken of the Buddha nature, and with very nearly the same words. It is emptiness: "Empty and tranquil, and without any sign, and yet all things are luxuriantly present."[1] Ju Xi later said of Li, "The Great Ultimate is nothing other than Principle [Li]."[2] Even heaven and earth existed by means of Principle, and that Principle was even before them. By its means yin and yang were generated.

Although Neo-Confucianism placed a high value on ritual as the pattern of properly ordered, harmonious human relationships, proper behavior had its origin in a purely ideal, absolute realm of Li. In Li all relationships exist virtually or potentially; outward observance only exemplifies these absolutes. This ideal realm, though immanent in all things, was approachable primarily by means of inward experience in meditation. Thus Neo-Confucians, unlike their Confucian predecessors, were concerned to probe the human mind for insight into its mechanisms. For example, one seeming paradox they pondered was how the mind in the ideal state might be both tranquil and, while working in the everyday world, active. The Buddhists had wrestled with this problem when attempting to understand the mind of the bodhisattva. The Neo-Confucians' answer was similar to the Chan Buddhists': both sought a state of tranquillity in activity.

This psychological concern also thrust the Confucian notion of the sage again into the foreground. In the thought of Confucius, the sages were all powerful men in the distant past. Neo-Confucian sagehood, however, was closer to the Mahāyāna Buddhist bodhisattva—it was a state of being to which the religiously gifted could aspire here and now. The sage would achieve a state of **enlightenment** that would set him or her apart from ordinary humans. This enlightenment was sometimes understood as a powerful mystical experience that transformed the personality. Further, both the sage and the bodhisattva were expected to engage in activities in the world for the benefit of others. Yet there were differences too: unlike the bodhisattva, the sage, though able in periods of meditation to regain his or her essential and original tranquillity, was not thought capable of maintaining such a state while active. Further, when active the sage would exhibit a typical Confucian array of virtues and attitudes, including some very non-Buddhist emotions. Ju Xi says:

> [Man's] original nature is pure and tranquil. Before it is aroused, the five moral principles of his nature, called humanity, righteousness, propriety, wisdom and faithfulness, are complete. As his physical form appears, it comes into contact with external things and is aroused from within. As it is aroused from within, the seven feelings, called pleasure, anger, sorrow, joy, love, hate, and desire, ensue. As feelings become strong and increasingly reckless, his nature becomes damaged. For this reason the enlightened person controls his feelings so that they will be in accord with the Mean. He rectifies his mind and nourishes his nature.[3]

Thus the great Confucian virtues, here called the five moral principles, are present eternally in the ideal and absolute realm of pure Principle. They constitute essential human nature, the original nature. Emotions are grounded in Li, the absolute, Principle, and are aroused by the activities of everyday affairs. In themselves, emotions—even anger and hate—are not considered bad. But when the emotions become overstimulated, a disparity may appear between one's inner, essential nature and one's outer, conscious life. Then one's actions, guided by overly active emotions, will no longer be in accord with Principle, and a return to Principle in a meditative experience of renewal is required.

This new emphasis on controlling emotions had a notable impact on the new orthodoxy's view of women. Males remained the focus of Neo-Confucian thought, and the primary threat to their emotional quietude was often associated with women. Rather than taking this as a call to males' self-control, Neo-Confucianists emphasized the need for a strict standard of chastity for women, so as to free men from the possibility of harmful emotional involvement. This emphasis transformed the moral code for women from a restrictive but balanced combination of virtue, personal cleanliness, and domestic work to an almost obsessive preoccupation with chastity. This was particularly significant for widows, whose chaste devotion to their husbands was to continue, sometimes leading to the ultimate act of devotion, suicide.

In addition to its emphasis on emotional control and female chastity, Neo-Confucianism retained an old Confucian political and moral stance. It continued to emphasize the regulation of public and private lives, keeping everything in its proper place, and ritualized social patterns. Yet it also offered its constituents the fulfillment of religious needs hitherto available only in Buddhism or Daoism. Accompanying a well-regulated social life was inner harmony and the direct experience of the ultimate, Li.

The School of Mind

This inner experience was especially vivid and dramatic in the Neo-Confucian School of Mind. An extraordinary biography of the Ming period philosopher and statesman Wang Yangming, its traditional founder, has been preserved. It shows in detail how much Neo-Confucianism owes to Buddhism and Daoism, while at the same time remaining loyal to old Confucianism. In his youthful quest for religious fulfillment, Wang immersed himself in both Buddhism and Daoism. Although he eventually gave them up, his thought, both in its content and in the dramatic way he discovered it, is strongly reminiscent of Buddhism. During a period in which he was temporarily out of favor at court, he went into retreat with a few disciples. Living the life of a Chan monk, he meditated on life and death, humbly chopping wood and carrying water for his students. He was plagued by the question of what a sage was, and he devoted himself to becoming one.

> One night it suddenly dawned upon him in the midnight watches what the sage meant by "investigating things for the purpose of extending knowledge to the utmost." Unconsciously he called out, got up and danced about the room. All his followers were alarmed; but the Teacher, now for the first time understanding the doctrine of the sage, said, "My nature is, of course, sufficient. I was wrong in looking for Principle in things and affairs."[4]

Wang was thus "enlightened" about his own nature, in which he discovered nothing less than Principle itself. That is, he had solved his and Neo-Confucianism's most fundamental problem, how to reconcile within his own life and experience the old Confucian concern for external things and affairs with the Buddhist concern for the inner life and inner experience. In a dramatic, Buddhist-like experience of enlightenment, he found the truth of Confucian principle. This set him on an intellectual course in which he identified Principle with Chan's "original mind" and insisted that for the sage there can be no disparity between thought and action.

Toward the end of the Ming period (fourteenth through seventeenth centuries) there lived Gao Panlong, another Neo-Confucian philosopher-statesman. Though from another school, Gao's autobiographical writings are similar to the School of Mind. As a young man, Gao set out to become a sage, by which he meant a perfected human being who, through deep insight into his own nature, perfectly exemplified the Confucian virtues of humaneness (ren), righteousness, decorum (Li), and wisdom. Gazing at a beautiful panorama, Gao asked himself how he could have remained unmoved by meditation on such a setting and concluded that his efforts so far had been a failure. Dividing his time between study of the classics and disciplined meditation, Gao's efforts culminated in a powerful enlightenment experience of the sort often referred to as "oceanic trance." He described it thus:

> Suddenly it was as if a load of a hundred pounds had fallen to the ground in an instant. It was as if a flash of lightning had penetrated the body and pierced the intelligence. Subsequently I was merged with the Great Transformation until there was no differentiation.[5]

Gao not only described his own experience but also wrote several short pieces on meditation technique and described a special meditation house he had built for himself in tranquil surroundings, the effect of which was for him profound and lasting; it established for him a lifelong meditative regime of re-creative self-cultivation.

TRADITIONAL CHINA UNDER CONFUCIANISM

China's social and religious structure changed astonishingly little from the eleventh century through the nineteenth. It was dominated by Neo-Confucianism; even the Mongol invasion and dynasty (1260–1368) hardly affected its dominance of the elite. Confucians continued to promote their religious values and curbed Buddhism and Daoism by monopolizing and controlling the governmental bureaucracy. This led it to clear domination of the intellectual life of the nation. Yet Confucianism, for all its power, never tried to root out other religious practices or institutions. This is partly because Confucianism was always an elite tradition and did not appeal to the masses. Its stress on scholarship, government service, and the maintenance

COMPARISON

Religion and the State

In the Islamic empire and medieval Christendom we see a synthesis of religious and administrative elements similar to the Neo-Confucians'. In all three worlds the ruling elite ran the state on the basis of their religious values. In Neo-Confucianism, the absolute Principle, Li, expresses itself in moral principles, from which are derived the rules of behavior and decorum. These were reinforced by such institutions as the family, the occupational guild, and the state. In the medieval Christian structure, the popes and their representatives were Europe's primary juridical (legal) arbiters. Their judgments were based on the principles and traditions they traced back to their scriptures. The medieval Muslim empire's standards were thought to be grounded ultimately in the word of Allāh, as found in the Qur'ān, and in Muḥammad's behavior, as documented in the Ḥadith literature. The directions were largely determined by the priestly men responsible for the law and the Ḥadith.

Often the ruling group saw itself as a distinct social group, uniquely qualified to interpret the scriptures. It is also noteworthy that this same group—frequently the society's only literate members—often wrote down its religions' texts. In so doing, whether consciously or not, the elite often oriented the texts' teachings to reflect their own beliefs and values.

of a rigidly hierarchical social structure kept any popular Confucianism from developing. The zhunzi ideal of the exemplary figure was itself elitist, inasmuch as it saw the masses as the passive recipients of a harmony imposed from above and fully lived only by the few. Thus the Confucian attitude toward Daoist, Buddhist, and folk religious practices was one of bemused toleration, ripening into active persecution only if these groups threatened political stability or the Confucians' special position.

Thus Confucianism promoted its own religious values by reinforcing ritual, moral codes, and legitimization of authority within such institutions as the family, the village, the occupational guild, and the state. This has meant that for many, and not just Confucians, religion in China has been an expression of a quality felt to be inherent in all human endeavors rather than a specialized activity more or less insulated from the rest of life. Perhaps nowhere in Chinese life beyond the government has Confucianism exerted more influence than on the family, especially the literati and merchant families of comfortable means. The hierarchical Chinese family, with its ritualistic system of unequal but supposedly mutually beneficial relationships, was seen not only as the foundation of human society but also as the model for government (see the accompanying box, "Religion and the State"). Just as the parents nurtured their children, the emperor nurtured his subjects; and just as the children were expected to revere their parents, the nation was expected to revere its emperor.

Even though we have been referring to Neo-Confucianism monolithically, in fact it had different effects at various levels of society. We shall examine the several layers of the imperial or official level, the popular level, the family, and the Buddhist and Daoist sects.

The Imperial or Official Level

During this period there were three elements at the imperial, or official, level of religion in China.

The Imperial Palaces still stand today in Beijing. Walls and a moat surround what is actually a group of palaces, the home of Chinese emperors for over five hundred years. During this time, the emperor acted as the people's representative to their deities, carrying out elaborate rituals in and near the palaces. (Eastfoto)

The Imperial Cult The set of religious activities under the direct control of the court was known as the imperial cult. Rituals included the seasonal sacrifices in which the emperor himself played a central, priestly role. Here the division of religious labor inherent in the hierarchical principle was exemplified to the most extreme degree: the people were not permitted even to witness the rituals that were carried out on their behalf and most clearly expressed the common identity of the Chinese nation. The emperor was the people's representative to their deities.

The most important imperial ritual of the year was the worship of Heaven and the imperial ancestors at the time of the winter solstice. A large, open mound of earth composed of three circular terraces still stands south of the imperial palace in Beijing where the emperor, acting as chief priest, conducted this rite. After purifying himself, he mounted the terrace, and at various levels he would kneel and pray before tablets inscribed with the names of the celestial and spiritual powers, such as the sun and moon and the spirits of specific stars thought to constitute a kind of heavenly bureaucracy. Other tablets bore the names of the imperial ancestors and the ultimate power, Sovereign Heaven, Supreme Deity. One nineteenth-century observer described this solemn occasion thus:

> The service opens by peals of music. The Emperor in his robes of azure ascends the altar by the steps on the south, and advances to his place at the center of the round altar in front of the tablet to Heaven. . . . There he stands while the whole burnt offering is consumed in the furnace southeast of the altar. The "three kneelings and nine prostrations"—three prostrations with the head to the pavement at each kneeling—are now performed before the tablet to Heaven and before each of the tablets to his Ancestors. The libations are presented, and the written prayer is read.[6]

The Educated Elite The literati, composed of the powerful bureaucrats who ran the government offices, would-be officeholders, and members of the rich gentry class, practiced Confucian rituals. Twice a year in towns and cities, local officials offered prayers, incense, and food at the temples of Confucius and his ancestors. Instrumental music, the singing of hymns extolling Confucian virtues, and stylized dancing also accompanied these commemorative rites. These rituals reinforced both the literati's loyalty to the state and their sense of responsibility as culture bearers whose very way of life was the model of civilized behavior.

Local Officials In county seats the magistrates presided at many rituals throughout the year. They regularly offered prayers to Confucius, to gods of war and of literature, to the local city god, to agricultural deities, and, incorporating some popular elements of Buddhism, to "Father Buddha" and certain bodhisattvas.

The Popular Level

An intermediate level of popular religion flourished; it mixed Confucian components with Buddhist, Daoist, and folk elements. It consisted of village or neighborhood ceremonies celebrated throughout the year, usually on the birthdays of the gods being honored. Many of these deities were the same as those included in the official cult, but many local deities were also celebrated. Typically these rites would draw people from the countryside to the temple located in the town. A parade of such pilgrims, carrying banners identifying their home village and accompanied by music and fireworks, would snake through the streets to the temple, where each village group would make offerings and pray for the deities' boons. Often fortune-tellers and diviners would join the festivities, offering their services to the devout. Sometimes one or two of them might even become possessed by the spirit of a deity, thereby providing direct communication with him or her.

Also at this popular level were other individual religious activities not carried out within the family group: personal petitions to local shrines, campaigns for personal moral rectification, and individual participation in meditation and physical exercises thought to promote health and long life.

The Family Level

At the family level, the ancestral cult held pride of place. The ancestors received the most solemn and most regular attention; all important family events were ritually announced to them, and marriages were performed in their presence. The great ancestral remembrances were occasions for the many branches of a family to gather, so they strengthened the authority of the head family and its patriarch. Filial piety kept alive this feeling of solidarity, and all family members felt responsible for the family's wealth and honor. In addition, such worship must have brought a sense of connection to a timeless realm of the sacred dead. It represented a repeated experience of ultimacy, transcendent in that the dead were godlike in their power and wisdom and immanent in that one's own destiny was someday to join in that awesome company.

Specifically Religious Institutions

Given that the dominant political group was the Confucians, it is not surprising that Buddhism and Daoism were both waning and, from the ninth century on, periodically oppressed. The Buddhist Saṅgha was persecuted with the most zeal. It had a tightly knit organization, marked by impressive initiation rituals for monks and nuns. Its adherents wore unusual clothes and hairstyles, which differentiated them from the ordinary people. Some monasteries owned land, making them economically independent. Above all, the loyalty of these monks and nuns to the Saṅgha was known to weaken their commitment to the distant imperial establishment. Despite the Buddhists' denials of political aspirations, these features made them a threat in the Confucians' eyes. And indeed, lay Buddhist secret societies, which followed a quasi-monastic pattern of initiation and rituals, did sometimes express religious and political protest.

China in a Period of Revolutionary Change

CONTACT WITH THE WEST

The events and movements of religious significance in recent centuries in China have come largely as a response to contacts with the Western world. The story is complex, involving not only religion but also politics, economics, and technology—the entire cultural spectrum. In general, it is a story of the clash of cultures during which Chinese indifference gave way to curiosity, which was in turn replaced by growing anger and fear and finally culminated in the twentieth century in what might be called a passionate ambivalence. Many Chinese, especially among the elite, have hated the West for its threat to traditional (primarily Confucian) values, and many at all levels of society have grown angry at Western colonization and economic exploitation. But the West has also been loved, especially by the less powerful and also the more liberal segments, because it offered a previously unknown degree of political, economic, and religious freedom and material progress.

Although the adventures of Marco Polo in the thirteenth century sparked the European imagination, the first important contacts came when the Spanish and Portuguese expanded their empires into East Asia in the sixteenth century. At first the Chinese court regarded these few "Western barbarians" with scant interest. This attitude is understandable. The very sophistication of Chinese culture, its customs, thought, and values, had always helped it to maintain its historical and cultural continuity against other cultures. Foreigners they viewed as barbarians, and barbarians had nothing to offer the civilized. But with the coming of the Jesuit missionaries, things began to change. From the first the Jesuits adopted a policy of deemphasizing their strangeness. They learned Chinese, studied the Confucian classics, and impressed the literati by entering into their philosophical discussions and praising Confucian morality and love of learning. The Chinese literati perceived Christianity mainly as a moral system consistent with Confucianism. They also admired the missionaries' useful disciplines of mathematics and astronomy. So successful were these missionaries that some were even given official posts.

But the very policy of deemphasizing differences and seeking harmony by accommodating to Chinese ways, which had served the Jesuits so well, ultimately proved to be their undoing. The Jesuit missionaries had allowed Chinese Christians to continue to participate in the state cult and ancestor veneration, classifying these practices as nonreligious "civil ceremonies." This changed in 1706, when the church hierarchy barred Chinese Christians from such ceremonies, effectively stopping them from participating in a practice that the Manchu emperor regarded as essential. This sparked the famous Rites Controversy, for the angry emperor demanded that the more permissive Jesuit practices again be followed. When the church again refused, the Christian missionaries were expelled from China. Christianity had come into conflict not only with the deeply held attitudes of the Chinese people but also with the power of the emperor and his Confucian literati.

CULTURAL AND RELIGIOUS CRISES IN THE NINETEENTH AND TWENTIETH CENTURIES

The restless and, some would say, reckless creativity of the West had produced by the middle of the nineteenth century not only superior armaments and economic exploitation through colonialism but also intellectual and religious movements of far-reaching consequences. The secular scientific worldview had developed, and new ideologies such as socialism and communism were being formulated. China could no longer maintain its aloof isolationism now that the world had, uninvited, forced its way in. And the world was itself in a state of agitation.

The Confucian elite attempted to keep the West's intellectual influence at a distance, just as the imperial government tried to do in the economic and military spheres. One of the most persuasive spokesmen for the traditionalists was the government official and Confucian scholar Feng Guifen (1809–1874). Feng coined the term *ziqiang* (**"self-strengthening"**) as the proper attitude of the Chinese toward the Western threat: Western science and technology had much to offer, and in fact, he proposed, translation centers should be set up and the best students sent there to learn Western mathematics, physics, and medicine. But the Chinese must be very selective in their borrowings: according to Feng, "What we then have to learn from the barbarians is only the one thing, solid ships and effective guns." Apart from this, the West had little to offer: "Those [books] which expound the doctrine of Jesus are generally vulgar, not worth mentioning." In 1860 Feng clearly set down the formula that was to dominate Chinese thinking until the end of the century:

> If we let Chinese ethics and famous [Confucian] teachings serve as an original foundation, and let them be supplemented by the methods used by the various nations for the attainment of prosperity and strength, would it not be the best of all procedures?[7]

This attempt to accept but limit change exhibits China's ambivalence: earlier it could be Westernized in such a way that these foreign elements could be harmonized with a traditional Chinese framework of values and attitudes. But it was not to be, since technology came embedded in a foreign culture with alien values and beliefs that increasingly sang a siren song to Chinese of all social strata. It was a question not just of finding a place in the Chinese order for things Western but of which order would prevail.

By 1898 China had fought and lost short wars with Britain, France, and Japan and had lost political and economic control of portions of its own territory to Russia, Japan, Germany, France, and Britain. With the increased economic and military penetration of China by the Western powers came a renewal of Christian missionary activity. This time it was predominantly British and American Protestant denominations. Especially through their schools, orphanages, and hospitals, Christianity had a noticeable impact. Some Chinese observers were nonetheless optimistic about this Western incursion. If the Confucian essence were truly strong, such secondary problems would disappear by themselves. After all, it had worked before with Buddhism.

The Tai Ping Rebellion

While the literati were wrestling with the impact of Western learning, a synthesis of East and West was being formulated on the popular level out of elements of Christian and Chinese religiosity. Instead of the aesthetic and detached humanism of early Confucian flirtations with Christianity, it was the popular culture that was most affected. This led to the **Tai Ping Rebellion**, which devastated China and almost toppled the Manchu dynasty.

Ironically, *tai ping* means "great peace," and it harks back to the popular Daoist movements that had sought to overthrow the Han dynasty. The leaders of this revolt believed that the Daoist utopian vision of har-

The splendor of the imperial court (above) contrasts sharply with the bare existence of the common people like this shopkeeper's family. Dissatisfaction with this inequality led first to the Tai Ping Rebellion and culminated in the Communist victory in 1949. (Religious News Service)

mony and simplicity would be established on earth as the biblical kingdom of the Christian God. Furthermore, without being restrained by the tradition of interpretation of Christian teachings and a culture based partly on them, the Tai Ping leaders applied Christian concepts to their own society with revolutionary zeal. They tried to establish their religious utopia by military force, and they very nearly succeeded.

The founder of the Tai Ping movement was Hong Xiuchuan (1814–1864). As a young man he had taken the civil service examinations, only to fail twice. After an extended period of nervous collapse, he recalled a vision of divine beings and heaven. Eventually he encountered some Christian missionaries and, after reading some of their religious tracts, interpreted his visions as showing that he was Jesus's younger brother, now called on to complete Jesus's work as a second messiah. Hong taught that the great evil in the world was Confucian teaching, and having successfully struggled against Confucius and the various demons in heaven, he had been sent down to earth again with a sacred sword to restore Christ's true teaching. Thus Hong came to view the religion of the threatening West as having been originally Chinese.

The Tai Ping vision of a heavenly kingdom on earth was derived as much from centuries-old peasant frustrations as from the Christian gospel. Its leaders sought racial egalitarian social structures: all people would be equal, including women; the old hierarchical system would be abandoned, and property would be held in common; and all would be members of the same family. Confucian notions of the world as a family were mingled with Christian millennialism and folk religious ideas of a struggle against demonic forces. The form of organization of the old Buddhist secret society was given a Christian content: instead of the future Buddha (Maitreya) who would renew the Dharma and thereby inaugurate a new golden age, a new messiah would appear—in fact had already appeared in the person of Hong—who would establish a permanent reign of justice and plenty.

Curiously, the barbarian demons against whom Hong's sword was sent were not the westerners but the Manchu rulers who had taken China from the Chinese and thus perverted God's heavenly kingdom. The Great Peace (Tai Ping) and God's universal kingdom would come with the overthrow of the Manchus.

From 1850 to 1864 Hong and his generals were at constant war with the Manchu regime. It was a double irony that native Chinese troops under native Chinese leadership finally stopped the Tai Ping advances after the Manchu troops had failed and that the intervention of the "Christian" powers of the West, notably Britain, led to the rebels' ultimate destruction. The great dream of peace had brought death to an estimated 20 million people.

CHINA IN THE TWENTIETH CENTURY

The dissatisfactions of the peasantry that had led to the Tai Ping Rebellion had not died with them. Their frustrations and the brittleness of the old Chinese system led to progressively weaker governments and civil war, culminating in the Communist victory in 1949. During this period one event stands out as most significant to later Chinese history: the emergence of Mao Zedong (Mao Tse-tung, 1893–1976) as the leader of the Communists in the famous **Long March** of 1934. The national government under Jiang Jieshi (Chiang Kai-shek, 1887–1975) began its notorious "bandit extermination" campaigns against the Communists in 1927, eventually surrounding the Communist guerrilla bases in southern China. The Communists managed to break out and escape to the north; although thousands died on this exhausting 6,000-mile Long March, the result was a strengthening of the Communist movement. In their survival, the peasants, frustrated by the centuries of domination by a small elite, saw the hope of salvation. After Japan's defeat in World War II, the Communist armies were able to sweep Jiang's forces out of the mainland and into exile on the island of Taiwan. In October 1949, before cheering throngs in Beijing, Mao Zedong proclaimed the People's Republic of China.

Religion under the Communist Regime

The official attitude of the Communist government toward traditional religion should come as no surprise. Karl Marx wrote in the nineteenth century that religion was the opiate of the masses, an instrument used by oppressive regimes to divert the attention of the people from their true enemies and even to enlist them in the willing service of their own exploiters.

Therefore, religion should not exist in a truly communist society and should at best be only tolerated.

Indeed, it has survived to the extent that the rulers of the new China have made freedom of religion a part of their constitution; yet the government has mounted a number of campaigns against citizens who practice it. Sometimes these campaigns have been verbal: Confucianism is identified with a repressive "feudal" system; the people should "struggle against Confucius." Some campaigns have gone further, denouncing and prohibiting many popular Buddhist, Daoist, and folk religious practices as superstition. Often religious institutions have been closed, churches and temples destroyed or confiscated, and priests and ministers sent to forced-labor camps. But most telling is the fact that former monasteries are now shoe factories, and temples have been abandoned or converted into showpieces to bolster national pride and increase tourism. To the Communists, fossils of religion are useful only in teaching the masses about the evils of the past.

Religious Aspects of Maoism

For some time scholars have pointed out that any modern ideology functions much like a traditional religion. Thus an ideology like Marxism provides a world of meaning and a way of life for its followers: it organizes their energies, defines what is worth doing, constructs a mythology of struggle and saintly heroism, and establishes rituals designed to reinforce these values. For this reason, many scholars have called Marxism a pseudoreligion. Like traditional religions, Marxism attempts to transform people into its own image of perfection. When it is successful, it engenders a sense of awe and reverence, of exhilaration or guilt, in the presence of what it holds to be sacred and of

This photo shows the National Day Parade, October 1, 1950. Workers celebrated the first anniversary of the founding of the People's Republic of China, marching with posters of their leader, Mao Zedong. There is much evidence that Maoism became an enemy of traditional religions partly because it appropriated many of the functions of religion. (Eastfoto)

ultimate value. We will consider the evidence that the Maoist form of Marxism is an enemy of traditional religions partly because it appropriates many of the functions of religion.

From the Maoist point of view, the traditional religions of China were not wrong in presenting descriptions of the structure, order, and harmony inherent in reality. The religions' error was in the specific content of their vision. For example, Confucianism advocated social and economic inequality, believing that such inequality was part of the very fabric of reality. The error of Buddhism and Daoism was that their monastic life styles harnessed the labor of others to support the monks. Moreover, Daoism believed in a transcendent reality that was ultimate both in the sense of "mysterious and undefinable" and in the sense of "most important." No one could capture this ultimate Dao in words, and no other value could take precedence over it. But Maoism sought to apply the sense of ultimacy to its *own* values by inducing a powerful personal experience of Marxism and associating its values with this experience.

The values and goals that Marxism proclaims are liberation of the masses from the capitalist yoke, unlimited material progress, and creation of a classless society. In its Chinese version, it should be seen as the inheritor of many of the fundamental values of China that we have repeatedly encountered. The state was to be one in which everyone had a valued place and would be supported in that place. Its society was to be absolutely democratic, and everyone's place was to be regarded as equally valued and rewarded. This utopian society would be of such natural harmony that the state itself would eventually cease to exist. But this meant that all self-centered tendencies toward individual privilege and pride must be quashed. Here Maoism was in accord with the old Confucian and Daoist emphasis on selfless performance, though its aggressive methods of bringing this about—thought control and brainwashing—were new.

Other features of Maoism also point to its quasi-religious character. It cherished and often recited its "holy history." The Moses-like figure of Mao is portrayed as leading the Communist armies on the Long March. They encounter many difficulties along the way, with enemies on all sides. Many holy martyrs fall during this period of "salvation history," but finally the victory is won. The foreign devils (imperialists) are thrown out of China, and the domestic demons (landlords and capitalists) are punished.

Also like many religions, Maoism has its holy book. The famous "little red book" containing the thoughts of Chairman Mao held all wisdom and was to replace all philosophies, theologies, and scriptures. In every spare moment, people were expected to read, memorize, and ponder his thoughts. The People's Liberation Army, which "had the deepest love for Chairman Mao and constantly studied his works," helped to organize family study sessions on the holy book. Typically, families held regular meetings to study and implement Mao's teachings and "make self-criticisms and criticisms of each other."[8] One possible result of all this is described in ritual terms: a meal was prepared of wild herbs and ordinary food, the former to represent the past and the latter "as a token of our present happiness." Then the family stood before Mao's picture and pledged renewed allegiance to him.

Maoism and the Transformation of Culture

Holiness, or ultimate value, was found not only in the person and works of Chairman Mao but also in the Chinese masses. It was the people, especially the peasants, who instinctively knew the correct doctrine and who felt the need for communism long before the actual organizers and leaders of the movement emerged. And it was to these same people that the leaders, including Mao himself, always had to return. As Mao once stated:

> Our god is none other than the masses of the Chinese people. . . . When we say, "We are the Sons of the People," China understands it as she understood the phrase "Son of Heaven." The People have taken the place of the ancestors."[9]

Like the ancestors, the people provided the fundamental direction to life and shaped social values.

This view has had far-reaching consequences for modern China, and the Maoist vision of cultural transformation took its first step here: culture begins with the masses; what is correct comes from the masses. But they are inarticulate, so Mao must interpret for them. Furthermore, no amount of mere study of words or abstract ideas can substitute for actual experience. Intellectuals and urban youths must be

Though freedom of religion is a part of the constitution, the Communist regime mounted a number of campaigns against citizens who practice it. During the 1980s, however, a cautious rapprochement with Confucianism was seen. This photo is of dancers performing the ancient "Liu Yi" dance as part of a memorial ceremony for Confucius. (Eastfoto)

sent to the countryside and live the life of a rural peasant in order to grasp and internalize the true mass perspective. The so-called **May Seventh schools** attempted to do just this with study sessions at school alternating with periods of agricultural work.

The ongoing task of each generation, then, is the transformation of the individual's personal, selfish, and urban outlook to the peasant's collective, self-sacrificing attitude. Even artistic and literary activity must show this peasant attitude; it too must be socially relevant and "correct."

Maoism's quest for purity of attitude was sometimes resisted, even within the ranks of the faithful. For example, the strengthening of the nation demanded the development of a strong military and a powerful economy. This in turn required the development of a modern industrial base, applying modern technology and management skills. But the need for expertise in these modern skills could and often did run counter to the desire for revolutionary purity. The usual way of discussing this problem was to distinguish between being "red" (politically correct) and "expert" (expert at a modern skill). Since 1949 China has oscillated between these two poles, emphasizing now one and now the other.

The most zealous, emotional, and disruptive period of emphasis on ideological purity ("redness") was during the Cultural Revolution. During this time (from 1966 to the early 1970s), the production of goods was allowed to suffer greatly in the service of purity. Purges not only of intellectuals and managers but also of Communist party bureaucrats were carried out on an immense scale by roving bands of youths known as the Red Guards. Clearly, to be red was of supreme importance, and all had to be sacrificed for it. This chaotic rite of purification stopped only when the army finally stepped in to restore order.

By the time Mao Zedong died in 1976, Maoism had

spent its crusading zeal. The emphasis of the Cultural Revolution on red at the expense of expert had already begun to wane, and the late 1970s saw a further shift away from the emphasis on ideological purity.

The Present Situation

The 1980s and early 1990s have seen an increase in China's willingness to open itself to the world, especially to the West. Although some private enterprise is now possible, and the press is a little freer, the specter of the red-versus-expert dichotomy still broods over China. The leadership tentatively experiments with increased individual freedom while at the same time attempting to maintain state and ideological control. A particularly shocking example of this may be seen in the government's response to the student protests that erupted in the spring of 1989. Refusing to attend classes, thousands of university students held mass meetings in several major cities. At first it appeared that their demands for greater individual freedom, political democracy, and an end to official corruption might in some way be met. But the slaughter of hundreds of protesters on June 3–4 in Tiananmen Square in Beijing quickly put an end to such hopes. Many since have been arrested and some reportedly put to death. University students must now spend many hours in studies designed to engender ideological purity and to purge them of Western liberal ideas.

Maoism is for the moment quiescent—even a limited amount of criticism of Mao has been permitted, and his birthplace, once a busy pilgrimage destination, is now largely deserted. There is some speculation, however, that among the peasants, if not government leaders, Mao still lives in the hearts of many. In the present climate of cautious toleration, the government has relaxed restraints sufficiently to allow Christians once again to practice their faith openly, although severe restrictions still prevail, and the number of functioning congregations is limited. Daoism, except for the most elementary folk beliefs and a small monastic community, has been all but destroyed. Buddhism is still a presence: some temples have been allowed to reopen, and perhaps with help from abroad the monastic tradition, now in utter ruin, may be rebuilt not just in form but also in practice.

As for the future, the collapse of Maoist idealism has left many Chinese with a hunger for values that some observers interpret as an expression of deep, unmet religious needs. Some Chinese scholars have even suggested that traditional religion is important to the stability of even a socialist society. This is apparently the thinking behind a cautious rapprochement with Confucianism as witnessed by an academic conference held in 1987 with government acquiescence in the hometown of Confucius. Some more adventuresome Chinese scholars have suggested that parts of the old teaching may still have relevance as a replacement for the discredited ideology of Marxism. If connection to what is believed to be ultimate is a part of every viable society and every fulfilled human life, then the Chinese, cut off from their traditional access to ultimacy, are facing a spiritual malaise far deeper than that of the West. In the modern West, despite its secular framework, religions continue to flourish, providing meaning and value to many, both as individuals and as part of voluntary religious communities. In China, however, the people face not only a public but also a private spiritual vacuum.

NOTES

1 Attributed to Cheng Yi by Ju Xi in *Chin-ssu Lu (Reflections on Things at Hand)* 1.32, in *A Source Book in Chinese Philosophy*, trans. and comp. Wing-tsit Chan (Princeton, N.J.: Princeton University Press, 1963).

2 Ibid., 48:8b–9a.

3 Ibid., 2.3.

4 Frederick Goodrich Henke, trans., *The Philosophy of Wang Yang-ming* (La Salle, Ill.: Open Court, 1916), p. 13.

5 Rodney L. Taylor, trans., *The Cultivation of Sagehood as a Religious Goal in Neo-Confucianism* (Missoula, Mont.: Scholars Press, 1978), p. 128.

6 Henry Blodgett, "The Worship of Heaven and Earth by the Emperor of China," *Journal of the American Oriental Society* 29 (1899): 65–66.

7 Ssu-yu Teng et al., *China's Response to the West* (Cambridge, Mass.: Harvard University Press, 1954), pp. 53, 52.

8 Donald E. MacInnis, ed., *Religious Policy and Practice in Communist China* (New York: Macmillan, 1982), p. 341.

9 Ibid., pp. 16–17.

RELIGIONS OF JAPAN

CHAPTER 15

JAPAN'S RELIGIONS: FROM PREHISTORY TO MODERN TIMES

THE JAPANESE RELIGIOUS CHARACTER

As we trace the history of religion in Japan, we will come to see many similarities to religion in China. We will see, in fact, that Japan has borrowed many religious ideas and practices from the Chinese. Yet we will also become aware of sometimes subtle differences. Like the Chinese, the Japanese have valued harmony in nature and in human society. But while the Chinese have viewed the world as a naturally orderly and thus harmonious place susceptible to disruption by ill-considered human actions, the Japanese have regarded the world as a place of natural and enduring tension: forces tending toward order and harmony contend with forces tending toward disorder and disharmony. Thus the native Japanese deities (**kami**) themselves were characterized by a degree of freedom, even caprice, not envisioned by the Chinese. To the Chinese, both nature and human society resulted from the dynamic interplay of yin and yang; these were in turn governed by the mysterious and ultimate harmony, Dao. But to the Japanese, nature and society resulted from the interplay of ultimately unpredictable kami. Moral categories apply to these deities and hence to the world only imperfectly. The kami—and humans by extension—are neither good nor bad but, depending on the situation, a mixture of both. Some kami may even be predominantly destructive.

The readiness to live with dynamic tension may also be seen in the way Japan has adopted foreign elements. When it welcomed Chinese ideas—Confucianism, Buddhism—and later Western technology and culture, it never adopted any in their entirety. For example, elements of Confucianism and Buddhism were allowed to remain side by side with indigenous Japanese elements, especially Shintō, their inconsistencies and tensions unresolved.

Both the Chinese and the Japanese have valued ritual, but in different orientations. Whereas Confucian ritual seeks to embody and celebrate a harmony that already exists, Shintō ritual seeks to create a temporary island of harmony within a chaotic and dangerous world. Thus the Japanese may perform a ritual to ask a destructive deity to leave the area or to invoke protective kami to ward off destructive ones.

Also, mystical experience has been put to a different use in Japan. In a trance state, the Japanese shaman does not seek a permanent transformation of personality or personal salvation. This contrasts with the Daoist mystic, who sought a permanent loss of self so as perfectly to embody the ultimate Dao. The Shintō shaman sought (temporary) loss of self in order to be possessed by the capricious kami so that their unique messages could be transmitted to humans. Their goal, like so much of Japanese religion, was to protect this world from unpredictable dangers.

OVERVIEW OF JAPANESE RELIGIOUS HISTORY

Japanese history can be divided into four periods. First is the protohistoric period from around the third century C.E. through the middle of the seventh. Our knowledge of it is fragmentary and based largely on myths and legends preserved for many decades only in memory. During most of this time, when the people of the relatively isolated Japanese islands knew no writing system, what came to be called the Shintō religion was taking form, as were many of Japan's folk religious beliefs and practices.

A legend from the seventh century tells of the gift from a Korean king of the first Buddhist artifacts. These images and texts opened Japan to the richness of Chinese civilization, with its writing system and vast literature of poetry, history, philosophy, and religion. That embracing of things Chinese was the key feature of the second period, the classical (mid-seventh through twelfth centuries). It was characterized by the rapid assimilation of Chinese ideas and the tension that resulted from the only partly successful attempt to restructure Japanese society after Chinese models. At first these "modern" ideas and practices, including Buddhism and Confucianism, affected only the top echelon of society, the aristocrats who clustered around the imperial court, but by the end of the period, they had reached the ordinary villagers. Also during this period, Shintō became a recognizable religion and achieved official sanction at court; many of its myths and rituals were written down for use by government-supported priests. Indeed, the religious landscape of the time contained elements of Confucianism, Buddhism, and Shintō scattered about in what often seems bewildering confusion. In short, the classical period witnessed a melding of foreign and indigenous religious traditions.

The third, or medieval, period (thirteenth through eighteenth centuries) saw the triumph of Buddhism in the rise of new and popular sects that tended to subordinate Shintō. Pure Land Buddhism came to dominate the common people, while Zen was especially popular among the upper classes. At the same time, Confucianism became so intimately incorporated into both Buddhist and Shintō practices that it ceased to exist as an independent tradition. But it once again became a serious subject of study toward the end of the period, first among Zen monks and later among government-supported scholars who thought of themselves as Neo-Confucians. Shintō also enjoyed a revival during the later medieval period, first among **national scholars** who modeled themselves on the Confucians and then among the people themselves, who made frequent pilgrimages to Shintō shrines.

The modern period (nineteenth and twentieth centuries) has been a time of rapid cultural and religious change during which Japan evolved from a decentralized, isolated, feudal society to a self-consciously modernizing nation that successfully assimilated Western technology, economic organization, and political power. Socially and religiously, the modern period has been characterized by disruption of traditional patterns of life and consequent confusion and uncertainty. This situation has led not only to changes in the relative importance of older religious groups but also to the formation of numerous "new religions."

In general, the Japanese have sought to preserve old values while at the same time assimilating foreign elements, sometimes with painful results. Confucianism and Buddhism, dominant at the end of the medieval period, quickly gave way to a rejuvenated Shintō, which was increasingly molded by the government into a civil cult of patriotism. With the destruction of that artificially created edifice after World War II, contemporary Japan can be described as existing in an uneasy equilibrium made up of contending religious sects, especially the very visible new religions; a noticeable show of secularism; and an underlying and often unconscious attachment to customary religious observance involving elements of folk religion, Shintō, and Buddhism.

THE SHINTŌ SUBSTRATUM OF JAPANESE RELIGIOSITY

Just as we argued for a substratum of commonly held religious ideas in China, so we will present a set of religious ideas and attitudes that form the foundation of much of the religious behavior of the Japanese. Although we will call this substratum *Shintō,* it includes the vaguely defined and disorganized Japa-

Japanese women are seen here coming to pray for the well-being of their families at the Shintō shrine Mitsumine Jinja, as their ancestors have done for nearly two thousand years. (Religious News Service)

nese folk beliefs and customs as well as the more articulate later "official" myths and rituals. Examination of the central concept of *kami,* together with the myths and rituals associated with it, will help us to form a picture of the Japanese religious character.

SHINTŌ AS A "LITTLE TRADITION"

Even today, Shintō, along with Buddhism, enjoys the allegiance of most Japanese. Rather than a system of dogmatic beliefs or a definite code of ethics, Shintō is a diverse set of traditional rituals and ceremonies. It has no founder; no all-powerful deity; no inclusive, canonical scripture; and no organized system of theology. Moreover, Shintō has incorporated many folk religious customs. It has also been influenced by Confucianism, Daoism, Buddhism, and, in modern times, Christianity. Nevertheless, certain attitudes and practices have persisted from the earliest times to the present, and these form much of the substratum of Japanese religiosity.

No written documents survive from before the seventh century, Shintō's most important formative period. Historians have had to draw on later folklore, archaeological findings, and oral traditions written down long after their original formation. Even in more recent periods, the development of Shintō has been difficult to ascertain beyond vague outlines. This is due to the very nature of Shintō, which has been for much of its existence what some scholars call a "little tradition," a set of customary activities lived by the common folk rather than a body of thought and practice carried by the learned and powerful.

This does not mean that Shintō has no structure or internal coherence: there are many common assumptions about the nature of the world and human life and destiny. These assumptions and the Shintō they influenced became, so to speak, the vessel into which everything else was poured. They thereby bestowed a peculiar Japanese shape onto all of its contents.

THE NATURE OF THE KAMI

The term *Shintō,* sometimes called *kami no michi,* means "the way of the gods." Some scholars derive the term *kami* from a word meaning "above, high, lifted up"; by extension, it means something unusual, special, and powerful; finally, it can also connote something august, awe-inspiring, mysterious, divine. The kami constitute an immanent ultimate, found within all things. It is similar to the notion of *mana* on other Pacific islands—an undifferentiated power inherent in all things that gives each its peculiar nature, efficacy, and attributes. The undifferentiated character of kami may be seen in the fact that many local shrines house kami whose names are not known and about whom no myths exist. Such shrines are merely local places of reverence rather than evidence of attempts to establish a relationship with a particular deity.

When this undifferentiated power becomes concentrated, however, it sometimes manifests itself as a sac-red object, an event, or, especially, a person, with a name and a distinct personality. Thus myths, legends, and folk tales sprang up around the kami, and *matsuri* (festivals) were celebrated in their honor. These kami are similar to the gods of Greek or Hindu polytheism (see the accompanying box, "Belief in Many Gods and One Principle"). Usually well disposed toward humanity, many kami are thought of as protective spirits. Yet, as noted earlier, there are also disruptive and destructive kami who have to be placated and kept at a distance. Indeed, any kami can become dangerous if good relations are not maintained through ritual activities. Japanese folk religion views the world as an often unpredictable interplay of dangerous and beneficial forces.

There are three main types of kami: deified powers of nature or abstract mental attributes, clan ancestors, and souls of the celebrated dead.

Deified Abstract Powers To the early Japanese, the kami were primarily the superhuman powers that animated the world around them. Most kami are associated with nature; they include the deities of heaven, earth, the seas, and the underworld. Their names suggest that they were deifications of natural or human forces. **Amaterasu**, the most important kami, whose name means "heavenly shining one," is in part a manifestation of the sun. Myths tell of "creative" kami who are identified with the power of growth and reproduction, "straightening" kami who are responsible for setting things right, "bending" kami who bring misfortune, and "thought-combining" kami who confer wisdom. Other kami are associated with such natural objects as heaven and earth, the stars, mountains, rivers, fields, seas, rain, animals, plants, and minerals.

Clan Ancestors These kami are also sometimes thought of as nature kami but are revered primarily as the first ancestors of family lines. For aristocratic families (the great clans), these were probably the most important kami, for their existence reflected and legitimized the clans' claims to social and political preeminence. The most famous of the ancestral kami is Amaterasu, the sun goddess, the founder of Japan's ruling family. For many centuries Amaterasu was served at her primary cult site at Ise by a priestess who was an imperial princess. Originally each clan preserved its own myths about its clan ancestor and maintained a shrine at which this kami was regularly worshiped. Usually these kami had their primary shrines at the local center of clan power, though a powerful clan might move its shrine to an important political center. (This suggests the political importance of such shrines.)

Souls of the Dead Humans venerated for their high office, extraordinary personality, or great deeds (either constructive or destructive) might also be honored as kami. All the deceased emperors and many war heroes are kami, as the elaborate imperial tombs and numerous shrines testify. In Tokyo today, the Yasukuni shrine is famous as a place where the people go to revere the war dead. Potentially this type of kami can arise when anyone has died in forlorn circumstances, that is, when the spirit of the dead has some reason for being troubled and unfulfilled. Other such kami have more benign origins; for example, a saintly religious person might be enshrined and become a means by which the person's "kami power" may be tapped for human benefit.

SHINTŌ MYTHOLOGY

A rich source for enlarging our understanding of the Japanese religious character is the myth collections

COMPARISON

Belief in Many Gods and One Principle

Polytheism—literally, "belief in many gods"—refers to a religious system that has, typically, numerous gods. Such gods are often depicted as personifications of forces of nature and aspects of human life, either social or mental.

If is often overlooked that in many polytheistic systems, the deities are themselves understood to be manifestations or emanations of a single deeper principle. In Japan, for example, there are many kami that are in part manifestations or representations of certain natural forces, including the sun, the earth, mountains, the wind, plants and insects, trees, and grass. Some kami represent abstract mental attributes: straightening, bending, and so on. But these personalized deities are manifestations of a single undifferentiated power, also called kami. This deeper principle is an ultimate power that is immanent within all things.

Another famous polytheistic system was the Vedic religion in India. Many of its devas (gods) in part personified natural forces: Agni, the fire; Soma, the juice of a certain plant; Sūryā, the sun; Vāyu, the wind. Vedic scholar Joel Brereton argues that some deities in part personified social attributes—for example, Mitra was the god of alliance, Aryaman was the god of custom, and Varuṇa personified authority. But Vedic thinkers came to believe that all these gods were themselves manifestations of something deeper. In a famous late hymn we read: "They call him Indra, Mitra, Varuṇa, Agni, and he is heavenly nobly-winged Garutmān. To what is One, sages give many a title" (Ṛigveda 1.164.46).*

On another continent the Native American Navajo people see the universe acting according to an ultimate set of preexisting and unchanging laws that center on the term *hózhó,* universal harmony, order, or destiny. They also speak of many so-called Holy People and hence have been considered polytheists. Many of these Holy People are personifications of natural phenomena (mountains, rivers, clouds). But they are themselves expressions of this underlying order and must follow its laws. Scholar Gladys Reichard thus sees the Navajo system more as "monism rather than any kind of theism."†

Thus polytheism is in many cases a cover, masking a belief in a deeper underlying reality.

*Ralph Griffith, *Hymns of the Ṛigveda* (Varanasi, India: Chowkhamba, 1971), p. 227.

†Gladys Reichard, *Navajo Religion* (New York: Bolingen Foundation, 1950), pp. 75–76.

assembled at imperial command early in the eighth century. Inspired by Chinese historical writings, Shintō scholars collected their oral myths and historical traditions into two important official "histories," the *Kojiki* ("Records of Ancient Matters"), which appeared in 712, and the *Nihon-shoki* ("Chronicles of Japan"), published in 720. Many myths were woven together in these texts in such a way that religion buttressed the political legitimacy of the Japanese state. In addition, the state conferred on Shintō the status of a great tradition through ideological and financial support. Shintō's position was later overshadowed by Buddhism, but the Shintō revival carried out by Japanese intellectuals in the Tokugawa period (1600–1868) once again gave Shintō, and especially its myths, a dominant position among Japan's religions.

A Creation Myth: The Primordial Parents

The dynamic tension in Japanese religions is seen in a major theme in these myths: creativity. The myths tell of the creation of the world out of chaos. Such creation took many forms: sexual union from which kami were born, cutting up or subdividing existing kami, and releasing the blood of kami. Each drop of this sacred life fluid was believed to have the power to generate new kami and thus new phenomena, things, and powers. Certainly a sense of *mana* is overwhelming in these early myths, in which even a kami's most casual activity produced new deities. Three of the major Shintō divinities were created as the result of ritual performance, in this case a rite of purification.

To explore the Shintō sense of the world's dynamic tension, let us look at the myth of the Primordial Parents. It holds that the first kami arose from the primordial chaos and dwelt on the high plain of heaven. Next were created the kami of birth and growth. Finally, the original parents—**Izanagi**, the male principle, and **Izanami**, the female principle—descended from heaven along a rainbow bridge. Standing on the tip of this bridge, Izanagi thrust his jewellike spear into the ooze below. When an island emerged, the two kami stepped down to it, mated, and produced the eight great islands of Japan. Many kami were born to the couple, but when the fire kami was born to Izanami, she was killed by the flames. Izanami thus went to Yomi, the land of the dead beneath the earth, and in his grief Izanagi followed his wife. Despite the warning of Izanami, whose body was now corrupt, he could not keep himself from looking at her. They quarreled, and Izanagi fled back to the upper world, pursued by the polluting forces of decay, disease, and death. These forces turned into the thunder demons, kami who bring disease and death to humanity. Seeking to repair the harm he had inadvertently caused, Izanagi vowed to create life even faster than the thunder demons could destroy it. Thus was established the tenuous balance between death and life.

In this tale, the tension between male and female is used to reinforce the tension between creativity and destruction. The union of husband and wife in love leads to both birth and death, and love turns to hate when the death taboo is broken. What is achieved is a kind of balance between the positive and negative forces: life dominates death but can never be wholly victorious. Such tensions—between life and death, male and female, chaos and order—are part of the structure of reality and can never be resolved entirely. Both sides are necessary for the world to function properly. They exist in a state of dynamic tension.

This dualism of cosmic forces, like the yin and yang of China, influenced Japanese differentiation of gender roles. As the Shintō myths show, women were associated with blood (particularly birth blood), death, chaos, and other polluting, negative forces. Men, by contrast, were identified with purity, life, and order. In one respect, this dichotomy suggested that women were a source of pollution to men and should be kept under the strict control of males (as fathers, husbands, and sons). Thus social and political power belonged exclusively to men, and women's activities were confined to the domestic sphere. In this context, Japanese culture imposed on women extreme standards of chastity like those of Neo-Confucian China. Yet women's association with mysterious phenomena like birth and death also rendered them religiously essential, and they became shamans capable of communicating with venerated dead ancestors and kami.

SHINTŌ RITUAL

The Japanese, like the pre-Buddhist Chinese, apparently had no notion of an afterlife as a place of reward or punishment. Certainly, the ancestors were honored as the source of family life, and among aristocrats the first ancestor was celebrated in myth as a great kami. But death and the land of the dead were regarded as the primary source of pollution, and contact with the dead required ritual cleansing before one could recommence social or religious activities. The reward for a significant life was a cult established in one's honor in this world, not a happy state in the next. Moreover, there was no concept of the perfectability of humanity, nothing like enlightenment or the Confucian sage. Shintō cultic activity was directed solely toward ensuring a viable existence in this world of dynamic, delicately balanced, and often unpredictable forces.

Matsuri

Shintō knows two distinct types of ritual action. Both seek communication with the kami who order and animate the world. The first and more

The Great Torii (gates) of Itsukushima shrine. The gate to this shrine, dedicated to the three daughters of the Shintō god Susano-ō, stands offshore the sacred Miyajima Island. At high tide, the gate is surrounded by water; at low tide, it can be reached on foot. (Consulate General of Japan)

common type is called **matsuri**, or celebrations. Matsuri are usually scheduled according to a regular ritual calendar of yearly and monthly rites. Priests preside at the services, which seek basically to ensure continued order in the cosmos. Humans wish to influence the sacred powers so as to keep the world favorable to human life and prosperity. Matsuri are basically rites of hospitality, analogous to inviting honored guests to one's home. Kami are entertained, offered food and drink, and praised or flattered, and promises are made to them.

A matsuri typically has five parts. The shrine area is considered a sacred space, established by its characteristic *torii,* or gates. The kami are thought to have descended to the shrine buildings, which are therefore never entered, not even for ritual purposes. First, the priests undergo purification rituals like bathing, eating special foods, and abstaining from sexual intercourse to prepare themselves for the presence of the kami. Then the kami, who dwell in heaven, must be called down to the ceremony. Once present, they are given offerings of food and drink, such as rice, sake, or fish.

Music, dancing, and praises are also offered. Next the priest dips a branch of the sacred *sakaki* tree, a kind of evergreen, in holy water and waves it over the assembly, sprinkling all with the kami's blessings. Finally, a meal of the food offered to the kami is eaten by the priests and others.

The relationship between humans and kami is one-way: we are dependent on them as children are on their parents. Thus the communication of these rituals is also one-way: from the human priests to the kami. The gestures and order of these rituals are fixed; innovation and spontaneity are strongly discouraged.

One might perform a matsuri for specific purposes: to usher in the new year, to guard the spring planting, or perhaps to ensure a generally harmonious relationship with these powerful beings. In other matsuri gifts are offered in the hope of driving away destructive kami, thus creating a temporary oasis of order and safety.

Shamanic Rituals

The second type of Shintō ritual is shamanic, involving communicating with the kami by falling into a trance. The kami is considered to possess the shaman, or **miko**, and to animate her body, speaking through her mouth. (Although men can also become kami-possessed, from earliest times professional miko have been women.) Communication in shamanism is primarily from kami to human, although an interpreter is usually present in order to question the kami when it "descends." This kind of ritual is often used in what we might call crisis situations—special, nonroutine circumstances when the will of the kami seems unclear but important. In ancient times, when shamanism was practiced by the elite levels of Japanese society, such a situation might be a decision about war or an attempt to understand the cause of a natural disaster such as an epidemic or an earthquake.

There is evidence that prior to the eighth century, the empress herself often served as miko for important matters of state. According to the *Nihon-shoki,* Empress Jingū acted as the miko when the emperor sought the will of the kami in his plans to punish unruly subjects in border areas. The emperor played the *koto,* a stringed instrument, to call down a kami who took possession of the empress and identified herself as Amaterasu. The kami told the emperor instead to mount an expedition against Korea, where riches were to be had. But because the emperor refused to believe

Matsuri (celebrations) are one type of Shintō ritual. They include music and dance, as seen in this procession that dates from the Heian era (794–1185). These rituals are fixed; innovation and spontaneity are strongly discouraged. (Shashinka Photo Library)

and act on the kami's words, he soon met an untimely death, and the shaman empress came to rule in his stead. The story as recorded stood as a clear warning to anyone who might be tempted to disobey the commands of the kami.

Among the common people, shamanic rituals are still performed. In rural areas, people might seek out the miko to ask the kami for advice on important decisions, such as the choice of a marriage partner, or to determine the cause of a disease or other misfortune. Answers to such questions often state that someone has offended one or another kami through an improper ritual performance or simply neglect, thus reminding us of the kami's unruly character.

Religion and Society in Early Japan

Having surveyed the Shintō religious substratum, we can begin to understand the events of Japanese religious history. The social structure of early Japan was dominated by the heads of the great clans. These clans held most of the land by hereditary right, giving it to the cultivation of peasants who were themselves bound to their tasks by heredity. Certain families of peasants, called *be,* were attached to the land and thus to the landholders. Just as members of the aristocratic clans were born to their position, so were the members of the be. There were also be of artisans, such as potters and metalworkers. Even shrines had their be of priests. Everything in this early feudal society was tied by the twin cords of heredity and place.

The religion of the clans was a form of Shintō centered on a family shrine. The deities worshiped there seem to have been partly the clan's ancestral kami and partly agricultural kami of the place itself. In the earliest times, a chieftain probably oversaw the clan in a paternalistic way, supervising the clan's affairs and rewarding and punishing individuals and subclans. Although the chieftain probably had priestly duties within the ancestral shrine, his wife appears to have been the principal religious figure. Serving the kami directly as priestess and sometimes as shaman, she perhaps oversaw subordinate priestesses. As shaman she would have had considerable influence in clan affairs, since she spoke for the kami.

The clan heads, their immediate families, and their more closely related cousins formed the aristocracy, the more important members of which gathered around the emperor at his palace. Indeed, the imperial family was but another clan, one that had inherited, along with land and be, the right to rule and to perform Shintō rituals for the benefit not only of its own clan—the usual pattern—but also for the nation as a whole. The aristocracy seems to have paid little attention to the common people, so long as their labor resulted in wealth for the clan. The religious practices and beliefs of the common people have not been recorded except in distorted form as folklore; they seem to have followed practices similar to those of the aristocrats.

Sometime during the sixth century, Chinese forms of Buddhism were introduced into Japan by way of Korea. Eventually, Buddhism brought with it the splendors of Tang dynasty Chinese civilization, including a system of writing that opened the gates of Chinese literature, Confucian theories of government and ethics, and Daoist lore. For the most part, the Japanese aristocrats were dazzled by things Chinese, which were regarded as being of utmost value and prestige. The elite wrote their poetry and official government documents in Chinese. This also allowed the Japanese entry into the greater Asian cultural sphere, since China was at its center. The common people, however, were for some time quite unaffected by these developments among the elite, further distancing the aristocracy from the rest of the people.

RELIGION IN THE CLASSICAL PERIOD

Confucianism, which was a part of the package of Chinese civilization, made itself felt especially in the political arena. Confucianism promoted the centralization of power on the Chinese model of a bureaucratic state with the emperor at its head, leaving little or no place for the old clan-centered aristocracy. Had this been fully implemented in Japan, it would have destroyed the power of the clans by centralizing power in the hands of the imperial court. In fact, a system of provincial administration did officially replace the old clan structures, although neither the clans nor their traditional Shintō cults were abolished. Instead, the clans became unofficial organizations whose internal loyalties and cohesion kept them at odds with the central authority. Confucianism even indirectly enhanced the prestige of Shintō since the development of an official mythology that focused on the imperial court served the Confucian goal of the centralization of national life.

The centralized government also required a capitol to house the large bureaucracy and to symbolize the new order. The emperor in 710 built a splendid palace at Nara, which became in the Confucian way the symbolic pivot around which the rest of the universe revolved. Both Nara and the later capital at Heian (present-day Kyōto) were laid out in the Chinese fashion in a grid pattern oriented to the four compass points. The palace was situated at the northern end of the city, and clustered around the palace were the houses of the aristocracy. The courtiers, increasingly separated from the land and their old clan seats, became the bearers and cocreators of the new culture. Much of the flowering of poetry, pottery, weaving, architecture, gardening, elegant dress, and court ritual characteristic of the classical period was the result of this Confucian influence. Although the Confucians tried to impose the Chinese sense of harmony, the Japanese never adopted it completely. Rather than bringing an overarching order to Japanese society, its bureaucracy simply became one more element in Japan's dynamic and complex structure.

THE CONFLUENCE OF SHINTŌ, BUDDHISM, CONFUCIANISM, AND DAOISM

By the end of the ninth century, the pattern of classical Japan had become well established. There was considerable religious diversity, especially among the elite under the patronage of the court and noble families. This diversity was manifested not just as religious sects contending for the exclusive loyalty of individuals; rather, these loyalties contended within each individual. Virtually no one felt that worship at a Shintō shrine precluded devotion to a Buddhist deity or practice of Confucian filial piety. And this was true almost as much of religious professionals—Buddhist monks and nuns and Shintō priests—as it was of anyone else. No aristocrat of this time would think of dealing with illness only with medicine: Buddhist priests were always called to chant the sūtras as powerful means of exorcising disease-causing spirits. And funerals were invariably conducted by Buddhist priests. Yet no one would neglect duties toward one's ancestors or toward the traditional Shintō clan kami.

The ritual calendar of that time reveals many Shintō, Buddhist, and Confucian festivals and even a few Daoist ones. Despite the practice of Buddhist rites by many aristocrats and emperors, rituals performed at the palace were predominantly Shintō. Though supported by the court, Buddhist rites were usually conducted not in the palace but at various temples around the city and in distant shrines in the provinces. Yet Buddhism grew ever more powerful. In both Nara and Kyōto, Shintō shrines had to share space with Buddhist temples and monastic houses. Pious emperors and wealthy aristocrats endowed monastic centers both in the capital and in the provinces. The government established and regulated a national Buddhist hierarchy of priests and supported many Buddhist temples.

Buddhism was part of the Chinese cultural heritage that Japan borrowed and adapted to its own ends. This meant that, in the Confucian way, Buddhism needed to be carefully regulated and restricted by the government. Leaders saw Buddhism as a powerful civilizing force that would bring education and the literary arts to Japan, as well as direct benefits such as effective intervention with the sacred powers. To serve these ends, in the mid-eighth century the government built official Buddhist temples in each province throughout the nation. The eighth-century Buddhist center at Nara became an especially important center of political, intellectual, and artistic life. Its arresting Tōdai-ji temple housed the Daibutsu (Great Buddha), a 45-foot statue of the Vairocana Buddha, the great sun Buddha (a reminder, perhaps, of the imperial family's claimed descent from the sun goddess, Amaterasu), which may be seen and worshiped there even today.

The main work of these temples was the same as that of those in the capital: the preservation of the nation —its peacefulness, its harvests, and its emperors. Monks and nuns appointed by the government offered prayers day and night. In addition, many Buddhist temples served as centers of Chinese, not just Buddhist, learning. Moving beyond its appeal to the elite, Buddhism, like other Chinese cultural and religious elements, was slowly adopted by the common people. It was included in official policy, and its temples, monasteries, and art were intended in part to support the centralizing of the elite culture.

Perhaps the most revealing document from the beginning of the classical period is the seventh-century Seventeen-Article Constitution. Not really a constitution in the legal sense, this brief edict set forth a fundamentally Confucianist philosophy of life. Indeed, it was basically a Japanese adaptation of the zhunzi ideal—a handbook for producing the ideal government bureaucrat. It was written by Prince Regent Shōtoku, who is still revered today as the first great champion of Buddhism in Japan. Yet of the 17 articles, only one is devoted to Buddhism (it urges support of the Buddha, Dharma, and Saṅgha), and only one even alludes obliquely to Shintō. In fact, this is the first clear statement of what may be called the prevailing spirit of the classical age: the compartmentalization of religious and cultural elements into more or less separate, specialized spheres of life. Shōtoku was typical of his era in assuming that these religions were not incompatible. Each represented a valuable specialty and could contribute something to Japan's dynamic conglomeration of elements. Confucianism encouraged loyalty to the government and an ethic of family cooperation. Buddhism protected the future of the individual in the next world and could wield great ritual power to ensure the stability of the state in this world. Shintō offered the best means of placating natural forces, thus ensuring plentiful harvests and a minimum of natural disasters.

The common people adopted Chinese elements much more slowly. There is evidence that the imperial court even sought to prevent Buddhist elements from reaching the peasants for fear that its religious powers might be used against the central authority. Nonetheless, by the end of the classical period in the late twelfth century, more practical elements of both Buddhism and Daoism had filtered down to the peasants. But here, too, the native Japanese tradition continued to shape religious life: foreign elements tended to be molded into a Shintō shape and were often considered simply to add force to the already established practices. For example, practitioners of Daoist divination used a Shintō miko to communicate with the native kami and sought to deal with the same spiritual problems as Shintō. The Buddhist chant invoking the name of Amitābha (in Japanese, Amida) was used in a similar way to cure ills and to ensure the chances of a good harvest.

SHINTŌ-BUDDHIST SYNCRETISM

The impact of all this Buddhist activity in and around Nara and Kyōto, especially on the aristocracy, was tremendous. But since few people saw religions as exclusive, Shintō continued to flourish, with many Buddhist elements. The mixture of Shintō and Buddhism proceeded along several paths. In this process it is clear that despite inherent tensions, devout Buddhists continued sincerely to believe in the reality and power of the Shintō kami.

The Jingū-ji System

As early as the middle of the eighth century, an emperor had built a shrine to the local kami within the precincts of the Buddhist Tōdai-ji temple in order to pacify the local spiritual powers. This eventually became common practice in Buddhist temples. It recognized the prior claim of the kami to the land and to the allegiance of the people; the Buddhists were rather like guests of the kami.

The reverse attitude was also present: the Shintō kami were thought to need the Buddhist Dharma, like any other sentient being. The kami should be taught the way to enlightenment, just like humans. To this end, Buddhist sūtras were chanted at Shintō shrines, and eventually it became a common practice to establish a small Buddhist temple within Shintō shrines. Typically nothing was lost and nothing thrown away; the old was supplemented by the new in this ***jingū-ji*** ("shrine-temple") **system.**

From this position it was a small step to the idea that the kami were already enlightened and were in fact disguised manifestations of the various Buddha and bodhisattva figures mentioned in the sūtras. This notion of identity or equivalence was easy and even natural at the folk level, since kami were known more for their location than for their theological definition. Since even the names of the kami enshrined at a particular spot might not be known or agreed on, they might easily be thought of by Buddhist names. Some were thought to be bodhisattvas who had intentionally

This statue of Buddha is the largest in Japan. Located in Kamakura near Tokyo, the twelfth-century statue stands 11.5 meters high (over 37 feet). People from all over Japan travel to see and worship at the statue. (Tass from Sovfoto)

disguised themselves to bring about people's conversion or enlightenment.

Tendai Saichō (Dengyō Daishi, 762–822) sought to make his new Tendai sect the national form of Buddhism. It would unify the nation under a single sect closely allied with the imperial court; all others would be assimilated into it. Although he never accomplished this goal, Tendai did become the most important Buddhist denomination, a position it maintained until the end of the classical period. It attempted to include all Buddhist ideas, texts, and practices, unified under the leadership of the Lotus Sūtra, which it viewed as the culmination of Buddhist thought. The Lotus Sūtra greatly emphasized the notion of *upāya* (expedient means) by which the Buddha had taught that there were many ways or vehicles to salvation. All were useful and in a relative sense "true." But the text also presented the ultimate, absolute truth, which was the central way of Tendai.

Perhaps the most important idea stressed by Saichō and subsequent Tendai masters was the bodhisattva. The Lotus Sūtra taught that all Buddhas were in fact bodhisattvas; none had actually gone to nirvāṇa; all remained active in the world, leading all beings to nirvāṇa rather than selfishly enjoying nirvāṇa alone. This image of active bodhisattvas tirelessly working in the world for the benefit of all beings helped to make Tendai appealing to the Japanese court. The government awarded subsidies for training "bodhisattva monks" who would not only penetrate to the abstruse secrets of the Lotus Sūtra doctrines and achieve enlightenment but also become teachers of the nation as a whole. They would study not only Buddhism but the Confucian classics as well. Not only would they study and practice religion in its narrow sense, but, out of compassion for all, they would become engineers, craftsmen, and laborers in the service of the state. Cheerfully putting their hands to the construction of schools, roads, bridges, irrigation systems, and other useful things, they would at the same time bear witness to the truth of the Lotus Sūtra and of Buddhism. Saichō even equated the bodhisattva monk with the Confucian zhunzi, the true gentleman or ideal government bureaucrat!

Shingon Kūkai (Kōbō Daishi, 774–835) had similar ambitions for his Shingon Buddhism, which, rather than basing itself on the Lotus Sūtra, was grounded in Tāntric or Vajrayāna Buddhism. Shingon centered on elaborate rituals and meditations focused on visualizations of maṇḍalas, complicated paintings of the Buddhas, bodhisattvas, helpers, and demons that populate not only the external realms but also the inner psychological and spiritual realms.

Shingon's elaborate rituals appealed to all levels of society, since all could participate, even if only as spectators. Indeed, Tendai Buddhism found room for many of these esoteric practices within its broad, inclusivist philosophy. Although to more sophisticated Tendai and Shingon monks and nuns these practices were often understood to be forms of meditation leading to ultimate religious experience, to the popular mind they held the power to affect the external world in useful, this-worldly ways. Salvation in the ultimate sense of personal transformation was of less concern to them than immediate utility. Such a reorientation is again reminiscent of Shintō, which had always stressed ritual and had never had an unworldly, personal notion of salvation.

THE MEDIEVAL PERIOD

After the relatively stable classical period, dominated by the emperor and several powerful clans, medieval Japan was tumultuous. The dominant groups were military: samurai warriors led by their shōguns (generals). These military groups were actually clans of lower rank, sometimes distant cousins of the various emperors. As military men are wont to do, they fought frequent and bloody battles for power, though there were several long periods of relative stability during the early medieval period.

With struggles so frequent, these were difficult times for most of the Japanese people. The aristocracy was impoverished and politically irrelevant. At the same time, the common people were at the mercy of the samurai, who ruled by force, exacting high taxes from them and enlisting them also in the fighting.

THE RISE OF NEW BUDDHIST SECTS

Despite—or perhaps because of—the political instability and social and economic disorder, this period was one of vitality for Buddhism. Under these circumstances, at all levels of society a sense of insecurity and helplessness seems to have overtaken people. Many people came to agree with Buddhism that ordinary life was caught in an all but endless cycle of impermanence and suffering. And by now the common people too had accepted the Buddhist ideas of karma and reincarnation.

The commoners had neither the leisure nor the education to follow the Buddhist monastic regimens. The samurai, however, did have the time and the skills. And despite their new power and prestige, they felt the relevance of the Buddhist teachings. Impermanence and suffering were part of their constant experience because as warriors they must be ever ready to face the horrors of wars. Insecurity and a sense of helplessness were also theirs because, despite their power as a class, as individuals they were bound by ties of loyalty to superiors who could, at any moment, ask of them their lives.

New religious movements arose in the early medieval period to meet these new religious needs. Three new types of Buddhism took form: Pure Land Buddhism, which emphasized devotion to the Buddha Amida; Nichiren, which regarded the Buddhist monk Nichiren as an incarnation of a bodhisattva; and the highly disciplined, monastic Zen. The first two sects became popular movements that adapted monastic practices for use by the laity, allowing them to continue their life in the world while performing rites that offered them hope for salvation from their sufferings. Faith became the new key to salvation.

Pure Land Buddhism This sect was of course not new to Japan. Devotion to Kannon (in Chinese, Guanyin) and to Amida had been mentioned in the Lotus Sūtra. Indeed, devotion to Amida had long been an important practice among Tendai monks. But now the texts devoted exclusively to Amida seemed increasingly relevant, for they described in detail the paradisiacal Pure Land into which the fortunate might be reborn. Moreover, commentaries written in China emphasized that in degenerate times and for people with little merit or spiritual ability, entrance into this happy land could be gained through the *nembutsu* chant or prayer. This was no more than the simple repetition—aloud, under the breath, or mentally—of Amida's name, in the formula *Namu Amida Butsu* ("Hail to the Buddha Amitābha").

The Tendai monk Hōnen, late in the classical era, began popularizing this devotional practice among the laity as a means to ensure rebirth in the Pure Land. His disciple Shinran (1173–1262) became an especially persuasive preacher of this practice. Eventually new and independent Buddhist sects grew up among people who traced their religious lineage to one or the other of these two men. The Jōdo (Pure Land) sect, following Hōnen, emphasized both good works (merit) and the *nembutsu* chant as a means of salvation. The more radical *Jōdo Shin* (True Pure Land) sect, following Shinran, disparaged merit and even the nembutsu as a means, arguing that ordinary people were *absolutely* dependent on the power of Amida. Even the chanting of the nembutsu did not lead to salvation because the impulse to chant it itself came from Amida. Faith alone was required.

Nichiren The much less numerous Nichiren sect, though similar in many ways to Pure Land, bore the stamp of the unusual personality of an ex-Tendai monk, Nichiren (1222–1282). This charismatic and eccentric man became convinced that he was the reincarnation of one of the bodhisattvas described in the Lotus Sūtra. As such he was empowered to impart the true meaning of the sūtra. This alone was the way to salvation. Abandoning the idea of upāya and the toleration and syncretism it implied, he declared that all other forms of religious practice, including Buddhist forms, were evil. His practice borrowed from Pure Land forms in that he required his followers to chant the formula *Namu myō hō renge kyō* ("Hail to the Sūtra of the Lotus of the True Dharma") as a way of achieving both enlightenment and this-worldly benefits such as wealth, health, and safety. His followers hoped that they could convert all of the Japanese people, thus making the nation into a Buddhist utopia, a Pure Land on earth.

With this era's pessimistic outlook, the dynamic tension so characteristic of Japanese religiosity throughout the classical period apparently reached nearly intolerable intensity. There were several reasons for this. First, the old, relatively optimistic appraisal of life in this world could not be maintained in the face of such hardship and uncertainty. Second, the classical Japanese had assumed a unified world, a kind of harmony that subsumed the tensions and thus kept them at a tolerable level, but in medieval times it was difficult to accept such an overarching harmony. Thus the proliferation of Buddhist sects at this time indicates both earnest attempts to solve the religious problems and at the same time symptoms of the failure to do so completely. Separate sects sought in their own ways to overcome this tension and allay the sufferings of the people. But each fragmented the religious world even more and moved further away from a unified worldview. Pure Land emphasized almost exclusively the next life, leaving this life to mere custom, a void that folk Shintō and Nichiren Buddhism tended to fill. Nichiren Buddhism increasingly specialized in the healing arts to minister to that dimension of the practical life. Moreover, even within their own specialized spheres, these sects were only partly successful. Ironically, even as Pure Land Buddhism sought to allay the anxiety of the masses about the future life, new forms of uncertainty and tension emerged within this religious movement itself. For example, when Shinran, the founder of the True Pure Land sect, took off his monastic robes and married, he declared the monastic life to be useless in the quest for salvation. Only the great compassion of Amida could save such a wretch as he. Such desperation and extreme humility was characteristic of many of his followers. He taught that one had only truly and with utter earnestness to cast oneself on the mercy of Amida to be assured of rebirth in paradise. Yet how could one be sure of one's earnestness? And how could one achieve utter humility if one did not entirely feel it at every moment? Anxiety on such points continued to trouble many.

Zen Zen (in Chinese, Chan) was the last Buddhist sect founded in the early medieval period, and unlike the other new sects, it was transplanted directly from China. A form of Zen had been known earlier but had been seen merely as an optional emphasis within a crowded field of Buddhist monastic practices. Clearly, conditions were only now favorable for it to take root in Japan as an independent sect. Zen established itself primarily as a monastic movement, and as in China, the monks came from all segments of society. But in addition, in Japan, Zen's austere meditative disciplines appealed particularly to the new elite, the samurai class. Two forms were transmitted directly from China, the Rinzai form by Eisai (1141–1215) and the Sōtō form by Dōgen (1200–1253). Both emphasized simplicity and practical guidance toward enlightenment *(satori)* here and now.

The Zen monastery became a place of intense effort in meditation, and although some samurai actually became monks, many more spent temporary retreats at monasteries or engaged monks as private tutors. They wished especially to learn the techniques of concentration and self-forgetfulness that could reinforce their ideals of loyalty and service to their military superiors.

These are the hands of a Zen Buddhist monk at a monastery of the Sōtō sect in Japan. In this posture of "Kyosakku," or "awakening spirit," the long stick is often held for hours. (Paolo Koch/Photo Researchers)

For good reason, they increasingly came to believe that Zen concentration could make them superior in battle: to lose the sense of self was at the same time to lose the fear of death; to increase concentration could enhance archery and swordsmanship skills by disengaging the mind from any inhibiting fear of failure or attempts consciously to control the body. Just as Zen monks sought the spontaneity of egoless enlightenment, the samurai sought the spontaneity of the egoless exercise of fighting skills. The dynamic tension characteristic of Japanese religiosity is especially striking here, for the samurai used the techniques of Mahāyāna Buddhism—the way of the bodhisattva dedicated to an enlightenment suffused with compassion—to kill more efficiently in the loyal service of their samurai master.

Like the common people, the samurai were subject to feelings of peril, suffering, and impermanence. But whereas the common people often felt helpless and became passive in the face of adversity, the samurai used Zen to enhance direct action and self-control. These attitudes, together with their warrior ethic of loyalty and determination, were approaches to life that had won them their high station.

Zen, through its success as the preferred religious practice of the new elite, also came to exercise tremendous influence in the arts. Indeed, despite the troubled times, a new flowering of culture came about. The arts of Nō drama, *haiku* poetry, and the tea ceremony all emerged through Zen, and a new Zen-inspired emphasis on simplicity, asymmetry, and naturalness came to dominate such older arts as painting, architecture, and landscape gardening.

THE REUNIFICATION OF JAPAN

Toward the end of the sixteenth century, Japan experienced a series of wars that eventually resulted in the establishment of a strong central government, though still under samurai control. The many small power centers were gradually consolidated by force and alliance until 1603, when the Tokugawa clan emerged victorious in a final battle. From the fortress at Edo (modern Tokyo), the Tokugawa clan led the nation through a long period of armed peace that lasted until just before the restoration of imperial rule in 1868.

The Tokugawa period was a time of religious consolidation and even routinization rather than creativity. The shōgunate sought to unify the nation by promoting Neo-Confucianism as the justification of its rule and the organizing principle of society. The goal of unity, so hard won on the battlefield, was to be preserved by establishing a Confucian-style harmony. The shōgun was the head of the nation, understood as a single family with a hierarchical organization and strong ties of loyalty and obedience. On the basis of this model, the peasants were for the first time bound to the land, and rigid class distinctions among the samurai, farmers, and merchants were established. Everyone was to have a place as established by law, and that law was enforced by Tokugawa swords.

The Tokugawa period also brought the first contacts with the West. First to appear were Spanish and Portuguese traders and Jesuit missionaries. The Japanese were at first quite interested in trade and in European firearms and medicine. Christianity, seen by some as a symbol of technological and cultural advancement, gained a small but loyal following in some areas. Indeed, during the wars of unification, some samurai leaders actually promoted Christianity as a counterpoise to the politically powerful Buddhist sects. But by the end of the sixteenth century, rumors of Western imperialistic intentions had reached the Japanese leaders. As early as 1587, the most powerful *daimyō* (feudal lord) issued an edict prohibiting foreign missionaries from operating in his domains and "interfering" with Shintō and Buddhist teachings. Little effort was made to enforce this until 1597, when 26 Japanese and European Franciscans were crucified at Nagasaki. Then in 1614 the Tokugawa regime, in an attempt to tighten its grip on the reins of power, issued an edict banning the practice of Christianity. This led eventually to a Christian uprising in Kyūshū, where several Christian daimyō had constructed strongholds. In 1639 the Christian forces were defeated, and the shōgun closed Japan to virtually all foreign contacts. Japanese Christians were hunted down and forced to recant or suffer martyrdom.

Effects of the Closing of Japan

The closing of the nation to foreign trade and ideas only served to make the social, political, and economic structure more rigid. Confucian ideas were used to strengthen loyalty to superiors and family ties. Moreover, Buddhism was used as an arm of the state to keep watch on the people through a "parochial system" in which every household was ordered to affiliate with a particular Buddhist temple. By government order, every Japanese became a Buddhist at a single stroke.

The effect of this extraordinary policy was at first mixed. Even Shintō priests had to become Buddhists, and some chose to leave the priesthood altogether.

Another result of making Buddhism the state religion was a proliferation of Buddhist temples and new academies. Yet in the long run Buddhism suffered greatly from this deceptive windfall. Buddhist religious life tended to become hollow and formalistic; many priests were attracted to their profession not by piety or zeal but by its financial security. As a result, the prestige of Buddhism steadily declined. Among the elite, Buddhism was seen as inferior to Confucianism; the common people turned increasingly to Shintō.

Among the educated classes, however, the study of Confucian philosophy eventually had an additional and unexpected result: it reawakened an interest in classical literature and history, at first the Confucian classics but later works that came to be considered classics of Japanese history, culture, thought, and religion. Shintō was increasingly seen as the bearer of the ancient and therefore classical Japanese value system and way of life. Thus the stage was set for a Shintō revival.

The National Scholar Movement

In 1728 a priest of the Inari shrine in Kyōto submitted a petition to the Tokugawa rulers in which he pleaded for patronage to establish a school of "national learning" *(kokugaku)* for the study of Japanese classical literature. This was the beginning of a renewal movement that sought to strip Shintō of its foreign (that is, Chinese) elements and establish it as an intellectual force rivaling the dominant Buddhist and Confucian schools of the time. Although in the beginning the movement was concerned only with religious and philosophical matters, it later became a political cause as well. National scholars Motoori Norinaga (1730–1801) and Hirata Atsutane (1776–1843) established a set of texts as a basis for Shintō theory and produced commentaries on such Japanese classics as the *Manyōshū,* the *Kojiki,* and the eleventh-century novel of Japanese court life, *Genji monogatari* ("Tale of Genji"). These works were presented as sacred scriptures to the newly awakened Shintō intellectuals.

An early work by Motoori called *Tama kushige* ("Precious Comb Box") became the manifesto of the movement. In it Motoori attached special importance to the descent of the imperial prince in the myth that established the descendants of the sun goddess as Japan's emperors:

> In the Goddess' mandate to the Prince at that time it was stated that his dynasty should be coeval with Heaven and Earth. It is this mandate which is the very origin and basis of the Way. Thus, all the principles of the world and the way of humankind are represented in the different stages of the Age of Kami. Those who seek to know the Right Way must therefore pay careful attention to the stages of the Age of Kami and learn the truths of existence.[1]

Hirata made even stronger claims for nationalism, and his views on the uniqueness and superiority of the Japanese national spirit *(kokutai)* were later made the basis for the ultranationalist ideology of the 1930s. In 1811 he wrote *Kodō taii* ("Summary of the Ancient Way"), in which he asserted:

> People all over the world refer to Japan as the Land of Kami, and call us the descendants of the kami. Indeed, it is exactly as they say: our country, as a special mark of favor from the heavenly kami, was begotten by them, and there is thus so immense a difference between Japan and all other countries of the world as to defy comparison. . . . We, down to the most humble man and woman, are the descendants of the kami.[2]

During the Tokugawa period, when this statement was written, the emperor, as the standard-bearer of the old tradition and direct descendant of Amaterasu, was an obscure figure living in seclusion in Kyōto; the real seat of government was 400 miles away at Edo in the hands of samurai. To express such ideas at that time was not only religiously innovative but also possibly politically dangerous. It was no accident that in the nineteenth century the leaders of the Meiji Restoration, who swept away the feudal regime, did so in the name of this same *kokutai,* which implicitly supported the emperor as the only legitimate ruler of Japan.

THE MODERN PERIOD

By the middle of the nineteenth century, the disparity between official ideology and the realities of social, political, economic, and religious life in Japan had seriously weakened and discredited the Tokugawa regime. Many people recognized the need for change, and when an American naval flotilla sailed into Tokyo Bay in 1853 demanding diplomatic and trade relations, it was a sufficient catalyst to bring about radical change. Military rule was ended, and direct imperial rule was restored in 1868. Like the early classical period, the modern period was a time of cultural disruption and innovation brought about by the rapid assimilation of foreign elements, this time from Western rather than Chinese civilization.

Once again the Japanese embraced the new while cleaving to the old. Again they borrowed selectively and experienced a dynamic state of cultural and religious tension. To be sure, this period of rapid change was not accomplished without pain, especially the pain of disorientation in social structure and religious values. Even so, by the standards of the age, Japan rose to the challenge with amazing energy: by the early years of the twentieth century, the nation had gone far toward transforming itself into a technologically advanced industrial nation with great military power and extensive colonial possessions, and by the century's end it had become a technological and economic marvel.

Seeking both to dissociate itself from the discredited Tokugawa regime and to build a new basis for national unity and identity, the new government soon launched an attack on Buddhism while at the same time promoting Shintō. In the reform edict of 1868, Shintō shrines were required to purge themselves of all Buddhist influences. Buddhist priests attached to Shintō shrines were forced to return to lay life. The Shintō-Buddhist priesthood had to choose one or the other religion, and in 1872 it became illegal for Buddhists to teach that kami were manifestations of Buddhist figures. The people blamed Buddhism for many of the evils of the past, and in their reformist anger they destroyed many Buddhist temples.

But as always, it was not easy to forge a new cultural synthesis out of disparate elements in so short a time. The quest for a viable national identity that was both modern and continuous with tradition proved especially difficult. To gain the respect of the world, it was necessary to embrace both religious freedom and democratic government; yet to remain true to Japanese tradition, both had to be modified. The modifications actually wrought led to a new emphasis on Shintō traditions and values.

In the new state ideology, the emperor, as the direct descendant of Amaterasu, was promoted as a divine person who symbolized Japan's national origins and unity. His religious status meant that he could not rule directly, participating in everyday political affairs, for this would jeopardize his sacred dignity. Yet a parliament, as a deliberative body, could hardly be thought of as being able to perceive the imperial will. Thus the constitution drawn up in 1889 provided for both an emperor and a parliament but gave real power to neither. Rather, real power was held by a small group of men operating behind the scenes and without legal standing or accountability. Japan wanted ultimate religious sanction in political affairs but bought it at the price of a government unresponsive to the people and sometimes arbitrary in its exercise of power.

A similar dilemma existed more directly in the realm of religious affairs. Just as the new rulers of Japan

Shintō priests at Mitsumine Jinja. The Allied military occupation of 1945–1952 sought to put an American stamp on postwar Japan. As part of this attempt, the Shintō Directive of 1946 disestablished state Shintō, converting the many shrines into independent, private religious institutions. Because certain aspects of Shintō are felt to be an essential part of the Japanese identity, many people believe that these aspects should be declared not religious, thereby circumventing the religion-state separation directive. (Religious News Service)

wanted religious sanction in politics, they also wanted religion to serve political ends. Shintō had in effect been made the national religion, although the constitution guaranteed religious freedom. The problem was "solved" by separating what was now termed state Shintō from sectarian Shintō. The former was declared to be nonreligious and the duty of every loyal citizen. The latter was organized into several sects that did not receive government patronage. Reverence for the emperor and respect for his authority, as well as reverence for many national heroes and the mythic kami, was required of every Japanese and was taught in the government schools under the guise of state Shintō.

The success of this educational policy can be seen by noting that the Japanese people, by 1941, had been molded into a powerful technological and military force. Embued with a sense of great national purpose, most were amenable to almost any policy that their leaders, wrapped in the cloak of sacred, imperial authority, initiated. Most impressive of all, perhaps, is the fact that the leaders themselves seemed to have genuinely believed that they were carrying out the will of the emperor and expressing the Japanese *kokutai,* or national essence. It is significant that when the nation lay in ruins in 1945 with the war lost, the leaders of Japan feverishly tried to negotiate a peace that would respect that same mysterious and sacred principle of national identity and significance.

State Shintō

We have seen that the official position of the Japanese government from early in the Meiji period to

1945 was that state Shintō was not a religion. However, this so-called civil cult retained its religious character. It became a system in which the ultimate values of the ancient religion of Japan were harnessed by the central authority to promote loyalty to itself, social solidarity, and patriotism. It was a powerful tool in the hands of those who in the nineteenth century had undertaken the difficult task of creating a modern nation out of the feudal domains of the Tokugawa period. By the twentieth century, it had become the tool of militarists who brought the nation to ruin in World War II.

JAPAN'S NEW RELIGIONS

During the nineteenth and twentieth centuries, many new religious groups sprang up in Japan and organized themselves as independent religious bodies. These so-called new religions began as closely knit sectarian groups, many hundreds of which still exist. Most continue to emphasize group solidarity, and many combine Shintō, Buddhist, Confucian, Daoist, and even Christian and other Western elements, though most may be classified as primarily Shintō or Buddhist. They undoubtedly represent in part a religious response to the tensions inherent in the rapidly changing cultural and political situation.

In general, perhaps the single most important characteristic of such cultural transformation is the feeling of having been cut off from one's religion and thus from the source of life's meaning. This absence of continuity is particularly dangerous for ritual, which depends heavily on past models that are repeated, imitated, and celebrated. In Japan, as elsewhere, one response to the destruction of traditional models has been to establish new ones. But no parliament or executive decree could suffice to gain the allegiance of the people. The religious category for innovation and devising new models is revelation, and the model must have sacred origins. In the Japanese case, the Shintō pattern of communication with the sacred kami was employed by many new sects, most often in the form of shamanic possession.

One of the most dramatic examples of modern shamanic possession in the service of new revelation comes from Tenrikyō ("religion of divine wisdom"). Its founder, Nakayama Miki (1798–1887), was possessed by Tentaishōgun and nine other kami, who proclaimed through her:

> Miki's mind and body will be accepted by us as a divine shrine, and we desire to save this [seen and unseen] world through this divine body. Otherwise, and if you all refuse our desire, the Nakayama family shall completely cease to exist.[3]

Among Miki's most impressive achievements are the many poems she composed under the inspiration of the kami. Taken together, they constitute a new mythology, a new understanding of the origins and meaning of the cosmos.

Although hundreds of new religions have appeared, especially since the defeat of 1945, they all have similar characteristics regardless of whether they are of primarily Shintō or Buddhist origin. Besides their dependence on shamanic revelation, they include an emphasis on healing the ills of body and mind, a dependence on myth rather than philosophy as the locus of meaning, an appeal to the nonintellectual and lower socioeconomic levels of society, a propensity for congregational worship and other group activities unusual in older forms of Japanese religion, and a strong allegiance to a single founder or to later charismatic leaders.

The largest and most highly visible of the new religions is Sōka Gakkai ("value-creation society"). Also known as Nichiren Shōshū because of its later affiliation with the medieval Nichiren sect of Buddhism, this group claims millions of followers, both in Japan and abroad. Its political party, the Kōmeitō ("clean government party"), has managed to elect several members to the Japanese Diet. Along with an authoritarian internal organization and militant conversion tactics, Sōka Gakkai has a utopian scheme to convert Japan into a Buddhaland. It is particularly noted for its practice of chanting the name of the Lotus Sūtra as a means of gaining power to achieve whatever goals the individual may have. Its ultimate goal it calls happiness in this life, which it believes to be the true meaning of nirvāṇa.

The appeal of the new religions, especially apparent in the case of Sōka Gakkai, stems in large measure from their genius in providing a sense of belonging to a supportive group and a mutually reinforced sense of meaning through structured ritual, ethical, and social behavior. In a world increasingly typified by the breakdown of traditional family and community ties in the face of urbanization and industrialization, this ability to give the individual a sense of belonging is clearly important. The Japanese, so recently deprived of the supportive environment of a very traditional society with its unquestioned loyalties and highly structured life and troubled by questions of identity of self and nation as a result of their defeat in war, are obviously attracted by such religious movements. Individuals can find in the new religions the reinforcement of like-minded people who together create a small world of their own, a world in which each person has a role and a meaning in relation both to the kami or other deities and to the community as a whole. This small world of order, predictability, and support then allows the individual to cope with the larger world of change and unpredictability, of work and family, of international threat and economic vulnerability. These two worlds again exhibit the old pattern of dynamic tension by which the Japanese have sought religiously to come to terms with life.

Yet another significant characteristic of many of the new religions of contemporary Japan is the importance of women in their creation. We have already mentioned Tenrikyō and its founder, Nakayama Miki. Other examples from the Shintō-oriented new religions include Ōmotokyō ("teaching of the great origin"), jointly founded by a husband and wife. Jiyūkyō ("freedom religion") was founded by a woman who announced that she was the incarnation of Amaterasu. Another prominent female religious figure is Kitamura Sayo (born 1900), founder of the Kōtai Jingū sect, a revitalized Shintō group with a feminist slant.

JAPANESE RELIGION SINCE WORLD WAR II

Perhaps a dozen of the hundreds of new religions, both Shintō and Buddhist, have dominated Japan since the war, and they are noted for their missionary zeal and vitality. Even so, a number of traditional religious groups claim significant memberships. In addition to shrine Shintō, there are traditional Buddhist groups that make up various branches of Tendai, Shingon, Nichiren, Pure Land, and Zen Buddhism. Yet it must be admitted that the primary function of many of the priests of these groups is to conduct funerals. Religious activities include regular rituals and the social and spiritual support functions common to neighborhood religious establishments everywhere. A number of Zen monasteries continue rigorous meditative discipline in the training of new priests, and some even cater to lay retreats where nonpriests can for a few days live the life of a monk. Moreover, a number of Western Zen masters have been trained in Japan to serve as missionaries in North America, where Zen centers have sprung up in recent decades. Still, Japanese Buddhism is known internationally today more for the outstanding quality of its historical scholarship than for the rigor of its practice.

Shrine Shintō

Among all the religions of Japan, Shintō was the most directly affected by defeat in war. The Allied military occupation, which lasted from 1945 to 1952, sought to put an American stamp on postwar Japanese society. The constitution that took effect in 1947 tried to make Japan a bastion of democracy and individual freedom in the Western pattern. War was made unconstitutional; so were armed forces for any purpose but self-defense. As a part of this policy, the Shintō Directive of 1946 disestablished state Shintō in a sweep, converting the many shrines into independent, private religious institutions relying solely on private and voluntary contributions for their continued existence. Public officials were prohibited from participating in religious ceremonies in their official capacities, and the emperor was made publicly to deny his divinity.

Events since 1952 have frequently reminded both government and citizens of the special relationship between Shintō and the Japanese national identity. The imposition of the American insistence on strict separation of religion and state has been a problematic source of tension for the Japanese nation and for Shintō leaders. For example, to this day, the position of the emperor and the meaning of the imperial institution have resisted clarification because the traditional Japanese conception of the emperor and of national identity clearly run counter to the American scheme. To pretend that the emperor is not a religious figure or that he exercises his religious functions purely as a private person is as misleading as it would be to pretend (like the prewar government of Japan) that shrine Shintō is not religious.

Yet shrine Shintō has shown considerable vitality in

spite of its difficult position. Soon after the issuance of the Shintō Directive in 1946, the Association of Shintō Shrines was formed to coordinate the programs of the newly independent shrines. This group has been active in setting up education programs, raising money, and providing an effective united voice for shrine Shintō. The association managed to prevent the destruction of the Yasukuni shrine in 1946, and it even helped to arrange for the emperor and empress to be present at ceremonies there in 1952. It has attempted again and again to reestablish the great Shintō shrines at Ise and Yasukuni as national shrines. The association has also tried to have the constitution rewritten in order to safeguard the position of the emperor as the head of state and to have the imperial household rites recognized as national religious ceremonies. It has been successful in litigation to permit the performance of Shintō ceremonies at the various traditional points in the construction of government buildings. And the association has induced the government to underwrite the maintenance of certain Shintō ceremonies as important "cultural properties." What cannot be done in the name of religion can sometimes be accomplished in the name of culture.

With the death of Hirohito, the Shōwa emperor, in January 1989, a new era, Heisei ("achieving peace"), was inaugurated, and a new emperor reigns. The funeral of the old emperor and the official ceremonies of accession of the new emperor, held in November 1990, again brought about heated argument in the Japanese press regarding the issue of religion-state separation. As a way out of this dilemma, even today there are people who favor the old formula of a governmental declaration that certain aspects of Shintō are not religious because they are felt to be such an essential part of the Japanese identity.

NOTES

1 Ryusaku Tsunoda, William T. de Bary, and Donald Keene, *Sources of Japanese Tradition* (New York: Columbia University Press, 1964), vol. 2, pp. 16–18.

2 Ibid., p. 39.

3 Hori Ichirō, *Folk Religion in Japan* (Chicago: University of Chicago Press, 1968), p. 237.

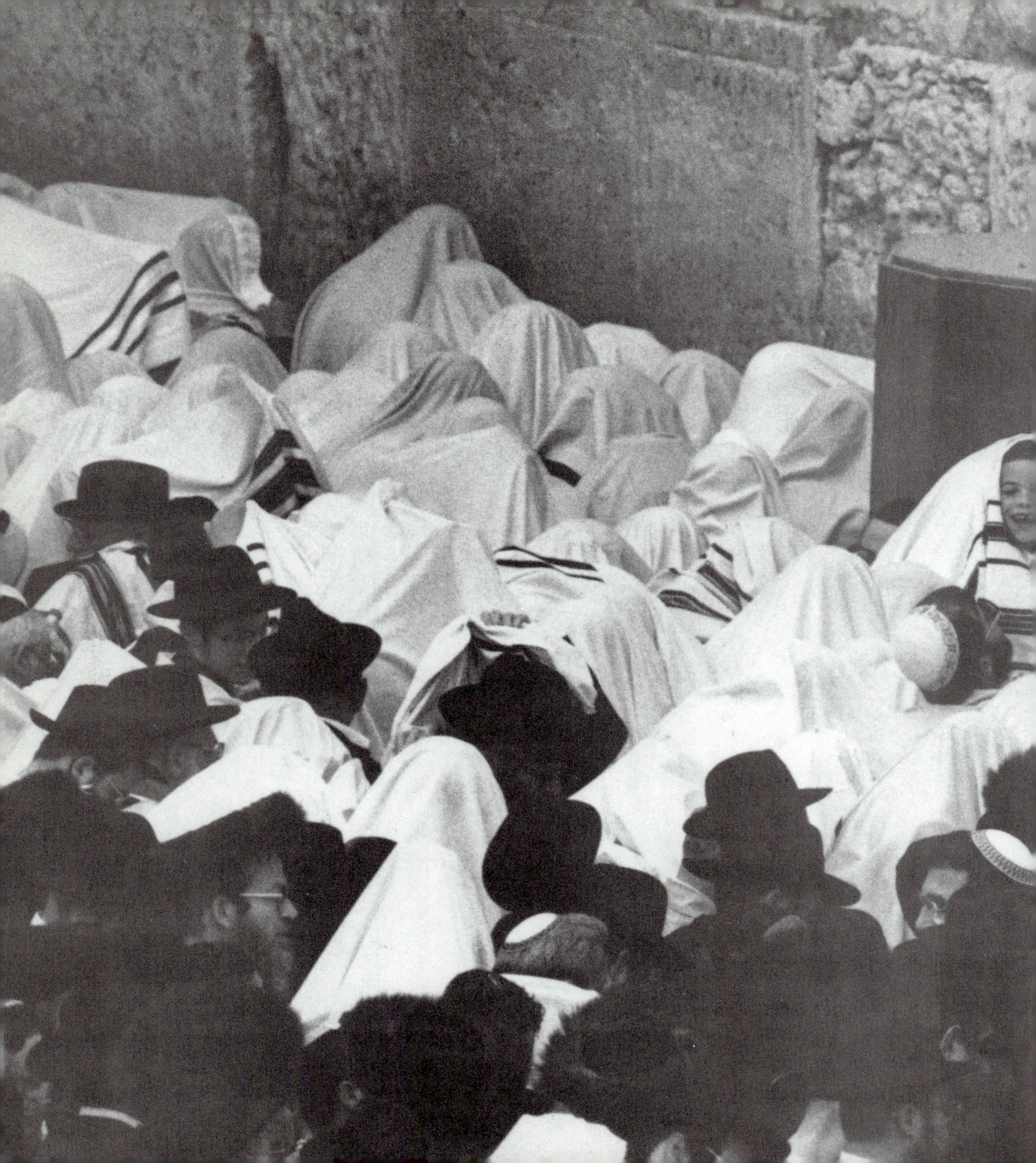

PART FIVE

JUDAISM

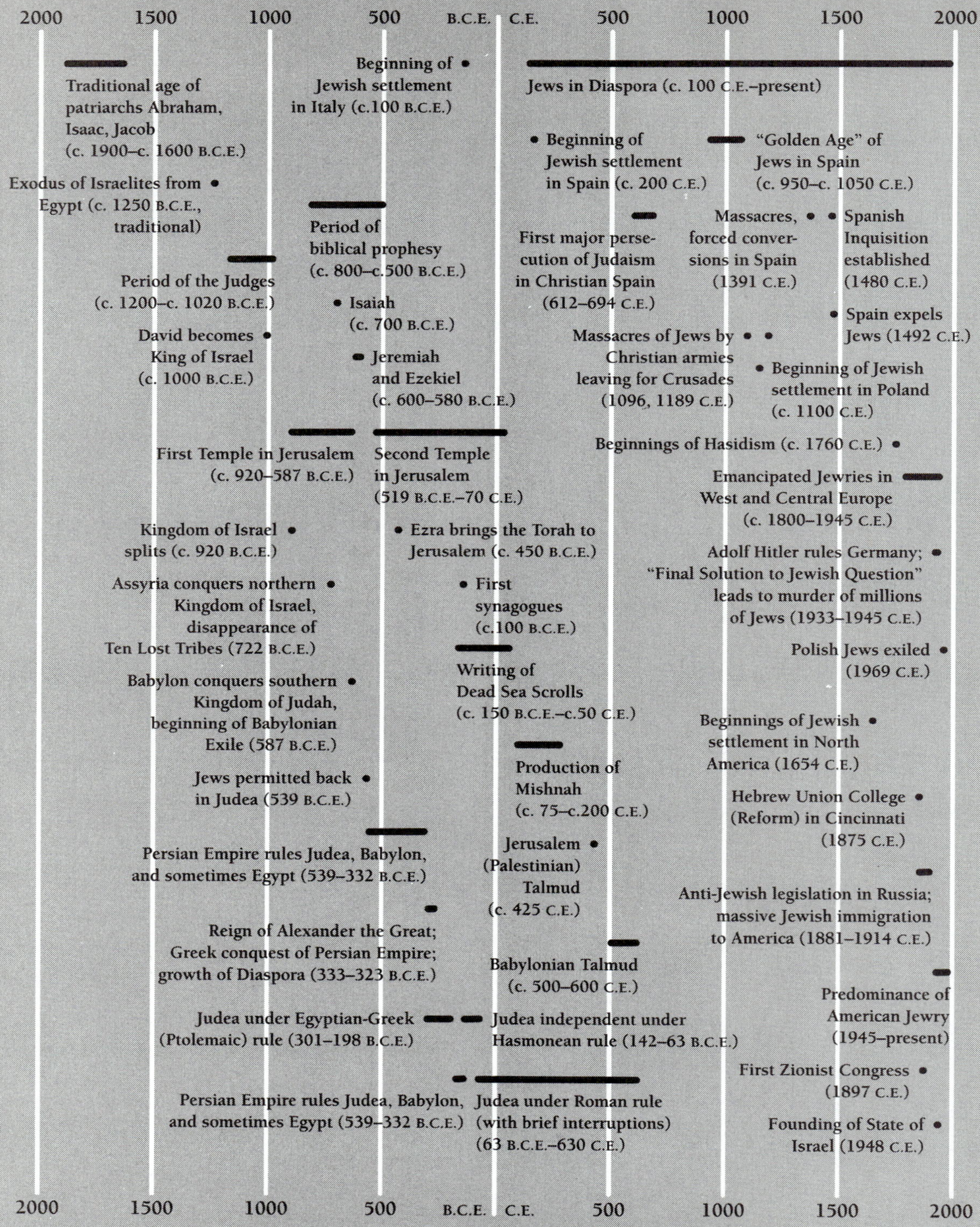
2000
1500
1000
500
B.C.E.
C.E.
500
1000
1500
2000
Traditional age of patriarchs Abraham, Isaac, Jacob (c. 1900–c. 1600 B.C.E.)
Exodus of Israelites from Egypt (c. 1250 B.C.E., traditional)
Period of the Judges (c. 1200–c. 1020 B.C.E.)
David becomes King of Israel (c. 1000 B.C.E.)
First Temple in Jerusalem (c. 920–587 B.C.E.)
Kingdom of Israel splits (c. 920 B.C.E.)
Assyria conquers northern Kingdom of Israel, disappearance of Ten Lost Tribes (722 B.C.E.)
Babylon conquers southern Kingdom of Judah, beginning of Babylonian Exile (587 B.C.E.)
Jews permitted back in Judea (539 B.C.E.)
Persian Empire rules Judea, Babylon, and sometimes Egypt (539–332 B.C.E.)
Reign of Alexander the Great; Greek conquest of Persian Empire; growth of Diaspora (333–323 B.C.E.)
Judea under Egyptian-Greek (Ptolemaic) rule (301–198 B.C.E.)
Persian Empire rules Judea, Babylon, and sometimes Egypt (539–332 B.C.E.)
Beginning of Jewish settlement in Italy (c.100 B.C.E.)
Period of biblical prophesy (c. 800–c.500 B.C.E.)
Isaiah (c. 700 B.C.E.)
Jeremiah and Ezekiel (c. 600–580 B.C.E.)
Second Temple in Jerusalem (519 B.C.E.–70 C.E.)
Ezra brings the Torah to Jerusalem (c. 450 B.C.E.)
First synagogues (c.100 B.C.E.)
Writing of Dead Sea Scrolls (c. 150 B.C.E.–c.50 C.E.)
Production of Mishnah (c. 75–c.200 C.E.)
Jerusalem (Palestinian) Talmud (c. 425 C.E.)
Babylonian Talmud (c. 500–600 C.E.)
Judea independent under Hasmonean rule (142–63 B.C.E.)
Judea under Roman rule (with brief interruptions) (63 B.C.E.–630 C.E.)
Jews in Diaspora (c. 100 C.E.–present)
Beginning of Jewish settlement in Spain (c. 200 C.E.)
"Golden Age" of Jews in Spain (c. 950–c. 1050 C.E.)
First major persecution of Judaism in Christian Spain (612–694 C.E.)
Massacres, forced conversions in Spain (1391 C.E.)
Spanish Inquisition established (1480 C.E.)
Spain expels Jews (1492 C.E.)
Massacres of Jews by Christian armies leaving for Crusades (1096, 1189 C.E.)
Beginning of Jewish settlement in Poland (c. 1100 C.E.)
Beginnings of Hasidism (c. 1760 C.E.)
Emancipated Jewries in West and Central Europe (c. 1800–1945 C.E.)
Adolf Hitler rules Germany; "Final Solution to Jewish Question" leads to murder of millions of Jews (1933–1945 C.E.)
Polish Jews exiled (1969 C.E.)
Beginnings of Jewish settlement in North America (1654 C.E.)
Hebrew Union College (Reform) in Cincinnati (1875 C.E.)
Anti-Jewish legislation in Russia; massive Jewish immigration to America (1881–1914 C.E.)
Predominance of American Jewry (1945–present)
First Zionist Congress (1897 C.E.)
Founding of State of Israel (1948 C.E.)
2000
1500
1000
500
B.C.E.
C.E.
500
1000
1500
2000

JUDAISM TIME LINE

JUDAISM

CHAPTER 16

GOD, TORAH, AND ISRAEL: THE BEGINNINGS

Judaism means, literally, "religion of the people of the southern Israelite realm of Judah."* Judah was a small nation, and the Jews have never been either numerous or powerful: there are but 18 million Jews today, scattered on all continents. Yet in the history of religions their influence has been remarkable. The Hebrew belief in one God laid the cornerstone for both Christian and Muslim monotheism, and its emphasis on morality and ethics permeates Western and Middle Eastern society.

The history of Judaism can be divided into three periods. The first, which we have called the time of beginnings (before the second century B.C.E.), began in ancient Israel and ends with the writing of the newest book in the Hebrew Bible. Though much of this period is shrouded in myth, the religion of this era came to center on the cult and temple of a particular deity, **Yahweh**. Stories told about these early days eventually emerged as the early books of the Bible, and in these stories we can see the outlines of thought and attitude that later came to characterize Judaism. Toward the end of this period, with many of its people away from their homeland, Judaism began to take the shape that it was to maintain for centuries. Thus ensued Judaism's second period, classical Judaism (second century B.C.E.–eighteenth century C.E.). During this time the Jews were unlike any other people and their faith unlike any other religion in history: for some 2,000 years, these people, most of them no longer living in Israel, retained their unity as a distinct "nation" solely by means of their religion. The **rabbis** (teachers) and their followers, as we shall see, developed a behavioral pattern and an explanation for it that, despite significant adaptations, remained remarkably constant for

*It is important to define at the outset some terms that will be used in Part Five. The people who profess Judaism have been known as Hebrews, Israelites, and Jews. *Israelite* means "a descendant of the patriarch Jacob," who was given the name Israel ("one who has striven with God"). *Hebrew* seems to have been the name the ancient Israelites used for themselves when speaking with outsiders or outsiders used when referring to the Israelites. *Jew* comes from the Latin *Judaeus,* derived from the Hebrew *Yehudi,* meaning "one who lives in Judah." The tribe of Judah eventually absorbed the remnants of the other legendary tribes of Israel into its own structure and so became equivalent in people's minds to the Israelite nation as a whole. Thus the religion that developed out of the traditions of ancient Israel came to be known as *Judaism.*

The land that the ancient Hebrews believed was promised to them by God has been known in history by the following names: *Canaan,* the name used by one of the major groups of inhabitants before the arrival of the Hebrews; *Israel;* and *Palestine,* after the Philistines, a people who fought the Hebrews for possession of the land.

Pronouncing Hebrew
Hebrew can be transcribed in several ways. We have used a simple style. Letters are pronounced as they are in English, with one exception: *ch* represents a guttural sound in the back of the throat, much like the German or Scottish *ch.*

centuries, whether the believers were in Jerusalem, Babylon, Berlin, or Brooklyn. That way of life and view of the world found itself driven to fundamental change only in the past two centuries, in the third period, the one we call modern Judaism. And each of these developments, as we shall see, came as a creative response to this people's situation and needs.

Yet Judaism has retained exceptional unity. It centers in its people's view of themselves—their belief that this whole nation and its scriptures are conjoined to the one God. As one medieval text put it, "God, Torah and Israel are bound together."[1] To be a Jew is to feel part of the history of a people, Israel; to perceive that history as having been shaped by a special relationship with God; and to acknowledge that because of that relationship, one should fulfill the obligations derived from a sacred text, the **Torah.** Jews thus see their entire history in terms of God and the Torah and have a sense of being part of a sacred continuum spanning many generations. Human history, not nature, is critical; acting as God commands, not just believing, is essential. These tenets, central to Judaism, invest Jewish life with transcendent meaning.

Hebrew Beginnings (c. 2000–1000 B.C.E.)

From its beginnings Judaism has centered on its God, identified as the one supreme deity and the source of righteous living. A sense of God's uniqueness led the Jewish leaders, at least from the time of Moses (thirteenth century B.C.E.), to condemn the worship of all other gods as idolatry. The Torah forbade the making of images to represent God, and all forms of polytheism were rejected. In general, Judaism has not been impersonal or other-worldly, like Hinduism and Buddhism, but has stressed that human history is a dialogue between God and humanity.

God's primary relation to his chosen people has been described throughout the religion's history in terms of the Torah. The early rabbis continually asserted that Israel's special **covenant** with God was grounded in the people's commitment to accept and observe the Torah.

To this day the Torah remains the central symbol of Judaism, and at least one Torah scroll is found in the ark of every synagogue.* A Torah scroll is a collection of parchments sewn together, wrapped around two wooden rollers, on which is handwritten a version of the first five books of the Hebrew scripture. It contains not only the terms of the covenant (prescribed cultic observances and ethical norms) but also the story of Hebrew origins and an account of the relationship of each successive generation with the one God who singled out Israel.

Judaism has been characteristically world-affirming, charging its adherents with the mandate to sanctify earthly life. It lacks the speculative metaphysical concern of Greek or Hindu thought.

The spoken and written word, not the visible image, has been primary; the Hebrew God is revealed only through specific divine commandments to his chosen people. The leaders of the religion have been more concerned with defining how Jews ought to act than with what they should believe. The Torah itself is more a *mitzvah* (commandment) than a prescription for faith.

Judaism as a Middle Eastern Religion

The Hebrew religion arose in the context of the ancient Middle East: rituals of sacrifice, seed time and harvest, and the New Year were celebrated throughout the area. Yet whereas many of the local religions focused on the sacred or divine presence of nature and the cycle of birth and rebirth, the religion of the Hebrew Bible does not. The scriptures of ancient Israel interpret the world in terms of one God, Lord of nature and history, whose will was made known to them on various occasions.

Most people of the Middle East symbolized aspects of their deities through natural phenomena, such as the sun, stars, or mountains, or in animals such as the bull. Stories preserved in the books of the Hebrew Bible reveal that many of the ancient Israelites shared these attitudes, but the authors of those books did not. The biblical writers saw their one deity as a personal patron bound to their nation by ties of mutual loyalty,

***Synagogue*, a Jewish house of worship, comes from a Greek word for "assembly." The term *ark* refers both to the container in which the original tablets of the covenant were to be carried around (Exod. 25:10–16) and to the chest in modern synagogues in which the scrolls of the Torah are kept.

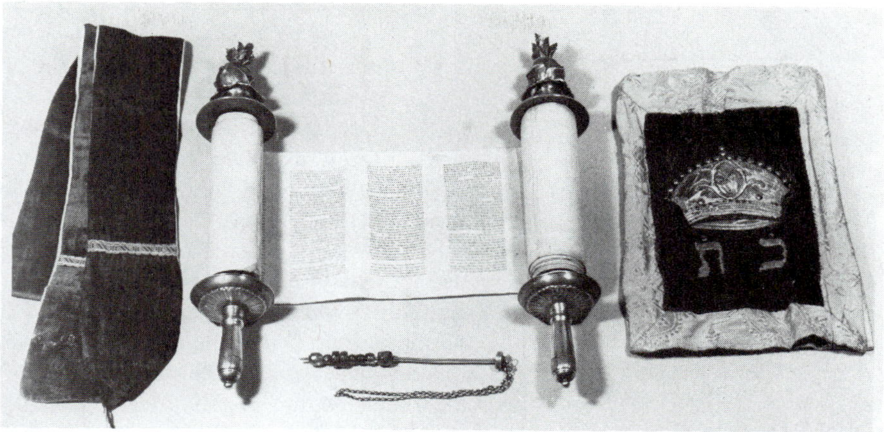

A Torah scroll is a collection of parchments sewn together, wrapped around two wooden rollers, on which is handwritten a version of the first five books of the Hebrew scripture. At least one Torah scroll is found in the ark of every synagogue. (The Jewish Museum. Harry G. Friedman Collection)

a covenant dating back to the earliest ancestors of the tribes of Israel, and this view came to form the basis of Judaism.

Though they described him anthropomorphically—like their neighbors, they thought of Yahweh as male, for example—early Jews saw God as sharply differentiated from themselves. In the Bible none of the ancestors of Israel is given a divine lineage or is credited with moral perfection. The world described in the Hebrew Bible is not mythical, and the universe is not seen as divine or as peopled with heavenly beings. Rather, the world is seen as the handiwork of God, created and sustained by him. God, in turn, is not seen as dependent on earthly or heavenly creatures. The God of the biblical account commanded the loyalty of the people but did not look to them for sustenance.

Biblical religion was not, as a rule, concerned with life after death. The divine promise to the faithful sons and daughters of the covenant was not immortality or other-worldly bliss; rather, God promised to sustain his descendants and provide for them a good life in Canaan. Neither was the Greek dualism of soul and body present in biblical thought. When Jews of a later time did develop a concept of life after death, they did not see this life as an immortal soul apart from the body but rather as a resurrected body.

From the time of Moses until 587 B.C.E., when the elite of the kingdom of Judah were captured and taken to Babylonia, the Hebrews' strong sense of group identity was expressed in doctrines of collective guilt and punishment. It was only during and after this exile that the prophet Ezekiel proclaimed an individual responsibility: "The soul that sins shall die. The son shall not bear the wickedness of the father, neither the father the wickedness of the son" (Ezek. 18:20).[2] Yet the sense of group responsibility never left them.

THE HEBREW BIBLE: SOURCE OF THE TRADITION

Since women in ancient Hebrew society were valued almost exclusively for their familial and domestic contributions, the early history of Judaism was told primarily in terms of the activities of God (conceived of as male) and his male worshipers. The foundational stories thus revolve around the patriarchs, beginning with Abraham's journey to a new land in response to a divine command, Moses's encounter with the Egyptian pharaoh, and Israel's liberation from Egyptian slavery. All are interpreted by biblical accounts as events in which God was directly involved.

The Bible also reveals how the ancient Hebrews saw themselves and how later editors of the texts perceived them. But these narratives also contain mythical and legendary embellishments and were written and edited over a period of centuries. Historical research has determined that the sagas of the early centuries of Judaism were transmitted orally and elaborated by the religious imagination over hundreds of years before they were "reduced to writing" and reshaped by the editors. Although the patriarchal narratives in the Book

COMPARISON

Books of the Bible

The canon of the Hebrew Bible (which is known to Christians as the Old Testament) was established during the early centuries of the Common Era. It consists of the following books and groups of books: (1) The Torah or Pentateuch (Genesis, Exodus, Leviticus, Numbers, and Deuteronomy); (2) the Prophets (Joshua, Judges, 1 and 2 Samuel, 1 and 2 Kings, Isaiah, Jeremiah, Ezekiel, and the minor prophets: Hosea, Joel, Amos, Obadiah, Jonah, Micah, Nahum, Habakkuk, Zephaniah, Haggai, Zechariah, and Malachi); and (3) the Writings, consisting of Psalms, Proverbs, Job, Song of Solomon, Ruth, Lamentations, Ecclesiastes, Esther, Daniel, Ezra, Nehemiah, and 1 and 2 Chronicles.

The following books or parts of books appear in the Greek-language Septuagint but not in the corrected Hebrew-language Masoretic text of the Bible: 1 and 2 Esdras, Tobit, Judith, Esther 10:4–16, Wisdom, Ecclesiasticus, Baruch, Daniel 3:24–90 and Daniel 13–14, the Prayer of Manasses, and 1 and 2 Maccabees. Both Jews and Protestants follow the Hebrew tradition of regarding these works as uncanonical and group them separately from the "inspired books." In the King James version of the Bible they are listed as the Apocrypha ("hidden books"). Roman Catholics, following a different tradition, regard them as divinely inspired and do not dissociate them from the other books of the Bible.

of Genesis are set in the second millennium B.C.E., the first books of the Hebrew Bible did not acquire their present written form until about the fifth century B.C.E. The entire Bible, which includes the Prophets, Psalms, Proverbs, Job, and several smaller books, was not canonized until possibly as late as the second century C.E. (see the accompanying box, "Books of the Bible").

Although the Pentateuch (the first five books of the Hebrew Bible) recounts how God was revealed to Moses under the name Yahweh ("I am who I am"), there is evidence that these books are a blend of at least two different sources, one calling this god Yahweh (later erroneously transcribed as *Jehovah*) and the other calling him Elohim ("all gods"). For example, in the opening chapters of the first book, Genesis, one can identify both the Elohist and Yahwist sources in the description of the creation. (The Yahwist tradition is simpler and begins in Genesis 2:3b.)

The Pentateuch is an account of various events that was compiled at different times and in different places over the centuries. The first 11 chapters of Genesis in particular contain very old tales and myths, but earlier traditions were often changed at a later time to conform to prevailing concepts. Usually the later materials were ascribed to earlier Hebrew figures. Accordingly, the books of the Pentateuch are said to have been written by Moses. The Psalms are attributed to David, Moses, and Solomon, among others, but actually many of them were taken from the hymn book of the second temple, which was rebuilt several decades after Cyrus the Great of Persia captured Babylon in 538 B.C.E. and allowed the Jewish exiles to return home. Both the Book of Proverbs, a compilation of commonsense sayings, and the Song of Songs, a collection of love poems, are traditionally ascribed to King Solomon.

Distinctive Themes

Several biblical themes were decisive in shaping Judaism. The first, the Exodus, provided the principal symbol of divine action for later generations.

This wood engraving depicts Moses descending Mount Sinai after receiving the Ten Commandments, God's instructions on how the people should comport themselves. (The Granger Collection)

The biblical account of the Exodus is that a group of Hebrew slaves under the leadership of **Moses** escaped from Egypt through the Sinai peninsula to the borders of Palestine. The slaves credited their liberation to their God, Yahweh, who guided them by means of a cloud by day and a fiery pillar by night. At Mount Sinai, the site of revelation in the desert, Moses received from Yahweh the Ten Commandments, or Decalogue, on which were written God's instructions on how the people should comport themselves. This account has not been confirmed by archaeological evidence or from stories told outside the Bible. It was nevertheless accepted by later generations of Israelites, both descendants of the escaping slaves and newer converts. The story provided a model of divine intervention on behalf of the nation, and this model shaped the Jews' view of history. It connoted hope for future divine salvation whenever later events took a cruel turn.

The second theme, of a nonnaturalistic deity of a particular people, took far longer to develop. Scholars have noted that, as presented in the texts, Abraham, Isaac, and Jacob, the traditional founders of the faith, did not explicitly deny the reality or power of the gods embraced by other peoples. Nor is there in the earliest writings the full-blown polemic against idolatry that appears centuries later in the Book of Isaiah. Instead, the early narratives suggest an exclusive bond between a particular deity, El-Shaddai, and Abraham, Isaac, and Jacob.

Many later Israelites were strongly attracted to the prevailing religious customs of their neighbors: the Canaanites who surrounded the Hebrew newcomers had evolved an impressive civilization that the backward Israelites were naturally tempted to emulate. Canaanite nature rites were based on a polytheistic fertility cult that joined the cycle of human generation to that of the seasons. But Hebrew religion resisted adopting this naturalistic polytheism.

It was the prophets, who were active in Israel as early as the time of King David (c. 1000 B.C.E.), who prevented it from moving toward naturalism. And it was the prophets also who prepared the Hebrew people for the third basic theme, exile and redemption. Their understanding of God's judgment and mercy enabled the people and their religion to survive a crushing military defeat and exile. The Hebrews had built a small nation in the Fertile Crescent between the great powers of Assyria and Babylonia to the northeast and Egypt to the southwest. When this land was overrun and conquered by these powers, the prophets depicted this as an act of Yahweh, who was bringing his people to judgment for their sins, not the least of which was their age-old willingness to worship other gods. But God would in time restore and redeem them, they promised. After defeat and exile, the nation was divided between a faithful remnant who accepted this interpretation of the recent terrible events and those who rejected it; these latter found it easier to believe that the gods of the conquerors had defeated their own. Such people abandoned the covenant, assimilated into the surrounding peoples, and disappeared from the history of Judaism.

In the end, however, the Jews' capital city of Jerusalem was again destroyed, by the Romans in 70 C.E. Sacrifice and temple worship came to an end, and the people lost their symbolic center. Since that time, the Jewish community has preserved its traditions and identity in the **Diaspora** (the community of Jews living outside Israel) and in exile, led by rabbinic teachers rather than by priests. In its isolation, Judaism has had a history separate from that of other religious traditions for nearly 20 centuries. This isolation of Judaism in a world perceived as alien is the final basic theme of biblical religious thought.

THE PATRIARCHAL AGE

Who were the Hebrews, the people we read about in the Genesis stories of Abraham, Isaac, Jacob, and their descendants? Although the biblical narratives cannot be confirmed in detail, archaeologists and textual scholars have pieced together much about the world they reflect.

Abraham was commanded by God to offer his own son, Isaac, as a sacrifice. Just as he was about to take his beloved son's life, a ram appeared in a nearby thicket, to be offered in Isaac's stead. In this Rembrandt etching, an angel of the Lord stays Abraham's hand at the last moment. (Zionist Archives and Library)

Abraham and the Nomadic Life

The lives of people like the Hebrew patriarch **Abraham** and his relatives were determined by their desert surroundings. They had a few domestic animals, lived in tents, and centered their existence on the available sources of water. In times of drought or pressure from marauding tribes, whole families migrated with their herds hundreds or even thousands of miles. Genesis ascribes such a migration to Abraham, starting from Haran in upper Mesopotamia and continuing through Canaan all the way down to Egypt (Gen. 12:4–10).

The community of people like Abraham was organized into a loosely knit tribe made up of clans that in turn consisted of individual families. The male head of the tribe was the leader by right of birth, and his authority, though circumscribed by the tribal elders' advice and by established custom, was supreme. Women were valued as the caretakers of the family tent, but their primary function was to bear children to ensure the continuation of the tribe.

The Covenant

Early Hebrew religion traced itself back to a covenant between God and Abraham:

> This is my covenant with you: you shall be the ancestor of a company of nations. . . . I am establishing my covenant between myself and you and your descendants after you throughout their generations as a perpetual covenant, to be God to you and your descendants. I will give you and your descendants after you the land in which you are now only an immigrant, the whole of the land of Canaan as a possession for all time, and I will be their God.
>
> (Gen. 17:4–8)

The word *covenant* means "contract" or "treaty." Applied to ancient Israeli religion, it reflects the fundamental belief that the God of the Israelite nation had entered into a contractual relationship with Abraham and his descendants: God would protect these people in their wanderings and give them a land of their own, and they would in turn remain loyal to God throughout their history. This bond was symbolized by the circumcision of all Hebrew males shortly after birth (Gen. 17:10–13), a custom that survives to this day. This covenant of mutual obligation was to be reflected in the everyday life of the Israelite community through its formal worship, its legal code, and its ethical values. It gave rise to the idea, central to nearly all later Jewish thinking, that obedience to the law is a religious value because the law itself comes from God.

The tales in Genesis, describing events said to have occurred long before the nation was organized, cannot reveal much about the realities of later Israel. But they do introduce and reinforce three ethical and religious themes that have shaped Jewish thinking: human dignity, loyalty to the covenant, and God's shaping of events.

Human Dignity If God was willing to enter into a covenant with humans, he must have valued us very highly. This attitude is expressed in the story of Abraham's challenge to God's announced intention to destroy the wicked city of Sodom (Gen. 18:23–32). When Abraham argues with God, God listens to his arguments; clearly, God values the people he has chosen.

Loyalty to the Covenant Israelites are to remain loyal to the covenant. Abraham was commanded by God to offer his own son, Isaac, as a sacrifice (Gen. 22:1–2). But just as he was about to take his beloved son's life, a ram appeared in a nearby thicket, to be offered, Abraham was told, in Isaac's stead. Abraham's willingness to give up what he cherished most has served the Jews as a model for their loyalty to God.

God's Shaping of Events God is shown repeatedly shaping events to ensure the people's continuity and the fulfillment of God's purposes. For example, God protects Joseph, son of Jacob, whose brothers sold him into slavery in Egypt. God ultimately elevates Joseph to a position of authority from which he is able to save many Hebrew lives, including those of his brothers (Gen. 50:19–21).

THE AGE OF MOSES

According to the biblical account, the Egyptian pharaoh invited **Jacob** (son of Abraham's son Isaac) and his family to live in the region of Goshen, and there they prospered. According to the Book of Exodus, however, a new pharaoh incited his people against the Israelites, setting taskmasters over them and forcing them into slavery. When even this did not satisfy his ill will, he decreed the death by drowning of all newborn Israelite males (Exod. 1). As the Israelites began to cry to their God to save them, one Israelite woman hid her infant in a cradle and placed it along the shore of the Nile. The pharaoh's daughter found the infant, named him Moses, and reared him in palatial splendor (Exod. 2:1–10).

As an adult, Moses became an exiled fugitive from

According to biblical accounts, the Exodus was finally permitted following a series of plagues that broke the pharaoh's resistance. This woodcut from the Cologne Bible of 1478 illustrates the final plagues, darkness and the slaughter of the firstborn. God passed over the Israelite doorsteps when the plague of death was visited upon the Egyptians. The celebration of Passover commemorates these legendary events. (The Granger Collection)

pharaoh's court. Having slain an Egyptian taskmaster, Moses did not dare remain in the land; he settled in Midian, married Zipporah, and became the shepherd of his father-in-law's flocks. While tending the flock at Mount Horeb (also known as Mount Sinai), Moses received his divine commission: he beheld a burning bush that was not consumed by the flames, and he heard a divine voice say:

> "I have indeed seen the plight of my people who are in Egypt . . . and I have come down to rescue them from the Egyptians and bring them up out of that land to a land, fine and large, to a land flowing with milk and honey, to the country of the Canaanites, Hittites, Amorites, Perizzites, Hivvites, and Jebusites. . . . So come now, let me send you to Pharaoh, that you may bring my people the Israelites out of Egypt. . . .
>
> "I am who I am. . . . Thus shall you say to the Israelites: 'I am' has sent me to you."
>
> (Exod. 3:7–14)

Moses responded to the divine call, but only after a series of plagues broke the pharaoh's resistance were the Israelites permitted to leave. The Torah relates that the waters of the Red Sea parted so that the Israelites could cross without getting wet, but when the Egyptians pursued them, the sea closed over their chariots, and the pharaoh's army drowned. This great victory was perceived as a display of Yahweh's redemptive power, and under the leadership of Moses and his sister, the prophetess Miriam, the newly liberated slaves danced and chanted:

> *"Sing to the Lord, for he has completely triumphed;*
> *The horse and its rider he has hurled into the sea."*
>
> (Exod. 15:1)

Moses now led the people to the sacred mountain (Horeb or Sinai), where he had first been commanded to lead the Israelites out of Egypt. There he now received a revelation from Yahweh: the covenant was sealed, and its essential demands, the Ten Commandments, were inscribed on stone tablets. The family covenant between Abraham and his God was now reconceived as a covenant between God and an entire people: the people of Israel were to give their loyalty to Yahweh in return for the assurance that God would guide them to the land promised earlier to Abraham and preserve them in it for as long as they kept their pledges to God.

In a sense Moses's work was now done. The story relates that he continued to lead the people for 40 years more, while they wandered in the desert on their way to the promised land. Many stories are connected to those years; a golden calf that the people built and worshiped even before Moses had come down the mountain with God's laws (Exod. 32) foreshadows the stubborn refusal of later Israelites to abandon the worship of other gods once and for all. In the end, however, Moses himself did not lead the people into the promised land. He was destined to catch only a glimpse of that land from a distant mountaintop and then to die and be buried in an unmarked grave.

The narratives of the Exodus came to form the core of the Israelite national legend. The saga of slavery, lib-

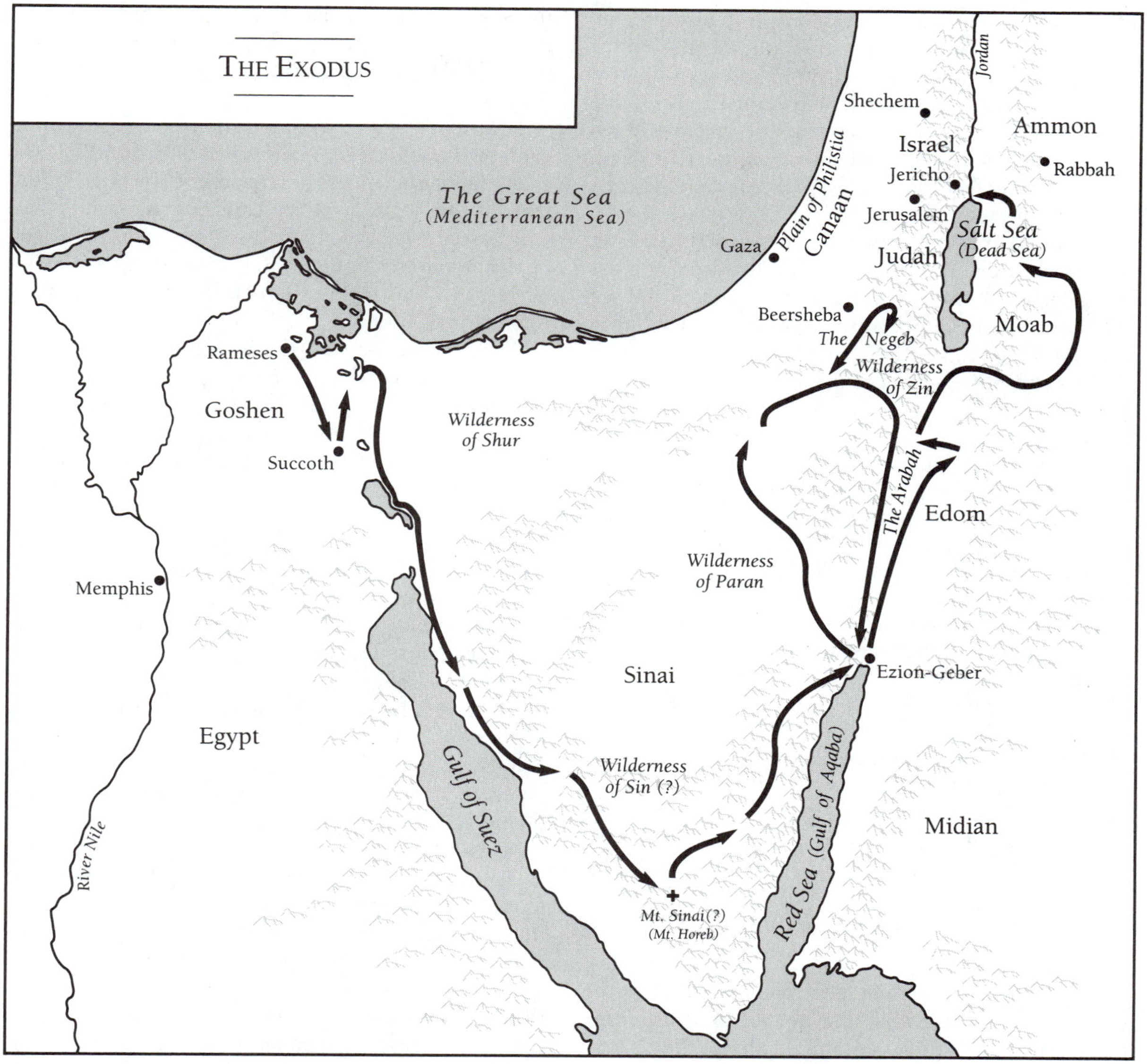

eration, and collective covenant with a redemptive deity has remained central to Jewish religious experience.

THE GOD OF THE MOSAIC COVENANT

According to Exodus, Moses, as God's designated servant, communicated the Lord's will to the people of Israel and thereby renewed the covenant God had entered into with Abraham, Isaac, and Jacob. The covenant was sealed with a sacred meal that God witnessed from afar. Although Yahweh's presence was manifest there, not even Moses could gaze directly at the divine face, "for no man shall see me and live."

Yahweh was the ultimate hero of the biblical saga. As Lord over nature, God singled out individuals and peoples for special relationships and service. Even

Moses, for all his stature, was only a transmitter of divine will. The powers Moses had, such as the ability to change a rod into a serpent, were given to him by Yahweh and were intended only to dramatize Yahweh's presence and purposes. These divine purposes transcended the role and life span of any mortal; when new servants were required, Yahweh did not hesitate to commission them.

Although Yahweh was associated with specific natural sites such as Mount Sinai, he also accompanied the people of Israel in their wanderings. Moses communed with Yahweh in a portable tent that contained the Ark of the Covenant, the sacred chest built to house the tablets of the Ten Commandments. There Yahweh spoke to Moses "as one man would speak to another" (Exod. 33:11). The ark and the tent of their meeting contained no image of Yahweh, only a set of tablets bearing witness to the covenant and setting forth its terms (Deut. 10:4).

An abridged version of the Ten Commandments reads as follows (Exod. 20; Deut. 5):

1. I, the Lord, am your God, who led you out of the land of Egypt, out of the house of bondage.
2. You shall have no other gods besides me.
3. You shall not invoke the name of the Lord your God with malice.
4. Remember the Sabbath Day and keep it holy.
5. Honor your father and your mother.
6. You shall not murder.
7. You shall not commit adultery.
8. You shall not steal.
9. You shall not bear false witness against your neighbor.
10. You shall not covet your neighbor's wife or anything else that is your neighbor's.

The Ten Commandments reflect the memory of events that distinguished the people of Israel from other groups. Its prologue affirms that Yahweh was entitled to Israel's loyalty because "I . . . brought you out of the land of Egypt, out of a state of slavery; you must have no other gods besides me." God demanded exclusive loyalty. Although the wording of the Ten Commandments does not deny other gods, the demand for undivided loyalty was evidently unparalleled in the religions of the region. Egypt, for example, was polytheistic. Some scholars have regarded Mosaic monotheism as derived from the Pharaoh Ikhnaton's exclusive worship of the sun (Aton); others respond that Aton's worship was directed to a natural object, the sun. The biblical narratives lack other important features of the ancient Egyptian religion as well: worship of a deified ruler, a biography for the god, and images of the deity.

Also unlike those of other groups, Israelite rituals expressed gratitude for being saved from bondage. For example, the shepherd's sacrifice of the first spring lamb became a way of remembering the time when God passed over Israelite doorsteps to visit the plague of death on the firstborn Egyptian children (Exod. 12:12–14). This is the origin of the Jewish celebration of Passover.

The recollection that the Israelites had once been strangers and slaves in a foreign land led to another of the covenant's atypical demands: "You must not ill-treat another stranger, nor oppress him, for you were once strangers yourselves in the land of Egypt" (Exod. 22:21).

The Ten Commandments also mention the observance of the Sabbath, the seventh day of the week, from sunset Friday to sunset Saturday. The commandment to rest on the Sabbath applied to all creatures, including slaves and domestic animals. In one account, the Sabbath rest was seen as a symbol of human dignity and as a celebration of God's liberation of the Hebrews from Egypt. Elsewhere the Sabbath rest was explained as a way of enabling Yahweh's creatures to imitate the divine pattern of creativity and rest. Thus the religious observance in Judaism of a weekly day of rest became a symbolic affirmation of many of the tradition's most important beliefs.

To confirm the covenant, Moses built an altar at the foot of the mountain and sprinkled sacrifical blood on the altar and on the people. The people then pledged that "all which the Lord has spoken we shall do and we shall obey," and Moses declared, "Behold the blood of the covenant which the Lord has made with you on the basis of all these regulations" (Exod. 24:8).

The biblical account insists that to the Israelites who left Egypt and wandered in the wilderness for 40 years, Yahweh was the sole power who had liberated them from Egyptian bondage, had given them the Torah to govern their lives, and would guide them toward the fulfillment of his declared purposes by bringing them to the land he had promised to Abraham. This faith that the particular history of their own nation was the work of a universal God has remained a central principle of Judaism throughout its history.

ISRAEL IN CANAAN: THE JUDGES (1200–1020 B.C.E.)

After Moses died, Joshua, one of the scouts who had spied out the promised land, became Moses's successor and led the people in a war of conquest. In reconstructing Israel's entry into Canaan, historians have noted discrepancies in the biblical account. The Book of Joshua records a definitive Israelite victory over the Canaanites, but the very next book states that at the time of Joshua's death, the people were still in need of someone to "go up for us against the Canaanites to fight against them" (Judg. 1:1). There is some evidence that the Hebrews who invaded Canaan under Joshua merged with a people of similar stock already settled on the land.

During the two centuries following the death of Joshua, the Israelite tribes were led by charismatic figures on whom "the spirit of Yahweh rested." These were the *shoftim,* or judges, who exercised military and judicial power. Their authority derived from their claim that they had been sent by Yahweh, a claim that did seem valid in times of military victory. But political instability was more usual, or as the biblical source itself indicates: "In those days there was no king in Israel. Every man did what was right in his own eyes" (Judg. 17:6). Archaeological confirmation of an Israelite presence in the land begins during this period.

Canaanite Influences

When the Israelites settled in their land, the question of Canaanite influence became a persistent concern. The seminomadic immigrants met an established, complex, agricultural society whose religious cults simultaneously bewildered, fascinated, and attracted them. Although the Canaanites' greatest impact on the Israelite settlers was cultural, the biblical writers agonized chiefly over the question of Canaanite religious influence and loyalty.

First among the Canaanite deities were the Baals (possessor-owners), male and female gods who had the power to "impregnate" the soil so that it might yield its fruit. The Baals, who were represented in human, animal, and hybrid sculptures, answered to a higher and more remote divine couple, the males to El and the females to Asherah.

In keeping with the activities of these deities, the cult focused on three harvest periods, fall, spring, and summer. By contrast, Yahweh had no female consort and was not depicted in human or animal form; because he was a jealous god, he was not prepared to share his people with other deities. His altars of unhewn stone contrasted sharply with the elaborate temples constructed by the sedentary inhabitants of Canaan, and the desert wanderers had no structured class of priestly functionaries.

Over time, however, the Canaanites' religious practices did influence the shape and substance of Israelite worship. As the new settlers became sedentary farmers, dependent on the yield of the soil, they were strongly attracted to the various fertility cults. The story of Gideon tells of the struggle against Baalism: Gideon, a farmer, offered unleavened cakes to Yahweh and received a sign that his gift was acceptable. Gideon then built an elaborate altar, dedicated it to Yahweh, and led a night raid on a neighboring Baal altar, destroying the image of the fertility goddess, Asherah. With an appropriate sacrifice, he rebuilt and rededicated the altar to Yahweh (Judg. 6).

This story preserves a response to the challenge of Canaanite religion. The Israelites integrated elements of Canaanite worship (unleavened cakes, burnt offerings, elaborate altars) into an expanding concept of Yahweh, who was henceforth also honored as the god of fertility. In so doing, the Israelites incorporated into their one God the powers and characteristics previously divided among male and female deities, thus moving away from polytheism and toward a nonanthropomorphic God.

The Canaanite language also left a mark. Once the Hebrews had settled in Canaan, they adopted the local alphabet and dialect.

The influence of Canaanite ritual is most evident in the Jewish agricultural festivals. The spring lamb sacrifice, which dated from the wilderness period, was now combined with the Canaanite feast of unleavened bread, though the Israelites reshaped it. Together these festivals became the feast of **Passover**, which now commemorated Yahweh's deliverance of his people from Egypt. Similarly, Shavuot, the Feast of Weeks (Exod. 34:22), was observed in midsummer at the end of the barley harvest, and Sukkot, the Feast of Tabernacles (Exod. 23:16), was celebrated during the fall harvest season. Both borrowed significantly from the Canaanites and became celebrations of Yahweh's bounties. Thus did the God of Israel come to be regarded as the bestower of the earth's bounties.

King David captured the hill city of Jerusalem and made it the capital of his realm. In this modern photo, both the old city and the new city can be seen. (Dan Porges/Peter Arnold, Inc.)

The Struggle against Assimilation

In many ways, however, a bitter struggle against Canaanite customs went on. Intermarriage is expressly forbidden in numerous biblical passages; foreign wives, it is claimed, will "cause your son to crave for their gods" (Exod. 34:16). From the repetitiveness of this prohibition we may conclude that it was a very real issue.

Some of the early prohibitions were probably a response to prevailing Canaanite practices. Some scholars believe that the biblical command not to "boil a kid in its mother's milk" (Exod. 23:19, 34:26; Deut. 14:21) was a reversal of the custom of the Canaanites. Another purpose of these dietary restrictions might have been to minimize social contact between the Israelites and their neighbors. Indeed, many Israelite laws reflected this determination to disallow Yahweh's people from adopting Canaanite cultural and religious practices.

The ancient Israelites' efforts to retain their separateness are symptomatic of the struggle to build a society that would preserve their own heritage in new surroundings. Yet because Jews lived among other peoples for so long, they found it consistently difficult to reach consensus on certain basic matters: How much might they borrow from their neighbors, and which features of their neighbors' way of life should they avoid? These questions remained unsettled for many generations and would arise again and again throughout the history of Judaism.

MONARCHY, EXILE, AND THE RESTORATION OF JUDAH (C. 1000–200 B.C.E.)

During the first two centuries of settlement in Canaan, the Israelites lived in a loose confederation of clans bound together by their commonly accepted covenant with Yahweh. Although Yahweh was worshiped at many local shrines, the central sanctuary was at Shiloh, where, in a tentlike structure called the Mishkan, or tabernacle, the Ark of the Covenant was housed. At least once a year the members of the various clans converged on Shiloh to observe a sacred feast (Judg. 21:19), probably at the time of the autumn harvest festival.

This loose confederation seemed adequate until new pressures required a united kingdom. By the middle of the eleventh century B.C.E., the Philistines, a seafaring people who migrated from Crete to Canaan shortly after the Israelites entered the land, were attacking in force. Armed with iron weapons, the mighty Philistines became the dominant power in the region after the collapse of the Egyptian Empire around 1100 B.C.E.

The Philistine threat made apparent to Israel the need for stronger central leadership. Earlier the concept of kingship had been foreign to the separate clans, and the reigning judge, Samuel, is recorded as having been strongly opposed to the coronation of a king.

Indeed, the narratives of 1 Samuel preserve a sense of ambivalence toward kingship that even Yahweh is said to have shared (1 Sam. 8:7). Nevertheless, Samuel heeded the people's cry for stronger leadership and anointed Saul as Israel's first king.

King Saul's efforts to unite Israel were dogged by tribal resistance, the superiority of the enemy forces, his own emotionally volatile temperament, and the emergence of the young warrior **David.** David was a youth from the small town of Bethlehem who confronted Goliath, a Philistine giant who had terrified the Israelite army. David's unexpected victory over Goliath made him an instant hero. He was elevated to the kingship when Saul's army was defeated by the Philistines, a battle in which both Saul and his sons died.

Under the leadership of King David (ruled 1000–962 B.C.E.), Israel dealt the Philistines a crushing blow. Capturing the Jebusite hill city of **Jerusalem**, the new king made it the capital of his realm. David's forces annexed large territories, from Syria in the east to the Gulf of Aqaba in the south. This expansionism was due in part to David's ingenuity but even more to the disarray of the larger kingdoms surrounding Israel: Babylonia, Assyria, and Egypt were temporarily in eclipse, and David's forces were able to exploit the power vacuum.

By the tenth century B.C.E. the Canaanites had been partly exterminated, partly assimilated, and partly reduced to serfdom as agricultural laborers. Some of their near kin also became Israel's allies: during the reigns of David and Solomon, his son and successor, the Phoenicians to the north concluded favorable military and trade pacts with Israel.

Under King David, Israel became a powerful monarchy with effective taxation and a considerable priesthood. The Ark of the Covenant was transferred to Jerusalem, and before David's death plans had been made for a royal chapel to house it. Under Solomon (ruled 961–922 B.C.E.) the first temple was built, using plans and materials provided by the Phoenicians, including cedars from Lebanon. Although this monumental structure revealed a Canaanite architectural influence, it housed no divine image.

Jerusalem thus became in a special sense Yahweh's city, and its temple was Yahweh's abode. God's power and favor, it was believed, would secure the kingdom and the dynasty. The holy ark was housed in the temple's "Holy of Holies," a windowless chamber within which the priest communed with God on behalf of the people. To the east of it, animal and plant offerings were made at an elaborate altar.

The splendor of the royal city reached its peak during Solomon's long and prosperous reign. Literary activity flourished, and oral traditions were set down in written texts now contained in the scrolls of the Torah. At the same time Israel's newly cosmopolitan character encouraged far-flung social contacts, which in turn

Thousands of orthodox Jews are seen here praying at the Western (Wailing) Wall during the Passover holiday. The Wailing Wall is a surviving section of the enclosure of Solomon's temple near the Holy of Holies. It is a site where Jews gather for prayer and religious lament. (Reuters/Bettmann)

resulted in cross-cultural marriages and some religious intermingling. Solomon's diplomatic marriages with foreign princesses (1 Kings 11:1) and his consequent dedication of shrines to their pagan deities undermined to some extent the exclusive worship of Yahweh.

Solomon's opulence, built on a foundation of forced labor and higher taxes, inevitably led to discontent, and his death marked the end of the heyday of the Israelite kingdom.

Israel was soon split into a northern kingdom called Israel and a southern one called Judah. Neither ever approached the power of Solomon's united Israel, for soon Assyria gained in strength, and Israel was reduced to the status of helpless vassal. The northern kingdom was overthrown in 721 B.C.E.; the southern kingdom, loyal to the dynasty of David, managed to endure longer. Less prosperous and smaller, Judah was also easier to administer, and its geographic location made it strategically less attractive to its foes. Its survival was purchased by paying heavy tribute to the surrounding nations, especially Assyria. Caught in a struggle between rival empires, however, Judah ultimately fell to the invading Babylonians led by Nebuchadnezzar. In 587 B.C.E. the temple was destroyed, and most of the aristocracy was carried off to exile in Babylonia.

THE RISE OF THE PROPHETS

The period of the monarchy—both the united kingdom of Israel and the separate kingdoms of Israel and Judah—was a pivotal age in Jewish history. These four centuries owed their distinction and abiding influence to a group of remarkable persons known as the **prophets**. *Prophet* is the Greek translation of the Hebrew *navi,* a person who communicates the divinely inspired word and speaks for God. The word *navi* sometimes also meant "seer." Such persons often lived in groups or guilds and could be requested by clients to foretell the future or to recover lost articles.

The biblical *navi* Samuel—the judge who somewhat reluctantly established the monarchy in Israel—was thought to be endowed with such clairvoyance. Later, the prophet Elisha was able to predict enemies' plans. Such spiritual personalities were not unique to Israel, but only there did the image of the *navi* shift from soothsayer to an authoritative moral presence.

Nathan

One of the earliest such moralizing *neviim* was Nathan, David's court prophet. Nathan challenged the lustful king's right to the voluptuous Bathsheba, whom David had admired from the roof of his palace. The monarch had dispatched her husband, Uriah the Hittite, to the front lines, fully intending that he be killed and hoping to take Bathsheba into his harem. The new style of *navi* can be seen in Nathan's challenge in the name of Yahweh to the king's prerogatives:

> Nathan said to David, ". . . Thus says the Lord, the God of Israel, 'I anointed you king over Israel . . . and I gave you the house of Israel and of Judah. . . . Why have you despised the word of the Lord, to do what is evil in his sight? You have smitten Uriah the Hittite with the sword, and have taken his wife to be your wife. . . . Behold, I will raise up evil against you out of your own house. . . .' "
>
> (2 Sam. 12:7–12)

David admitted his wrongdoing. Nathan's insistence that David obey the word of Yahweh became typical of later prophets, who insisted that every person obey Yahweh's demands.

Elijah

A century later, in about 875 B.C.E., the prophet Elijah condemned in the name of Yahweh the greed of a king after the monarch had expropriated the field of a poor man and plotted the man's death (1 Kings 21:1–29).

Elijah articulated another leading motif of classical prophecy: a zealous resistance to the worship of other gods. After King Ahab married the Phoenician princess Jezebel and permitted her to erect altars to Baal, Elijah vehemently objected (1 Kings 18).

THE WRITING PROPHETS

By the middle of the eighth century B.C.E., the transition from soothsayer and clairvoyant to communicator of Yahweh's demands culminated in the prophet Amos, and the age of classical prophecy began. Its leading figures differed from the seers and prophetic

Elijah in contest with the prophets of Baal, in this woodcut from the Nuremberg Bible, 1482. In the biblical texts, Elijah emphasized zealous resistance to the worship of other gods. (Jewish Theological Seminary of America)

guilds in a number of respects. First, the utterances of these prophets were written down, either personally or by a faithful scribe; their words in Yahweh's name have come down to us in the biblical books that bear their names. Although their words were heavily edited before reaching their present form, the prophets clearly possessed great poetic gifts. They defended and refined the character of the covenant, clarifying Yahweh's demands on his people. They portrayed Israel's history as God's continuing activity and placed new emphasis on the people's responsibility to obey God.

A divine initiative summoned the prophets to speak out, often against their will. Neither employees of the kings nor apologists for their royal patrons, most of the writing prophets were solitary figures. Almost without exception, they portrayed a God who required unqualified obedience and was concerned with righteousness and justice. Their prophecies were related to an understanding of God's justice and love.

But the biblical prophets were not social reformers armed with a detailed blueprint for institutional change. Rather, they were people seized by a radical vision of a God who demanded from them and from Israel nothing less than total commitment. They believed that Yahweh's power determined the fate of nations and that God would not permit his will to be violated with impunity, even by those to whom he was bound by a special covenant.

*Amos (783–743 B.C.E.)**

Amos was the first of the writing prophets whose words have been preserved. Gripped by a divine summons to go "prophesy to my people Israel," Amos's fiery message was that the covenant was conditional and that Yahweh demanded social justice—a righteous God could not be bribed by mere propriety or ritual observance.

Amos accused the affluent Israelites of being complacent as they made their sacrificial offerings. While the wealthy gentry consolidated their holdings into vast estates, he roared, the poor were dispossessed by creditors, and some were even sold as slaves. To the aristocrats assembled at the royal sanctuary at Beth El, Amos issued an angry warning in Yahweh's name:

> I hate, I spurn your feasts, and I take no pleasures in your festal gatherings. . . . And the thank-offerings of your fatted beasts I will not look upon. Take away from me the noise of your songs, and to the melody of your lyres I will not listen. But let justice roll down like waters, and righteousness like a perennial stream.
>
> (Amos 5:21–24)

To a people who found security in God's special covenant with Israel, Amos explained that Yahweh

*Approximate dates established for the writings.

The shepherd prophet Amos's fourth vision, a basket of ripe summer fruit, symbolized the immediacy of Israel's end. (The Bettmann Archive)

acted in the life of other people as well. Amos denied that Israel had any exclusive claim on Yahweh. Indeed, if a special bond existed, it was grounded not so much on special favor as on added expectations: "You only have I known of all the families of the earth; therefore will I punish you for all your wrongdoing" (Amos 3:2).

To those who expected Israel's well-being to endure regardless of the way its people lived, Amos predicted that the nation would be destroyed. He envisaged Assyria as a divine instrument to punish the nation to whom Yahweh was especially bound. Could the tide of destruction be stemmed? Perhaps, but not by additional offerings. There was only one hope: "Seek good and not evil that you may live. . . . Hate evil and love good and establish justice at the gate; perhaps the Lord, the God of hosts, will be gracious to a remnant of Joseph" (Amos 5:14–15).

The message scandalized and terrorized its hearers. The royal priest Amaziah reported to the king: "Amos has conspired against you in the midst of the house of Israel," and to the prophet the priest intoned, "O seer, go away, off with you to the land of Judah, and there earn your living, by prophesying there" (Amos 7:10, 12).

Isaiah (c. 742–701 B.C.E.)

Isaiah, who witnessed the Assyrians' destruction of the northern kingdom, articulated a new vision. No longer only the God of this one people, Isaiah's God becomes the Lord of all history. Isaiah's call was a model of the religious experience:

> In the year that King Uzziah died [usually dated 742 B.C.E.], I saw the Lord sitting upon a throne, high and uplifted, with the skirts of his robe filling the temple. Over him stood seraphim, each having six wings, with two of which he covered his face, with two he covered his loins, and with two he hovered in flight. And they kept calling to one another, and saying "Holy, holy, holy, is the Lord of hosts; the whole earth is full of his glory. . . ." Then said I, "Woe to me! for I am lost; for I am a man of unclean lips, and I dwell among a people of unclean lips; for my eyes have seen the King, the Lord of hosts." Then flew one of the seraphim to me, with a red-hot stone in his hand, which he had taken with tongs from the altar; and he touched my mouth with it, and said, "See! this has touched your lips; so your guilt is removed, and your sin is forgiven." Then I heard the voice of the Lord saying, "Whom shall I send, and who will go for us?" Whereupon I said, "Here am I. Send me."
>
> (Isa. 6:1–8)

Unlike the shepherd Amos, Isaiah was an aristocrat; he frequently attended the court as a counselor of the kings. Yet he did not endorse the kings' political alliances. If Judah was to be spared, Isaiah advised, its kings must desist from political strategies. The southern kingdom, he declared, could be saved only by trusting God: "For thus, said the Lord God, the Holy One of Israel: By returning and resting shall you be saved. In quietness and confidence shall be your strength" (Isa. 30:15).

In Isaiah's vision Yahweh was a holy God who demanded a standard of spiritual excellence from his

This undated engraving depicts Isaiah's call. One of the seraphim touched his mouth with a red-hot stone taken from the altar. (The Bettmann Archive)

covenant partner. Since most of the people had demeaned the covenant by their actions, Judah would fall. Isaiah envisaged that some would survive the tragedy and bear the seeds of a restored and faithful kingdom, and indeed, the prophet's son was named Shear Yashuv, "a remnant will return." "For though your people, O Israel, be like the sand of the sea, only a remnant of them will return" (Isa. 10:22).

This idea of some people surviving echoed in the Jewish consciousness through the centuries and held out hope that from the anguish of exile and the ashes of destruction Yahweh would appear to help the survivors, renew the covenant, and restore the people to the land. The Book of Isaiah contains a far-reaching vision of the "end of days." That vision, which was surely congruent with Isaiah's hope for survivors, described a time when Judah and the Davidic monarchy would be restored, with Mount Zion in Jerusalem as its center. On that day nations would no longer contend with each other: "For the land will have become full of the knowledge of the Lord as the waters cover the sea" (Isa. 11:9; cf. 2:1–4).

Jeremiah (628–c. 586 B.C.E.)

Jeremiah's life and ministry must be viewed against the background of Judah's final years. Toward the end of the seventh century B.C.E., King Josiah instituted significant reforms. Besides outlawing the altars of Baal, he centralized all worship in the temple at Jerusalem. Josiah's reforms were justified in part by the "book of the law," which the high priest claimed he found during the recent renovation of the temple. Historians generally agree that this book contained the outlines of the Book of Deuteronomy.

The Book of Deuteronomy reflects Josiah's other reforms: festival offerings were to be made only in Jerusalem, and the worship of heavenly bodies was prohibited (Deut. 17:3). Historians have noted a striking resemblance between Deuteronomy's structure and the treaties between Assyrian rulers and their vassal states. Indeed, the treaty between Assyria and Judah itself may have served as the model for the biblical writers' descriptions of Yahweh's covenant with Israel.

Following that model, Deuteronomy enumerates the ruler's (Yahweh's) acts of beneficence ("I brought you out of the land of Egypt"), the code of laws that lay out the covenant's requirements ("give heed to the statutes and the ordinances . . . and do them"), and the blessings or curses resulting from honoring its terms ("if you act corruptly . . . you will soon utterly perish from the land" [Deut. 4:1, 25]). The tablets delineating the agreement's terms were to be deposited in the divine ark, and the covenant's obligations were to be regularly read to the public (Deut. 10:31).

The people, however, did not respond to Josiah's call for reform, and the disappointed king fought the Egyptians and was killed around 608 B.C.E. It was against this background of political and social disintegration that Jeremiah received his prophetic call.

Jeremiah's message reaffirmed the righteousness of Yahweh and the impending destruction of Judah. During those last years of the southern kingdom, Jeremiah's words were harsh and unsparing. In Yahweh's name he denounced Judah for idolatry, social

Jeremiah is shown with God speaking to him in a vision. Themes of his prophecy are shown, including the warring armies and the worship of idols. (The Bettmann Archive)

oppression, and failing to learn from the experience of the northern kingdom: "For all the adulteries that apostate Israel had committed, I put her away, and gave her a writ of divorce, yet her faithless sister Judah was not afraid" (Jer. 3:8).

Jeremiah's words also added to the prophetic literature the record of his personal struggle. Despite his love of his family and his people, his divine call destined him to a life of solitary anguish. His message angered and disappointed his kin, and he was alternately harassed and shunned as a traitor. He accused Yahweh of having deceived him and demanded to know why his persecutors prospered. More than any other book of the Bible, Jeremiah portrays a soul's struggle between faith and despair.

Jeremiah defended himself by contending that he would not have announced such dismal tidings had not the word of Yahweh come to him. Furthermore, in time Jeremiah could point out that his prophecies had come true in his own lifetime: the walls of Jerusalem were breached by the Babylonians, the temple was burned, and the Judean monarch was exiled with the aristocracy in 586 B.C.E.

Once Judah was actually overthrown, however, the prophet's message was transformed from reproach to encouragement and hope. He assured the people that God's covenant was still valid and that God's presence would attend them even in exile. The exile would be only temporary, he said, and it demonstrated not Yahweh's weakness but rather his power. Yahweh had sent his people to a strange land; yet he could be worshiped outside Jerusalem and beyond the borders of Judah. In God's name Jeremiah counseled the exiles to "call me, and I will answer you; you shall pray to me, and I will listen to you" (Jer. 29:12). The prophet foretold a time when Yahweh's covenant with his people would be fully observed: "I will put my law within them, and will write it on their hearts; and I will be their God, and they shall be my people" (Jer. 31:33). Toward the end of his life Jeremiah took refuge in Egypt; he is believed to have died there.

It seemed that the people of Yahweh had reached their lowest ebb. From that period of exile, we have this lament:

By the waters of Babylon,
There we sat down and wept,
When we remembered Zion.
Upon the poplars, in the midst of her,
We hung up our harps.

For there our captors
Demanded of us song,
And our tormentors, mirth:
"Sing us some of the songs of Zion."
How could we sing the songs of the Lord
In a foreign land?
If I forget you, O Jerusalem,
May my right hand fail me!
May my tongue cleave to my palate,
If I do not remember you;
If I set not Jerusalem
Above my highest joy!

(Ps. 137:1–6)

The Second Isaiah (550–539 B.C.E.)

In Babylonia the exiles found themselves in a triumphant and prosperous land. Under the leadership of Nebuchadnezzar (ruled 605–562 B.C.E.), it dominated much of southwestern Asia. Nebuchadnezzar sponsored lavish building projects that slaves from Judah helped to construct; the upper-class Jewish exiles were given more freedom. But after the middle of the sixth century B.C.E., the power of the Babylonian Empire was overwhelmed by Persia. Led by Cyrus the Great (ruled 550–529 B.C.E.), Persia exceeded the size of earlier empires, and Judah became its province of Judea.

At this time a new voice was raised. The poetic utterances of this anonymous prophet were appended to the biblical Book of Isaiah; hence the name "Second Isaiah." Like the first Isaiah, he affirmed that Yahweh was the Lord of history. The Second Isaiah viewed Cyrus's ascendance as divinely ordained and predicted that Cyrus would repopulate the land of Israel with his Judean captives in fulfillment of Yahweh's covenant with the people.

The Second Isaiah brought to a peak the concept of Yahweh's exclusive power. With irony and eloquence he declared that all other gods were naught:

> I am Yahweh, and there is no other; beside me there is no God. I will gird you though you knew me not, that men may know from the east and from the west, that beside me there is none. I am Yahweh, and there is no other—who forms light, and creates darkness, who makes weal and woe—I Yahweh am he who does all these things.
>
> (Isa. 45:5–7)

Yahweh, who had exiled his people because of their sins, would now restore them:

> "Comfort, O comfort my people," says your God, speak to the heart of Jerusalem, and call to her, that her time of service is ended, that her guilt is paid in full, that she has received of Yahweh's hand double for all her sins.
>
> (Isa. 40:1–2)

The Second Isaiah developed most fully the concept of Israel's role as Yahweh's witness and servant among the nations. The entire people was perceived as a prophet proclaiming the divine truth:

> Thus says Yahweh, the God, who created the heavens, and stretched them out, who made the earth and its products, who gives breath to the people upon it, and spirit to those who walk in it: I, Yahweh, have called you in righteousness, and have grasped you by the hand, I have kept you, and made you a pledge to the people, a light to the nations.
>
> (Isa. 42:5–8)

Earlier prophets had insisted that Israel should have no other gods besides Yahweh; the Second Isaiah declared that in fact there *were* no other gods. The Israelites had originally been cautioned to obey Yahweh's teachings in order that the Israelites themselves might endure and prosper; the Second Isaiah suggested that by its loyalty to Yahweh, Israel was performing a mission for the whole world: Israel's witness helped to bring nearer the time when God's sovereignty would be acknowledged by all nations.

The Historical Role of the Prophets

The Bible records a seemingly endless struggle of the prophets to redirect the attitudes and practices of their nation. From its pages we can learn much of the attitudes and religious hopes that shaped Israelite life and thought in the generations before the Babylonian exile. Many Israelites, it seems, shared the common religious viewpoint of their region and era. Awed by the powers that they believed controlled nature, they understood that to secure an abundant harvest and a stable life, one should worship as many divinities as possible; not least among these gods and goddesses were those to whom neighboring peoples were equally devoted. However, a frequently embattled

COMPARISON

The Axial Age

Many scholars have noticed that within roughly a century of 500 B.C.E.—a period sometimes called the Axial Age—religions and cultures all over the world went through major transformations. In Greece during the sixth through fourth centuries B.C.E., Greek philosophy, the great dramatists, and the mystery religions all appeared. In Judaism in the sixth and fifth centuries B.C.E., Ezra, Nehemiah, and their colleagues began to codify the Torah, and the prophets' pure monotheism began to achieve widespread acceptance. Zarathustra, the founder of Zoroastrianism, is held to have lived during the seventh or sixth centuries B.C.E. This was also the period of the warring states in China and the corresponding period of the Hundred Philosophers, out of which came the two main Chinese religions—Confucianism (founded by Confucius, 551–479 B.C.E.) and Daoism. In India this was a period of great religious and social turmoil out of which grew several religions to replace waning Vedic religion. The upanishads, though very hard to date, probably had their first sages in the sixth or fifth century B.C.E. The founder of Buddhism, Gautama Buddha, is traditionally dated 563–483 B.C.E., though some scholars place him a century later. Jainism was given its general shape by Mahāvira, also commonly placed in the sixth century.

Why do we see such transformations across so many cultures? Several answers have been offered, though none has won general acceptance.

TECHNOLOGICAL ADVANCEMENTS

Technology had advanced on several fronts. Writing had developed; it had existed for centuries among some ruling and priestly elites, but during this era in some places it spread to a wider population. (Religions were perhaps drawn to put themselves on record, and those records became the earliest texts of many religious groups.) Road and bridge building, vehicles, and horsemanship had been mastered. Thanks to such developments, communication and transportation reached new heights, and

group, small but growing, fervently believed that the destiny of the people of Israel required that they devote themselves exclusively to one God alone, their own national God, Yahweh. He alone had rescued them from slavery in Egypt, given them a land of their own in which they might live, and taught them a way of life. This group was led by prophets who continually brought new messages from their God, messages sometimes of warning and sometimes of encouragement. The prophets labored ceaselessly to convince the rest of the nation that adopting the ways of their neighbors would lead to disaster. Only Yahweh, not the fertility cults, could ensure abundant flocks and harvests, they argued. Only by maintaining a distinctive way of life—in particular, only by worshiping their own God and no other—could they achieve the prosperity and security for which they longed. This latter group, bearers of the prophetic teaching that gave meaning to their lives, eventually prevailed and set the history of Judaism on its course.

RELIGIOUS FAITH AFTER EXILE

After Cyrus conquered Babylonia, he authorized the recolonization of part of Judea as a buffer state against this may have increased cross-cultural fertilization.

ECONOMIC AND POLITICAL CHANGES

Wrought in part by these technical advancements, the material circumstances of many people changed. The era was one of increasing wealth, for the improved roads and ridership made more trade possible with a wider prospective purchasing population. Not unrelated, cities also developed during this period, with both their problems and possibilities. Indeed, many of the new religions arose in an urban setting.

Roads and improved transportation also made larger empires possible. Around this period the Persians, the Greeks, and certain Indian kings were able to establish great empires. As a result of the increased trade and political contact within and among these empires, many of the world's people lived in more cosmopolitan and polyglot circumstances than before.

NEW RELIGIOUS NEEDS

In general, changes in social situation often are accompanied by changes in cultural and religious structures, and it is here that the third set of answers enters. The pressures, needs, and social dislocation wrought by these new circumstances must have been enormous. The needs of the empires and large states were also often addressed by the new religious systems: Confucianism undoubtedly helped the Chinese emperors rule, as Zoroastrianism helped Persian emperors. The Hindu notion of *dharma* (duty), also appearing during this era, probably also helped to stabilize India.

Emerging in part to address the changed circumstances, some new religions—notably the Chinese Daoist, Greek mystery, Indian upanishadic, Buddhist, and Jain religions—offered mystical teachings, providing their constituents a new kind of salvation based on self-discipline.

CHANGES IN HUMAN CONSCIOUSNESS

The fourth answer, which like the others has not enjoyed broad agreement, is that something happened around this period to the human mind, the psyche, or human consciousness to allow for such advancements.

Whatever their causes, the religious and cultural transformations of the sixth and fifth centuries B.C.E. are even now still being felt.

Egypt. Many of the Judean exiles went back to Jerusalem. Then in 538 B.C.E. Cyrus allowed the return of the sacred symbols of the temple and the reconstruction of the sanctuary itself. However, many of the exiled Judeans, thriving in Babylonia, declined to return. The criticisms of their decision by the prophets Haggai and Zechariah show that in fact a considerable number had chosen to remain in Babylonia.

In Judea, Persia generally supported religious autonomy as long as it posed no threat to its sovereignty, and a priestly group led by Joshua received permission from the new Persian ruler, Darius the Great (ruled 522–486 B.C.E.), to rebuild the temple at Jerusalem.

Ezra and Nehemiah

Developments in Judea in the half-century following the new temple's completion in 515 B.C.E. are obscure, but in the middle of the fifth century B.C.E. Judaism began to change dramatically in the direction of its present form. Two leaders from the period stand out: Ezra, priest and scribe, and Nehemiah, official of the Persian court, governor of Judea, and devout Jew.

Ezra was authorized by the Persian king to go to Jerusalem and reorganize the community. He took with him "a book of the law of Moses," which parallels the Pentateuch. Reports of the impressive covenant

Dietary laws, as outlined in Leviticus, prohibit the eating of anything with blood. Through the centuries to this day, meat for Jews who keep kosher must be properly butchered. In this illumination from an Italian Hebrew manuscript (dated 1435 C.E.), the ritual slaughter of chickens and oxen is shown. (The Granger Collection)

renewal ceremony that Ezra performed mention a reading from the Torah, and some scholars believe that it was he and his colleagues who began to codify this text, giving it much of its present form (see the accompanying box, "The Axial Age").

Now firmly under Persian control, Judea became a theocracy, ruled by priests. Temple worship flourished. In part inspired by the Second Isaiah's message of the "mission of Israel," both Ezra and Nehemiah, like the ruling priests, sought to protect the identity of the Jews, who were surrounded by Gentiles (non-Jews). Both men forcibly curtailed intermarriage, fearing, much as earlier Jews had, that it would weaken the covenant community. Similarly, they sought to bring every aspect of their people's lives under the governance of Yahweh's religious law. Combining the various legal codes that had survived from preexilic years, they supplemented and revised them to form a single law code. The priests instructed the people in this law, enforced compliance, and broadened its provisions through interpretation.

The nineteenth chapter of Leviticus is a good example of the new comprehensiveness of the law. The command "You shall be holy for I the Lord your God am holy" (Lev. 19:2) was carefully explained: fidelity to the holy covenant required acceptable sacrifices at the temple; a corner of each field was to be left for the poor; the righteous were to refrain from theft; and they were to be considerate of the hired hands. In observance of the command "You must not eat anything with blood," the people were to respect the dietary laws. To this day a Jew who "keeps kosher" (observes the dietary laws) salts and drains meat before it is cooked to remove the blood.

Worship in the Temple

By the fourth century B.C.E. the Torah probably existed in its present form. Serving as the constitution of the reformed Judean community, it defined among other things the responsibilities of the priesthood, which reached its height during this period.

The priests' role developed over many centuries. In the period of the judges, priestly functions were performed by every Israelite male. At the time of the monarchy, the kings appointed their own priests (1 Kings 12:31), and still later all men of the tribe of Levi served as priests. The functions of the priesthood included using oracular objects to discern the will of Yahweh, rendering judgment in disputes, and offering sacrifices.

After the temple was restored, those who could trace their ancestry to Moses's brother Aaron were identified as the *Kohanim,* the permanent custodians of priestly privileges (Num. 25:6–13). Under the supervision of the high priest, the Kohanim presided over elaborate animal and grain offerings in the restored temple. In the morning and evening as well as on holidays, congregations of the devout assembled to worship Yahweh and to seek forgiveness for their sins.

During this period many of the Bible's great psalms were composed and chanted as part of the temple worship. Particular psalms were designated for various occasions and were often sung to instrumental accompaniment. They expressed trust in Yahweh, praise for his mighty acts, and yearning for the renewed manifestation of his power and glory.

Also in this period the Jewish calendar was assembled into nearly its present form. The New Year (Rosh Hashanah) was observed at the new moon of the seventh month (usually September). Ten days later the covenant community celebrated **Yom Kippur**, the Day of Atonement. This day of fasting, intended to reconcile the sinful community with Yahweh, included an intricate sacrificial ceremony (Lev. 16). Five days later the community observed the joyous harvest festival of Sukkot (Tabernacles).

Most important was the spring pilgrimage festival, Passover. As explained earlier, this celebration recalled the Exodus from Egypt and the coming to freedom. Lambs were sacrificed in the temple as a reminder of the blood of the lambs sprinkled on the doorposts of the Hebrew households in Egypt to permit the Angel of Death to pass over the Jewish homes and visit only those of their oppressors. Unleavened bread was consumed during the feast as a reminder of the haste with which the slaves had left Egypt: there had been no time for the dough to rise (Exod. 12:39). An elaborate supper was accompanied by recitation of the acts of divine deliverance by which the ancestors had been released from bondage.

The other pilgrimage festival, Shavuot (Pentecost), remained essentially an agricultural feast linked to the barley harvest. It came to a climax seven weeks after the Passover observance, usually in the early summer. (Many centuries later the rabbis transformed this festival celebrating God's bounty into an observance of God's revelation of the Torah.)

The minor festival of Purim ("lots") is traditionally dated from the period of Persian hegemony over Judea. According to the Book of Esther, Haman, the chief minister of the Persian ruler Ahasuerus, plotted to destroy the Jews of the kingdom. A Jewish princess named Esther and her uncle Mordecai interceded with the king. As a result, the day chosen by lot by Haman for the destruction of the Jews was decreed by the king as the day of Haman's execution. The holiday in honor of this story became one of feasting and merriment.

TENSIONS WITHIN THE COVENANT COMMUNITY

As noted, Ezra and Nehemiah were so concerned about the problem of intermarriage that they compelled men with foreign wives to send them away. This edict, and the tensions within the community that it reflects, may well have inspired the Book of Ruth. Ruth remained a faithful Israelite after the death of her Jewish husband. When her mother-in-law, Naomi, ordered her to return to her former life, Ruth declared, "Thy people shall be my people and thy God my God" (Ruth 1:16). A genealogy at the end of the book identifies Ruth, a woman of Moabite origin, as an ancestor of King David.

Because Judaism conceived of the world in terms of a creator who is at once powerful and just, nothing challenged the Jewish faith more fundamentally than two almost unanswerable questions: Why do the wicked prosper? Why do the innocent suffer? At a time when Zoroastrian dualism was widespread, the Second Isaiah continually reiterated the importance of believing in one God. The Deuteronomic and prophetic views affirmed God's sovereign justice: loyalty to the covenant yields long life, prosperity, and fertile soil. Suffering is the wages of sin. Infidelity invites disaster.

Some of the earlier prophets had wrestled with this problem. In contrast to the Deuteronomic claim that evil comes only to the wicked, Jeremiah demanded to know why the wicked prosper and the innocent suffer (Jer. 12:1). Isaiah spoke of a time when there would be no more wickedness, when people would "beat their swords into plowshares," when "the wolf will lodge with the lamb, and the leopard will lie down with the kid; the calf and the young lion will graze together, and a little child will lead them" (Isa. 11:6).

Isaiah prophesied that there would come a time of harmony among all creatures. It would be crowned by the reconciliation of brothers and sisters and would take place under a ruler who would combine power and goodness (Isa. 2:1–7). The Hebrew word *mashiach* ("anointed one") refers to anyone charged with divine office. It eventually came to denote the long-expected ruler who would usher in God's kingdom on earth, known as the **Messiah**.

Between the fourth and second centuries B.C.E., eloquent voices were raised against the conventional view of Yahweh as the just Lord of history. The author of Ecclesiastes denied the prophetic view of a messianic redemption: "I have seen everything that has been done under the sun; and lo, everything is vanity and striving for the wind. The crooked cannot be made straight, and that which is lacking cannot be corrected" (Eccles. 1:14–15). The author of the Book of Job resolutely rejected the view that if a person suffered in God's world, it was because he or she had sinned. Declaring his own innocence, Job demanded to know why he suffered. His challenge received no reasoned response, but ultimately he was persuaded to accept a God whose ways could not be fully comprehended by mortals.

During the latter centuries of the second temple, messianic fulfillment seemed remote. As civil strife and foreign pressures plagued the Judeans, a more urgent vision seized their imagination. This was expressed in a form of literature called **apocalypses** (Greek for "disclosures" or "revelations"). These writings depicted a dramatic confrontation between the forces of light and darkness. Divine intervention in human affairs was believed to be imminent, and the vindication of the righteous was anticipated. Like some of the prophetic literature, the apocalypses were replete with vivid and bizarre imagery and purported to reveal divine truth. Such writings showed a sense of irrevocable judgment, with little appeal to any moral regeneration that could alter the course of events.

The "Day of the Lord," a day of judgment and cosmic upheaval, was inevitable; the specific date was known only to a select few. The apocalypses anticipated a climactic shattering of the established order: the end of the world as it was known and the imposition of a totally new order.

In this outlook prophetic monotheism appears to have been influenced by Zoroastrian dualism. Angels were transformed from anonymous, featureless agents of Yahweh into distinct personalities with names (cf. Dan. 8:16; 10:13, 20). Satan went from being a member of the divine entourage to the chief of a kingdom of demonic spirits opposed to God. Indeed, he even acquired independent power. Rather than against sinful humanity alone, Yahweh was cast in battle against supernatural powers. Such notions became important to postbiblical Judaism, as well as to Christianity.

In fact, the apocalypses were yet another response to the conflict between faith and human experience. They expressed the belief that God would intervene to destroy the wicked and spare the righteous. In the Book of Daniel is an intimation of still another theological answer to the problem of evil—a life after death, a day of reward for the righteous and of reckoning for the wicked: "and many of those who sleep in the land of the dust shall awake, some to everlasting life, and others to everlasting reproach and contempt" (Dan. 12:2).

The Foundation of Judaism

The Book of Daniel, just quoted, is the latest work included in the canon, or official contents, of the Hebrew Bible. The collection of sacred texts around which the Jewish religion developed was now complete; Judaism's time of beginning was drawing to a close, and its foundation had now been set in place. It will be useful to review the chief elements of that foundation.

Participation in the Jewish religion was intimately tied to membership in the Jewish people, the people of Israel. This nation traced its origins back to the patriarch Abraham, and the Jewish way of life was believed to be the human side of a great covenant between the people of Israel and their God, the only true God, the creator and all-powerful ruler of heaven and earth. It was believed that in the time of Moses, after the Israelites had been freed from Egyptian slavery, this way of life had been inscribed in a sacred scroll of laws, the Torah. Now participation in the Jewish religion meant to live according to the Torah and to take part in the only community whose way of life was based on it, that of the Jews.

The divine part of this covenant was a double gift—the gift of the Torah itself, believed to be a perfect code of law upholding a perfect way of life, and the gift of the land of Israel as promised to Abraham and his descendants. In this land the Jews expected to be kept secure and prosperous so long as they obeyed their God, especially so long as they carefully avoided the worship of any other deities. In fact by the time the Book of Daniel was written the Jews already constituted a far-flung diaspora (dispersion) all the way from Babylonia and Persia in the east to Egypt and Asia Minor in the west, and they were in the process of spreading still farther across the Mediterranean basin. Nevertheless, everywhere they went, they kept an awareness of themselves as a separate nation, continuing to live by the sacred laws of the Torah and to visit the homeland whenever they could to worship in the great temple of Jerusalem.

The temple of Jerusalem became the worldwide center of Jewish life. At the great pilgrimage festivals of the year, especially Passover in the spring and Sukkot in the fall, hundreds of thousands of Jews from the diaspora would gather to bring sacrifices and witness the pageantry; in this way people could renew their ties to their nation and to their God at the same time. Even on ordinary days as the months of the year went by, the temple was a busy place, and a visit to it was a powerfully exciting event. On these occasions, the temple and the city of Jerusalem, with their splendor and their enormous crowds of worshipers, must have been one of the great wonders of the world.

In other respects as well, life according to the Torah marked off the Jews as a highly distinct group. Their calendar, especially the weekly celebration of the Sabbath; their dietary laws, especially their refusal to eat meat and milk at the same meal; and their dedication to the practice of circumcision were features of Jewish life that attracted much attention from others, sometimes respectful, sometimes contemptuous, sometimes hostile or fearful. Within the privacy of their own communities, Jews maintained these customs and waited for their God to gather them back into their homeland and reward them for having remained so loyal to this way of life.

NOTES

1 Maurice Simon and Harry Sperling, trans., *Zohar* (London: Soncino Press, 1956), p. 74.

2 All biblical quotations in Part Five are from J. M. Powis Smith and Edgar J. Goodspeed, trans., *The Complete Bible: An American Translation* (Chicago: University of Chicago Press, 1948, 1975).

JUDAISM

CHAPTER 17

FROM THE HELLENISTIC AGE TO THE DAWN OF MODERNITY: DIASPORA

With Alexander the Great's conquest of Israel in 332 B.C.E., Judaism entered a new phase that was to last for two millennia. From Alexander's era onward, Jews would virtually always live under foreign rulers. At first many Jews remained in their old homeland, Israel, under Greek and then Roman authorities. Once exiled from Israel, these homeless people settled all over the Western world: in Egypt, Babylonia (modern Iraq), medieval Spain, Italy, Germany, Poland, and a host of other countries. They were a nation without power and without land. In part as a response, they provided themselves with a consistent and nearly complete life style, gleaning it from their canon, especially the Torah and the record of their rabbis' interpretations, the so-called Oral Torah. Together these sources offered them instructions not only about how to pray but also about such mundane matters as what to eat and not to eat, how to behave around one's family, and how to earn a living.

As time went on and the Jews withdrew more and more into their own community, their host nations became progressively more aggressive toward them, venting this hostility in periodic outbreaks of persecution and even, at times, massacre. Yet somehow, being a part of a sacred story that told them that they were God's people—that "God, Torah, and Israel are bound together"—was enough to sustain and unite them.

THE HELLENISTIC AGE

After Alexander conquered the Mediterranean basin, the Jews—especially the more affluent ones—came to be influenced by the Greek (Hellenic) culture in terms of language, dress, popular ideology, and education. Few could resist the appeal of its sophistication. There were even priests in Jerusalem who saw no conflict between offering sacrifices to Yahweh in the morning and participating in Greek games in the afternoon.

WISDOM LITERATURE

The impact of Hellenization can be detected in some contemporary commentaries on the Torah and even in books that eventually found their way onto the list of canonized Hebrew scriptures. Ecclesiastes, for example, was influenced by the reflective, individualistic, and sophisticated mood cultivated in the Greek schools. Its author's world-weary contention that "nothing is new under the sun" was at variance with the community-centered, cult-oriented piety of the Torah as well as with the biblical hope of Isaiah for a future when people "will beat their swords into plowshares."

Hellenic influences on the Jewish community can be summarized on a variety of levels. Greek rationalism, mystery cults, and morality all had an impact on the peoples conquered by Alexander and ruled by his successors. Some intellectuals struggled to reconcile the Torah with Greek concepts of body, soul, wisdom, and immortality. In the *Wisdom of Solomon,* for example, the author uses the Greek dualism between body and spirit to ponder how the soul might be freed from the prison of the body. Other thinkers were drawn to the Greek games, with their glorification of human nudity and worship of the gods of the host city.

THE MACCABEAN REVOLT

It was the upper-class Judeans, especially the priestly class, who had most embraced this Hellenistic life style and its new modes of thought. Fascinated with this culture, many Judeans, encouraged by their Greek overlords, sought to transform Jerusalem into a Greek city with Greek commercial laws, schools, an amphitheater, and even a Greek citadel.

This trend was troubling to many Jews, especially the common peasants and artisans, who had neither the leisure nor the wealth to adopt the new mode. Many of them disapproved of the changes their priestly leaders had begun, feeling that these changes ran counter to God's will. Zealous Jewish pietists stirred the people against the Hellenizers. This problem finally turned violent when King Antiochus IV, the Greek ruler of Syria and Judea (ruled 175–163 B.C.E.), concerned about the turmoil, demanded religious obedience from his Judean subjects. Antiochus forbade observance of the Sabbath, circumcision, and Torah study. When his officials demanded that Israel sacrifice to Zeus, the people were outraged. The Book of Maccabees tells how an elderly priest, Mattathias of Modin, openly defied this order, instead killing the Syrian official who had made the demand. Mattathias led his five sons and their followers in the ensuing battle against the Greek regime, and one son, Judah Maccabee, emerged as the leader of the successful resistance. The Hellenizers' retreat inspired the Maccabees to cleanse and rededicate the temple in 165 B.C.E. That occasion served as the historical basis for the Jewish festival of Hanukah ("dedication").

After Judah Maccabee's death, his brothers and their sons expanded the area of Jewish control beyond the Jordan River, forcing captive peoples to become adherents of Judaism. A brief period of independence (142–63 B.C.E.) ended with the coming of the Romans.

PHILO AND THE JEWS OF ALEXANDRIA

During the Hellenistic period, the largest Jewish center outside Israel was in Alexandria. By the first century C.E., an estimated 1 million Jews lived in Egypt. According to a later talmudic report, so vast was the place of worship in Alexandria that the leader had to wave a flag to signal the congregants' turn to respond (Sukkah 51b). The Jews of Alexandria attained eco-

The cleansing and rededication of the temple in 165 B.C.E. by the Maccabees is the historical basis for the Jewish festival of Hanukah. As seen here, Jews display a nine-branched candelabrum (menorah) and offer prayers of thanksgiving to God. On each of the eight days of the festival, an additional candle is lighted. (Religious News Service Photo)

nomic and social prominence. The majority of them had stopped speaking Hebrew; the Torah had had to be translated into Greek in the third century B.C.E. This translation (the Septuagint) made Jewish scripture accessible to non-Jews as well.

It was during this time that the first recorded instances of anti-Jewish prejudice appeared. An Egyptian named Apion wrote an attack against the Jews, accusing them of hating the Greek people and of sacrificing Gentile victims to Yahweh in the Jewish temple. Voicing charges that have echoed down to our own time, Apion denounced the Jews as a mysteriously different people and alleged that their rites and values threatened the greater society in which they lived.

The greatest thinker of the Hellenistic Diaspora was Philo of Alexandria (c. 15 B.C.E.–c. 45 C.E.). When the Roman emperor Caligula ordered his own image erected in the temple at Jerusalem, Alexandrian Jews appointed Philo to lead a delegation of Jewish notables to Rome. Philo's account of this mission in his *Legation to Gaius* makes clear his staunch espousal of Jewish belief.

Nevertheless, Philo was driven by a passion to reconcile the insights of contemporary culture with inherited Jewish piety. His philosophical interpretation of biblical laws and narratives was a Hellenization of scripture, reflecting his belief that he was discovering the symbolic or allegorical meaning of the Torah.

Philo identified the biblical term *Hochmah* ("wisdom") with the Greek term *logos* ("word, speech, reason"). Logos was the divine power that mediated God's creation of the world and bound human reason to God's reason. When the Torah spoke of humanity as created in the "image of God," Philo took this to mean that the divine Logos (the mind of the universe) was a model for the creation of the human mind.

Accepting the Greek dualism of body and spirit, Philo believed that the human body with its sinful passions lured human beings to the material world. However, the human soul, or reason, enabled them to aspire to illumination by God. The final goal was liberation from bondage to the body, together with the soul's reascension to its divine abode. Through mystical ecstasy, humans could experience such liberation even during their earthly lives. The Torah's commandments, in Philo's view, were to be used to achieve this higher state.

Philo reinterpreted the biblical stories as allegorical descriptions of human progress toward spiritual illumination. For example, Israel's liberation from Egypt symbolized the human emancipation from bodily passion. But Philo never forsook his belief in the special destiny of the people of Israel or in their obligation to observe the laws of the Torah.

Philo's attempt to reconcile biblical truth with Greek philosophy became a model for the Christian church fathers as well as for medieval Jewish thinkers.

DEVELOPMENTS IN JUDEA

The Romans conquered Judea, which they called Palestine, in 63 B.C.E. Until 1948, the date of the founding of the modern state of Israel, the Jewish community living there—and throughout the Diaspora—would never rule themselves politically. The Jews in Palestine, however, did enjoy a degree of religious independence. This allowed them to develop their religion in ways that helped them to adapt to being a disenfranchised, subject nation. As before, they were led by their priests. It was these priests who defined the terms of the evolving religion.

FACTIONS: PHARISEES AND SADDUCEES

Even before the coming of the Romans, the priests' situation had demanded change and adaptation. Because all Jews considered the Torah to be the source of authority, the key issue revolved around its scope and interpretation. What was to count as authoritative scripture? Who was qualified to interpret it? In addition, various oral traditions and interpretations, eventually called the Oral Torah, had appeared after the written scroll. Should these be considered authoritative?

One upper-class group that included many priests was the Sadducees, whose name may have come from Sadoq, King David's priest. The other principal party was the Pharisees. This name may have meant "separatists," and some scholars have suggested that they were a populist group that challenged the prerogatives of the privileged few. The Sadducees argued that the Torah (the teachings held to have divine authority) did not include the Oral Torah. They also insisted that the Torah itself must be interpreted by the proper authorities—the priests. The Pharisees claimed that their broader biblical interpretation was more in keeping with an oral tradition going back to the covenant at Sinai. They held that all Israelites, even nonpriests, were eligible to expound the Torah, as long as they had mastered both the written and the oral law and accepted it as divine. This broader conception of authority made the Pharisees the forerunners of the rabbis. (The title *rabbi* was not used until after the destruction of the temple by the Romans in 70 C.E.) The Pharisees expanded the set of people who could have a special relationship with the divine. They taught, for example, that all Pharisees should observe the laws of diet and ritual purity that the written Torah required only of priests.

With respect to belief, the Sadducees denied the existence of any afterlife, declaring that the soul perished with the body; the Pharisees interpreted the Torah to include a belief in resurrection and the "world to come." On an issue of free will, the Sadducees argued that human beings had the power to shape their lives. The Pharisees accepted the power of fate while at the same time acknowledging people's accountability for their actions: "All is foreseen [by God] but free will is given [to humanity]" (Ethics of the Fathers 3:16).

In sum, the Sadducees held to a distant God, accessible only to his appointed mediators, the priests themselves. Only they could interpret God's word, and only they could mediate the divine presence on earth. The more liberal Pharisees opened interpretation to the larger group of trained believers and insisted on the accessibility of God to all responsible Jews. Thus to them all Jews should be held responsible and accountable directly to God.

These disagreements were probably debated and at times adjudicated in the Sanhedrin, a legislative and judicial council that was formed in the Hellenistic period and included both the Sadducees and the Pharisees. Unfortunately, little is known of the composition, authority, or history of this body.

REBELLION AGAINST THE ROMANS

The era of Roman dominion was oppressive and turbulent. For three decades Palestine was ruled by Herod ("the Great"), a Roman appointee. Marshaling the support of the upper (priestly) class, Herod rebuilt the second temple at Jerusalem and maintained social order. But his taxes were oppressive and his rule was harsh. After his death, Palestine came to be ruled by a series of "procurators," the most renowned of whom was Pontius Pilate, who ruled for a decade until he was deposed in 36 C.E. In some ways Roman rule at this time was religiously sensitive. For example, Jewish men were not required to serve in the Roman armies, since under military conditions they would not be able to observe the Sabbath or their dietary restrictions. Nor were Jews compelled to worship the emperor.

Nonetheless, the Romans' heavy taxes and onerous demands were resented by most of the populace, and many of the Roman governors heaped additional indignities on the Jews. Pontius Pilate, for example, in addition to ordering public executions for relatively minor offenses, outraged pious Jews when he seized temple funds to build an aqueduct and smuggled soldiers bearing silver images of the emperor on their ensigns into Jerusalem, in violation of the Torah's ban on human images in the holy city. Not surprisingly, many Jews attempted military rebellion, which led to even crueler Roman reprisals. Those who despaired of political or military success against the hated Romans were increasingly sustained by the hope that God would soon send a messiah to redeem the people from their oppressors.

Jesus of Nazareth lived and preached in this period. He was one of many itinerant preachers who addressed these people, eagerly awaiting messianic redemption. In his teaching, Jesus was closer to the Pharisees than to the Sadducees. He was apparently also influenced by the ascetic and highly disciplined Essenes, a first-century B.C.E. Jewish communal group that had taken refuge from the political turmoil in Jerusalem and established communes at the edge of the Judean wilderness. (The discovery of the Dead Sea Scrolls in the late 1940s shed valuable light on the practices and beliefs of this sect, though many scholars remain unsure precisely which scrolls were actually composed by Essenes.)

A similar passivity seems to have been maintained by the increasingly popular Pharisaic group. But the oppressive brutality of a succession of Roman governors, together with provocative forays by revolutionary groups, raised sentiment to fever pitch. In 66 C.E., near the end of Emperor Nero's reign, full-scale war began. Although the initial resistance of the ragtag Jewish soldiers was fiercer than the Romans had expected, within two years virtually all resistance had been

Even after Jerusalem was destroyed in 70 C.E., a group of Zealots continued to resist the Romans at a fortification called Masada. Violating Jewish commandment, 960 men, women, and children took their own lives rather than surrender to the Romans. Archaeologists excavated the site, seen here, between 1963 and 1965, and it remains a symbol of Israel's determination to resist oppression and foreign domination. (The Israel Ministry of Tourism)

crushed, except in Jerusalem. Sending yet another army, the Romans breached the walls of Jerusalem in 70 C.E., mercilessly executing many of the defenders, some by crucifixion.[1] Worst of all, the Romans destroyed the great Jerusalem temple, which had been the religious center of Jewish life for centuries. The connection with God through the temple sacrifice had been brutally severed.

When, decades later, Emperor Hadrian (ruled 117–138) announced that he would erect a temple to Jupiter on the site of the old temple, Jews again rose in rebellion. They were led by Simon Bar Kochba, who would be, it was hoped, the messiah Israel had so long awaited. But after three years of vigorous combat (132–135), this rebellion too was crushed, and an even more punitive repression followed. Teaching the Torah, observing the Sabbath, and circumcising one's sons were made offenses punishable by death. Jerusalem was renamed Aelia Capitolina and was closed to Jewish entry except for one day a year, when Jews were permitted to visit the holy western ("wailing") wall and mourn the destruction of their nation.

THE GROWTH OF THE RABBINIC TRADITION

Thus the strategy of direct, violent confrontation with Rome did not succeed. All hope for military salvation was dashed. Yet an alternative response—a religious one—ultimately proved far more effective. Johanan ben Zakkai, a Pharisaic sage who had survived the destruction of the temple, was allowed to establish a center for teachers of the Torah in the village of Jabneh, which then became a vital center of Judaism's renewal.

The Beginnings of Rabbinic Leadership

Following the destruction of the temple, priestly authority dissolved. The Pharisaic scholars, now called *rabbis* ("teachers"), claimed leadership over the Jewish people in Palestine. As their claim gained wider acceptance, rabbinic influence over Jewish life steadily grew. The rabbinic conclave, first in Jabneh and then elsewhere in Palestine, formed not only the center of Torah interpretation and rabbinic ordination but also the seat of the new Sanhedrin, the Bet Din, a body that expounded the terms of God's covenant. After reconciliation with Rome in the second century, the authority of the leader of the rabbis, known as the *patriarch* in Greek and the *nasi* in Hebrew, was extended by imperial legislation over all Jews in the Roman Empire. The Roman regime itself thus underwrote rabbinic authority in religious matters.

The Centrality of the Synagogue

The impact of the temple's destruction on Jewish consciousness cannot be overstated. The elaborate pageant of sacrifice could no longer be enacted.

Pilgrimages during the three great festivals of the year ceased. Indeed, the very symbol of God's presence in the midst of his people lay in ruins. Did obliteration of the temple and ignominious exile signify the end of the covenant? The restoration of Pharisaic morale, if not the survival of Judaism itself, rested on the shoulders of Johanan ben Zakkai and his descendants.

One of Rabbi Johanan's most significant teachings was that worship through prayer was an effective substitute for the ritual once carried out in the temple of Jerusalem. Now learned laymen—any Jewish males who had acquired the necessary skills—could preside at worship, and the reconciliation with God once effected by priests offering sacrifices on the altar could be achieved by earnest prayers for forgiveness and acts of penitence. (Women were not considered capable of so presiding by these rabbis.)

When the synagogue first came into being is not known. Some historians believe that the seed of the institution was sown as early as the Babylonian exile in the sixth century B.C.E. Having no access to Jerusalem, the exiles created little meeting places, perhaps especially for the Sabbath, where they could hear familiar prayers and psalms and receive instruction. Yet there is no unequivocal reference to a synagogue until Hellenistic times. The Palestinian synagogues may have begun as informal gathering places for Jews who could not be present in Jerusalem for the sacrificial service during the period of the second temple.

In any case, the destruction of the temple elevated the synagogue and the rabbinic sage to greater importance. Sages like Hillel, who flourished between 30 B.C.E. and 10 C.E., and Shammai (c. 50 B.C.E.–30 C.E.), who had taught and preached prior to the destruction of the temple, laid the groundwork for the rabbinic explication of the Torah. However, the flowering of the Oral Torah reached its fullness in the academy of Jabneh and its successors.

Bound together by a reverence for God's will, the members of the schools studied the oral traditions that had been preserved for centuries in the minds of teachers and disciples before ever being committed to writing. Through study, debate, and careful reasoning, the early rabbis applied the Torah to the problems and situations of their time and sought to bring this living tradition to the people.

Sometimes these deliberations were conducted in the midst of persecution. We have seen that after the Bar Kochba rebellion, study of the Torah was officially banned; noted sages were put to death for violating this prohibition. Thereafter, the center of Jewish life in Palestine moved to the Mediterranean coast and to northern Galilee.

This stone carving of the Ark of the Covenant survives from an early Capernaum synagogue. With the destruction of the temple, the synagogue was elevated to greater importance as a place to hear prayers and psalms and receive instruction. (The Granger Collection)

The leading rabbi at the time of Bar Kochba had been Akiba ben Joseph (martyred in 135 C.E.), and now the leading teachers in Galilee included Akiba's disciple Rabbi Meir and Meir's disciple Rabbi Judah the Patriarch (c. 135–c. 220). Rabbi Judah compiled an authoritative codification of the oral law called the **Mishnah**, which greatly facilitated the learning and discussion of the oral traditions in the academies of the Torah. It contained the teachings and opinions of some 148 scholars and was divided into six sections. One section, called "Seeds," contained agricultural laws and regulations dealing with prayers, blessings, and the rights of the needy. Another, called "Feasts," dealt with the observance of the Jewish holidays. "Women" summarized the laws of betrothal, marriage, and divorce; "Damages" dealt with civil and criminal law; "Sacred Things" preserved the memory of sacrificial worship; and "Purities" was concerned with matters of ceremonial purity.

No attempt was made to distinguish more important from less important covenant obligations. In fact, the section called "Sacred Things" dealt with the sacrificial cult that could no longer be practiced after the destruction of the temple. Its inclusion was based

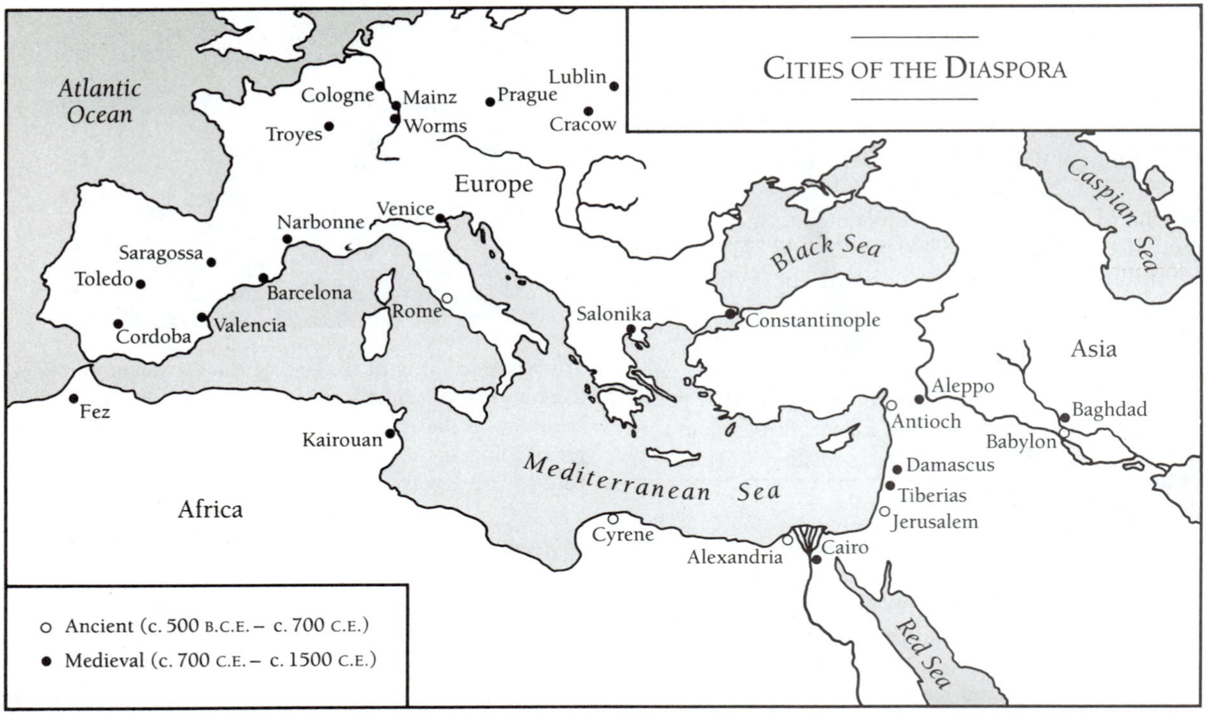

on the assumption that studying such matters was itself a covenant obligation that would hasten the coming of the Messiah and the restoration of the temple.

THE NEW BABYLONIAN DIASPORA

The academies in Palestine continued to function for two centuries after the codification of the Mishnah, but their glorious age of creativity had faded. Palestine declined economically and culturally. In 425 C.E. Emperor Theodosius II abolished the office of patriarch, but by this time the center of Jewish spiritual and intellectual life had shifted to Babylonia.

During the Hellenistic age, the Jewish community in Alexandria flourished, and after the destruction of the temple in 70 C.E., the Jewish community in Rome began to grow. Still, Babylonia was one of the oldest sites of the Jewish Diaspora. All during the period of the second temple, Babylonian Jews lived in the shadow of the Palestinian center, but many Jews whose families had been exiled to Babylon in the sixth century B.C.E. had remained in that land even after the edict of Cyrus, and over the years a large and well-established Jewish settlement had grown up there. Thousands of pilgrims from Babylonia came to Jerusalem three times a year to observe the great festivals of pilgrimage. Babylonian Jews made substantial annual contributions to the temple treasury, and some of the early great thinkers of the Palestinian academies had been raised in Babylonia.

By the middle of the second century C.E., the pendulum had begun to swing, and many Palestinian Jews, including scholars, sought a home in Babylonia, where they enjoyed greater freedom and autonomy. The civil head of the Jewish community, who was called *Resh Galuta* ("chief of the exiles"), claimed that his lineage went back to King David. But even more influential were religious leaders like Samuel and Rav Abba Areka, who had studied with Rabbi Judah the Patriarch in Palestine.

CREATION OF THE TALMUD

At first the Palestinian leadership struggled to maintain its centrality, prestige, and legal authority. No Babylonian teachers could be fully ordained, and they were called by the shortened title *Rav* ("master") rather than *Rabbi* ("my master"). For similar reasons, Palestinian authorities claimed the exclusive right to supervise the coordination of the Jewish lunar year with the solar cycle of the seasons. By the fourth century, however, Babylonian Jews were no longer dependent on the Palestinian authorities for the declaration of the new moon. This technical change, together with the steady decline of Palestine as a center of Jewish life, led to the independence of the Babylonian diaspora. Over the centuries this community developed many of its own distinctive traditions, including the custom of men's heads being covered during worship.

But the Babylonian diaspora did have problems. In the middle of the third century, the Parthians were overrun by a Persian dynasty, the Sassanids, who practiced a form of Zoroastrianism. Their clergy were often hostile to Judaism and persecuted its adherents. This stimulated efforts to codify the Torah traditions in the hope of providing readily available guidance for the beleaguered community. During the fourth and fifth centuries, a collection of commentaries on the Mishnah, known as the *Gemara* ("completion"), was assembled and written down. This massive compendium, completed only in the sixth century, became known as the Babylonian **Talmud.**[2] Although rabbinic literature came to include many collections and disputations, the Babylonian Talmud is the text that most influenced the shape of Jewish life for centuries.*

The 36 major divisions of the Babylonian Talmud contain an estimated 2.5 million words, recording the teachings of 2,000 sages over a period of 800 years. The Mishnah states the oral law in virtually every sphere of life from tithing to regulating marriages and divorces, from the proper blessings to recite over food and wine to the proper way to initiate a new male child into the covenant. A typical talmudic discussion begins by citing the Mishnah text. It then records various rabbis' attempts to clarify the text, to draw forth its full implication, to raise new questions, and to apply this text to a specific situation.

To the modern Western mind a talmudic discussion may seem in one section to be like a meticulously reasoned legal brief but in another to be like an unstructured stream-of-consciousness outpouring. Law and lore, biographical vignettes, and free flights of the religious imagination all are juxtaposed. To an outsider, the issues appear at times irrelevant or even trivial. But they all show the rabbinic reverence for the life of the mind: a sharply honed intelligence was regarded as an essential instrument in defining God's covenant with Israel.

*The Palestinian academies had earlier developed a compendium of their discussions on the Mishnah known as the Palestinian Talmud. Codified by the beginning of the fifth century, this Talmud was far less influential than its Babylonian counterpart.

THE RABBINIC MIND

The task confronting the Babylonian rabbis was complex. They had to meet the demands of the Jews in their new situation, the Diaspora, and they had to show that their teachings, which aimed to meet those needs, were legitimate and authoritative. They did so in a way that the Mishnah had not: they frequently grounded their teachings on biblical texts, subjecting the Bible to very creative interpretations. Teachings that had no obvious biblical support were regarded as part of the oral law transmitted from Sinai or were assigned biblical roots by ingenious interpretations called *Midrash*.

When a biblical passage clashed with their own sensibility, the rabbis found ways of reinterpreting it. For example, Deuteronomy 21:18–21 specifies that if a man has a "stubborn and rebellious" son, the son shall be put to death. The rabbis defined "stubborn and rebellious" so restrictively that they concluded: "Never has there been a stubborn and rebellious son in the biblical sense" (Sanhedrin 71a).

Some parts of rabbinic law expanded on the Bible. The stipulation in Deuteronomy 24:6 that no man should take the mill or upper millstone of a debtor as a pledge for a loan was intended to protect the subsistence of the person forced into debt. The rabbis extended this to include "all tools used in the preparation of food" (Mishnah, Baba Metzia 9:13). Another example of rabbinic elaboration is found in the dietary laws. The Bible clearly specifies that only animals that "part the hoof" (are cloven-footed) and chew their cud may be eaten (Lev. 11:4–7). In addition, whereas the

Bible prohibits cooking the meat of a young goat in its mother's milk (Exod. 23:19 and 34:26, Deut. 14:21), the rabbis extended this to prohibit the consumption of any milk product and meat together.

The rabbis restructured the observance of the sacred seasons. The New Year's festival (Rosh Hashanah) was transformed from Yahweh's enthronement ceremony to a day when God judges the deeds of men and women. The ten days between Rosh Hashanah and Yom Kippur (the Day of Atonement) were regarded as days of penitence. The fate of humanity for the year to come is sealed on Yom Kippur, when God determines who is to live or die in the year ahead.

Passover, the feast commemorating Israel's liberation from bondage, had long been joined with the beginning of harvest, when new, unleavened bread *(matzah)* was eaten (Lev. 23:5–6). On this foundation the rabbis developed an elaborate ritual for the Passover supper. The *Seder* ("order") is a structured meal in which the consumption of symbolic foods—matzah, bitter herbs, parsley, wine, salt water—is woven into the texture of a liturgical text *(Haggadah)* recounting the pilgrimage from bondage to freedom. The intention of the Passover home liturgy was to enable all Jews, especially the children, to remember God's great act of deliverance. Rabbinic teaching also reconceptualized Shavuot, the early summer festival that follows seven weeks after Passover. It became known as the anniversary of the sealing of the covenant between God and Israel at Sinai (Exod. 20).

By the middle of the fourth century, the rabbis had also mathematically fixed the Jewish calendar. They adjusted its length, based on the lunar year (354 days), to the longer solar year by adding an extra month every seven years.

Halacha and Agada

The rabbis focused their attentions not only on belief but also on observances, patterns of life, and conduct. Their deliberations and prescriptions for conduct were called *halacha* (law—literally, "the way to walk"). Halacha regulated sexual relations, business ethics, birth and death observances, responsibilities to the more and less fortunate, the order of worship, and relations with the Gentile world. Indeed, halacha extended to all human activity. A Jew could sanctify or profane the name of God by every deed during every waking moment.

The Passover supper or Seder consists of symbolic foods including bitter herbs, parsley, eggs, salt water, and wine. The consumption of these foods is woven into the texture of a liturgical text (Haggadah) recounting the pilgrimage from bondage to freedom. (UPI/Bettmann)

God had singled these people out, the rabbis maintained; in return he demanded obedience to his commandments. The Jews who observed the demands of halacha were deemed by the rabbis to have fulfilled their human destiny on earth and to have earned their place in the world to come. Though Rome claimed political dominion, Jewish faith affirmed that God was truly sovereign. God's messianic kingdom would be advanced if Israel adhered to his law. Although the futility of opposing Rome militarily was evident, life by the covenant could still ultimately affect the course of history.

Judaism has always been more concerned with regulating conduct than with regulating belief. The great rabbinic arguments were rarely doctrinal. To be sure, there are limits to acceptable belief, but rabbis were concerned more about defining acceptable behavior than about disciplining wayward souls. Thus the rabbis portrayed God as declaring: "Would that they [my children] forsook me and observed my commandments, for by observing my Torah will they come to know me" (Palestinian Talmud, Hagigah 1:7).

Whereas halacha defines the terms of the covenant, *agada* explores its nature and meaning. Agada is the language of Jewish theology. It takes many forms. For example, it recounts, with legendary embellishments, biographical vignettes from the lives of the rabbis, who are regarded as models of piety and faith. Another common form is the imaginative re-creation of a dialogue between God and biblical Israel. One agada reconstructs the event at Sinai as follows: God summoned Israel to be his people. Israel expressed reluctance, whereupon God threatened to overturn the mountain and suspend it over their heads if they did not accept the call. At that point Israel agreed to become God's covenant partner (Talmud, Shabbat 88a). Such stories have been used to interpret fundamental theological issues. Was the initiation of the covenant a voluntary act or a divinely ordained destiny? The acceptance of a variety of stories suggests the fluidity and even the acceptance of unresolved tensions in rabbinic Judaism.

One of the most important theological tensions recorded in agada is that between God's justice and mercy. Is the covenant a conditional bond, sustained only by Israel's fidelity? Yes, the rabbis sometimes said, Israel's merit helps to maintain the covenant, and Israel's disobedience threatens it. "As a dove is saved by its wings, so Israel is saved by mitzvot, by fulfilling God's commandments" (Ber 53b). According to other passages, however, the covenant is grounded in God's love and is thus unconditional. Israel is portrayed as praying to God: "Lord of the universe, though I am poor indeed, nonetheless I belong to thee, and it is within thy power to help me" (Pes 118b).

RABBINIC JUDAISM: THE RELIGION OF TORAH

When the temple in Jerusalem was destroyed, the Jewish world lost its focal center, and Judaism faced the greatest crisis of its early history. It has already been mentioned that the temple provided spectacular pageantry, but the temple served two more essential functions as well. By serving as a center of pilgrimage shared by Jews from all over the world, the temple linked Jews everywhere and gave them a sense of national unity and common destiny. And by offering continuous divine worship in the manner described in the Bible, the temple represented the continuing vitality of the covenant between God and the people of Israel. All this was now gone, and in its absence the very survival of Judaism hung in doubt. The greatest accomplishment of the early rabbis—the way in which they surmounted the crisis of the Diaspora and exile—is that they developed a new kind of center around which Jewish life everywhere in the world could revolve.

That center was the Torah. Previously the name of a book, the term *Torah* in rabbinic usage came to designate the entire range of rabbinic teaching; since rabbis claimed to know the will of God for every imaginable situation, the term *Torah* came to embrace every aspect of the Jewish religion. Ancient Hebrew has no word for *religion* or *Judaism;* the early rabbis' name for their way of life was *Torah.*

The rabbis taught that in his encounter with God on Mount Sinai, Moses had received a dual Torah, part written and part oral. The written part was known to all Jews, but the Oral Torah had been transmitted by Moses to a select group of disciples chosen both for their intellectual skills and for their dedication to this sacred trust. These disciples had in turn transmitted the "whole Torah" to the next generation, and so it had come down to the rabbis' own time.

Flowing from this basic conception was another, equally basic and, if anything, more radical: the commentaries, explanations, and applications that rabbis taught their students were not a mere supplement to Torah; they were Torah in their own right. Rabbinic teaching was a kind of divine revelation, no less than the written words of scripture.

This bold conception had fundamental meaning for Jewish life. It implied that the new rabbinic leaders of the Jews were the equivalent of the biblical prophets or Moses himself; they were people whose every word communicated direct knowledge of the will of God to a nation pledged to live according to that will. It implied that complete fulfillment of the will of God could not be achieved on the basis of scripture alone but required equal or perhaps even greater attention to the accumulated Oral Torah that rabbis taught alongside scripture. It thus implied the limitless proliferation of rules but also the exciting idea that every action could be an opportunity to fulfill a divine command and thus participate in the sacred covenant.

This was a successful solution to the problems of powerlessness and dispersion. Unlike the temple, the new sacred center of Judaism could not be destroyed by an invading army; it was not limited to one place in the world, nor was it necessarily under the control of a limited hereditary aristocracy like the Aaronide priesthood. The rabbis taught that Torah was the inheritance of all Jews (meaning all male Jews). It could be carried wherever the Jews' wanderings brought them, and since most of it was oral, it was written on their hearts, not on parchments that an oppressor might seize and destroy. Although the rabbis vehemently insisted that the ignorant must accept the authority of the learned (that is, the rabbis themselves) over Jewish life, they eagerly sought as many disciples as they could find, hoping to create a community in which everyone lived a life of constant Torah study and disciplined fulfillment of the Torah's commands.

For the rabbis themselves, the potential reward of this Torah-centered Judaism was even greater. For ordinary Jews, Torah offered the chance to come closer to God, but the scholar dedicated to the spread of Torah had the chance to become more like God, the chance to do repeatedly what God had done only once: give Torah to the Jewish people. The act of Torah study became a way to relive the original revelation at Sinai, and the act of teaching Torah was almost God-like in its power. No wonder that Judaism became perhaps the most text-based and studious of the major world religions! No wonder that "learning Torah"—the regular study of the sacred texts of the Mishnah, the Talmud, the Midrash, and their commentaries—became a religious ritual in its own right, perhaps the most absorbing ritual that Jewish life had to offer.

RESPONSE TO THE CHRISTIAN CHALLENGE

The centuries following the destruction of the temple were years of great creativity in both halacha and agada. These were also the years when Christianity emerged as a world religion, and some of the antagonism between the early church and the synagogue mirrored in the New Testament can be found in the talmudic literature. Although very few talmudic passages refer indisputably to Jesus, certain statements in the agada appear to be oblique Jewish responses to Christian claims. For example, a number of rabbinic passages take pains to assert that, unlike a mortal king, God had no son (Jerusalem Talmud, Shabbat 8). The omission of any reference to Moses in the Passover Seder, they wrote, was to dramatize that in Judaism, God's redemptive grace requires no human mediator. Without specifically referring to the Christian negation of "the Law," they asserted repeatedly that God's gift of the Torah and the Jewish people's obligation to fulfill it was God's greatest gift of love. To observe the Law faithfully was to reciprocate that love.

THE SYNAGOGUE LITURGY

The main elements of the Jewish prayer book acquired their essential form during the talmudic age. These prayers reflect the basic theological claims of rabbinic Judaism, and they are to be chanted by a leader, recited silently by the individual worshiper, or sung in unison.

A section of worship called the Shema features the declaration of God's oneness: "Hear, O Israel, the Lord our God, the Lord is One." The congregation acknowledges its covenant with God, who with great love has singled out Israel for the gift of the Torah and who has proved his redemptive power by liberating Israel from Egyptian bondage. A central portion of the liturgy includes a prayer for the establishment of God's messianic kingdom:

> Sound the great horn for our freedom . . . and gather us from the four corners of the earth . . . and to Jerusalem, Thy city, return in mercy, . . . rebuild it soon in our days . . . and speedily set up therein the throne of David.

These prayers, recited daily by observant Jews since the destruction of the temple, have kept alive the memory of Zion and the yearning for that sacred land.

Worship services on the Sabbath, holidays, and other days feature the reading of the Torah scroll. The conclusion of the worship service renews Israel's loyalty to the "King of Kings, the Holy One, Blessed be He," by whose power and purpose the world will one day be perfected under the kingdom of the Almighty. Until that day, Israel's witness must endure, for "on that day shall the Lord be One and His name One" (Zech. 14:9).

JUDAISM'S ENCOUNTER WITH ISLAM

Babylonia continued as the major center of Jewish life for several centuries, and the rabbinic leaders' influence spread. Jews of North Africa and Europe submitted questions to them, and their answers became a new form of rabbinic literature.

Around this time, the new religion of Islam established dominion over western Asia, North Africa, Sicily, and Spain. At first the Jews welcomed the Muslim conquest of Babylonia. Although Muḥammad himself had chafed at the Jews' refusal to embrace his faith, his followers allowed the Jewish academies to continue.

KARAISM

In the eighth and ninth centuries, the *Gaon* (rabbinic authority) and the *exilarch* (secular leader) had considerable power over the Jewish community, not only in Babylonia but also in Palestine, North Africa, and Spain. The Babylonian academies attracted students from all these communities. The Talmud was regarded as the standard of covenant fidelity, and the rabbinic authorities were accepted as the spiritual heirs of the talmudic sages.

In the eighth century, partly in rebellion against this rabbinic authority and partly as a reflection of trends in the Muslim community, a group of Babylonian Jews known as *Karaites* ("devotees of scripture") challenged the whole concept of a revealed oral law. The entire monumental compendium of the Talmud was, in their judgment, without divine sanction. To ascertain the terms of God's covenant with Israel, they insisted, Jews must read scripture, not rely on rabbinic exegesis.

In matters of halacha, the Karaites read the scriptures more literally. For example, the Talmud and the gaonic sages prohibited the kindling of fire on the Sabbath but not its use, provided that the fire had been kindled prior to sunset on the Sabbath eve. The Karaites held that scripture did not intend Jews to kindle or even have light during the Sabbath. Similarly, the rabbis had devised phylacteries *(tefillin)*, prayer boxes containing scriptural passages, that a male worshiper wrapped around his arm and forehead during morning devotions. They regarded this as a response to the command in Deuteronomy 6:8: "Thou shalt bind them for a sign upon thy hand and they shall be for frontlets between thine eyes." The Karaites rejected these ritual objects.

This challenge to talmudic Judaism has had several explanations, most of which center on the chasm that had opened up between the leadership and the people.

A contemporary Jewish man and his son are shown during morning devotions. Visible are the phylacteries (tefillin) or prayer boxes containing scriptural passages wrapped around his arm and forehead. These practices are a response to Deuteronomy 6:8, "Thou shalt bind them for a sign upon thy hand and they shall be for frontlets between thine eyes." The boy's head is covered with a yamulka. (Reuters/Bettmann)

The exilarch had come to reside in Baghdad, the Muslim caliph's capital, and had taken up an opulent style of living supported in part by public taxes—a fact not lost on the taxpayers. The Karaites advocated a simpler and more austere piety more congruent with the life that the common folk could afford. In addition, a language gap had developed: the rabbis taught in Aramaic, the language of the Talmud, of which the people knew little. The Karaites emphasized not authority but reason, which allowed access by all. They sought freedom from the overlordship of the exilarch by returning to what they took to be the original authority, the Torah.

By the tenth century, the Karaites' influence had waned considerably, in large part because of the giant of the age, Saadia ben Joseph.

SAADIA'S RESPONSE

Saadia (882–942) was born in Egypt but became the leading Babylonian rabbi. He spearheaded a vigorous, shrewd, and sophisticated response to Karaism. Recognizing the language gap, Saadia both translated the scriptures into Arabic and added a popular commentary so that Arabic-speaking Jews could follow the train of thought. Saadia's aggressive and cogent answers restored the credibility of the talmudic tradition to many people who had come to mistrust it.

The celebration of Passover is depicted in this illumination from the Rylands Haggadah from fourteenth-century Spain. During Muslim rule of Spain, Jews were allowed a great deal of religious freedom. (The Granger Collection)

Saadia was also the first major Jewish thinker since Philo to master the prevailing philosophical tradition and effectively harmonize it with Judaism. By the ninth century, a revival of Greek rationalism (made available in Arabic translations) had provoked learned Muslims and Jews to question the claims of revealed scripture. Saadia reasserted that there was no conflict between reason and revelation. If a biblical text appeared to contradict human reason, as when the Torah ascribed physical attributes to God, it was not to be taken literally.

In his major work, *The Book of Belief and Opinion,* Saadia taught that God had revealed the truth in the scripture. Yet God has also empowered humans to derive both metaphysical truth and moral laws by means of unaided reason. What then was the reason for revelation? Certain ritual laws of the Torah, Saadia asserted, were not derivable from reason, and revelation yielded truth in uncorrupted form. Moreover, the details of God's moral law would gain no consensus without the authority of revelation. In short, revelation demonstrated truth more rapidly and more persuasively than reason alone.

At the time of Saadia's death, Babylonia as the Jewish center was already on the wane. Jews in search of economic opportunity and intellectual and spiritual freedom began to turn westward.

JUDAISM IN MUSLIM SPAIN

The Muslim invasion of Spain in 711 was welcomed by the Spanish Jews. Smarting under the oppressive rule of the Christian Visigoths, the Jews believed that Muslim rule would bring relief and new opportunity. Their hopes were largely fulfilled. Under the Muslims, Jews were able to secure positions as physicians, merchants, and administrators to the Arab elite.

At first Spanish Jews turned to the Babylonian rabbis for leadership. But as the exilarch's influence waned, the Spanish community itself assumed the commanding place in world Jewry, much as third-century Babylonia had displaced Palestine as the center of Jewish life. Although the Spanish rabbis did not enjoy the governmental support that the rabbinate had had in Babylonia, the Muslim authorities did allow the Jews freedom to follow their religion's requirements, halacha. Along with this freedom, Spanish Jews became caught up in the sophisticated culture of their Muslim hosts, and the ninth, tenth, and eleventh centuries in Spain are generally regarded as a golden age in Jewish history. The great Arab philosophical schools of the day inspired Jewish thinkers to try to reconcile reason and revelation, freedom and determinism, and a belief in an incorporeal deity with the physical world.

Yet despite the considerable tolerance afforded them, and their success, even upper-class Jews still felt estranged. Jews were a minority, and they practiced a faith that was not shared by their neighbors. Judah Halevi and Moses Maimonides, the two greatest Jewish figures of their time, lived under a growing shadow of persecution.

Judah Halevi

Judah Halevi (c. 1075–1141) was born in Toledo, Spain, a Muslim city that was restored to Christian control during his lifetime. Early in life he had mastered the talmudic texts, but he then turned to secular poetry, becoming one of the leading writers of his time. He went from an exploration of the Aristotelian rationalism of his day toward a romantic, almost mystical defense of traditional Jewish piety. His most famous works show an impassioned yearning for intimacy with God and an identification with the Jewish people in Zion—a yearning that may be seen in part as a response to the persecution and estrangement of his people.

His most important work, the *Kuzari,* was the first major defense of Judaism to appear in the West. It was a semifictional account of the rulers of the Khazars, who lived along the west bank of the Caspian Sea and who converted to Judaism. Their conversion occurred after a Christian, Muslim, and Jewish philosopher had each spoken to them on behalf of their religions. Under this guise the book offered a philosophical defense of Judaism.

The most persuasive evidence of Israel's truth offered by Halevi's rabbi was the survival of God's people despite the traumas of history, the readiness of the people to die for their faith, and the unbroken tradition by which the Torah had been transmitted across many lands and generations. In his turning to the survival of his people as the key mark of God's favor, Halevi articulated a main principle of Jews' religious self-esteem: the miracle of the very survival of Judaism and the survival of its people despite the Diaspora.

Halevi believed that Christianity and Islam were only stages in the spiritual growth of humanity. Even when they appeared to reject Judaism, they reflected its influence, and their adherents would eventually acknowledge the authentic revelation that Judaism represented in its finest form.

Halevi yearned for the land of Palestine because it was a uniquely receptive environment for God's word. He did not feel content to await the messianic restoration of the Jewish people but declared: "Your love of Torah cannot be sincere if you do not make this place your goal, your home in life and death."[3]

Moses Maimonides

In the eleventh century, Spanish Jews were being caught in the crossfire of the Muslim-Christian contest for supremacy, and by the last quarter of the twelfth century they were no longer safe in Muslim Spain. The zeal of the Christian Crusaders was matched by Arab fanaticism, and non-Muslim "infidels" were compelled to convert, leave the country, or lose their lives.

When Maimonides, or Moses ben Maimon (1138–1204), was only 13 years old, the Muslims conquered Córdoba and closed the synagogues. Faced with the demand to convert to Islam, Maimonides's family remained for a while as secret Jews but then migrated to Morocco, Palestine, and eventually Egypt. A brilliant talmudist and physician to the Egyptian ruler, Maimonides was recognized as the unofficial leader of the Egyptian Jews. His *Mishneh Torah* (second Torah) was a 14-volume codification of talmudic and gaonic law. Written in readable Hebrew, it was intended to be a comprehensive survey of the demands of Jewish piety and included everything from the norms of sexual behavior and business ethics to the details of the temple service.

Although traditional Judaism had emphasized proper conduct more than doctrines of faith, Maimonides tried to define the essential beliefs of Judaism. His 13 principles, including the oneness of God, the revelation of the Torah, the coming of the Messiah, and the future resurrection of the dead, became a permanent part of the traditional Jewish liturgy but never attained the status of a creed.

Maimonides's *Guide for the Perplexed,* written in Arabic, attempted to adjudicate conflicts between Aristotelian philosophy and Judaism's revealed texts. He accepted Aristotle's proof of the existence of God but rejected the philosopher's view of the eternity of the world as contrary to the biblical idea of creation. Similarly, against the Neoplatonists, who conceived of the world as eternally proceeding from God, Maimonides argued that the world was God's free creation. At the same time, he reinterpreted biblical anthropomorphisms. Contrary to Halevi, Maimonides taught that the divine voice in scripture was not to be taken literally but rather as a symbol of rational prophetic comprehension.

Maimonides viewed biblical prophecy as a continuous flow of reason and inspiration from God to the human mind, a flow that was in proportion to the individual's disciplined preparation, though God could refuse inspiration even to those who prepared themselves. He identified the prophecy of Moses as different from all others: a perfect expression of the divine will.

He found reasons for the Torah's commandments. The biblical laws prescribing animal sacrifice, for example, were a practical way of weaning the people of that day from homage to pagan deities. The Sabbath was a way of cultivating a belief in God's creation of the world; the dietary laws were an antidote to gluttony; and circumcision was a way of keeping men's sexual desire under control.

Maimonides was, without question, the most commanding Jewish presence of his age. His rationalism did not meet the needs of the Jewish people in his own time or thereafter, but his reformulation of the terms of the covenant greatly influenced all subsequent interpreters. For Maimonides, to follow the demands of the Torah was a way of cultivating the virtues that make a decent society possible and of acquiring beliefs that qualify a person for immortality.

Opponents maintained that Maimonides's teachings were more Greek than Jewish and that his system of salvation was intellectually elitist. In the end, his philosophy could not offer the sense of intimate communion with the ultimate that was part of any vital religion.

By the thirteenth century, the Christian authorities in Spain were staging contentious and hostile public disputations offering Jews the choice of conversion or expulsion. Jews were formally expelled from Spain in 1492, as illustrated in this nineteenth-century engraving. (The Granger Collection)

The limitations of Maimonides's rationalism became more evident as conditions in Spain worsened. Jews were being persecuted with increasing fervor. By the thirteenth century, the Christian authorities were staging contentious, sometimes hostile public disputations. Increasingly, Jews were offered the choice of conversion or expulsion. They were formally expelled in 1492.

Under such harrowing conditions, it is not surprising that interest in Maimonides's dry rationalism yielded increasingly to a more mystical version of Judaism, the Kabbalah.

KABBALAH: JEWISH MYSTICISM

Jewish mysticism reached its peak of creativity and influence during the High Middle Ages. Like its Christian and non-Western counterparts, **Kabbalah** (the generic term for the mystical tradition in Judaism) asserted that the external world of visible reality was only a pale reflection of an invisible higher realm. The Kabbalist yearned for direct access to the higher spiritual realm, to experience its hidden splendor personally.[4]

Echoes of mysticism abound in biblical and talmudic Judaism. Moses's experience at the burning bush (Exod. 3–4), Isaiah's temple vision (Isa. 6), and Ezekiel's vision of the heavenly chariot (Ezek. 1–3) are considered precedents. The Talmud (Hagigah 14b) makes cryptic reference to four rabbis who "entered paradise," that is, who dabbled in mystical speculation, and notes that only one, Akiba, emerged unscathed.

THE ZOHAR

The main text of Kabbalah was the *Zohar,* a thirteenth-century commentary on the Pentateuch by Moses de León (1250–1305) of Granada. Its basic premise was that the Torah was the outer garment of an inner mystery. Persons properly instructed with the help of the Zohar might "unveil" the depths of spiritual truth. The Zohar viewed God in his transcendence as *Einsof,* the infinite, absolute reality beyond all human conceptualization or relation. God was "the most hidden of the most hidden"; he was also the creator of all forms of being and nurtured his creation with radiant power and grace. The vital links between the hidden self-sufficient God and the one who created, guided, and redeemed the world were the ten *sefirot,* the emanations and manifestations of God.

The richly complex structure of the divine inner life as described in the Zohar included masculine and feminine components. Such sensual symbolism, even though it seemed flagrantly pagan to its rationalist detractors, added popular appeal to Kabbalah. The structure of the divine life itself had an earthly counterpart in humanity; indeed, human beings had the power to affect it by performing certain acts, including the observance of the Torah. Through human initiative, the soul could be reunited with its divine source, and the unity of God could be restored. Thus Kabbalah offered a way to individual salvation and the salvation of God's world, all predicated on the assumption that human acts had cosmic implications.

During the fourteenth and fifteenth centuries, Kabbalah gained an ever increasing number of devotees. It reached its peak during the centuries after the Jews' expulsion from Spain, perhaps because the dispersed exiles needed a rationale for their condition that would rekindle their piety and renew their hope of redemption.

EUROPEAN COMMUNITIES OF THE DIASPORA

RENAISSANCE ITALY

After they were expelled from Spain, many Jews had the good fortune of finding a new home in Italy during the Renaissance, where the popes and the church were generally protective and discouraged excessive hostility toward the Jews.

To one Kabbalist, this mazelike pattern meant the way God rules the world. Kabbalah was the Jewish mysticism that reached its peak in the High Middle Ages.

Many Jews found a new home in Italy after being expelled from Spain. There the popes and the church were generally protective and discouraged excessive hostility toward the Jews. This Italian synagogue ark dates from the sixteenth century. (The Granger Collection)

But the issue of persecution—why it recurred, what it meant, how to respond to it—was now in the forefront of their minds. An Italian Jew, Solomon ibn Verga (late fifteenth and early sixteenth centuries), traced the history of Jewish persecution in his major work *Shevet Yehudah* ("Staff of Judah"). Ibn Verga rejected the then prevalent explanations that Jewish suffering was a sign either of God's special love or that messianic redemption was at hand. He viewed anti-Jewish hostility as the fruit of religious fanaticism and called on both Christians and Jews to respect each other's heritage. A Spanish exile, Samuel Usque (sixteenth century), also surveyed Jewish history. In contrast to ibn Verga, Usque revived the ancient idea that Israel's suffering could hasten the coming of the Messiah.

NORTHWESTERN AND CENTRAL EUROPE

During the centuries when Jewish life was flourishing in Muslim Spain and Renaissance Italy, Jews in France, England, and the several hundred states of the Holy Roman Empire were suffering great indignities.

Although the disunity of Germany made it possible for German Jews (known as Ashkenazic Jews)* harassed in one state to seek protection in another, the Crusaders' wars against Islam brought special suffering. Jewish communities in Mainz, Worms, Trier, and Cologne were virtually annihilated by Christian armies eager to defeat the unbelievers in their midst before venturing forth to reclaim the Holy Land. Under a papal edict of 1215, Jews were forced to wear yellow badges and hats.

Yet on occasion church leaders did try to restrain their communicants' anti-Semitism. When, in the thirteenth century, Jews were accused of ritual murder (purportedly killing Christian children to obtain their blood for Passover), the Catholic hierarchy refuted the accusation and ordered that the Jews be treated kindly.

During these centuries in which persecution and enmity were facts of daily life, Jews were compelled to draw on their own internal resources for comfort and sustenance. The *Kehillah,* or Jewish community, became more and more autonomous: an elaborate social welfare system was begun, and numerous synagogues, some magnificently appointed, were built. Within the Kehillah could be found bakeries for the Passover matzah, soloists (cantors) to sing the liturgy, kosher butchers, Jewish school systems, and a communal fund that provided dowries for poor brides and stipends for the unemployed.

Given its self-sufficiency, the Kehillah needed guidelines and laws. The rabbis generally satisfied this

*The German Jews and their descendants who migrated south or east (many ultimately to America) were called *Ashkenazim,* after Ashkenaz, a descendant of Noah (Gen. 10:3). They were distinguished from *Sephardic* (Spanish) Jews, who lived in Muslim Spain and later found refuge in the Ottoman Empire, Italy, and the Netherlands.

need, often functioning more as legal authorities than as pastors. For example, Rabbi Gershom ben Judah (960–1028), widely known as the "light of the exile," issued numerous ordinances. Most famous of these is his ban on polygamous marriages.

Another important teacher of this period was the French Jew Shlomo ben Yitschak, known as Rashi (1040–1105). His comprehensive commentaries are still used to make the Talmud and the Bible accessible to the average Jew. Whereas Maimonides codified the law according to his own categories, Rashi wrote a running commentary on the verses as they appeared. He clarified halacha and agada in simple Hebrew prose, interspersed with current French vernacular.

After the Crusades, Worms and Regensburg became centers of Jewish mysticism. Their most creative period was from the middle of the twelfth century to the end of the thirteenth. The most influential mystical work, *Sefer Hasidim* ("Book of the Pious"), has been attributed to Rabbi Judah ben Samuel of Regensburg (died 1217), who was known as Judah Ha-Hasid ("The Pious One").

Whereas Maimonides had accentuated aspects of talmudic ethics, the Kabbalists of Germany glorified the life of the saint. The Talmud itself alludes to the level of decency expected of the ordinary human being and the higher level attained by a Hasid, a saintly person.

Judah Ha-Hasid, like his contemporary Saint Francis of Assisi (1182–1226), stressed the importance of self-denial and extreme altruism but tempered it with the traditional Jewish affirmation of life. Thus he instructed the pious person to "drink, be happy with his lot, keep his body upright so that he may know God. For it is impossible to become wise in learning while he is sick or aches in one of his limbs."[5] At the same time Judah felt a strong sense of responsibility for the Jewish community as a whole. No Jew could profess piety who did not join the household of Israel in its troubles and fasts. Observance of the Torah remained the key to overcoming evil impulses and earning one's place in the world to come.

Some of the customs initiated or popularized by Ashkenazic Jews during these centuries have remained part of Jewish life. The custom of inviting a 13-year-old boy to read from the Torah in the synagogue, thereby becoming a *bar mitzvah* ("son of the commandment"), a full-fledged member of the congregation, probably dates from this period. The custom of reciting intercessory prayers for the dead also began among the Ashkenazim. Originally intended for the martyrs of the Crusades, the custom was extended to all the departed, with a special memorial prayer *(Kaddish)* recited at each anniversary of the death.

After the Crusades, Jews experienced a more peaceful period in Germany. This illuminated frontispiece to Genesis from the Schocken Bible dates from the early fourteenth century in Germany. (The Granger Collection)

EASTERN EUROPE

As oppression in Germany and France worsened, between the thirteenth and sixteenth centuries many Ashkenazic Jews migrated eastward to Poland. Poland became the new center of Jewish life. Bringing their German dialect with them, the immigrants' language developed into the mix of Polish, German, and Hebrew known as Yiddish.

The Shtetl

The Jewish *shtetls* (villages) of eastern Europe offered the community a rich symbolic life from the cradle to the grave, compensating in part for the hostility of the outside world. The Jews came to see themselves as players in a transcendent drama. Their self-esteem was not dependent on the opinions of the Gentile host nation but was rooted in their covenant faith. They regarded themselves as having been singled out by God for a special destiny on earth. By observing the Torah, they were assured a place in the world to come. They were also certain that God would punish their oppressors.

Besides working as artisans and merchants, Jews served as administrators of Polish nobles' estates and as tax collectors. As such, they became special targets of the Christian peasants, and in 1648 a band of Cossacks from the Ukraine, in rebellion against their Polish rulers, conducted a series of massacres of Jews.

In the face of this and further persecution, interest in Kabbalah, which offered a mystical hope, understandably soared. Polish Jews were especially attentive to leaders who promised redemption. Most notable among these would-be messiahs was Shabbatai Tzevi, a fervent student of Kabbalah born in Turkey in 1626. Performing certain acts (including pronouncing the ineffable name of Yahweh) and claiming to be the long-awaited Messiah, he attracted an impassioned following throughout Europe; thousands of Jews sold their property in preparation for their imminent return to Zion. In the end the Turkish sultan convinced Shabbatai to convert to Islam. Many Jews, desperately trying to maintain their faith in him, asserted that this was part of the messianic plan, but a great many more felt betrayed.

Hasidism

The most significant response to the terrifying events in eastern Europe was a movement of mystical piety called **Hasidism**. Beginning late in the eighteenth century, Hasidism transformed Kabbalah into a popular and joyous folk movement, engendered a renewed sense of community among the surviving Jews, and gave dignity and self-esteem to the untutored. Most of all, this movement fostered a new kind of religious leadership. Rabbinic Judaism had been Torah-centered rather than person-centered. In the biblical period, the

The Jewish shtetls or villages of eastern Europe offered a rich symbolic life from the cradle to the grave. Observance of the Torah assured a place in the world to come. Grandparents and parents taught children the laws of their ancestors. (The Bettmann Archive)

Hasidism survives today as seen here in this photo of Hasidic men dancing at the Western Wall in Jerusalem. Singing and dancing are incorporated into rituals as a celebration of life's joy. (UPI/Bettmann)

priest was the leader of the cult, and the prophet was the interpreter of the will of God. Although some talmudic rabbis were believed to be endowed with special powers to beg for God's mercy, rabbis generally feared that an emphasis on individuals might degenerate into idolatry. Hasidism featured a new kind of religious personality who was adored by his followers as a mediator of divine grace.[6]

This personality was modeled on the founder of Hasidism, Israel ben Eliezer (1700–1760). Born in the Polish village of Okup and soon orphaned, Israel grew up as a ward of the community. Not a scholar, he felt more at home talking to animals or telling stories to children. For years he and his wife eked out a living running a small inn in the Carpathian Mountains, where he became familiar with the therapeutic value of certain herbs and became known as the Baal Shem Tov ("Master of the Good Name," that is, the name of God), an allusion to his healing powers.

The Baal Shem Tov stressed the "hallowing of every day." One might worship God and help to redeem the scattered sparks of his holiness through virtually any act in one's daily routine (eating, working, even sexual activity) if performed with the proper intention. The most distinctive characteristic of Hasidism was the incorporation of singing and dancing in its rituals as a celebration of life's joy.

The Baal Shem Tov became the model for the leaders called *tzadikim* ("righteous ones"). These persons in whom the outpouring of divine radiance seemed to have been concentrated in turn became channels through which God's grace flowed to the community. The tzadik, who was believed to have attained the highest degree of communion with God, became the center of the community. Sharing a meal with a tzadik and eating the remnants on his plate, turning to him for personal counsel, and worshiping God in a synagogue graced by the tzadik's presence were cherished spiritual experiences.

For all its positive virtues, Hasidism was not without weaknesses. In subsequent generations, the hereditary leadership was transferred from the tzadik to a member of his family, regardless of that person's qualifications. Through its emphasis on simple piety, Hasidism might lead to a neglect of Torah study and Jewish law, though it did develop an intellectual dimension under the guidance of Rabbi Shneur Zalman (1747–1813), who made the tzadik more a sage than a performer of wondrous deeds.

THE VARIETIES OF MEDIEVAL JUDAISM

In sum, over the long course of the Middle Ages, the Jewish religion developed a great variety of emphases and styles. Groups of learned Jews—rabbis, mystics, and philosophers—cultivated different bodies of knowledge through which they sought personal fulfillment. Philosophers sought such fulfillment outside the boundaries of specifically Jewish learning, trying to meet Christian and Muslim thinkers on equal terms. Kabbalists agreed with Jewish philosophers that the truly meaningful realm of existence was hidden from ordinary view, but they sought the ultimate not through abstract thought but through uncovering the

Torah's secret meanings and rebuilding their way of life around those meanings. For most of the Middle Ages, both philosophy and Kabbalah remained the semisecret province of small groups of intellectuals following their particular quests.

More traditional rabbinic leaders continued in the meantime to build their lives on the older idea that the Jews were God's covenanted people committed to a life shaped by God's sacred Law. On this basis, rabbinic leadership continued to hold the loyalty of ordinary Jews, men and women who shared with the rabbis a willingness to follow what they took to be the dictates of the Torah even at the cost of growing isolation from European society and culture. Within their own communities, Jews preserved the Torah, obeyed its commandments, and waited for messianic redemption. As the Middle Ages advanced, Jewish isolation grew more pronounced, and perhaps partly as a consequence, the hostility of the Jews' neighbors increased. In 1492 the Jews were expelled from Spain, and in 1648 they were massacred in Poland. By the late eighteenth century, it was widely agreed that the Jewish people were poised for a new phase in their long history.

NOTES

1 Details can be found in Flavius Josephus, *The Jewish War*, trans. G. A. Williamson (London: Penguin, 1959), pp. 343–360.

2 For a useful discussion of the Talmud and a translation of some of its commentaries, see Judah Goldin, trans. and ed., *The Living Talmud: The Wisdom of the Fathers* (New Haven, Conn.: Yale University Press, 1955). The standard translation is Isadore Epstein, ed., *The Babylonian Talmud*, 18 vols. (London: Soncino Press, 1935–1948).

3 Adapted from H. Hirschfeld, trans., *Judah Halevi: The Kuzari* (New York: Schocken Books, 1964), p. 62.

4 For further reading on Kabbalah, see G. S. Scholem, *Major Trends in Jewish Mysticism* (New York: Schocken Books, 1941).

5 Sholom Singer, trans., *Medieval Jewish Mysticism: Book of the Pious* (Northbrook, Ill.: Whitehall, 1971), p. 52.

6 As a popular introduction to the lives and deeds of the Hasidic leaders, see Elie Wiesel, *Souls on Fire: Portraits and Legends of Hasidic Masters* (New York: Random House, 1972).

JUDAISM

CHAPTER 18

MODERN TIMES: PERSECUTION, DIVISIONS, NEW WORLDS

Rabbinic Judaism, the coherent set of beliefs and life patterns that had served the Jews well for two millennia, was forced to change radically when it entered the modern period. Modernity brought some of Judaism's most severe persecutions. It also brought emancipation to the Jews—political freedom, economic opportunity, and liberty to think in new ways. Ironically, freedom, the very thing that the Jews had lacked for so long, challenged their religion more deeply than many persecutions. For the first time, the Diaspora Jews were offered full citizenship in their host nations, and many Jews came to regard themselves no longer as exiles in their host countries but as Germans, French, or Americans. But if Judaism was no longer the faith of a distinct people with a distinct life pattern, what then was Judaism to be? For some Jews, it was an encumbrance, and they abandoned the religion altogether. But for most, Judaism offered a great deal if only it could be reinterpreted in a relevant manner. These recastings of the religion make up the history of modern Judaism.

GHETTOS AND THE DAWN OF MODERNITY

Jews had been living for centuries in restricted areas of their towns. The practice may have begun in medieval times when European Jews chose to live in separate neighborhoods. In Spain and Portugal, however, this practice was made obligatory, and by the sixteenth century, many European countries were confining Jews to special Jewish quarters, the so-called ghettos. (The term *ghetto* is probably derived from *geto,* a foundry or cannon factory that was near one of the first Italian ghettos in Venice.)[1]

Within the ghettos, the Jewish population was allowed a large measure of self-government and cultural autonomy. But the ghettos themselves were often surrounded by a wall with a gate that was closed each evening. Jews found outside during forbidden hours were subject to penalties. Those who ventured outside the ghetto walls were required to wear identification badges. Social interaction between Jews and Gentiles became less frequent, and Jewish life began to turn inward.

During this period a small but active Jewish community flourished in the freer political climate of the Netherlands. Yet even there the descendants of the Sephardic Jews expelled from Spain in the sixteenth century worried about maintaining the goodwill of their Dutch hosts. In 1656, when a member of the Amsterdam Jewish community, Baruch Spinoza (1632–1677), challenged many of the traditional tenets of Judaism (and of Christianity as well), he was banished from the community by the rabbinic leaders.

The first transforming winds of modernity blew in with the eighteenth-century Enlightenment, a philo-

In European cities, Jews lived in Jewish quarters or ghettos, first by choice and later by law. This 1880 engraving shows the Jewish quarter of Amsterdam. Though the Jewish population was allowed a large degree of autonomy within the ghettos, there were often walls around the areas and gates that were locked at night. (The Bettmann Archive)

sophical movement that questioned traditional values, stressed human reason, and expressed confidence in human progress. This emphasis on reason implied secularization of the social order and the separation of church and state. In such a state, people of any religion could be citizens, even Jews. This switch from the traditional exclusionary life to the modern inclusionary life was typified by Moses Mendelssohn and by the revolutionary emancipation of the Jews of France.

Moses Mendelssohn

Born in the ghetto of Dessau, Germany, Moses Mendelssohn (1729–1786) grew up a traditional Jew, studying the Talmud and following his rabbi to Berlin to pursue his education. There he steeped himself in classical philosophy and German language and literature. Because of Mendelssohn's charm and his gifts as a philosopher and man of letters, he became a popular figure in influential Gentile circles, thus straddling the line between the Jewish and Gentile worlds.

From his positive experience with the Germans, Mendelssohn came to believe that German Jews should come out of their cultural shell and interact with their host culture. To this end he translated the Hebrew scriptures into German. His treatise *Jerusalem* (1783) argued for further freedom of philosophical inquiry and of the individual conscience. Mendelssohn distinguished between revealed religion, or dogmas, and divine legislation, in keeping with the thought of the Enlightenment. Judaism had no dogmas, he asserted; its beliefs in divine omnipotence, freedom of the will, and immortality were all rationally self-evident. Yet he remained an observant Jew who held that the laws of the Torah—regarding diet, the Sabbath, and other matters—were revealed to Moses "in a miraculous and supernatural way."

In short, Mendelssohn maintained that it was possible to participate in the integrated social world of enlightened Europeans and to be a Jew at the same time. Thus he could write to his friend Gottfried von Herder, "not as Jew to Christian, but as person to person." He never lost his deeply felt bond with Judaism, yet for joining the host society in a way in which religion was irrelevant, he may be described as the first modern Jew.

The French Revolution and the Jews

The Jews had been officially expelled from France in 1394. Yet by the eighteenth century, there were about 50,000 Jews in southern and eastern France. Like all Jews in western Europe, the French Jews lived under a regime that enforced segregation and other demeaning measures.

The French Revolution of 1789 greatly affected Jewish life, not only in France but all over western and central Europe. At the request of the French Jews and with the support of liberal Gentile leaders, the French National Assembly formally emancipated all Jews.

As the armies of France carried the revolution across Europe, the ghettos were opened and the emancipation was proclaimed in Holland, Italy, and elsewhere. Although many Jews welcomed the promise of new economic and political freedom, others feared (with good reason) that they would now become estranged from the disciplines of classical Judaism and be completely absorbed into the culture of the Christian majority.

More than a decade after emancipation, Emperor Napoleon (ruled 1804–1815) convened an assembly of Jewish delegates in 1806 to determine whether the Jews were truly prepared to surrender their status as a semiautonomous people governed by talmudic law in return for the privileges and duties of French citizenship. The delegates assured Napoleon's representatives that traditional Judaism had always deferred to the prevailing law of the land. This had certainly been the case in Babylonia and Spain in all matters that did not conflict with the convictions of the faithful, they declared, and it would surely continue in the freedom of postrevolutionary France.

In previous centuries, rabbinic authority had rested on a double foundation: belief in the divine origin of the Torah together with the political support of the Gentile rulers. Now, however, the national European authorities had become less tolerant of the internal self-governing enclaves, and the scientific bent of the Enlightenment was challenging all belief in revealed religion and traditional faith, Christian and Jewish alike.

Nineteenth-century Jews felt that a new era of freedom and opportunity had begun. But it would demand a new definition of covenant loyalty. The redefinitions that were now required would be no less dramatic than those brought about by the Roman destruction of the Jerusalem temple. Now, as then, no less was at stake than the ability of Judaism to survive in drastically changed circumstances.

Growing numbers of western Jews now found the faith and life style of their fathers intellectually untenable and socially restricting; freed of the political obligation to obey traditions in which they no longer believed, they began to abandon their ancestral heritage. Between 1802 and 1812, for example, one-third of the members of the Berlin Jewish community converted to Christianity.

RESPONSES TO MODERNITY

Reform Judaism and Abraham Geiger

One response to defection was religious reform. Reformers sought to make the traditional synagogue more appealing to its middle-class members. In the traditional medieval synagogue there was no instrumental music, and formal preaching was confined to special Sabbaths. In some German synagogues, reformers introduced organ music, prayers in German as well as Hebrew, and weekly sermons delivered in German. These changes tended to make the liturgy of **Reform Judaism** more like worship in a German Protestant church, and for that reason many tradition-minded Jews resisted them.

Advocates of reform maintained that such alterations would make Jewish ceremonies more pleasing to modern Jews. Before the centuries of ghetto isolation, they said, Judaism had always interacted creatively with the external environment. Talmudic law showed the influence of Roman law, and Hellenistic thought was apparent in some of the agada.

Under the aegis of what came to be known as the "science of Judaism," scholars like Berlin Rabbi Abraham Geiger (1810–1874) justified the latest changes in ritual and belief. Geiger argued that Judaism had always been changing. What God had demanded under one set of conditions (for example, animal sacrifices in the ancient temple) might no longer be required in another. The halacha had to reflect God's progressive revelation in history.

Whereas the traditional synagogue had segregated the sexes, in the more radical Reform synagogues men and women sat together. Some synagogues discarded as unnecessary the prayer shawl (*tallit*) and head covering. Many reformers rejected some of the dietary restrictions as obsolete.

Downplaying Judaism's ritual dimensions, the reformers emphasized its ethical aspects. Whereas Mendelssohn had asserted that Judaism was revealed law, the reformers insisted that Judaism's ethical monotheism, its belief in a God of love and justice, was its noblest distinction. Reform Judaism rejected the messianic yearning for a return to Zion and the rebuilding of the ancient temple in Jerusalem. Peace and brotherhood became its goals, and the reformers believed that these could be achieved on European soil and in accordance with the principles of the Enlightenment.

Rabbi Samson Raphael Hirsch believed separateness was essential for a Jewish presence in the world. His separatist community was the beginning of modern Orthodoxy. (YIVO Institute)

Orthodoxy and Samson Raphael Hirsch

Many Jews regarded the new reforms as a betrayal of authentic Judaism. Rabbi Samson Raphael Hirsch (1808–1888) was one of the most vehement objectors. The leader of a separatist community in Frankfurt am Main, Germany, Hirsch viewed the Jewish emancipation as "a new trial, much severer than the trial of oppression." Though acknowledging the desire to be "at home" in the host nations of Europe, he refused to abandon the hope of ultimate restoration to Zion. Hirsch also maintained that observing traditional Jewish rituals remained the best way of training a *Yisroel-Mensch*—a Jewish person worthy of the blessings of God.

Both wishing to make the tradition's demands more attractive to modern Jews and insisting on the Torah's divine authority, Hirsch sought to define a way of life that was at once appealing and ritually scrupulous. Separateness, he asserted, was essential to maintaining a Jewish presence in the world. Jews should participate actively in secular life, yet not compromise their adherence to Jewish law. Thus was born modern **Orthodox Judaism**.

Positive-Historical Judaism and Zecharias Frankel

A third response to modernity—between the poles of Reform and Orthodoxy—was championed by Zecharias Frankel (1801–1875), another leading German rabbi. Frankel had participated in some of the conferences convened by the German reformers and sympathized with the concept of an evolving tradition. However, he distrusted Reform's readiness to discard some rituals on aesthetic or rational grounds. Change, he declared, must not be decreed by rabbinic confer-

Rabbi Zecharias Frankel saw ritual as the expression of the soul of the Jewish people. His "positive-historical Judaism" eventually emerged as Conservative Judaism in North America. (YIVO Institute)

ences but rather must develop gradually and organically out of the changing life style of the Jewish people.

Although the reformers emphasized ethical monotheism and judged rituals in terms of their relevance to the advance of that grand idea, Frankel saw ritual as the expression of the soul of the Jewish people. He also feared that Reform could become schismatic, and to him the preservation of Jewish unity was critical. His "positive-historical Judaism" would eventually emerge in North America as **Conservative Judaism**.

Haskalah in Eastern Europe

The 3 million Jews living in Russia in the middle of the nineteenth century were also affected by the changes in western Europe. The champions of *Haskalah* ("enlightenment") shared a renewed love for Hebrew literature as well as a consuming interest in Western culture from which their ancestors in the villages of Russia had been insulated. The "enlighteners" encouraged their people to speak Russian rather than Yiddish, to send their children to secular schools, and generally to adopt the ways of the Russian urban middle class.

But all the hopes for an end to political and economic discrimination were soon demolished. When the repressive Alexander III (ruled 1881–1894) came to the throne, he sought to consolidate his power over a disgruntled populace and openly encouraged *pogroms,* massacres of Jews. New restrictive legislation forced even assimilated Jews to feel like aliens on Russian soil.

The Rise of Zionism

The pogroms in Russia and the persistence of anti-Semitism in western Europe gave rise to **Zionism,*** a modern movement of Jewish national liberation. The inspiration for this movement came largely from Jews who had pursued the path of assimilation and felt betrayed by the false promise of emancipation.

The Zionists came to perceive the history of the Jews in the Diaspora as the saga of an outcast people. They saw the growth and intensification of modern nationalism as an ominous threat to a community without its own national home.

Theodor Herzl (1860–1904), a Viennese Jew, reached these conclusions as he covered the famous Dreyfus trial as a foreign correspondent. Herzl's personal encounters with anti-Jewish prejudice during his childhood and young adulthood were suddenly brought into focus when he saw Alfred Dreyfus (1859–1935), a captain in the French army, falsely convicted of treason in a trial with blatantly anti-Semitic overtones. The experience led Herzl to believe that the restoration of Jewish sovereignty was the only practical solution to the outcast status of the Jewish people. Herzl's influential book *The Jewish State* was published in 1896. In the following year he organized and became president of the World Zionist Congress.

*From Zion, a height in Northeastern Jerusalem that was the sight of Solomon's temple. Zionism was the modern movement advocating setting up a Jewish state or religious community in Israel.

Theodore Herzl (center) was the founder of the World Zionist Congress in 1897. Seen here en route to Palestine, Herzl and his followers believed that Jews needed a country of their own to assure their safety and gain the respect of other peoples. (Culver Pictures)

Cultural Zionism

To some Jewish thinkers, especially those in eastern Europe, Zionism promised more than a place of political refuge. The Russian Jewish educator and essayist Asher Ginsberg (1856–1927), who was known by his pen name, Ahad Haam ("One of the People"), viewed the creation of a Jewish center in Palestine as the way to cultivate and preserve historical Jewish values. Ahad Haam voiced the hopes of many Jews who had become estranged from the life of the synagogue and traditional religious concepts. Despite secularism, Ahad Haam and his followers remained proud of the Jewish people and their spiritual creativity. The crisis of modern Jewish life in the Diaspora was far more than just a matter of political insecurity or anti-Semitism. Centuries of exile as a fragmented minority had separated the Jewish body and soul, they argued, and Jews had lost touch with their distinctive ethos. A Jewish center in Palestine would create the necessary conditions to build a community grounded in biblical and talmudic values.

While devotees of Ahad Haam and Herzl debated the distinctions between political and cultural Zionism, hundreds of European Jews began resettling in Palestine. Support of such settlements inspired a zeal similar to that of some Christians for their foreign missions. Through contributions from the Jews of the Diaspora, land was purchased and the cost of settlement was subsidized. Immigrants were called *halutzim* ("pioneers") or *olim* ("those who go up to Zion").

To be sure, there were Jews in Europe and elsewhere who opposed the Zionist solution. Some Orthodox Jews regarded any attempt to precipitate the restoration of Zion as a violation of God's law. Many Reform Jews opposed Zionism as an anachronism in a world moving toward peace and brotherhood. Some felt that this nationalist movement was antithetical to the concept of Judaism as only a religion.

Hitler's extermination of 6 million European Jews during World War II made all such debate irrelevant. In the wake of this horror, for the first time in 2,000 years a Jewish nation was established in Israel.

JUDAISM IN AMERICA

During the nineteenth century the largest Jewish community was still in Europe, but by the middle of the twentieth century it had moved to the United States. The first Jewish settlers in North America, 23 refugees from Brazil, landed at New Amsterdam (New York) in 1654. Not until the failure of the liberal revolutions in Germany in 1848, however, did Jews in North America constitute a true community.

The United States insisted on the separation of church and state, meaning there was no official support for a Jewish community. The frontier spirit encouraged individualism; consequently, a voluntaristic, individual synagogue rather than an organized, all-embracing community became the focus of Jewish life.

Reform Judaism

By 1875 the German Reform movement had been transplanted to America. Rabbi Isaac Mayer Wise (1819–1900), an immigrant from Bohemia, converted Orthodox synagogues into Reform congregations, first at Albany, New York, and later at Cincinnati, Ohio. In 1875 he founded at Cincinnati the Hebrew Union College as a seminary for American rabbis.

The American Jewish reformers restated their faith in the dawn of the messianic age—the fulfillment of the American promise of "life, liberty and the pursuit of happiness." The Pittsburgh Platform of 1885 declared: "We accept as binding only the moral laws and maintain only such ceremonies as elevate and sanctify our lives, but reject all such as are not adopted to the habits of modern civilization."[2] A prayer book was drafted to unify the disparate Reform congregations. It included English translations of the prayers but omitted references to angels, resurrection of the dead (replaced by the immortality of the soul), and petitions for the restoration of Zion. The dietary laws were regarded as obsolete, as were the traditional prayer shawl and head covering.

The Conservative Movement

Reform Judaism in America responded primarily to the needs of the German Jews. But its model for American Jews was seriously challenged at the beginning of the twentieth century by a large wave of immigrants from eastern Europe. Steeped in the rich ceremonialism of traditional Judaism, many newcomers felt ill at ease in the austere and dignified Reform temples. The Conservative movement appealed to these Russian immigrants, and their children provided its basic constituency. By 1887, Conservative Judaism had established its own seminary, the Jewish Theological Seminary in New York City. The Conservative movement, like the Reform, was bent on creating a distinctively American synagogue. Unlike Reform, however, its leaders positioned themselves closer to the milieu of the new immigrants.

Solomon Schechter (1847–1915), a Hebrew scholar who became the leading spokesman for Conservative Judaism, affirmed, like Zecharias Frankel before him, that modification in Jewish ritual observance must grow organically from the life experience of the people. Conservative rabbis retained the head covering and prayer shawl and affirmed the importance of the dietary laws.

Orthodoxy in the United States

Some immigrants, alienated by Reform's radical accommodation to modernity, also found Conservatism too liberal. Inspired by Hirsch's teachings, they founded American Orthodoxy. In 1896 they established the Isaac Elhanan Yeshiva; at first dedicated exclusively to the traditional study of the Talmud, it later became America's principal Orthodox seminary.

Theologically, Conservative Judaism has been more ready than Orthodoxy to acknowledge the evolutionary nature of the Jewish tradition. It has also been more responsive to changes in ritual practice. Orthodox congregations generally maintain a separate section for male and female worshipers, whereas Conservative synagogues have mixed seating. Conservative Judaism permits driving to the synagogue on the Sabbath, but Orthodoxy insists that in observance of the Sabbath ban on work, its members must walk to worship.

The Diminution of Differences

Since World War II the distinctions among the major Jewish religious movements have blurred. All three have endorsed the rebirth of Israel and wrestled with the tension between change and continuity. Even Orthodoxy has been compelled to make some accommodations to the American ambience; for example, the Orthodox prayer books now have English translations. At the same time, the Reform movement has displayed a new openness to previously discarded observances. *Bar mitzvah*—the celebration of a Jewish male's coming of age—was once virtually abandoned by Reform congregations. Now it has been almost universally reinstated. (Indeed, many congregations have recently allowed Jewish females to perform this rite, calling it a *bat mitzvah.*) Generally, what continues to distinguish the three movements is their differing views of rabbinic authority. Orthodox and Conservative leaders insist that only a structured rabbinic authority may interpret the Torah; Reform regards the rabbis as guides rather than final authorities.

THE HOLOCAUST

No event since the destruction of the second temple by the Romans has had an effect on Jewish existence and faith equal to that of the Nazi Holocaust. Led by Adolf

During the Holocaust, German Nazis established death camps where they systematically and gruesomely murdered 6 million Jews, an astonishing one-third of all Jews in the world. Here the Gestapo are seen lining up Polish Jews in the Warsaw ghetto. (UPI/Bettmann)

Hitler, German Nazis established numerous death camps, at Auschwitz and elsewhere, which systematically and gruesomely murdered 6 million Jews, including 1 million children—an astonishing one-third of all Jews in the world! This attempt to annihilate the Jewish people (which the Nazis called the "final solution to the Jewish problem") led to the coining of a new word, *genocide,* literally "murder of a race."

Hitler's obsessive hatred of Jews bore some links to earlier manifestations of anti-Jewish prejudice. Like other demagogues before him, he sought to mobilize a dissatisfied people against a visible and vulnerable enemy. Hitler's war against the Jews added an unprecedented chapter to the history of anti-Jewish prejudice. During the Middle Ages and the early modern period, the anti-Jewish myths that erupted periodically in Christian Europe had been connected, at least theoretically, to an appeal for conversion and were based on the premise that if all Jews would accept Christ as the Messiah, there would be no "Jewish problem." Hitler's racist view, however, offered no way of avoiding the stigma of being Jewish: all persons of Jewish blood, he intoned, were members of an inferior and expendable race.

Many survivors of the Nazi slaughter experienced a major crisis of faith. Theologians and laypersons alike pondered the unanswerable question: If God was all-powerful and also ethical, why did he permit this savagery? Some Jewish thinkers like Martin Buber (1878–1965) spoke of the "hiddenness" or "eclipse" of God. Others redefined the God of the covenant: God had infinite love but only limited power. Still others found new meaning in the concept of Israel as the "suffering servant" of Isaiah 53 who bore witness to God in a world not yet prepared for the moral restraints of the Torah. And some Jews emerged from the Holocaust no longer able to believe in God at all.

In the United States, the main effect was to draw the Jewish community together: German and Russian Jews, religious and secular Jews, all felt united by a common fate and a renewed determination to survive. The Jewish philosopher and theologian Emil Fackenheim described this mood as a religious commitment:

> Jews are not permitted to hand Hitler a posthumous victory. Jews are commanded to survive as Jews lest their people perish. They are commanded to remember the victims of Auschwitz lest their memory perish. They are forbidden to despair of God lest Judaism perish. . . . For a Jew to break this commandment would be to do the unthinkable—to respond to Hitler by doing his work.[3]

THE REBIRTH OF ISRAEL

By the end of World War II, Jewish opposition to the creation of the state of Israel was dwindling. In the post-Holocaust world, it was obvious that Jews had to establish their own sovereign nation.

In theological terms, Israel's rebirth served as a desperately needed sign of grace. The people of the covenant, devastated by the Nazi scourge, were given some reason to celebrate anew the goodness of life. Realizing the hopes of Ahad Haam, a culture built on the distinctive Jewish ethos now began to take shape. Israel's civic calendar is determined by the feasts of the Bible and the Talmud (see the accompanying box, "The Jewish Calendar Year"). The Hebrew language is spoken, and biblical history is taught to Israeli children as their nation's saga.

The archetypal figure of Israel's rebirth was the nation's first prime minister, David Ben-Gurion (1886–1973), who combined Herzl's vision of a politically empowered Jewish community with Ahad Haam's vision of Israel as a new testing ground for the Hebraic spirit. Since the founding of the state after nearly 2,000 years of political subjugation, the Jews in Israel once again confront the challenges of power and the unfamiliar privileges and burdens of government. Israel's leaders have grappled with enormous problems of war and peace, as well as the constant challenge of meeting the needs of the country's Arab minority without endangering its security.

Israel has also dealt with Jewish religious diversity. In earlier times, Gentile authorities often determined which Jewish group gained official sanction—whether the Hasidim or their opponents, and later, Orthodoxy or Reform, would prevail. Today in Israel, Jewish authorities determine the legitimacy of a particular Jewish movement. At present Orthodoxy is granted special privileges not accorded Conservative and Reform Judaism. This issue is a major source of contention among Jews both in Israel and in the Diaspora.

The place of Israel in the life of the Jewish people as a whole has not yet been articulated in a way that satisfies all Jews. Some hold that a truly authentic

David Ben-Gurion was the first prime minister of the new state of Israel. He combined Herzl's vision of a politically empowered Jewish community with Ahad Haam's vision of Israel as a new testing ground for the Hebraic spirit. (Religious News Service)

Jewish life can now be lived only in Israel, where one can lead a life that fully embodies classical Jewish concepts of justice and love. Others believe that Israel must now serve as the spiritual center for the sons and daughters in the Diaspora.

MODES OF JEWISH WITNESS

The integrated and unified life of rabbinic Judaism has been lost in modern times. Freedom has brought diversity and pluralism. No longer do all Jews declare with a single voice the binding authority of the revealed Torah. One voice now heard is Orthodoxy's, which insists that God's will is embodied in the Torah and in talmudic texts but must be authoritatively interpreted by a particular group of rabbis in each generation. Other Jews contend that the Bible, however divinely inspired, remains a human response to the commanding presence of God. There are also many Jews who do not regard themselves as religious, do not belong to any synagogue, and yet remain proud of their heritage. They praise the cultural and ethical dimensions of Judaism and express hope that their children will remain proud of the Jewish people, its values, and its history.

Some Jews fear that the prevailing diversity of practice in matters of halacha seriously threatens the integrity of the covenant. Traditionally, a Jew is a person who is either born to a Jewish mother or has converted to Judaism through a process that includes ritual circumcision and/or immersion. At present many Reform rabbis also consider a child with one Jewish parent as Jewish if that child is being reared as a Jew. Orthodox and Conservative rabbis require a religious divorce before remarriage, whereas Reform rabbis generally accept a civil decree as adequate. Orthodox and Conservative rabbis will officiate only at a mar-

Many aspects of Jewish life meet in modern Israel as Jews confront the problems of war and peace and deal with the diversity of Jewish religious life. (Reuters/Bettmann)

The Jewish Calendar Year

Practicing Jews maintain a pattern of ritual observance that enables them to live by covenant (or sacred) time. Most of these observances commemorate events in the sacred history of Israel, occasions when God revealed himself to the people. Through ritual reenactment of these events, participants are urged to remember and be faithful.

The cornerstone of Jewish observance is the weekly Sabbath. Strict traditionalists refrain from all work and set aside the 24-hour period from sunset Friday to sunset Saturday for worship, study, and leisurely family fellowship. Many Jews who do not observe the prohibition against work nevertheless honor the Sabbath eve with a festive meal, the lighting of candles, and the recitation of a special prayer (*Kiddush*) praising God for ordaining the Sabbath as a commemoration of the creation of the world and the gift of life.

At each Sabbath morning service in the synagogue, a portion of the Torah scroll is read and interpreted by the rabbis. During the service boys and girls who have just reached the age of religious majority (13) may read from the Torah and pledge to be faithful to its teachings. The first performance of this ceremony marks a young person's status as a *bar* or *bat mitzvah* ("son or daughter of the commandment").

The Jewish year formally begins in the fall with Rosh Hashanah. Prayers in the synagogue emphasize humanity's accountability to a just God and the need for spiritual renewal. The high holy-day season concludes ten days after Rosh Hashanah with the observance of the great fast day, Yom Kippur, the Day of Atonement. Many Jews spend most of this day in the synagogue. The liturgy emphasizes humanity's moral frailty and need for God's reconciling love. Sins against others are forgiven by God, but only if the sinner seeks the forgiveness of the person wronged.

Five days after Yom Kippur comes the beginning of the weeklong Sukkot (Feast of Tabernacles). It is customary for booths to be constructed and gaily decorated with the fruits of the fall harvest. Each synagogue has a *sukkah* (booth), and many families build one adjacent to their

riage between two Jews, but many Reform rabbis will officiate at marriages in which one of the partners is not Jewish. Such issues are not likely to be resolved in the near future.

The Voice of Jewish Women

Recently a new mode of Jewish witness, that of Jewish women, has been heard. Many have noted that from Abraham, Isaac, and Jacob to the authors of the rabbinic Talmud, Judaism has presented itself and its momentous events in terms of the activities and concerns of men. The Bible and the Talmud are the central focus of Jewish religious life, and the exclusion of women's voices from them has shaped Jewish self-perception for centuries, they note. For example, when the Torah is read in a liturgical context, women are continually excluded, as over and over again they homes. Sharing meals in the sukkah is a way of fulfilling the biblical commandment in Leviticus 23:42–44. The decorated booth is a reminder of God's display of providential love to the ancient Hebrews living in precarious shelters during their years of wandering in the wilderness. Sukkot ends with the observance of Simchat Torah (rejoicing over the Torah). At this time the annual cycle of Torah reading has brought the congregation to the end of Deuteronomy, and the scroll is now rewound to the beginning of Genesis. This festival, which includes a joyous processional with the Torah scrolls, celebrates the renewal of the Torah reading cycle. In many synagogues it is also the time to consecrate children newly enrolled in religious school.

The Jewish calendar next brings Hanukah, the Feast of Lights, which occurs at the winter solstice. This festival is based on the story of Judah Maccabee's successful battle to free Judea from Syrian King Antiochus's religious persecution in 165 B.C.E. This victory was followed by a rededication of the temple to the service of Yahweh. According to a talmudic legend, the victors found a pitcher with enough oil to last only a day, but miraculously the oil lasted for eight days. In commemoration, Jews light candles at home in special candelabra for eight nights, offering prayers of Thanksgiving to God. A recent addition to the Hanukah observance is the exchange of gifts, a practice borrowed from Christians celebrating Christmas.

In late winter Purim is observed. Based on the Book of Esther, Purim commemorates the survival of the Jews despite the efforts of many enemies to destroy them. The scroll of Esther is read in the synagogue, and children masquerade in costumes based on characters in the narrative. A carnival atmosphere prevails.

The major spring festival is the weeklong observance of Passover. Centered in the home, Passover features a special meal (Seder) at which the family and guests recount the story of Israel's bondage in Egypt and God's mighty act of deliverance. A special prayer book (the Haggadah) tells the story, and edible symbols lend vividness to the account. For example, unleavened bread (matzah) is a reminder that the slaves left Egypt in such haste that their bread dough had no time to rise (Exod. 12:39).

Seven weeks after Passover is Shavuot (Feast of Weeks), which commemorates the covenant at Sinai and the divine revelation of the Torah. In many synagogues this is when 15-year-olds who have studied with the rabbis reaffirm their own covenant as part of a colorful service.

have heard a history that is centered on men and reflects male concerns. Judith Plaskow argued that

> when the story of Sinai is recited as part of the annual cycle of Torah readings or as a special reading for Shavuot, women each time hear ourselves thrust aside anew, eavesdropping on a conversation among men and between man and God.[4]

Such women have also noted that such Talmudic passages as the following prayer have shaped Jewish self-perceptions:

> *Blessed art thou, Lord our God, King of the*
> *Universe, who hast not made me a gentile.*
> *Blessed art thou, Lord our God, King of the*
> *Universe, who hast not made me a slave.*
> *Blessed art thou, Lord our God, King of the*
> *Universe, who hast not made me a woman.*[5]

As women have begun to speak out from the feminist perspective of the late twentieth century, they have attempted to bring about a change in such attitudes. They see themselves as following the model of the Babylonian rabbis, Maimonides and other leaders, who reinterpreted traditional Jewish texts to reshape their religion in response to the needs of their changing constituencies. Similarly grounding their claims on creative interpretations of scripture, many Jewish women have argued for a new understanding of God's covenant with *all* of the Hebrew people. In the innovative feminist Midrash, the concerns of women, so long absent from biblical commentary, are being expressed in stories, legends, and liturgical material. As a result of such efforts, some Jewish institutions have expanded: women have been ordained as rabbis, and, paralleling the boy's *bar mitzvah,* a 13-year-old girl may now become *bat mitzvah,* a "daughter of the commandment."

The feminist reconstruction of Judaism has met resistance. Orthodox Judaism, for example, still holds that women cannot be included in the *minyan*—the quorum of ten men traditionally required for a prayer service. Orthodox Jews also continue to define the understanding of the Jewish people in its traditional but patriarchal terms.

Jewish feminists respond that if significant changes are to come, such habits as using male gender language for God and assuming that men have the primary responsibility for the fulfillment of commandments, must be transformed. Though such assumptions lie at the heart of centuries of Jewish tradition, many Jewish women and men are acting to change them because they see them as contrary to the message of the covenant and as inappropriate in the modern Jewish community.

In American society, Jews both male and female are seeking ways to enjoy the blessings of social equality in civic life without losing the distinctiveness and continuity of their Jewish heritage. Grateful for the unprecedented openness and freedom of American life, Jewish leaders are nonetheless aware of the difficulties of promoting Jewish fidelity to a particular tradition in a society that attaches little significance to religion.

But recently, many observers have noticed a change in contemporary attitudes. Whereas people once believed that science, technology, and politics would offer solutions to their problems, few still have faith in these as ultimate answers or see them as satisfying frameworks for meaning. This loss of faith, combined with frustrations over the meaninglessness of the secular life, has led many people, both Jews and non-Jews, to a growing interest in and openness to spirituality and the religious life. As part of this movement, many modern Jews have turned with renewed seriousness back toward their tradition's symbols, stories, and religious observances. They have found new meaning in the continuity that has bound together God, Torah, and Israel for millennia.

Rabbi Sally Priesand, the first practicing woman rabbi, is seen here in 1972. Following the model of the Babylonian rabbis, who reinterpreted traditional Jewish texts and practices in response to the needs of the times, many women seek a feminist reconstruction of Judaism. (UPI/Bettmann)

NOTES

1 Edward H. Flannery, *The Anguish of the Jews: Twenty-three Centuries of Anti-Semitism* (New York: Macmillan, 1965), p. 304, n. 1.

2 G. W. Plaut, *The Growth of Reform Judaism* (New York: World Union for Progressive Judaism, 1965), p. 34.

3 Emil Fackenheim, *Quest for Past and Future* (Bloomington: Indiana University Press, 1968), p. 70.

4 Judith Plaskow, "Jewish Memory from a Feminist Perspective," in *Weaving the Visions: New Patterns in Feminist Spirituality,* ed. Judith Plaskow and Carol P. Christ (San Francisco: Harper & Row, 1989), pp. 39–40.

5 Judith Baskin, "The Separation of Women in Rabbinic Judaism," in *Women, Religion and Social Change,* ed. Yvonne Haddad and Ellison Findley (Albany: State University of New York Press, 1988), p. 6.

ASSOCIATION

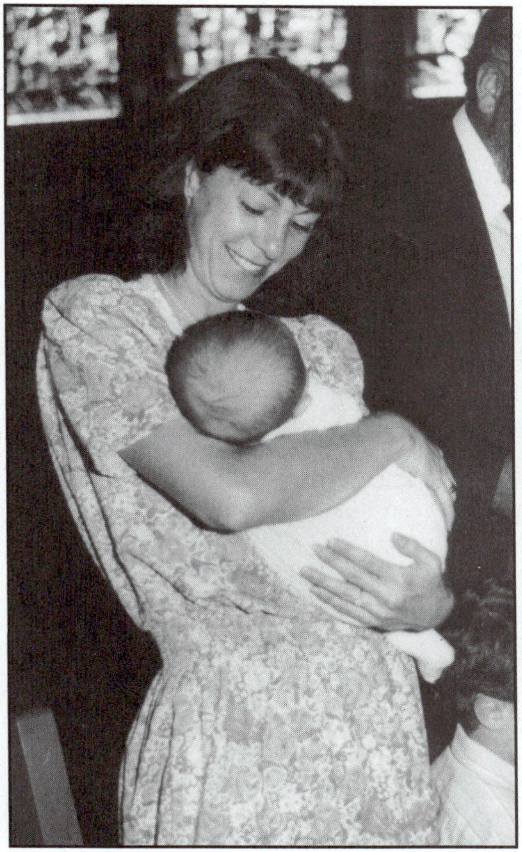

PART SIX

CHRISTIANITY

B.C.E.	C.E.		500		1000		1500		2000

● Birth of
Jesus of Nazareth
(c. 4 B.C.E.)

Coronation of ●━━━━━━━━━━━━━━━━━━━
Charlemagne   Dominance of the "Ideal of Christendom" (9th–16th centuries)
as emperor
of West (800)   ━● Great Schism (1378–1417)

● Legalization of   ━━━━━   Posting of ●
Christianity by   Viking raids on   95 Theses by
Edict of Milan   Christian centers   Martin Luther (1517)
(313)   in East and West
                     (9th and 10th   Publication of ●
                     centuries)   Calvin's Institutes
                                         (1536)

● Death of   Vatican ●
Paul of Tarsus   End of Iconoclastic ●   Council of Trent ●   Council I
(c. 60 C.E.)   Controversy (842)   (1545–1563)   (1869–1870)

━━━   Break between Eastern and ●   End of wars of   Vatican ●
Justin Martyr   Western Churches (1054)   religion by Peace of Council II
(c. 100–c. 165)   Westphalia (1648)   (1962–1965)

━━━   Capture of Jerusalem by ●
Irenaeus of Lyons   Western Crusaders (1099)   ━━━━━━
(2nd century)   Revival of classical ideals
                                               in Italy and gradual
● Conversion of   spread to northern Europe
Tertullian   (15th and 16th centuries)
(c. 197)
                     Establishment of Henry VIII as ●
                     head of Anglican church (1534)   ● Beginnings
━━━   of Oxford
St. Antony of the Desert   Toleration Act of 1689 in Britain ● Movement
(c. 251–356)   ━━━ in England
                                                               (1830s)
━━━   Rise of Puritanism in England; Development
Augustine of Hippo   of Pietism in Germany and Britain; Spread ● Voltaire's
(354–430)   of Anglicanism, Puritanism, and Pietism   Philosophical
                     to British North America (17th century)   Dictionary
                                                                 (1764)
● Formation of   Francis of Assisi (1182–1226) ━━━
New Testament   ● Immanuel
(late first century) Thomas Aquinas (1225–1274) ━━━   Kant's Critique
                                                                of Pure
                   Meister Eckhart (1260–1328) ━━━   Reason (1781)

                          Las Casas (1474–1566) ━━━

                       Teresa of Avila (1515–1582) ━━━

                 John Wesley's conversion experience (1738) ●

                          ━━━   Friedrich ●
Founding of Monte Cassino ●   Rise of Franciscan   Schleiermacher's
by St. Benedict (529)   and Dominican orders The Christian
                          (13th century)   Faith (1821–1822)

                          ━━━
                      Founding of many   Karl Barth's Epistle to ●
                      Western universities   the Romans (1919)
                      (13th century)

B.C.E.	C.E.		500		1000		1500		2000

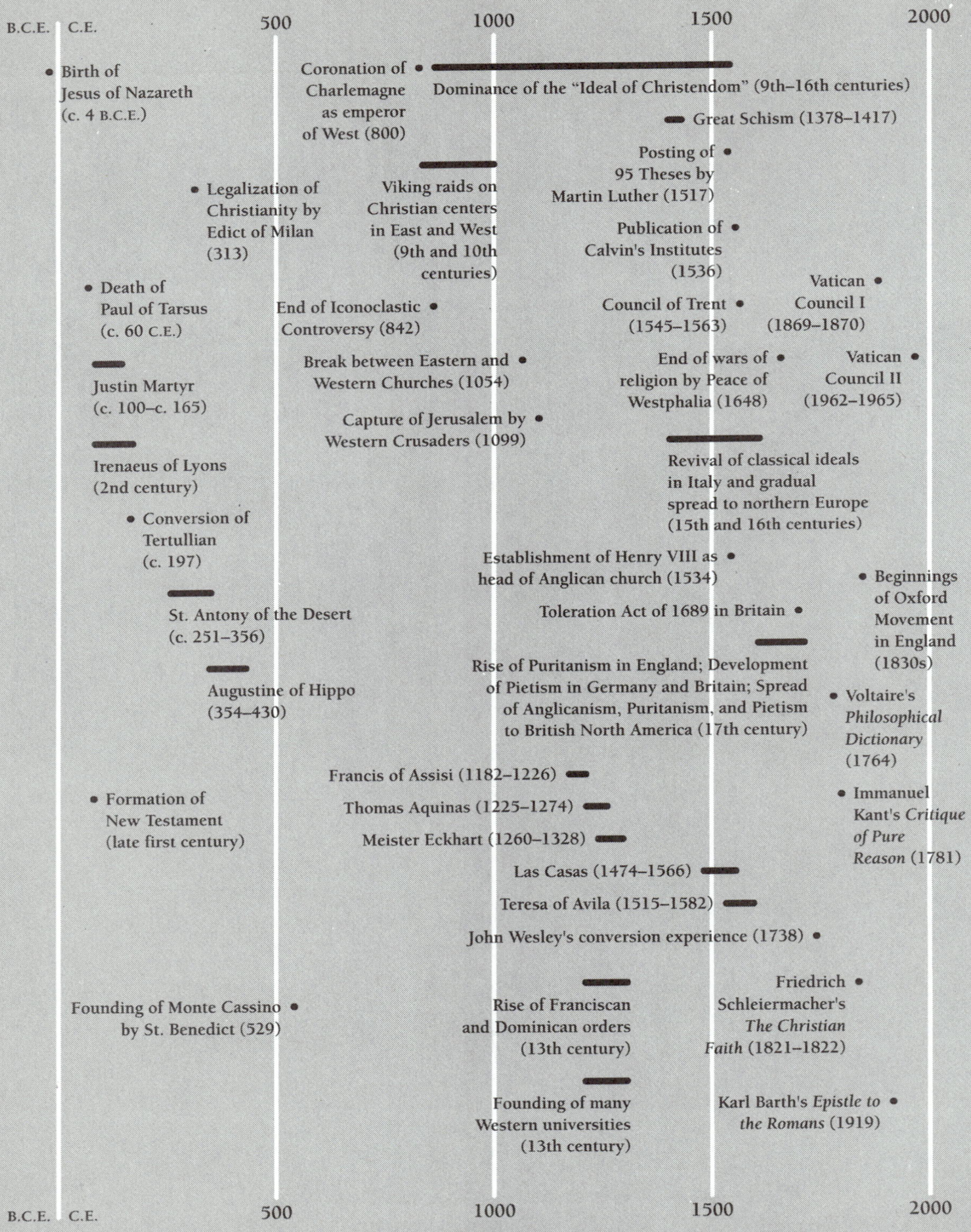

CHRISTIANITY TIME LINE

CHRISTIANITY

CHAPTER 19

THE FORMATION OF THE CHURCH

Christianity is the world's largest religion, with more than a billion and a half adherents, located on every continent. It gets its name from the figure on whose life and death it is centered, Jesus of Nazareth. Jesus was a historical figure, and Christianity is a religion oriented around history: Christians believe that God is the sovereign of history, present and active in historical events, directing history to its culmination. Christianity is also a revealed religion, with a set of scriptures believed to be divinely inspired (though understandings of that differ widely among Christians). Looking beyond Jesus's death to his resurrection, Christians see in Jesus not only a human man but also the revelation of God.

The tension between the historical and the revealed plays itself out throughout Christian history, especially in the church's relations with political powers and in its understanding of Jesus. Beginning as a persecuted sect under an unsympathetic Roman Empire, in less than four centuries Christianity came to dominate the empire, culminating as the most powerful force in medieval Europe. As its political power waned, however, followers called for a return to the revealed word of God, with less emphasis on the political structures of the church and more on Christ as the revelation of God.

As noted in the introductory chapter, religion does not develop in a vacuum but reflects the culture with which it is intertwined. As societies evolved and as worldviews shifted, crumbled, and formed anew, the understanding of the church, the interpretation of the sacraments, and the perceptions of Jesus also evolved and shifted. In Part Six we shall be looking at how Christianity evolved, how church and society have been related at different points, and how that relationship has been reflected in the conception of the person of Jesus and the sacraments of the church.

CHRISTIAN ORIGINS

BACKGROUND: ROMAN CONTEXT, JEWISH WORLDVIEW

In 63 B.C.E. a Roman army led by Pompey conquered Jerusalem, making Palestine a Roman province. Through annexation, conquest, and inheritance, Rome soon controlled the entire Mediterranean area, from Britain to North Africa. Roads, sea lanes, relay stations, and a common language all helped to unify the Roman Empire, permitting safe travel and the dispersal of ideas and thus smoothing the way for the spread of Christianity.

Excellent administrators with a passion for order and discipline, the Romans believed that the *Pax Romana* (Peace of Rome)—brought about and enforced by their military might—reflected the order and harmony of the universe. At the heart of Roman society lay a great reverence for tradition and custom, especially in Roman religion with its emphasis on duty and loyalty. Centered on the cult of the emperor, religion bound Roman society and its far-flung empire together. The Romans believed that the "genius" or divine guiding spirit of the emperor brought celestial peace to earth. As such the emperor became the symbol of Roman power, to be honored by all. On the whole the Romans were tolerant of other religions in conquered lands: as long as the peoples were willing to honor the emperor, they could continue to follow their own religions. As will be seen, however, Christianity proved an exception to the rule.

Christianity's Roots in Judaism

Christianity began as a Jewish sect, sharing the Jewish worldview. First and foremost, this included belief in a personalized monotheistic God who judges and rewards human actions. As opposed to Roman religion with its many gods, Judaism proclaimed one and only one God with an exclusive claim to worship. Polytheism, and thus Roman society, was seen as blasphemous and wicked. Only the law of God was considered absolute and true, not the law of the Romans; when the two came into conflict, Jews were to obey the law of God and be willing to die for it.

Second, this worldview also included the hope that God would save the Jewish people. For many, this salvation had political overtones, involving the overthrow of Roman domination and the establishment of a new order in which all people would worship the one God of Israel. This new order, the kingdom of God, was expected to come with a cataclysmic upheaval at the *eschaton,* or end of time, and would be ushered in by a messiah, or savior. Some expected this messiah to be a political figure like the revered King David; others looked for a semimythical "son of man" descending on clouds of glory from heaven. When Jesus appeared, his followers applied such titles and hopes for salvation to him.

In addition to monotheism and the expectation of a saving messiah, Christianity also inherited the Hebrew scriptures as the revealed word of God and the Jewish concern with ethical living. Not simply limited to special times or places of worship, Jews and Christians taught that one's belief in God should pervade one's whole life, resulting in acts of justice, mercy, and compassion.

To these Jewish tenets, early Christian interpreters added the belief that God sent a son, who is himself also God, to be born as a human being and to share human life. Jesus was believed to be the *incarnation* of God—God in human form. Thus the promise of the kingdom of God was reinterpreted in a new way: instead of arriving as either a mighty king or a mythical figure descending from heaven, God had come to earth as a humble human being. Jesus was thus called the Christ (from *Christos,* "anointed one," the Greek for "messiah"). Just how the incarnation should be understood, and how God could be present in Jesus yet still remain one God, has been a subject of debate throughout Christian history.

JESUS OF NAZARETH

Stories about Jesus

In Christianity's early days converts learned about the kingdom of God with its promise of salvation through the preaching of Jesus's followers and the stories they told about him, placed within the context of Israel's historical circumstances. Following the Roman conquest, Judea was ruled by an ambitious king from southern Palestine, Herod the Great (ruled 37–4 B.C.E.), who rebuilt the temple in Jerusalem and claimed the right to appoint the high priest of Judaism and to oversee Jewish activities. After his death Herod was succeeded by his son Archelaus, whose incompetence led Rome to appoint a series of imperial governors for Judea. The best known of these in Christian history was Pontius Pilate (governed 26–36 C.E.), whose misuse of temple funds and brutal repression of protesters increased the enmity the Jews felt toward their Roman overlords.

Jewish responses to Rome's oppression varied. The Sadducees, conservative members of the religious elite who controlled the temple priesthood, tried to protect Israel by placating its Roman rulers. The Pharisees, reforming rabbis who tried to remain faithful to God by adhering to the law of the Torah, resisted Roman control in matters of religion. Some groups, notably the Essenes, withdrew to a semimonastic life in the desert near the Dead Sea, while the Zealots, a party of fanatical nationalists, believed that only God should rule Israel and so worked to overthrow Roman rule militarily. Most Israelites did not resist openly but hoped that the Messiah promised by the Jewish scriptures would appear to save the situation.

PALESTINE AT THE TIME OF JESUS

Into this atmosphere of discontent came Jesus, an itinerant teacher from the town of Nazareth in the northern province of Galilee. Miracle worker, healer, preacher, and Jewish holy man, Jesus spoke in parables of the nearness of God, the need for change, and love of God and neighbor. A small band of followers became attached to him during his brief ministry. As his reputation spread, Pilate became concerned that he would stir up the flames of discontent and, perhaps fearing a riot, executed him in the gruesome Roman fashion: crucifixion, a slow and painful death by being nailed to a cross. His followers, dispirited and terrified at his demise, were astonished at reports of his resurrection (literally, "rising again"). This news, buttressed by a series of reported visions or visitations by Jesus to his followers, caught the people's imaginations; his resurrection and its significance became the focus of their early stories.

Just as Israel had long defined itself by its stories of the Exodus from Egypt and God's continuing action in human history, so Christians defined themselves through stories of Jesus. They recounted what he had said and done—the parables he had told, the miracles he and his followers had performed, the narratives of his death and resurrection. To his followers, Jesus's life and resurrection were signs of his divinity and pointed to the kingdom of God he would bring.

Originally circulating orally among early followers, these stories were gradually collected and edited into coherent narratives known as the **gospels** (Anglo-Saxon *godspel*, "good news"). Of the many gospel narratives in circulation, these communities eventually accepted four as trustworthy—Matthew (written c. 70–85 C.E.), Mark (c. 65–75 C.E.), Luke (c. 70–75 C.E.), and John (c. 85–95 C.E.)—attributed by tradition to close followers of Jesus.

Matthew and Luke begin with stories of Jesus's miraculous birth to a virgin, Mary, and her husband, Joseph, in a stable in Bethlehem and include genealogies to link Joseph to King David, from whom the Messiah was to come. Both take care to date Jesus's birth in order to tie their stories to a particular historical time—thus affirming Jesus's humanity as well as his divine origins.

The narratives of Jesus's public ministry begin with the prophet John the Baptist preaching in the wilderness. John announced that he was the forerunner of the Messiah, sent to preach the coming of the kingdom of God and the need to repent (literally, "turn around") and be baptized (**baptism** is a ritual cleansing by water). John baptized Jesus in the Jordan River, proclaiming him to be the promised Messiah and initiating his ministry. At this moment, according to the accounts, Jesus experienced a divine vision or call:

> And just as he was coming up out of the water, he saw the heavens torn apart and the Spirit descending like a dove on him. And a voice came from heaven, "You are my Son, the Beloved; with you I am well pleased." (Mark 1:10–11)[1]

Following this experience, Jesus retreated to the desert for a time, then reappeared preaching a message similar to John's: "Repent, for the kingdom of heaven has come near" (Matt. 4:17).

The large center panel of this sixteenth-century Greek work, "Great Deesis with Dodekoarton," depicts Christ enthroned in heaven. The side panels show scenes of his birth, ministry, crucifixion, and resurrection, events on which Christianity is based. (Elvehjem Museum of Art)

Jesus soon gathered followers, reportedly summoning fishermen such as Peter, James, and another John, who dropped their nets and joined Jesus in his wandering ministry. Though tradition speaks of 12 disciples, Jesus's close followers probably fluctuated in number and included women such as Mary Magdalene and Joanna. Although most of the immediate disciples were poor and uneducated, followers came from all social strata. Many of the women in particular had the means to feed and house Jesus and his disciples on their travels, and even a member of the Jewish Sanhedrin (ruling council), Joseph of Arimathea, was a secret admirer.

Prominent also among the gospel stories were accounts of healing, exorcism, and other miracles. These stories, plus those of the virgin birth, descent of the Holy Spirit of God in the act of baptism, and Jesus's charismatic authority, established Jesus's divine origins in Christians' eyes and affirmed their own identity as followers of God in Jesus Christ. Christians began seeing themselves in these stories both as recipients of God's favor and messengers of divine grace. The cry of blind Bartimaeus calling from the roadside—"Jesus, Son of David, have mercy on me" (Mark 10:47)—became a similar prayer for mercy on Christian lips. And the feeding of 5,000 people with a few loaves and fish symbolized Christ feeding Christians with his own body in the Eucharist.

Key Teachings of Jesus

It is hard to know how much of the gospels is historical fact and how much is interpretation developed to meet the needs of the worshiping communities. Modern scholars have debated which biblical passages most clearly convey the core of the historical Jesus's teachings, but most agree that at least the Lord's Prayer (Luke 11:2–4), parts of the Sermon on the Mount (Matt. 5–7), and the parables (for example, Luke 15:11–32) do so.

It was common for popular Jewish leaders to teach a special prayer as a sign of secret fellowship, and Jesus's prayer, now known as the Lord's Prayer, taught his understanding of the kingdom of God. The following reconstruction from Aramaic, the language used in Israel in the first century C.E., is believed to best approach the actual words of Jesus:

> *Dear Father,*
> *Hallowed be thy name,*
> *Thy kingdom come,*
> *Our bread for tomorrow give us today,*
> *And forgive us our debts as we also herewith forgive*
> *our debtors,*
> *And let us not fall into temptation.*[2]

The controlling image of this prayer is of a loving and protecting father whom worshipers address with child-like trust. Jesus's use of "Father" suggests the warmth, intimacy, and trust that characterize a close parent-child relationship, and he invited his followers into such a relationship with God.

The Lord's Prayer is part of Matthew's version of the Sermon on the Mount (Matt. 5–7; cf. Luke 6:17–49), probably a reconstructed account of what people remembered of Jesus's preaching rather than a verbatim record. Although Jesus's teaching often centered on the Mosaic law, Jesus reinterpreted it with a confidence and audacity that astonished his hearers:

> You have heard that it was said to those of ancient times, "You shall not murder"; and "whoever murders shall be liable to judgment." But I say to you that if you are angry with a brother or sister, you will be liable to judgment; and if you insult a brother or sister, you will be liable to the council; and if you say, "You fool," you will be liable to the hell of fire. (Matt. 5:21–23)

Here the Mosaic law remains valid but becomes extended, intensified, and internalized: not only is the act prohibited, but even the desire is condemned.

Jesus's commentary on the Mosaic law forms part of his larger teaching on the kingdom of God. Instead of the earthly kingdom sought by Jewish nationalists, the kingdom of God is a spiritual kingdom characterized by love of God and love of neighbor. All who truly repent and obey God's commands will be part of this new order; thus the gospels portray Jesus telling self-righteous religious leaders that the poor, the sinful, and the social outcasts will enter the kingdom of God before they will.

Much of Jesus's teaching about the kingdom of God was in the form of **parables**, short stories drawn from everyday life to surprise listeners into insight. Jesus compares God to a shepherd who seeks the one lost sheep until it is found or to a woman searching for a lost coin:

> What woman having ten silver coins, if she loses one of them, does not light a lamp, sweep the house, and search carefully until she finds it? When she has found it, she calls together her friends and neighbors, saying, "Rejoice with me, for I have found the coin that I had lost." Just so, I tell you, there is joy in the presence of the angels of God over one sinner who repents. (Luke 15:8–10)

In one of the best-known parables, that of the prodigal son (Luke 15:11–32), Jesus identifies God with a father who celebrates the return of a runaway son. God's overwhelming love, generosity, and mercy accept sinners and usher them into the kingdom. Because of his concern for sinners, Jesus's opponents often charged him with impiety, accusing him of breaking the law of God. In the parables Jesus typically counters these charges by emphasizing God's commands to care for the poor and the outcast.

The teachings preserved and presented in the gospels show a Jesus who is in continuity with the Jewish past yet radically reshapes it for the new age. Christians could point to the authority of Jesus as one sent from God in their own confrontations with Jewish leaders who insisted on the complete and literal fulfillment of the law. Parables demonstrating Jesus's compassion for the outcasts and invitation to sinners over the pious attracted the poor and downtrodden; those outside the law felt welcome in the new faith. And ultimately such stories justified Christianity's separation from its parent religion, for they showed that Jesus had greater authority than the rabbis.

One of the best-known parables of Jesus, that of the prodigal son, has inspired many works of art including this piece by Mastroianni. Jesus identifies God with a father who celebrates the return of a runaway son. (The Bettmann Archive)

Death and Resurrection

The stories about Jesus and the accounts of his teachings gained much of their significance when seen through the prism of Jesus's Passion—his suffering, death, and miraculous resurrection.

The Passion narratives begin with Jesus's last visit to Jerusalem. There his opponents tried to trap him into making a blasphemous or treasonous statement; parrying his enemies' challenges only angered them further. It was the time of the Jewish Passover, and the gospels record that Jesus gathered his followers around him to celebrate the Passover feast. During this evening meal—the famous Last Supper—Jesus blessed bread, broke it, and gave it to his disciples, saying, "Take, eat: This is my Body, which is given for you. Do this for the remembrance of me." After supper, he blessed the cup of wine and gave it to them, saying, "Drink this, all of you: This is my Blood of the new Covenant, which is shed for you and for many for the forgiveness of sins. Whenever you drink it, do this for the remembrance of me." [3] Though Jesus's blessing of the bread and wine accorded with Jewish tradition, his identification of himself with them was a startling departure from tradition and was interpreted by Christians as Jesus's identification of himself as the new Passover lamb who would die for the sins of the world. Again, the gospels present Jesus as the fulfillment and culmination of Jewish law, which in turn was recast as a foreshadowing of what would yet happen. Moreover, the Last Supper formed the model for the **Eucharist** (from the Greek for "thanksgiving"), the chief act of Christian worship, which recollects and re-presents Christ's giving of himself. How Jesus is identified with the bread and wine and what transpires during the Eucharist have been debated throughout Christian history.

After the meal Jesus went outside to pray in the garden of Gethsemane, where he was arrested, brought before the Jewish authorities, tried by the high priest, and found guilty of blasphemy. Pontius Pilate ordered the execution on a hill outside of Jerusalem, where Jesus and two other criminals were crucified at the same time. The account of the trial, scholars agree, is dangerously flawed and probably unfairly places responsibility on the Jewish authorities: Jewish court procedure demanded that capital crimes be tried only during the day and for more than one sitting, and there is no instance of the death sentence for blasphemy for merely claiming to be the Messiah.[4]

Jesus's arrest and trial terrified his friends—Peter denied knowing him, and most of the other disciples fled. Only Jesus's mother, a few women disciples, and the apostle John waited at the foot of the cross where Jesus died that Friday (later called Good Friday). Because the Sabbath would begin at sundown, they laid Jesus in a tomb borrowed from a wealthy admirer. On Sunday the women went to the tomb and, to their astonishment, found it empty. While there is some confusion over who was the first to see the resurrected Jesus, most narratives portray Jesus appearing to Mary

Jesus and his apostles gathered to celebrate the Jewish Passover feast. This Last Supper formed the model for the Eucharist. In this work by Volterra, Judas is depicted below the table with Satan represented as a creature with wings and a snake as an appendage. (Alinari/Art Resource)

Magdalene, commissioning her to tell the rest of the disciples the good news. Other followers reported seeing the risen Jesus several additional times.

These stories became the foci of the church's claims that Jesus was the incarnation of God. Jesus's life and teachings were interpreted in light of belief in the resurrection.

THE SPREAD OF THE FAITH

Christian missionaries traveled to the main cities of the Hellenistic world, telling of Jesus's life, death, and resurrection, claiming that he was the Messiah who would usher in the new age. They taught Jews first, especially in the far-flung synagogues of the Diaspora, but soon Gentiles (non-Jews) also joined the congregations.

Although the Acts of the Apostles and the letters of Paul provide some source material, we know little about most of these early activities. Clearly, these first followers believed that they had been commissioned by the risen Jesus to carry on his ministry, as seen in Matthew's account:

> And Jesus came and said to them, "All authority in heaven and earth has been given to me. Go therefore and make disciples of all nations, baptizing them in the name of the Father and of the Son and of the Holy Spirit, and teaching them to obey everything that I have commanded you. And remember, I am with you always, to the end of the age." (Matt. 28:18–20)

In another report Jesus instructed his followers to remain in Jerusalem and await the coming of the Holy Spirit of God. On Pentecost (Shavuot), Jesus's mother and disciples were meeting together in a room, praying:

> And suddenly from heaven there came a sound like the rush of a violent wind, and it filled the entire house where they were sitting. Divided tongues, as of fire, appeared among them, and a tongue rested on each of them. All of them were filled with the Holy Spirit and began to speak in other languages, as the Spirit gave them ability. (Acts 2:2–4)

Filled with the power of the Holy Spirit, Peter and the others began preaching to the Jews who had come to Jerusalem for the festival. The text says that about 3,000 people believed Peter's message and were baptized that day. In Christian tradition the events of this Pentecost mark the birth of the church.

Paul of Tarsus

Christianity started out as a Jewish sect—its first converts were primarily Jews. Very early in

Before his conversion, Paul, a learned Jew and Roman citizen, persecuted the Christians. In this painting by Raphael, Jesus is seen speaking to Paul from heaven. Paul is perhaps most responsible for taking Christianity beyond being a sect of Judaism. (The Bettmann Archive)

Christian history, however, the "good news" of the kingdom of God was extended to include Gentiles; and the man who preached this message most compellingly was Paul.

Born at Tarsus in Anatolia (in present-day Turkey) in the early years of the Common Era and called Saul until his conversion to Christianity, Paul was both a learned Jew who studied with the famed Rabbi Gamaliel and a Roman citizen. Initially perceiving the teachings of Jesus's apostles as dangerous to Judaism, Paul persecuted Christians, reportedly holding the coats of the people who stoned Stephen, the first Christian **martyr** (literally, "witness"; here one who bears witness to the point of death). But around 40 C.E., on his way to Damascus to arrest Christians, he had a vision in which Jesus appeared and called him to be an apostle:

> Now as he was going along and approaching Damascus, suddenly a light from heaven flashed around him. He fell to the ground and heard a voice saying to him: "Saul, Saul, why do you persecute me?" He asked, "Who are you, Lord?" The reply came, "I am Jesus whom you are persecuting." (Acts 9:3–5; cf. Gal. 1:13–17)

After withdrawing for a time to the Arabian desert, Paul returned to Damascus and started preaching the new faith in Syria. By 51 C.E. he was writing letters to Christian communities around the Mediterranean world. They show him as an itinerant missionary, preaching brilliantly to all who would listen and establishing Christian churches wherever he found a receptive audience. He journeyed from his home base in Syria to Asia Minor, Greece, and Italy.

Calling himself the apostle to the Gentiles, Paul took issue with the so-called Judaizers. They taught that to gain the new kingdom one must follow the requirements of the Mosaic law (circumcision, dietary rules, and so on), in effect becoming a Jew while becoming a Christian. Paul, however, taught that what saves a person is not obedience to the Mosaic requirements but faith—that is, trust in Jesus Christ. Jesus came to free people from the law, from its rigorous requirements and its judgment. To the church at Galatia Paul wrote:

> Christ redeemed us from the curse of the law by becoming a curse for us—for it is written, "Cursed is everyone who hangs on a tree"—in order that in Christ Jesus the blessing of Abraham might come to the Gentiles, so that we might receive the promise of the Spirit through faith. (Gal. 3:13–14)

Thus Paul transformed the new religion with a universal message of salvation for all who believe in Christ's death and resurrection.

Paul reinterpreted Greek as well as Hebrew thought. Concerned with justice, Greek philosophers sought to make people "good," that is, to help them realize their potential for virtue and to live according to reason. In his teaching on sin and grace, Paul denied that humans have the power to make themselves good apart from God. This teaching, later known as the doctrine of **original sin**, states that sin and death came into the world with Adam and Eve; their disobedience has affected their descendants, so that all human beings sin and are condemned to die. But God, who is both merciful and just, sent Jesus Christ to die in the place of sinful humanity. Through his sacrificial death we are redeemed; that is, we are forgiven for our sins and saved from eternal death. This free gift of God's, called **grace**, is ours through faith. To the church at Rome Paul wrote: "There is therefore now no condemnation for those who are in Christ Jesus. For the law of the Spirit of life in Christ Jesus has set you free from the law of sin and of death" (Rom. 8:1–2).

Paul set up a dichotomy between spirit and flesh, teaching that they are at constant war in human life. Only God's grace allows people to live in the spirit. By spirit Paul meant a life centered on God, and by flesh, a life centered on self. Later Christians were to identify flesh with the human body, inferring from this that the body itself is evil and must be rigidly controlled.

With his emphasis on God's grace and the power of the Messiah to free one from the law, sin, and death, Paul's message found favor especially among Jews who had tried to keep the whole law yet failed and among Gentiles who were attracted by Judaism's monotheism and ethical standards yet repelled by its cultic requirements. Paul's energetic preaching of this new doctrine was a major factor in the rapid spread of the faith, and Christian communities were soon established in all the major Mediterranean towns. Paul's last journey took him to Rome, where, according to tradition, he was executed around 65 C.E. during an early persecution of Christians by Emperor Nero.

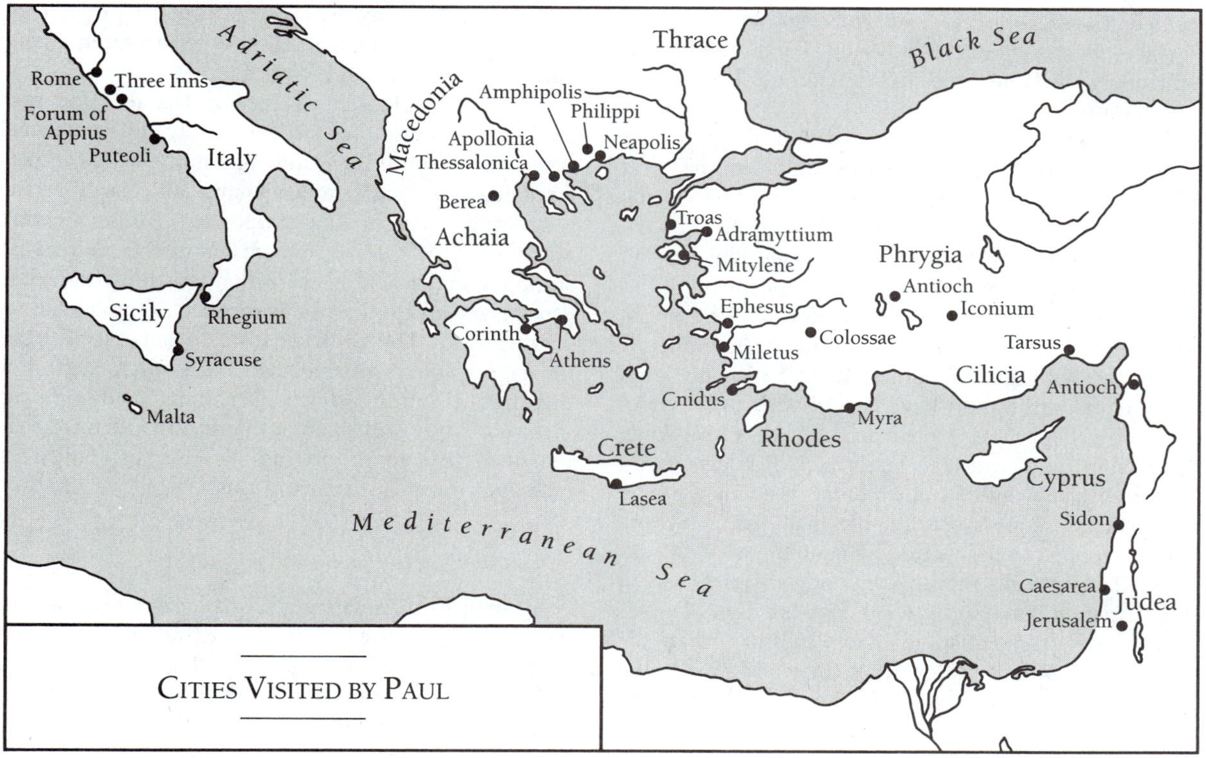

CITIES VISITED BY PAUL

The First Christian Communities

The early Christian communities were filled primarily with people from the lower classes—unskilled laborers, petty craftworkers, household slaves—attracted by the Christian ideal that all who are baptized in Christ Jesus are one, without the social distinctions that divide humans in the world: "There is no longer Jew or Greek, there is no longer slave or free, there is no longer male and female; for all of you are one in Christ Jesus" (Gal. 3:28).

Women figured prominently in these Christian congregations. Some of them were themselves merchants or relatively well-to-do, and believers often gathered in the homes of such women; others preached, taught, and performed acts of charity. Women occupied positions of leadership, such as Phoebe, who was deacon of the church at Cenchrae in Greece; Junia, whom Paul calls a prominent apostle, despite later Christian belief that only men could be apostles; and Priscilla who, together with her husband Aquila, helped to spread the gospel in Rome and Corinth. Christian attitudes toward women represented a radical break from Judaism, where legally women were under the husband's domination and spiritually had no role in the public life of the community.[5]

Christians became so identified with the poor and powerless that a critic of Christianity in the next century, the philosopher Celsus, characterized the church as fit only for children, slaves, and women, mocking Christians as saying, "Let no one educated, no one wise, no one sensible draw near. For their abilities are thought by us to be evils. But as for anyone ignorant, anyone stupid, anyone uneducated, anyone who is a child, let him come boldly."[6] In many ways early Christians would have agreed with this characterization. Paul himself preached status reversal when describing the Corinthian church: "Not many of you were wise by human standards, not many were powerful, not many were of noble birth. But God chose what is foolish in the world to shame the wise" (I Cor. 1:26–27). Instead, the poverty and powerlessness of the Christian community was taken as a sign of God's power and righteousness. This message that the kingdom of God would overturn the world's order and bring down earthly powers gave hope to the poor and disfranchised, contributing to the church's growth. Women, slaves, and lower-class workers found not only acceptance and welcome in the church, with the promise of hope for the future, but also opportunities for recognition and prominence in the present. Status in the church remained independent of status in the world, and thus those most powerless in Roman society could rise to positions of great power within the Christian community.

THE EARLY CHURCH

CHRISTIAN IDENTITY

Delay of the Parousia

Several of the narratives about Jesus portray him foretelling an imminent end of the world, preceded by the Parousia, or Jesus's own return. The first generation of Christians clearly expected Christ to return during their lifetime. But as that first generation of believers began to die out and Jesus did not return as expected, Christians were faced with the problem of the delay of the Parousia and how to make sense of it both theologically and practically.

Part of the problem lay in the fact that the first Christian communities were radically different from any churches of today—they had no New Testament, no creeds, no uniform leadership or clear lines of succession. The Christian scriptures were the Hebrew scriptures (the Old Testament), and the sources of authority and teaching were the apostles, those first proclaimers of the gospel, who were themselves now passing away. The church had to organize itself for a longer stay on earth than had been anticipated, and this meant settling down, becoming a disciplined institution, yet still maintaining a clear identity that remained true to its origins. A series of challenges helped to focus Christians in this task.

Challenges to the Faith

Responses to Judaism Christianity's relationship with Judaism set the first challenge. Initially Christians saw themselves in continuity with Judaism, inheritors of the promises contained in the Hebrew scriptures. Christians interpreted these scriptures Christologically, as pointing to Jesus as the Messiah foretold in prophecy, who would establish a new covenant between God and God's people.

In part because the situation of Judaism was growing more desperate in the face of Roman persecution, many Christians felt the need to establish an identity apart from their parent religion. When the Romans responded to a Jewish rebellion in Judea by destroying the temple in Jerusalem in 70 C.E., Christians consciously distanced themselves from these events. With the expulsion of the Jews from Jerusalem, the Jewish Christian community there also ceased to exist, and the church became predominantly Gentile. The Jews established an academy at Jamnia (outside Jerusalem in Palestine); around 85 C.E. the council at Jamnia expelled all followers of Jesus from the synagogues. The Hebrew canon of scripture was closed to prevent Christian additions or interpolations, and the rupture between Jews and Christians was complete.

Thus Christianity was separated from its predominantly Jewish milieu to make its own way in the Roman world. As Christians now sought to establish their differences from Judaism, talk shifted from being the "new Israel" to being "catholic" or universal. The Hebrew scriptures, now referred to as the Old Testament, remained the primary source of authority for the new faith, but Christian documents—gospels, letters, stories, sayings—also circulated and were beginning to be held as divinely inspired. Furthermore, anti-Jewish voices began to be raised in anger against the Jews who did not recognize their own Messiah, tragically setting the stage for later anti-Semitism.

Yet Christians never forgot that their roots lay in Judaism: for example, when Marcion, a second-century Christian teacher, tried to uproot Christianity and sever it altogether from its Jewish past, proclaiming that the God of Jesus Christ was a different being from the Jewish God of creation, he was firmly rejected. From Judaism Christians drew not only their monotheism, but also their belief in a God who is active in history and who demands ethical living from believers.

Gnosticism A second major challenge formative in the development of Christian identity was posed by **Gnosticism** (from the Greek *gnosis,* "knowledge"). There were actually many Gnostic groups, but they shared a common belief that salvation comes from knowledge, secret revelation not generally available to ordinary Christians. Gnostics were dualists; believing in a sharp dichotomy between spirit and matter, they rejected the material world as evil. In elaborate myths and cosmologies, Gnostics taught that creation was a mistake, the result of a great cosmic upheaval in the process of which fragments of spirit or sparks of divinity became trapped in matter. Humans are thus lost fragments of God and do not belong to this perishable world. To Gnostics, Jesus came down from heaven to teach the secret knowledge needed to return us to our true spiritual home. And because matter is evil, Jesus only appeared to be human; in reality he was a spiritual being, not sharing our physical existence at all. This belief, known as docetism (from the Greek *dokein,* "to seem or appear"), along with the understanding that salvation comes through secret knowledge, was rejected by the mainstream church.

The Catholic Response

Challenges such as those posed by Judaism and Gnosticism forced the church to become clearer about its identity: What is the church? Who is Christian? Where is the line drawn between what is and what is not acceptable in faith, worship, morality? In many ways this formative period is similar to an adolescence of the church as it struggled with questions of identity. In opposition to groups such as the Gnostics, most Christians considered themselves part of the catholic or universal church, in continuity with Jesus and the apostles and one with Christian communities around the Mediterranean world.

A number of noted Christian teachers led the fight against those whom they believed were leading the church astray; their writings contributed greatly to the development of orthodoxy (Greek *orthodoxos,* "right belief"). It is important to remember, however, that in any conflict it is the winners who write the history and set the standards. One such teacher was Irenaeus, bishop of Lyon. In a long treatise written in 185 C.E., *Against Heresies,* he attacked various Gnostic groups as dens of false teaching filled with perverted practices.

To teach Christians how to recognize heresy or false teachings, Irenaeus set forth standards that would assure them of a reliable truth. He pointed to three pillars or structures of authority that had grown out of the church's experience that would ensure continuity with the apostles and the ongoing presence of the Holy Spirit: (1) orders of ministry, (2) canon of scripture, and (3) the rule of faith.

Orders of Ministry Whereas the first Christian communities had a variety of ways of ordering themselves, the church during the second century settled, for the most part, on the threefold office of bishop, presbyter (later called priest), and deacon. The bishop was the head of the local church in each city, usually preaching and presiding over the worship; presbyters assisted him in this task, especially in large cities where there were several congregations; and deacons served the people at communion, distributed alms to the poor, and ministered to the sick and needy. There also were other offices, including special groups of widows and virgins with a recognized ministry of prayer and visitation and sometimes healers or exorcists. The bishops were considered successors to the apostles, receiving and preserving the tradition handed down to them. Irenaeus envisioned a great chain of bishops linking church to church and generation to generation, guaranteeing the authenticity of Christian teaching. He emphasized Rome as the oldest and best-known church, with whom all other churches should be in harmony. Such continuity across time and space, as seen in the person of the bishop, united the scattered Christian congregations, helping them to forge a common identity in the face of a hostile world.

Scriptural Canon The canon of scripture also developed over time, beginning with the Hebrew scriptures, then adding the letters of Paul, the four gospels, and the Acts of the Apostles. Additional letters attributed to other apostles and the Revelation of John were eventually accepted as authoritative as well, and various other Christian documents in circulation were eliminated. *Canon* means "measuring rod," and the scriptures provided a means by which to measure orthodoxy.

Rule of Faith This third pillar is harder to pin down; it refers to what most Christians considered the teaching of the apostles—the basic truths without which, Christians agreed, there would be no true church. The rule of faith preceded any formal creeds, though eventually these would emerge, but included creedlike phrases such as "belief in one God, Father Almighty, who created heaven and earth; in one Lord Jesus Christ, the Son of God, who was born, died, and rose again for our salvation; and in the Holy Spirit of God, who was present in the prophets and apostles."

These three pillars reinforced one another and found their form and expression in the worship liturgy. Every Sunday (in honor of the day of the Resurrection), Christians would gather to celebrate the Eucharist, initially part of a community meal based on Jesus's Last Supper. The service would include prayers and the reading of scripture, but the focus was on the ritual blessing and sharing of bread and wine. Consecrated or set apart as holy through prayers and blessings, Christians believed that the bread and wine became the body and blood of Christ, a memorial of his death and resurrection (see the accompanying box). The words of institution (the prayers and blessings) became standard early in the life of the church, and the Eucharist, along with the Lord's Prayer and baptism (whereby members were initiated into the faith), formed the basic ingredients of Christian worship. The liturgy connected Christians across the world in a common belief, embodying and teaching the faith through hymn and prayer. Right teaching and right worship went hand in hand in the formation of Christian identity. At the same time, the liturgy gave Christians a sense of belonging to an elect group, chosen by God out of the sinful world, to be holy.

PERSECUTION AND MARTYRDOM

The Church and the World

In addition to struggling with the internal challenges posed to Christian identity, a rocky relationship with the Roman Empire also shaped Christianity during this formative period. The New Testament scriptures reveal various attitudes among the different communities: Paul tells the Christians they are to be subject to the governing authorities because such have been instituted by God (Rom. 13:1); the gospels portray Jesus drawing a sharp line between God's kingdom and the earthly realm, in which each receives its due ("Give to the emperor the things that are the emperor's, and to God the things that are God's"—

This Roman mosaic from Libya shows an early Christian facing wild animals in the arena. The martyrs helped unify the early church with a common standard of behavior. (The Granger Collection)

Mark 12:17); and in the Revelation of John, written during a time of persecution, the world and its rulers are irredeemably evil and will be destroyed. In many ways these three attitudes also characterize Christianity's relations with political powers at different times of its history. As we shall see, the church seesawed back and forth between the extremes of assimilation and antagonism toward the world, from sharply opposing Christ and Caesar to blending the two. Perhaps because extremes are more readily recognizable and easier to follow, Christianity has had a harder time finding the middle way of giving each realm its due.

During the first three centuries of its existence, Christianity remained aloof from the world. Roman society was imbued with polytheism at every level: shrines and images lined the roads, art and theater portrayed stories of the gods, and rites accompanied all civic and even social events. Christians, worshiping only one God and condemning Roman religion as idolatry, refused to participate in civic life and so were criticized as haters of humanity.

Christian indifference to society and contempt for the Roman religion infuriated devout Romans who believed that their gods were responsible for peace and the blessings of life. Tensions rose between Roman and Christian believers. Rumors circulated that Christians were cannibals and atheists engaged in incest, for, according to the rumors, they ate the body and blood of their God, they refused to worship Roman gods yet had no visible God of their own, and they called one another brother and sister and greeted with a kiss. Such tension in turn led to persecution and the martyrdom of Christians.

Though educated Romans did not believe the cannibalism and incest stories, the charges of atheism were much harder to dispel, as seen in the case of Polycarp, the aged bishop of Smyrna, who was martyred in 155 C.E. Because he was elderly and highly revered, the Roman proconsul tried to save Polycarp's life, telling him: "Swear by the fortunes of Caesar; change your mind; say, 'Away with the atheists!' " According to an eyewitness account, Polycarp looked around the arena, motioned with his hand at the gathered crowd, and said: "Away with the atheists!"[7] Atheism was the main charge that the Romans leveled against Christians, and Christians, in turn, flung it back at the Romans.

Persecutions during the second century were sporadic, often the result of mob violence arising from the clash of cultures. The official Roman policy is found in

THREE ACCOUNTS OF THE EUCHARIST

Following are three descriptions of the Eucharist from the second century. The first is by Ignatius of Antioch, a bishop who was martyred in Rome. He writes to the church at Philadelphia, warning them against schism ("observe a single Eucharist") and proclaiming the unity of the church with Christ in the elements of the Eucharist.

Be careful, then, to observe a single Eucharist. For there is one flesh of our Lord, Jesus Christ, and one cup of his blood that makes us one, and one altar, just as there is one bishop along with the presbytery and the deacons.

(Ignatius, *Letter to the Philadelphians,* c. 107 C.E.)

The second passage comes from the *Didache,* a church manual probably from second-century Syria. In its instructions and Eucharist prayers, it again notes that the bread symbolizes the church's unity.

Now about the Eucharist: This is how to give thanks: First in connection with the cup:

"We thank you, our Father, for the holy vine of David, your child, which you have revealed through Jesus, your child. To you be glory forever."

Then in connection with the piece [broken off the loaf]:

"We thank you, our Father, for the life and knowledge which you have revealed through Jesus, your child. To you be glory forever.

"As this piece [of bread] was scattered over the hills and then was brought together and made one, so let your Church be brought together from the ends of the earth into your Kingdom. For yours is the glory and the power through Jesus Christ forever."

You must not let anyone eat or drink of your Eucharist except those baptized in the Lord's name. For in reference to this the Lord said, "Do not give what is sacred to dogs."

After you have finished your meal, say grace in this way:

"We thank you, holy Father, for your sacred name which you

an exchange of letters between Pliny, the governor of Bithynia, and Emperor Trajan around 110 C.E. Trajan commanded Pliny neither to seek out Christians nor to accept anonymous accusations against them. Yet people denounced as Christians and found guilty were to be punished, whereas those who denied Christ, thus proving their innocence, were to be released. No specific crime was necessary; simply proclaiming the name of Christ warranted punishment.

This remained standard policy until the third century, a troubled time for Rome. It was being attacked by the Germanic Goths in the north and the Persians in the east, its economy was shaky and its currency debased, and its leadership was unstable, one emperor following another in rapid succession, often through assassination. Though the empire was not yet crumbling, its foundations were shaken and confidence was low. Emperor Decius, with a vision of a renewed, strengthened Rome, tried to unite and stabilize the empire through a crusade to return to traditional Roman values. He issued an edict calling for formal acknowledgment and sacrifice to the Roman gods and imprisoned or executed all who refused. Thus began the first systematic empirewide persecution of *have lodged in our hearts, and for the knowledge and faith and immortality which you have revealed through Jesus, your child. To you be glory forever.*

"Almighty Master, 'you have created everything' for the sake of your name, and have given men food and drink to enjoy that they may thank you. But to us you have given spiritual food and drink and eternal life through Jesus, your child.

"Above all we thank you that you are mighty. To you be glory forever."

(Didache 9.1–10.4, second century C.E.)

Our third selection is by Justin, a second-century Christian teacher who was also martyred in Rome. In this defense of the faith, Justin tries to make Christianity understandable to the Romans. Note that as in the *Didache,* Justin specifies that the Eucharist is a holy meal, in which only baptized Christians are permitted to partake.

On finishing the prayers we greet each other with a kiss. Then bread and a cup of water and mixed wine are brought to the president of the brethren and he, taking them, sends up praise and glory to the Father of the universe through the name of the Son and of the Holy Spirit, and offers thanksgiving at some length that we have been deemed worthy to receive these things from him. When he has finished the prayers and the thanksgiving, the whole congregation present assents, saying, "Amen." "Amen" in the Hebrew language means, "So be it." When the president has given thanks and the whole congregation has assented, those whom we call deacons give to each of those present a portion of the consecrated bread and wine and water, and they take it to the absent.

This food we call Eucharist, of which no one is allowed to partake except one who believes that the things we teach are true, and has received the washing for forgiveness of sins and for rebirth, and who lives as Christ handed down to us. For we do not receive these things as common bread or common drink; but as Jesus Christ our Savior being incarnate by God's word took flesh and blood for our salvation, so also we have been taught that the food consecrated by the word of prayer which comes from him, from which our flesh and blood are nourished by transformation, is the flesh and blood of that incarnate Jesus.

(Justin, *First Apology* 65–66, c. 155 C.E.)

Source: Cyril C. Richardson, trans. and ed., *Early Christian Fathers* (New York: Macmillan, 1970).

Christians (250–251), which was followed by further persecutions under Emperors Valerian (257–260) and Diocletian (beginning in 303).

The Christian Response

Christians responded to persecution in a number of ways, the most highly valued of which was martyrdom. Jesus was the prototypical martyr, and his death set the example for Christian discipleship. One of the best-known martyrs was Ignatius, bishop of Antioch, who was marched to Rome from Syria to face wild animals in the arena. Writing to the churches in Rome, he begged his friends not to save him from execution:

> I am corresponding with all the churches and bidding them all realize that I am voluntarily dying for God—if, that is, you do not interfere. . . . Let me be fodder for wild beasts—that is how I can get to God. I am God's wheat and I am being ground by the teeth of wild beasts to make a pure loaf for Christ. . . . When I have fallen asleep . . . I shall be a real disciple of Jesus

> Christ. . . . Pray Christ for me that by these means I may become God's sacrifice. If I suffer, I shall be emancipated by Jesus Christ; and united to him, I shall rise to freedom.[8]

In addition to the call of discipleship, Christians believed that martyrdom demonstrated the reality of Christ's death as well as their own contempt for death and for this world and its rulers. The extraordinary courage of the martyrs and their willingness to die for their faith commanded respect and reinforced the certainty among believers that their God and their future heavenly abode transcended their pain and even death itself. The martyr accounts often tell of pagans who, witnessing the courage and steadfastness of the martyrs, became Christians themselves. In the famous statement of Tertullian, a Christian defender, the blood of the martyrs was the seed of the church.

Christian martyrs also helped to unify the church with a common standard of behavior. Diverse Christian groups found familiar ground and a common identity in the martyr accounts, which were carefully crafted to portray the martyrs as following in Christ's footsteps, scorning death, and teaching persecutors the truth of the gospel by word and deed. The church honored its martyrs in story and ritual, commemorating the days of their deaths. Their burial sites were deemed holy, places where heaven touched the earth, and in later centuries churches such as St. Peter's in Rome would be built atop their graves. Because of the danger involved in being a Christian, the church developed a lengthy indoctrination process known as the *catechumenate* to teach Christians what would be expected of them and to strengthen them in case of persecution.

Of course, not all Christians responded with the martyrs' courage. During the Decian persecution many Christians lapsed—they either renounced their Christianity and made the required sacrifice to the gods, or they obtained false certificates saying that they had sacrificed. When the persecution ended, the church faced a demoralized and decimated flock clamoring for readmission. This was a major crisis, leading to a schism between those who believed that the church should remain pure and would be polluted by the return of the lapsed and those who believed that the church should be forgiving and take back the penitent. Mercy won over purity as Christianity declared that Christ's forgiveness extended even to those who had denied him.

During the second century a number of educated Christians tried to reason with the Roman government in an effort to end the persecutions. In open letters addressed to emperors and governors, these Christian **apologists** (from the Greek *apologia,* "defense") defended Christianity, refuting rumors and explaining Christian practices and beliefs. The most famous of the apologists, Justin Martyr (c. 100–160, so called because he was himself executed for the faith), wanted to build a bridge between Christianity and classical culture by using Greek philosophical language to show what they had in common. Justin argued that the wisdom of the Greeks had been a form of revelation, an activity of the divine Logos ("word" or "reason") of God, whom Christians identified with Jesus. Since Christ is identified with wisdom, Justin claimed, Christ as the Logos was present in human beings before the incarnation, and there were Christians (among whom he included Socrates, Plato, and Moses) before the birth of Jesus.

The work of apologists and teachers such as Justin extended Christianity, making it more accessible and acceptable to the educated classes. It also took Greek and Roman thought seriously, instead of dismissing philosophy as inimical to God. Serious thinkers and seekers would no longer have to reject their previous learning or be content with a simple, unexamined faith. Christian teachers, in the tradition of Greek and Roman instructors, became a respected force in the church.

Constantine and the Edict of Milan

The final persecution of Christianity, known as the Great Persecution, took place under Emperor Diocletian, who, like Decius before him, wanted to stabilize a shaky empire. The church had just experienced 40 years of relative peace and had grown immensely during the latter part of the third century, gaining converts, acquiring property, and achieving a degree of acceptance among the general population.

Suddenly, in 303, the emperor ordered all the churches destroyed, their property confiscated, and the scriptures burned. Many Christians were executed in a harsh oppression that continued for nine years. Then an important political change took place. As part of

In 312, before the battle with Maxentius to decide the emperor of the West, Constantine had a vision of a cross in the heavens. Placing the symbol on his army's shields, Constantine won the battle. The following year Constantine met with the emperor of the East and issued the Edict of Milan, ending persecution of the Christians. (The Granger Collection)

Diocletian's reorganization plans, it became customary to have two emperors, one in the east and one in the west. Two generals, Constantine and Maxentius, disputed the title of emperor of the west; their armies met outside Rome in 312. Before the battle, it was reported, Constantine had a vision of a cross in the heavens bearing the words *In hoc signo vinces* ("You will conquer in this sign"). Placing that symbol on his army's shields, Constantine won the battle and became the western emperor.

The following year (313) Constantine met with Licinius, emperor of the east, and issued the Edict of Milan, which ended persecution, restored church property, and granted freedom of worship to Christians. For a time Constantine continued to promote toleration of all religions; upon becoming sole emperor, however, he gave strong support to the Christians, appointing them tutors to his children and counselors to himself.

The Imperial Church

Assimilation to the World

Church and State

The accession of Constantine and the Edict of Milan formed a watershed for the church. Almost overnight Christianity moved from a maligned and persecuted sect to the most favored religion of the empire, dramatically shifting relations between Christianity and the political powers. The church was supported financially and politically. As Christians moved into highly visible positions in the government, conversion became a means to advance in imperial service. Christians were no longer up against the world; they now *were* the world. And as the new holders of power, they understood their task as Christianizing the culture they had, in effect, conquered. There have been many opinions, both then and now, as to whether this shift in Christian fortunes was good or bad. How was the relationship between the church and the empire to be worked out? Would the church become an arm of the state, with its bishops serving as government ministers? Would the state become an arm of the church, a theocracy with the emperor subordinate to the bishops? Or would the church and the state be coequal, with different responsibilities and spheres of authority yet cooperating together?

In the eastern half of the empire the state dominated the church. Constantine set the tone by considering himself "bishop to the bishops," calling church councils and mandating doctrine. His successors continued this policy, often exiling outspoken bishops who dared to challenge them.

The opposite situation existed in the western half of the empire, where bishops were strong and emperors weak. One of the greatest of these bishops was Ambrose of Milan, who successfully stood up for what he believed to be the interests of God and the church against the state. In 390 there was a riot in the port town of Thessalonika in which imperial troops were killed. In anger and haste, Emperor Theodosius ordered that the local citizens be convened and executed. He thought better of this action and sent out a second message to halt the killing, but too late: 7,000 people were massacred. Ambrose insisted that Theodosius make public confession and repentance before he would be allowed back in church. The empire witnessed the unprecedented sight of an emperor doing public penance for a deed performed in office.

There are two ways of looking at this incident. From the perspective of the government, was it unwarranted interference by the church in affairs of state? Or, as the church claims, was it the appropriate use of authority by a bishop for a member of his flock who had sinned? The emperor's power was temporal, but the bishop's was perceived as both temporal and eternal. The threat of **excommunication** (banishment from the church) that Ambrose held over Theodosius would not only have deprived him of eternal salvation but, perhaps more important, would have caused him to lose the approval of God in the people's eyes. The old pagan understanding of the emperor as the one who brings divine peace to earth had not disappeared; it had merely changed shape. An emperor perceived in disfavor with God was also seen as an object of God's wrath and thus a danger to the empire. Fear of riots and assassination, if not of God directly, kept most emperors within the confines of the church. This tenuous balance between the authority of the church and the authority of the state was a key issue that arose repeatedly during the Middle Ages and remains an issue even today.

Worship

As the church grew in imperial favor it also grew in wealth and power, reflected both in the classes of people who now belonged and in the external trappings of worship. No longer was this simply the church of uneducated women and slaves, as Celsus had mocked; instead, the wealthy and the ambitious flocked to its doors as Christianity became a recognized road for public advancement. Because of the crowds, large churches known as *basilicas,* modeled after Roman public buildings, were erected in the major cities of the empire. These were richly ornamented with polished marble, lamps, tapestries, and especially mosaics of Christ the King, the Virgin Mary with the Christ Child, and the reigning emperor and empress. The service, too, became more ornate, with long processions, clouds of incense, and rich vestments for the clergy and assistants, also modeled after the protocol and adornment of the imperial court.

Assimilation to the Roman world was seen not only in the huge basilicas and their ornate worship but also in the structure of the church. The clerical hierarchy became rigid with several layers or orders, including doorkeeper, lector, and subdeacon, in addition to deacon, presbyter, and bishop. Women were gradually excluded from any public role as the church adopted the standards of existing society, and their earlier ministries of prayer and visitation were sharply curtailed outside of the monastic life.

THE ASCETIC MOVEMENT

Early Christian Asceticism

From its earliest beginnings Christianity had a tradition of asceticism and renunciation. The word *asceticism* (from the Greek *ascesis,* "training, exercise") comes from the Greek athletic world, with its training for competitions. Christians believed that they were training for the kingdom of God, warring against passions and desires that kept them from single-minded devotion to God. Virginity and vowed celibacy (not marrying and remaining sexually chaste, possible even for those who were no longer virgins) were highly exalted as a superior way of life. With the example of Jesus, believed to be born of a virgin and himself celibate, and Paul's commendation that the duties of marriage distracted from ministry, virginity came to be regarded as more "spiritual" than marriage. In addition, such an attitude undermined traditional Jewish and Greco-Roman views of the family, demonstrating Christian freedom from the strictures of society. From the Roman perspective this was one more indication of the hostile nature of Christianity. Rather than an expression of freedom, the Romans saw it as one more display of contempt toward everything the Romans held dear—religion, state, family. For the population of the Roman Empire to remain stable, it is estimated that every woman needed to produce an average of five children. By refusing to fulfill this civic duty, Christians proclaimed that their true allegiance was to their heavenly home and not to the Roman world.

Virginity as a chosen life style was an especially important option for women, who were thus freed from many of the constraints fettering other women: authority of father or husband, arranged marriages, physical abuse, dangers of childbirth. Virgins and widows assumed a special role as intercessors, their task being to pray constantly and, in some communities, to join the clergy in performing the liturgy. In the fourth century, widows and virgins in Rome and Palestine formed communities to study scripture and live ascetically. Unlike their married sisters, whose education often stopped when they turned 12 (the usual age of marriage) and whose lives were narrowly limited to home and children, these women were able to study and teach, forming friendships with men based on mutual interests and concerns. The ascetic practices of these communities, such as those founded by the rich Roman widows Paula and Macrina, focused on voluntary poverty and extremely simple living. Macrina, for example, persuaded her very wealthy mother and others to live as simply as their servants did as a means of achieving solidarity with them. Such elevation of poverty as a superior way of life eventually led to standard monastic vows of poverty (along with chastity and obedience).

Monastic Foundations

With the end of persecution and the legalization of the faith, martyrdom too ceased, thus removing Christianity's most powerful act of discipleship. Some believers, seeking heroic acts of piety, fled to the desert. There are three main reasons why Christians retreated into the wilderness. First, it was a reaction against the newly powerful and wealthy Constantinian church, which to many seemed compromised to the world. During times of persecution Christians had hidden in the desert; now the desert became a place to flee what many considered a more subtle form of persecution: assimilation to the world. Second, this was a lay movement against an increasingly hierarchical church. There was a deep anticlerical element as people fled into the desert to escape ordination with its temptations to pride. Stories abound of monks hiding in caves at the approach of a bishop. Finally, the movement into the desert was taken as a way of following Christ and of recapturing the spirit of primitive Christianity. Asceticism became the new martyrdom, a living martyrdom—some of the authority that had resided with the martyrs now passed to the ascetics. Ordinary Christians with families and jobs in the cities would make the hard trek into the desert, not to stay but to sit at the feet of the desert mothers and fathers (as these hermits were called) and listen to their teaching.

The best known of these hermits, considered the father of eremetical ("desert place") monasticism, is Antony of Egypt (c. 251–356, said to be 105 at his death). As a young man Antony adopted Jesus's instruction: "Sell all that you own and distribute the money to the poor, and you will have treasure in heaven; then come, follow me" (Luke 18:22). Antony sold his possessions and moved into the desert for a solitary life of prayer. After many years he emerged again with a reputation for holiness and wisdom and spent the rest of his life alternating between teaching his many visitors and retreating further into the desert for solitude and prayer. Athanasius, the bishop of Alexandria and younger contemporary of Antony, wrote the *Life of Antony,* which quickly became popular, influencing many to follow Antony's example in the ascetic life.

Not all who lived in desert solitude fared as well as Antony, however. The dangers of living alone were many, ranging from physical dangers to a loss of Christian community and awareness of its teaching, to the danger of pride from a belief in one's own spiritual prowess. To remedy this a former military man named Pachomius (286–346) established monasteries in the desert where groups of monks would live together, sharing food, labor, and times of common prayer. The one responsible for bringing monks fully into communal life, however, was Basil of Cesarea (330–379), who wanted to harness the spiritual energy of the monks for the good of the greater church. He wrote a set of rules governing communal monasticism, placing the monasteries under episcopal (the bishop's) authority. Some monks were now ordained, bringing monasteries into the full sacramental life of the church as well. Monasteries and the secular (nonmonastic) church became resources for each other, with a rich cross-fertilization of leadership, prayer, and theology.

The Rule of Saint Benedict

The most significant form of monasticism for western Christianity was that established by Benedict of Nursia (c. 480–550) at Monte Cassino in northern Italy. The famous *Rule of Saint Benedict,* with its clear instructions, practical outlook, and humane standards, took the insights of eastern monasticism and transformed them to fit the conditions of the west. Described as a "little Rule for beginners,"[9] it calls for moderation in ascetic practice, economic self-sufficiency for each house, an orderly program of common prayer, private devotional reading and contemplation, and manual labor—all as a means to spiritual growth. Benedict calls the monastery a school for God's service; through obedience, stability, and the monastic life, one learns to surrender self-will and become humble, growing in love of God and neighbor. Benedictine monasticism became the model for future religious communities, playing a key role in the development of medieval Christianity.

Saint Benedict's *Rule of Saint Benedict* contained clear instructions for monks. Here Benedict is depicted presenting his book of rules to an abbot; the angel behind Benedict represents the divine inspiration believed to be present in the instructions. (The Bettmann Archive)

ISSUES AROUND THE PERSON OF JESUS CHRIST

With the conversion and accession of Constantine, the attention of the church shifted from the threat of persecution and concern with survival to the further development of its doctrine. The main issues during the fourth and fifth centuries surrounded the person of Jesus Christ: Who is Jesus in relation to God? And what do Christians mean when they speak of Jesus as both human and divine?

Arianism

A dispute arose when Arius, a priest of Alexandria in Egypt, challenged his bishop whom he believed was confusing Jesus, the Logos of God, with God, thus compromising monotheism and divine transcendence. Arius taught that the Logos was subordinate to God the Father—a perfect creature made in the image of God, but not eternal or one with God. The Logos, according to Arius, is the greatest of all created beings, who in turn created all other creatures, finally becoming incarnate in Jesus Christ.

A violent controversy erupted across the newly Christian empire. Preachers and bishops argued over whether Jesus was fully divine or created, whole regions opting for one side or the other. Dockworkers sang popular songs about it, and the issue was argued over in the marketplace. Constantine, who had hoped to use Christianity to unite and strengthen the empire, saw it splintering over theology. In 325 he called for a

From the Council of Nicea came a clear exposition of the Christian doctrine of the Trinity: God is one essential being, eternally existing and subsisting in three persons, Father, Son, and Holy Spirit. This eleventh-century miniature illustrates the interconnection of the Father (center) with the Son (Jesus, at left) and the Holy Spirit (represented as a dove, at right). (The Bettmann Archive)

council of the whole church, inviting bishops to come to Nicea, near Constantinople, to discuss the matter. Some 318 bishops assembled and ultimately condemned Arianism. They adopted the following statement for purposes of doctrinal clarification:

> We believe in one God, the Father All Governing, creator of all things visible and invisible; And in one Lord Jesus Christ, the Son of God, begotten of the Father, . . . God from God, Light from Light, true God from true God, begotten not created, of the same essence as the Father, through whom all things came into being, . . . Who for us and for our salvation came down and was incarnate, becoming human. He suffered and the third day he rose, and ascended into the heavens. And he will come to judge both the living and the dead. And [we believe] in the Holy Spirit.[10]

The critical anti-Arian affirmation was that the Son is "of the same essence" or of one substance *(homoousios)* with the Father, affirming an identity between the Father and the Son.

Despite its promulgation of a statement of faith or creed, the Council of Nicea left many people dissatisfied. Controversy continued for another 50 years over the precise meaning of *homoousios* and over the salvific necessity for Christ's identity with God. The key proponent of the Nicene position was Athanasius, now bishop of Alexandria and known as the "champion of orthodoxy." His understanding of Jesus was tied closely to his perception of the human condition. Human beings, Athanasius taught, were created in the image of God and to be in relationship with God; as long as they were turned toward God, they shared the divine life. When they disobeyed, however, humans turned away from God toward nothingness—they fell from life into death, and the image of God was lost. To halt the fall, God took on human flesh, being born in the person Jesus, to die in the place of sinful human beings and defeat death. Only the Creator can re-create the lost image, and only the one who is Life itself has life to give. Thus, Athanasius argued, it is essential that the Logos incarnate, Jesus Christ, be one with God the Father if we are to be saved.

Other theologians took up this argument, refining the theological language. Out of this debate came a clear exposition of the Christian doctrine of the Trinity: God is one essential being, eternally existing and subsisting in three persons, Father, Son, and Holy Spirit. A second council held in 381, the Council of Constantinople, defined this language and reissued the creed of Nicea with an additional paragraph affirming the full divinity of the Holy Spirit and its activity in the church and the world. This Nicene-Constantinopolitan Creed (usually known simply as the Nicene Creed) is still used in many Christian churches today.

Christology

Following Constantinople, the controversy shifted to issues of Christology, that is, questions about Christ and how his divinity is related to his humanity.

In Michelangelo's *Pietà*, Mary is seen holding the crucified Christ. Two cherubs hold a crown above Mary's head. The distinction between Jesus's human and divine natures has created much debate through the centuries. Included are questions regarding Mary's role as "Mother of God." (The Bettman Archive)

Two parties or schools, centered in the cities of Alexandria and Antioch, dominated the debate. The Alexandrian school emphasized Christ's divinity (God took human flesh) and essential unity (Jesus was only one person); the Antiochene school emphasized Christ's humanity (God was joined to a human person) and the distinction between his human and divine natures. The debate grew heated when Nestorius, the bishop of Constantinople, preached a sermon against the use of *Theotokos* ("God-bearer" or "Mother of God") as a popular title for the Virgin Mary. Mary only gave birth to Jesus's human nature, not his divinity, Nestorius insisted, because God cannot be born.

In 431 Emperor Theodosius II called the Council of Ephesus to deal with this issue. The bishops confirmed the union of human and divine in Christ, condemned Nestorius, and affirmed the title *Theotokos* for Mary. The first of several schisms followed this council as churches in the Middle East and Persia followed Nestorius, withdrawing from the catholic communion and establishing separate Nestorian churches that eventually spread as far as China.

As the conflict continued, the emperor once again convened a general council in Chalcedon, a city near Constantinople, in 451. The bishops adopted a statement of Leo I of Rome *(Leo's Tome)* and issued a "definition of faith" concerning the union of the two natures of Christ. This was not a creed and did not attempt to explain the mystery; instead, it was a statement outlining the parameters of catholic belief. The definition stated that Christ is one with God concerning his divinity and one with us concerning his humanity; the union is without confusion, change, separation, or division. In doing this, the bishops excluded views not in accord with the emerging orthodoxy, thereby increasing their own authority and that of the church.

As the gates of orthodoxy narrowed, the power and authority of the bishops correspondingly increased. Lay teachers had flourished in the early church, eagerly exploring the seemingly limitless bounds of the Christian faith. Now such teachers were closely scrutinized, charges and countercharges of heresy resounded within the hierarchy, and lay participation was severely curtailed at all levels. Bishops were given authority over the founding of monasteries, with all monks subject to them; clergy were not to meet or travel apart from the bishop's permission; only those approved by the bishop could practice exorcism. Gradually the power of the bishops spread to cover more and more aspects of corporate and individual life under episcopal oversight.

A number of churches could not accept the Chalcedonian statement and also withdrew. These included most congregations in Egypt, Ethiopia, and Armenia and some in Syria, Palestine, and India. These churches are called Monophysite ("of one nature"), since they believe that despite his human body, Christ had a wholly divine nature.

The schisms following Ephesus and Chalcedon weakened both the church and the eastern Roman

Empire (often called the Byzantine Empire); when Muslim crusaders in the seventh century occupied large parts of the east, many Christians welcomed the Arabs as delivering them from the persecution of the Orthodox.

AUGUSTINE

Whereas Christological issues dominated the theological debates of the east, the western part of the empire found itself more concerned with questions about sin and grace. The doctrines of original sin and salvation through the grace of God in Jesus Christ were formulated most clearly by Augustine, bishop of Hippo (354–430).

Augustine, though raised by a Christian mother, Monica, had put aside biblical teachings as too simple and childish. He began a long quest for wisdom, evolving through Stoicism, Manichaeism (a Zoroastrian Gnostic religion founded by the Persian prophet Mani), and Neoplatonism. None of these ideologies answered his primary question: Where does evil come from? This was basically a Christian question, and Augustine finally found his answer in Christian thought.

Drawing from the Greek philosophical concept that identifies goodness with being and evil as the absence of being and from the Christian understanding of a good God who created all things good, Augustine argued against the Manichaean identification of matter with evil. To have existence, Augustine argued, is to be created by God, and to be created by God is to be created good; therefore, evil cannot have any independent existence. Instead, evil is the absence of good, as sickness is the absence of health. Human evil, or sin, results from people placing lesser goods above God, their supreme good.

After Augustine's conversion, he, several friends, and his illegitimate son all received baptism and returned to North Africa to live a monastic life. Consecrated bishop of Hippo in 395, he reluctantly abandoned his quiet existence and plunged headlong into the life of the church and its controversies. Most of his writings come from his time as an active churchman. In addition to three major works—*Confessions, The Trinity,* and *City of God*—he wrote numerous sermons, letters, and tracts opposing heresies or addressing pastoral problems. He died in 430 during a siege of Hippo by Vandal invaders.

The Nature of Sin and Grace: The Pelagian Controversy

Augustine's interest in the nature of evil naturally led to the issue of sin, though the question was first raised by a British monk, Pelagius. Horrified by Augustine's prayer—"Give what you command, and command what you will"[11]—and basing his argument on ideas of God's fairness and justice, Pelagius taught that a loving God would not have commanded people to obey moral laws if they were unable to do so. The power to do good, Pelagius argued, was given to human beings in creation and remains with them still, usually lying dormant but ready to be awakened and strengthened through instruction and moral effort.

Pelagius focused on sinful acts that could be repented of and forgiven, thus cleansing the soul to an original righteousness. Augustine, by contrast, understood sin not merely as individual misdeeds but as a deep and pervasive alienation from God resulting from Adam and Eve's disobedience—a condition into which

Scenes from the life of St. Augustine are depicted in this fifteenth-century Flemish painting. (The Metropolitan Museum of Art, The Cloisters Collection, 1961)

all human beings are born. Because of this original sin, no human acts are good apart from the grace of God, because all are based ultimately on self-love and human pride, not love of God. Augustine felt keenly the great fractures in the universe and in human souls and saw that these could be healed only by God, not by human effort. In his death and resurrection, Christ broke the chains of sin that enslave us, freeing us once again to love God.

The Nature of the Church: The Donatist Controversy

Before closing this section on Augustine, it is important to look at one last controversy and its implications for the church of the Middle Ages. Following the Great Persecution of Diocletian, a number of lapsed Christians were restored to the communion of the church, including a deacon who was accused of handing over the scriptures to the Roman authorities. When this deacon was later ordained bishop, a group of Christians who believed strongly in the purity of the church withdrew to form their own church. The Donatists, named for their leader Donatus, believed that a lapsed Christian had lost the Holy Spirit and remained outside the true church; thus he could not validly administer the sacraments. Augustine countered that the state of the celebrant makes no difference to the validity of the sacraments, which are of God, not of human beings. The Donatists' insistence on a pure church, Augustine argued, overlooked the persistence of human sin; until the Last Judgment, the church is a mixed body, containing saints and sinners. By including the full range of human beings, this teaching buttressed the church's claim to universality or catholicity.

But Donatists were too numerous to be defeated merely by doctrinal debate, especially in North Africa where the Donatist church was larger and more powerful than the Catholic church. Ultimately Augustine had to call on imperial troops for aid in destroying them. His justification for the use of force in the service of the church added to the church's growing claims of authority, setting the precedent for the violent repression of all those whom the church judged deviant from the straits of orthodoxy.

NOTES

1 Except where noted, all biblical quotations in Part Six are taken from The New Oxford Annotated Bible, New Revised Standard Version (New York: Oxford University Press, 1991).

2 Joachim Jeremias, *The Lord's Prayer,* trans. John Reuman (Philadelphia: Fortress Press, 1964). Jeremias gives a remarkably clear exposition of the text and its probable history.

3 This version is a composite of Matthew 26:26–28, Mark 14:22–24, and Luke 22:17–19 used in the Episcopal *Book of Common Prayer,* pp. 362–363; cf. 1 Cor. 11:23–25.

4 Günther Bornkamm, *Jesus of Nazareth,* trans. Irene and Fraser McLuskey (New York: Harper & Row, 1960), p. 163.

5 See Constance F. Parvey, "The Theology and Leadership of Women in the New Testament," in *Religion and Sexism: Images of Women in the Jewish and Christian Traditions,* ed. Rosemary Radford Ruether (New York: Simon & Schuster, 1974), pp. 117–149.

6 Celsus in Origen, *Contra Celsum* 3.44, trans. Henry Chadwick (Cambridge: Cambridge University Press, 1986), p. 158; cf. *Contra Celsum* 3.55.

7 *Martyrdom of Polycarp* 9.2, in *Early Christian Fathers,* ed. Cyril C. Richardson (New York: Macmillan, 1970), p. 152.

8 Ignatius, *To the Romans* 4.1–3, in *Early Christian Fathers,* p. 104.

9 *The Rule of St. Benedict* 73, trans. Antony C. Meisel and M. L. del Mastro (New York: Image Books, 1975), p. 106.

10 "The Creed of Nicaea," in *Creeds of the Churches,* ed. John H. Leith, 3rd ed. (Atlanta: John Knox Press, 1982), pp. 30–31.

11 *The Confessions of St. Augustine* 10.29, trans. John K. Ryan (New York: Image Books, 1960), p. 255.

CHRISTIANITY

CHAPTER 20

THE VISION OF CHRISTENDOM

EARLY MIDDLE AGES

THE FALL OF ROME AND THE RISE OF THE CHURCH

The imperial church of Constantine and his successors grew powerful and wealthy but ultimately failed as a means of holding the Roman Empire together. East and west grew apart: the eastern half, known as the Byzantine Empire and administered from Constantinople (the city founded by Constantine) remained intact until 1453, when it was conquered by the Muslim Ottoman Turks. The western portion of the empire, however, was subject to continued attacks from northern Germanic tribes; Rome itself was sacked in 410 and 455. The traditional date for the "fall" of Rome is 476, when Roman rule over the empire ended.

As Rome's political and social institutions collapsed, church leaders stepped into the vacuum. The bishops with their ecclesiastical organization were usually the only ones capable of bringing order in the face of invasion and disintegration. When the civil courts ceased functioning, church courts took their place, and when Roman secular education disappeared, monastic schools passed down Latin language and literature. The power and prestige of the bishops of Rome increased, as Pope Leo I (440–461) negotiated with the Huns and Pope Gregory I (590–604) with the Lombards when the invaders were poised to destroy Rome.

As the power of the papacy grew, an understanding of the historical roots of that power was lost. Until the rift between east and west, the bishop of Rome was one of five principal ecclesiastical authorities, known as patriarchs. The others were located in the cities of Jerusalem, Antioch, Alexandria, and Constantinople—all in the east. When the empire split, the four eastern patriarchs shared power, whereas in the west the bishop of Rome enjoyed lonely preeminence. This, plus the necessity forced on the church hierarchy to pick up the pieces when civil government collapsed, added to the power and prestige of the papacy. Initially any bishop could be called pope (from the Latin *papa,* "father"), but eventually the title was reserved in the west for the bishop of Rome alone. The key claim was that he had inherited Saint Peter's preeminence among the apostles, granted by Jesus himself:

> You are Peter, and on this rock I will build my church. . . . I will give you the keys of the kingdom of heaven, and whatever you bind on earth will be bound in heaven, and whatever you loose on earth will be loosed in heaven. (Matt. 16:18–19)

As the Vicar of Peter (and thus ruling in Peter's stead), the pope came to be seen in the west as head of the church, responsible directly to Christ. The historical circumstances that pushed the bishop of Rome and the

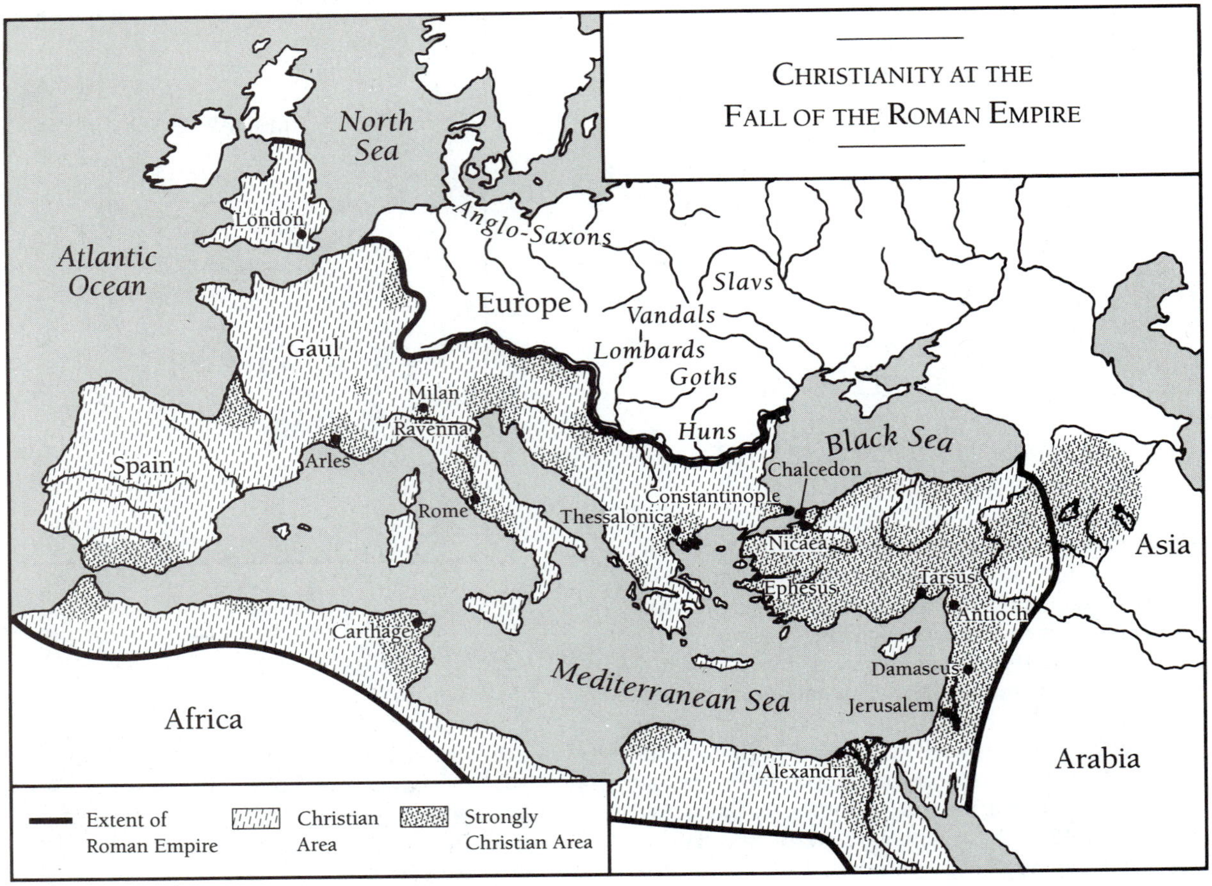

clerical hierarchy as a whole to the forefront were forgotten, and the "tradition" of Jesus's deputation to Peter and the pope's inheritance to such eventually led to claims of almost limitless power.

Missions and Missionaries

During the heyday of the Roman Empire, Christianity was primarily an urban religion, flourishing in the cities and towns of the Mediterranean world. With the Germanic invasions, however, the cities of the Roman world, with their sophisticated, literate urban classes that had filled the great basilicas, were depopulated. The church, built and sustained by one kind of culture, had to change its direction and vision for a wildly new and different society composed of poor peasants and a military aristocracy.

The task of expanding Christianity beyond its urban base into the countryside fell to a number of missionaries who left their homes and families to preach the gospel among the Germanic tribes. The general mission strategy was to seek a tribe that already had some contact with Christianity and work at converting the king. Because the Germanic view held the king to be a mediator between the tribe and its gods, once the king was converted, the rest of the people would follow. Often this task was simplified by the presence of a Christian queen who brought extra pressure on her husband. Such was the case with Clothilda, a Catholic princess from Burgundy, and Clovis (c. 466–511), king of the Franks (in present-day France). Clothilda reputedly urged Clovis to adopt her faith as she prepared for their son's baptism:

> The gods whom you worship are no good. . . .
> They haven't even been able to help themselves,

> let alone others. They are carved out of stone or wood or from some old piece of metal. . . . You ought instead to worship him who created at a word and out of nothing heaven, and earth, the sea and all that therein is; who made the sun to shine, who lit the sky with stars, who peopled the water with fish, the earth with beasts, the sky with flying creatures, at whose nod the field became fair with fruits, . . . by whose hand the race of man was made.[1]

Clovis remained unaffected by her appeal, and when the child died, he blamed the death on the baptism. However, great losses during a battle with a rival tribe, the Alemanni, moved him to try this new God of his queen's:

> Jesus Christ, . . . you who Clotilda maintains to be the Son of the living God, you who deign to give help to those in travail and victory to those who trust in you, in faith I beg the glory of your help. If you will give me victory over my enemies, and if I may have evidence of that miraculous power which the people dedicated to your name say that they have experienced, then I will believe in you and I will be baptized in your name. I have called upon my own gods, but, as I see only too clearly, they have no intention of helping me.[2]

Soon after, the Alemanni turned and fled. When Clovis told Clothilda of all this, she was overjoyed and sent for Remigius, bishop of Rheims, who instructed Clovis in the Christian faith. The people too were prepared to follow the new God, and a grand baptismal ceremony was immediately organized in which Clovis and more than 3,000 members of his army were baptized.

Because Clovis had become the only Catholic Germanic chief (several were Arian Christians), the bishop of Rome forged a strong alliance with him. Capitalizing on such early inroads, Pope Gregory I began sending monks out as missionaries to convert other northern peoples, such as the Angles and Saxons in Britain (596). In addition to concentrating on the tribal king, Gregory's mission strategy also included converting indigenous temples and festivals for Christian use. The people were already accustomed to gathering at these holy sites; by continuing the practice, the local culture was Christianized without being destroyed. A number of current popular traditions, such as the Christmas tree and Easter eggs, are Christian adaptations of indigenous customs.

After great losses in battles with a rival tribe, Clovis, king of the Franks, tried the Christian God. When the enemy fled, Clovis converted and was baptized by Remigius, bishop of Rheims. More than 3,000 members of Clovis's army were baptized in a grand baptismal ceremony. (The Bettmann Archive)

Eastern Christianity was also involved in the missionary enterprise. In the ninth century the patriarch of Constantinople sent two brothers, Cyril (826–869) and Methodius (c. 815–885), to the Slavs of Moravia. They preached in Old Slavonic and prepared a sacred liturgy in that language, still used by Orthodox churches of eastern Europe. Though converting few people themselves, they laid the foundation for many conversions during the next generation in Serbia, Bulgaria, and Russia.

In the tenth century the baptism of Prince Vladimir of Kiev led to the Christianization of Russia. No doubt influenced by his Christian mother, Vladimir plunged eagerly into Christian life and, moved by the beauty of the liturgy, allied himself with the Greek Orthodox church. Not all of the Slavs became Orthodox: the Poles, Czechs, Slovaks, Croats, and Slovenes became Roman Catholic.

As can be seen by Clovis's prayer, conversion was not necessarily based on an inner conviction of sin or a sense of God's mercy, as in classical Pauline or Augustinian theology, but on the need for a powerful protector. The Christian God was believed to be more powerful than the Germanic gods; hence Clovis and his people adopted that God for their own. It is clear from later descriptions of Clovis that his conversion meant little in terms of his life. He remained a bloodthirsty warrior who took great delight in cleaving the heads of his enemies. Thus when we speak of the conversion of Europe during this period, it should not be understood as people suddenly committing heart and soul to Jesus Christ and living lives based on Christian principles but rather as people seeking the most powerful deity as their patron and protector in a harsh and brutal world.

The Rise of Islam

Early in the seventh century an Arab merchant named Muḥammad had a series of visions in which he perceived God calling him as a prophet to proclaim God's justice and mercy and teach obedience. The new faith, Islam, began in what is now Saudi Arabia. Because of their common tradition and belief in a single God, Muslims respected both the Jewish and Christian faiths, teaching that Jesus Christ was one of a series of great prophets that included Moses, Abraham, the Hebrew prophets, and Muḥammad himself. However, they believed that by worshiping Christ the prophet as a deity, Christians demeaned God.

Shortly after Muḥammad's death, Muslim armies expanded into the whole of North Africa, converting its inhabitants to Islam. By 750 Syria, Egypt, Libya, parts of Asia Minor, the Persian Empire, and the Iberian peninsula (modern Spain and Portugal) had fallen to Muslim swords, and it was feared that France would fall as well until the Franks under Charles Martel defeated them at Tours (732). The Byzantine emperor, Leo III (717–741), also beat back Muslim attackers besieging Constantinople, thereby preserving a smaller but still flourishing empire. Defeated at Tours and stalemated over Constantinople, the Muslims temporarily lost interest in Christian Europe, which was left to develop on its own.

Muslim dominance of the Mediterranean and occupation of so much formerly Christian territory had a twofold effect on European civilization. First, trade between the Christian east and Christian west virtually ceased. Without trade, the basic differences in language, culture, theology, and political theory that had always divided east and west intensified. Second, the constant and recurring threat of conquest by Islamic forces terrified all Christians, east and west. Medieval Christians viewed Muslims as godless heretics, while Muslims regarded Christians as mistaken idolaters. Warfare between Christians and Muslims, once begun, became a fact of life for centuries.

THE VISION OF CHRISTENDOM

Following the Muslim expansion, Europeans developed the overarching ideal of **Christendom**, a single political entity headed by an emperor but under the authority of the church. This dream became reality when Charlemagne (c. 742–814), heir to the Frankish kingdom of Clovis, conquered most of Europe and forced conversion on the defeated tribes. On Christmas Day in the year 800, Pope Leo III crowned Charlemagne "Emperor of the West," clearly symbolizing that the emperor ruled under the authority of the pope. Charlemagne's rule raised hopes that the unity and peace of the Roman Empire of the first century might be revived. A new political entity, the Holy Roman Empire, came into being. Although the empire crumbled after Charlemagne's death, the vision of a united Christendom remained, reasserting itself under future powerful monarchs and continuing as a political ideal until the rise of nation-states in the sixteenth century.

The Feudal World

The concept of a Christendom unified under the papacy was reinforced by the character of the

The new political entity, the Holy Roman Empire, came into being under Charlemagne's rule. Here he is depicted in a sixteenth-century stained-glass panel. (The Metropolitan Museum of Art, Gift of William H. Riggs, 1913)

feudal system, which flourished between the ninth and fifteenth centuries. Because money and trade had almost disappeared, land, which was owned by powerful local lords, was the primary measure of wealth. People without resources of their own became vassals of the local lord, pledging homage and allegiance in exchange for land rights. The lord's manor estates were essentially self-contained villages and included the manor house, the peasants or serfs who were permanently attached to the land, workshops, church, and fields. The lords were themselves vassals to higher nobility, and on up the pyramid to the king.

This social structure was reflected in the church as well, which played an important role in feudal society. Parish boundaries in many places were coterminous with those of the manor estate, and the lord of the manor often had the right to appoint the local priest. The church's own wealth increased as nobles made generous bequests. Thus the church, with its huge landholdings, became an intricate part of the feudal system; its bishops and abbots became feudal lords with great temporal power, themselves vassals to kings and princes. Popes found themselves administering vassals, fighting wars, and negotiating over secular issues with secular rulers. Such responsibilities required liquid wealth, which the church sought from everyone in the form of tithes, taxes, and military service. Eventually the church came to offer ecclesiastical positions to children of the nobility in exchange for donations, in effect selling offices. Such clergy were essentially secular lords and often neglected their duties, some never even visiting the churches under their care. Such practices were roundly condemned and the subject of repeated attempts at reform by both clergy and laity.

Medieval Theology

The medieval worldview of an ordered, hierarchical society was mirrored not only in the outward organization of the church but also in its theology and worship. God was perceived as the supreme feudal monarch to whom all Christians owed fealty as loyal vassals. One of the great theologians of this time, Anselm of Canterbury (1033–1109), used this image to explain why God became human in the incarnation of Jesus Christ.[3] By disobeying God, Anselm explained, human beings have, in effect, broken their feudal oath and dishonored God. When a vassal breaks fealty, that person owes a debt to the lord above that owed as part of the original allegiance. But humans already owe God all that they have, including life itself, by virtue of their original relationship in creation; they are incapable of paying the additional satisfaction and so face the penalty of death. Only God has the resources to pay what is owed, but only humans owe it; therefore, it was necessary for God to become human in order to pay the debt, restore God's honor, and save human beings from the penalty of death. What we have here is a restatement of the theology of the Council of Chalcedon—Christ is fully human and fully divine—in language that reflects the social structure and worldview of the time. Theology and the feudal system mutually reinforced and affirmed each other.

The medieval understanding of the sacraments of the church—the rituals believed to mediate the grace of God, such as baptism and the Eucharist—also reflect this feudal worldview. For example, the sacrament of **penance** for the forgiveness of sins was divided into three components: contrition (feeling sorry for sin), confession (naming sins before a priest), and satisfaction (doing good acts as a sign of contrition and in payment for sins). Satisfaction in particular was understood as repaying part of the debt owed God for sin. Any debt left over at death would be discharged in **Purgatory**, a "way station" between earth and heaven where a person was purified of sin before entering the presence of God. The idea of temporal satisfaction, an earthly penalty owed for sin, led to the idea of payment by substitute (to be discussed shortly) and the practice of indulgences, scripts issued by the pope that pardoned the temporal satisfaction owed for sin in exchange for some meritorious act, such as a pilgrimage to Rome or going on a Crusade. Initially a means of easing human fears and the burden of penance, indulgences became abused by those who sought to sell them for profit; the outcry against such abuse was a leading cause of the Reformation of the sixteenth century.

Interpretations of the Eucharist

Debates over what actually happens during the Eucharist broke out between those who held a realist-metabolic interpretation and those who held a symbolic one. The realists believed that during the consecration, when the words of institution were said, the bread and wine actually became the body and blood of Jesus Christ; that is, there was a real and metabolic change in the elements. Thus when one ingested what appeared to be bread and wine, one was in reality eating Christ. The symbolic interpreters said that Christ was spiritually present in the eating but that the bread and wine remained bread and wine.

The realist-metabolic interpretation, later known as transubstantiation, became the dominant view. One of the consequences of this was that an aura of mystery surrounded the Eucharist and extended to the priest as the person who had the power to make Christ present. The altar became a place of power. Masses (worship services) multiplied as wealthy patrons paid for clergy to say them for their dead relatives and for their own souls following death. Actual communion lost its importance—what mattered was the moment of sacrifice when the priest would say *Hoc est enim corpus meum,* "This is my body," and make Christ real on the altar.

Lay Religion

A second consequence of the new sense of the mystery of the Eucharist was that the chasm between clergy and laity widened even more. Communion was considered so awesome that ordinary people ceased communing. Unable to follow the Latin Mass, commoners spent the time in private devotions unrelated to what was happening at the altar. Even the phrases of institution became "magical": *Hoc est . . .* became reduced in common parlance to the words *hocus-pocus.* Priests prayed some parts of the Mass privately, so that even worshipers who understood Latin could not hear. This added to the celebration's air of mystery, reinforcing, in popular belief, its other-worldly, magical character.

The impressive majesty of the priest standing before the altar resacrificing Christ for the sins of the world often left the people with feelings of awe and terror. No longer the gentle savior, Christ became the stern judge. The people turned to Mary and the saints as intercessors and mediators better able to sympathize with human frailty and thus plead their case before Christ.

Medieval people also made pilgrimages to various saints' shrines. The poor journeyed to nearby shrines, and people with means headed for faraway places. The Holy Land had been a favorite goal of pilgrims since the fourth century, but after the Muslims occupied it, travel there was difficult. Pilgrimages continued, however. In Spain, after the Spaniards drove the Muslims out, the shrine of Saint James of Compostuela became quite popular.

The Apocalypse of St. John, **to whom the Book of Revelation is attributed, by Albrecht Dürer. Periodic waves of apocalyptic fervor swept Europe during medieval times. The doctrine of Purgatory and penance gave people a sense of hope that they could work through their punishment and someday be with God.** (Photo by Robert Sietsema)

Based on references to Christ's return in the Book of Revelation, waves of apocalyptic fervor periodically swept Europe. Many Christians prepared for Christ to return to earth, judge the living and the dead, bring history to an end, and achieve the perfection of all things. This apocalyptic consciousness undergirded many people's piety. Since they viewed life on earth as a battle between God and Satan that would end in a cataclysm, they believed that only with the help of Christ, the church, and the sacraments could their souls be saved. Each person's judgment would come immediately upon dying, they believed; all would be punished or rewarded for their deeds on earth. Those who died in a state of mortal (serious) sin would be condemned to hell, a place of eternal suffering. The sacrament of penance—confession and absolution followed by praying, doing charitable deeds, and making donations to the church—could, through Christ's power as administered by the church, help to eradicate the effects of sin. Even after such penance, however, sinners might still need a period in Purgatory to work out their punishment. After being transformed by the suffering of Purgatory, the freed souls would then ascend to heaven, where they could enjoy forever the beatific vision of God.

The doctrine of Purgatory and penance gave medieval people a sense of hope that at death they would not be left in a state of mortal sin to face the wrath of God. Purgatory and the penitential system offered a way to work out temporal punishment so that one might someday be with God. Practitioners also enjoyed a sense of the power of their prayers—and especially the prayers of the saints on their behalf—to help both themselves on earth and souls in Purgatory.

Medieval Monasticism

The structure of feudal society and its concern about sin and satisfaction had a profound effect on monasticism as well. Although monasticism started with the individual desire for perfection, it rapidly moved beyond the pious aims of monks such as Antony and Benedict to become a leading medieval institution. Instead of existing primarily for people seeking personal salvation, monasteries filled a vital spiritual, economic, and social role in the Middle Ages. Wealthy nobles founded and endowed monasteries to pray, fast, and fight spiritual battles on their behalf. An example of this can be seen following the battle of Soissons in 923. The Frankish bishops imposed a three-year penance on all participants that entailed fasting on bread, salt, and water for three 40-day periods each year. Such an action, though not impossible, would have rendered most of the Frankish knights incapable of further military action for at least 120 days a year. Instead, the knights or their lords could pay monks to undergo the privation—and thus pay the satisfaction—in their place. Sin and its payment were not internal states like guilt but rather objective and quantifiable entities—weights on a scale. Thus payment could be made, or weight added, on

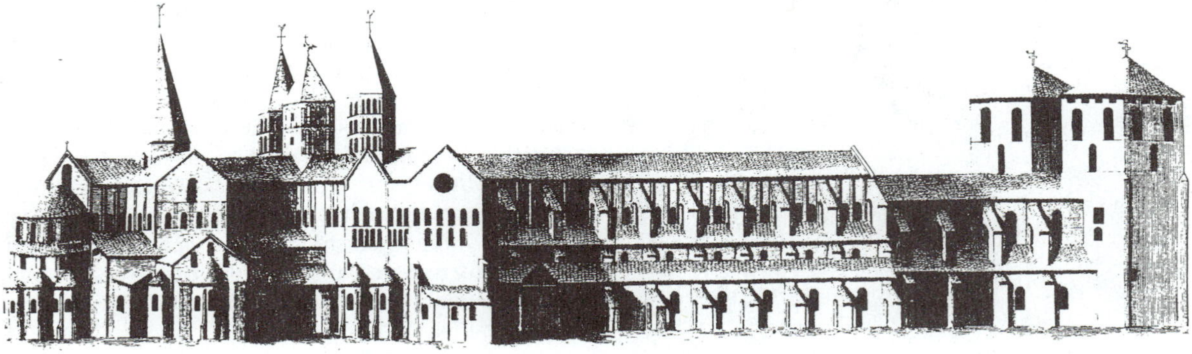

The most powerful of the monasteries was Cluny, whose name became synonymous with the splendor and grandeur of the medieval church. The Romanesque third abbey church (shown here) was built between 1080 and 1225 and was the largest church in Europe when completed. (The Granger Collection)

behalf of someone else. What was necessary was that the debt owed to God was paid.

In addition to fulfilling this penitential function, thus alleviating the burden placed on the military aristocracy, monasteries also helped to relieve economic and family pressures. Many feudal societies had restrictions against splitting property, and so families were faced with the problem of how to care for extra children in a society where land was the primary source of wealth. The oldest son would inherit the estate, a second son could become a squire to a higher lord, but often third or fourth sons would be enrolled in the church, either as priests or as monks. Extra daughters for whom there was insufficient dowry for a "good" marriage, widows without remarriage prospects, and even very young children might be placed in monasteries, sometimes against their will. No personal sense of vocation was necessary; monks and nuns filled a societal need, and sons and daughters who entered were often fulfilling family obligations.

As an unintended result, monasteries, with their continuous endowments, grew extremely powerful and wealthy, becoming great landowners themselves. They became havens for the aristocracy, admitting only the nobility. The manual labor that Benedict had specified as an essential part of the monastic life was relegated to the monasteries' servants and to the peasants who were part and parcel of the land.

The most powerful of the monasteries was Cluny, whose name became synonymous with the splendor and grandeur of the medieval church. Founded in 910 by Duke William of Aquitaine, who wanted to make up for a life of warfare by building what he believed was a bridge from earth to heaven, Cluny rapidly expanded into a monastic empire with "daughter houses" spread across Europe. With its international status, Cluny helped to promote the idea of a united Christendom, its monks transcending local mentalities to forge a European identity.

Cluny was also involved in the political life of society. Feudal Europe during the tenth and eleventh centuries was chaotic, characterized by the unceasing warfare between competing local lords. In an effort to control the fighting and protect the fabric of society, Cluny issued a decree in 989 known as the Peace of God, which declared monks, clergy, women, children, laborers, and farm animals and implements off-limits to warring knights, in effect protecting all noncombatants. In 1017 a second decree, the Truce of God, was issued; this prohibited fighting from noon Saturday to Monday morning. No single ruler was strong enough to control the warfare; only Cluny with its growing empire was powerful and respected enough to step into the breach.

By the end of the eleventh century some monks believed that the Cluniac order, with its emphasis on elaborate ceremony, beautiful carvings, and complex liturgy, had become too rich and concerned with outward appearances. Led by Robert of Molesme, in 1098 a group of reformers left the order to form a new monastery at Cîteaux in Burgundy, desiring to return to the simplicity of Benedict's *Rule*. Known as the Cistercians (after *Cistercium,* Latin for *Cîteaux*), this new order emphasized austerity, simplicity, humility, and retirement. They wore habits (the monastic dress) of undyed wool, ate simple vegetarian meals, and refused the valuable gifts and endowments granted to other monasteries. Because they wished to escape the world, the Cistercians settled on frontier land, clearing wilderness areas. Their wish for the simple life backfired, however, as their productive settlements became prime agricultural land during a time of rapid population growth. In trying to leave the world, the Cistercians found that the world had followed them. Like the Cluniacs, the Cistercian movement also grew immensely and came to play an important role in political and ecclesiastical affairs.

EMPEROR AND POPE

Gregorian Reform

During the tenth and early eleventh centuries the papacy degenerated into a morass of political intrigue. Because high ecclesiastical offices—bishoprics and abbacies—carried land and tithes with them, they became prized assets for powerful and wealthy lords and valuable sources of revenue for the popes who disposed of them. The practice of simony—the buying and selling of offices—proliferated; excommunication—cutting a person off from the sacraments of the church—became a weapon for political and personal gain; and the papal throne was occupied by a series of men who often obtained their positions through treachery and assassination, having little concern for the moral or spiritual life of the church.

Led by monks from Cluny, a great call for reform arose. Pope Leo IX set out to reform the papacy by regulating papal elections. He appointed a number of cardinals (from the Latin *cardo,* "hinge") who would meet in the *curia* or papal senate when needed to elect a new pope. The cardinals were thus the hinge on the door leading to the papacy and, despite periods of ineffectiveness, are still responsible for selecting the pope.

The reform movement took its name from Pope Gregory VII, its leading proponent. Intent on reforming the morals of the clergy, Gregory tried to end simony and to enforce monastic norms of life on all clergy. He decreed that married clergy must no longer celebrate Mass and forbade the laity from hearing Mass from them. Enforcement proved difficult, however, since many if not most of the lower clergy were married; nonetheless, thousands of clerical wives and children were cast aside into grinding poverty as clergy obeyed. Others lived in concubinage in nominal but not actual obedience to papal decrees.

Gregory also aimed to change the feudal relationship that had gradually developed between church and state, claiming papal supremacy not only over the whole church but also over the emperor. He decreed that popes alone, not the emperors, may depose or reinstate bishops, create new bishoprics and monastic orders, and rearrange diocesan lines to suit economic needs. With regard to secular rulers, the pope "alone may use the imperial insignia"; "the pope may absolve subjects of unjust men from their fealty"; "he may depose emperors."[4] Undergirding these astonishing assumptions of absolute authority was his assertion that "the Roman Church has never erred, nor ever, by the witness of Scripture, shall err to all eternity."[5]

Gregory opposed especially the practice of lay investiture. Because of the close ties between church and state in feudal society, the great lords of the church—bishops and abbots—were also secular vassals, receiving land and power from the emperor and powerful nobles and owing them allegiance in return. Naturally, the aristocracy wanted to ensure the loyalty of their vassals and so insisted on the right of appointment and investiture. Gregory VII wished to end this practice, insisting that only the pope had the right to appoint and depose bishops and to invest them with the insignia of office (ring and staff). When the powerful Emperor Henry IV tried to appoint his own candidate as archbishop of Milan in 1075, assuming the right of investiture, Gregory VII excommunicated him. Excommunication involved more than simply keeping Henry from the sacraments of the church, serious as this was believed to be; it also dissolved the allegiance of his nobles, leaving him politically vulnerable. The famous story of the repentant Emperor Henry standing barefoot in the snow begging forgiveness from

Pope Gregory in January 1077 was stamped into the European imagination.

Gregory's claims to absolute power did not last. In 1084 Henry organized an army to depose the pope. Gregory fled, dying in exile a year later. The controversy over lay investiture was eventually settled by the Concordat of Worms in 1122. Pope and emperor met to work out a compromise whereby there would be canonical elections of bishops and abbots, free from the evils of simony and violence. From the king the candidate would receive the regalia, the tokens of temporal office, signifying his duty as a secular lord, while from the pope he received ring and staff, the symbols of spiritual office. This double investiture—royal and ecclesiastical—indicated the dual nature of the bishop as minister of the church and lord in the secular realm, reflecting the realities of feudal power.

The Crusades

Despite the tensions between popes and emperors, the overarching ideal of Christendom directed that the church and feudal lords work together for what they believed to be the expansion and protection of the faith. This common vision and mission was especially evident in the Crusades, a succession of ventures to liberate the Holy Land from its Muslim conquerors. Speaking in 1095 before a large open-air gathering of French churchmen and nobles, Pope Urban II proclaimed a holy war against Islam. In an effort to recruit men, the pope promised that all who undertook the journey to free the Holy Land from the "pagans" would receive the immediate remission of confessed sins. This decree of the first indulgence marked a major point in papal doctrines. To the cry *Deus vult!* ("God wills it"), many knights from France, Germany, and Italy set out to rescue the shrines of the Holy Land from the Turks. Traveling via Constantinople, the warriors fought their way south through Asia Minor into Palestine, capturing Jerusalem after a bloody struggle in 1099.

Despite the victory of the First Crusade in Palestine, the Muslims repeatedly threatened the Christian position, recapturing Jerusalem in 1187. As new military groups arrived almost yearly from Europe, the original religious idealism gave way to a lust for booty. The Venetians deflected the Fourth Crusade, originally bound for Egypt, toward Constantinople, where they hoped to help the deposed Byzantine emperor to regain power. In 1204 these Crusaders sacked Constantinople, placing a western prince on the throne and embittering the Byzantines.

The Crusades dragged on for almost 200 years, with armed bands drifting in and out of the Holy Land. Kings and popes did little to stop them, and great lords probably enjoyed having their more bellicose knights occupied elsewhere. The so-called Children's Crusade was the most bizarre episode in the crusading annals. Children from all over Europe set off to take the Holy Land, believing that the power of innocence would succeed where armed might had not. Against his better judgment, the bishop of Brindisi, a southern Italian seaport, allowed them to leave, but they never reached the Holy Land. A great storm sank their ships; many of the children drowned, and the survivors were captured and sold into slavery.

The Crusades had several goals: to win back the Holy Land from the "infidels," to reunite the eastern and western portions of Christendom, and to bring personal salvation to the knights and their supporters. By the time the Crusading spirit had passed, however, the movement had lost its momentum and popular support. Ultimately, the Crusades could not stop the resurgence of Muslim military strength and resulted instead in increased enmity and distrust between Muslims and Christians. The papacy, which at first had gained prestige for sponsoring the Crusades, was discredited by both the west's defeat and the debasement of the movement's seemingly lofty aims. Finally, the hope of reunion between the Eastern Orthodox and Catholic churches was forever put to rest by the cruelty and rapaciousness of the western knights during the sack of Constantinople.

LATE MIDDLE AGES

THE NEW URBAN WORLD

Although the stated goals of the Crusades were never accomplished, the movement between Europe and the Middle East did lead to a renewed awareness and knowledge of lands beyond Rome. As sea and land routes became safer and more heavily traveled, trade increased, and goods and ideas were exchanged across cultures. Money returned to circulation; a middle class of artisans, merchants, and bankers appeared; and methods of agricultural production improved. With the land able to support a larger population and with the increase of trade, cities also grew, leading to new sets of needs, concerns, and aspirations in an urban environment.

New Religious Orders

At the end of the Roman Empire the church had been forced to shift from primarily an urban institution to one capable of meeting the needs of a rural, feudal world. Now, approximately 600 years later, the church once again found itself facing a changing situation—the rise of the town and the needs of its inhabitants. One way the church had met the earlier demand was through the spread of monasteries, which served as centers for mission and evangelism. Now a new form of monasticism was again in the foreground of the church's outreach, with new orders formed especially to meet the needs of a changed society.

The best known and most admired of these pioneers was Francis of Assisi (1182–1226), who founded the Franciscan order in reaction to an overly powerful and wealthy church that was unresponsive to the urban

St. Francis of Assisi (left), following a sudden conversion, renounced his wealth and began preaching, inspiring many to adopt his ideals of poverty. A wealthy townswoman, Clare of Assisi (right), joined his movement, establishing a contemplative women's order, the Poor Clares. (The Bettmann Archive)

JEWISH-CHRISTIAN RELATIONS

Although Judeo-Christian relations during the early Middle Ages appear to have been cordial, that situation changed dramatically in the eleventh century when persecutions and expulsions broke out in cities across France. The critical event, however, was the First Crusade (1096), when religious excitement mixed with greed as Crusaders plundered the Jewish quarters in French and German towns on their way to Palestine, murdering the inhabitants. Enmity was formalized in the Fourth Lateran Council (1215), which ordered all Jews to wear a distinguishing mark, often a yellow patch (an idea adopted with deadly relentlessness by Nazi Germany).

The theological justification for such actions—that Jews were enemies of God because they had crucified the Son of God and thus were identified with the power of evil—appeared in the late-first-century gospels of Matthew and John. Furthermore, the church claimed to be the new Israel, the inheritor of the promises of God; how then could old Israel continue to exist except as servants to the new?

But socioeconomic reasons also lay behind rising anti-Semitism. The revival of European economic life in the twelfth century depended on the rise of banks and the lending of money. Forbidden by canon law to charge interest, Christians turned to Jewish bankers for their financial needs. But no one likes the moneylender; the Jew, who was already stigmatized as the infidel and Christ killer, was now also depicted as the greedy stranger holding his Christian victim in thrall. As international trade and finance grew and Christians entered the banking business, the kings and princes who had borrowed from Jewish sources now turned against them. King Edward I of England expelled all Jews from the land in 1290, followed by expulsions from

poor. The son of a wealthy cloth merchant, Francis was enthralled by adventure and romance. Following a severe illness, he underwent a sudden conversion, renouncing his wealth and proclaiming his marriage to "Lady Poverty." Receiving a revelation in which the Lord told him to restore the church, Francis and a small band of followers set out to rebuild dilapidated church buildings near his home. Eventually he began to rethink his vision and decided that the Lord wanted him to restore the church by returning it to its primitive ideals of poverty. As he preached in towns and countryside, his magnetic personality and the strength of his message inspired many to emulate him and his understanding of the life of Christ. A wealthy townswoman, Clare of Assisi, joined his movement, establishing a contemplative women's order known as the Poor Clares.

The second of these new orders, the Dominicans, was founded as a response to a movement that the church deemed heretical. In the twelfth century a new kind of preacher began roaming the cities, espousing a form of Manichaeism that regarded the material order as evil and reserved salvation for a spiritual elite. One of its main centers was the town of Albi, in southern France, which organized its own clergy, refusing to listen to the bishop or papal representatives. Pope Innocent III, determined to crush this heresy, asked one of his bishops to visit the so-called Albigensians. The bishop traveled in typical pomp and glory. In his retinue was a young Spanish cleric, Dominic (c.

France in 1306 and banishments and massacres in German towns throughout the fourteenth century. In fifteenth-century Spain, all Jews were offered the choice of banishment or conversion to Christianity. Many of those who remained and "converted" continued to practice their Jewish faith secretly; when discovered, they were tried, tortured, and burned.

Despite the increasing anti-Semitism of the time, medieval Christianity owed a great intellectual debt to Judaism. Many of the new ideas that sparked the intellectual fervor of the late Middle Ages, including the rediscovery of Aristotle, came by way of the Jewish and Muslim worlds, enriched by fruitful theological discussions between Jewish and Christian scholars.

Although Jews achieved partial freedom during the Enlightenment and following the French and American revolutions, anti-Semitism reappeared in its most virulent and demonic form in the twentieth century with the deliberate extermination of most of European Jewry in the Holocaust. How much the Vatican knew about the "Final Solution" and whether the pope's silence implied consent remain a hot topic of debate. Nevertheless, Pius XII's policy of neutrality during the war and his failure to protest Nazi atrocities even when urged to do so by knowledgeable authorities such as the president of the Polish government in exile, the bishop of Berlin, and the chief rabbi of Palestine have severely damaged the reputation of the wartime papacy. In sharp contrast stand the actions of several papal nuncios in eastern Europe and Turkey who were involved in rescue missions, among them Monsignor Roncalli in Istanbul, later known as Pope John XXIII, who helped to save several thousand lives.

Following World War II, a mood of deep contrition has marked Christian attitudes toward Judaism, marked by debate on whether or not the conversion of the Jews is a legitimate part of the Christian mission and support for the founding of Israel in 1948. Cooperative efforts between Christians and Jews have led to the removal of anti-Semitic sentiments from church textbooks and liturgies.

1170–1221), who saw that this show of wealth was itself alienating the people. Dominic undertook to address them in simplicity with a life style that they could support. From his success there, Dominic established an order of preaching friars to promote "pure doctrine." The Dominicans became a widespread order, preaching in the cities and living simple lives, unattached to any particular monastery or property.

Despite Dominic's limited success, civil war broke out between Catholics and Albigensians. In 1215, at the Fourth Lateran Council, Pope Innocent III ordered a Crusade against the heretics, and a Catholic army from northern France captured the Albigensian strongholds. The church then set up ecclesiastical tribunals to punish those found guilty of heresy on the principle that it is permissible to burn the body in order to save the soul. This was the beginning of the **Inquisition**, for centuries a means of enforcing religious conformity (see the box "Jewish-Christian Relations").

Despite some misgivings about new orders, Innocent saw the value of the Franciscans and Dominicans. He approved the formation of orders of friars and preachers to work in the cities, preaching the gospel and helping the poor, especially important in an era when the laity had little preaching and no religious education. The orders attracted followers from all social classes, inviting laity to join as "third orders" (after monks and nuns), in which they would take simple vows of charitable works and regular prayer within the context of ordinary life.

Cathedrals

The economic burst that characterized the twelfth century and the renewal of city life led to the building of magnificent cathedrals in most European cities. First built in a style called Romanesque, the cathedrals were massive structures built on a plan of a great cross rather than in the rectangular style of the basilicas. Eleventh-century cathedrals, baptisteries, and even the Leaning Tower of Pisa adapted the classical pillars, rounded arches, and multicolored marbles of the Roman basilicas.

In the twelfth century a daring method of building known as the Gothic style began in northern France. Pointed rather than rounded arches were developed, allowing greater height on less stone. The taller arches permitted larger window spaces, many of which were filled with stained glass, bathing the interior of the church with an ethereal light. Sculptors adorned the portals with scenes from scripture; statues of prophets, apostles, and saints filled niches along the walls and columns; and fantastic creatures known as gargoyles brooded down from the roofs. The light and height of the Gothic cathedrals suggested to many the merging of heaven and earth: lofty ceilings reached to heaven, their great piers planted firmly in earth.

Built for the glory of God, the cathedrals were also great public works, providing employment for townspeople and prestige for the city. The people were justifiably proud of their cathedrals. Medieval chroniclers reported that all classes of the population—nobles, merchants, and artisans, men and women, rich and poor—helped to pull the carts of stones used to construct the cathedral of Chartres in France. With astonishing speed, the Gothic style spread from France to other parts of Europe and England.

The great cathedrals became the centers of town life. Cathedral clergy called canons lived together under the direction of the bishops and deans. Cathedral schools, established initially to train clergy, began to educate lay children, thus contributing to a resurgence of literacy. Food and alms were distributed to the poor, and markets were set up alongside the cathedral walls, becoming gathering places for the exchange of ideas and gossip.

Universities and Scholasticism

In the twelfth century the Christian scholars of Europe were introduced to previously unknown Greek and Roman works brought back by the Crusaders from the east and from Muslim and Jewish scholars and translators in Spain. These new ideas worked like intellectual yeast to change the shape of medieval theology.

In conjunction with the new learning and in response to the needs of a growing merchant class, major universities developed in cities such as Oxford, Bologna, and Paris. Franciscans and Dominicans in particular staffed the faculties, and students received

In the twelfth century, Gothic architecture began in France. The taller arches permitted larger windows, many of which were stained glass, bathing the interior of the church with an ethereal light. The Cathedral at Rheims is seen here with its pointed arches and flying buttresses. (Photo Researchers)

ecclesiastical status as clerics in minor orders. An international spirit pervaded the universities. Latin formed a common bond as professors and students from all over western Europe gathered and exchanged ideas.

Europe had rediscovered ancient thinkers, in particular the Greek philosopher Aristotle, by way of Jews and Spanish Muslims. Their philosophies and the stimulating university life led to a new way of thinking known as Scholasticism. The Scholastics set out to synthesize faith and reason, applying philosophical techniques to theological inquiries in a question-and-answer format. The questions ranged widely from philosophical issues about how human beings know things to theological problems about creation, salvation, and the existence of God.

The use of reason to demonstrate God's existence can be found first in the work of Anselm (1033–1109), the forerunner of Scholasticism, whose theory of atonement was discussed earlier. Anselm's ontological argument for the existence of God depended on the definition of God as "that than which nothing greater can be conceived." In short, Anselm argued: One can conceive of God existing in one's thought and one can conceive of God existing in reality. But to exist in reality is greater than to exist merely in thought. Therefore, since God is "that than which nothing greater can be conceived," God must exist in reality as well as in thought. Anselm never intended his proof to convince nonbelievers; rather, he formulated it as an intellectual exercise to express the depths of his own faith.

Thomas Aquinas (c. 1225–1274), considered the greatest of the Scholastic theologians, was born to a noble family near Naples. Intended for a prestigious ecclesiastical career, he joined the newly formed Dominican order over his family's protests. Teaching theology at the universities of Paris and Naples, Thomas engaged in theological disputes with fellow scholars over the relationship between faith and reason and the correct use of philosophy—that of Aristotle in particular—in theological inquiry. He wrote two huge compendiums of philosophical and theological thought, *Summa contra Gentiles* and *Summa Theologica,* in an encyclopedic attempt to synthesize all knowledge.

Thomas took a more positive view of the human capacity to do good than his famous predecessor Augustine. Though he agreed that people inevitably sin, he insisted that they are inclined to do good and avoid evil. Human beings have a large measure of free choice once God's grace restores the virtues lost in Adam and Eve's fall (specifically, faith, hope, and love). Even without grace, people can exercise the classical virtues of prudence, fortitude, temperance, and justice. Since people have the capacity to do good, Thomas taught, they must do so if they are to achieve the highest good: the Beatific Vision, or union with God.

Thomas Aquinas was considered the greatest of the Scholastic theologians. Here he is seen as depicted in a fresco by Giovanni da Fiesole, known as Fra Angelico. (The Granger Collection)

But morally good actions are only one part of human communication with God and only a step on the way to the Beatific Vision. Another important part is reception of the sacraments, especially the Eucharist. Thomas wrote of the doctrine of transubstantiation using Aristotelian categories of substance and accidents. Substance defines what something really is in essence; accidents describe what that thing looks like in appearance. According to this concept, the bread and wine are changed in substance into the body and blood of Christ, only retaining the outward appearance or accidents of bread and wine. Thomas had a deep reverence for the Eucharist and wrote several hymns of adoration that are used in Roman Catholic, Anglican, and Protestant churches today. One of his best known explores the mystery of Christ's presence in the bread and wine:

> *Now, my tongue, the mystery telling*
> *Of the glorious Body sing*
> *And the Blood, all price excelling,*
> *Which the Gentiles' Lord and King,*
> *Once on earth among us dwelling,*
> *Shed for this world's ransoming.*
>
> *Word-made-flesh, true bread he maketh*
> *By his word his Flesh to be,*
> *Wine his blood; when we partaketh,*
> *Though the senses fail to see,*
> *Faith alone when sight forsaketh,*
> *Shows true hearts the mystery.*[6]

Aquinas hoped that applying reason to faith would lead to wisdom and the Beatific Vision. Starting with an unformed faith, a person uses rational powers or intellect to investigate the world. The culmination of natural knowledge and divine revelation produces a formed faith, which, in turn, should lead to wisdom and the vision of God. Thomas was never able to reach this final step, to cross from formed faith to the Beatific Vision. Instead, at the end of his life he fell silent, saying that what he had seen in the light of revelation made all that he had written seem as chaff.

Controversy swirled around Thomas's work for many years, but his influence gradually increased when he was canonized (declared a saint) by Pope John XXII in 1323. In the sixteenth century he was named "Universal Doctor of the Church," and Thomism, the systemization of his thought, became the standard for Roman Catholic theology until the mid-twentieth century.

Mysticism

When Thomas Aquinas fell silent, the path toward union with God was left to the mystics, who, not sharing the Scholastics' optimism about the power of reason, focused instead on self-denial, prayer, and mystical contemplation (see the accompanying box, "Mysticism"). Bernard of Clairvaux (c. 1090–1153), a Cistercian abbot and monastic theologian who preceded Aquinas, developed a mystical theology of love in which he asserted that the only human desire that could be satisfied was the desire to know and love God. Its consummation was union with God, who is love:

> The reason for our loving God *is* God. . . . He is himself the Lovable in his essential being, and gives himself to be the object of our love. He wills our love for him to issue in our bliss, not to be void and vain.[7]

It is ironic that Bernard, the theologian of love, was also the foremost preacher of the Second Crusade. He believed that it was necessary to wage war to convert the Muslims and save them from eternal damnation.

Meister Eckhart (c. 1260–1327), a noted Dominican preacher, taught that each person has a divine spark of God within; one need only free oneself from attachments and images to find this connection with God. His claims of such direct access to God, however, threatened the established authorities, and he was later tried for heresy. This experience led the church to examine mystical works and their authors carefully, and later mystics became quite circumspect.

Compounding the problem for bishops charged with "defending the faith" was the fact that many noted mystics were women. In a society that strictly limited women's religious callings, it is not surprising that mysticism appealed to them. Visions gave a woman authority directly from God when no authority outside the cloister was recognized by the church. Hildegard, abbess of Bingen (1098–1179), experienced mystical visions most of her life. In addition to these experiences, she also composed music, penned poetry, and wrote books on medicine and natural philosophy, showing keener scientific observation than was common in her day. Elaborate illuminations depicting her visions illustrated her writings.

Catherine of Siena (1333 or 1347–1380) was an Italian woman known for both mysticism and heroic works of charity. She joined the Third Order of Saint Dominic, continuing to live in her parents' home. Her *Dialogue* records her descriptions, dictated while in ecstasy, of her remarkable visions. Though not trained in theology, she knew enough to remain within the

COMPARISON

MYSTICISM

When scholars have attempted to identify commonalities among the world's religions, one subject that often comes up is mysticism. Some twentieth-century scholars, including Aldous Huxley and Rudolf Otto, have claimed that mystical experiences from around the world are often identical. There are two fundamental kinds of mystical experience, says Otto. First is the Inward Way, in which one withdraws from all outward things and, beginning to tap an intuitive sense, experiences the ground of one's own soul. There in the soul one finds that which contacts the infinite, Meister Eckhart's "spark of God." A similar experience is found in eastern mystics, like the Hindu monist Śaṅkara, who calls it Ātman, which is identified with Brahman. The second kind of experience is the Outward Way or the Way of Unity. Otto calls this an experience of seeing the fundamental unity of all outward things as well as inward ones: "They see all not in process of becoming but in Being, and they see themselves in the other. Each being contains within itself the whole intelligible world. Therefore all is everywhere" (Otto, quoting the *Fifth Ennead* 8). This, he says, is parallel to the Hindu experience of the One, from which comes the many, that is, the world.

In the 1970s and 1980s, such scholars as Steven Katz, Robert Gimello, and Wayne Proudfoot criticized these authors, saying that such parallels overlook the very real differences in language, claim, and nuance among mystics from different traditions. Since the words we use in our experiences are part of those actual experiences, then when one has a mystical experience of God, for example, all that one has learned about God enters into that experience. Since the meaning of "God" is not the same as the meaning of "Brahman," they argue, two mystical experiences of different religious "objects" must differ.

More recently, the scholars Donald Rothberg, Donald Evans, and Sallie King, among others, have criticized this second position as missing the unusual nature of the process leading to mystical experiences and the experiences themselves. Mysticism involves, in part, letting go of one's concepts and language and coming to an experience that may not be entirely shaped by thought and language. They argue that inward experiences of Brahman, like those Otto spoke of, *do* have key features in common with inward experiences of God. If this is so, it may be that certain experiences across many traditions are indeed of a single type or a few types.

The debate is far from resolved.

orthodoxy of her day. Her works of charity and remarkable spirituality attracted many disciples. A voluminous correspondent, she was actively involved in the affairs of the church. She wrote reverently yet sternly to Pope Gregory XI, urging him to leave Avignon, France, and do his duty by returning to Rome. During the Great Schism, which began in 1378, she supported Urban VI, the Roman pope, urging kings and cardinals to support him as well. Canonized in 1461, she is one of only two women to be named "Doctor of the Church" in Roman Catholicism.

Another revered mystic of the late Middle Ages was

attached to the church of St. Julian in Norwich, England, and thus is known to us as Julian of Norwich (c. 1342–1416). Julian experienced a series of intense visions during a severe illness as a young woman and then spent the next 20 years reflecting on what she believed God had shown her. Her account of the visions and subsequent theological reflections, *Showings, or Revelations of Divine Love,* is written in English, not Latin, and is extraordinary for its theological depth and spiritual insights, such as her description of the mystery of the Triune God, in which she used both male and female language:

> Greatly ought we to rejoice that God dwells in our soul; and more greatly ought we to rejoice that our soul dwells in God. Our soul is created to be God's dwelling place, and the dwelling of our soul is God, who is uncreated. . . . For the almighty truth of the Trinity is our Father, for he made us and keeps us in him. And the deep wisdom of the Trinity is our Mother, in whom we are enclosed. And the high goodness of the Trinity is our Lord, and in him we are enclosed and he in us.[8]

Julian taught that the love of God created and sustains all living creatures. When her inquiring mind questioned God about the problem of sin and human salvation, she was shown that Christ's compassion is greater than human sin and was assured with these now-famous words: "All will be well, and all will be well, and every kind of thing will be well."[9] Julian was aware that occasionally the revelation given to her contradicted the traditional teaching of the church. Although outwardly she conformed to the church, she appears inwardly to have reserved her own judgment and clearly trusted that God would make the truth plain.

CHALLENGES TO CHRISTENDOM

Decline of the Papacy

Papal power and prestige reached their height in the thirteenth century with the reign of Pope Innocent III (1198–1216). The first pope to use the title Vicar of Christ, Innocent exercised the temporal powers of the papacy with greater sweep and efficacy than any pope before or since. He exerted his authority over kings and emperors, claiming that as Vicar of Christ he stood in the place of Christ, imbued with both priestly and royal authority. Innocent involved himself in the political affairs of many lands, placing all of England under interdict when King John refused to accept the pope's choice as archbishop of Canterbury. The churches were closed, no sacraments were performed, and John's subjects were absolved of their allegiance until the king capitulated, acknowledging the pope as his feudal lord.

The Fourth Lateran Council in 1215, the most significant of the medieval councils, was the crowning event of Innocent's papacy. It called for the education and moral reform of clergy, episcopal oversight and regulation of monasteries, prohibition against selling relics or charging for the sacraments (both of which had become moneymaking schemes), and suppression of heresy. Baptism, confirmation, penance, the Eucharist, marriage, holy orders, and extreme unction were defined as the official sacraments of the church, and the laity was required to go to confession and receive communion at least once a year.

The last of the politically powerful popes was Boniface VIII (1295–1303), a proud man whose claim of absolute supremacy presaged the eclipse of papal power. In a dispute with Philip IV of France in 1302, Boniface issued a proclamation stating that temporal authority is subject to spiritual authority, which in turn is subject only to God. "Therefore," Boniface said, "we declare, state, define and pronounce that it is altogether necessary to salvation for every human creature to be subject to the Roman Pontiff," the pope.[10] The next year Philip kidnapped and humiliated Boniface, parading him sitting backward on a horse. When he died shortly thereafter, the papacy moved to Avignon, where it remained firmly under French control, a tool of the French state with French popes and cardinals, for 70 years.

In 1377 Pope Gregory XI returned to Rome but died the next year. Following a dispute over the papacy, both Italian and French cardinals elected replacements, and for almost four decades, a time known as the Great Schism, there were two and even three papal courts. Each pope vied for supremacy, and each regarded the other as an antipope. In 1415 the Council of Constance finally resolved the schism, deposing all others and electing Martin V pope.

This quarrel over papal authority caused some to renew efforts to establish the general council as the ultimate authority in Christendom. Several theorists, backed by legal reasoning and traditional precedent and mirroring thought in the east about councils, claimed that a general council held ultimate authority and could be called without the pope's authorization. Though they did not prevail, the counciliarists succeeded in pressuring popes to call several councils during the fifteenth century to tackle the twin tasks of reforming the church and clarifying doctrine.

Despite the Great Schism and the councils, the popes of the late Middle Ages still sought to maintain the ideal of a Christendom unified under their authority. But even as they strove to rekindle the vision, it was being replaced in the minds of kings and emperors by a new vision of the nation-state. Where Innocent was able to bend a king to his will, Boniface failed. The power of excommunication and interdict had been used so frequently by the church for political purposes that they no longer held much weight, either with feudal lords or with their subjects. Furthermore, national pride was replacing church membership as the chief source of identity—the common people were beginning to consider themselves primarily as English or French or German and not simply as members of Christendom. Eventually popes had to work merely to defend their own holdings in Italy against invasion from foreign kings and Italian princes; the vision of a united Christendom began to splinter against the reality of the independent state.

During the Renaissance, Popes expended great wealth in lavish patronage of the arts, employing artists to embellish buildings and squares all over Italy. This detail is from Raphael's *Christ's Charge to St. Peter,* a cartoon for the walls of the Sistine Chapel. (The Granger Collection)

Renaissance

Yet even at the end of this era the papacy remained a dominant and sometimes creative force. Popes expended great wealth in lavish patronage of the arts, employing artists such as Michelangelo and Raphael, whose magnificent works embellished buildings and squares all over Italy. The murals of the Sistine Chapel and other buildings, statues of David and Moses, and much more attest to the vivid genius of these artists of the era known as the Renaissance ("rebirth").

Literary arts also flourished as humanist scholars rediscovered the ancient world. (Humanism is the study of the humanities or liberal arts; Renaissance humanists were concerned with reviving classical antiquity.) Erasmus, a prominent humanist who hoped to renew the church by returning to its source, studied and published the New Testament in Greek. Vernacular languages also came into their own, and we find great poets such as Dante and Chaucer writing in Italian and English instead of Latin.

Also during this time, Europe began to expand, both literally and figuratively, after centuries of being closed in on itself. Following Columbus's astonishing voyages of exploration, Spain and Portugal unleashed waves of conquistadors, ultimately claiming the entire Western Hemisphere as part of Christendom, backed by the pope, who divided South America into Spanish and Portuguese spheres. Vast wealth flowed into Spain, which under Ferdinand and Isabella became the most powerful new nation-state in Europe. Franciscans, Dominicans, and members of other religious orders were sent out with the explorers and conquistadors, baptizing the conquered peoples of the New World and occasionally trying to save them from slavery and extermination. Portuguese voyagers opened trade routes around Africa to the fabled East, where new missionary ventures were launched. The discovery of vast lands and peoples who had never heard of Jesus Christ shattered the illusion of a united Christendom, despite papal efforts to expand it.

The Call for Reform

In this era of vigorous changes, it is not surprising that many European Christians grew discontented with the religion that had served the old feudal structure so well. John Wycliffe (c. 1329–1384), a theologian at Oxford University, attacked the power of popes, bishops, and monks and attempted to improve the position of poor parish priests. Known as the "Morning Star of the Reformation," he denied the doctrine of transubstantiation, maintaining that the substance of bread and wine remains after consecration. He also taught that the church belongs to the people, not the clerical hierarchy, and believed that the Bible should be available in local languages for all to read and study. Wycliffe was much admired by the English poet Geoffrey Chaucer, who modeled the figure of the parson in *The Canterbury Tales* after him.

A second important reformer at this time was John Huss (1369–1415) in Bohemia, who was dean of the philosophical faculty and rector of the University of Prague. Influenced by Wycliffe, Huss also preached against clerical abuses and called for a reform of the church, beginning with the papacy and its vast wealth. The pope is only a holy father, Huss said, if he lives a holy life, following Christ in poverty. Despite having been promised safe conduct by Emperor Sigismund to present his views at the Council of Constance in 1415, the Council in an act of treachery overturned the safe-conduct pledge and burned Huss at the stake as a heretic.

Church reform had to wait another hundred years for Luther and Zwingli, and then it was accomplished only by tearing Christendom asunder.

NOTES

1 Gregory of Tours, *The History of the Franks,* trans. Lewis Thorpe (New York: Penguin, 1974), pp. 141–142.

2 Ibid., p. 142.

3 Anselm, "Why God Became Man," in *A Scholastic Miscellany: Anselm to Ockham,* ed. Eugene R. Fairweather (Philadelphia: Westminster Press, 1956), pp. 100–183.

4 Gregory VII, *Dictatus Papae,* trans. S. Z. Ehler and J. B. Morrall, in *Church and State through the Centuries* (London: Berns & Oates, 1954), pp. 43–44.

5 Ibid., p. 44.

6 Thomas Aquinas (1263), in *The Hymnal of the Protestant, Episcopal Church, 1940* (New York: Church Pension Fund, 1940), hymn 199.

7 Bernard of Clairvaux, "On the Love of God," in *Late Medieval Mysticism,* ed. Ray Petry (Philadelphia: Westminster Press, 1957), pp. 54–60.

8 Julian of Norwich, *Showings,* trans. Edmund Colledge and James Walsh (New York: Paulist Press, 1978), p. 285.

9 Ibid., p. 225.

10 Boniface VII, *Unam Sanctum,* ed. E. Friedberg, in *Corpus Juris Canonici* (Leipzig, 1881).

CHRISTIANITY

CHAPTER 21

THE SPLINTERING OF THE VISION

REFORMATION MOVEMENTS

STATE OF THE CHURCH

We have seen that Christianity, especially after Constantine, often mirrored society, sharing its worldview and adopting its norms and customs. As the feudal world disintegrated and the centralized power of the Holy Roman Empire dissolved into that of the individual nation-states, the Catholic church shared that dissolution, losing the power and prestige of a centralized papacy with its unifying vision of Christendom. And just as feudal society replayed itself within the doctrine and organization of the medieval church, so too the growing world of banking and commerce found a home in the Renaissance and Reformation church. Head of a vast institution, the pope was in constant need of money to support the ecclesiastical bureaucracy, to negotiate with princes and kings from a position of strength, to sponsor great building projects, and to live in a style commensurate with royalty. This need for money cascaded down the ecclesiastical structure as every high office had to be paid for through taxes, tithes, and moneymaking projects such as selling indulgences or showing relics.

On top of this, the highest offices were often filled with men rumored to have obtained their positions through bribery, intrigue, or even murder, who used them for their own advantage and aggrandizement. Typical of the day were Pope Sixtus IV (1471–1484), the builder of the Sistine Chapel, who approved his nephew's assassination of rival Giovanni de Medici, and Pope Innocent VIII (1484–1492), who sired 16 children, whom he acknowledged and elevated to prominent positions as cardinals of the church. In the eyes of many people, such ambition, corruption, and blatant disregard for moral virtues tarnished the church, putting it almost beyond reform.

At the other end of the spectrum, the parish churches in small towns and villages were filled with men who were no better off than their poorest parishioners. Often illiterate and uneducated in theology or scripture, these parish priests were barely able to make their way through the Latin Mass, ignorant of the meaning of the words they were parroting, and offering little education or inspiration to their parishioners. As a result, much of the European peasantry, though nominally Christian through baptism, remained unaware of Christian teaching and practiced an odd mixture of half-remembered pagan traditions and half-forgotten Christian rites.

Beginning as a call for moral and doctrinal reform of the church, the sixteenth-century Reformation dramatically transformed the face of Christianity as numerous groups broke away from Roman Catholicism to form separate protest or Protestant churches. Outgrowing its religious beginnings, the Reformation movement came to encompass European political and social life as well. For over 100 years religious concerns dominated the scene until, by the mid-seventeenth century, a war-torn and exhausted continent shook itself free from the last vestige of the yoke of Christendom.

MARTIN LUTHER AND REFORMATION IN GERMANY

The sound of nailing on a quiet day at the University of Wittenberg, October 31, 1517, marked the beginning of the Protestant Reformation. Martin Luther, an Augustinian friar who served as professor of scripture at the university and preacher in the local parish church, was concerned when his parishioners began buying indulgences that they were told promised the complete forgiveness of all sin without the need for repentance and would free souls from Purgatory. In response, he nailed a list of propositions to the university's chapel door, requesting academic debate. Though the debate never took place, the *Ninety-five Theses* were reprinted and circulated to the public, unleashing a storm of protest and popular indignation.

Martin Luther, a charismatic preacher and a colorful writer, served as a catalyst for reform, beginning with his *Ninety-five Theses*. (Courtesy the Busch-Reisinger Museum, Harvard University)

Justification by Grace through Faith

A charismatic preacher and a colorful writer, Luther served as a catalyst for reform, his religious insights stemming from his own experience of God's wrath and mercy. Intended by his parents to be a lawyer, Luther left law school to enter the Augustinian friary at Erfurt, a strict order where he at first found peace in following the routines of the cloister. Troubled, however, by the late medieval understanding of salvation and grace, which said, in effect, that God would not deny grace to any who do the best they could, and ruled by an overscrupulous conscience, Luther's frequent confessions failed to assure him that he was, indeed, gaining salvation. In short, he lived in dread of God's righteous wrath. His superior, Staupitz, sent him to study scripture and, upon receiving his doctorate, to teach at Wittenberg.

Studying the Psalms and Romans preparatory to teaching, Luther pondered the problem of the righteousness of God:

> I hated that [expression], "the righteousness of God," which, according to the custom and use of all teachers, I had been taught to understand in the philosophical sense with respect to the formal or active righteousness . . . with which God is righteous and punishes the unrighteous sinner. I did not love, indeed I hated the righteous God who punishes sinners and secretly . . . I was angry with God.[1]

As he continued to study and lecture, however, Luther broke through to a radically new understanding of the righteousness of God: it is the righteousness that God gives to believers to make them just in God's eyes. Instead of having to earn grace through pious acts or good works, sinners have only to trust in God's mercy, given in Jesus Christ. Justification by grace alone through faith alone became the guiding principle of the Reformation.

Luther further developed this theme in *The Freedom of the Christian* (1522), which discusses the relationship between faith and good works. Holding the two in dynamic tension, Luther wrote: "A Christian is a perfectly free lord of all, subject to none. A Christian is a perfectly dutiful servant of all, subject to all."[2] Human beings can do nothing to merit salvation, which is the utterly free gift of a merciful God, but are freed from the law and its demands through faith in Christ. At the same time, however, Luther explained, Christians respond to God's love by loving in return and by serving their neighbor in need.

Authority of Scripture

A voluminous writer, Luther's most monumental work was his translation of the Bible into German, thus opening the scriptures for people to read for themselves and, in the process, shaping the modern German language. Suspicious of new translations, the Catholic church placed the Bible in the vernacular on its list of prohibited books, arguing that only people trained in theology could interpret the scriptures properly, and in addition upheld unwritten (Catholic) tradition as equally authoritative. To this Luther responded that only the gospel has final authority, for it reveals the Word of God, Jesus Christ. All Christians, guided by the Holy Spirit, ought to be able to read and interpret the Bible. Not a biblical literalist, Luther read scripture through the interpretive lens of Saint Paul's justification by faith; the letter of James, for instance, which advocates works along with faith, Luther dismissed as of "straw."

Priesthood of All Believers

Along with the doctrine of justification by grace through faith and the authority of scripture, Luther also taught the priesthood of all believers. All occupations and vocations are blessed by God, and all can be used for the service of God; priests and monks are no holier than lay people, and the monastic life offers no greater promise for salvation than life in the world. Nevertheless, the church has to order itself; although all Christians are kings and priests before God, not all Christians can preach or celebrate the sacraments without creating pandemonium. To this end the Christian community should choose promising leaders to be ministers of word and sacrament for the congregation. The gulf between clergy and laity would no longer be one of presumed quality (Catholicism held that ordination was a sacrament conveying its own special grace) but rather one of training and vocation.

One result of this teaching, encouraged by Luther, was the closing of monasteries and the return of monks and nuns to secular life. In this monks fared better than nuns, since many ordained monks had the opportunity to serve as parish ministers. Though some former nuns married, many others found themselves without means of support. Although Luther helped to arrange marriages for former monastics, he himself remained unmarried until one determined ex-nun, Katharina von Bora, refused all his suggestions of possible suitors, agreeing only to marry Luther himself. Katie, as Luther called her, was a strong-minded woman who worked well with her husband, running a household filled with children, students, and friends.

The Course of the Reformation

When Luther invited debate on indulgences, he did not realize that the issue was far more complex than simply the theological understanding of penance; the attack on indulgences also attacked the pope and the church's financial structure underlying their sale. In an effort to raise money for building St. Peter's in Rome, Pope Leo X sold the archbishopric of Mainz to Albert of Brandenberg (who was underage and already in possession of two other episcopal sees), giving him the right to sell papal indulgences with the understanding that Albert and the pope would split the proceeds. Unaware of these unspoken economic and political motives, Luther believed that genuine debate was possible and would demonstrate the validity of his position. Instead, an assembly of church and state officials of the emperor summoned Luther to appear before the Diet of Worms in 1521. Ordered to recant his writings without debate, Luther refused, saying:

> Unless I am convicted of error by the testimony of Scripture or (since I put no trust in the unsupported authority of Pope or of councils . . .) by manifest reasoning I stand convicted by the Scriptures . . . I cannot and will not recant anything.[3]

Pope Leo X excommunicated Luther, and the Holy Roman emperor, Charles V, declared him an outlaw. Luther's prince, Frederick the Wise, spirited him away to Wartburg Castle. While there he translated the New Testament into German, but he did not stay long in hiding; he returned soon to his parish and the university, where he assumed leadership of the reform movement in Germany.

Why did the Protestant Reformation succeed when so many earlier attempts at reform had failed? When John Huss tried to reform the church, he was betrayed and burned; Luther defied papal authorities and carried much of Germany with him. One reason, discussed earlier, was the rise of the nation-state and the growing sense of national identity. The electors and princes of the German estates saw in Luther's cause an opportunity to bolster their own political position and to end the drain of their country's resources to Rome. This is not to say that they were not genuinely interested in church reform but rather that political and religious motivations cannot be sharply distinguished.

One other crucial element in the Reformation's success was the printing press—it revolutionized the world, for the first time making cheap, easily reproduced writings available to the masses. Luther consciously took advantage of this new technology, writing 30 pamphlets during the years 1517–1520, of which 1 million copies were in circulation by 1524. In addition, itinerant preachers traveled around teaching and preaching to the illiterate, and town governments hired "reading women" to read the latest Luther sermon to the peasants who came into town on market day.

In sum, through his doctrine of justification by grace alone through faith alone, widely dispersed in writing and preaching, Luther opened the door to the immediacy and authority of direct encounter between human beings and God. His translation of the Bible, use of the vernacular, abolition of the penitential system, and shrinking of the chasm between lay and clergy all focused on this end. An unforeseen consequence of his new teachings was the further splintering of the church. Without a pope, there ceased to be any single authority who could decide on doctrinal matters; thus the Protestant denominations proliferated, with virtually every region's religious story becoming distinctly its own.

REFORMATION IN SWITZERLAND

Zwingli and the Lord's Supper

Luther's writings and reforms sparked interest, debate, and new thinking all over Europe. Ulrich

Ulrich Zwingli, a humanist and preacher in Zurich, agreed with Luther's teachings except in regard to the Lord's Supper, which he believed to be a memorial. He did not believe that Christ was present in the bread and wine of communion. (The Granger Collection)

Zwingli (1484–1531), a humanist and preacher at the Great Minster Church in Zurich, agreed with much of Luther's teachings but split over the understanding of the Eucharist. Luther taught that the Sacrament of the Altar, or Lord's Supper, "is the true body and blood of the Lord Christ in and under the bread and wine which we Christians are commanded by Christ's word to eat and drink."[4] Because of Christ's promise, when the words of institution are proclaimed, the Word of God is joined to the elements of bread and wine, granting forgiveness of sins to those who receive with faith.

Zwingli, by contrast, believed that the Lord's Supper was a memorial, a remembrance commanded by Christ. The risen Christ, according to Zwingli, is up in heaven at the right hand of God; therefore, he cannot be present in the bread and wine of communion. The argument between Zwingli and Luther centered on the words "This is my body." Luther argued that Jesus's words are to be taken literally, thus identifying the body with the bread. Zwingli insisted that the *is* is metaphorical: the bread merely represents the body of Christ. These differences created a rift between Luther and Zwingli that was never healed, the first of many fissures to divide Protestantism. Zwingli died in battle near Zurich as he led a Protestant army in civil war against the Catholics.

Calvin and the Sovereignty of God

John Calvin (1509–1564), a French humanist and lawyer who became the most influential reformer in Switzerland, was fascinated by Luther's teachings. When King Francis I ordered a persecution of French Protestants, Calvin fled, ending up in Geneva, where he was persuaded to stay and lead the budding Protestant movement. In 1536 Calvin published his first edition of *The Institutes of the Christian Religion,* a landmark theological work (its final and definitive revision appeared in 1559). The *Institutes,* described by Calvin as a guide to reading scripture, systematized Reformed thinking in a way that Luther's tracts, written to meet specific situations, did not.

John Calvin, a French humanist and lawyer, became the most influential reformer in Switzerland. While his teachings concerning predestination are best known, Calvin was far more interested in God's involvement in the world. (Snark/Art Resource)

The key to Calvin's teaching is the absolute sovereignty of God, whose providence directs the world. Reflecting on this sovereignty, Calvin became interested in questions of election and how people are saved, ending up with what is known as "Calvin's horrible decree," or the doctrine of double predestination: God chooses to save some people; God chooses to damn others. Although this occupies only a small section toward the end of the *Institutes,* it became an identifying mark of Calvinism, especially in the eyes of non-Calvinist detractors. Calvin himself was far more interested in God's involvement in the world, especially in the person of Jesus Christ, through whom we come to know God and God's mercy. For Calvin, God's sovereignty was not something to be feared but a "blessed assurance" that the world, nourished and preserved by God, has meaning; faith in God leads to joyful obedience. The later (1647) *Westminster Catechism* summarizes this perspective with its leading question: "What is the chief end of man? . . . To glorify God and to enjoy him forever."[5]

Calvin's emphasis on God's sovereignty had important consequences for church and society. Because God is the true Lord, theoretically no institution or individual should have absolute authority over others. Nonetheless, the elect need to preserve order, educate the young, and prevent those who are not of the elect from creating chaos. But even the elect can be corrupted by power and hence should not hold it for too long; this led Calvin to favor divided authority and the rotation of government office. Modern democracies, with their rotating rulers, owe Calvin a vast, though largely unacknowledged, intellectual and practical debt.

For Calvinists, earthly life brings struggle, the elect never being really at home. But unlike other Reformation thinkers, Calvin thought that humans, with God's grace, can improve themselves and society. In this a measure of individualism pervades his outlook. The rise of capitalism and the development of a prosperous middle class coincided with the rise of the Reformed faith in northern Europe and, indeed, may have been aided by Calvinism's optimistic emphasis on individual effort. Believing that God alone properly rules, Calvin set to establish a godly commonwealth in Geneva, ruled by laws based on the Bible. Citizens risked punishment if they missed sermons or even laughed in church, magistrates banished several for witchcraft or adultery, and Calvin supported the death of the Spanish physician Michael Servetus, who was burned at the stake for denying the doctrine of the Trinity.

Worship

An important distinction between Lutheran and Reformed (churches following Zwingli and Calvin) Protestantism centered on the reform of worship. Luther declared that although the gospel contains all that is necessary for salvation, it does not dictate how services should be run. Therefore, unless certain practices are forbidden in scripture or detract from the centrality of the gospel (leading Christians to place their trust in custom or works), they are allowed. Thus Lutheran services retained candles, clerical vestments, and crucifixes as aids to simple faith and piety. Hymn singing with musical accompaniment filled the worship (Luther wrote many hymns himself); scripture reading and preaching became the focal point of the service. Although Luther wished to retain the centrality of the Eucharist, many Lutheran churches practiced only monthly or even quarterly communion.

Zwingli and Calvin took the other tack: unless something is specifically mentioned in the Bible, it is forbidden in church; hence they stripped the churches of all external signs. Calvinist services centered on sermons with simple Eucharistic ceremonies celebrated quarterly. Believing that Christ is present in the hearts of believers, Calvin maintained the ancient outline for the Eucharistic liturgy but included instructions to communicants about the meaning of the rite. Simple music, principally settings of the Psalms, replaced elaborate polyphonic hymns or anthems, and organs were forbidden as nonscriptural. Reinforcing the sense of human responsibility and obligation to God, the services became more austere and serious affairs in which human beings came into direct but somber contact with their severe Deity.

Whereas Lutherans centered primarily in Germany and Scandinavia, Calvinism became an international movement. From Geneva the teachings of Calvin spread to an influential group of French nobles, the Huguenots, who, persecuted by Catholic rulers, were eventually expelled from France. Calvinists also established churches in Germany, the Netherlands, England, and Scotland. John Knox (1513–1572) reformed the Catholic church in Scotland along Calvinist lines, from which came Presbyterianism, strong especially in Scotland, England, Northern Ireland, and the United States.

Protestantism and the Laity

The rapid spread of Protestantism meant monumental changes for the common worshipers. The availability of scripture in the vernacular opened doors formerly closed to them, and the corresponding increase in education opened even more. Gone was the Latin Mass, with all its mystery, now replaced by lengthy vernacular sermons. Gone was individual confession before a priest, replaced by "godly counsel" from elders. Gone from the Reformed churches were the stained-glass windows depicting Bible stories and saints' lives; gone too were the statues, relics, incense, and elaborate priestly vestments as the churches became plainer, if no less noble, structures. Gone from many sects were bishops and priests, now replaced by preaching and teaching elders. Now were heard calls for individual and social morality as a way to gain the simple, worthy life. Restrictions on amusements, especially on Sundays, similarly curbed self-indulgence. Although the disappearance of religious processions, festivals, and pilgrimages may have robbed life of some of its fun, more citizens heard the Word of God more often, attendance at church being mandatory. And as both Lutheran and Calvinist laypersons participated more fully in worship services and the clergy shared in family life, the gap between them narrowed.

ROYAL REFORMATION IN ENGLAND

Political Reform

The course of reform in England proceeded along a different track from that in Germany or Switzerland; taking its direction from the ruling monarch, the Reformation was mandated from above

Henry VIII of England, here in a portrait by Hans Holbein, established the Church of England as a result of a quarrel with the pope. Henry had sought to divorce his wife in order to marry another in a desire for a male heir; the pope refused to grant an annulment. (Alinari/Art Resource)

rather than rising from the commoners, as in Germany. The dynastic concerns of King Henry VIII (ruled 1509–1547) and his desperate desire for a male heir triggered the eventual break of the English church from Rome. Henry, anxious to divorce his wife Catherine of Aragon and marry another, applied to Pope Clement VII for an annulment of the marriage, but after years of legal wrangling the pope denied Henry's petition. Disgusted with Rome, Henry turned to his English Parliament for action. At the king's behest Parliament passed a series of acts separating England from Rome, culminating in the Act of Supremacy (1534):

> Albeit the King's Majesty justly and rightfully is and oweth to be the Supreme Head of the Church of England, and so is recognized by the clergy of this realm . . . , yet nevertheless for corroboration and confirmation thereof, and for the increase of virtue in Christ's religion within this realm of England, . . . be it enacted by authority of this present Parliament, that the King our Sovereign Lord . . . shall be taken, accepted, and reputed the only Supreme Head in earth of the Church of England.[6]

The language of the act implies that the monarch has always been head of the church—Parliament simply granted official recognition to that status, calling on all others to do likewise. In actuality, with the passing of the act, the headship of the church shifted from pope to king, and the church in England became the Anglican church, the Church of England.

As the new head, Henry had the power to punish heresy, visit clergy, define doctrine, and correct abuses. In an act that changed the complexion of English life, Henry dissolved the monasteries, seizing their property and ousting their inhabitants. Although loose discipline was offered as the excuse for the dissolution, Henry's true motivation was his desire for their wealth. To this day the countryside of England is dotted with the shells of ruined abbeys, whose lead roofs Henry stripped to make cannons.

But Henry's interest in reform was limited almost exclusively to the political. Deeply conservative at heart, Henry allowed initial reforms, such as placing the Bible in English in every parish church and encouraging preaching from scripture, but soon his dislike of Lutheranism led him to reiterate traditional Catholic doctrines and Eucharistic practices. Denial of transubstantiation was declared a heresy, punishable by burning. The final settlement of Henrician Anglo-Catholicism was essentially the Catholic church without the pope.

Theological Reform

When Henry died in 1547, he left three surviving children, each of whom shaped England's religion: Mary (daughter of Catharine of Aragon), Elizabeth (daughter of Anne Boleyn), and Edward (son of Jane Seymour). With the accession of Edward VI (ruled 1547–1553) the Reformation entered its second and most Protestant phase. The regency council for Henry's young son Edward included the archbishop of Canterbury, Thomas Cranmer, who was in correspondence with Calvin in Geneva. Cranmer, chief architect of the *Book of Common Prayer,* also wrote a series of homilies to be read in churches across the land that preached the Reformed faith. The more austere Calvinist model of worship was followed: candles, images, and vestments were eliminated; a table of thanksgiving and remembrance replaced the altar of sacrifice in the Eucharist; and even the words "the Body of Christ given for you" were dropped in favor of "Take, eat in remembrance of me."

Never a strong child, Edward died after a brief reign, and his half-sister Mary, a staunch Roman Catholic, became queen of England (ruled 1553–1558). Mary faced the supreme irony of being head of the Church of England, a position she despised, and having to use her power to pass an act through Parliament that deprived her of that very leadership and restored supremacy to the pope. Under Mary all of Henry's and Edward's reforming legislation was repealed. England again became Roman Catholic, and the churches were filled once more with incense, vestments, statues, and the sounds of the Latin Mass. Many who resisted were accused of heresy—about 300 Protestants were burned, including Archbishop Cranmer. Cranmer was caught in the dilemma of believing both that the monarch had the right to order religion and also that only the Reformed church was preaching the true faith. Under torture he recanted his Protestant views, but when tied to the stake he publicly repudiated that recantation, holding the hand that had signed the recantation into the flames first. Many other Protestants fled, often to Geneva, where they remained absorbing Calvinism and determined to return after Mary's death to continue the Reformation.

Under the long rule of Elizabeth I (ruled 1558–1603) the church in England once again turned Protestant, solidifying its position in what is known as the Elizabethan Settlement. When Elizabeth took the throne, she found a nation sick of religious fanaticism and longing for a peaceful solution. She also faced a Parliament divided between an upper house full of Mary's Roman Catholic lords and a House of Commons with many reformers pushing for a more extreme Calvinist Protestantism. Gradually Elizabeth succeeded in establishing a church that was a *via media,* a middle way between the Protestant and Catholic extremes. The 1559 *Book of Common Prayer* included both sets of Eucharistic words ("This is my body given for you"; "Take, eat in remembrance of me"), the wearing of vestments, and the reappearance of some saints' days. A set of 39 Articles of Religion, written toward the end of Edward's reign, was reissued, but with a less Calvinist bent. Internationally, England allied itself with the Protestant cause, but at home Elizabeth wanted to welcome those who were secretly Catholic in their hearts. According to Francis Bacon, Elizabeth had no wish to "make windows into men's hearts and secret thoughts."[7]

Under the rule of Elizabeth I the church in England once again turned Protestant in what is known as the Elizabethan Settlement. Elizabeth succeeded in establishing a church that found the middle way between the Protestant and Catholic extremes. (Snark/Art Resource)

THE RADICAL REFORMATION

The translation of the Bible into the language of the various peoples of Europe opened the floodgates to private interpretation based on personal revelation and experience of God. Several small groups of such Christians formed, preaching a new, radical form of Christianity. In the eyes of these reformers, all mainstream denominations, both Protestant and Catholic, were compromised and corrupted by the world; instead the church should be a gathered community of the faithful, separated from unbelievers and uninvolved in world affairs. Many of these groups practiced adult believers' baptism as a sign of incorporation into the community and so were called Anabaptists (literally, "rebaptizers") by their detractors. The radical reformers urged a return to what they believed was the simplicity of the early church based on a literal reading of the gospels. They rejected government involvement, refused to take oaths, and, for the most part, preached nonviolence.

One Anabaptist group gathered around a formerly Catholic Dutch priest named Menno Simons (1496–1561). Despite severe persecution by both Catholics and other Protestant groups, Simons preached pacifism, which he considered an essential part of true Christianity. His followers ended up in the United States and elsewhere, where they formed a number of Mennonite churches, marked by believers' baptism as a sign of faith and entrance into the gathered community and often respected for their staunch pacifism.

CATHOLIC REFORMATION

The currents of reform streaming through Europe did not spring entirely from within Protestantism; indeed, more than a decade before Luther's *Ninety-five Theses,* Queen Isabella of Castile (ruled 1474–1504), lamenting the degenerate moral state of the church, instituted a program of reform. Working with Cardinal Francisco Jiménez de Cisneros, later archbishop of Toledo, she sought the best candidates to fill high ecclesiastical positions, choosing men known for their incorruptibility and their desire for reform. Together they visited monasteries, called for renewed obedience, punished immoral clergy and monks, and encouraged learning and scholarship.

The concern was primarily with moral reform and doctrinal deviation was sternly discouraged. The infamous Spanish Inquisition, placed by the pope under the control of Isabella and Ferdinand, became a much-feared instrument of ensuring orthodoxy, especially among Jewish converts. In 1492 Isabella and Jiménez decreed that all Jews must either accept baptism or leave Spanish territories. Most were exiled, but of those who remained, many continued to practice Judaism in secret, knowing that discovery meant torture and death by the Inquisition.

Council of Trent

From the start reformers like Luther had repeatedly called for a general council of the church to discuss and instigate doctrinal and ecclesiastical re-

Isabella and Ferdinand of Spain as depicted in a woodcut from Ludolphus of Saxony's *Vita Christi cartuxano* by Alcala de Henares, 1502. The infamous Spanish Inquisition, placed by the pope under the control of Isabella and Ferdinand, became a much-feared instrument of ensuring orthodoxy. (The Granger Collection)

form. Pope and emperor refused to act until Protestantism threatened to engulf much of the European church. Finally, with the schism between Protestantism and Catholicism firmly entrenched, Pope Paul III convened a council in Trent, Italy, so that reform and clarification of doctrine could begin at last. The council met in three sessions between 1545 and 1563. Protestant representatives refused to attend.

The Council of Trent declared that the Bible and church tradition were equal sources of truth, rather than the scriptures alone, as Protestants contended. The delegates upheld the authority of popes, the seven sacraments, celebration of the Mass in Latin, and transubstantiation. Its decrees on **justification**, or God's action making humans righteous, are perhaps its finest work, outlining clearly and succinctly the overarching nature of grace as divine aid, while requiring humans to cooperate with grace and do good works for **sanctification**. The council instituted many long-demanded reforms, including the recommendations that bishops live in their sees and that clergy be educated and attentive to their parishioners. Catholic theology was clarified, and the Latin Vulgate was pronounced the authoritative scripture. By clearly outlining Catholic teachings, the Council of Trent ruthlessly excised once-useful ambiguities. At the beginning of the sixteenth century, Martin Luther could in good conscience declare that his teachings accorded with Catholic tradition, as could his opponents. By the end of the council, such latitude had disappeared. Motivated by a reaction against Protestantism, Trent gave birth to the modern Roman Catholic church. Major rethinking did not take place again until the Second Vatican Council of the 1960s.

Monastic Reform

Deeply concerned with the apparent laxness of monastic life, Protestant and Catholic reformers took sharply different approaches to remedying the problem. While Protestants disavowed monasticism altogether, claiming that all Christians were equal in God's sight on the basis of their baptism, Catholics followed the path of earlier reform movements, either revitalizing old orders or founding new ones.

Teresa of Ávila (1515–1582), a famed mystic and leader in the Spanish reform movement, restored the strict observance of the Carmelite rule despite fierce opposition. Teresa wrote several renowned texts on the spiritual life and the life of prayer (see the accompanying box), hoping to allay the suspicions of the Inquisitors, who generally took a dim view of mysticism as direct revelation to individuals without mediation by the church. Many of her writings, including *Interior Castle, The Way of Perfection,* and the autobiographical *Life,* have remained significant Christian devotional works. In 1970 Pope Paul VI declared her a Doctor of the Church, an honor she shares with only one other woman, Catherine of Siena.

The second significant religious order resulting from a renewed zeal was the Society of Jesus, founded by Ignatius of Loyola (c. 1491–1556). Hoping to win Europe away from the Protestants, Ignatius, a former Spanish soldier, organized his highly disciplined order along military lines. The Jesuits, as they were called, founded schools all over Europe to educate leaders in philosophy, theology, and spirituality.

A four-week program known as the *Spiritual Exercises,* written by Ignatius, forms the core of Jesuit spiritual formation. Through rigorous self-examination and meditations on the life of Jesus, the exercises are designed to purify a person from inordinate attachments to this life and to create soldiers of Christ. Through the exercises, Jesuits aimed to conquer their passions and give themselves wholly to God. Although initially intended specifically for Jesuit formation, Ignatian retreats adapted for laity have become popular with both Protestants and Catholics interested in spiritual growth.

Missions and Missionaries

With their concern to combat heresy and preach the gospel, the Jesuits produced a number of outstanding missionaries who traveled to Protestant Europe, Asia, and the Americas. Francis Xavier and Matteo Ricci opened new fields in the Far East, where they hoped to convert people by accommodating the Christian message to the ancient cultures of the East. Although few people left their own Hindu or Neo-Confucian religions in India and China, the Jesuits laid the groundwork for future missionaries and greatly expanded Western knowledge about the religions and cultures of Asia. Initial success in China and Japan by Jesuit and Franciscan missionaries crumbled after those countries' rulers violently suppressed Christianity in the seventeenth and eighteenth centuries (see Chapter 14). Only a few Christian communities survived.

Teresa of Ávila, *Interior Castle*

Teresa of Ávila wrote *Interior Castle* to help her nuns reach spiritual perfection. She compared the human soul to a beautiful crystal, made in the shape of a castle and containing seven mansions. In the innermost of these mansions was Jesus Christ, the King of Glory, illuminating the whole castle with his splendor. The nearer that one came to the center of the castle, the stronger the light was, but outside "everything was foul, dark and infested with toads, vipers and other venomous creatures." In the following excerpt, Teresa describes the close relationship that should exist between the soul of a believer and Christ.

Now if we think carefully over this, sisters, the soul of the righteous man is nothing but a paradise, in which, as God tells us, He takes His delight. For what do you think a room will be like which is the delight of a King so mighty, so wise, so pure and so full of all that is good? I can find nothing with which to compare the great beauty of a soul and its great capacity. In fact, however acute our intellects may be, they will no more be able to attain to a comprehension of this than to an understanding of God; for, as He Himself says, He created us in His image and likeness. Now if this is so—and it is—there is no point in our fatiguing ourselves by attempting to comprehend the beauty of this castle; for, though it is His creature, and there is therefore as much difference between it and God as between creature and Creator, the very fact that His Majesty says it is made in His image means that we can hardly form any conception of the soul's great dignity and beauty.

It is no small pity, and should cause us no little shame, that, through our own fault, we do not understand ourselves, or know who we are. Would it not be a sign of great ignorance, my daughters, if a person were asked who he was, and could not say, and had no idea who his father or his mother was, or from what country he came? Though that is great stupidity, our own is incomparably greater if we make no attempt to discover what we are, and only know that we are living in these bodies, and have a vague idea, because we have heard it and because our Faith tells us so, that we possess souls. As to what good qualities there may be in our souls, or Who dwells within them, or how precious they are—those are things which we seldom consider and so we trouble little about carefully preserving the soul's beauty. All our interest is centred in the rough setting of the diamond, and in the outer wall of the castle—that is to say, in these bodies of ours.

Let us now imagine that this castle, as I have said, contains many mansions . . . and in the centre and midst of them all is the chiefest mansion where the most secret things pass between God and the soul.

Source: Teresa of Ávila, *Interior Castle*, trans. and ed. E. Allison Peers (Garden City, N.Y.: Doubleday, 1961), pp. 28–30.

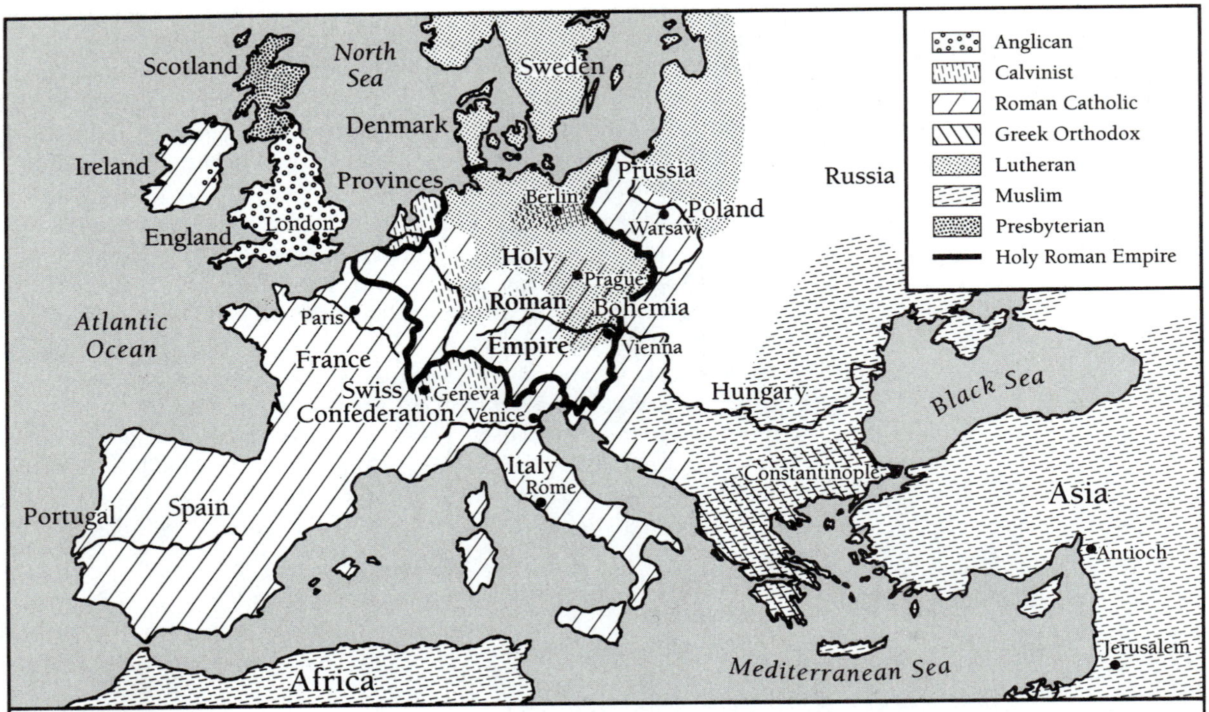

CHRISTIANITY AT THE TREATY OF WESTPHALIA, 1648

In the Americas missionaries from several orders effected mass conversions of Native Americans and African slaves, firmly establishing Catholicism in the Spanish and Portuguese colonies. Since the conquerors thought themselves part of a holy mission to spread the gospel, conquest and conversion proceeded almost simultaneously. Conversion by conquest meant little instruction, so religious practices soon bore traces of Native American and African beliefs, producing a highly syncretized Catholicism that blends native deities with Christian saints.

THE AGE OF ABSOLUTISM

Our story now returns to Europe, where bitter enmity and religious intolerance between Catholics and Protestants during the sixteenth and seventeenth centuries convulsed the area in a series of religious wars. The Peace of Augsburg in 1555 temporarily alleviated the situation with its declaration of *cuius regio, eius religio* ("whose king, his religion"), in which, at least for Lutherans and Catholics, the religion of the ruler determined the religion of the land. But religious issues combined with rising national sentiments to create powerful and violent conflicts; the Thirty Years' War (1618–1648) devastated central Europe.

Finally, the exhausted population saw peace restored by the Peace of Westphalia (1648), which redrew the map of Europe. According to this treaty, Calvinism, Lutheranism, and Roman Catholicism were afforded equal status within the Holy Roman Empire. The Catholics came to dominate western and southern Europe; the Protestants controlled most of northern

Europe. This religious alignment has remained practically unchanged ever since.

A rigid and intolerant age followed the Peace of Westphalia. Marked by absolutist governments and religious orthodoxies, the divine right of monarchs paralleled growing dogmatism in the churches. Both claimed a God-given authority to rule their respective subjects. As we have seen so often, church and society reflected one another: both were shaped by and responded to historical and cultural forces, both saw themselves as ordained by God, and both became in human imagination changeless and eternal realities.

DEVELOPMENT OF THE ORTHODOXIES

The early years of the Reformation were heady days, filled with excitement and anticipation about the newness of the gospel and God's action on earth. The reformers debated issues of faith, argued over the meaning of the Eucharist, and fought about the organization of the church. Caught up in the heat of the moment and consumed with the urgency of the task, they wrote as the occasion demanded. It was left primarily to their successors to systematize Protestant theology and delineate more clearly the differences between the denominations that emerged from the fray.

Eucharistic Theology

The first great systematizer of Lutheran thought was Philipp Melanchthon (1497–1560), Luther's principal collaborator and friend. Where Luther emphasized correct doctrine over Christian unity, Melanchthon introduced a more humanist spirit that elevated church unity above total doctrinal agreement. The old dispute between Zwingli and Luther over the meaning of the Eucharist irrupted within Lutheran circles as strict Lutherans accused Melanchthon and his supporters of being crypto-Calvinists. At issue was the understanding of how Christ is present in the Lord's Supper. Lutherans believed that because of the inseparable union between the divine and human natures of Christ, the properties of Jesus's divinity are transferred to his humanity (a sharing or communication known as the *communicatio idiomatum*), so that the body of Christ may be present in many places—that is, in many Eucharistic meals—at the same time. Reformed doctrine, by contrast, held for a greater distinction between Jesus's human and divine natures; it restricted the *communicatio idiomatum,* insisting it impossible for Christ's body to be present both in heaven, "at the right hand of God," and in the communion bread of innumerable churches on Sundays.

The Formula of Concord (1577) established a clear line of demarcation between Lutheranism and Calvinism regarding the Eucharist, declaring that the body and blood of Christ are truly and essentially present, distributed with the bread and wine.

Predestination

While Lutheran orthodoxy centered on Christ's presence in the Eucharist, within the Reformed churches controversy swirled around predestination and limited atonement, or who is saved and why. Calvin himself had relegated predestination to the end of his *Institutes;* later Calvinists, however, placed it front and center in their theology. A Dutch Reformed theologian, Arminius (1560–1609), disagreed with the strict Calvinist position that God decreed the election of some and the reprobation or damnation of others, teaching instead that predestination is based on God's foreknowledge of who will have faith, repent, and be saved. Christ died for the salvation of the whole human race, freely offering grace to all; human beings have the freedom to accept or reject that grace. The acronym TULIP summarized the conclusions of the Synod of Dort (1618–1619), convened to decide the issue:

Total depravity: the belief that every human faculty is tainted by sin
Unconditional election: there are no conditions to predestination, no foresight governing who is elect
Limited atonement: Christ died only for the elect, not for all human beings
Irresistible grace: God gives grace to the elect who are unable to reject or resist it
Perseverance of the saints: once saved, always saved—an extension of irresistible grace

PURITANS IN ENGLAND

The intimate connection between the course of religion in England and the current monarchy continued with Elizabeth I's successors. During her long reign, Elizabeth maintained a deliberate balance between the more traditionally minded and the more reform-minded

John Bunyan, *The Pilgrim's Progress*

Whereas Catholic spirituality as found in mystics like Teresa of Ávila focused on sacraments and the process of spiritual formation, aiming toward union with God, Protestant piety centered on the Christian as a sinner in need of God's grace. One of the greatest expressions of the Protestant life of faith is John Bunyan's *Pilgrim's Progress,* written while he was imprisoned for preaching the Puritan faith against the established Church of England in the 1660s.

A rich and fascinating allegory of the Christian life, *The Pilgrim's Progress* portrays the journey of Christian from the City of Destruction to the Celestial City. On his way Christian encounters heavenly guides who help to open his eyes to the true nature of sin and grace:

Then he took him by the hand, and led him into a very large parlour that was full of dust, because never swept; . . . now when he began to sweep, the dust began so abundantly to fly about, that Christian had almost therewith been choked. Then said the Interpreter to a damsel that stood by, "Bring hither water, and sprinkle the room," which when she had done, was swept and cleansed with pleasure.

Then said Christian, What means this?

The Interpreter answered: This parlour is the heart of a man that was never sanctified by the sweet grace of the Gospel; that dust is his original sin, and inward corruptions that have defiled the whole man. He that began to sweep at first is the Law, but she that brought wa-

parties in the church. Upon her death, however, the Puritans, as English Calvinists were called, steadily increased their demands for a more reformed church, objecting especially to the episcopal system of church government.

Conflict broke out between the king, Charles I, and the Puritans, who were influential in the House of Commons. When William Laud, the archbishop of Canterbury, enacted harsh measures against the Puritans, civil war (1642–1646) erupted. The triumphant parliamentary and Puritan forces deposed the king, beheaded both him and Laud, and established a Puritan dictatorship. The Puritans abolished the episcopacy, banned the *Book of Common Prayer,* closed theaters and other places of amusement, and tried to force the whole population to live according to their strict moral code.

But the people soon wearied of Puritan rule. Parliament welcomed Charles II as king (ruled 1660–1685), restored the episcopacy, reissued the *Book of Common Prayer,* and punished Puritan dissenters (see the accompanying box). In 1689 Parliament passed the Toleration Act, giving limited freedom of worship to all Christians except Catholics and Unitarians (a small group who rejected the idea of the Trinity).

One group, the Society of Friends, known as the Quakers, profited from the new toleration. Its founders, George Fox (1624–1691) and Margaret Fell (1614–1702), taught that the light of the living Christ resides in all people. They developed a democratic model of Christian living in which men and women are equal, without hierarchy or professional priesthood. Worship services are quiet—the community sits awaiting revelation from the Holy Spirit, who is *ter, and did sprinkle it, is the Gospel. . . . The Law, instead of cleansing the heart (by its working) from sin, doth revive, put strength into, and increase it in the soul, even as it doth discover and forbid it, for it doth not give power to subdue.*

Again, as thou sawest the damsel sprinkle the room with water, upon which it was cleansed with pleasure: this is to show thee that when the Gospel comes in the sweet and precious influences thereof to the heart . . . so is sin vanquished and subdued, and the soul made clean, through the faith of it; and consequently fit for the King of Glory to inhabit.

Then I saw in my dream that the Interpreter took Christian by the hand, and led him into a place where was a fire burning against a wall, and one standing by it always, casting much water upon it to quench it: yet did the fire burn higher and hotter.

Then said Christian, What means this?

The Interpreter answered: This fire is the work of grace that is wrought in the heart; he that casts water upon it, to extinguish and put it out, is the Devil: but in that thou seest the fire, notwithstanding, burn higher and hotter, thou shalt also see the reason of that. So he had him about to the backside of the wall, where he saw a man with a vessel of oil in his hand, of the which he did also continually cast, but secretly, into the fire.

Then said Christian, What means this?

The Interpreter answered: This is Christ, who continually with the oil of his grace maintains the work already begun in the heart, by the means of which, notwithstanding what the Devil can do, the souls of his people prove gracious still. And in that thou sawest that the man stood behind the wall to maintain the fire, this is to teach thee that it is hard for the tempted to see how this work of grace is maintained in the soul.

Source: John Bunyan, *The Pilgrim's Progress*, ed. Roger Sharrock (New York: Penguin, 1965), pp. 61–64.

thought to dwell in the hearts of believers as the ultimate authority, superseding even the Bible. Only when moved by the Spirit does someone stand and speak. The Quakers gradually won respect for their tolerance, pacifism, and eagerness to help the poor and the oppressed.

BRITISH NORTH AMERICA

During the seventeenth century, English settlers began establishing colonies in North America. Those who left for economic reasons or the desire for adventure often remained loyal to the established Church of England; however, others migrated for the express purpose of establishing "godly" commonwealths. John Winthrop (1588–1649) and other Puritan leaders founded the Massachusetts Bay Colony in 1630, hoping to make this "Zion in the wilderness" into a community governed by biblical precepts that would set an example for the rest of the world.

Intolerant toward religious diversity, Puritan magistrates banished most dissenters and executed the few recalcitrants. Anne Hutchinson (1591–1643), a Boston matron and mother of 16 children, stood trial for heresy because she had criticized the clergy for what she believed to be lax theology. Perhaps even worse in the eyes of the colony patriarchs, who thought that the Bible prohibited women from teaching, she had held meetings at her home on Sunday evenings to discuss the sermon of the day. Found guilty and banished, she and her family wandered into the wilderness, where they were killed by marauding Indians. In 1660 Mary Dyer, a Quaker friend of Hutchinson's, was hanged on

Anne Hutchinson, a Boston matron and mother of 16, is shown here standing trial for heresy for criticizing the clergy. Perhaps worse in the eyes of the colony patriarchs, she broke the prohibition against women teaching. (The Granger Collection)

the Boston Common for returning to Massachusetts in defiance of a writ of banishment.

While Protestantism's emphasis on lay leadership and married clergy opened the doors for greater participation by men, the religious options for women, ironically, were lessened. Religious communities and convents gave Catholic women opportunities for leadership, ministry, and mission. Their Protestant sisters' choices, however, were usually limited to marriage, home, and family or a lonely and often-ridiculed life as a spinster. Women who did venture into religious prominence were often persecuted.

Women and men from a variety of faiths were drawn to the American colonies by dreams of religious tolerance. Roger Williams (c. 1603–1683) founded Providence, Rhode Island, as a haven for victims of religious persecution in Massachusetts. When his church became Baptist, its members baptized one another. Williams himself, in part through contact with Native Americans, moved toward a radical spiritualism, concluding that all churches were false and that one did not have to become Christian to be saved. Maryland was founded in 1634 as a colony for English Catholics, and in 1682 William Penn founded Pennsylvania as a refuge for Quakers. In his original charter, Penn had guaranteed freedom of worship; however, as settlers from the Church of England came to outnumber Quakers, that denomination became the official religion. Yet despite such setbacks, a seed of religious freedom had been planted that later came to fruition in the American Revolution.

In all non–Roman Catholic colonial churches, preaching replaced the Eucharist as the principal focus of worship. Even the Church of England's parishes tended to be nonsacramental, not necessarily by choice but because there were not enough priests to celebrate the Eucharist often.

EVANGELICAL REVIVAL

Pietism and the Great Awakening

The rediscovery of the gospel message of salvation through faith in Jesus Christ deeply touched human hearts and sparked excitement for Bible study, prayer, and simpler Christian living during the early years of the Reformation. The next generation of reformers, however, became preoccupied with highly intellectual theological wranglings over doctrinal minutiae that alienated many Christians who wished to return to a simple and vibrant faith of the heart rather than the head. **Pietism**, born of this longing for a deep personal faith, emphasized a life of devotion and study among small groups of Christians or "colleges of piety" in order to attain a closer relationship with God. Appearing first in Moravia and parts of Germany, the movement spread to England and North America, seeking to revitalize Protestantism by empowering the laity.

Beginning among German immigrants in the 1720s, a series of religious revivals led by itinerant preachers, known as the Great Awakening, drew huge crowds whose emotional excitement often reached fever pitch. Jonathan Edwards (1703–1758), an American theologian and preacher from Connecticut, played an important role when he presided over a spontaneous religious revival in the Congregational church where he was the pastor in 1734. The revival soon spread.

Edwards firmly believed that the Holy Spirit might descend on people during a revival and that conversions at such time were not temporary phenomena induced by group pressure but lasting, transforming experiences. His vivid imagery in sermons aimed at encouraging repentance, such as "Sinners in the Hands of an Angry God," had an electrifying effect on his congregants. Although Edwards believed that emotion was important, he discouraged excessive emotionalism, teaching instead the need for right doctrine and a virtuous life as outward signs of inward repentance and grace.

Like a comet, the Great Awakening blazed across the colonial scene; it lasted only a few years but had a profound effect on the American religious psyche. Because revivalists often preached outside of established churches, drawing people across denominational lines, they planted the seeds of religious volunteerism, in which each individual chooses a church on the basis of personal preference rather than ethnic or family loyalty. This in turn encouraged client-centered churches where the clergy tailored their ministry to the needs and desires of the laity. In addition, the Great Awakening aroused interest in missionary and humanitarian endeavors as Christians tried to spread their beliefs and translate their faith into social action.

Evangelical Revival in England

Back in England, Anglicanism reigned supreme as the state religion. Formal, liturgical, centered on the old county parishes, and headed by the aristocracy, the Church of England failed to meet the needs of a growing industrial society—coal miners, mill workers, and the urban poor found neither comfort nor welcome in the established church. Into the misery of the common people came John Wesley (1703–1791), preaching the love of God and the need for conversion and a transformed life.

Brought up in a strict but loving family, John and his brother Charles felt the call to God's service early in life. Ordained priests in the Church of England, they traveled as missionaries to the Native Americans but soon returned, discouraged and disconsolate. On the outward voyage, however, John had met a group of Moravians whose quiet faith and calm spirit, even in the midst of a fearful storm, impressed the young cleric immensely. Upon his return to England, John felt sharply his lack of loving trust in God; attending a meeting of the Moravian society, he experienced his own moment of conversion:

> In the evening I went very unwillingly to a society in Aldersgate Street, where one was reading Luther's preface to the Epistle to the Romans. About a quarter before nine, while he was describing the change which God works in the heart through faith in Christ, I felt my heart strangely warmed. I felt I did trust in Christ, Christ alone, for my salvation; and an assurance was given me that He had taken away my sins, even mine, and saved me from the law of sin and death.[8]

Influenced by the evangelical faith of Luther through the pietism of the Moravians, Wesley combined the teachings of the gospel with a passion for social concerns. Whenever possible he preached in churches, desiring to awaken and cultivate faith within the Church of England, not establish a rival denomination. Rejection by the church, however, forced him into the fields and towns, where he organized societies for study and prayer. The members of these societies became known as Methodists. Women played a new and prominent role in Methodism as traveling evangelists, preachers, and teachers. Wesley never intended to break with the Church of England; to his dying day he remained an Anglican priest, urging his followers to worship and receive the sacrament in their parish churches. But when the church did not meet the common people, in his view, Wesley began ordaining ministers himself (a right reserved to bishops in an episcopal system); the breach became inevitable.

In the United States most Anglican clergy, who were loyalists, returned to England following the War of Independence. When the bishop of London refused to ordain priests for the former colonies, Wesley stepped in and ordained the needed ministers. Methodism enjoyed great success as it spread westward with the settlers; soon its leaders considered themselves independent from the Anglican church, no longer bound by Wesley's desire for unity. Following his death in 1791, his followers in England also acknowledged the inevitable, and Methodism became a separate denomination alongside the Church of England.

NOTES

1 Martin Luther, *Luther's Works,* ed. Jaroslav Pelikan and Helmut T. Lehmann (St. Louis: Concordia/Philadelphia: Fortress, 1960), pp. 336–337.

2 Ibid., p. 344.

3 Henry Bettenson, ed., *Documents of the Christian Church* (New York: Oxford University Press, 1963, 1967), pp. 282–283.

4 Martin Luther, "Large Catechism," in *The Book of Concord,* ed. Theodore G. Tappert (Philadelphia: Fortress, 1959), p. 447.

5 John Calvin, "The Westminster Shorter Catechism," in *The Creeds of Christendom,* ed. Philip Schaff, vol. 3 (Grand Rapids, Mich.: Baker Book House, 1966), p. 676.

6 A. B. Wickens and Dorothy Carr, eds., *The Reformation in England* (London: Arnold, 1967), p. 65.

7 Christopher Hibbert, *The Virgin Queen* (Reading, Mass.: Addison-Wesley, 1991), p. 89.

8 John Wesley, *The Journal of John Wesley,* ed. Percy L. Parker (Chicago: Moody Press, n.d.), p. 64. Entry for May 24, 1738.

CHRISTIANITY

CHAPTER 22

CHRISTIANITY IN THE MODERN WORLD

REVOLUTION AND RELIGIOUS REVIVAL

Unlike the Reformation, which began with the quiet of Martin Luther nailing a piece of paper to a chapel door, the modern era began with smoke and noise. The noise of Massachusetts gunfire in 1775 marked the beginning of the American Revolution; the smoke of the explosions of 1789 announced revolution in France. Modern times began as well with the smoking coal and metallic clangings of factories, the enormous harbingers of the industrial revolution.

For Christianity the smoke of the political upheavals meant the separation of the church from political authority. In France, for example, the Catholic church had been associated with the royalist *ancien régime*, and after the revolution that intimate association and the important role it had given to the church came to an end. In the United States, the separation between church and state was permanently enshrined in the Constitution.

Such separation from the state and the new freedom of religion led to a difficult set of circumstances for the churches. First, they were no longer needed to legitimize the new political structures, founded on more egalitarian principles. That meant, among other things, that the churches were no longer financially supported by the state; some, as in France, even had much of their property confiscated. Second, in the context of religious freedom, the churches fractured and split into countless variations, especially in the United States. Third, with religious freedom came the freedom to not attend church, and the churches lost much of their influence over people's lives.

The smoke of the industrial revolution brought new social problems as well. The newly expanded cities were unprepared for the sudden influx of farm workers. Laborers lived in terrible poverty, working intolerably long days for absurdly low wages. Because the old-fashioned rural-style parishes were inadequate to meet their needs, workers simply turned away from them and never heard the Christian message at all.

With the cacophony of the intellectual debates arising from the scientific revolution came difficult doctrinal problems for the churches. Theories of evolution, history, and, later, psychology led theologians and biblical scholars to ponder how their message should be preached in the new climate.

In short, whereas the church had been the dominant institution in medieval and reformation life, linked by property and power to the civil authorities, in modern times it had no central role. Confronting the needs of a vast new population—the dislocated poor—the churches had little economic or political power to help them. And whereas in medieval times church doctrines were relatively well integrated into the general view of the world, in the modern age religious views were challenged from many directions.

During the Enlightenment, thinkers such as René Descartes (top) and John Locke agreed that the physical universe is constructed on an orderly basis, governed by simple laws capable of being discerned by human reason. However, they remained convinced Christians, seeing God's hand beyond the workings of the universe. (The Granger Collection)

Enlightenment and Secularization

When the dust and the smoke of the political and industrial revolutions settled, Christianity found itself in a radically new relationship with respect to the rest of the world. Religion was no longer a powerful directing force in people's lives, nor were the churches the primary focus of national attention. Instead, religion in general, and Christianity in particular, became simply one of many options around which to center life. This quieter revolution in attitudes began with the scientific discoveries of the sixteenth and seventeenth centuries that this world and its human inhabitants are not the center of the cosmos but simply one small planet revolving around a sun that is itself just one of billions of other stars in an infinite expanse of space.

In astronomy, Nicolaus Copernicus (1473–1543) and Galileo Galilei (1564–1642) discovered that the earth circles around the sun, which challenged the old picture that placed the earth at the center of the universe. In physics, Isaac Newton (1642–1727) discovered how physical objects could operate by themselves in a lawlike way, which removed the active hand of God from the running of the universe. In biology, Charles Darwin (1809–1882) showed that different species had evolved from one another, which contradicted the biblical story of creation. All of these scientists and others like them effectively challenged traditional Christian teachings and seemed to threaten humanity's cherished existence as the crown of God's loving care.

This was a time of intellectual ferment as new scientific and philosophical ideas mixed to produce the rich and heady period known as the Enlightenment. Based on laws of empirical observation, new thinkers like René Descartes (1596–1650) and John Locke (1632–1704) agreed that the physical universe is constructed on an orderly basis, governed by a few simple laws capable of being discerned by human reason.

While Descartes and Locke remained convinced Christians, seeing God's hand beyond the workings of the universe, philosophers such as Voltaire (1694–1778) attacked Christianity as an intolerant, superstitious faith, contrary to reason. Still others proposed a middle ground between scientific skepticism regarding religion and traditional acceptance of church authority, centering religious knowledge and practice in ethics. Immanuel Kant's (1724–1804) famous maxim, known as the *categorical imperative,* states that human beings should judge the way they act toward one another by one question: Is this action worthy of becoming a universal law? It rests on the assumption that humans have the innate capacity to recognize good and evil and to do good, contrary to Saint Paul's assertions of human sinfulness and the necessity of God's grace.

The Enlightenment provided a period of transition from the age of faith, dominated by the church, to our modern secular society. During the process of secularization various spheres of human life were removed from religious norms and controls, so that government, business, intellectual endeavor, social life, and other areas were no longer viewed from a religious perspective. Following the Peace of Westphalia (1648), political struggles and wars were no longer fought for ostensibly religious reasons, economic life was no longer regulated by Christian regulations about profit and interest, and culture ceased to be dominated by the clergy. God became increasingly a "God of the gaps" with fewer and fewer gaps, invoked to explain whatever still remained outside human understanding. A privatized religion resulted, where one's relationship with God became personal, private, and often restricted to a few areas of life, no longer formative to one's identity. Finally, secularism contended that human society has the right to control its own destiny based on reason, without concern for revealed religion.

The Second Great Awakening

In response to this secularization process, Christian preachers tried to reawaken religious life by proclaiming an emotional and personal religion marked by conversion to Christ and changed habits of life. The first phase of the second Great Awakening, associated with Timothy Dwight, president of Yale and grandson of Jonathan Edwards, was a late-eighteenth-century evangelical, intellectual movement. A modified Calvinism, it downplayed predestination, stressing human responsibility in responding to God's initiative.

Conversion produced a reform-minded people eager to stamp a Christian character on the United States by correcting social ills and promoting good habits. A benevolent empire of voluntary societies, drawn primarily from the established New York–New England elite, worked to spread the gospel. Interested in promoting Bible reading, the American Sunday School was founded in 1824 to educate children who worked during the week. The American Bible Society, which still translates and prints Bibles, widely distributed inexpensive editions. Temperance (limiting drinking), prison reform, and abolition were also targeted as worthy causes by the evangelical social consciousness of the awakening. The strongly divisive anti-slavery movement, spearheaded by Lyman Beecher, president of a Cincinnati seminary, and popularized by his daughter Harriet Beecher Stowe in her novel *Uncle Tom's Cabin,* brought to an end the unanimity of the evangelical movement.

Whereas the awakening in the east was associated with the educated, intellectual elite, on the western frontier it was marked by the emotional revivalism of the tent meeting. In 1801, in Cane Ridge, Kentucky, a local minister organized a "camp meeting" to renew faith. Thousands of people gathered, and revival fever spread—overcome with emotional excitement, people began to jerk, laugh uncontrollably, run around, and even bark. Soon revivals became an important element of frontier life, offering an opportunity to socialize, court, and trade as well as find God. The Cane Ridge Revival also marked the beginning of an anti-intellectual reaction in American Protestantism that called people back to the "fundamentals" of the Christian faith, the language of later fundamentalism.

The Temperance Movement

By taking a closer look at the nineteenth-century temperance movement, we can see how social and reform movements have been interwoven with society, reflecting the political and cultural norms and aspirations of the day. Nineteenth-century reformers zeroed in on drinking as a special target of reform. Before the Revolutionary War there were legal controls on drinking; however, following independence these sanctions ceased—alcohol consumption increased, especially among the growing immigrant population, and public drunkenness and brawling became commonplace. In 1826 the American Temperance Society was founded by New England Congregationalists and Presbyterians, soon shifting its position from temperance to abstinence. Some scholars believe that temperance, ostensibly a movement of moral reform, was also a symbol of the shifts in nineteenth-century American class status. With the increase of non-English, lower-

This cartoon from an American newspaper of 1874 shows members of a temperance society praying outside of a saloon. The caption read "The Temperance Crusade—Who Will Win?" There are many theories as to what led to and fueled the temperance movement. (The Granger Collection)

class, and Catholic immigrants, many of the older, established social elite saw a decline in their own status. Some historians theorize that this shift was a major impetus behind the reforming zeal of the temperance movement:

> The Federalist saw his own declining status in the increased power of the drinker, the ignorant, the secularist, and the religious revivalist. During the 1820's, the men [and women] who founded the Temperance movement sought to make Americans into a clean, sober, godly, and decorous people whose inspirations and style of living would reflect the moral leadership of New England and Federalism. If they could not control the politics of the country, they reasoned that they might at least control the morals.[1]

The temperance movement reflected the nation's social values; the symbol of the rising middle class, it became a way of distinguishing the hard worker from the ne'er-do-well. Following the Civil War many former abolitionists joined the temperance cause, possibly out of genuine concern for the poor and downtrodden, possibly as a means of maintaining status in the reform movement. The Eighteenth Amendment establishing Prohibition (1920) marked "the high point of the struggle to assert the public dominance of old middle-class values. It established the victory of Protestant over Catholic, rural over urban, tradition over modernity, the middle class over both the lower and upper strata."[2] Temperance rapidly lost support, however, as resistance to Prohibition solidified. The repeal of the Eighteenth Amendment in 1933 also marked the decline of the old middle-class values, reflecting the shift from a commercial society to an industrial one, in which self-control, renunciation, discipline, and sobriety were no longer "hallowed virtues."[3]

LIBERALISM AND CONSERVATISM

The course of Christianity in a nation and in the world is not a single thread that can be followed through the complex patterns produced by the weaving of various peoples, cultures, and ages. Rather, it resembles more the intricate tracing of streams in the desert that appear and disappear with the rain, but without direct connection between the streams. At the turn of the twentieth century many of the concerns of the evangelical awakening reappeared, divided into liberal and conservative streams. Liberal Christianity reflected the confidence and air of hopeful optimism prevalent in the American social consciousness during the decade before World War I. It retained the high Enlightenment evaluation of the capacity of human reason and the perfectibility of society through education and economic growth, emphasizing the role of the church as a vehicle for social reform. Conservative Christianity, by contrast, distrusted liberalism's optimistic hope in human capabilities, stressing instead the primacy of revelation over reason. Individuals could not save themselves; they needed salvation through personal faith in Jesus Christ.

Social Gospel

Considered by many to have been the American churches' most distinctive contribution to Christianity, the Social Gospel attempted to create a new heaven on earth by applying Jesus's teachings and the power of the church to social problems in a spirit of confidence and hope. One forceful voice was Walter Rauschenbusch, a Baptist minister whose 1907 book *Christianity and the Social Crisis* electrified the nation and propelled him to the forefront of the movement:

> If the twentieth century could do for us in the control of social forces what the nineteenth did for us in the control of natural forces, our grandchildren would live in a society that would be justified in regarding our present social life as semi-barbarous. . . . If at this juncture we can rally sufficient religious faith and moral strength to snap the bonds of evil and turn the unparalleled economic and intellectual resources of humanity to the harmonious development of a true social life, the generations yet unborn will mark this as that great day of the Lord for which the ages waited, and count us blessed for sharing in the apostolate that proclaimed it.[4]

Essentially a Christian socialist, Rauschenbusch criticized capitalism in light of Christian ethics "as an unregenerate part of the social order, not based on freedom, love, and mutual service, . . . but on autocracy, antagonism of interests, and exploitation."[5] Because capitalism idolizes profit and places private advantage over public good, he argued, it bears responsibility for many of the problems plaguing society: poverty, injustice, prostitution, corruption,

Walter Rauschenbusch's 1907 book, *Christianity and the Social Crisis,* propelled him to the forefront of the Social Gospel movement, considered by many to have been the American churches' most distinctive contribution to Christianity. The Social Gospel movement saw capitalism as a system that impoverishes the many and enriches the few, and therefore as sinful.
(The Granger Collection)

class warfare. Any social system that impoverishes the many and enriches the few is sinful. Sin and salvation are not only individual but also social, and social systems need redemption as much as individuals. Instead, Rauschenbusch proclaimed, Christians should strive to establish the reign of God, characterized by justice, freedom, and love.

Working with the immigrant settlements of Chicago, fighting for child labor laws, preaching women's suffrage (right to vote), and standing for pacifism in the midst of war, Jane Addams (1860–1935) perhaps best embodied the spirit of the Social Gospel. Although not a theologian—indeed, she cared little for formal doctrine—Addams shared the concept of Christian progress and the reform of human society. In 1889 she founded Hull House Settlement in the slums of Chicago to assist new immigrants by teaching children and adults, finding jobs for the unemployed, and even delivering an illegitimate baby that the neighbors refused to touch. Addams identified three motives for undertaking settlement work: (1) the desire to extend democracy beyond politics into the whole of society, (2) the hope that all could share the goods of civilization, and (3) the renewal of Christianity's early humanitarian roots. Explaining this last point, she wrote:

> The impulse to share the lives of the poor, the desire to make social service, . . . [to] express the spirit of Christ, is as old as Christianity itself. . . . Jesus had no set of truths labelled "Religious." On the contrary, his doctrine was that all truth is one, that the appropriation of it is freedom. . . . I believe that there is a distinct turning among many young men and women toward this simple acceptance of Christ's message. They resent the assumption that Christianity is a set of ideas which belong to the religious consciousness, . . . that it is a thing to be proclaimed and instituted apart from the social life of the community. They insist that it shall seek a simple and natural expression in the social organism itself.[6]

The Conservative Response

In the 1920s the alliance between social reform and revivalism that had marked the early part of the century dissolved. Whereas the Social Gospel was the rallying cry of liberal Protestants, revivalism, along with the literal interpretation of the Bible, became the hallmark of conservatives. Individual conversion had long marked rural revivalism in America, but in the late nineteenth century, revivalists turned their attention to the burgeoning cities, where preachers such as Dwight Moody (1837–1899) promoted individual salvation as the solution to the city dwellers' problems. Moody, an unschooled Congregationalist businessman, stirred millions with his vivid preaching, using embellished Bible stories and homey anecdotes to emphasize his conviction that God forgives and loves even the worst of sinners. Persuading music leader Ira Sankey to join him, the new team introduced the gospel song into their revival meetings, teaching and popularizing the gospel hymns that have remained hallmarks of revivalism ever since. Moody cared for and preached to the urban poor as well, working among Chicago's needy in the Young Men's Christian Association. But he remained convinced that once these poor people converted to Christianity, their problems would end.

Toward the end of the nineteenth century, conservative Christians adopted a much harsher antiliberal tone. Rejecting social programs, they condemned the theory of evolution as antibiblical, espousing instead conservative nationalism and narrow biblical literalism. Several groups emerged at this time, each with its own particular ideology. Around 1900 the Christian Fundamentals movement pushed for agreement on a set of basic Christian beliefs, but doctrinal conflicts and charges of heresy threatened to and sometimes did split seminaries apart. Though most Protestant denominations eventually rejected **fundamentalism**, it remains an active force in American Christianity, still shaking the foundations of some churches.

A second group coalesced around the doctrine of perfection associated with John Wesley. The Holiness movement believed that a life-transforming experience of perfection completes conversion; following this one lives in a state of perfection and holiness. The movement divided into two streams, the first taking its cue from Wesleyan holiness and best exemplified by the Church of the Nazarene. The second, more radical stream, emphasizing the charismatic gifts of the spirit such as prophecy, healing, and speaking in tongues, adopted the name Pentecostal after the Pentecost experience described in the Book of Acts. At a time when most denominations are decreasing in size, Pentecostal churches such as the Assemblies of God are among the fastest growing Christian groups in the United States.

John Wesley's doctrine of perfection led to the Holiness movement that divided into two streams, the first exemplified by the Church of the Nazarene and the second represented by the Pentecostal churches. Pentecostal churches such as the Assemblies of God are among the fastest growing Christian groups in the United States today. (The Bettmann Archive)

REACTION AND RENEWAL

Throughout the nineteenth and twentieth centuries, movements of renewal and reform have repeatedly irrupted in Christian churches around the world. Liturgical and doctrinal renewal is usually based on an attempt to recover Christianity's ancient roots and restore its rich inheritance. But renewal movements are seldom isolated antiquarian exercises; rather, they reflect and respond to changes in the outside world. At times they have been as much reactionary as renewing.

Liturgical Renewal

During the nineteenth century, Catholics and Protestants each worked to restore vitality to Christian worship. Enchanted by romantic notions of medieval customs, Dom Prosper Louis Pascal Guéranger restored the Roman rite in France in the 1830s, teaching the clergy to sing the service. Monks studied ancient plainchant, believed to have come from Pope Gregory's sixth-century reformation, studying also the history of Christian worship; as the revival spread into Germany, England, and the Netherlands, their scholarly discoveries fueled the twentieth-century liturgical movement.

In England liturgical reform became the agenda of a group of High Church Anglicans. Responding to a number of moves by Parliament that they believed threatened the autonomy of the Church of England, Oxford professors John Keble, Edward Pusey, and John Henry Newman wrote a series of pamphlets titled *Tracts for the Times,* in which they explained the nature of the church and its relationship to the state. For two centuries the Anglican church had understood itself as the *via media,* the "middle way" between Protestantism and Catholicism. The Oxford theologians, however, moved from *via media* to the *branch* theory of the church, which saw the Church of England in the tradition of the Roman Catholic and Orthodox churches as equal branches of a single universal church. Eventually some of the reformers, most notably John Henry Newman, abandoned the Church of England altogether for the Roman Catholic fold, Newman himself eventually being made a cardinal by the Vatican.

The Oxford movement contributed to the life of Anglicanism in two significant ways: it reestablished monastic orders and reformed the liturgy. Monasticism in England had ended when Henry VIII dissolved all the monasteries in 1536. During the intervening centuries a few experiments in communal living had been attempted, but none succeeded until 1845, when women involved in the Oxford movement formed the Sisterhood of the Holy Cross. Women's religious orders proliferated over the next several decades, and men's orders were founded as well.

The sisterhoods offered opportunities for women that were unavailable elsewhere in Victorian society, where the usual options for women were either to marry or to remain at home as a spinster. Capable and caring women found in these orders a place to expend their passion and energy by helping the poor, teaching, or nursing. Many streamed against the tide of societal norms, cut off from family and friends. At a time when few people cared for the poor, the women's orders were an active witness of Christianity's mission to the outcast.

Liturgically, the Oxford movement introduced a

medieval flavor in the church, reviving the use of candles, incense, and elaborate vestments. Responding to the solemn and sermon-oriented Reformation services, the Eucharist was restored as the focal point of worship, emphasizing the real presence of Christ in the Eucharist and weekly communion. Worshipers in a High Church parish now found themselves amid a highly complex ritual. Swinging incense braziers hallowed the space, choristers sang hymns to ancient Gregorian melodies, and a spirit of deep reverence marked reception of the Eucharistic meal.

As interest in liturgical renewal increased, the aims and concerns of the movement deepened. Researchers discovered that the life of the early church differed considerably from the forms and piety of nineteenth-century Christianity. Immersed in modern concepts of individualism, Christians had adopted a subjective view of one's relationship with God that centered on the self. Catholics engaged in private, individual devotions; liberals tried to shape themselves after Jesus as a moral exemplar; pietists focused on their inner and personal sense of Christ. Lost was the belief of the early church that God's incarnation as Jesus Christ transformed the community of believers into the so-called body of Christ or that since God saves us, human efforts are unnecessary.

Twentieth-century liturgical reformers tried to recapture early concepts of the Eucharist that highlighted the transformation of the church community into the body of Christ. Worshipers who take communion were thought to participate in an objective divine act rather than in subjective, individual acts. The body of the faithful, they held, becomes the body of Christ, charged with carrying on Jesus's ministry to the poor and the forgotten.

New communities formed around this image of Christians as the body of Christ doing Christ's work in the world. In France, Britain, and the United States, groups of clergy and laity formed missions hoping to revitalize churches with worship shaped to reflect the ancient corporate idea of the church. An example of such is the Taizé community in France, which works toward reconciliation across denominational lines. With members from the Lutheran, Reformed, Anglican, and Catholic traditions, the community follows a simple rule of life:

Throughout your day let work and rest
be quickened by the Word of God.
Keep inner silence in all things
and you will dwell in Christ.
Be filled with the spirit of the Beatitudes;
joy, simplicity, mercy.[7]

The most sweeping changes occurred as a result of the Roman Catholic Second Vatican Council (1962–1965) and the adoption of a new *Book of Common Prayer* by the Episcopal church in the United States in 1979. Similar revisions and reforms emerged in the 1980s in United Methodist, United Presbyterian, and other churches. Today, in the final decade of the twentieth century, Protestants and Catholics alike celebrate Christ's death on the cross in liturgies that depend heavily on models from early Christianity. They have made lay participation fuller and more meaningful, symbolize the sacraments as objective acts of God, and envision the church as a people corporately called to do God's work in the world.

Theological Renewal

The twentieth century has witnessed an outburst of renewed theological thought, in part as a reaction to the overly optimistic Social Gospel dream of ushering in the kingdom of God on earth by ending social injustice. Such hopes were called into serious doubt not only by the inequalities of capitalism and the ethical questions raised by the rapidly changing industrial society but also by the traumas of first one world war and then another and later by the threat of atomic annihilation.

Had the liberals with their belief in the perfectibility of human society been wrong? Karl Barth (1886–1968) thought so. This Swiss theologian became disillusioned when the German scholars he had studied under signed a document supporting German war aims. Barth told Christians that they had gone astray by concentrating on humanity and claiming an understanding of God based on human analogy, instead of depending on God as the Wholly Other, who comes to us from outside ourselves. Human beings know God only through the divine revelation of God's own self in the life, death, and resurrection of Jesus Christ.

In his attack on liberal Christianity, Barth disposed of its optimism as a mere episode in Christian history, insisting that Christ, not humanity, forms the center of the faith. Though enslaved to sin, people can be drawn into faith through God's gift of Christ. Barth tried to reconcile predestination with ultimate universal salvation, hoping to retain the liberals' optimism about the worth of humanity while correcting their overemphasis on human concerns and abilities. Election (selective redemption) takes place in Christ, but since Christ is representative of all of humanity, in one sense all human beings are God's elect.

In the United States, Reinhold Niebuhr (1892–1971) applied Barthian theology and faith to social issues. Concerned with labor conflicts in Detroit while serving as pastor there, Niebuhr concluded that the Social Gospel message of Rauschenbusch was too simple, based on a misapprehension of human relations and human sinfulness. Sin, Niebuhr taught, lodges not only in destructive social systems but in human beings themselves. People relate to one another in terms of power—who has power over whom. In *Moral Man and Immoral Society* (1932), Niebuhr used Marxist analysis to examine society, concluding that all social classes are motivated by self-interest, tainted with a sense of their own power. Marxism fails, he said presciently, because it is not cynical enough about human motivation, expecting the worker class to act altruistically for the good of the whole. Utopian experiments are all doomed to failure; improvement in social justice is possible and should be striven for, but we will never have the kingdom of God here on earth.

Liberation Theology

After World War II, many Protestant scholars sought to assimilate and consolidate the wealth of new theological thought while exploring its implications. The horrors of the Holocaust, in which 6 million Jews perished along with an equal number of non-Jewish "undesirables," further sobered thoughtful Christians. Dietrich Bonhoeffer (1906–1945), a German theologian executed by the Nazis, moved many people by his letters from prison (see the accompanying box, "Christianity in a Time of Crisis") and especially by his *Cost of Discipleship*. He believed that the world had now "come of age," no longer needing the concept of a father God who provides for and protects his children.

Similar discontent with classical theology and its academic provenance led black, Latin American, Native American, and feminist theologians to question the methods and presuppositions of Christian thought. The social systems of Europe and North America that had influenced theology had little relevance for the poor, the oppressed, and the powerless. In Latin America thinkers such as Gustavo Guitiérrez began to reexamine explanations of the faith, discovering that scripture actually portrays God as favoring the poor. God's "preferential option for the poor" means that poverty is not a sign of personal sin and rejection; rather, the spiritual insights of the poor may be equally or even more valid than those of the ecclesiastical establishment and should not be ignored. Forming so-called ecclesial base communities, groups of villagers meet together to study scripture from the perspective of the poor. Convinced that if the oppressed of the world took charge of their destinies God would empower them to correct society's imbalances and injustices, liberation theologians encourage grassroots spirituality and self-determination. Conflict between liberationists and many of the Roman Catholic hierar-

Liberation theologians believed that if the oppressed of the world took charge of their destinies, God would empower them to correct society's imbalances and injustices. Martin Luther King, Jr., a Baptist minister, focused attention on racial injustice in America during the civil rights movement of the 1960s. The link between African-American Christians and civil rights activists was very close. (Religious News Service)

Christianity in a Time of Crisis

The German theologian Dietrich Bonhoeffer was highly respected as a teacher and pastor, but in 1936 he was forbidden by the Nazis to lecture or publish. Arrested later on suspicion of treason, he was executed by the Gestapo shortly before the end of World War II. From prison he sent the following reflections to a friend.

Man has learnt to deal with himself in all questions of importance without recourse to the 'working hypothesis' called 'God'. In questions of science, art, and ethics this has become an understood thing at which one now hardly dares to tilt. But for the last hundred years or so it has also become increasingly true of religious questions; it is becoming evident that everything gets along without 'God'—and, in fact, just as well as before. As in the scientific field, so in human affairs generally, 'God' is being pushed more and more out of life, losing more and more ground.

Roman Catholic and Protestant historians agree that it is in this development that the great defection from God, from Christ, is to be seen; and the more they claim and play off God and Christ against it, the more the development considers itself to be anti-Christian. The world that has become conscious of itself and the laws that govern its own existence has grown self-confident in what seems to us to be an uncanny way. False developments and failures do not make the world doubt the necessity of the course that it is taking, or of its development; they are accepted with fortitude and detachment as part of the bargain, and even an event like the present war is no exception. Christian apologetic has taken the most varied forms of opposition to this self-assurance. Efforts are made to prove to a world thus come of age that it cannot live without the tutelage of 'God'. Even though there has been surrender on all secular

chy who favor the status quo has marked Latin American Christianity for several decades.

The vibrant atmosphere of African Christianity is producing its own theologies of liberation, focusing heavily on biblical interpretation while still seeking to address inequities of many kinds. In South Africa church leadership has been crucial in the struggle to abolish apartheid. The work of Anglican Archbishop Desmond Tutu and Reformed writer Allen Boesak continues to stir world opinion, helping to bring about change. Now that South Africa is making substantial steps toward ending apartheid, the churches are stepping back from the struggle to allow the government to work, now focusing on healing their strife-torn nation.

The Women's Movement

Although women in the early church served as apostles, elders, prophets, and deacons, within a century the church had succumbed to societal mores, and women were barred from most leadership roles. Only in the heavenly next life would women "become male" and thus gain full equality. Over the ensuing 1,900 years, as we have seen, a few groups such as certain spiritualists, Quakers, and Methodists broke with tradition, incorporating women into full partnership with men, but they were roundly criticized for this by mainstream Catholic and Protestant churches.

The women's movement in the United States arose out of the abolitionist movement. When women *problems, there still remain the so-called 'ultimate questions'—death, guilt—to which only 'God' can give an answer, and because of which we need God and the church and the pastor. So we live, in some degree, on these so-called ultimate questions of humanity. But what if one day they no longer exist as such, if they too can be answered 'without God'? Of course, we now have the secularized offshoots of Christian theology, namely existentialist philosophy and the psychotherapists, who demonstrate to secure, contented, and happy mankind that it is really unhappy and desperate and simply unwilling to admit that it is in a predicament about which it knows nothing, and from which only they can rescue it. Wherever there is health, strength, security, simplicity, they scent luscious fruit to gnaw at or to lay their pernicious eggs in. They set themselves to drive people to inward despair, and then the game is in their hands. That is secularized methodism. And whom does it touch? A small number of intellectuals, of degenerates, of people who regard themselves as the most important thing in the world, and who therefore like to busy themselves with themselves. The ordinary man, who spends his everyday life at work and with his family, and of course with all kinds of diversions, is not affected. He has neither the time nor the inclination to concern himself with his existential despair, or to regard his perhaps modest share of happiness as a trial, a trouble, or a calamity.*

The attack by Christian apologetic on the adulthood of the world I consider to be in the first place pointless, in the second place ignoble, and in the third place unchristian. Pointless, because it seems to me like an attempt to put a grown-up man back into adolescence, i.e. to make him dependent on things on which he is, in fact, no longer dependent, and thrusting him into problems that are, in fact, no longer problems to him. Ignoble, because it amounts to an attempt to exploit man's weakness for purposes that are alien to him and to which he has not freely assented. Unchristian, because it confuses Christ with one particular stage in man's religiousness, i.e. with a human law.

Source: From Dietrich Bonhoeffer, *Letters and Papers from Prison,* Revised, Enlarged Edition, ed. Eberhard Bethge (New York: Macmillan, 1971), pp. 325–327.

working to free the slaves came to realize that they too lacked many of the same civil rights, they shifted their attention to issues of suffrage and equality with men. Sarah Grimké, a nineteenth-century Quaker who spoke out on both abolition and women's rights, interpreted scripture from a feminist viewpoint when addressing her more traditionally minded male colleagues of the Congregational Association:

> The Lord Jesus defines the duties of his followers in his Sermon on the Mount. He lays down grand principles by which they should be governed, without reference to sex or condition: "Ye are the light of the world." . . . But the influence of women, says the Association, is to be private and unobtrusive; her light is not to shine before men like that of her brethren; but she is passively to let the lords of the creation, as they call themselves, put the bushel over it, lest peradventure it might appear that world has been benefitted by the rays of her candle. . . . But women may be permitted to lead religious inquirers to the PASTORS for instruction. Now this is assuming that all pastors are better qualified to give instruction than woman. This I utterly deny. I have suffered too keenly from the teaching of man, to lead anyone to him for instruction.[8]

The campaign to increase women's participation in the churches continued, leading first to the right to vote in church legislative bodies and then to ordain women ministers. The liberal Protestant churches that developed out of the reform crusades proved more receptive than the more conservative denominations. In the 1980s Methodist Marjorie Matthews became the first woman elected bishop of a major church, followed by the 1989 election of Barbara Harris as assistant bishop of the Massachusetts Episcopal church. Such advances did not occur without dissent, however. Many Episcopal bishops refused to recognize the ordination of women, declared Harris's election invalid, and formed a separate nongeographic synod with an all-male clergy.

Although the Roman Catholic church does not ordain women, nuns have long occupied positions of leadership and dignity. Many have served as teachers, nurses, administrators, and missionaries; in many respects, Catholic sisters were the first career women. Yet many women have decried the church's patriarchal structure.

In 1980, the United Methodist Church elected Marjorie Matthews the first woman bishop of a major church. (John C. Goodwin/United Methodist News Service)

Many Christian women strive for what they see as equality within their churches through the use of nonsexist language and feminine images for God. Metaphors such as Mother, Lover, and Wisdom complement traditional Father, Son, and Holy Spirit language. At the same time, theologians and liturgists seek to preserve the theological and Christological underpinnings to the classical expression of the Trinity in order not to end up with a modalist God who simply shows different faces throughout history. Still other women, declaring Christianity inherently patriarchal, have left the church altogether, some forming new sects dedicated to the Goddess and celebrating what they call woman-life.

THE MODERN ROMAN CATHOLIC CHURCH

At the beginning of the modern era, in the nineteenth and early twentieth centuries, Catholic intellectuals had to work against a background of papal conservatism, as the leadership of the Roman Catholic church remained defensive toward Protestantism, secularism, and other modern challenges. Despite resistence, however, change proceeded quietly, and Catholicism reestablished itself, gaining acceptance in predominantly Protestant nations like the Netherlands and Great Britain.

Although the papacy lost its last vestiges of political power when Italy was unified in 1870, Pope Pius X (1846–1878) achieved increased spiritual authority at the First Vatican Council, convened in 1869. A majority of the council fathers announced their belief in papal infallibility, despite spirited opposition from Catholic liberals in France, Germany, and Britain. The concept is actually very limited in scope and means that when the pope speaks *ex cathedra* (that is, as bishop of Rome on behalf of the whole church) regarding matters of faith and morals, his teachings are without error.

During World War II, Pope Pius XII (1939–1958) had the difficult task of trying to maintain diplomatic relations with both warring sides. He was later criticized for not taking a firm public stand against the Holocaust and other horrors perpetuated by the Nazis. After the war Pius XII emphasized the growing importance of the laity within the church and encouraged Catholic scholars engaged in biblical studies.

Pope John XXIII, seen here attending the opening of Vatican II in 1962, envisioned a renewed and reformed church reaching out to the modern world. (Religious News Service)

John XXIII (1958–1963) surprised the entire world by his willingness to leave the Vatican, visiting churches, hospitals, prisons, and other institutions. When he convened the Second Vatican Council in 1962, the response to his vision of a renewed and reformed church was thundering approval.

The Vatican II delegates discussed a wide range of subjects. The official documents of the council included constitutions on justification, liturgy, the role of the laity, and religious freedom. Often eloquent, these statements were the work of many minds and reflected the unity of sentiment evident at the council. Written in nontechnical language, they indicated John's vision of a church that could speak to all people and have been well received.

Two primary goals were achieved by the bishops before the council ended in 1965: (1) the reform of church governance to promote collegiality (that is, to give responsibility and power to the bishops at the expense of the Roman curia and the Vatican bureaucracy), and (2) changes in religious practice to encourage lay participation in church matters.

Vatican II opened windows to the modern world, introducing many far-reaching changes. Mass was no longer said in Latin but in the local language. Members of religious orders were encouraged to participate in and to improve the world around them—many priests and nuns replaced their religious garb with secular dress, and some were highly visible in the American civil rights and antiwar movements. Members of the laity have organized parish councils and participated in other new forms of church activity.

In the 1980s numerous disputes arose as Pope John Paul II, elected in 1978, pursued conservative policies. His positions on liberation theology, the clergy in public life, and women's ordination have caused discontent, especially among liberals who have called for open discussion of such issues as birth control and abortion.

A serious decline in men joining the priesthood following Vatican II has led to a shortage of priests. Large parishes tended by a single priest now often turn to lay people in place of clergy. Married deacons perform weddings; lay ministers distribute communion at Mass and bring it to the sick; laity function as trained spiritual directors and teachers.

THE CHURCH IN RUSSIA

The conversion of Prince Vladimir of Kiev (ruled 980–1015) in about 988 marked the "baptism of Russia." Prince Vladimir's decision to embrace Eastern Orthodoxy was logical in view of Kiev's trade connections with Constantinople and Byzantine cultural superiority. After the fall of Constantinople in 1453, the czars (emperors) of Russia declared Moscow the "third Rome." Phileothos of Pskov, a monk of the sixteenth century, described this view to the czar:

> The Old Rome fell because of its church's lack of faith . . . and of the second Rome, the city of Constantinople, the pagans broke down the churches with their axes. . . . And now there is the Holy synodal Apostolic church of the reigning third Rome, of your tsardom, which shines like the sun. . . . Listen and attend, pious tsar, that

> all Christian empires are gathered in your single one, that two Romes have fallen, and the third one stands, and a fourth one there shall not be.[9]

Moscow became the main center of Eastern Orthodox Christianity.

The church contributed greatly to the Russian sense of national unity and purpose. The people proudly viewed their country as Holy Russia, the site of the third Rome. Though loyal to Byzantine Christian formulations, the Russian church produced its own icons, hymns, church architecture, and saints' lives, each with a distinct national character.

In 1917 the Russian Revolution overthrew the Romanov dynasty, and after a period of civil war a Communist dictatorship took over. Its leader, V. I. Lenin (1870–1924), imposed on Russia a materialistic and atheistic communist system. Because the Orthodox church had been closely tied to the state and a powerful supporter of the absolutist system, the new regime tried to destroy Russian Orthodoxy: churches were desecrated, seminaries were closed, and many church leaders were killed, imprisoned, or exiled. When the patriarch protested the government's attacks on the church, Lenin ordered his imprisonment. Later released, he agreed to cooperate with the new Soviet Union. His successors followed his action, believing it better for the church to profess loyalty to the state than risk total destruction.

Although the Soviet government did not outlaw all practice of religion, it deprived the Orthodox church (as well as other religious bodies in the Soviet Union) of all legal rights, including the right to hold property. Despite active persecution under Soviet governments, the Russian church remained alive, emerging again into the light of freedom with the collapse of communism in 1991. With the advent of democratic institutions and attempts to introduce a market-based economy, the churches in the former Soviet republics face the danger of identifying religious freedom too closely with political and economic freedom, at a time when Western churches are wrestling with the problem of divesting their Christian faith from societal norms.

Mother Teresa's Missionaries of Charity tend to the needy rather than proselytize. (UPI/Battman)

RESPONSE TO THE GLOBAL VILLAGE

The world has been shrinking rapidly since World War II. Instantaneous communication broadcasts world plights and problems into millions of homes, easy transportation opens new corners of the earth to millions more, and the intricate network of commerce and industry ties us all together in ways we can barely begin to fathom.

With the sudden wealth of knowledge about other peoples and cultures, Christianity, with its Western bias and seemingly antiquated myths and creeds, strikes many people as irrelevant at best or at worst a harmful instrument of oppression. Christians are asking themselves, in the light of our late-twentieth-century global village, what Christianity has to say and offer to the world.

Expansion of Christianity

Christianity spread rapidly during the nineteenth and twentieth centuries, first through an expansive Western-directed missionary effort, followed by the emergence of native leadership and growth of indigenous churches that reflected the local cultures.

Protestant missions grew out of the evangelical revivals and social reform movements of the nineteenth century, depending largely on voluntary associations such as the Church Missionary Society that recruited and supported missionaries. The Catholic missionary effort revived under Gregory XVI (1831–1846), who encouraged the old missionary orders—Jesuits, Dominicans, and Franciscans—to reenter the mission field. Later specifically missionary orders such as the Maryknoll Fathers and Sisters formed, serving especially in Latin America and Asia. Instead of the mass conversions that characterized mission efforts during the Middle Ages, modern missionaries have emphasized individual conversions. They have also worked hard on improving local living conditions by establishing schools, hospitals, orphanages, and other institutions.

The relationship between missions and colonialism, which also proceeded at a rapid pace at this time, was involved and complex. It has become commonplace to accuse Western missionaries of being mere agents for imperialism, looking to their own governments for protection while forcing ancient cultures, especially in Asia, to open their doors to Western ideas backed by foreign might. While it is true that the Treaty of Nanking, following the infamous Opium War (1839–1842) between China and Britain, forced concessions for missionary work in Chinese territory, in other parts of the world missionaries opposed their own governments' imperialist policies. The British East India Company, for example, opposed missionary work in India for fear that preaching would arouse the people and hinder trade.

Although missionaries initially hesitated to train and support indigenous leadership in the new churches, they eventually heeded the call to prepare native African, Indian, and Asian leaders. With the end of colonial rule following World War II, a truly remarkable expansion of Christian churches began under African leadership. Despite persecution from dictators such as Idi Amin in Uganda, Christianity in Africa has proved durable and vital. While traditional European denominations continue to grow in Africa, African Christians within them have developed many new forms of worship and thought, frequently assimilating local beliefs to ancient Christian ideas. Many elements of indigenous religions appear in the worship and hymn forms used in African churches. Charismatic groups also contribute enormous fervor, and African theological seminaries are thriving and creating a distinctively African theology.

Missions to Asia produced far fewer converts than missions to Africa, though two notable exceptions are Korea, where the Presbyterian church in particular is popular, and the Philippines, which remains primarily a strong Roman Catholic land.

Roman Catholic missions in China enjoyed early success with the work of the Jesuits in the sixteenth century. Although the Jesuits were expelled following the Rites Controversy (1706), a conflict between the pope and the Chinese emperor, Catholics and other missionaries later returned (Chapter 14). In the nineteenth century, as Catholic mission work suffered from internal disputes, the balance shifted to the emerging Protestant missions. But following the Communist revolution in 1949, all missionary activity ceased, and many churches were shut down. Faced with the apparent alternatives of rejecting their country or rejecting their faith, Chinese Christians sought new ways to understand the Christian gospel apart from its Western cultural trappings, rather than adopt wholesale the Western Christian antagonism toward Marxism and rejection of Chinese society. Under the leadership of Y. T. Wu (1890–1979), described by an anonymous missionary as "the man who saved the church in China,"[10] Chinese Christians established their identity through the Three-Self Movement: churches should be self-supporting, self-administering, and self-propagating. K. H. Ting, bishop of the Anglican church in China, writes about Wu's vision of a Jesus who is present in the midst of the struggle:

> In his speeches Y.T. presented a Jesus who stood with the masses of the suffering people, ready to go through the torture of the cross and to shed his blood for their liberation. . . . In his vision of the immanence of the transcendent God in nature, in history and in people's movements, Y.T. was not only drawing on classical Chinese notions—which were therefore evangelistically important—but also playing, both theologically and politically, an enlightening and liberating role. He opened up a sluicegate, allowing many Chinese Christians to take their place in the movement for national salvation with their faith intact, as well

as allowing intellectuals mindful of the nation's fate to take their place among Christians.[11]

Pluralism

Like Wu and Ting, Third World Christians around the globe have pondered how to separate the gospel from its Western cultural context. Is the gospel a kernel contained within cultural husks that can be stripped away to reveal the truth of the Christian message, or is the gospel-culture relationship more like an onion where, if one keeps peeling, eventually nothing is left? Can the gospel be translated from culture to culture without either imposing the culture of the bearers or annihilating the culture of the receivers?

Those of us who live in the West have grown up, whether we recognize it or not, in a society imbued with the Jewish and Christian heritage. The preaching of such religions in Western nations is, for the most part, a call for people to return to their ancestral religion. But people in many non-Western nations perceive the call to Christianity as a call to reject traditional beliefs and thus to turn aside also from their own society and culture. This is the problem of religious pluralism. Does the fact that Christ was Jewish or Christianity was Western necessarily mean that God is not present and active in other religious traditions? Does acceptance of the gospel imply wholesale rejection of all other faiths? And if so, then how is Jesus the Christ to be understood as the universal savior that Christians proclaim?

Two general models have dominated Christian attitudes to other religions: (1) the conservative, exclusivist approach states that salvation is found only in Jesus Christ and that other religions have little value; (2) the liberal, inclusivist attitude recognizes the richness of other faiths but believes that their fulfillment is found in Christ. Currently, theologians are pushing beyond these two approaches to come to a new understanding of the relationship between Christianity and other religions, in which the universality of God's action and presence in the world is the basis for a theological understanding of other faiths. Theologian Christoph Schwöbel suggested the following approach:

> The religions therefore have to be seen as human responses to God's all encompassing presence and activity in which God is active . . . as the source and end of its fulfillment. . . . It must, however, be emphasized that this understanding of the universality of God's presence to his creation and of the universality of God's reconciling and saving love for his creation is for Christian theology never independent of God's self-disclosure in the particularity of the Christ event as the particular Trinitarian God—Father, Son, and Spirit.[12]

The debate continues, and as Christians learn more about other peoples and enter into dialogue with them concerning their beliefs, they will move in new directions of Christian thought and practice.

Ecumenism

Christians are also talking more with one another in a growing climate of **ecumenism**, the cross-denominational exchange of ideas, practices, and even pulpits. During World War II support for the Confessing church in Germany (which opposed the pro-Nazi state church) and efforts to save Jews in danger of extermination under Nazi rule strengthened networks of Christians on both sides of the conflict. In 1948 these contacts bore fruit in the establishment of the World Council of Churches (WCC), which included both Protestant and Eastern Orthodox groups. Roman Catholics refused to join but have sent observers and consultants in recent years. The WCC works at promoting understanding among its members, sponsors conferences, and relates issues of peace and justice to the gospel.

On a smaller scale, many denominations divided by historical and geographic circumstances have merged, forming stronger churches with a renewed sense of Christian mission. Dialogues between denominations have also led to an appreciation of the differences, celebrating the uniqueness of various expressions of Christian belief. Less concerned with issues of doctrine and more involved with the active expression of faith, ecumenism's greatest triumph is on the local level as churches gather together to run food pantries, shelters for the homeless or for battered women, refugee relief, day care centers, and a wide variety of community support groups. At a time when membership in many churches is dropping, Christian outreach in the community continues to bear witness to the ancient Christian concern for the poor and the needy.

CONCLUSION

As Christianity enters the twenty-first century of its existence, it is clear that conservative and liberal attitudes continue to divide Christian approaches to issues of faith and practice. Conservative Christians reiterate that the best hope for humanity lies in a return to the gospel message of faith in Jesus Christ. Issues such as new inclusive God-language, pluralism, and liberation theology, they aver, must not be allowed to detract from the gospel or dilute the faith.

Yet issues of inclusiveness dominate contemporary liberal Christian thought—spreading a gospel uncontaminated by Western cultural imperialism, resolving the tensions that still exist between women and Christianity as a traditionally patriarchal religion, working for justice and peace in troubled places around the world, and ministering at home to the poor, friendless, and needy. The medieval vision of Christendom has been shattered beyond repair; not only is the one, holy, catholic, and apostolic church divided, but Christianity again finds itself in a non-Christian world. The basic message of new life in Jesus Christ remains, but the old wineskins of a traditional Christian orthodoxy that regulates a primarily Christian society have burst. If the church is to survive effectively, it must find new wineskins to contain the message in a rapidly changing and pluralist world.

NOTES

1 Joseph R. Gusfield, *Symbolic Crusade: Status Politics and the American Temperance Movement* (Urbana: University of Illinois Press, 1963), p. 5.

2 Ibid., p. 7.

3 Ibid., p. 8.

4 Walter Rauschenbusch, *Christianity and the Social Crisis* (New York: Harper Torchbooks, 1964), pp. 421–422. Originally published in 1907.

5 Walter Rauschenbusch, "Christianizing the Social Order," in C. Howard Hopkins, *The Rise of the Social Gospel in American Protestantism, 1865–1915* (New Haven, Conn.: Yale University Press, 1940), p. 223. Originally published in 1912.

6 Jane Addams, "The Subjective Necessity for Social Settlement," from *Philanthropy and Social Progress,* in *The Social Thought of Jane Addams,* ed. Christopher Lasch (Indianapolis: Bobbs-Merrill, 1965), pp. 40–41. Originally published in 1893.

7 J. L. Gonzalez Balado, *The Story of Taizé,* 3rd rev. ed. (London: Mowbray, 1988), pp. 23–24.

8 Sarah Grimké, "Letter 3," *Letters on the Equality of the Sexes and the Condition of Woman* (New York: Franklin, 1970). Originally published in 1838.

9 M. Chernivasky, " 'Holy Russia': A Study in the History of an Idea," *American Historical Review* 63 (April 1958): 619.

10 Mary Austin Endicott, *Five Stars over China* (Toronto: Canadian Far Eastern Newsletter, 1953), p. 433.

11 K. H. Ting, "A Pioneering Theologian," in *No Longer Strangers* (Maryknoll, N.Y.: Orbis Books, 1989), p. 154. First published in 1982.

12 Christoph Schwöbel, "Particularity, Universality, and the Religions: Toward a Christian Theology of Religions," in *Christian Uniqueness Reconsidered,* ed. Gavin D'Costa (Maryknoll, N.Y.: Orbis Books, 1990), p. 39.

PART SEVEN

ISLAM

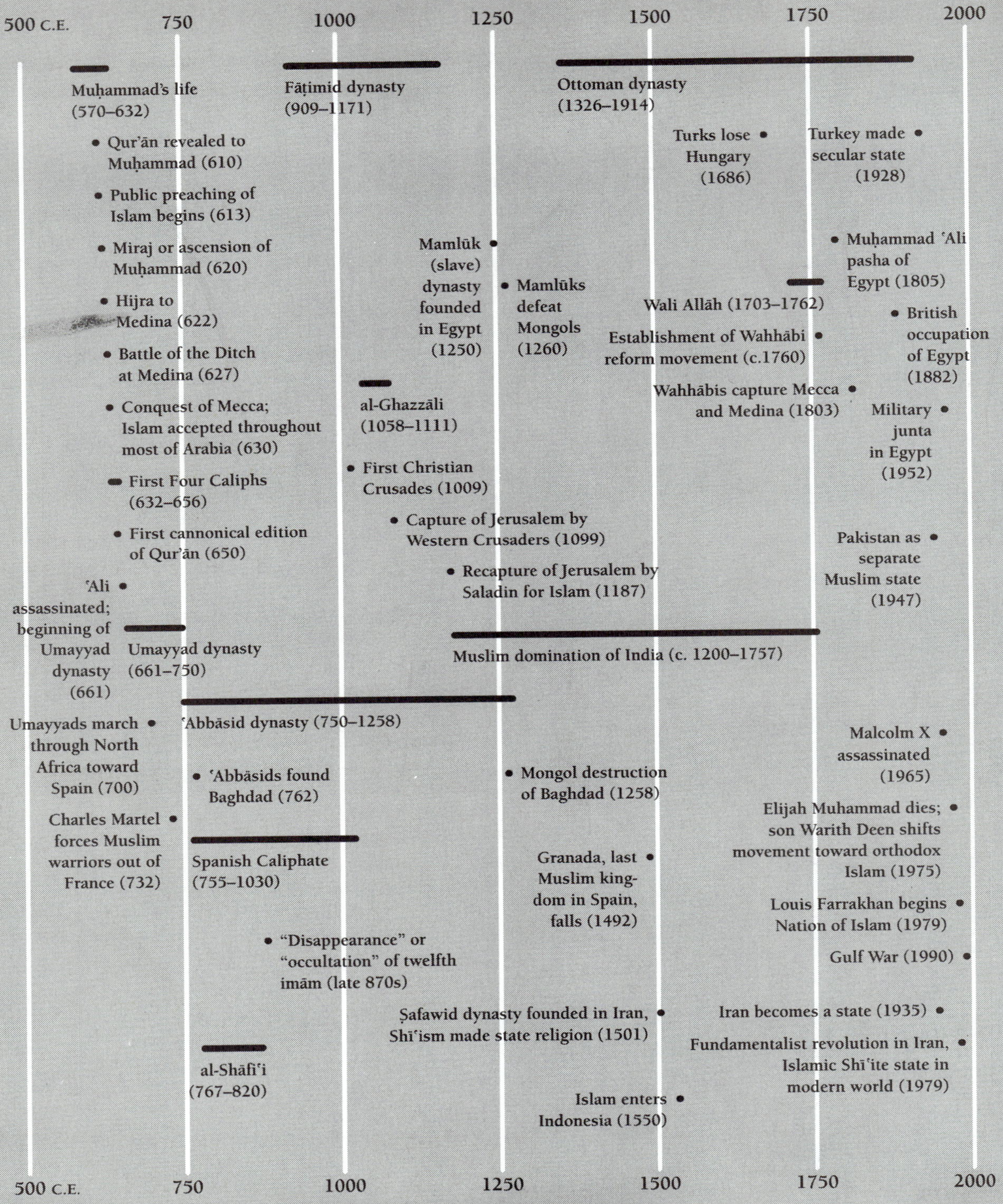
500 C.E.
750
1000
1250
1500
1750
2000
Muḥammad's life (570–632)
Qur'ān revealed to Muḥammad (610)
Public preaching of Islam begins (613)
Miraj or ascension of Muḥammad (620)
Hijra to Medina (622)
Battle of the Ditch at Medina (627)
Conquest of Mecca; Islam accepted throughout most of Arabia (630)
First Four Caliphs (632–656)
First cannonical edition of Qur'ān (650)
'Ali assassinated; beginning of Umayyad dynasty (661)
Umayyad dynasty (661–750)
'Abbāsid dynasty (750–1258)
Umayyads march through North Africa toward Spain (700)
'Abbāsids found Baghdad (762)
Charles Martel forces Muslim warriors out of France (732)
Spanish Caliphate (755–1030)
"Disappearance" or "occultation" of twelfth imām (late 870s)
al-Shāfi'i (767–820)
Fāṭimid dynasty (909–1171)
al-Ghazzāli (1058–1111)
First Christian Crusades (1009)
Capture of Jerusalem by Western Crusaders (1099)
Recapture of Jerusalem by Saladin for Islam (1187)
Mamlūk (slave) dynasty founded in Egypt (1250)
Mamlūks defeat Mongols (1260)
Muslim domination of India (c. 1200–1757)
Mongol destruction of Baghdad (1258)
Granada, last Muslim kingdom in Spain, falls (1492)
Ṣafawid dynasty founded in Iran, Shī'ism made state religion (1501)
Islam enters Indonesia (1550)
Ottoman dynasty (1326–1914)
Turks lose Hungary (1686)
Turkey made secular state (1928)
Muḥammad 'Ali pasha of Egypt (1805)
Wali Allāh (1703–1762)
Establishment of Wahhābi reform movement (c.1760)
British occupation of Egypt (1882)
Wahhābis capture Mecca and Medina (1803)
Military junta in Egypt (1952)
Pakistan as separate Muslim state (1947)
Malcolm X assassinated (1965)
Elijah Muhammad dies; son Warith Deen shifts movement toward orthodox Islam (1975)
Louis Farrakhan begins Nation of Islam (1979)
Gulf War (1990)
Iran becomes a state (1935)
Fundamentalist revolution in Iran, Islamic Shī'ite state in modern world (1979)
500 C.E.
750
1000
1250
1500
1750
2000

ISLAM TIME LINE

ISLAM

CHAPTER 23

THE BEGINNING: THE WORLD OF MUḤAMMAD

Islam is an Arabic word meaning "surrender" or "obedience" to God. *Muslim*, "one who has surrendered," comes from the same root. Surrender is believed to be humanity's proper response to God. Fazlur Raḥman, a modern Muslim intellectual, explained that humanity is to "surrender to the will of God," that is, to carry out God's commands fully and faithfully. As in many other religions, these commands touch on nearly every aspect of life—dress patterns, eating habits, behavioral codes, and so on. Where Islam differs is that the commands of God have been thought to extend even to the political arena. From very early on, politics, behavior, and theology have been profoundly intertwined. From the heights of the ruler's court down to the meanest laborer, all are understood as connected to the divine picture and simultaneously to the political drama. Thus the history of Islam is intertwined with the history of the Muslim empire, its legal system, and other matters frequently thought of as secular. Islam has grounded an entire civilization on what it believes to be the commands of God.

That civilization has been enormous. Founded by Muḥammad in Arabia in the seventh century C.E., by late medieval times it extended from eastern India to Spain and from North Africa to the Caspian Sea. It is thought to be today's fastest-growing faith, with 1 billion adherents, or about 20 percent of the world's population, primarily in countries in southern and western Asia and northern Africa.

To understand how this religion and its civilization came to be, we must look in detail at its birthplace, the Arabian peninsula, and at its founding figure, Muḥammad (c. 570–632).

Pronouncing Arabic
Arabic letters with accent marks over or under them may generally be pronounced as in English. But there are several exceptions: a long vowel, such as *ā*, is held longer than a short one, *a*—thus *Allāh* is pronounced "allaaa"; *ḥ* represents a soft guttural sound, like *ch* in the Scottish *loch; q* is a "k" sound made at the back of the throat. The *hamza* (') indicates a glottal stop, for which you briefly close the throat—thus *Qur'ān* is pronounced not "ko-ran" but more like "core, on." The *ʿayn* (ʿ) indicates a strong guttural sound made with a compressed throat—to begin *ʿAbbāsid,* tighten the throat and then release it on "ah."

ARABIA ON THE EVE OF ISLAM

Two key aspects of the Arabian peninsula shaped Islam: its geography and the nature of the cities in which Muḥammad lived.

The Arabian peninsula is a big, arid, and mostly empty place. On the west, a jagged range of mountains, some reaching to 12,000 feet, forms a protective barrier along the Red Sea. To the east, an enormous desert slopes down toward the other natural border, the

Bedouins of Muḥammad's time lived in tents, much like these twentieth-century Bedouins. Several features of Bedouin life influenced Islam, though Muḥammad's challenge to the importance of its kinship structure was one of the most controversial aspects of his preaching. (Jeff Rotman/Peter Arnold, Inc.)

Persian Gulf and the Indian Ocean. Thus the inhabitants' way of life was able to develop in relative isolation from the rest of the world. Until very recent times, agriculture was possible here in only a few areas—along the coasts, in the mountains, and at scattered oases. Most of the inhabitants, the so-called Bedouins, survived as best they could in the desert. Living in worn tents, they followed their camels, sheep, and goats from oasis to oasis and occasionally engaged in limited trade. Known to be a tough people, they bolstered their income by raiding one another and the settled towns and selling protection to the merchants' caravans passing through their territories. Because needed trade routes crossed these areas, distant governments frequently sought agreements with Bedouin tribes, much to the latter's advantage.

The Bedouins' social units were kinship groups: the tribe and, within it, the clan. An individual was not identified by place or citizenship but by ancestry and kinship group. One's personal prestige and security rose and fell with the prestige and power of one's tribe and clan.

No central government controlled tribal Arabia. Occasionally, tribes formed alliances with each other, but these tended to be short-lived, ending in intertribal competition. Rather than a government, the main restraint on intertribal conflict was the blood feud. If someone killed a member of your clan, it behooved you to avenge that death. Thus killing a man could lead to a war with his kinsmen, sometimes lasting generations. Such threats saved the lives of many people who found themselves confronting superior forces from another tribe, but as deterrents they worked very unevenly. Tribal Arabia was torn almost constantly by costly blood feuds.

Several features of Bedouin society influenced Islam. First, the tribe was governed by a participatory system in which every mature and able male had the right to be heard on critical issues affecting the tribe. The leader of the tribe was its **shaykh**, a man of proven ability. The shaykh was chosen by a consensus of the tribe's ranking males. He was not the despot usually suggested to westerners by the word *sheik* but rather first among equals, able to persuade but not to dictate. When Muḥammad came to lead his people, he too was originally taken not as a dictator but only as the first among equals.

Second, the tribes had no written laws but lived according to traditional values transmitted through the generations by word and example. Normative behavior was commonly called the **sunna** ("well-trodden path") of the ancestors, who embodied the honor and glory of the group. Muḥammad's behavior and the pattern of life he established also came to be called the *sunna*.

Third, honor was important to the Bedouin, as it would be to Muḥammad. Everything a Bedouin male did represented his clan. Thus his behavior would enhance or besmirch the collective honor of his kinsmen, living and dead. As Toshihiko Izutsu, a Japanese interpreter of Islam, put it:

> We are accustomed to think of moral virtues as personal qualities inherent in the individual. This was not the case with the pagan Arabs. For them, moral virtues were rather precious communal possessions inherited from fathers and forefathers. A man's honor or glory . . . always came to him as an inheritance within the tribe. He felt himself charged with the sacred duty of transmitting it unharmed, or even greatly enhanced, to posterity.[1]

The nomads' values reflected their situation. An existence filled with the threat of violence placed a premium on martial skills and bravery. The ideal man was fierce and independent. He would bow to no man, win glory through successful aggression, and be known as an implacable avenger of his kinsmen. In such an atmosphere of machismo, men sought fame for having colossal appetites for life's fleeting pleasures (especially wine and sexual conquests) and the love of one's family. One's image as a great and powerful man became all-important.

Reflecting its macho ideals, Bedouin culture was dominated by its males. We know little about the lives and aspirations of Bedouin women. We do know that they minded the home and that hospitality to kin and strangers was highly valued—natural in an environment in which one might find oneself dangerously alone at any time. Also, in a land without courts, keeping one's word was an essential trait. Generosity in supporting weaker tribe members and fairness in distributing tribal resources were fundamental to the solidarity needed for the group's survival and were thus endlessly praised. (This foreshadowed Islam's emphasis on charity to needy believers.)

Finally, the Bedouins loved poetry. It was recited and memorized, not being committed to writing until well after the rise of Islam. The Bedouin poets were believed to be possessed by spirits that gave them their marvelous creative powers. Poets were among the great assets of the tribe. They celebrated the virtues of their tribe and its great men and blasted its enemies with devastating satire. Muḥammad would come to be praised as the greatest Arabic poet—high praise indeed.

In several ways, Bedouin beliefs and practices were the patterns that Islam reversed. First, Bedouins believed in no personal survival after death. The only kind of immortality the male sought was to be honored as a great man by later generations. Muḥammad would introduce the notion of an afterlife.

Second, the pre-Islamic Arab was given to grand gestures and ostentatious displays of virtue. For example, one Arab watched his son be slaughtered rather than surrender personal property left in his care by an acquaintance who then died. Early Islam came to see such displays as destructive and egocentric.

PRE-ISLAMIC RELIGION

The religion of pre-Islamic Arabia can be described as a mixture of polytheism and animism. A supreme god was commonly recognized, but he was not alone. There were gods associated with rocks, trees, and springs. Some deities were associated with heavenly bodies like the sun and various stars, others with abstract concepts like fate and time. The Arabs also acknowledged the existence of a multitude of lesser spirits who could trick, inspire, or inform human beings.

Pilgrimages were sometimes made to sacred precincts, where one could worship or consult the deities. Sometimes these pilgrimages were large-scale affairs, especially during sacred months when intertribal warfare was prohibited.

Mecca, the birthplace of Islam, owed much of its security and prosperity to its being a major pilgrimage center. It is located in a circular valley, in the center of which stands a cube-shaped shrine, the Kaʿbah. The lord of the Kaʿbah was called **Allāh**, which means simply "the god." Allāh was the high god, creator of the world, and the tribal god of Muḥammad's tribe, the Quraysh, to whom the tribe turned in times of great stress.

Although Allāh may have been regarded as the ultimate or highest god, he was probably not particularly important in most Bedouins' daily lives. Of the Meccan sanctuary's many deities—360, according to later Islamic tradition—Allāh was probably not even the most popular.

A COMMUNITY IN TRANSITION

Muḥammad lived virtually his entire life in Arabian cities, especially Mecca, which was situated among west central Arabia's mountains and hills. In addition

COMPARISON

Religion and the Growth of Cities

It is striking how often new religions appear in association with social restructuring, especially the growth and development of cities. Muḥammad's Mecca, on active trade routes, had only recently grown in size and wealth. Although Jesus grew up in small towns, Paul and most early adherents of the young Christianity were city dwellers in the northeastern Mediterranean basin.* Protected by the Roman state, many of those cities had only recently expanded. The transformation of Christianity begun by Martin Luther took place in recently urbanized northern Europe. During the centuries immediately preceding Luther, such cities as Paris, London, and Cologne had blossomed. Northeastern India in the time of the Buddha, too, was a society in transition, moving out of a tribal structure toward a new, more cosmopolitan society characterized by increased commerce, a money economy, the beginnings of a rational bureaucracy, and a new and increasingly wealthy merchant class.

Something about towns and cities raises new problems and requires new answers. The French sociologist Émile Durkheim suggested that it centered on *anomie,* social dislocation. With the loss of the old social patterns and a village's or a tribe's group cohesion, the individual often loses a sense of belonging. In the face of this, one begins to long for deeper meaning, a meaning often provided by a new religious structure.

Other features of cities may also play a role. A merchant population often becomes literate, if only to keep track of shipments. That often leads to an increasingly inquisitive population, one that asks new questions. In addition, towns and cities attract people from a variety of backgrounds and cultures. Muḥammad's Mecca and Medina, for example, were home not only to Bedouins and Arabs but also to Abyssinian Christians and Jews. Paul's cities were home to Jews, Greeks, Romans, and other peoples. Contacts between people with such different backgrounds often lead to a cross-fertilization of ideas.

*Wayne Meeks, *The First Urban Christians* (New Haven, Conn.: Yale University Press, 1983), pp. 9–32.

to being a pilgrimage center, Mecca sat astride the major north-south caravan routes through western Arabia, connecting the spice markets and ports of southern Arabia with the countries of the Mediterranean Sea. Increased trade along these routes had led to an increase in Mecca's size and power during the century before Muḥammad's birth. His tribe had only recently settled in Mecca. Developing a complex system of alliances with nomadic tribes to protect the caravans, the Quraysh came to dominate this trade and thus became wealthy and powerful.

Sociologists have described Meccan society on the eve of Islam as a transitional community (see the box "Religion and the Growth of Cities"). Although many of the nomadic patterns, values, and social mechanisms remained, urban commerce-based life was causing major changes in values and relationships. Tribal solidarity was breaking down, being replaced by a sometimes rapacious economic individualism. In a nomadic tribe, the economic gap between the richest shaykh and the poorest person was comparatively small, and wealth was distributed fairly equitably. But in Mecca wealth had come to be concentrated in a group of wealthy merchants who conspired to maintain their advantages and who shared little with their poorer kin. "The breakdown of the tribe or clan led to the oppression of weaker members of the community such as widows and orphans. The successful merchant thought only of increasing his own power and influence."[2]

In the emerging ethos, people were increasingly ranked in terms of private wealth and power. Although the traditional sense of kinship responsibilities among this new commercial aristocracy did not disappear, it was weakened. The richest people were now the "best" people in Mecca, and status and wealth could be handed down from one generation to the next and from husband to wife. We know from the story of Muḥammad's first wife that women could be wealthy and to some extent powerful. Marriage into a powerful family was a goal avidly pursued by the ambitious.

In the commercial society of Mecca, orphans, widows, and the weak were soon picked clean. The less successful merchants faced usurious interest rates on borrowed funds and unfair trade advantages. The poorest residents were often left to starve.

Major changes in the lives of individuals or of societies invariably cause anxiety and stress. As old forms of social cohesion break down, the way is opened for a new definition of community in which individualism can be joined with social responsibility. One of Islam's many contributions to Arab life was to offer such a definition.

As a conduit for trade, Mecca was also a conduit for religious influences, for it was culturally and religiously diverse. Arabian cities were home not only to Bedouin polytheists but also to Abyssinian Christians, Arabicized Jews, and people from distant lands. Indeed, Muḥammad presupposed that his audience had heard a great deal about both the Old and New Testament figures he cited as examples.

MUḤAMMAD'S LIFE AND MESSAGE

As was stated at the outset, Islam attempts to integrate all aspects of life into a single cohesive tradition. The model for this cohesive life is the founder, **Muḥammad** (c. 570–632). In his life and teachings, all of the history of Islam finds its foundations; where questions arose, the tradition came to look in extremely close detail at his biography.

Muḥammad, shown here in a traditional portrait, was the prophet and leader of the community of worship, its supreme judge and highest political officer. Islam attempts to integrate all aspects of life into a single cohesive tradition. (The Granger Collection)

He was born into the Ḥāshim clan of the Quraysh tribe, which had recently become dominant and wealthy in Mecca. His father, ʿAbd-Allāh, died before Muḥammad was born, and his mother, Āmina, died when he was 6. The youngster became the ward of his grandfather, ʿAbd-al-Muṭṭalib. When ʿAbd-al-Muṭṭalib died two years later, Muḥammad became the responsibility of his uncle Abū-Ṭālib, the new head of Ḥāshim. In the socioeconomic pecking order in Quraysh, Ḥāshim was somewhere in the middle.

We know little about Muḥammad's young adulthood. He seems to have had some success as a commercial agent. At 25 he married Khadīja, a wealthy widow 15 years his senior. Although the marriage was undoubtedly to Muḥammad's economic advantage, the relationship was far more than a commercial convenience. Islamic tradition presents him as devoted to her; Khadīja is shown as an ideal woman who supported Muḥammad in his religious calling and was his first convert. He took no other wife while she lived, and he was emotionally devastated by her death. Of their several children, the sons did not survive their father, but one of the daughters, Fāṭima, became important in Islam's history.

Muḥammad was deeply troubled during his early adulthood, according to Muslim accounts. He was one of a growing number of people in newly urban Mecca who sought a more satisfying perspective than that offered by the old Bedouin religion. Muslim biographers show him seeking a value system other than his contemporaries' pursuit of wealth and power and searching for a principle of community that might transcend feuding tribal particularism. Muḥammad became increasingly convinced that the only true and living God was Allāh, the Lord of the Kaʿbah, and that the ruthlessness and oppression in his society were affronts not to the old ideals of tribal solidarity but to Allāh, the God. In fear and trembling, Muḥammad concluded that time was running out, that a terrible divine judgment was about to descend on his people.

EARLY REVELATIONS

Deeply troubled by such questions, Muḥammad began going into the caves in the mountains near Mecca for solitary meditation. Wrapping himself with his shawl for warmth, he would sit for hours. On one of these retreats he heard what he knew to be a divine voice speak to him. Here is Arthur J. Arberry's translation of what may have been that first revelation:

Recite: In the Name of the Lord who created,
created Man of a blood-clot.

Recite: And thy Lord is the Most Generous,
who taught by the Pen, taught man that
he knew not.

No indeed; surely Man waxes insolent,
for he thinks himself self-sufficient.
Surely unto thy Lord is the Returning.
(96:1–8)[3]

After receiving this revelation on what would later be called the Night of Power, Muḥammad rushed home in awe and excitement. Half believing and half doubting the authenticity of what had just happened, he told only his wife and closest family members. After a few more, the revelations ceased. This brought on an agony of self-doubt, resolved only when the revelations began occurring again.

Muḥammad was probably 40 years old when he had the first of his revelations. They would continue periodically for more than 20 years. Ultimately, they came to be collected in the **Qur'ān** ("Recitation"), Islam's scripture.

Muḥammad had no conscious control over the timing or the content of these divine speeches. He apparently felt seized by a power outside himself that rendered him oblivious to his surroundings. They were wrenching divine invasions that, paradoxically, always left him with clear verbal messages when he returned to normal consciousness. The overwhelming majority of Muḥammad's revelatory experiences were auditory, but there were exceptions. One passage from the Qur'ān clearly describes a vision, either of Allāh himself or of some other superhuman being:

By the Star when it plunges,
your comrade is not astray, neither errs,
nor speaks he out of caprice.
This is naught but a revelation revealed,
taught him by one terrible in power,
very strong; he stood poised,
being on the higher horizon,
then drew near and suspended hung,
two bows'-lengths away, or nearer,
then revealed to his servant that he revealed.
His heart lies not of what he saw;
what, will you dispute with him what he sees?
(53:1–12)[4]

The most common Muslim interpretation of these verses is to identify the "one terrible in power" with the angel Gabriel, who is identified in the Qur'ān and in Islamic tradition as the angel of revelation who delivers God's messages to his prophets. Sometimes the prophet sees Gabriel (in Arabic, *Jibrīl*) during the revelatory experience, and sometimes he does not.

For a long time after the revelations had started, Muḥammad's intermittent conversations with God remained a private piety that had no impact on the larger Meccan society. This would change in 613, when Muḥammad was ordered to "warn" the people of Mecca, the "Mother of Cities," of the guidance and good news that was now being offered them. "O you wrapped in your cloak, arise and warn!" (74:1–2).[5]

MUḤAMMAD AND MONOTHEISM

It has often been remarked that *Allāh* has no plural in Arabic. Muḥammad proclaimed the absolute unity and uniqueness of Allāh. The prophet's message depicted the ultimate as a unique "thou" unlimited by space, time, or form. Although Allāh was consistently spoken of with male pronouns, Allāh cannot be represented by any image or likened to anything created. The creator of all things was absolutely sovereign over all.

The Arabic word for polytheism is ***shirk,*** the "association" of one thing with another. Polytheism obscures God's unique status by ascribing various "associates" worthy of human worship. The Qur'ān declares this to be a monstrous delusion. Allāh has no consort, no sons, no daughters, no "associates" of any kind. "Say, 'He is Allāh, one. Allāh, the Eternal. He has not begotten nor was He begotten, and He has no equal' " (112:1–4).

The Qur'ān has much to say about unbelief and unbelievers. The Arabic word for unbelief is ***kufr,*** a term that is difficult to translate. The "unbelievers" with whom Muḥammad was dealing were not theoretical atheists. On the cognitive level, their unbelief consisted of denying the sovereignty of Allāh, God's revelation via Muḥammad, or the Last Judgment.

But *kufr* may also mean denying the truth or denying one's obligation to someone else; hence it is often translated as "ingratitude." According to the Qur'ān, the polytheists are guilty of colossal ingratitude. They acknowledge Allāh as creator, yet they refuse to give him the loyalty and service that he deserves.

> O people, serve your Lord Who created you and those who were before you; maybe you will yet fear Him: Who made for you the earth as a couch, and the sky as a dwelling and sent down rain from the sky by which He brought forth fruit for your sustenance. So do not knowingly ascribe partners to Allāh. (2:21–22)

The Qur'ān blasts members of the Quraysh tribe who ignored the Lord of the Kaʿbah, upon whom they depended:

> In the name of God, the Merciful, the Compassionate. For the forming of Quraysh, for their forming the winter and summer caravans, let them serve the Lord of this House, who has fed them when they hungered and secured them from fear. (106:1–5)

Because they are ungrateful, polytheists can expect no mercy from Allāh. "Truly Allāh will not forgive that anything be associated with Him. Anything else He may forgive to whomever He wishes. Whoever associates anything with Allāh has invented a monstrous crime!" (4:48).

Muḥammad did not introduce monotheism to the Arabian peninsula. Both Christians and Jews inhabited Arabia. Where Muḥammad's monotheism differed from theirs was, first, contrary to the lush iconography of seventh-century Christianity, there could be no image, depiction, or characterization of this deity. Allāh was utterly above and beyond all names and all things. "Say," says one of the revelations, "He is God, One, / God, the Everlasting Refuge, / who has not begotten, and has not been begotten, / and equal to him is not any one."[6] The Qur'ān differed from Judaism in that, although it used covenant imagery, its God had no special relationship with any particular community. All human beings were equally subject to the one God.

Second, this new religion emphasized the key role of the prophet or apostle as a spokesman. Unlike the Christian doctrine, the prophet was not presented as a son of God or an equal to God. That would be a form of *shirk,* associating something with God. Instead, this sole deity had taken on a messenger through whom to speak. "It is [Allāh] who has sent his Messenger with the guidance and the religion of truth. . . . Muḥammad is the Messenger of God" (48:28).

The Meaning and Purpose of Human Existence

According to the Qur'ān, human life reaches its fullest potential only when it is thoroughly theocentric (centered on God). The ultimate purpose of human existence is to serve God: "I created jinn* and humanity only to serve Me" (51:56).

The human being was put on this earth to be Allāh's

**Jinn* (singular, *jinni*) are invisible spirits neither human nor angelic credited with the ability to inform soothsayers and inspire poets. The jinn were called to serve God. The English word *genie* is derived from the Arabic *jinni.*

khalīfa ("successor" or "representative"), to govern and enjoy the world on its creator's terms, and to reflect God's commands. Serving the one true God should be the driving principle of human existence. And as we have said, this is the basic meaning of *Islam:* surrender, submission, obedience to the will of God; serving God in every sphere of life; and doing whatever God commands. A man who makes such a commitment is a **Muslim** (a woman, a *Muslima*). Hence Islam is not an isolated act; it is an ongoing, dynamic relationship that requires constant renewal and touches on every aspect of daily existence. It is, Muslims are fond of saying, a way of life.

Human beings know who Allāh is and what he would have us be and do because he has told us in revelation about himself and about the consequences—both temporal and eternal—of obedience and disobedience to his imperative. Allāh has told all these things through the divine revelations delivered by his prophets and preserved in scripture. The true Muslim, then, is above all a *believer.* Such belief has both intellectual and emotional components. Intellectually, one accepts the truth of monotheism ("There is no God but God") and accepts the divine revelations as authentic ("and Muḥammad is his apostle"). Emotionally, one surrenders completely to the one who "sent down" that revelation and takes on the way of life he has commanded through his prophet.

Social Reform

From the first, serving Allāh has meant striving to serve him in one's relationships with other people. The only reliable basis of personal and social value, teaches the Qur'ān, is the will of God. One is to model oneself on God, who is, among other things, compassionate, protective of the weak, just, and implacably opposed to evil in all its forms. Human beings cannot, of course, fully match God in any of these positive attributes. But as God's potential successors or representatives, human beings should strive to reflect such qualities, however imperfectly, in their social relationships. Consider this passage in which Muḥammad is directed to treat the orphan and the poor with some of the same kindness with which Allāh had treated him:

Did He not find you an orphan and shelter you?
Did He not find you erring and guide you?
Did He not find you poor and give you wealth?
So as for the orphan, do not oppress him.
And as for the beggar, do not scold him.
As for the Lord's blessing, proclaim it!
(93:6–12)

In one Qur'ānic narrative, human beings are explicitly urged to imitate the ethical behavior of Allāh:

Do good, just as God has done good to you!
And do not try to spread corruption in the world.
Surely God does not love those who corrupt.
(28:77–78)

The Qur'ān summarily dismisses the authority of the old Bedouin sunna. One's ancestors cannot be guides to proper conduct. They are models only for how to earn eternal damnation: "And when it is said to them, 'Follow what God has sent down,' they say, 'No, but we will follow what our ancestors used to do.' What? And if their ancestors were unguided?" (2:165).

Muḥammad's attack on the ancestors and their "well-trodden path" was one of the most controversial and explosive aspects of his preaching. Included in this attack was a challenge to the excessive importance the Bedouins gave to kinship. If human beings were created to serve God, then the most important thing about a human being is his or her relationship to God, not the blood relationship to family, clan, or tribe. True Muslims are "brothers" who share a religious loyalty that may take precedence over their loyalty even to their own families: "O believers, if your fathers and brothers prefer unbelief to belief, do not take them as friends. Whoever takes unbelievers as friends, they are the transgressors" (9:23). Being a Muslim in the early days inevitably led to family conflicts of the most heartrending kind.

Yet the new value system could also be enormously liberating. The true Muslims no longer needed to respect every aspect of the old social order of either desert or town. As devoted servants of Allāh, they were the best of people, regardless of their place in the old order. The social, economic, and political dead ends of kinship society were exchanged for new and open-ended bases for community, social status, and responsibility.

We have seen that in Mecca, Muḥammad lived and preached in a transitional society in which tribal values were gradually giving way to economic individualism. Muḥammad's preaching reinforced this trend toward individualism. In his unremitting attack on the breakdown in social responsibility, he appealed neither to kinship nor to the old sunna. Allāh, he contended, who gives us our lives and everything that we enjoy, holds each of us personally responsible for sharing our wealth with the needy, for protecting the rights of society's more vulnerable members, and for dealing justly in every human transaction, personal or otherwise. Countering the trend toward greed, he asserted that the greater the wealth, the greater the responsibility. Selfish and stingy people are desperately clawing at fleeting joys while forgetting their responsibility to the creator. Muḥammad called on the greedy and the powerful to repent of their selfishness before time runs out for them and for everybody else.

Eschatological Visions

According to the Qur'ān, people who pursued worldly ends did so out of their belief that there would never be a day of reckoning. After all, they thought, they had nothing else to hope for or to fear: "There is nothing but our present life; we die, and we live, and we will not be resurrected" (23:39). Muḥammad, however, declared that what a human being believes and does in this life has eternal significance. The God who created and sustains the universe will soon call all to judgment. The end of the world, variously called the Day of Judgment, the Hour, and the Last Day, seemed to Muḥammad to be very near, although only Allāh knew the exact time it would arrive. On that awful day, the dead will be resurrected, raised up after death to a new life. All humanity, past and present, will stand before God to be judged. Unbelieving or selfish people face eternal damnation in hell. Those who respond to the revelation of Allāh before it is too late are promised everlasting life in paradise.

Muḥammad's traditional critics found the notion that the long dead could be raised a ridiculous fable. Muḥammad's reply was to refer the Meccans to their own belief in Allāh as the creator of the universe. If he created it the first time, why would it be difficult for him to do it again?

> The unbelievers asked, "Will we be resurrected as a new creation when we have become just bones and crumbled pieces? Don't they see that Allāh, who created the heavens and the earth, is capable of creating the life of them?" (17:98–99)

Muḥammad declared that what a person does in this life has eternal significance. This fifteenth-century Turkish manuscript illumination shows Muḥammad on a tour of the infernal world of shadows. Women, who have let strangers see their hair, now hang by their hair over flames as punishment. (The Granger Collection)

The Qur'ān does not offer a doctrine of natural immortality. The human essence is not an imperishable spirit that automatically escapes the body at death, to rise to a higher plane of existence. The human being does not "have" a body and a soul; the human being *is* a body and a soul—one aspect does not live without the other. Presumably, this will be as true in the hereafter as it is now. One implication of this view of the nature and destiny of humanity is that neither paradise nor hell excludes physical or sensory experience.

Muḥammad's early emphasis on judgment and the hereafter was not the beginning of a sustained campaign to pull people out of the world into lives of ascetic withdrawal. This life, in the worldview of the Qur'ān, is neither a mirage nor a trap. It is God's creation and therefore real and good. The world becomes a snare and a delusion only when human beings make it or any part of it their ultimate concern. In comparison with the views of his opponents, Muḥammad's message makes this life less valuable by contrasting it with everlasting life. At the same time, Muḥammad's message makes this life radically more serious by making it a testing ground for eternity rather than an end in itself. With Allāh's help, the Muslim can live *in* the world without being *of* the world because his ultimate concerns reach beyond the sphere of death and decay. If necessary, the Muslim should sacrifice goods, family, and even life in service to God, in the sure and certain promise of eternal fellowship with Allāh in paradise.

The Muslim Community

Early Development

After 613, when Muḥammad was commanded to "arise and warn" the people of Mecca, he began to preach, first to his family and then to the broader community. At first he attracted the poor and disaffected elements of society to his new teachings: slaves, poor people, women, children. But he also succeeded in winning over a number of able and energetic young men, some of them from the most influential clans of Quraysh. Scholar W. M. Watt describes Muḥammad's most important followers as coming from the level of society immediately below the topmost stratum of rich and powerful merchants.[7] These were men who were frustrated in their drive to reach the top and who were more than willing to see the old order turned upside down.

Together they began to build a new society, loyal no longer to the clan or the tribe alone but to Allāh and, by implication, to his prophet. They began to develop their own sunna, which ranked people not in terms of wealth or kinship but in terms of religious and moral values. To them, the men best suited to leadership were not the wealthy merchants but the Muslims. They were, in short, developing a complete and independent community.

As Muḥammad's influence gradually increased and with it the potential for social unrest, the leaders of the old order felt compelled to act.

Early Meccan Opposition to Muḥammad

Mecca was governed by a loose-knit council of elders from the disparate clans of Quraysh. Muḥammad's opponents could call on no political or police authority to squelch him, and fear of a blood feud restrained those who might otherwise have had Muḥammad assassinated. But they did accuse him of being guided not by God but by a jinni and of using wild claims to support personal ambition.

Although Muḥammad was attacking the old beliefs and values, he was at first protected by his clan. Abū-Ṭālib, while remaining true to the old religion, refused to withdraw clan protection from his nephew. He made it clear that if Muḥammad were killed, he would be avenged.

Ibn-Isḥāq (died 767), one of the earliest biographers of Muḥammad, recounts that the leading merchants initially tried to buy him off. When this failed, they persecuted and even tortured the slaves and other vulnerable members of his entourage. Some of Muḥammad's followers were forced to leave the peninsula and seek refuge temporarily among the Christians of Abyssinia. But Muḥammad remained in Mecca, and the leading merchants decided to try a commercial boycott as a means of depriving him of the protection of his Ḥāshim clan. The boycott lasted two largely ineffective years.

The year 619 marked a turning point for Muḥammad. The death of both his wife Khadīja and of his uncle and protector Abū-Ṭālib made it difficult for him to remain in Mecca. Abū-Lahab, the new leader of Ḥāshim, and another of Muḥammad's uncles despised both Muḥammad and his religious ideas. Abū-Lahab at first continued the protective policy of Abū-Ṭālib, but ultimately he concluded that Muḥammad's continual attacks on his own polytheistic ancestors and kinsmen were too disloyal and so withdrew clan protection. As a result, Abū-Lahab earned the distinction of being cursed by Allāh himself in the Qur'ān (sura 111).

Although Muḥammad had enough followers to ensure that his enemies did not have the freedom to kill him with impunity, Abū-Lahab's new policy left Muḥammad and his people in a very insecure position. Muḥammad sought protection outside Mecca. He attempted to negotiate an alliance with a neighboring town and with Bedouin tribes around Mecca. When these efforts failed, Muḥammad in 620 began secret negotiations with representatives of the oasis town of Yathrib, about 250 miles north of Mecca. Yathrib would later become known as Medina, from the Arabic *Madina al-Nabi,* "City of the Prophet."

Unlike Mecca, Medina was a water-rich oasis and an agricultural community. Its inhabitants included members of two important Arab tribes, as well as some Jewish clans that were allied with one or both of those. The Medinans had long been divided by a power struggle among various factions, and they hoped that in Muḥammad they had found an outside arbiter who might resolve their differences. Thanks to their large Jewish community, they were also more receptive to Muḥammad's monotheism.

After two years of secret talks, a large group of Medinans agreed in June 622 to accept Muḥammad as the prophet of Allāh and to fight on Allāh's behalf. They committed themselves to defend Muḥammad as they would their own kinsman, and Medina became Islam's new center. Over the next months, small groups of Muslims slipped out of Mecca and made their way to Medina. Muḥammad remained behind as long as possible to detract attention from this ***hijra*** (flight or emigration). Just as the enemies of the prophet were about to seize and kill him, he made his escape and reached Medina on September 24, 622. For this reason, the Muslim calendar begins on the first day of the lunar year of Muḥammad's *hijra* to Medina. A new stage in the history of the Islamic movement had begun.

THE MEDINAN YEARS

The followers of Muḥammad who made the trek from Mecca to Medina are known as the Emigrants, and the hosts who received the refugees from Mecca are referred to as the Supporters. Together they formed the community ***(umma)*** of Islam. Unlike the old clans and tribes, the umma was a community based more on a common faith than on a common ancestry. It soon developed its own government, economy, and army.

Muḥammad's new polity at Medina was in a precarious position. Although the Emigrants provided it with a deeply committed core of tested Muslims, they had neither military nor economic strength. Among the Medinan Muslims, some quickly developed an understanding of the Islamic movement and committed themselves to it, though many maintained only a nominal connection. The factionalism that had prompted the search for an outside arbiter did not evaporate, and the agreement to take disputes to Muḥammad for settlement was often ignored. To many Medinan Arabs, the new arrivals from Mecca were an economic burden, and the peculiar religious authority asserted by the prophet was seen as a threat to the personal ambitions of their leaders.

Besides problems of internal discipline and cohesion, the new community also faced external threats. In the oasis itself were Arabs who did not even pay lip service to the new way of life. In addition, the Medinan Jews were affiliated with the umma through alliances with its Arab elements, and despite whatever they may have expected of Muḥammad before the hijra, according to Muslim accounts, they made every effort to subvert the Islamic movement after his arrival. Outside the oasis, there were both actual and potential enemies.

In effect, a state of war already existed between Muḥammad's people and the Meccan Quraysh. As the Islamic movement grew into new territory, it challenged the intricate system of tribal alliances through which the Meccans secured the safety of their caravans. The Islamic understanding of life was a direct challenge to tribal independence and tradition, and even tribes unaffiliated with the Meccan Quraysh could not be expected to welcome the new religion.

Historians often note that Muḥammad had only limited political authority during the first years of the Medinan period. His followers responded to his revelations and participated in the worship he led, but in daily political, economic, and military matters, the prophet's view was but one important opinion among several. In the early years, he acted in most matters like a tribal shaykh, able to lead and persuade but not dictate.

In Medina the prophet carried out a sustained and eventually successful effort to increase his political authority as well as the internal discipline of the expanding community. His political drive in Medina, as well as in the wider Arabian peninsula, was not a diminution of his religious impulse but an expression of it. As we have seen, from the outset his verbal assaults on the old organization of life in Mecca implied a quest for a new and total community embodying the religious worldview that was its principle of formation. Having failed to organize and direct the energies of the Meccan community, Muḥammad tried again in Medina.

The Struggle against Mecca

On the eve of the *hijra,* according to traditional accounts, God gave Muḥammad permission to fight his enemies. Never again would the prophet rely exclusively on preaching and example to move the people of the Arabian peninsula.

In 623 Muḥammad began a series of raids against Meccan caravans. This strategy resulted in the first major clash between the Muslims and the army of the Meccan Quraysh. Trying to intercept a major caravan, Muḥammad and his forces encountered a Meccan relief battalion twice their size. Muḥammad's forces won the encounter nevertheless. This decisive victory at the so-called Battle of Badr, fought on March 15, 624, was a major turning point, for the Meccan Quraysh lost much of their prestige among the nomadic tribes.

Historians have identified many causes for the Muslims' success, including the Medinan forces' superior dedication and tactics and the Meccans' generally weak leadership. According to the Qur'ān, the battle was a demonstration of God's sovereignty. Many of the doubtful in Medina were impressed by the battle, as it gave new weight to the prophet's revelation as well as to his words on all matters. The superior morale of his followers at Badr was inseparable from their conviction: they fought as representatives of an irresistible power at work in human events.

The Meccan Quraysh made two major efforts to eradicate the Muslim challenge. In March 625 at Uḥud, the Meccans inflicted severe losses on Muḥammad and his followers but were unable to achieve a decisive victory. Two years later, in 627, the Meccans and their allies advanced on Medina with a large army. When the defenders dug a trench across the only approach to the oasis that the cavalry could use, Quraysh military superiority became useless. The Battle of the Ditch, as Muslims call it, became a long siege in which the tribal alliance assembled against Medina gradually disintegrated. Finally, the Quraysh were forced to withdraw, their prestige gone and their power to threaten the Islamic movement lost.

By 628, Muḥammad's authority in Medina was consolidated. The power of his unfolding religious message, the force of his personality, and the resounding success of his policies had won. His enemies were disgraced, their tribal alliances in disarray. When the Jewish community in Medina became opposed to the Islamic movement, Muḥammad destroyed and expelled it. Following his victory at Badr, Muḥammad

Muḥammad proclaimed the rite of pilgrimage to Mecca to be one of the five pillars of service to God. Today, as in early Islam, Muslims come to Mecca to participate in the sacred ritual and to share their ideas and their goods. This aerial view shows the Grand Mosque at Mecca in Saudi Arabia. (The Granger Collection)

extended his influence over the nomadic tribes, using religious missions, military demonstrations, and economic incentives in an effort to secure allegiance, alliance, or neutrality. After 628 he was less disposed to permit tribal alliances with the umma without conversion to Islam.

Although Muḥammad had acquired the military power to defeat Mecca, he turned instead to conciliation. In word and deed he proclaimed the rite of pilgrimage to Mecca to be a proper service to God. The people of Mecca were thus assured of the continuing importance of their town in any new Islamic order, but they were warned that the pilgrimage must be purged of its pre-Islamic polytheistic character. In 628 the prophet entered into a peace treaty with the Meccans that seemed remarkably favorable to his old enemies. After this arrangement broke down in 630, Muḥammad was able to capture Mecca with little resistance.

Muḥammad's Triumph

Muḥammad triumphantly led his armies into Mecca on January 11, 630. His long military, diplomatic, and economic campaign had not been intended to destroy the Meccan Quraysh but to integrate them into his community. He promptly declared a general amnesty. According to tradition, Muḥammad himself cleansed the Meccan sanctuary of all symbols of polytheism, including the 360 idols.

In March 632, Muḥammad led the great pilgrimage (ḥajj) to Mecca and surrounding religious sites. The ḥajj became a Muslim rite, and only professed Muslims were permitted to perform it. Every aspect of the old rite was reshaped and reinterpreted in strictly monotheistic terms. The pilgrimage of 632 is called in tradition the Farewell Pilgrimage because it occurred shortly before the prophet's death. His words and actions on this pilgrimage provided a ritual model later Muslim pilgrims sought to imitate.

Three months after the Farewell Pilgrimage, Muḥammad fell ill. He was cared for in his mosque-house in Medina by his favorite wife, ʿĀ'isha, the daughter of Abū-Bakr. Abū-Bakr led the communal prayers during Muḥammad's final illness. On June 8, 632, Muḥammad died. His death came as a great shock to his community. But that community would survive his death. As Abū-Bakr said at the time: "Muḥammad is dead . . . ; God is alive, immortal."

ISLAM AT THE DEATH OF THE PROPHET

At Muḥammad's death, his authority was established over much of the Arabian peninsula. It was still comparatively weak in the southern and eastern regions. Yet already the expansionist tendency of the new faith was clear. Muḥammad had indicated long-range expansion plans by sending out a series of military, diplomatic, and commercial missions to surrounding kingdoms, as well as to the Byzantine and Persian empires.

Muḥammad had immense personal power. He was the prophet and leader of the community of worship, its supreme judge and highest political officer. As we have stressed, according to classical Muslim thought the state is a community of faith organized as a polity, and citizenship, in the fullest sense of the term, is acquired by professing Islam and assuming its obligations. The state's basic function is to express, protect, and extend the faith, and God's will is the first basis of public life as well as humanity's guide in more private matters. The sections of the Qur'ān revealed at Medina—the later revelations—represented God as speaking in every area of life, though specific regulations for religious rites and for economic, social, and military matters fell short of a comprehensive system of commands and prohibitions.

THE QUR'ĀN AND THE FIVE PILLARS OF ISLAM

The Qur'ān is Islam's holy book. Its name comes from the Arabic *qara'a,* "to read or recite," and it is the compiled record of the recitations or revelations Muḥammad received from Allāh over more than 20 years. Though during his Medinan period many of Muḥammad's prophetic speeches were written down soon after they were uttered, no authoritative, organized edition of the revelations had been made at the time of his death. Many of his first revelations were probably preserved only in the memories of his earliest followers.

After Muḥammad died, his followers tried to gather and write down all that he had proclaimed as the speech of God. At least four collections of his revelations—different in arrangement and in some of the content—became widely known, but it was not until the tenth century that a definitive edition emerged.

THE QUR'ĀN

The Qur'ān is about equal in length to the New Testament and is divided into 114 *suras,* which are anywhere from a few lines to many pages long. The origin of the word *sura* is unclear, and it is misleading to think of a sura as a chapter in the usual sense. Most of the longer suras are loose collections of originally independent prophetic revelations or fragments; there are many abrupt changes of subject in the text. Only some of the shorter suras form tight literary units. Furthermore, some parts of the text have ritual uses; the opening sura, for example, a prayer addressed to Allāh, is recited during the daily prayers.

The Qur'ān is not chronological or thematic. It was assembled, roughly, in order of decreasing sura length (short suras at the end). Since Muḥammad's revelations generally became longer over the years, much of the material received at Medina is at the beginning, and many of the Meccan revelations are at the end.

When it was written down, only consonants were shown, as was customary in Semitic writing. The names of the suras, the numbering of the verses, and even the vowels and diacritical marks were added long after Muḥammad's death.

The Qur'ān's style, particularly its repetitiousness, must be understood in accordance with its function. Divine guidance to human beings is not to be read passively and silently but should be proclaimed and heard. It is understood primarily as speech, since the suras existed first as speech. The revelations were heard first by Muḥammad's early followers, and even after Muḥammad's death they were transmitted as proclamations rather than written texts.

To be sure, the Qur'ān abounds with references to revelation as writing or scripture. Yet in the Islamic view, scripture is a record of divine speech. It is to be read aloud, chanted, or heard as God's continuing message to humanity. Even when Muslims meditate on the Qur'ān, they typically describe their experience as the internalization of speech. The poetry, rhythms, wordplays, and repetition are intended to be spoken and heard as well as read. For the Muslim, the marvel of the Qur'ān is not only what is said but how it is said.

The Problem of Interpretation

The essence of Islamic studies is the understanding of what the Qur'ān means to people who accept it as true and as a guide to life. This leads to the

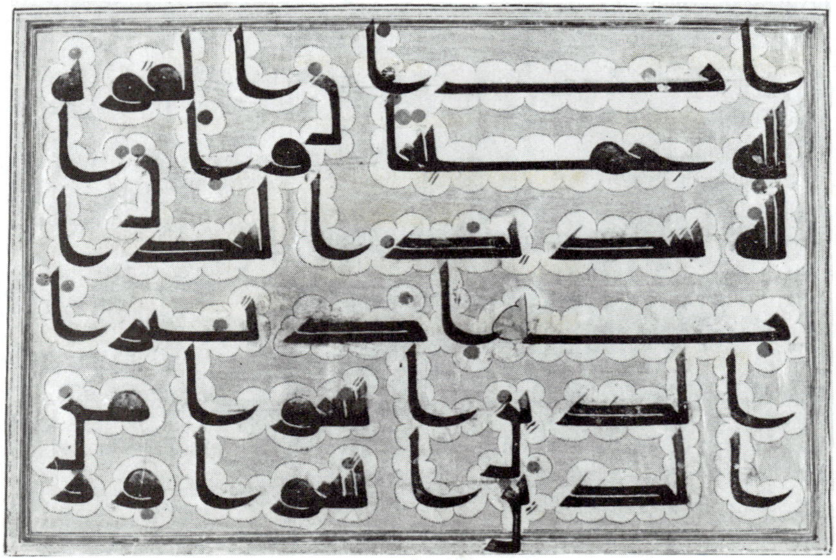

The Qur'ān is Islam's holy book. This page from the eleventh or twelfth century shows the angular Kufic script, the richly ornamental script devised in the seventh century for use primarily in the Qur'ān. (Los Angeles County Museum of Art)

question of hermeneutics—that is, how has the revelation been interpreted? The many varieties of Muslims all claim to draw inspiration from the Qur'ān and to be true to its fullest meaning. The various schools—the legalists, philosophical theologians, mystics, and modernists that we will discuss in later chapters—never saw themselves as being untrue to the text's original meaning but rather as discovering its hidden implications for particular situations and needs. Indeed, that it has thrived in so many cultures and ages is a tribute in part to the text's creative ambiguity and the techniques of hermeneutics used to reveal its meanings. The careful historian, however, will first try to determine its original meaning for the early community; only with this as a baseline can one understand the historical development of Islamic religious thought and practice.

The Qur'ān describes itself as words taken from a heavenly archetype or model and as one of God's eternal attributes. Thus it has a meaning internal to God and beyond division and time. The physical book and its human recitation then become concrete expressions of God's eternal speech, the eternal made manifest. Thus in no way, in orthodox belief, was it affected by Muḥammad's personality; its divine content was transmitted to humanity through him in concrete words and images that human beings can understand.

That revelation in Islam is primarily verbal does not mean that there are no other types of revelation. The verses of the Qur'ān are called *āyāt* ("signs"), and there are many kinds of divine signs: historical events (such as those that happened to Muḥammad), miracles, and the wondrous features of the cosmos and the human soul are all portrayed as filled with divine messages. But the verbal revelations recorded in the āyāt are especially significant, for they clarify God and human life in *conceptual* terms.

The message in divine speech places all other signs in their proper perspective and gives them their true meaning. But what are we to think of Christian claims that the revealed truth is embodied in the life of an individual?

The Human Example

Scholars of comparative religion have observed that in comparing Christianity with Islam, the parallel should not be between Jesus as the Messiah and Muḥammad but rather between Jesus as the Messiah and the Qur'ān. Islam sees God being revealed not in a person but in speech.

In the orthodox Muslim view, it is blasphemy to speak of any finite being, including Jesus, as God incarnate, although it is legitimate—indeed, required—to recognize Muḥammad as the ideal human response to God. Muḥammad's life exemplified how people should conduct themselves when they surrender to the divine claim, and his example provides an authoritative commentary on and supplement to the Qur'ān. Thus in all things except Muḥammad's prophetic mission itself, Muslims should follow the prophet's way *(sunna);* the majority of Muslims call themselves **Sunnis** in recognition of this command.

THE FIVE PILLARS

The tradition holds that there are five "pillars" of Islam that together form the first duties owed by humanity to God; they are the essence of a life of *islām* (submission). Although the Qur'ān offers much advice on the pillars, their structure was clarified only by later authors, in records that claimed to preserve the prophet's sunna. The **Five Pillars** are intended as the focus of a total life orientation, and they are understood as the gateways to a presence who forgives, sustains, and transforms.

The Qur'ān repeatedly contrasts believers with nonbelievers. The true Muslim, it asserts, is first of all a *mu'min,* a person who believes and trusts God and his word. External obedience to Islamic ordinances is mere hypocritical display if it is done without *īmān* (belief, faith, trust).

The Profession of Faith

The first pillar is the profession of faith. In its simplest form, it is to utter the *shahāda:* "There is no God but God, and Muḥammad is his apostle." Even more simply, it is to utter *"Allāhu akbar"* ("Greater is God," greater than all that could conceivably be compared to him). To utter the shahāda before Muslim witnesses is to gain entrance into the community. Thereafter it is repeated many times a day, reaffirming the religious relationship with both Allāh and one's fellow believers.

Orthodox Islam has resisted tendencies to privatize its faith. People can, of course, profess a faith that they

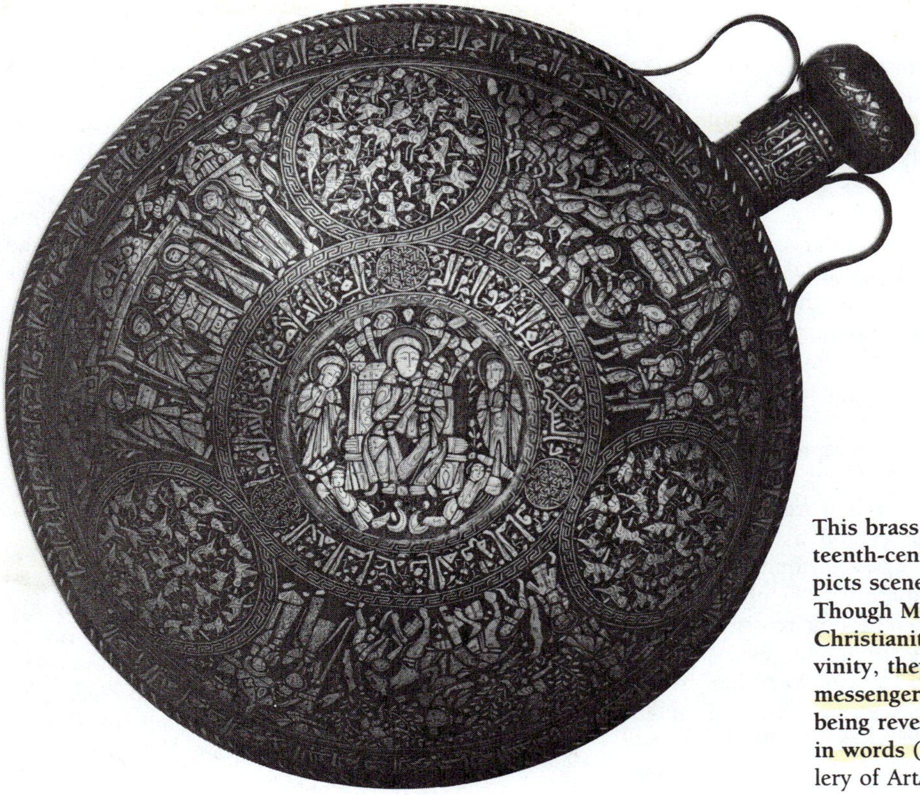

This brass canteen from thirteenth-century Islamic Syria depicts scenes from Jesus's life. Though Muslims do not accept Christianity's claim of Jesus's divinity, they do accept him as a messenger of God. Islam sees God being revealed not in a person but in words (the Qur'ān). (Freer Gallery of Art/Smithsonian Institution)

do not hold, but Muslims contend that authentic faith or conviction will drive its holders to declare themselves publicly. Islam stresses public confession of faith.

Ritual Prayer

To enter the community of Islam is to enter a life of prayer, and so the second pillar of the religion is the ritual prayer *(ṣalāt),* which is performed at least five times a day. It is a formalized process of specific words and physical movements, although individual and extemporaneous elements can be added.

Five times a day Muslims focus their attention on the One who gives proper meaning and direction to all life. The most dramatic physical act of the ritual prayer is full prostration, in which believers touch their foreheads to the earth, symbolizing total submission to the One who has created them from dust. Ideally, ṣalāt is an intimate conversation with God, in which the worshipers' intentions, words, and actions are heard, seen, and accepted by the One to whom they are offered.

The word *mosque* is derived from *masjid,* "place of prostration (before God)." It is considered preferable for Muslims to perform the ṣalāt in a mosque, in community with other believers. The words and actions of the assembled community in prayer are coordinated in the mosque by an **imām**, literally, the "one who stands before" the people and leads them in common worship, as the prophet himself did in his mosque-house in Medina.

At the appointed times of required prayers, a functionary called the *mu'adhdhin* (often transliterated as *muezzin*) summons the surrounding community to its devotions, often from a high minaret (tower) above the mosque.

Although it is better to perform the ṣalāt in a mosque, Muslims can fulfill the obligation of prayer wherever they find themselves. When Muslims pray, they face toward Mecca, thus producing a geographic symbol of the unity of the worshiping community and of the object of their worship. The Qur'ānic instruction states:

We have seen thee turning thy face about*
in the heaven; now We will surely turn thee
to a direction that will satisfy thee.
Turn thy face toward the Holy Mosque [in Mecca];
wherever you are, turn your faces toward it.
(2:144)

A special effort is to be made by all to attend a mosque for the noon prayer on Friday, when, in addition to the ṣalāt, a religious leader often delivers a sermon. Although these leaders help to organize the religious community, Islam emphasizes that no priesthood is needed to mediate between ordinary worshipers and God. The individual believer is thought to have direct access to God and bears the responsibility to seek that intimacy.

In addition to the five daily required performances of ṣalāt, there are numerous such prayers for special occasions, and believers may perform any number of voluntary ones. Intimate conversation with God is not limited to a fixed number of ritual performances. Besides being a communication between worshipers and God, ṣalāt is also an entrance into the Muslim life of meditation. As Muslims meditate and recite the Qur'ān, they are to be confronted by an immediate address from God. Ritual prayer requires turning away from all concerns save the ultimate concern, from all identities save the important identity. Islam has a vast devotional literature and practice aimed at fostering and directing this energy.

The Ramaḍān Fast

The third of the Five Pillars of Islam is the fast *(ṣawm)*. Daily throughout the month of Ramaḍān, the ninth month of the Islamic lunar calendar, every Muslim whose health permits it must refrain from food, drink, tobacco, and sexual activity between the time of first light and the onset of full darkness. Ramaḍān is particularly holy for Muslims, for it was the month when Muḥammad received his first Qur'ānic revelation.

The month of Ramaḍān, wherein the Qur'ān
was sent down to be a guidance
to the people, and as clear signs
of the Guidance and the Salvation
So let those of you who are present
at the month fast it; and if any of
you be sick, or if he be on a journey,

Although it is preferred to perform the ritual prayers in a mosque, Muslims can pray wherever they find themselves. To symbolize and enhance the unity of the worshiping community, Muslims face toward Mecca during prayer. (Bruno Barbey/Magnum)

*The plural pronoun refers to Allāh. This plural is an expression of respect, not number.

then a number of other days; God desires
ease for you, and desires not hardship for you; and
that you fulfill the number, and
magnify God that He has guided you, and haply
you will be thankful.
(2:185)

In such a fast, as in much else, Islam adopted a preexisting religious practice and invested it with new meaning.

Because the Islamic lunar year differs from the solar year, the fast does not always come at exactly the same time of year. It is followed by the great feast of *ʿId al-Fiṭr,* the Festival of the Breaking of the Fast, and for three days there is great feasting and rejoicing.

Ramaḍān is a time to restrict the flesh, yet it is also understood as a celebration of freedom from the worldly and a time for inner contemplation of God and the hereafter.

Almsgiving

The fourth pillar of Islam is almsgiving *(zakāt):*

They will question thee concerning what they
should expend [for charity]. Say: "Whatsoever
good you expend is for parents and kinsmen,
orphans, the needy, and the traveler; and whatever good you may do, God has knowledge
of it." (2:215)

Islam instructs its members to give part of their worldly wealth to help people in need and to further the cause of truth. Those who have received abundance should respond in gratitude, and in imitation of God they should return part of that abundance. The enjoyment of material blessings is purified only by acceptance of the social responsibilities that the giver of all good things imposes on us.

The alms required by law is not to be regarded as a free private gift but instead as a mandatory minimum tax. From the time of the prophet, zakāt has been gathered and dispensed under the auspices of the Islamic state. From the beginning of the religion, the social responsibility of the believer has been understood to extend throughout the entire community of believers, and zakāt was considered the minimum expression of this responsibility.

Pilgrimage to Mecca

The last and by far the most elaborate of the Five Pillars of Islam is the ḥajj, the pilgrimage to Mecca and nearby sacred sites:

The Pilgrimage is in months well known; whoso undertakes the duty of Pilgrimage in them shall not go in to his womenfolk or indulge in ungodliness and disputing in the Pilgrimage. Whatever good you do, God knows it. And take provision; but the best provision is Godfearing, so fear you Me, men possessed of minds! (2:197)

The ḥajj is another practice adapted from pre-Islamic times; it became associated with both Abraham's life and alleged religious practices and those of Muḥammad. The pilgrims enter a state of ritual purity during which they wear special gowns and do not shave or cut their hair, thus distancing themselves from their ordinary life.

Arriving at the sanctuary in Mecca during the twelfth lunar month, pilgrims perform their ablutions and enter the most sacred of mosques. There they perform the first circumambulations of the Kaʿbah, the cube-shaped building at the center of the sanctuary. Each rite of circumambulation consists of seven circuits of the Kaʿbah in which the first act is touching or kissing the black stone set in one corner. According to legend, the black stone was delivered to Abraham by Gabriel, the angel of revelation. Originally white, tradition holds, the stone has been blackened by the sins of humanity. (The black stone predated Muḥammad as a symbol for one of Arabia's many gods.)

After the rite of circumambulation, pilgrims together run between two low hills near the central mosque. This rite too may have been adapted from an earlier tradition but was given an Abrahamic interpretation. The story goes that Abraham's wife Sarah, who was unable to bear a son, gave her servant Hagar to Abraham as a concubine to produce an heir. But when Hagar bore a son, Ishmael, Sarah, in a jealous rage, persuaded Abraham to expel both mother and child. Dying of thirst after wandering in the wilderness, Hagar and Ishmael came to the site of the Meccan sanctuary. There Hagar ran back and forth between two hills crying out for divine assistance; the well of Zamzam, which produces water holy to Muslims, miraculously appeared. And so Muslims repeat Hagar's

Pilgrims circumambulating the Kaʿbah during a ḥajj (pilgrimage). The shrine at the center of the Grand Mosque in Mecca is sheathed in embroidered black silk, and pilgrims kiss or touch the black stone that is set at one corner. (Saudi Arabian Information Office)

running, taking it as a symbol of humanity's need and God's ready response.

The culmination of the ḥajj does not take place at Mecca but at ʿArafāt, a plain 14 miles to the east. Here all pilgrims perform the rite of "standing" before God, and some experience a liminal and overpowering sense of the divine presence and of unity with all other believers. It was on a nearby hill that Muḥammad delivered his final sermon shortly before his death.

The ḥajj today, as in early Islam, is one of the great unifiers of the Islamic community. Muslims by the thousands from all over the world come to Mecca to share their ideas and their goods. Although every Muslim is supposed to make the ḥajj once in his or her lifetime, only a very small percentage of them have the time and the wealth to do so.

With the death of Muḥammad, the writing of the Qur'ān, and the fixing of the Five Pillars and the ritual patterns, the first phase of Islam's history drew to an end. Within 12 years of Muḥammad's death in 632, Islam's soldiers had, astonishingly, captured Damascus, Jerusalem, Egypt, and Persia. With these victories, its second phase began. The religion found itself transformed: once the faith of the disenfranchised few in an unimportant corner of the desert, it became the religion of a world power. Though its circumstances had changed, what did not change was the desire to carry out God's will as articulated in the Qur'ān and the example of Muḥammad. The tradition's next problem became how to specify God's dictates in such a way that its millions of new adherents in their respective cultures could be certain of them.

NOTES

1 Toshihiko Izutsu, *Ethico-religious Concepts in the Qur'ān* (Montreal, 1966), p. 62.

2 W. Montgomery Watt, *Muḥammad: Prophet and Statesman* (London: Clarendon Press, 1961), p. 49.

3 Arthur J. Arberry, *The Koran Interpreted* (New York: Macmillan, 1955), vol. 2, p. 344.

4 Ibid., p. 244.

5 Unless otherwise indicated, translations from the Qur'ān are by Paul McLean.

6 Arberry, *The Koran Interpreted,* vol. 2, p. 353.

7 Watt, *Muḥammad,* p. 39.

ISLAM

CHAPTER 24

ISLAM'S CLASSICAL PERIOD: RELIGIOUS LAW, THEOLOGY, AND MYSTICISM

THE EARLY EXPANSION: ARABIA TO SPAIN

Muḥammad left no instructions for the leaders after him, but the *caliphate* (succession) came to be based on his model. One man (or **caliph**, "successor"), continued to oversee the community's political and religious affairs, combining the offices of chief executive, commander in chief, chief justice, and leader of public worship (imām). The caliphate began on an ad hoc basis; only much later was a theory of the institution worked out.

THE FIRST FOUR CALIPHS (632–661)

The first four caliphs had all been early converts to Islam and trusted companions of the prophet throughout most of his career. Their closeness to Muḥammad undoubtedly gave them an aura of reflected charisma, and their knowledge of the prophet's message could be assumed to be comprehensive. But the four orthodox and rightly guided caliphs, as they were called by the later orthodox tradition, were in no sense prophets.

Nor were they despots. They had no independent army with which to coerce their people, no elaborate bureaucracy behind which they could hide from popular demands. Compared with the later holders of the office, Muḥammad's first successors were remarkably accessible, and they followed the prophet's example of seeking counsel on issues of practical policy instead of dictating to the community. By carefully considering all factors, including worldly and religious aims, the first caliphs tried to foster unity of vision and direction. Partly through their ability and partly through good fortune, Islam survived the centrifugal tendency that set in after the prophet's death.

The reigns of the first two caliphs, Abū-Bakr (ruled 632–634) and ʿUmar ibn-al-Khaṭṭāb (ruled 634–644), were dominated by expanding Islamic power in the Arabian peninsula and northward into the Byzantine and Zoroastrian Persian empires. They continued Muḥammad's policy of holding together their growing community by turning outward the aggressive energies of the Arab tribes in military campaigns. These efforts were aided by the fact that both the Byzantine and Persian empires were weakened from their own wars. As a result, between 635 and 641 the Islamic community conquered Egypt, Syria, and Iraq; they conquered the Iranian plateau under the third caliph.

That caliph was ʿUthmān ibn-ʿAffān (ruled 644–656), who was of a clan that was soon to play a major role in Muslim history: the Umayyad clan of the Quraysh. The Umayyads had been late converts to Islam and had produced some of its most energetic

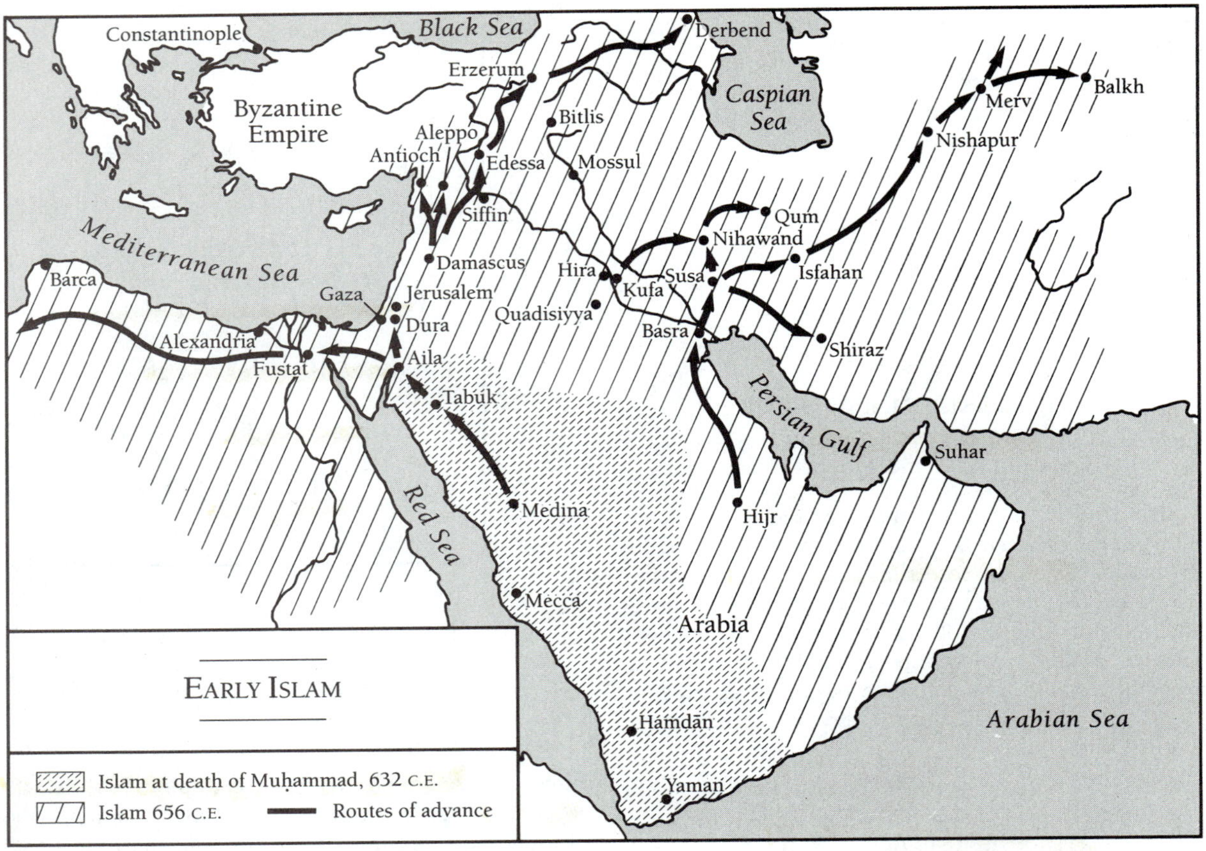

early opponents. In contrast to most of his clan, ʿUthmān had converted early, became a companion to the prophet, and even married Muḥammad's daughter. Once in office, however, ʿUthmān incurred charges of nepotism and corruption by relying heavily on Umayyad kinsmen to govern his vast domain. To many older Muslims it appeared that the pre-Islamic aristocrats were returning to their former positions under the protection of easily manipulated relatives.

Though ʿUthmān had the credentials of an "old believer," he did not retain the support of his most influential peers, and he eventually found himself with little backing in his own capital. An armed force of Arabs from the province of Egypt came to Medina to confront him with a list of grievances, vocally supported by a mob of Medinans. Though the precise details are sketchy, we know that the caliph was assassinated. Tradition holds that he was killed by insurgents in his own house. Tradition further states that ʿAli ibn-abi-Ṭālib, his successor, neither took an active part in the assassination nor came to ʿUthmān's aid.

The story of ʿAli (ruled 656–661) is particularly important for later Muslim history. ʿAli became caliph in Medina but never received universal acceptance. Two other leaders began a revolt against him. Trying to put down his enemies, ʿAli transferred his base of operations to Kūfah in Iraq, a momentous move, for it shifted the political center of Islam permanently away from the Arabian peninsula. ʿAli was able to defeat his challengers in battle but was soon dealt a far more serious challenge by Muʿāwiyah ibn-abi-Sufyān, the powerful Umayyad governor of Syria. Muʿāwiyah refused to submit to ʿAli's authority under the pretext that ʿAli must purge himself of complicity in ʿUthmān's death by producing ʿUthmān's murderers for punishment. ʿAli attempted to crush the Syrians through military action, but with victory almost within his grasp, he decided to submit the conflict to arbitration, which eventually went against him.

A puritanical group in ʿAli's army promptly withdrew and declared war on both ʿAli and his Umayyad opponent. The dissident group and their spiritual heirs have been known ever after to the wider Muslim community as the **Khārijites** (Seceders). In the Khārijite view, ʿAli sinned by submitting his dispute with the Syrians to human arbitration; it should have been settled by God—that is, on the battlefield. ʿAli's sin disqualified him as a leader; even worse, it discredited him and his supporters as Muslims.

The Khārijites rejected all aristocratic pretensions, whether pre-Islamic or based on kinship or an alleged special relationship with the prophet. They claimed that the Qur'ān sorted out human beings in moral terms, and they therefore felt justified in arguing that the community of true believers could choose anyone as caliph, provided that he passed the tests of piety and consistent moral rectitude. ʿAli, they felt, had failed these tests.

ʿAli suppressed the first Seceder revolt but was unable to destroy the movement, for he was fighting fanatical elements that had once been part of his own army. He may have been preparing for another campaign against the rebels when a Khārijite slew him as he was going to a mosque at Kūfah, thus clearing the way for the Umayyad dynasty.

EARLY POLICY TOWARD NON-MUSLIMS

The official attitude of Muḥammad and his immediate successors toward followers of pre-Islamic polytheism was harsh and uncompromising. When the first waves of Arabs overran non-Muslims outside the Arabian peninsula, they imposed Arab-Muslim political and fiscal domination, not Islam itself. ʿUmar's policy was to keep his armies largely intact and treat the conquered territories as a source of revenue. In this ʿUmar was following the example of Muḥammad during his final years; when he made treaties with Jewish and Christian groups in Arabia, he granted them Muslim protection in return for financial tribute and political subjugation. Similarly, in newly won lands ʿUmar granted protection in exchange for tribute.

This fifteenth-century Turkish miniature shows Muḥammad with four men, probably the first caliphs. The four had all been trusted companions of the prophet throughout most of his career. In the miniature, flaming halos surround Muḥammad's head and the Qur'ān that lies open in the center. (Bodleian Library/Oxford University)

THE UMAYYAD DYNASTY (661–750)

The Umayyad dynasty began in difficult times. The Islamic community had become enormous, yet it had little institutional structure to counter the inevitable regional competition. Furthermore, the Khārijites were more than ready to wage a guerrilla war against what they took to be a pseudo-Muslim society. Yet despite these internal challenges, Umayyad rulers expanded the Abode of Islam, as they called their empire, into North Africa, the northern reaches of India, and Spain. They would have taken France had not Charles Martel turned back a raiding party at Poitiers in 732. (Their penetration of Spain gave rise to a rich Iberian-Islamic culture that for seven centuries was a conduit through which classical Greek and Islamic science and philosophy were transmitted to Europe.) Byzantium, however, survived repeated efforts to conquer its capital, Constantinople.

One of the most important ways in which the Umayyads tried to bring unity to their fractious empire was religion. Questions of practical theology were

Built as a mosque in the eighth century, the cathedral at Córdoba is graced by over eight hundred columns supporting two tiers of arches. Córdoba was the center of a brilliant Islamic culture that flourished in Iberia. (Spanish National Tourist Office)

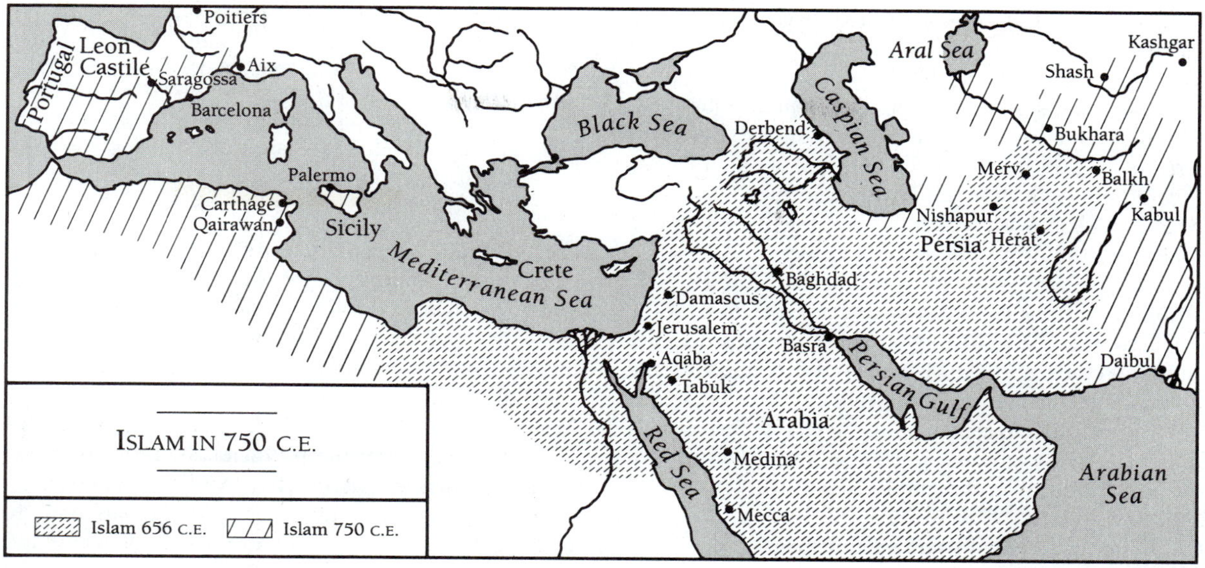

ISLAM IN 750 C.E.

debated, and the first independent schools of religious law began to organize and systematize the ethical and legal content of Islamic revelation. They also reviewed Umayyad administrative, fiscal, and judicial practices according to what they felt were the explicit and implicit prescriptions, prohibitions, and recommendations of the prophetic deposit, the record of Muḥammad's life and revelations.

This review was carried out by scholars isolated from the practical problems of running a government, so their findings often unfairly criticized the Umayyad administration and provided the regime's enemies with much religious ammunition. Among their enemies were the ʿAbbāsids, the descendants of Muḥammad's uncle al-ʿAbbās, who carefully cultivated the leaders of the new scholarship. The Umayyads were increasingly condemned for departures from ideal systems of Islamic law that were not even in existence until long after they came to power.

During the Umayyad period, the number of non-Arab converts gradually increased, as did the dissension between the Arab Muslims and the new converts over the latter's full social and fiscal rights. Iranian Muslims, proud of Iran's long tradition of civilization, objected to second-class status. In particular, they resented having to pay taxes from which Arab Muslims were exempt. The Umayyad reforms were too little and too late, and in 750 an ʿAbbāsid revolution toppled and almost annihilated the Umayyads.

THE ʿABBĀSID CALIPHATE (750–1258)

The ʿAbbāsid caliphs moved the political center of Islam east to Baghdad in Iraq. For the next 500 years this dynasty, at least in name, ruled the Islamic world. The ʿAbbāsids modeled their administration on the Sassanids' Persian Empire; the caliph, now called the "shadow of God on earth," came to be insulated behind an elaborate bureaucracy and court ritual and protected by a standing army.

Although the ʿAbbāsids themselves were Arabs, most of the troops that had supported them in their struggles against the Umayyads were non-Arabs, especially Iranians. The drive of these non-Arabs for political, social, and cultural liberation had been made under the banner of Islam as a universal faith. In part as a result, the ʿAbbāsids conceived of a multiracial and multicultural empire united by religion. Trying to integrate the non-Arab cultures that were now part of the empire, the early ʿAbbāsids actively encouraged the religiocultural synthesis that had begun under the Umayyads.

It was in this context that the religious "sciences" of law *(fiqh)* and systematic theology *(kalām)* flourished. Islamic mysticism *(taṣawwuf,* or Ṣūfism) also flowered. Driven in part by the ideal of Islam as a universal religion, its leaders were motivated to make orthodox or Sunni Islam, with which the ʿAbbāsid caliphate was identified, uniform in faith and practice.

Sunni Islam grew in three main strands: law, theology, and the ascetic way. First we will look at the sciences of law and theology, which developed under the Umayyads and flourished in the context of the ʿAbbāsid vision of a universal religion. Muslim thinkers were at pains to articulate the details of their beliefs and ways of living both clearly and authoritatively for all of the faithful in the empire. Then we will turn to the ascetics' path.

We emphasize that Islam's scholars articulated both belief and ways of life, for Islam does not draw a sharp line between the secular and the religious. The goal of early Muslim leaders was to organize all of the community's life and thought around a single system of faith. Just as God is one, they believed, every aspect of life must be subject to the orders of the **sharīʿa**, the road God wishes human beings to walk.

Religious Law (*Fiqh*)

Westerners tend to separate law from religion; Islam makes no such distinction. The tradition has considered Allāh to be the ultimate source of human direction of every kind, and it developed a very sophisticated tradition of **fiqh**, usually translated as "jurisprudence," to understand humans' rights and obligations according to God's definitions. Thus fiqh embraces not only what is commonly known as law and constitutional theory but also what in the West is known as religious ethics, moral duty, and public and private worship. Fiqh is even concerned with manners, dress, and personal appearance.

Fiqh scholars attempt to classify all human actions in the following categories: (1) acts that are absolutely required, (2) those that are recommended but not required, (3) those that are indifferent, (4) those that are discouraged but not forbidden, and (5) those that are absolutely forbidden. Muslim legal scholars also commonly divide the divine imperative into duties owed to God (*ʿibādāt,* or acts of worship) and duties owed to other human beings *(muʿāmalāt)*.

SOURCES OF FIQH

The Qur'ān, together with the example of Muḥammad's leadership and way of life, built on the Arabs' pre-Islamic tradition to create a distinctive worldview and life style. But these did not constitute a comprehensive system of ethical or legal norms. Such was not needed, for as long as Muḥammad lived, questions about proper conduct could be answered by God himself through the prophet. The need for more precise guidelines arose after Muḥammad's death, when the prophetic revelation came to an end; it intensified in the context of the ʿAbbāsids' drive for unity.

The scholar most responsible for establishing the science of fiqh was Muḥammad ibn-Idrīs al-Shāfiʿi (767–820), who was active in the Hejaz, Baghdad, and Cairo during the early ʿAbbāsid period. Al-Shāfiʿi helped to develop Islam's rigorously systematic approach to the law. He declared that fiqh had four sources: (1) the Qur'ān; (2) the *sunna,* or the normative practice or precedent of Muḥammad preserved in the reports *(aḥādīth)* of his companions; (3) analogical reasoning *(qiyās)* based on a principle or cause *(ʿilla)* found in the other sources; and (4) the consensus *(ijmāʿ)* of the Muslim community.

This theory of sources addressed the central issue early Islam faced: how fallible human beings could determine the correct way to live in accord with God's will. Verbal revelation had ended when Muḥammad died, and most Muslims considered the caliphs who followed him only as leaders carrying out executive functions, not as infallible messengers of God.

The Qur'ān

The first source of fiqh was the Qur'ān, taken to be the speech of God himself. Very early in Islamic history, the compilers of the Qur'ān took pains to discern every shade of its meaning, and many non-Arab converts, especially in Iran, took up the study of Arabic just to be able to understand the work.

Muḥammad's Sunna and the Aḥādīth

The second source was Muḥammad's patterns of action, his sunna. His life and the history of the early Islamic community were subjects of intensive historical research. Early biographers were especially interested in discovering the situations in which specific revelations were made. Many obscure points in the Qur'ān seemed to be clarified when viewed in their original setting, making the masses of reports about Muḥammad and his companions essential to understanding both the Qur'ān and God's commands.

Many early Muslim scholars considered Islam's sunna to be a cumulative tradition. As a source of law, it might include not only specific precedents set by the historical Muḥammad but also later adjustments of Islamic values held to be fully authoritative and in agreement with the prophet's teaching. Al-Shāfiʿi argued that Muḥammad's sunna was the only reliable one. Muḥammad should be recognized as the ideal human response to God. Muḥammad's example became the authoritative commentary on the Qur'ān as well as a supplement to it.

Al-Shāfiʿi lived nearly two centuries after Muḥammad. By that time, a large number of oral accounts of the prophet's life were in circulation. There were purported eyewitness reports of his utterances, his acts, and even his silent approval of decisions. This mass of oral traditions (***aḥādīth;*** singular, *ḥadīth*) offered a day-to-day picture of the prophet's life. In al-Shāfiʿi's view, an authentic ḥadīth of Muḥammad was a secondary form of revelation inspired and protected by God, even though it was not God's own speech.

To compile the complete and authoritative record of this sunna, scholars during the early ʿAbbāsid period traveled thousands of miles and engaged in countless interviews with persons said to have aḥādīth about or from Muḥammad. These scholars tried to weed out unreliable aḥādīth: reports that could not be verified by an unbroken chain of dependable reporters were dismissed or treated with suspicion. The most reliable reports were those corroborated independently by several chains of tradition.

During the ninth century, a number of large written collections of aḥādīth concerning the prophet were accepted by Sunni Muslims as interpretations of the Qur'ān and supplements to it. Muslims often refer to them simply as the Six Books. They were assembled by many men; the collections of Muḥammad ibn-Ismāʿīl al-Bukhāri (died 870) and Muslim ibn-al-Ḥajjāj (died 875) were regarded as especially authoritative because their compilers had eliminated all but the most solidly substantiated oral traditions.

A ḥadīth consists of two parts. The first is the *isnād,* or chain of guarantors. *Isnād* means "making something rest (on something else)"; it is the guarantee on which the authority of a ḥadīth rests. Here is an example of a ḥadīth whose primary source was ʿĀ'isha, the prophet's widow and source of several verbal traditions. Between the prophet and the compiler Muslim ibn-al-Ḥajjāj there was presumably an unbroken chain of reliable transmitters:

> Bishr ibn al-Hakam al-ʿAbdī told me [Muslim ibn-al-Ḥajjāj] that ʿAbd al-ʿAzīz ibn Muḥammad told him from Yazīd ibn ʿAbd Allāh ibn al-Hād, who got it from Abū Bakr ibn Muḥammad, who heard from ʿĀ'isha that she heard the Prophet (may God bless him and give him peace!) saying, "The hand of a thief is cut off only for [the theft of] a fourth of a dinar or more."[1]

This ḥadīth is concerned with the prophet's statement about the penalty for theft. Qur'ān 5:41 reads: "And the thief, male or female: cut off the hands of both, as a recompense for what they have earned, and a punishment exemplary from God; God is the All-mighty, All-wise." Though seemingly clear, this verse does leave unanswered some questions about its application: should this penalty be applied equally to someone guilty of grand theft and to one guilty of petty theft? The ḥadīth resolves this by stipulating that petty theft should not receive the full penalty mentioned in Qur'ān 5:41. According to the proper method of interpretation, those who seek the right conduct should move from the consideration of a passage in the Qur'ān to the search for a ḥadīth offering an authoritative commentary.

Although this first prophetic example answers how the Qur'ānic penalty for theft should be applied, it also opens up new questions. Is it God's will that no penalty should be applied to the petty thief? If this is not the case, what should the punishment be? Before Muslim scholars would use their own judgment in such matters, they would search for further relevant examples from the prophet's life.

The many thousands of surviving aḥādīth pertain to every part of the Qur'ān. Notice that in our example, an allegedly prophetic action or comment offers a decisive answer to an important question of belief or practice. For most of Islam's history, the aḥādīth have told Muslims how to understand the Qur'ān, and certainly the details of traditional Islamic law pertain more to the aḥādīth than to the Qur'ān.

Qiyās, or Analogical Reasoning

The Qur'ān and the aḥādīth were often not comprehensive enough, however. In their new situations, Muslims faced ethical or legal questions that these sources had not directly addressed. In such cases, legal scholars were to seek indirect or implicit guidance through the use of qiyās, or analogical reasoning. Basing their thoughts on an analogous issue mentioned in either the Qur'ān or the sunna, scholars were to work out the implications for a particular case. Let us consider some examples.

Verses 2:219 and 5:93 of the Qur'ān describe the drinking of wine and a specific form of pre-Islamic gambling as sinful or unclean. Verse 4:43 enjoins believers from approaching the ritual prayer in a state of intoxication so that they do not know what they are saying. Clearly these verses direct believers to avoid specific beverages and games of chance. But at the same time they contain an ʿilla, a cause or principle that can be extended to new or different situations. The principle here is that the pleasures to be derived from intoxication and games of chance are far outweighed by their socioreligious liabilities. The underlying principle behind the Qur'ān's prohibition of wine and a particular form of gambling can thus justify the prohibition of all forms of alcoholic beverages and gambling.

The Qur'ān does not directly call for any temporal penalty for drinking and gambling, but we may extend the principle and say that for the discipline and good order of Islamic society, drinking and gambling should be punished.

Although the tradition needed a legal method that could deal with new issues, qiyās was always regarded as dangerous by the tradition. The Qur'ān and Muḥammad's sunna were considered reliable, but the judgments of legal scholars or rulers were not. Qiyās could never override a Qur'ānic law or the sunna; it could extend the cumulative legal tradition but not recast it.

Ijmāʿ, or Consensus

In the drive for reliable sources of law, much of the divine imperative is clear enough from the Qur'ān and the sunna. Yet there were many areas of ambiguity that could and did provoke disagreements—the loose ends, gaps, and conflicts in the aḥādīth and the Qur'ānic record. Furthermore, Muslim legal scholars were aware that in the process of defining and applying the commands of the prophetic deposit, they were inevitably making a great many personal judgments about the meaning of Qur'ānic verses and about which verse or ḥadīth should be given priority in the face of an apparent conflict. What guarantee was there that the scholars of religious law would not misinterpret some of the principal issues?

The Sunni majority rejected the idea that any individual or succession of individuals could claim infallible authority to interpret and apply the prophetic revelation. Although a legal scholar might engage in a struggle *(ijtihād)* to reach a conclusion about a legal issue, that conclusion would be only one person's belief or opinion, and it could be challenged by other thinkers.

How could Muslims be certain of God's intention on a point of law? According to one tradition, the prophet told his followers: "My community reaches no agreement that is an error."[2] In other words, those definitions, interpretations, and applications of the prophetic deposit on which the learned Sunnis had agreed could be accepted as the will of God and were not to be challenged.

To speak of consensus may conjure up images of large councils. But **ijmāʿ** as a source of religious law worked in a far less organized manner. The consensus of the community was discovered by looking into the past: if past scholars had resolved a particular issue, that resolution was to serve as a starting point for later scholars.

From one angle, ijmāʿ was a dynamic principle authenticating change. The foundation and responsibilities of the caliphate were authenticated by the community's consensus. So too, consensus gave a kind of legitimacy to many of the mystics' ideas and practices. But from another angle, ijmāʿ was conservative or even regressive. This became especially true in the tenth century, when the Sunni consensus was that the fundamental methodological and substantive rules of Islamic law had become fixed. The door of ijtihād was considered closed, and the proper attitude of the legal scholars was to be unquestioning adherence to the precedent of their schools of law.

This new conservative attitude was both symptom and cause of the progressive conversion of fiqh from an active to a largely passive intellectual discipline. This intellectual atrophy affected other areas of scholarly life as well: the legal scholars succeeded in establishing a strong position in Muslim society and worked hard to integrate all intellectual activity into a single overarching and relatively unchanging religious framework.

THE FOUR WAYS OF CONDUCT OR SCHOOLS OF LAW

After many conflicts, some of them explosive, the Sunni community agreed to disagree on several points, both minor and important. These came to be known as the ways of conduct or schools of law, four of which still exist and are emphasized in different regions. The Ḥanafite school, founded in Baghdad, used qiyās as a basis for a wide interpretive freedom; it is regarded as the most liberal and flexible of the Sunni schools. The Mālikite school of Medina, which is popular in North Africa, supports the tradition of Medina as Islam's first capital; it emphasizes the centrality of Muḥammad's sunna. The Shāfiʿite school, which is popular in southern Arabia, East Africa, and East Asia, devised the classical theory of fiqh; it attempted to standardize a vocabulary and method. The Ḥanbalite school, also founded in Baghdad and popular in Saudi Arabia today, is the most conservative of the four.

H. A. R. Gibb pointed out that traditional Islamic law is relatively underdeveloped regarding political theory, criminal law, and the regulation of financial matters on a large scale.[3] Yet it is remarkably detailed with respect to ritual practice, family and sexual relationships, issues concerning the personal status of individuals, and a wide range of social issues. The legal scholars succeeded in creating an ideal of personal and social conduct that cuts across all political and cultural boundaries; it provides the spine, if not the heart, of the universal body of Islam.

A SYSTEM OF THEOLOGY (*KALĀM*)

The second large issue that Muslim thinkers had to confront in their new situation concerned the details of Islam's theology: its beliefs and understandings about God's being and God's many relationships with the universe. Despite the Qur'ān's many theological statements, early Islam saw no need for a theology. Theological issues were met on an ad hoc basis and were interpreted in relatively narrow terms. But as contact between Arab conquerors and their subjects in Egypt, Syria, and Iraq increased, serious Muslims became aware of the precision, comprehensiveness, and consistency of Greek thought. They realized that for Islam to survive and spread in this setting, it would need a systematic intellectual expression of its theology.

THE MUʿTAZILITES

To meet this challenge, Wāṣil ibn-ʿAṭā (died 748) founded at Basra an intellectual movement that laid the foundation of Islamic theology (**kalām**). Wāṣil and his followers came to be known as **Muʿtazilites** (Withdrawers).

The Problem of the Divine Attributes

The Muʿtazilites focused on what they understood to be Islam's two main themes: God's absolute unity and his absolute justice. They attempted to develop all the logical implications of these themes and to demonstrate that Muslim beliefs were superior to all others on the bases of textual and purely rational argument.

The Qur'ān often speaks of God in humanlike terms. Not only is God referred to as male, but he is said to have a face and hands and to sit on a throne. Several verses suggest that on the Day of Judgment the resurrected dead will meet God face-to-face. Qur'ān 75:22–23 comments, "Upon that day faces shall be radiant gazing upon their Lord." If taken literally, such a statement could inspire people to imagine God as a being having physical characteristics and located in space. Most strict literalists at that time were content to assert the literal accuracy of the Qur'ānic passages and to refuse to discuss the problems raised by the Muʿtazilites.

The Muʿtazilites drew their arguments from the Qur'ān itself, which describes God as immeasurably higher than the highest creatures and utterly unlike any creature: "There is nothing whatever like him." The Qur'ān also speaks of God as unseen and yet everywhere present, infinitely distant and yet closer to us than our own jugular vein. Interpreting these concepts rationally, the Muʿtazilites declared that God was above and different from his creation. They found it irrational to ascribe finite parts to God: Qur'ānic references to his feet and hands were only metaphors for which a rational theological meaning could be supplied. God's "hands," for example, were simply a metaphor for his power or solicitude.

According to the Muʿtazilites, the Qur'ān's descriptions of God as the eternal knowing and seeing being had led untrained people to understand the divine attributes—eternity, knowledge, vision, power—as real attributes of God. Such attributes were incorrectly viewed as distinguishable from one another and from the divine essence. This thinking, argued the Muʿtazilites, violated the basic theme of Islam: the absolute unity of God *(tawḥīd)*.

The Muʿtazilites rejected the general Muslim view that the Qur'ān was God's eternal word uncreated in time. Clearly the Qur'ān was not God but was created in time as God's revealed guidance. The Muʿtazilites labeled the assertion of the eternity of the Qur'ān as the worst blasphemy and campaigned to purge Islam of this heresy. The early ʿAbbāsid caliphate adopted the Muʿtazilite view of the Qur'ān. Leaders who refused to accept it were subject to imprisonment and torture. But later in the caliphate the eternity of the Qur'ān again became the official position, and a counterpersecution began.

God's Justice

Muslims commonly believed that everything that happened was predetermined or decreed by God. This appalled the Muʿtazilites, who argued that God had granted human beings the freedom to choose between good and evil. To suggest that God punishes or rewards creatures for choices and acts that God himself has predetermined was to declare God to be unjust—indeed, it was to undermine God's absolute justice. Evil acts are not God's specific will and determination. They flow from the free choice of human beings.

The Muʿtazilites were eventually defeated, but their ideas and methods greatly stimulated the intellectual development of Islam. In fact, many of their ideas influenced the orthodox theology that arose to combat the Muʿtazilites themselves.

THE RISE OF SUNNI THEOLOGY

Although the Muʿtazilites considered themselves champions of Islam and defenders of the faith, Sunni leaders regarded them as heretics. Sunni intellectuals called for the creation of an orthodox theology that would lay down the true doctrine and defend it intelligently. These theologians would recognize that revelation was the limit and the guide of human reason. If an element of the prophetic deposit did not yield to rational explanation, it had to be accepted on authority.

The two most renowned leaders in establishing a Sunni orthodoxy were abu-al-Ḥasan ʿAli al-Ashʿari (died c. 922), of Baghdad, and abu-Manṣūr Muḥammad al-Maturīdī (died c. 944) of central Asia. Both men founded continuing schools of theology in the ʿAbbāsid period. In the controversy over the Qur'ān's references to God's hands and face, they denied that such features could be likened to their human counterparts and said that it would be blasphemy to do so. Yet if God had intended such references to be mere metaphors, he would have said so. Thus believers had to affirm that (1) this language was accurate and that (2) the form or modality of God's hands and face was a question beyond human understanding.

The formula suggested for dealing with such passages was "without asking how and without likening [to human features]." Similarly, the orthodox theologians insisted that the divine promise that human beings would see their Lord with their eyes in the hereafter was to be affirmed, even though the modality of such a vision could not be described or imagined.

With regard to divine qualities, the orthodox school of theology concluded that they existed eternally in God and had no existence apart from that reality except in the abstractions of human reasoning. Using the analogy of a human being, the orthodox theologians pointed out that a human being was still one person, even though he or she had many qualities.

Orthodox theology made a series of distinctions between the physical Qur'ān as written or recited and the eternal attribute of God's word or speech, which had always existed in God. The fleeting sounds of a reciter of the Qur'ān and the collection of pages from which the Qur'ān was read were created. But the message that was recited or read was God's eternal speech to humanity.

In the main, orthodox theology developed in a strictly deterministic direction. The orthodox theologians were as quick to defend God's absolute sovereignty as the Muʿtazilites were to defend his justice. In the orthodox view, to say that anything could occur that God did not directly will and create was to imply that God was either heedless or impotent. Thus even the most careful Muʿtazilite efforts to define a limited sphere of human freedom were treated by the orthodox as blasphemous diminutions of God's sovereignty and freedom. The idea that God might *freely limit* his sovereignty to grant a measure of freedom to his creatures was absent from the orthodox theological discussion.

But if God wills all, does this make God the willer and creator of evil? The orthodox theologians willingly accepted this burden. God decrees and creates evil in and for human beings, but this does not make God evil or unjust. The commandments of God fixed the value limit for human beings. In terms of those revealed norms, people could be said to obey or transgress. But those limits were not applicable to God. The very character of God is that he is unlimited. Al-Ashʿari put it this way:

> The proof that He is free to do whatever He does is that He is the Supreme Monarch, subject to no one, with no superior over Him who can permit or command, or decide, or forbid, or prescribe what He shall do and fix bounds for Him. This being so, nothing can be evil on the part of God. For a thing is evil on our part only because we transgress the limits set for us and do what we have no right to do. But since the creator is subject to no one and bound by no command, nothing can be evil on His part.[4]

While using rational and scriptural arguments negatively to assault all notions of autonomy in the created universe, orthodox theologians thus used rational arguments positively to prove many of the fundamental doctrines of the faith.

But there are limits. Some of God's attributes, for example, are only possible, not necessary. That they exist is accepted on the authority of revelation. Or again, rational demonstrations can show that it is possible for God to send prophets, but no rational argument can prove that this or that individual *must* be God's prophet. Most fundamentally, the detailed structure of the sharīʿa cannot be built from rational arguments alone. The sharīʿa's ordinances are reliable because they were revealed. But how was revelation itself validated? Muḥammad's authority was validated in part by the "miracles" he performed or that occurred in connection with him. Here is the orthodox theologian ʿAbd-al-Qāhir al-Baghdādī (died 1037) on the question of the prophetic miracle *(muʿjizah)*:

> The full meaning of the term *muʿjizah* among theologians is as follows: It consists in the appearance of something contrary to the customary order of this world which manifests the veracity of the possessor of prophethood. . . . The miraculous occurrence is occupied by the shrinking of any opponent [of the prophet] from attempting any opposition [by trying to produce a similar miracle].[5]

THE PHILOSOPHERS AND THE ORTHODOX REACTION

The question of miracles was further sharpened by what Montgomery Watt has called the "Second Wave of Hellenism," the first wave being constituted by the Muʿtazilites.[6] In the tenth and eleventh centuries, Islamic philosophers attempted to square Islam and Greek thought. The Islamic philosophers developed elaborate theories of being, drawing mostly from Neoplatonic and Aristotelian concepts. Ultimate reality was not the omnipotent personal will of orthodox theology, which creates the world out of nothing. The ultimate for the philosophers was the necessary being by whose self-intellection dependent being is caused or from which it emanates. Each level of dependent being is the necessary and automatic effect of the one above it and in turn causes the level below it, the bottom rung on the causal-emanational ladder being the sublunary sphere of growth and decay, which we presently occupy.

Abū-Hāmid Muḥammad al-Ghazzāli (died 1111) achieved distinction both as a theologian and as a mystic (Ṣūfī). Born at Tus in Khurasan, he traveled widely and became familiar with all phases of Islamic thought. In *The Confusion of the Philosophers,* al-Ghazzāli emerged as the great champion of orthodox theology against the challenge of the philosophers.

Al-Ghazzāli saw the philosophers' concept of causal necessity as simply an extension and elaboration of the earlier Muʿtazilite arguments. Here is al-Ghazzāli's summary of the implications of the Islamic philosophers' view of causation:

> Their [the philosophers'] postulate is that the connection observed to exist between causes and effects is a necessary connection and that it is not possible or feasible to produce a cause which is not followed by its effect, or to bring into existence an effect independently of the cause.[7]

Some philosophers indeed argued for the eternity of the world because if the cause (the ultimate) exists, its effect must exist. Thus the one has a logical and ontological but not temporal priority over the world of dependent being.

Orthodox theology presented the image of a universe largely devoid of positive being. A. J. Wensinck had stated that the orthodox theological tradition early showed itself conscious of being essentially monistic.[8] God is not simply the supreme being. He becomes very nearly the only real being. This "essential monism" was given great and varied development in Ṣūfism, the mystical tradition of Islam.

Philosophers like Ibn-Sīnā (Avicenna; died 1037) and Ibn-Rushd (Averroës; died 1198) became well known in the Christian West. These Muslim intellectuals and a host of lesser Muslim philosophers were important in the intellectual life of the West not only in themselves but also as channels through which Western thinkers became aware of—and came to be influenced by—Aristotle and other Greek philosophers.

While the philosophers helped to lay the groundwork for an intellectual renaissance in Europe, their labors did not produce the same result within Islam. Al-Ghazzāli dealt heavy blows to speculative philosophy, striking at its basic assumptions. Though it continued in the eastern empire, after Ibn-Rushd speculative philosophy in the Arabic-speaking Muslim world, always a highly elitist activity, quickly died out. Thereafter, Muslim theology tended to concern itself less with the substance of theology than with its methodological prolegomenon (preliminaries). Concern with elaborate classifications of the types of knowledge and with the forms of reasoning and

"A Mechanical Device with Two Drinking Men" from the fourteenth-century *Book of Knowledge of Ingenious Mechanical Devices* by al-Jazari. Muslim scholars had made great advances in science and philosophy when Europe was still backward. These Muslims helped to lay the groundwork for an intellectual renaissance in Europe. (Freer Gallery of Art/Smithsonian Institution)

argument became increasingly dominant. Matters of substance returned to the foreground only after Islam came into contact with the non-Muslim West.

THE MYSTICAL PATH

At al-Ashʿari's death in the early tenth century, religious law (fiqh) was nearing completion, and theology (kalām) was well on its way to general recognition as a necessary pursuit of all Muslim legal scholars. Around this time, the third major strand of Islam, its meditative spiritual wing, **Ṣūfism** (*taṣawwuf* in Arabic), reached maturity. This ascetic and mystical form of Islam was to become increasingly distinct, self-conscious, and controversial.

THE EARLY ASCETICS

As early as the Umayyad dynasty, when the Islamic Empire had become quite powerful and wealthy, some devout Muslims began to protest what they saw as its worldliness, corruption, and spiritual shallowness. Drawing on Christian monastic models, these ascetics devoted themselves to fasting, long vigils, and meditation on the Qur'ān. In imitation of Christian monks, some began wearing garments of coarse wool (*ṣūf*), hence the name of their movement.

Ṣūfīs saw asceticism as a way to overcome humanity's domination by the transitory joys and fears of earthly life, seeking spiritual freedom through devotion to God. As the Ṣūfī Masrūq put it, the Ṣūfī "is controlled by nothing other than God."[9] For some Muslims the quest for purity required surrender of all worldly possessions; others sought to purge their thoughts and feelings of all attachments. The famous mystic al-Kimaud (died c. 810) sought to have "hands empty of worldly possessions and hearts empty of attachment."[10]

The Ṣūfīs trembled before the wrath to come, the awesome terrors that they predicted in the mosque and the marketplace. Some early ascetics were known for their almost constant weeping as they combined a passionate love of God with a hatred of the world, an attitude quite opposed to the Qur'ān's view that the world is to be enjoyed on God's terms.

Ṣūfism as the Inner Dimension of Prophecy

Ṣūfīs held that their movement began with Muḥammad, whom they considered an intimate of God. Muḥammad's consciousness, they maintained, was radically altered through his long meditations and revelations. Furthermore, he had initiated several early followers into the mystical path. Ṣūfīs thus saw themselves as explaining and elaborating the mystical side of the path he began.

Muḥammad's night journey to Jerusalem and his ascent to the presence of God are familiar to all Muslims. Most assume that he saw God that night, if not with his eyes then with his heart. But Ṣūfīs took this communion with God as a mystical archetype to be repeated through their spiritual exercises. One need not wait for the next life to encounter God, as most Muslims hold: the Ṣūfīs believe that one can experience God here and now.

Love of God

Later Ṣūfīs went beyond the negativism of the early ascetics to discover a more positive frame of reference. In their view, what drew the mystics out of their bondage to the things of this life was their love of God, which became their consuming passion. Love for anyone or anything other than God was acceptable only as a symbol of the love for God.

After the great theologian al-Ghazzāli became a Ṣūfī, he declared that human perfection lies in the "conquest" and "complete possession" of the human heart by the love of God.[11] Without love, religion became a dry and empty formalism. Moreover, the Qur'ān described God as the lover of believers. Numerous aḥādīth quoted by Ṣūfīs stated that the love of God and his prophet were fundamental to the faith. The following extract from a poem by the Persian mystic al-Rūmī (1207–1273) suggests the Ṣūfīs' passion:

The man of God is drunken without wine,
The man of God is full without meat.
The man of God is distraught and bewildered,
The man of God has no food or sleep. . . .
The man of God is not learned from book.
The man of God is beyond infidelity and religion,
To the man of God right and wrong are alike.

The Dome of the Rock, shown here, was built in 691. Muḥammad is said to have ascended to heaven from the rock in Jerusalem on which this mosque is built. Muslims also believe this to be the rock on which Abraham was prepared to sacrifice his son Isaac and where the temple of Solomon was built. (David Skolkin)

The man of God has ridden away from Not-being,
The man of God is gloriously attended.[12]

Some legalistic theologians rejected as blasphemous the notion that any real intimacy was possible between God and human creatures, assuming that the human love of God mentioned in the prophetic deposit was only a synonym for obedience to God's law. But Ṣūfīs were resolute that intimacy with God was possible to those who sought him in total commitment. For those seeking God with a pure heart, there was a mystical path (*ṭarīqah*) straight into his presence. (See the accompanying box, "A Famous Mystic.")

Most Ṣūfīs believe that the mystical path begins by following the sharīʿa, the rules laid down by God. The first stage requires avoidance of sin and acceptance of obedience to God. Would-be mystics are to break free of all external forms of attachment to earthly things.

I have separated my heart from this world
My heart and Thou are not separate.[13]

Ṣūfīs emphasized that one should never pursue the ṭarīqah without the guidance of a shaykh, a spiritual master. Yet the ṭarīqah is considered an inner meditative path. It involves becoming free from even the consciousness of things, including the awareness of self. In the end, those who persist along this path will be absorbed into consciousness of the reality of God.

Over time, the Ṣūfīs devised a ritual called *dhikr,* which became an important element of their spiritual discipline. Basically it entails remembrance of God and repetition of his name. Through dhikr, Ṣūfīs progressively empty their psyches and turn away from all other things except the one transcendent being on whose name all their attention is focused. Eventually, they hope, the name of God will give way to absorption into the One who is named.

Ṣūfīs see spiritual breakthroughs as acts of grace. In a metaphorical way, God rushes to meet pilgrims seeking him in love, and at the end of the path he draws them out of themselves into a state of ecstasy. Self-consciousness is obliterated; only God remains. In this bliss Ṣūfīs are totally unaware that they are contemplating God. Every vestige of their separate selves is swallowed up in an immediate experience of God. No words can express the infinite majesty, beauty, and essence of this extraordinary condition.

Like mystics in other traditions, the Ṣūfīs try to suggest this peak experience by means of an esoteric language that uses metaphors and references to nothingness. The union of the soul with the divine was compared to the blending of a drop of water with the sea or to the incineration of a moth in a candle's flame. For many, poetry has been the best medium for describing the intense experiences of mystical reality. Here is how al-Rūmi expressed his joyful nearness to God:

A Famous Mystic

With the development of the love theme in the eighth and ninth centuries, Ṣūfism became a truly mystical movement to live in, with, and for the divine Beloved.

Rābiʿah al-ʿAdawīyah (died 801), a woman from Basra in Iraq, was one of the first to describe the Ṣūfī love theme.

To her, the ideal love of God was "disinterested" love—love free of any egocentric elements. Ordinary Muslims might worship God out of fear of hell or hope for paradise, but Rābiʿah strove to rid herself of such "selfish" motives, as one of her famous prayers makes clear:

*O God, if I worship thee for fear of Hell, burn me in Hell and if I worship thee in hope of Paradise, exclude me from Paradise; but if I worship Thee for Thy own sake, grudge me not thy everlasting beauty.**

Rābiʿah reportedly declared that the love of God so filled her heart that she could not even hate the devil himself.

*Farīd al-Dīn al-ʿAttār, *Muslim Saints and Mystics: Episodes from the Tadhkirat al-Awliyā'*, trans. Arthur J. Arberry (London: Routledge & Kegan Paul, 1966), p. 51.

She found even the veneration of Muḥammad to be in conflict with her exclusive devotion to God.

Many pious men sought Rābiʿah's hand in marriage, but she refused all of them, giving the following explanation to one disappointed suitor:

The tie of marriage applies to those who have being. Here being has disappeared, for I have become naughted to self and exist only in Him. I belong wholly to Him. I live in the shadow of His control. You must ask my hand of Him, not of me.†

In a male-dominated society, many Muslim women followed the Ṣūfī path in one way or another, but only a few matched Rābiʿah's achievements.

†Ibid., p. 46.

Happy the moment when we are seated in the palace, thou and I,
With two forms and with two figures but with one soul, thou and I . . .
Thou and I, individuals no more, shall be mingled in ecstasy,
Joyful and secure from foolish babble, thou and I
All the bright-plumed birds of Heaven will devour their hearts with envy
In the place where we shall laugh in such a fashion, thou and I.[14]

Liberated by God's love from the domination of this world, Ṣūfīs who have reached their goal are free to serve the world. Even though essentially heedless of their separate egos, they return to normal life in order to work for God. Al-Ghazzāli posed the following test for the individual claiming to love God:

> If his [the mystic's] love is really strong, he will love all men, for all are God's servants, nay, his love will embrace the whole creation, for he who loves anyone loves the works [God] composes and [God's] handwriting.[15]

Ṣūfī history is replete with fighters for Islam, missionaries, helpers of the weak and needy, and confronters of tyranny.

Ṣūfīs strive to merge their will totally with God's, subordinating their own personalities to God's. To explain this kind of personal revelation, Ṣūfīs often use the analogy of the light and the mirror:

How can the heart be illumined
while the forms of creatures are reflected in its mirror?
Or how can it journey to God
while shackled by its passions?
Or how can it desire to enter the Presence of God
while it has not yet purified itself
of the stain of forgetfulness?
Or how can it understand the subtle points of mysteries
while it has not yet repented of its offenses?[16]

The disciplines associated with the mystical path are a "polishing" of the self's mirror, a progressive removal of all attachments and thoughts that impede reception of the divine illumination. But Ṣūfīs, like other great mystics, never draw the religious focus to themselves but direct it always to the transcendent One who has blessed them.

THE CRISIS OF ṢŪFISM

Some Ṣūfīs were led by their mystical love of God into making statements that seemed to be pantheistic or "incarnationist." In 922, Manṣūr al-Ḥallāj, a Persian mystic, was publicly flogged, crucified, and then beheaded for declaring, "I am the Truth." (Truth is one of God's names.) To his critics this seemed to assert either that he was equal to God, which was blasphemous, or that he was above the moral law, which was dangerous. Yet indeed some Ṣūfīs did disobey the law in order to lose social acceptance and thus free themselves from worldliness.

Most followers of the mystical path regarded al-Ḥallāj as a saint. They blamed his martyrdom on those unable to understand his views. Ṣūfī al-Qushayri gave the following explanation:

> The seekers of the ultimate goal have a serious problem.* It lies in the fact that there appears on occasion in the deepest recesses of their inwardness a speech that they do not doubt comes from God. Out of his kindness he speaks secretly and intimately with his friends. Then the innermost being of the man responds, and the man hears the response of his own inwardness and the statement from God. . . . The man knows by mystical intuition, as though he saw himself in sleep, and he is not God, while he does not doubt that this is truly the speech of God. But if this subtle intuition of distinction should be temporarily obscured in the man, the sense of human identity is momentarily removed in the state of mystical unification. It is for this reason that one of the Ṣūfīs may say, "I am the Truth," while Abu Yazid† said, "Praise be to me." In these cases, the men were not making claims for themselves. Rather God was speaking directly through them in a state in which the finite individualities of the men have been effaced.[17]

In the end, Ṣūfism was considered not heretical but orthodox; indeed, to many Muslims it was the crown of Islam. As the form of Islam that most fully expressed human feeling and creative imagination, Ṣūfism spread throughout the Islamic world and played a major role in Islam's becoming a world religion with broad appeal.

Ibn-ʿArabi's Speculative Mysticism

The most articulate voice of medieval Ṣūfism was that of a Spaniard, Muḥyi al-Dīn ibn-ʿArabi (1165–1240). His speculative mysticism (*waḥdat al-wujūd,* or "transcendent unity of being"), expressed in several hundred books, has been described as the full and final disclosure of mystical Islam, an assertion that ibn-ʿArabi himself made and that has been accepted by many Ṣūfīs over the centuries.

For ibn-ʿArabi, the Islamic profession of faith that there was absolutely no God but God became "There is absolutely no Reality but God." Considered in terms of absolute transcendence and unity, the one being comprised not only the abstract but also the concrete and not only the underlying unitary essence of being but also its multiplicity of limited forms. Speaking poetically and mythologically, ibn-ʿArabi described the longing of the absolute being to enter into internal distinctions and relations and the reason for this longing: infinite being, beauty, and wisdom were driven toward self-manifestation, and all determina-

*The problem is that ecstatic utterances are often misinterpreted and thus considered blasphemous by conventional Muslims.

†A famous Ṣūfī of the ninth century noted for his controversial ecstatic utterances.

tions, concrete or ethereal, were within the One, being the *maẓāḥir* (theaters of manifestation) of his infinite possibilities. This philosophy is essentially monistic, holding that all reality is a single substance or essence.

Humanity occupies a special place in this divine plan of self-expression: we can experience the secret of the world's multiplicity in God's unity and see the unity in multiplicity. Every human being is a potential microcosm of the divine self-expression, but only those who realize the ultimate unity actually become microcosms. The mystics' goal is to realize the unitary essence underlying the plurality of the world and thus to eliminate their ego isolation. They are then able to return to the world as a manifestation of the unity underlying and integrating it. In this system, according to ibn-ʿArabi, "the prophet Muḥammad is . . . the perfect human being, the total theophany [divine manifestation], the prototype of creation."[18]

Though he remains influential, ibn-ʿArabi's triumph was never complete. Many legal scholars and theologians attacked his position as monstrous, an attack on the fundamental Islamic doctrine of the transcendence of God. Among Ṣūfīs themselves, ibn-ʿArabi had vocal critics who argued that the subjective experience of unity could not be the basis for a monistic or pantheistic theology. True Ṣūfism, these critics argued, overcame divine-human distance, but God and his human creatures remained essentially distinct.

ṢŪFĪ BROTHERHOODS

Ṣūfism first was organized around a master and a small group of disciples. In the tenth century, monastic retreats were started, but at that time Ṣūfīs were still considered a spiritual elite. This feeling changed, and during the eleventh century many Ṣūfī monasteries were founded in different parts of the Islamic world as Ṣūfism acquired greater acceptance. In the twelfth and thirteenth centuries the loosely organized monastic communities were succeeded by a system of more highly organized brotherhoods. These had places for full-time monastics and lay supporters and were supervised by shaykhs and a council of senior members.

Each order or brotherhood was founded by a saint *(wali)* whose memory was revered, and each had a specific form of dhikr (rite for remembering God) and way of dressing. In some orders, music, dancing, swaying, and complex litanies became a part of the worship.

There were no separate orders for women, though some orders reserved special convents for them. In others, the women members, both novices and teachers, were separated from the men, and during rites the women might be screened off by curtains.

The more organized Ṣūfī life represented by the brotherhoods marked a major change in Ṣūfism's relationship to the wider community. Ṣūfī leaders strove to reach a larger body of believers, and a Ṣūfī order with a devoted following in the community could not only increase its missionary efforts but also accumulate much wealth and influence. To lay associates, the rites of the orders offered a level of emotional involvement that ordinary forms of Islamic worship could not provide. Moreover, in large cities, association with an order offered entry into an intimate religious community that was not possible in a public mosque. The brotherhoods also provided amenities such as schools, contact with professional guilds, and help for travelers and the destitute. Some Ṣūfī brotherhoods, where military authority had collapsed, became the dominant political force.

The rise of religious brotherhoods testified to the success of the Ṣūfī movement. But success brought danger: legal scholars and government officials tried harder to regulate the movement, and as the orders gained prestige and power, the old freedom and spontaneity of the early Ṣūfīs was lost.

An important element of later Ṣūfism was its devotion to great mystics of the past. Not all Muslims had the aptitude or religious strength required for the highest spiritual calling. But could the average Muslim derive benefits from supporting long-dead mystic heroes and heroines? Medieval Ṣūfism answered with a resounding yes. From the thirteenth century onward, Ṣūfī orders drew much popular support from the belief that the spiritual leaders of the past could bestow worldly and spiritual favors on ordinary believers who approached them in faith and reverence. The saints were considered not only recipients of God's special grace but also channels through which his grace could help others along the path. The saints might intercede for all who appealed to them for help. Thus saints' tombs became revered places of pilgrimage and of elaborate rites.

ṢŪFISM IN THE MODERN WORLD

Even before the impact of the West was felt in the Islamic world in modern times, several attempts were made to reform Ṣūfism. For the most part the reformers tried to recover the original nature of Islam, which seemed to have been corrupted by its many innovations. During the eighteenth century, the puritanical Wahhābis led massive attacks against the saints' tombs and shrines, condemning this kind of devotion as a form of idolatry.

In recent times, Muslim modernists, both stunned and stimulated by Western thought, have rejected the complex and often obscure systems of later Ṣūfism, perceiving them as gross distortions of Islam and irrelevant to Islam's desperate attempt to cope with Western aggression. Religious orders too have been criticized as wasting energy urgently needed to confront other problems. Despite such attacks, the beliefs and practices of popular Ṣūfism continue to shape the lives of many Muslims today.

THE SPIRIT OF ISLAM

Guided by the ideal of a universal religion, Islam became a great empire under the Umayyads and the ʿAbbāsids. Its leaders attempted to organize the entirety of its community's life and thought around a unified religious worldview. The community and its thinkers tried to develop a way of life, a sophisticated system of jurisprudence, and even precise codes for behavior based on the divine revelations and the example of Muḥammad. Its theologians developed a subtle theology around those revelations, based on their claim of the absolute sovereignty of God. Its caliphs oriented their political structure around this framework as well. Finally, its mystical path and Ṣūfī brotherhoods also saw their beginnings in Muḥammad's experience and oriented themselves around the direct experience of Allāh.

How did this affect the ordinary Muslim? Just as the political authorities sought unity within their far-flung empire, individual Muslims sought unity amid the diversity of life. The ordinary Muslim's life was guided by the divine law, the spiritual path, and Allāh's truth, which shaped and directed both. The divine law, as defined by the Qur'ān and Muḥammad's sunna and delineated by the legal scholars, formulated the relations among God, humans, and the community on the level of action. In some contexts it dictated precisely what to do and how to act; in others it set limits on action. Providing context and direction, it melded human activities with the attitudes and values of the Qur'ān. The contours of outer life were thus felt to be shaped by the one God.

A pilgrim is seen before the Shrine of a Hair of the Prophet, New Delhi, India. During the eighteenth century, the puritanical Wahhābis led massive attacks against the saints' tombs and such shrines, condemning this kind of devotion as a form of idolatry and contrary to true Islam. (Ron Vawter)

The inner life was exemplified to the ordinary believer by the Ṣūfī saints, who were believed to remember God constantly. Though few nonascetics could maintain that exalted state, the daily prayers, yearly fasts, and other practices frequently reminded the believer of God. The mu'adhdhin's call to prayer punctuated life five times a day, reminding all of the presence of God. Prayers could bring a sense of calm, harmony, and equilibrium. But Islam penetrated as well into other aspects of activity—dress codes, eating patterns, the arts: "Whithersoever you turn, there is the Face of God" (Qur'ān 2:109). Art, especially the grand unity of the dazzling mosaics on the mosque walls, became a support for the spiritual life, a reflection of the divine unity.

To be a Muslim, then, was to live in a culture and a civilization deeply imbued with spiritual values. This unity was felt to stretch from the distant rulers to the local village; to live within it was to participate in a harmonious and God-centered world. It offered a sense of nearness to the true prophet, Muḥammad, and to the One, the source. By reflecting on God's speech and by striving to deny self-centeredness, each person was to surrender wholly to God's community and thus move toward Allāh. As Ṣūfī al-Ghazzāli wrote, "By getting rid of the obstacles in the self and . . . stripping off its base characteristics . . . the heart may attain to freedom from what is not God and to constant recollection of Him."[19] Through such a life of submission and remembrance, Islam could offer a taste of God's unity.

SEEDS OF DISUNITY

But despite such attempts at unity, Islam was never a monolithic faith. We have seen divergences in doctrine, variations in ways of conduct, political divisions, and theoretical disagreements. We have not yet seen the deep rifts that would also characterize later centuries. Shīʿite Islam offered a sectarian alternative to the main Sunni tradition from a very early date. Other divisions emerged after the great Islamic synthesis began to wane. These deeper divisions become the subject of our next chapter.

NOTES

1 Muslim ibn-al-Ḥajjāj, *Ṣaḥīh,* vol. 5, p. 112.
2 Abū-Dā'ūd, *Sunan,* vol. 2, p. 131.
3 H. A. R. Gibb, *Modern Trends in Islam* (Chicago: University of Chicago Press, 1947), p. 89.
4 Abū-al-Ḥasan al-Ashʿari, *The Theology of al-Ashʿari,* trans. Richard J. McCarthy (Beirut: Imprimerie Catholique, 1953), p. 99.
5 ʿAbd-al-Qāhir al-Baghdādī, *Kitāb Uṣūl al-Dīn,* p. 170.
6 W. Montgomery Watt, *Islamic Philosophy and Theology* (Edinburgh: Edinburgh University Press, 1962), pp. 37, 91.
7 Abū-Ḥāmid Muḥammad al-Ghazzāli, *Tahāfat al-Falāift,* ed. M. Bouyges, pp. 270–271.
8 A. J. Wensinck, *The Muslim Creed* (Cambridge: Cambridge University Press, 1932), p. 62.
9 Abū-Bakr Muḥammad al-Kalābādhī, *Kitāb al-Taʿarraf li-Madhhab Ahl al-Taṣawwuf,* p. 93.
10 Ibid.
11 Abū-Ḥāmid Muḥammad al-Ghazzāli, *The Alchemy of Happiness,* trans. Claude Field (Lahore: Ashraf, 1964), p. 117.
12 Reynold A. Nicholson, trans., quoted in John A. Yohannan, ed., *A Treasury of Asian Literature* (New York: Harper, 1956), p. 337.
13 Abū-Nu'agam al-Isfahāni, *Ḥilyat ul-aliyā'* 10:310.
14 Reynold A. Nicholson, trans., *Rūmi: Poet and Mystic* (London: Allen & Unwin, 1950), p. 35.
15 al-Ghazzāli, *Tahāfat al-Falāift,* p. 134.
16 Ibn ʿAtā ʿIllāh, *The Book of Wisdom,* trans. Victor Danner (New York: Paulist Press, 1978), p. 49.
17 F. J. Streng, ed., *Ways of Being Religious* (Englewood Cliffs, N.J.: Prentice Hall, 1973), p. 296.
18 Annemarie Schimmel, "Islamic Mysticism," *Encyclopaedia Britannica,* 15th ed. (Chicago: Encyclopaedia Britannica, 1973–1974), vol. 9, p. 946.
19 W. Montgomery Watt, *The Faith and Practice of al-Ghazali* (London: Allen & Unwin, 1953), p. 54.

ISLAM

CHAPTER 25

SHĪʿISM, REGIONAL DEVELOPMENTS, AND THE MODERN PERIOD

Although their ideals and pretensions were universal, the ʿAbbāsids never exercised effective political or religious control over the entire Islamic community. In Spain the Umayyad prince who had escaped the original ʿAbbāsid revolution had maintained his political autonomy. In the provinces various overlords began to set up independent dynasties as early as the ninth century; many of these rulers were recognized by the caliphs as their deputies. But after the ninth century the centrifugal forces inherent in the huge empire overtook the ʿAbbāsid caliphs, and they were forced to accept political arrangements they could not prevent.

THE SHĪʿITE ALTERNATIVES

The greatest religious challenge to Islam's unity came from **Shīʿism**, the major sectarian alternative to Sunni Islam. Despite their diversity, all Shīʿite sects claim loyalty to the cause of Muḥammad's cousin and son-in-law, ʿAli, and ʿAli's descendants. The word *Shīʿa,* meaning "party" or "faction," is an abbreviation for the expression *Shīʿat ʿAli* ("party of ʿAli").

Shīʿite and Sunni Muslims have much in common, but they differ on matters as fundamental as the nature and source of religious authority, the meaning and end of Islamic history, and the content and sources of the the prophet Muḥammad's sunna.

THE CALIPHAL CLAIM OF ʿALI AND HIS DESCENDANTS

When Muḥammad died, a small group of Muslims supported ʿAli as his successor. ʿAli was a member of the prophet's family, the "people of the house," as his supporters called them. Some believed that Muḥammad had said and done things that clearly indicated his preference for ʿAli as his successor (see the accompanying box, "Ghadīr al-Khumm"). When ʿAli became caliph in 656, after having been passed over three times in the selection process, he was forced to fight almost incessantly against his opponents and was finally murdered in 661. But the support of his followers smoldered after his death, and their cause flamed up in support of his sons against the Umayyads. The elder son, Ḥasan, was soon bought off by the first Umayyad caliph; the younger son, Ḥusayn ibn-ʿAli, was annihilated with a small band of his followers near the town of Karbala in 680.

The horror of these events lent an air of martyrdom to ʿAli's family and vehemence to the Shīʿite cause against the Umayyads. That the people of the house had the right to rule became the rallying cry of anti-Umayyad movements, and one after another rose and fell in attempts to topple them. Despite very strong support for their cause, the Shīᶜites were never able to bring a member of ᶜAli's family to empirewide power. Some Shīᶜites supported the ᶜAbbāsids, another branch of the people of the house, but were again disappointed.

Beginning thus in political and military rebellion, Shīᶜism became a religious alternative to the Islamic orthodoxy. Eventually it split into a number of distinct sects, some of which became explosively political.

When exploring the doctrines and practices of the Shīᶜite sects, keep in mind that the Shīᶜite alternatives did not split off like splinters from an already mature trunk of Sunnism. The great alternatives within Islam developed in parallel and in constant interaction. The interaction between Sunni and Shīᶜite Islam took myriad forms and was sometimes positive, more often negative. Neither Sunnism nor Shīᶜism would be what it is today without the other, and the dynamic interaction of the two strands of Islam continues.

THE TWELVER TRADITION

The largest Shīᶜite sect of the present day is the so-called Twelver sect *(ithnā ᶜashariyya)*. Twelvers make up approximately 10 to 15 percent of the world population of more than 1 billion Muslims.

The Twelve Imāms: Their Status and Functions

As their name indicates, the Twelvers recognize 12 true imāms, the first being ᶜAli and the last the **Mahdi**, the messianic imām of the future. After ᶜAli the imāms can all claim descent from Muḥammad through his daughter Fāṭima. However, the Twelver tradition stresses that the spiritual relationship between the imāms and the prophet is immeasurably more important than the physical kinship.

Just as Muḥammad clearly designated ᶜAli as his successor, Twelver Shīᶜites believe, each of the 12 later imāms also received the clear designation of his predecessor. Since the imāms were divinely guided in their choice of a successor, all of the true imāms can be said to have been appointed by God. Thus Twelver Shīᶜites place enormous emphasis on belief in the imāms: to die while denying them is to die in a state of unbelief.

This Shīᶜite worshiper in Isfahan, Iran, prays at the Shah Mosque. The glazed tiles form intricate linear patterns typical of Muslim ornamentation. Shīᶜism, which claims that ᶜAli and his descendants are the rightful successors to Muḥammad, is the state religion of Iran. (United Nations)

Some of the short-lived Shīᶜite sects of the Umayyad and early ᶜAbbāsid periods placed ᶜAli above the prophet in rank, and some even talked of various ᶜAlis as incarnations of the deity. Twelver doctrine does not follow these "exaggerators," but it does present a very exalted picture of the imāms.

The same divine illumination that shone through Muḥammad is available after him in his designated

GHADĪR AL-KHUMM

Ghadīr al-Khumm is the name of a pool or bog between Mecca and Medina. According to Shīʿite tradition, that is where Muḥammad publicly designated ʿAli as his successor. The Shīʿites believe that the words and deeds of the prophet at Ghadīr al-Khumm left no room for doubt and that God had told Muḥammad that ʿAli should succeed him. At Ghadīr al-Khumm, Muḥammad spelled out this divine command to a host of Muslims, including such leaders as ʿUmar ibn-al-Khaṭṭāb.

The incident at Ghadīr al-Khumm occurred shortly before Muḥammad's death. He had just finished his so-called farewell pilgrimage and was traveling from Mecca to Medina when he stopped at the spot on the eighteenth day of the lunar month of Dhū-al-Ḥijjah.

A respected Shīʿite intellectual gave the following account of what happened:

When the ceremonies of the pilgrimage were completed, the prophet, attended by Ạli and the Muslims, left Mecca for Medina. On reaching Ghadīr Khumm he halted, although that place had never been a halting place for caravans. The reason for the halt was that verses of the Qur'ān had come upon him, commanding him to establish Ạli in the Caliphate. Before this he had received similar messages, but had not been instructed explicitly as to the time of Ạli's appointment. He [the prophet] had delayed because of opposition that might occur. But if the crowd of pilgrims had gone beyond Ghadīr Khumm they would have separated and the different tribes would have gone in various directions. This is why Muḥammad ordered them to assemble here, for he had things to say to Ạli that he wanted all to hear. The message that came from the Most High was this: "O Messenger, deliver that which has been sent down to Thee from thy Lord; for if thou dost not, thou wilt not have delivered the message. God will protect thee from men. God guides not the people of the unbelievers" (5:71). Because of this positive command to appoint Ạli as his successor, and perceiving that God would not countenance further delay, he and his company dismounted in this unusual stopping place.

The day was hot and he told them to stand under the shelter of some thorn trees. He then commanded that they should make a pulpit platform out of the pack-saddles about which the people were assembled. Many had fastened their cloaks about their feet to protect them from the heat of the sun. And when the crowd had gathered, Muḥammad walked up on to the platform of saddles and called Ạli to stand at his right. After a

successors. Mythologically speaking, the preexistent essences of Muḥammad, ʿAli, and the succeeding imāms were all created from the same light. That light was the first creation, and its manifestation is the meaning and end of the whole creative process. This being the case, a cosmos without an imām would be impossible and unthinkable. The prophets and the imāms are sinless and infallible. The knowledge possessed by the imām is essentially the same as that possessed by the prophet. Although Twelvers maintain that Muḥammad holds a special place as the deliverer of the final scripture, they believe that imāms too have access to the mystery and power behind the universe. And they too can work miracles.

Like the Sunnis, the Twelvers believe the Qur'ān to be the speech of God. They revere it no less than the *prayer of thanks he spoke to the people, informing them that he had been forewarned of his death, and saying, "I have been summoned to the Gate of God, and I shall soon depart to God, to be concealed from you, and bidding farewell to this world. I am leaving you the Book of God, and if you follow this you will not go astray. And I am leaving you also the members of my household, who are not to be separated from the Book of God until they meet me at the drinking fountain of Kawthar" [that is, in paradise]. He then called out, "Am I not more precious to you than your own lives?" They said, "Yes." Then it was that he took Ali's hands and raised them so high that he showed the white of his armpits, and said, "Whoever has me as his master has Ali as his master. Be a friend to his friends, O Lord, and be an enemy to his enemies. Help those who assist him and frustrate those who oppose him."*

*When the prophet descended from the pulpit it was time for the noon prayers, after which he went to his tent. Near his own tent he [Muḥammad] had another tent pitched for the Commander of the Faithful (i.e., the Caliph to be). When Ali was seated in this tent, Muḥammad ordered the Muslims, group by group, to go and congratulate him on his succession to the imamate and to salute him as Commander of the Faithful. Both men and women did this, and ᶜUmar [ibn-al-Khaṭṭāb] was as much pleased as anybody.**

In the Shīᶜite perception, only the most colossal moral failure could have caused ᶜAli to be passed over three times by the self-styled leader of the Muslim community.

The eighteenth day of Dhū-al-Ḥijjah became a holiday for Shīᶜite Muslims, and on this day pastry dolls are filled with honey, which represent Abū-Bakr, ᶜUmar, and ᶜUthmān, who "usurped" ᶜAli's rightful place as the prophet's successor. The blood of the usurpers, represented by the honey, is symbolically shed as the dolls are cut into pieces.

But Sunni tradition did not deny all aspects of the Shīᶜite accounts of Ghadīr al-Khumm. On the basis of alleged aḥādīth from the prophet, many Sunnis have held that Muḥammad did indeed declare, "Whoever has me as his master has ᶜAli as his master. Be a friend to his friends, O Lord, and be an enemy to his enemies. Help those who assist him and frustrate those who oppose him." But Sunni authorities deny that this speech by Muḥammad, whether made at Ghadīr al-Khumm or elsewhere, carries a sectarian Shīᶜite meaning.

In the Sunni perception, ᶜAli was a trusted lieutenant of the prophet, and all that the prophet was doing at Ghadīr al-Khumm was celebrating the close relationship between a leader and his loyal representative. The Shīᶜites have exaggerated ᶜAli's status, they say, reading into the prophet's speech meanings that the prophet may never have intended.

*D. M. Donaldson, *The Shīᶜite Religion* (London: Luzac, 1933), pp. 5–6. Translation of the Qur'ān by Arthur J. Arberry; Shīᶜite authority is Muḥammad al-Bāqir (died 1700).

Sunnis. The Sunnis and the Shīᶜa agree that deluded and erring humans need revelation for guidance. But many Sunnis have argued that the need is fully met in the plain sense of the Qur'ān and the sunna. True believers do not need an allegedly infallible person standing between them and the prophetic deposit.

Twelvers respond that without the imāms, Muslims have only a limited and distorted fragment of the Qur'ān's meaning. The imāms can clarify its many obscurities and profundities and answer new questions. It is an abstruse and elliptical text; they can illuminate its deeper, spiritual meanings, such as its hidden allusions to the status and intimacy between God and ᶜAli and the imāms. And the imāms have illuminated the mystical journal it depicts. In short, to Shīᶜites the imāms are absolutely reliable interpreters.

The Shīʿites find it ironic that their major opponents call themselves Sunnis. By rejecting the imāms, the Sunnis rejected the very heart of the prophet's sunna. In trying to gather traditions about the prophet, the so-called Sunnis largely depended on companions who rebelled against God by depriving ʿAli and his heirs of their rights. Thus their definitions of the prophet's sunna were based on false assumptions and unreliable sources. Moreover, by ignoring the prophet's designation of ʿAli, the Sunnis denied the fact that the sunna of the prophet points beyond itself to the *continuing interpretive revelation* available through ʿAli and his heirs. The continuing light was available, but most Muslims tragically denied it.

The Twelvers also attacked some of the basic Sunni positions not by appeal to the prophet's alleged words and deeds but by reasoned arguments. For example, the Sunnis had maintained that in seeking answers to questions of correct doctrine and practice, the caliph was to consult the **ʿulamā'**, the learned scholars of the community. But this, the Twelvers said, was a blasphemous denial of God's benevolence. Was it reasonable to suggest that a benevolent God would leave such matters to the opinions and arguments of fallible humans? If the divine benevolence means anything, it means that God would never leave the world without an imām. Prophets come and go, but the imāmate remains. There is always in this world a personal "presence" who provides divine illumination and ultimate transformation. To say otherwise is to mock God's kindness.

In Twelver doctrine, the imāmate is a spiritual office, not a political one. Twelvers hold that the imāms had the divine right to political power, but historically imāms ruled only small groups of faithful followers in a largely hostile Muslim Empire. Shīʿites expect, however, that temporal and religious authority will be reunited when the time is ripe, but this will require that large numbers of Sunni Muslims convert to the true faith of Shīʿism.

To protect the Shīʿite minority from its enemies, Shīʿites had been allowed by God, they believed, to practice religiopolitical expediency, or dissimulation *(taqiyyah)*. That is, in order to assume public positions inoffensive to Sunnis, it is legitimate to misrepresent their beliefs.

The Hidden Imām

The doctrine that the true imām was always designated by his predecessor was widely accepted among the Shīʿis. But it did not result in a unification of Shīʿism: sects proliferated as Shīʿis debated which of several candidates had really received the designation of a departed imām. The Zaydites recognize four; the so-called Seveners recognize seven; and the Twelvers, the sect dominant in Iran, recognize twelve.

The figure of the twelfth imām is one of the most remarkable phenomena in the history of Islam. Abū al-Qāsim Muḥammad, the twelfth imām, was allegedly born in about 868 in Iraq as the son of a slave girl and the eleventh imām, al-Ḥasan al-ʿAskari. Shortly after his father, the eleventh imām, died, this young Muḥammad disappeared mysteriously. His followers hold that rather than experiencing a normal death, he underwent an "occultation" and became the "hidden imām." Concealed from human sight, he has continued to guide his human followers from this occult status through a series of living agents. He can do so because his life has been supernaturally prolonged by God. When he comes out of concealment, Muḥammad will emerge as the Mahdi, the "rightly guided one," a messianic caliph-imām who will reunite human perfection with invincible power and vindicate the rights of the holy line of imāms.

The hidden imām still guides Muḥammad's followers in the world by appearing to various members of his community in dreams and visions. He is believed to receive messages left at the tombs of the imāms. More fundamentally, he continues to guarantee through his mysterious influence that the scholars and legal experts of the Twelver community will not lead the faithful into error. For centuries the Twelver ʿulamā' have claimed to be collectively the "general deputy" of the hidden imām.

The Martyrdom Motif

Martyrdom, held to be an act of great merit, is close to the surface in Twelver piety. To meditate on the imāms is to meditate on a succession of martyrs. All of the first 11 imāms were murdered, according to Twelver tradition. The martyrdom theme reaches a yearly climax in the month of Muḥarram, when the story of Ḥusayn's martyrdom is emotionally recounted and sometimes dramatized in "passion plays." The self-sacrifice of the perfect person brings home to the faithful the depths of the human predicament and the need for repentance and rededication. Muḥarram is to be a time of self-examination, overwhelming guilt, tearful repentance, and renewed commitment to following the imāms—even unto death. This celebration of martyrdom has enhanced the resolve of Shīᶜite soldiers in Iran, Lebanon, and elsewhere.

Law, Theology, and Ṣūfism

Like their Sunni counterparts, Twelver legal scholars have sought to articulate the sharī'a. We have seen the great differences between the Twelvers and the Sunnis on questions of the imāmate and religious authority. In other areas of law, we find a large number of differences in detail, some of them important. For example, Shīᶜite inheritance laws are more favorable to women than common Sunni practice, perhaps because of the role of Fāṭima in Twelver piety.

For obvious reasons, the Twelvers do not use the same collections of prophetic traditions that are used by Sunni jurists. Twelver collections of traditions include not only traditions of the prophet but also those of the imāms, which are equally authoritative. The Twelvers do not reject ijmāᶜ (consensus) as a source of law, despite their criticism of the Sunni use of it. Because the hidden imām is a living part of the Twelver community (and may be disguised as one of its scholars), the Twelvers believe the scholars cannot possibly agree in error.

In theology, the Twelvers eventually incorporated the basic positions of the Muᶜtazilites: the Qur'ān is the speech of God, but it was created, not eternal. The attributes are not real distinctions in God. Human beings' acts are free and responsible, not predetermined by God.

The relationship between Shīᶜism and Ṣūfism in the history of Islam is complex. We have seen the imāms described as intimates of God as well as intimates of the prophet. Many Ṣūfīs outside the Twelver community took ᶜAli and other imāms as mystical models to be followed and considered ᶜAli the founding father of the Ṣūfī way.

Yet current Twelver Shīᶜism is anti-Ṣūfist. Whereas the Ṣūfīs of the Sunni community have given an important place to ᶜAli, the Sunni Ṣūfīs have never been willing to accept the entire Twelver package. The Twelvers commonly regard the Ṣūfīs as usurpers of roles that belong exclusively to the imām. True mysticism in the Twelver view must be guided by the imām. The Ṣūfī shaykh without the imām will lead the spiritual pilgrim into delusion. But like the Ṣūfīs, Twelver imāms can also intercede for their followers, and so pilgrimages to the tombs of the imāms are seen as meritorious. Indeed, the invisible hierarchy of Ṣūfī saints is seen as a misappropriation of the roles of the hidden imām.

Twelver Shīᶜism and Politics

For most of the history of the sect, the Twelvers have lived under political regimes that they have viewed as profane usurpations of the rightful power of the imām. If legitimate government is government by the imām, it follows that such government will next be experienced when the twelfth imām emerges in triumph at the end of the age.

This position is easy enough to maintain in a hostile or neutral political environment. But what about government that proclaims itself Shīᶜite and officially endorses the true faith, as in Iran since the early sixteenth century? There, government was said by the Twelvers to be legitimate when it was dedicated to the implementation of the sharī'a (in its Shīᶜite version). Such a government would, of course, accept the direction of the ᶜulamā'.

We have noted the claim of the Shīᶜite ᶜulamā' to be the general representative of the hidden imām. In theory, this doctrine gives the ᶜulamā' the right to represent the twelfth imām politically as well as spiritually. Until very recently, however, the relationship of the ᶜulamā' to the temporal authorities remained dialogic. The rulers attempted to win the support of the ᶜulamā'; the ᶜulamā' attempted to guide the use of rulers' power.

This reciprocity between rulers and religious leadership was challenged by the last shah of Iran, deposed in 1979. Seeking to modernize his state, he attempted to circumvent the authority of the ᶜulamā'. But in a

Ayatollah Khomeini led Shīʿites in a revolution against the last shah of Iran, declaring that the only legitimate constitution is the sacred law of Islam. (UPI/Bettmann)

revolution led by Ayatollah Khomeini, Shīʿites overthrew the shah, declaring that the only legitimate constitution was the sacred law of Islam. Any modernization, said the religious leaders, should be guided by the revealed truth and directed by leaders of the ʿulamā'. Under Khomeini and his successor, Ayatollah Ruholla Khumayni, the ʿulamā' have now become Iran's political leaders as the representatives of the hidden imām.[1]

THE ISMĀʿĪLĪS OR SEVENERS

The Seveners are the Shīʿite sect that recognizes only seven imāms; they either stop with Ismāʿīl (died 760), or they recognize his son Muḥammad ibn-Ismāʿīl as the last imām who was to return as the messianic Mahdi.

In Egypt at the end of the ninth century, ʿUbayd Allāh al-Mahdi claimed the imāmate and took the messianic title of Mahdi, stating that all the promises associated with the Mahdi would be fulfilled during his reign and that of his successors. He led a successful revolution, eventually establishing the Fāṭimid dynasty (claiming descent from the prophet through his daughter) in Egypt. Though their hope to unify the Muslim world did not succeed, the Fāṭimid caliphate endured for more than two centuries (901–1171), ruling at its height Egypt, North Africa, and Syria. But many Ismāʿīlī groups rejected the claims of the Fāṭimids and continued to wait for the return of Muḥammad ibn-Ismāʿīl.

Not only did the Fāṭimids of Egypt fail to unify the Muslim world, but their line continued to generate new and independent sects. One of the most important of these has been the Druze, named for its alleged founder, Darāzi, who reportedly proclaimed the divinity of the Fāṭimid caliph al-Ḥākim (996–1021). According to historians, the founder of the Druze movement was Ḥamza ibn-ʿAli, who claimed to be the Lord of the Age and imām. Ḥamza preached that al-Ḥākim was a manifestation of God. Since God was now openly in the world, there was no longer any need for formal law or even for esoteric teaching.

The Druze in Egypt did not long survive al-Ḥākim, but the sect survived elsewhere. It developed into a well-organized, closely knit, and rather introverted religious community, with several levels. Druze eschatology anticipates the triumphant appearance of al-Ḥākim and Ḥamza and the universal vindication of the Druze religion.

The Druze today number about 200,000 in Syria, 150,000 in Lebanon, and 50,000 in Israel. They are fiercely independent, and though they arose historically from an Islamic-Ismāʿīlite environment, they cannot be readily subsumed under either heading.

Egypt returned to Sunni control in 1171. The great majority of the Egyptian population had remained Sunni at heart throughout the Fāṭimid period.

Some Characteristic Ismāʿīlite Doctrines

Some of the teachings of the Ismāʿīlites are obvious from the historical sketch. They shared with the Twelvers the belief that the true imām is designated by his predecessor. Both the Twelvers and the Ismāʿīlīs admit the possibility of a child holding the imāmate. The doctrines of occultation and return (or reappearance) are encountered frequently. In all of the Ismāʿīlite systems, the imām, whether visible or not, was represented by large numbers of agents who called themselves "deputies," "callers," or "proofs" of the imām. Like the Twelvers, the Ismāᶜīlīs insist that there is never more than one true imām at a time and that humanity cannot achieve political and spiritual well-being without an infallible leader and guide.

The Ismāᶜīlīs emphasized the distinction between the outer and inner dimensions of all things. The outer aspects of religions are the obvious meanings of the scripture and the obvious requirements of the law. These are but the superficial and changeable aspects of revelation. But to gain true spiritual realization, the individual must reach the inner or esoteric dimension of revelation. That dimension is revealed, to those capable of understanding it, by the imām.

The inner truth that Ismāᶜīlīs sought to discover largely consisted of modified Neoplatonic and Gnostic cosmologies and related prescriptions for self-realization. In one such Ismāᶜīlite system, God is said to be above all attributes or relations, above even the distinction between being and nonbeing. God first created the universal intellect, and from this intellect everything emanated in a descending order of being. As a result, the human soul has a fundamental affinity with the universal intellect and seeks to rejoin it.

With their emphasis on the inner spiritual meaning behind religious law, some Ismāᶜīlīs held to an antinomian doctrine, believing that the law was necessary only for those unable to appropriate the inner truth. Some held that when the messianic Mahdi arrived, the changeless spiritual truths would be openly manifested and the sharī'a would be no longer necessary.

THE ZAYDITES

The Zaydite Shīᶜite sect, founded by Zayd ibn-ᶜAli Zayn al-Ābidīn (died 740), established states in the ninth and early tenth centuries on the shore of the Caspian Sea and in Yemen. It comprises roughly 55 percent of today's population of northern Yemen.

The main differences with the other sects concern the imāmate. Unlike the other two sects, Zaydites hold that ᶜAli, Ḥasan, and Ḥusayn were designated by the prophet but that after these three, there was no binding designation of one imām by another. The true imām must be a descendent of Ḥasan or Ḥusayn. He must openly call the community to allegiance and will also rebel against usurpation and tyranny. Most important, the true imām will actually exercise political authority. Thus he will not be a child, and cannot practice dissimulation *(taqiyyah)*.

The Zaydites preserve much of the flavor of early political Shīᶜism. They are by far the closest to Sunnism on the questions of religious and political community and leadership, for their imām is both a religious and a political leader.

CHALLENGES TO ᶜABBĀSID UNITY

To review, the unity of Islam under the ᶜAbbāsid caliphs and the Sunni orthodoxy was challenged from early on by the various Shīᶜite theologies, legal systems, and dynasties. But after the middle of the tenth century, Islam began to fracture. For the next 100 years, an Iranian Shīᶜite dynasty dominated most of Iran and Iraq, reducing the ᶜAbbāsid caliphs to the status of puppets in their own capital. Meanwhile, the Sevener Fāṭimid caliphate controlled Egypt, North Africa, and Syria from 901 to 1171.

The Umayyad ruler of Córdoba, ᶜAbd-al-Raḥmān III, adopted the title of caliph in 929. In fact, for more than three decades leading up to the end of the caliphate of Córdoba in 1030, there were three self-proclaimed successors to the prophet, despite the fact that nearly all pious theorists agreed that there could be only one legitimate caliph at a time.

Late in the tenth century, the ᶜAbbāsid caliphs of Baghdad had to contend with the Saljūq Turks, a nomadic tribe from the Eurasian steppes. After settling in lands of the ᶜAbbāsid realm, the Saljūqs converted to Islam. Soon they put an end to the rule of the Iranian Shīᶜites, became dominant in Syria and Palestine, and seized most of Asia Minor from the Byzantine Empire. Declaring themselves champions of orthodox Islam, the Saljūqs recognized the ᶜAbbāsid caliphs but allowed them no real temporal power.

After the Saljūqs, Islam's empire was further threatened by the Christian Crusaders, who took Jerusalem in 1099. Jerusalem was reconquered in 1187 by Muslim forces led by Ṣalāḥ al-Dīn (Saladin), a warrior from Kurdistan, who had overthrown the Fāṭimids and set up his own dynasty in Egypt.

Soon new invaders posed an even greater danger to

the ʿAbbāsid caliphate: under the leadership of Chinghiz Khan, Islam was attacked by the Mongols from central Asia. In 1258 they sacked Baghdad and killed al-Mutaʿṣim, the last ʿAbbāsid caliph. For a time they threatened to overrun the entire Middle East and North Africa. They were finally turned back by the Mamlūk or "slave" dynasty—its members were originally non-Arab slaves used as soldiers by the Egyptian sultans. The Mamlūk sultan placed on the throne of Egypt a prince of the ʿAbbāsid dynasty. This pitiable remnant of the once great caliphate and his weak descendants continued to exercise nominal power in the Middle East until the Ottoman Turks defeated the Mamlūk sultanate in 1517.

The Mughul and Ottoman Empires

During the sixteenth century, a series of wars and political upheavals restored a measure of stability to the Islamic world. In 1502 the Ṣafawid dynasty, claiming descent from the seventh imām, came to power in Iran and openly supported the cause of Twelver Shīʿism. Iran has ever since been ruled by a series of dynasties that have supported Twelver Shīʿism.

About the same time, two great Muslim empires were established by military conquest. In India, the Mughuls ruled over a vast population of Hindus, Muslims, and followers of other religions. The Ottoman Turks controlled a diverse group of peoples living in western Asia, northern Africa, and eastern Europe.

THE DELHI SULTANATE AND THE MUGHULS

Toward the end of the tenth century, Muslim warriors of Afghan and Turkish origin conquered northwestern India. In 1206 they established the Delhi sultanate, which ultimately controlled northern India (1206–1388). The first Muslim invaders pursued a harsh policy toward the local population. Hindus and Buddhists, with their elaborate temples and devotion to many gods and saints, were obviously not "true believers," and so the Muslim warriors plundered and destroyed many of the local shrines and killed or drove off the monks and nuns. Buddhism in India never recovered from this blow, but Hinduism survived and created new forms of devotion. In time, local Muslim rulers granted tolerance to the Hindus, but there were still many conversions to Islam, some forced and some voluntary. In this way some members of Hinduism's lower castes were able to escape the social discrimination of traditional Indian society.

After the Delhi sultanate had been weakened by the devastations of Mughul invaders (1398), the Mughul leader Babur (1483–1530) was able to conquer northern India with his army of Muslim warriors from Turkestan and establish the Mughul Empire. This realm, founded shortly after the Ottoman Empire, peaked faster than the latter and declined more rapidly. Yet at its height the Mughul Empire created a culture that left a permanent mark on the Indian subcontinent.

Babur's grandson Akbar (ruled 1556–1605) extended the empire's territory. By the time of his death, the Mughuls controlled almost all of India, including Kashmir in the north and much of the Deccan in the south.

Akbar was a nominal Muslim who never openly repudiated Islam but, in the interest of the well-being of all his subjects, refused to force Hindus to become Muslims. Akbar revoked all laws that discriminated against Hindus and decreed universal religious toleration. Clearly this policy went far beyond traditional Islamic law pertaining to non-Muslims. By discarding the laws that had given different treatment to adherents of different religions, Akbar was in effect disestablishing orthodox Islam. While he lived, Akbar cowed the orthodox ʿulamāʾ into submission and even induced scholars to subscribe to an infallibility decree that gave him the almost unlimited power to disregard any feature of Islamic tradition he considered incompatible with his political requirements.

An ardent though illiterate student of comparative religion, Akbar found much merit in traditions other than Islam but was impatient with the narrowness of all of them. At his court he sponsored discussions among representatives of Islam, Hinduism, Zoroastrianism, Jainism, and even Christianity. Finally the emperor concluded that a new religious synthesis was needed. This new faith, which Akbar called simply the Divine Faith *(Dīn-i-ilāhī),* was a form of monotheism

Muslims are seen in the upper gallery of the main mosque in the old walled city of Delhi celebrating the end of the holy fasting month of Ramaḍān. During Shah Jahan's reign (1628–1658), Delhi was decorated with magnificent palaces, forts, and mosques. (Reuters/Bettmann)

that combined elements of several traditions. He thus attempted to develop a religion that could appeal to all of the various subjects of his empire, but his new faith failed to have much impact.

Two generations later, Shah Jahan (ruled 1628–1658) restored Islam as the state religion, and his reign is regarded as the golden age of Mughul art. Delhi, the seat of government, was decorated with magnificent palaces, mosques, and forts. The emperor had the Taj Mahal built in Agra as a monument to a favorite wife. But when he fell ill, his sons fought over the succession, and Shah Jahan was subsequently imprisoned for the rest of his life by the victor in this struggle, his son Aurangzeb.

Sons of Shah Jahan

Dārā Shikōh One of Shah Jahan's sons, Dārā Shikōh (died 1659), was deeply influenced by Ṣūfism's mystical worldview, and at his request several Hindu scriptures were translated into Persian. The prince collected the results of his religious studies into a book titled *The Mingling of the Two Seas.* In Dārā Shikōh's view, despite their linguistic and symbolic differences, both the Ṣūfī path and Hindu mysticism led to the same reality.

By its very nature, monistic Ṣūfism had been forced to look beyond Hinduism's many symbols and practices and to recognize the essentially monistic character of much of its higher thought and mysticism. However, when the tolerance of Akbar's reign gave way to Aurangzeb's revival of traditional Islamic practice, Dārā Shikōh was executed for heresy. His name was reviled by Mughul Muslim historians, who described him as a lover of Hinduism and an enemy of Islam. In their eyes, his execution was fully justified.

Aurangzeb Another of Shah Jahan's sons, Aurangzeb (ruled 1658–1707), was a man of enormous energy and military skill. He expanded the Mughul Empire beyond the limits of his predecessors, but at the time of his death the huge state was on the verge of explosion. An avowed and energetic champion of orthodox Islam, Aurangzeb reintroduced the system of discriminating among religious communities in favor of Islam. A poll tax was reimposed on non-Muslims, and mass conversions were enacted by force. Many Hindu temples were razed, and in 1675 the Sikhs' ninth guru was executed for refusing to convert to Islam, earning for the empire the lasting enmity of the powerful Sikh community.

THE DECLINE OF MUGHUL POWER

In the end, Aurangzeb's efforts to impose Islam weakened rather than strengthened the imperial bond. Only two generations after his death, his empire was in decline. Corruption among government officials and oppression of the people led to widespread revolts against the central power. Invaders from Iran plundered Delhi in 1739 and were followed by a band of marauders from Afghanistan in 1757. The Sikhs seized power in the Punjab, and Hindu and Muslim princes set up quasi-independent states within the empire. The British ultimately took over the "protection" of the Mughul Empire. Yet for many Muslims and Hindus, the Mughul emperor at Delhi continued to symbolize India's lost unity.

The reign of Shah Jahan (1628–1658) is regarded as the golden age of Mughul art. This example, a painting of an old Ṣūfī crossing the water on a prayer mat, is from an Mughul book of 1629. (The Granger Collection)

Shah Wali Allāh's Religious Reform

As the Mughul Empire disintegrated, Muslim revival movements sought to revitalize the Islamic community and to reestablish its power in India. One of the leaders of this effort was Shah Wali Allāh (1703–1762), a Ṣūfī intellectual in Delhi who used Ṣūfī organizations as instruments of reform. Eager to unify the Indo-Muslim community, he tried to mediate the squabbles among the four rival Ṣūfī schools.

To unite the fractious Muslim community, Wali Allāh promoted a morally aggressive form of Ṣūfism that was concerned with all aspects of the community's life. In his view, Islam united in one community all kinds of people, from simple believers to spiritually refined mystics. The mystics, the Ṣūfīs, could help to bind the community together: their spiritual knowledge could drive them to become active in the ordinary world, bringing about a unified Islamic community that was the reflection of Allāh's unity. To this end, Ṣūfīs should participate in Islam's ritual and social obligations, bringing to them a special depth of understanding.

Wali Allāh called for a fresh approach to the Qur'ān and the sunna as a means of resolving conflicts among Muslim scholars. To make the meaning of the Qur'ān more accessible to all Muslims, he took the controversial step of translating the Qur'ān into Persian. (Since the Qur'ān that God had given to Muḥammad was in Arabic, translation into other languages was regarded as irreligious, even blasphemous.)

Muslims, he stressed, should consider the underlying intention of the prophetic deposit's commands and prohibitions. Properly understood, the sharī'a could produce not only an integrated life for individuals but also a happy, stable community whose members could enjoy social and economic justice. The sharī'a's values were rationally defensible because they met the needs of the human community, but none of its aims could be achieved if the law was conceived or applied too rigidly. As political, social, and economic conditions changed, the application of the law also had to change, or the value of the sharī'a would be lost.

Wali Allāh had developed a form of revivalism, the movement to restore early forms of belief and practice as a way of meeting the growing crisis within the Muslim world. Unlike many later Islamic revival movements, which would turn to early Islam, Wali Allāh had turned to the mystical and intellectual traditions of medieval Islam as authentic and valuable. It is a tribute to his thought that many later reform movements—Ṣūfī and anti-Ṣūfī, intellectual and activist, modernist and revivalist—have acknowledged their debt to him.

Sayyid Ahmad and the Way of Muḥammad

The militant struggle for freedom from the "alien" rule of the Sikhs and the British was led by Sayyid Ahmad of Rae Bareli (1786–1831). Sayyid Ahmad was a disciple of Shah ᶜAbd-al-ᶜAzīz, the eldest son of Shah Wali Allāh. Beginning as an itinerant preacher in India, Sayyid Ahmad set out in 1822 to make the pilgrimage to Mecca. On his return to India two years later, he organized a holy war *(jihād)* against the non-Muslims who were taking control of the subcontinent. He died fighting the Sikhs.

Sayyid Ahmad launched a movement called the Way of Muḥammad. Like Wali Allāh's, this was a revival movement, but unlike the earlier one, Sayyid Ahmad's turned to the faith and practices of the very earliest generations of the prophet's followers as the ideal. The Way of Muḥammad extolled what it called "true Islam" as a pure and simple monotheism that proclaimed a transcendent God. Proper adherence to this form of Islam would give rise to a morally rigorous and total community (umma) in which all human beings were essentially equal. Through this approach, the Way of Muḥammad hoped to counter Ṣūfī and Hindu influences that had crept into popular religious practices.

Sayyid Ahmad was also critical of the Shīᶜites, whom he regarded as schismatics. The family of the prophet deserved respect, but not in the exaggerated way demanded by the Shīᶜites. Though the great Muslims of the past could legitimately be regarded as exemplars of Islamic life, not even the prophet himself could solve the problems of individuals in this earthly life. Muslims had to strive to attain righteousness and to avoid any tendency to idolize other human beings, even the heroes of Islam.

In sum, Sayyid Ahmad and Wali Allāh agreed on four important aims: a return to the Qur'ān and the prophet's sunna, elimination from Islamic life of ideas and practices derived from alien influences, the need to create a unified Islamic community, and the creation of an Islamic government in India. Where they differed was in their means: Wali Allāh had turned to medieval Islam and mystical Ṣūfism as his ideal, whereas Sayyid Ahmad gazed back further, to the earliest period.

The movement started by Sayyid Ahmad continued after his death. Throughout most of the nineteenth century, the northwestern frontier of India nurtured an Islamic rebellion against the British. Like other strands of thought in India whose origin can be traced back to Wali Allāh, the Way of Muḥammad was a religious doctrine that inspired other movements among Muslims in search of similar goals.

THE EXPANSION AND LONG DECLINE OF THE OTTOMAN TURKS

Late in the thirteenth century, the Ottoman Turks began their rise to power among the Turkish tribes of Asia Minor. (The term *Ottoman* or *Osmali* comes from Osman, who is believed to have founded the dynasty. Osman died in 1326.) The Ottomans identified themselves as warriors fighting for the holy cause of Islam. After consolidating a strong position in Asia Minor, they launched a campaign of military and political expansion across the Bosporus in Europe. In 1453 Constantinople fell to their armies. Within 100 years, the Turks controlled territory from Hungary to North Africa. By the end of the sixteenth century, they had absorbed the ancient heartland of early Islam and of the Umayyad and ᶜAbbāsid caliphates and were the guardians of the holy cities of Mecca and Medina. When they took Constantinople (which they renamed Istanbul) and established their capital there, the Ottomans had effectively replaced the Byzantine Empire.

In building and ruling their great domain, the

The Byzantine Empire collapsed in 1453, when the Ottoman Turks captured Constantinople and renamed it Istanbul. As this mosque illustrates, the flattened domes that typified Byzantine architecture still embellish the city's skyline. (Turkish Government Information Office)

Ottomans showed remarkable military and administrative competence. To offset the centrifugal tendencies of military feudalism, they developed a strong central government and an army consisting largely of civil and military officials owned by and therefore loyal to the sultan.

Ottoman Religious Policies

The Ottomans wielded their power on behalf of Sunni Islam. This was not new in the history of Islam. What was new was the degree to which the Ottoman system was able to fuse religious and temporal authority. Niyazi Berkes, perhaps the leading expert on the emergence of modern Turkey, explained it as follows:

> The Ottoman polity . . . succeeded more than any other in maintaining Islam and its representatives, the *ʿulamāʾ,* within the framework of the state organization. The religious institution . . . was merely a segment of the ruling institution, and was organized into an order. . . . Its role lay mainly in the cultivation of jurisprudence, the giving of opinions on legal matters, and the execution of the *Sharīʿah* law and the kānūn [temporal or administrative law]. . . . The *madrasah* [theological seminary] was not primarily a school of theology, but was chiefly a training center of jurisprudence. Through its judiciary, the state had adopted Sunni orthodoxy . . . and thus limited the possibilities for theological controversies.[2]

The implications of this synthesis were many and complex. The men of the sword and the men of religion had come together in a kind of symbiosis. On the one hand, the ʿulamāʾ and their value system were elevated and given specific channels and areas of authority in the Ottoman system. But on the other hand, the ʿulamā', at least at the center of the empire, lost that independence or distance from political pressures and vicissitudes that they had for so long managed to maintain. As a clerical bureaucracy within the Ottoman system, the ʿulamā' became almost totally identified with that wider system and dependent on it.

The Ottoman government approached the Ṣūfī religious brotherhoods in various ways. In general, the orders were free to function and grow as popular religious institutions, offering emotional purification, intuitive satisfaction, and an elaborate cult of the saints. As long as the leaders avoided theological controversy, disruptive political activity, and blatant violation of social norms, they were not only tolerated but even received government support.

Early Confrontations with Modernity

The first signs of the decay of the Ottoman Empire came in the late seventeenth century, when the Turks failed to take Vienna and had to cede Hungary to Austria. They suffered a series of losses in Europe and the near total destruction of their navy by a Russian fleet in the eighteenth century. One of the main reasons for the halt in Ottoman expansion was the improvement of Europe's sailing technology and its resultant revolution in naval tactics, which reduced Muslim control of international trade. In addition, the colonization of the New World brought a flood of gold bullion from the Americas, which caused runaway inflation in the Ottoman Empire, impoverishing much of the population.

At first the Turks were slow to understand the process of modernization and the technological revolution taking place in Europe, and they responded by trying to make their political and economic systems work with their old efficiency. But the system was geared to continuous expansion; once it began to slow, its demonstration of military decline led to even further weakening.

After the military defeats of the late eighteenth century, many Ottoman leaders began to think that some borrowing from the West might be necessary. But those early modernization efforts were small in scale and limited to the military. Struggling against the inertia of the entrenched medieval system, Ottoman modernization did not gather momentum and scope until well into the next century. The aim of the reforms was to match the West in military power as quickly as possible, but in fact the empire was never able even to approach the developmental curve of the West.

Modernity in the West was associated with a progressively greater understanding and control of the environment. Each discovery in one area of life caused adjustment, sooner or later, in the entire system. The modern mind demanded innovation and change because it assumed that its new knowledge and power were unlimited. It was thus the antithesis of the medieval mind, which was essentially conservative and geared to a much slower rate of change.

The Ottoman leaders failed to grasp the meaning of modernity. But they could not be faulted on this account, because it was poorly understood or controlled even in the West. In retrospect, it is clear that the Ottoman effort to close the gap in secular power was doomed from the beginning. The Turks could import modern weapons and Western officers to train their military elite, but they could not import a self-sustaining, accelerating process of modernization.

Even as the Ottomans began their first, haphazard reforms in the nineteenth century, the invention of the steam engine gave the West yet another strong push into the industrial revolution. This in turn created its voracious appetite for raw materials and markets and unleashed its capacity to produce new and terrible military machines.

THE WAHHĀBI MOVEMENT

While military disasters in Europe convinced the Ottoman rulers of the need to modernize their armies, a challenge of a different sort was brewing beyond the southeastern fringes of the empire. In the hinterlands of the Arabian peninsula, Muḥammad ibn- ʿAbd-al-Wahhāb (1703–1792) founded a militant puritanical revival movement that eventually affected the religious climate of almost every part of the Muslim world.

The Ottoman Empire had never controlled the area of the Arabian peninsula in which the Wahhābi revival first gathered momentum. Born in the remote Najd region, Wahhāb traveled and studied in the Hejaz, Iraq, and Syria. He was influenced by the conservative Ḥanbalite school of law and the writings of ibn-Taymīyah (1263–1328), a fundamentalist teacher in

Damascus who protested against such medieval innovations as devotion to the saints, vows, and pilgrimages to the shrines of famous Muslims.

Wahhāb sought to revive and spread what he regarded as the pure, original Islam of Muḥammad and his companions. To him, pure Islam was to be realized through strict and exclusive adherence to the plain sense of the Qur'ān and sunna. The **Wahhābis** held that rationalistic and esoteric interpretations of the Qur'ān did not illuminate the speech of God but simply diverted or obscured its impact. Wahhāb's form of original Islam was a militant, radical monotheism that set itself against every form of idolatry, immorality, and innovation.

The Wahhābi movement also campaigned against Ṣūfī thought and practices. The Ṣūfīs, they felt, had blasphemously blurred the distinction between the creator and the created. They were pantheists or monists, according to this school, and had misunderstood the radical transcendental nature of Allāh. The Ṣūfīs' esoteric method of interpreting the Qur'ān was no better than unbelief, since it refused to accept the plain sense of God's speech. Also the cult of the saints that had grown up in Ṣūfism was based on a faith in creatures besides God and hence a form of idolatry; it too was alien to pure and true Islam.

In theology the Wahhābis' literalism renewed the concept of individual involvement with God, as shown in the concrete language of the Qur'ān. Wahhābi revivalism directed believers' energies toward an active life devoted to building and extending a religious and moral order.

From the perspective of the entrenched Muslim establishment, the Wahhābis were dangerous innovators, attacking thought and practices hallowed by countless Muslim generations. But Wahhābis saw themselves as restoring the original straightforward and coherent message of the Qur'ān and Muḥammad's sunna. To them the plain Arabic speech of the Qur'ān spoke against the misguided institutions and leaders of the wider Muslim world: the wider community needed nothing less than conversion to the original Islam.

The Wahhābi movement soon became a tight, highly disciplined, egalitarian community that was at once an army, an economic system, and a community of worship. Its political and military effectiveness became evident when Wahhāb won the powerful Suʿūdi (Saudi) chiefs of the Najd to his cause. Indeed, the coupling of Islamic puritanism and the house of Suʿūd has continued to the present day.

The Wahhābis sought to develop a community based on what they perceived as original Islamic principles. They came to control major portions of Arabia during the early nineteenth century, and their soldiers campaigned into Syria and Iraq. Wherever they went, they instituted programs of religious indoctrination, destroyed shrines to the saints (which to them were idolatrous), and enforced a rigid code of public conduct.

The Ottomans crushed their early rule in Arabia in 1818, but this merely drove the movement underground. By the end of the nineteenth century, the Suʿūdis, still intent on building a government based on early Islamic principles, began the political expansion that eventually produced the modern state of Saudi Arabia.

Wahhābism reached every area of the Muslim world and inspired, shaped, or reinforced many militant revivalist movements. Modernizing forces were challenging traditional beliefs, late medieval institutions were failing, and Islamic societies were losing their sense of direction. The cures offered by Wahhābi revivalism generated in many Muslims new commitment, energy, and hope.

Islam and the Modern World

The period from 1800 to the beginning of World War II was the heyday of Western colonialism. Europeans went out first as traders and missionaries and later as colonists and imperial officials to Asia, Africa, and the Americas. The Islamic world was deeply disturbed by the West's aggressive advance, which shattered the self-esteem of all classes of Muslims throughout southern and central Asia and much of North and East Africa.

The Challenge of the West

The Dutch, who began to displace the Portuguese traders in Indonesia during the seventeenth century, took control of the rich Spice Islands, and the British entrenched themselves in Malaya. In the nineteenth century, Muslim control over central Asia was overthrown by the troops of czarist Russia.

After the Great Mutiny of 1857, in which native troops revolted against the British in India, the British authorities threw out the ineffectual Muslim administration and took control of India. In 1876, Queen Victoria was proclaimed empress of India.

Iran was never formally annexed by a European power, but in 1907 it was divided into spheres of influence. The Russians claimed a free hand in the north, and the British in the south, though neither felt it necessary to consult the government of Iran. Nearby Afghanistan was similarly split into Russian and British zones of influence, but the mountainous terrain and tough spirit of the Afghans were not easily conquered.

As all Africa was opened up to Western influence, the Islamic areas of North Africa became an amalgam of European colonies, dependencies, and protectorates. By the outbreak of World War I, the British were in Egypt and the Sudan, and French, British, and Italian forces held the Horn of Africa. Across the Strait of Bab el Mandeb, the British had been in control of Aden since 1839.

Throughout the nineteenth and early twentieth centuries, the Ottoman Empire limped along, the "sick man of Europe," beset by massive external pressures and internal disintegration. Turkish control of the Balkans eroded as the Christians of that region, with the encouragement of the European powers, expelled their Muslim overlords and formed independent nations.

REGIONAL DEVELOPMENTS

Modern Egypt

Egypt was invaded by Napoleon's French army in the early nineteenth century. The French were driven out by the Ottomans, who eventually installed Muḥammad ʿAli (c. 1769–1849) as *pasha* (viceroy) of Egypt. An energetic leader and effective military commander, ʿAli led the Ottoman force that contained the first wave of the Wahhābi revolt in Arabia. When he began expansion into the Sudan and Syria, both the Ottomans and the European powers became alarmed at his ambitions, and the Europeans intervened, forcing ʿAli back to Egypt. In the process, Ottoman suzerainty was reduced to a mere formality in his realm, and he became ruler of an independent Egypt. Although the British became Egypt's de facto rulers in 1882, ʿAli's dynasty remained its nominal rulers until 1952.

The Ottoman Empire and Pan-Islamism

The last effective ruler of the Ottoman Empire, ʿAbd-al-Hamid II (ruled 1876–1909), inherited a realm that was disintegrating both from internal forces and from the external aggression of the European powers. He tried to strengthen his grip by asserting that he was not only the Ottoman sultan but also the true caliph, defender of the Islamic umma against the common European enemies. His claim to be the true caliph and his pan-Islamism were welcomed by Muslims in many lands, especially those living under European colonial rule.

This movement toward pan-Islamism was seconded and trumpeted far and wide by Jamāl al-Dīn al-Afghāni (1837–1897), an Afghan religious activist who summoned Muslims everywhere to recover the purity and solidarity of early Islam. He directed his attacks not only against the Western colonialists but also against Islamic governments too weak to resist Western influence. His stirring speeches and articles encouraged a rebellion in Egypt and a constitutional movement in Iran.

But eventually this pan-Islamist movement, and the Ottoman sultans' claims to be the successors of Muḥammad, could not contain the growing separatist tendencies of the Arabs. The reasons for this separatism were several: Arab peoples had been provoked by the long history of Ottoman corruption and failures, they were inspired by Egypt's short-lived independence, and Wahhābi puritanism, which contrasted its own "true" Islam with the Ottoman version, offered a new religious ideal.

For these and other reasons, many Arab leaders allied themselves with the British and French during World War I; Arabs fought and eventually defeated the Ottoman Empire. But rather than giving them the freedom they had hoped for, the victorious Western powers established their own mandates over Arab lands. France was given responsibility for Syria and Lebanon; Great Britain for Palestine, Transjordan, and Iraq. In addition, the Arab leaders discovered to their horror that in the Balfour Declaration of 1917 the

French and English had promised Zionist leaders a Jewish homeland in Palestine. Having thrown off the yoke of one empire, they had fallen victim to a more alien imperialism: the Western powers, Arabs felt, had used the Muslims and then betrayed them.

Saudi Arabia

Now under the dominance of the British, the old Wahhābi-Suʿūdi alliance came to power, forming Saudi Arabia in 1932. Time had given Wahhābism a measure of tolerance and moderation toward other Muslims, but the movement retained its puritanical rigor. The Saudi government was established on very conservative Islamic principles: no belief was to be held as true that was not confirmed by the Qur'ān, authentic aḥādīth, or conservative reasoning; houses and clothes were to be simple; diversions like joking, music, and gold ornaments were prohibited. Even certain games were ruled out as distractions from prayers. The enormous oil deposits of the peninsula came to light in the 1930s but had little economic impact until after World War II.

Unlike the Saudi government, established on puritanical and conservative Islamic principles, Mustafa Kemal (pictured) led Turkey toward modernization and secularization, severely limiting Islam's influence. (Wide World)

Palestine

Between the two world wars, Arabs' nationalism, fanned by bitterness over their treatment by the European powers, developed. One focus of their bitterness was Palestine. Part of the problem was that the Balfour Declaration had been, for political reasons, quite vague. It clearly called for the "establishment in Palestine of a national home for the Jewish people." Yet it also called for the protection of the resident Arabs: "Nothing shall be done which may prejudice the civil and religious rights of existing non-Jewish communities in Palestine." In short, in order to garner support from both Jews and Arabs, the declaration had been left ambiguous.

To Arabs, Zionism became a symbol of the West's contempt for them, as well as a reminder of Arab inability to cope with the forces of modern history. But Jews also felt that the British were not supporting their cause energetically enough. Matters were settled only after the Holocaust mounted by Nazi Germany during World War II, which gave a new, desperate, and tragic urgency to political Zionism. Israel was founded in 1948.

Turkey

Unlike the Saudis' conservative turn to an early Islam, the Turkish response to modernity was toward modernization and secularization. This turn was led by Mustafa Kemal (1881–1939), later called Atatürk ("Father of the Turks"). After the Ottomans and the Central Powers were defeated in World War I, the once-enormous Ottoman Empire was squeezed into the area of roughly the modern state of Turkey. Responding to this disaster, Atatürk started a revolution that Westernized and secularized his nation. Vehemently attacking the institutions and symbols of traditional Islam, the Turks aggressively separated religion from the state. Excluding the ʿulamā' from any role in the new state, they established secular education and legal systems. Organized Ṣūfism was legally eliminated from public life. Although the government maintained and staffed the mosques, even Islamic worship forms felt the pressures of the revolution. Arabic was replaced by Turkish in both education and religious ceremonies; the Qur'ān was translated into Turkish. The *fez* (the traditional head covering) was outlawed, and clerical dress was banned outside the mosques. Even Western-style surnames were introduced.

One of the most dramatic social changes was the emancipation of urban Turkish women. Turkey's modern family code legally abolished such traditional institutions as polygamy. The revolution opened social and educational opportunities to women and granted them the right to vote and to hold political office.

The caliphate was formally abolished in the early 1920s, and Turkey became a republic. The end of the caliphate marked the end of state sponsorship of pan-Islamism in Turkey. Yet even with this loss, to many Muslims outside Turkey, the success of the Turks in maintaining their independence in a world dominated by the West was a source of pride. Some viewed Turkey as a champion of Muslims living under colonial rule.

To many observers, however, it was not clear whether the Turks were seeking to give new expression to Islam or abandoning it. Defenders of the Turkish revolution argued that there was a great difference between being anticlerical and being antireligious. They distinguished between the religion of the Qur'ān, which could meet the spiritual needs of modern men and women, and the religion of the ᶜulamā', which was inflexible and traditionalist. They condemned the ᶜulamā' as unwilling to take a fresh look at the prophetic deposit and as unable to understand modern issues. Coupled with this anticlerical attitude, they argued for an increased role of the laity under the rallying cry "No priesthood in Islam."

RETHINKING THE BASES OF ISLAM

The expansion of Western colonialism increased the Muslim understanding of Western civilization, but it also deprived Muslims of confidence and self-respect. The attack from the West was framed in both secular and religious terms: some Western secularists suggested that the Muslims' devotion to Islam and its way of life was what had placed them outside the mainstream of human progress in the first place. If the Muslims wanted to share in the wonders of the modern world, they had to move away from Islam. Some Christian apologists, secure as a result of Western dominance, redoubled their criticism of the teachings of Islam and the person of Muḥammad.

Muslim thinkers attempted to demonstrate not only that Islam was compatible with modern progress but also that it had created, directly or indirectly, much of what was called the modern spirit. As these Muslim thinkers began to reformulate the truth of Islam in the light of modern conditions, they admitted that there was much to imitate in Western civilization. But what they admired in the West they found also in one way or another in the original or essential Islam. Where Muslims might have imitated the West, they instead revived lost elements of their own Islamic revelations, for they believed that the West's intellectual vitality, including its science, philosophy, and universities, had been sparked by early Islam. In contrast, the present backwardness of the Islamic world had come about despite Islam. We will trace the development of this viewpoint in the work of three influential intellectuals and see how it has affected modern Islamic law.

Muḥammad ᶜAbduh of Egypt

One of al-Afghāni's influential students was Muḥammad ᶜAbduh (1849–1905), a liberal Egyptian jurist and educator. Heeding al-Afghāni's call to defend the Islamic world militarily, he participated in the revolution that led to the British occupation of Egypt in 1882. After a period of exile, Muḥammad ᶜAbduh was permitted to return to his homeland, where he came to terms with the British administration. With British support he became Egypt's chief *mufti* (Muslim legal consultant), and he also was active in the administration of al-Azhar, the seat of Islamic scholarship in Cairo.

As a respected member of the ᶜulamā', ᶜAbduh pointed out to them that traditional learning was inadequate for intellectual or moral leadership in the modern age. He supported educational reform in Egypt and attempted to modernize the curriculum of al-Azhar in order to produce ᶜulamā' who would be solidly grounded in both the religious sciences and modern thought. Declaring that the perspective of the original Islam had been at once rational and religious, he asserted that Muslims had nothing to fear and everything to gain from plunging into scientific study. Although faith and reason operated on different levels, he argued, they were complementary and mutually supportive.

ᶜAbduh rejected the authority of the medieval

schools and called for the right to reconsider the Qur'ān and the corpus of prophetic tradition in the light of modern conditions. He insisted that legal interpretation and practice focus on the law's ethical principles or intentions and take into account the effects on society of any legal decision or doctrine.

ʿAbduh produced a strong defense of Islam. In his view, the original Islam was dynamic and effective in all areas of life, including science and philosophy. Indeed, the Qur'ān had ordered Muslims to transform the world and seek knowledge wherever it might be found. As a result, they were at one time at the vanguard of human understanding of the universe. They later provided medieval Christians with the foundations of modern science and philosophy.

ʿAbduh felt that the Muslims would have adopted modern ways easily if they had remained faithful to the Qur'ān. If Muslims were now intellectually backward, this was in spite of Islam's original impulse, not because of it. ʿAbduh depicted Christianity as an other-worldly tradition teaching an unnatural ethic of love that had been honored only in the breach and offering a theology that was the enemy of rational thought. To him, Europeans had moved to the leading edge of history only when their intellectual life broke free of ecclesiastical bonds. In his opinion, Christianity, not true Islam, was incompatible with the modern age.

Amir ʿAli

The book *The Spirit of Islam,* written by Amir ʿAli (1894–1925), a Shīʿite lawyer in India, has been praised as the bible of Islamic modernism. It is addressed both to Muslims struggling with the problem of modernity and to cultivated westerners prejudiced against Islam.

Let us consider Amir ʿAli's thinking on two important issues for modern Islam: the definition of the Islamic political community and the status of women.

Arguing that a liberal political spirit was part of the essence of Islam, Amir ʿAli tried to fit the position of Muḥammad as a political liberator into a historical context:

> Seven centuries had passed since the Master of Nazareth had come with his message of the Kingdom of Heaven to the poor and the lowly. A beautiful life was ended before the ministry had barely commenced. And now unutterable desolation brooded over the empires and kingdoms of the earth, and God's children, sunk in misery, were anxiously waiting for the promised deliverance which was so long in coming.
>
> In the West, as in the East, the condition of the masses was so miserable as to defy description. They possessed no civil rights or political privileges. These were the monopoly of the rich and the powerful, or of the sacerdotal classes. The law was not the same for the weak and the strong, the rich and the poor, the great and the lowly.[3]

After depicting the dismal state of humanity in the seventh century, Amir ʿAli then described the liberating role of Muḥammad. His basic message, which had been preached by the other prophets, was the unity of God and the brotherhood of all human beings found in an active concern for every member of society. During Muḥammad's lifetime, this liberal political spirit was effectively conveyed without the need for elaborate institutions, as the prophet was immediately accessible to everyone and took counsel with his people on every major issue. His concern for the security and moral freedom of non-Muslims was shown in his efforts to integrate the Jews of Medina into his commonwealth and his generous guarantees to the Christians of the oasis of Najrān.

In the 30 years after the prophet's death, the Islamic "republic" embodied in primitive form many of the values and institutions fundamental to liberal democracy:

> An examination of the political condition of the Moslems under the early Caliphs brings into view a popular government administered by an elective chief with limited powers. The prerogatives of the head of state were confined to administrative and executive matters, such as the regulation of the police, control of the army, transaction of foreign affairs, disbursement of the finances, etc. But he could never act in contravention of the recognized law.
>
> The tribunals were not dependent on the government. Their decisions were supreme; and the early Caliphs could not assume the power of pardoning those whom the regular tribunals had condemned. The law was the same for the poor as for the rich, for the man in power as for the labourer in the field.[4]

Amir ʿAli recognized that in the later political history of Islam, the liberal political spirit of the faith was at times dimmed but never entirely lost. With Islam's great expansion, people were invariably blessed with more freedom, more opportunity, and greater prosperity than they had known under earlier rulers. The record of Islam regarding the treatment of religious minorities, Amir ʿAli believed, was much better than that of the Christians.

Instead of contenting himself with an ineffective idealism, Muḥammad moved the primitive society as far as it could be moved toward perfection, and at the same time he laid down the principles necessary to inspire and guide later progress. Modern Muslim political and religious leaders had to recover the spirit of their master and free that spirit from archaic forms that no longer reflected it. At the same time, liberal idealism had to interact with an intelligent and realistic assessment of what was really possible in the present state of any given Islamic society.

According to Amir ʿAli, Muḥammad had enacted legal improvements in the status of women and established the principles for future progress in women's rights. Qur'ān 4:3 had long been cited as tolerant of polygamy, and in the Arberry translation it reads: "If you fear that you will not act justly towards the [orphan girls], marry such women as seem good to you, two, three, or four. But if you fear you will not be equitable, then only one." Amir ʿAli interpreted this passage as having the following meaning: "You may marry two, three, or four wives, but not more. But if you cannot deal equitably and justly with all, you should marry only one." Like many other modernists, he maintained that a literal interpretation of this verse amounted to prohibiting polygamy, since no man could possibly treat four women equally, a fact that the Qur'ān states elsewhere.

Amir ʿAli pointed out that Muḥammad had offered a progressive message to all kinds of human communities. In primitive societies plural marriage may have been the only effective way of protecting women from sexual exploitation or destitution, and veiling and secluding them may have been a part of Muḥammad's principle of showing women respect. However, maintaining such practices when they were no longer needed would have been a flagrant disregard of the prophet's liberal tendency. Amir ʿAli blamed inflexible traditionalism for the failure of the Islamic world to abolish polygamy and other practices abusive to women.

Later modernists who rejected many of Amir ʿAli's specific conclusions happily accepted his general method, which had such goals as the brotherhood of all Muslims, respect for women, and government for the people. The specific laws and institutions required to realize these goals could vary with time and local conditions. In this perspective the sharīʿa was no longer seen as a detailed set of prescriptions and prohibitions but rather as timeless principles or goals—values toward which individuals and societies should strive. Modern Muslims were free to adopt whatever laws and governments might promote this movement.

Muḥammad Iqbal

The most recent of our intellectual modernists was Muḥammad Iqbal (1876–1938), an Indian poet and philosopher whose ideas contributed to the creation of the Islamic state of Pakistan in 1947. His intellectual and spiritual roots were in Persian mysticism and philosophy, his education included Western philosophy, and his thought was a fascinating blend of Ṣūfī themes and elements of Western vitalistic and process philosophy.

Iqbal produced a daring metaphysics that emphasized human power, freedom, and responsibility. Life, divine or human, was a continuous creative flow, and the finite human ego was internal to the divine life and endowed by God, the infinite and perfect ego, with spontaneous and creative freedom. Human freedom was not an external limitation on God but rather an expression of God's own creative freedom. Love drove the universe, moving every finite self to realize its possibilities and to seek the infinite personality of God in prayer, to commune with him, and to absorb his qualities.

But love also motivated the human self to a passionate service to God in the world of normal consciousness. The human self could attain a unity of wills with its Lord and could manifest divine qualities in the world of space and serial time, but the individual nonetheless endured. Spiritual progress produced the power to overcome and to transform the world, rather than the impulse to withdraw from it. Iqbal's person of faith would combine material and spiritual power and overcome the world as God's servant. Muḥammad, who did indeed overcome the world, was the archetype of Iqbal's mysticism.

Because of the integrative nature of his worldview, Iqbal was concerned with the political future of the Islamic community in India. Since Muslims could not expect to dominate a future independent India, they were faced with the political alternatives of accepting minority status in a predominantly Hindu secular state or insisting on partition and the establishment of a Muslim state. Iqbal spent his last years as a supporter of partition, but he warned that if an Islamic state in the subcontinent were to be truly Islamic, it had to reach out to the entire world community of Islam. Iqbal envisioned an Islamic League of Nations transcending both nationalism and imperialism.

Iqbal saw the West as an engine of destruction because it had no effective spiritual roots. Although the West had ideals, it lacked the spiritual energy to move toward them. Thus the West that had created the wonders of modern science, technology, and medicine was also the civilization that had produced nationalism, imperialism, capitalistic exploitation of the poor, godless secularism, and materialistic communism. Iqbal therefore did not want Muslims simply to copy Western modernity.

What was the result of such attempts to rethink the bases of Islam? As a group, the ʿulamāʾ did not respond positively, and neither did the grand masters of Ṣūfism or the majority of Muslims. The modernist approach remained an elitist phenomenon, and only the surface of educational reform was scratched. Nonetheless, modernist intellectuals were able to provide spiritual direction and an intellectual defense to a growing group of Westernized Muslims who were rising to the top of many Islamic societies.

THE MODERNIST CHALLENGE IN LAW

During the nineteenth and twentieth centuries, the traditional sharīʿa law, regulations based on the Qurʾān and Islamic tradition, has gradually been replaced in the Muslim world by modern legal codes based on Western models. In the area of family law, reform governments have exercised restraint and have attempted to reinterpret the traditional law instead of openly repudiating it. Only Ḥanbalite Saudi Arabia has been a consistent exception to the general trend toward legal modernization.

The modern Muslim evaluation of the medieval schools of law has been comprehensive. The medieval scholars have been accused of allowing Islam to be corrupted by elements opposed to its original dynamic character, a corruption that was then fixed by the acceptance of the doctrine that the door of ijtihād was closed. This doctrine destroyed the vitality of Muslim legal thought and deprived it of freedom and flexibility.

According to the liberal modernist version of qiyās, the principles, goals, and fundamental purposes of religious law are unchanging. But the specific forms in which the eternal principles of sharīʿa are expressed must, in contrast, change constantly in the face of the continuing changes in human circumstances. Within this analytical framework, modernists argue that modern commercial, civil, and criminal codes are more adequate articulations of the eternal principles of sharīʿa than are the outmoded traditional rules.

The liberal-modernist argument has often used Western analysis and evaluation of the ḥadīth literature. Though the collections of aḥādīth have provided students of early Islam with much information about the development of Islamic thought and practice, they have not offered many reliable details about the words and deeds of the historical Muḥammad. This sort of analysis has threatened much of the traditional religious law, particularly elements not developed in the text of the Qurʾān itself. For Muslim modernists, however, it has offered interpretive freedom; instead of being bound by the structure of the traditional sunna, they can seek a fresh appreciation of the Qurʾān and the true Muḥammad.

The modernist tendency in law has not gone unchallenged. The edifice of law constructed by the medieval schools contains rules and principles solidly rooted in the text of the Qurʾān itself, and modernist appeals to principle and general purpose are seen by conservative Muslims as attempts to suspend the very letter of the Qurʾān in order to articulate its alleged "spirit." To traditional Muslims, this modernist qiyās is simply a route to a system of law made by human beings rather than by God. A massive and growing antimodernist reaction is currently seeking to reestablish purified versions of ancient Islamic law throughout the Islamic world.

THE END OF WESTERN COLONIALISM

By the beginning of World War II, Western imperialism was declining in some areas of the world, and after peace was restored in 1945, an irresistible wind of freedom swept around the globe. In predominantly Islamic regions, the nationalist struggle took on religious overtones—reminiscent of ancient Islamic militancy—and in the postwar years one Muslim people after another gained political independence. Sometimes independence came with a rush and the cooperation of colonial administrators, but at other times it was achieved only after a long and painful struggle.

Arab Nationalism, Israel, and Oil

Most of the Arab peoples emerged from colonial rule as underdeveloped, militarily weak nations. Independence appeared to many Arab leaders an empty sham, since they remained dependent on economic, technological, and military help from the West. Britain, France, and the United States were quite willing to use their leverage to guide the new nations along lines that met Western interests.

A continuing focus of Arab frustration was the state of Israel, which achieved independence in 1948. In the Arab view, it had been the West's anti-Semitism that had brought about the Holocaust in which millions of European Jews perished. The Arabs blamed both the West's moral failure and political Zionism for the creation of Israel and the disruption of the Arab-Muslim world, as well as the displacement of the Palestinian Arabs from their homeland. The survival and subsequent expansion of the Jewish state also demonstrated the inability of the Arabs to unite in defense of their Palestinian blood relatives.

Arab morale has waxed and waned with the progress of the struggle against Israel. The performance of the Arab armies in the 1967 Six-Day War, which expanded Israel's territory, disappointed the Arabs, but the military standoff of the 1973 Yom Kippur War did boost their confidence.

The concentration of much of the world's petroleum in the Middle East has increased the wealth and power of many Islamic states. The West's desire for continued access to the petroleum, the moderately pro-Western stance of certain Arab governments, the sudden upsurge of oil prices during the energy crisis of 1973, and the Arab attempts to present a united front to the West have given Arab states even greater power. But some of that unity was threatened in 1991, when one Muslim nation, Iraq, invaded another, Kuwait. The Arab community was split during this Gulf War: half the Arab countries fought Iraq while the other half sympathized with it. By the end of that year, the vision of achieving unity through a strengthened Islam was also threatened. Some regimes appeared to be drifting toward a renewed Islamic fundamentalism, while some states continued their more moderate approach to the modern world. Some Arab governments entered into peace talks with Israel while Palestinian leaders still advocated a holy war against Israel. With the fall of the Soviet government, which had supported much of the Arab warfare against Israel, this attitude has changed somewhat, and it is not clear where the Arab world will emerge in the new world order.

Pakistan

In 1947 the Indo-Muslim dream of a separate Islamic state was realized through the creation of Pakistan. The establishment of this new state entailed huge migrations of Hindus, Sikhs, and Muslims and was marked by bloody riots. Pakistan was an undeveloped country plagued by ethnic diversity and bizarre geography. West Pakistan, the political and military center, was separated from East Pakistan, the site of much of its population and resources, by hundreds of miles of Indian territory.

Although the main force behind the creation of a separate Pakistan was devotion to Islam, religion soon became a source of conflict among the Pakistanis themselves. There were old and new forms of sectarian conflict, as well as conflict between Sunni modernists and Sunni traditionalists. In 1971 the Islamic society of Pakistan split in two, and after a civil war between East and West Pakistan and a war between West Pakistan and India, East Pakistan proclaimed itself the new and independent nation of Bangladesh.

Black Nationalism in Africa

Since the thirteenth century (and perhaps earlier), Islam has been expanding into sub-Saharan Africa. In the fourteenth and fifteenth centuries, Timbuktu in West Africa was the site of 100 Qur'ānic schools. Conversions to Islam increased rapidly during the colonial period as Islam became a vital force in the African nationalist movements of the modern era. As a result, several new nations in sub-Saharan Africa have Muslim majorities, and others have growing Muslim communities. Although Christian missionaries have had considerable success among the followers of tribal religions, today they are not increasing their rate of conversion at the same pace as the Muslims.

THE BLACK MUSLIMS OF THE UNITED STATES

In the United States in the 1950s and 1960s, many black Americans became Black Muslims, who sometimes refer to themselves as the lost nation of Islam. Their founder was Elijah Muhammad (1897–1975). Born in Georgia as Elijah Poole, he became an assembly line worker in a Detroit automobile factory, where he met a salesman named W. D. Fard, whom Muhammad described as his source of truth about Islam. Fard mysteriously disappeared around 1934.

Calling himself the messenger of Allāh, Muhammad announced that American blacks were descended from the ancient tribe of Shabazz that had originally settled the holy city of Mecca. Blacks in the United States, he believed, were members of a great black nation that included all people of color—black, red, brown, and yellow—but the enemy of the black nation of Islam had always been the white race.

Black Muslim racial mythology is basically a mirror image of white racial mythology. Whites are seen as aberrant derivatives of the original black people. Because whites are clever but essentially demonic and not fully human, there can be no real community that both blacks and whites can share. Blacks must pursue separate development because even the lowest blacks are immeasurably superior to all whites. The racial mythology of the original Black Muslim movement is liberally sprinkled with Arab-Islamic terms and references to the Bible and the Qur'ān.

An important leader of the Black Muslims was Malcolm X (1925–1965), who was born in Omaha as Malcolm Little. Through his dynamic personality he was able to attract a large personal following of his own and to become one of Elijah Muhammad's closest collaborators. After a quarrel between the two men in 1964, Malcolm X was suspended from his functions. He then went on a pilgrimage to Mecca. During his ḥajj he was impressed to see people of every race, including

The Bādshādi Mosque, built in the seventeenth century by the Mughul ruler Aurangzeb, is one of the splendors of Pakistan. Although the main force behind the creation of a separate Pakistan in 1947 was devotion to Islam, religion continued to be a source of conflict in the region, resulting in East Pakistan becoming Bangladesh in 1971. (United Nations)

whites, worshiping side by side. This experience did not lessen Malcolm X's resentment of wrongs suffered by blacks in the United States, but it taught him the hopelessness of racism, as well as the true meaning of the Islamic community. Converted in Mecca to orthodox Islam, he returned to the United States and founded the Organization of Afro-American Unity, a group preaching black nationalism but opposed to black separatism. While speaking to a large gathering in New York City, he was shot and killed.

After Elijah Muhammad's death in 1975, his son and successor, Warith Deen Muhammad, radically transformed the Black Muslim movement. Renamed first the World Community of Islam and more recently the American Muslim Mission, it now is open to whites. In 1979 the charismatic but sometimes inflammatory Louis Farrakhan broke away from the Mission, establishing the more radical Nation of Islam. Membership in the Nation is restricted to blacks, and it advocates a separate black social structure. Both groups have expanded, demonstrating an ability to answer the religious needs of urban blacks.

Malcolm X was an important leader of the Black Muslims. Converted to orthodox Islam during his ḥajj, he continued to resent the wrongs suffered by African-Americans in the United States but realized the hopelessness of racism. He then founded the Organization of Afro-American Unity, preaching black nationalism but opposed to black separatism. (UPI/Bettmann)

MILITANT REVIVALISM

The Islamic world is currently in a state of flux that has affected all areas of life. As many Islamic societies achieved independence from colonial rule, they often abolished parliamentary democracy and political pluralism as hindrances to the rapid attainment of national strength. Nationalist leaders—many of them dictators—have devoted themselves to constructing educational systems, and although religious education has received state support, it also is under state control. Even in family law and laws regulating the personal status of individuals, the principles of traditional Islamic law have often been set aside to achieve pragmatic goals. Many of the new regimes have restricted the activities of the ʿulamā', Ṣūfī orders, and lay religious associations that could become centers of political power.

The continuing revolution in world transportation and communication, the education of thousands of Muslim students in Western universities, and the political and economic interdependence of states and communities around the globe have all caused culture shock in Islamic societies. The result has been a series of conflicts and confusions regarding moral values and life styles. The West is accused of cultural imperialism and is identified with the rise of materialism, individualism, permissiveness, and the destruction of family life. Industrialization, urbanization, and the departure of thousands of Muslims to alien lands in search of work have further eroded the network of family bonds that has for centuries kept Islamic societies together.

One response to the problems of the modern world has been the spread of the militant Islamic revivalism begun by the Wahhābi puritans of the eighteenth century. Muslims in all parts of the world have heeded the call to return to a rigorous, literal, pristine form of Islam. In theory, the new puritanism does not mean the rejection of science, technology, and modern innovations in politics and economics, but all efforts at modernization have to be adjusted to the enduring absolutes of a purified religious traditionalism. Great emphasis is placed on "de-Westernization," the systematic removal from Islamic societies of values and cultural symbols regarded as alien to a divinely ordered life.

Modern puritanism is more than just a widespread sentiment; it is found in many disciplined and politically active organizations. One of the best known is the Muslim Brotherhood, founded in Egypt in 1928 by Ḥasan al-Bannā'. It later spread to the Sudan, Syria, Lebanon, Iraq, and North Africa. Its first members were mainly teachers and preachers who founded schools, cottage industries, medical facilities, and paramilitary groups. During the 1940s the group fought the British in the Suez Canal Zone and Zionist groups in Palestine.

The tensions between the modernizing reform and puritanical revival movements are manifest in the status of Muslim women. Wealthy, educated, upper-class women push for reform of the laws oppressive to women. However, in countries headed by traditionalist leaders, women such as these in Iran are forced by law to cover their faces. (Marc Riboud/Magnum)

The Muslim Brotherhood maintains that the plain meaning of the Qur'ān, the sunna of Muḥammad, and the pattern of early Muslim life provide humanity with a rule of life that is good for all times and conditions. According to Ḥasan al-Bannā', "Islam is dogma and worship, fatherland and nationality, religion and state, spirituality and action, Qur'ān and sword."[5]

For followers of the Brotherhood the primary nation of Muslims is the umma, or universal community of faith. Western-style nationalism is illegitimate, and regional governments are allowable only until a universal Islamic order can be established. In this perspective, the problem of Arab unity is not that the Arabs are not Arab enough but that they are not Muslim enough; this is why they have failed to achieve real unity. The Brotherhood program is like Atatürk's reforms in Turkey in reverse: it would like to replace law codes derived from European models with a purified restatement of traditional religious law. The state cannot legislate in any area preempted by revelation.

If the Muslim Brotherhood were to achieve its goals, every Muslim's way of life would be changed. De-Westernization would be applied to details of everyday clothing, forms of greeting, language, and cultural expression; it would be the antithesis of a liberal, permissive society. An extremely rigorous religious education would instill personal, family, and communal discipline. The ruler would be elected by the people and would be responsible to them, though on a day-to-day basis he would exercise authority in conjunction with a representative assembly. A truly Islamic state would fight for the liberation of all Muslims and would serve the cause of justice everywhere.

Few national leaders in the Islamic world have welcomed the recommendations and political activism of such revival movements as the Muslim Brotherhood. However, some non-Arab Muslims have proved receptive to these concepts. Despite differences in detail, the politically powerful Jamā'at-i Islāmi (Islamic party) of Pakistan is similar to the Brotherhood in its general aims and tone. Even Turkey has its own National

Salvation party, which promotes revivalist goals. The revolutionary regime in Iran is a Shīᶜite version of Sunni revivalist movements like the Brotherhood and Jamāᶜat-i Islāmi. It is unclear how these countries or Islam as a whole will resolve the tensions between the conservative revivalists and those militating for greater modernization.

The tensions that arise from these complex waves of modernizing reform and puritanical revival movements are manifest in the changing religious and social status of modern Muslim women. In the twentieth century, wealthier, educated, upper-class women have pushed for reform of the laws—regarding seclusion, marriage, divorce, and professional status—that they regard as oppressive to women. By pushing for greater educational opportunities and by refusing to wear the veil, which they regard as paternalistic, these women see themselves as struggling for equal rights and as attempting to enter the mainstream of public life.

Several counterforces, however, have led many Muslim women to return to the veil. In countries headed by traditionalist religious leaders, such as Iran, women have been forced by law to cover their faces. Some women elsewhere have personally chosen to don the veil in the belief that God requires it, to avoid conflict with male relatives who deem it fitting, or to affirm traditional Muslim values over Western-style social ways. Some women enjoy the privacy the veil affords or consider it fashionable. But more modernist women decry the practice as demeaning.

The militant, puritanical trend in Islamic societies is growing, creating much tension both inside and outside the Muslim world. The trend is likely to continue, and the puritans will win many concessions from modernizing governments even if they fail to seize or dominate the political apparatus.

All this reflects more than a phase of social transition. The Muslim peoples have been offered a multitude of options by the West and the now defunct Communist bloc. The leaders of the militant revival want Islam to become a major force in the modern historical drama. They see the old-style modernists as adjusting Islam to fit imported ideas and institutions of dubious value and are convinced that exactly the reverse is needed. If Muslims are not to lose their roots and their souls, modernization must be shaped and controlled by the basic values and structures of their traditional faith.

NOTES

1 This treatment of recent developments in Twelver Shīᶜism is based largely on Moojan Momen, *An Introduction to Shīᶜi Islam* (New Haven, Conn.: Yale University Press, 1985).

2 Niyazi Berkes, "*Iṣlāḥ* (in Turkey)," in *The Encyclopaedia of Islam,* new ed. (Leiden, Netherlands: Brill, 1960), vol. 4, p. 167.

3 Amir ᶜAli, *The Spirit of Islam* (London: Methuen, 1967), p. 268.

4 Ibid., p. 278.

5 G. Delanque, "Al-Ikhwān al-Muslimūn," in *The Encyclopaedia of Islam,* new ed. (Leiden, Netherlands: Brill, 1960), vol. 3, p. 1069.

GLOSSARY

Abhidharma name of a Theravādin Buddhist school and its series of seven scholastic works (the *Abhidharma Piṭaka*). Well-known for enumerating mental and physical constituents of the experienced world.

Abraham The traditional founder of the Jewish people; the man who recognized the existence of one God and entered into a covenant with him.

adhvaryu A priest in the Vedic sacrificial ritual who performed manual jobs in the ceremony, including the offering and pouring of oblations.

Adi Granth The principal Sikh scripture, assembled by Guru Arjan (1581–1606), preserving the writings of Guru Nanak (1469–1539), the founder of Sikhism.

aḥādīth The mass of oral traditions or sayings attributed to the prophet Muḥammad. (Singular, *ḥadīth*.)

ahimsā Noninjury and nonviolence toward any living being, emphasized by Jains and Buddhists.

Ahura Mazda ("Wise Lord") God of Zoroastrianism, the highest supreme sovereign over all creation; later known as Ormazd.

alchemy In popular Daoism, the partly chemical art of concocting the elixir of immortality. As presented in the work of Go Hong, it consists of making a compound of gold and mercury to be taken as a pill and is to be accompanied by good deeds and meditation.

Allāh ("the God") The one God of Islam.

Amaterasu The Shintō sun goddess from whom the Japanese emperors are purported to be descended.

anātman No self; no soul; in early Buddhism, the denial of the existence of an ultimate substantial soul.

ancestor Any of the deceased persons of one's family, generally of honorable social standing, who are venerated for having set moral precedents or laid the foundations of culture. In Chinese religions, ancestors are venerated in themselves; in African religions, they serve as intermediaries to the divine.

apocalypse Vision of heavenly secrets allegedly granted to a biblical ancient of unusual piety or wisdom. These secrets, written in books that began to circulate during the second century B.C.E., tended to focus on the irresistible unfolding of God's plan for history and on hidden knowledge of the heavenly realms. Apocalyptic speculation fed an intense anticipation of the end of history during the period 200 B.C.E.–200 C.E.

apologists Defenders of early Christianity who wrote reasoned explanations of Christian practices and beliefs to Roman government officials; defenders of a specific religion.

Aryas An Indo-European people who from the middle of the second millennium B.C.E. dominated northern India. Developed the Vedas.

Ārya Samāj ("Aryan Society") Society founded by Dayananda in 1875 that undertook to reform Hinduism by rejecting all post-Vedic scriptures and their ideas.

āśrama Hindu stage of life. Traditional āśramas for males were brahmacārin (student), gṛihastha (householder, during which one worked and raised a family), vānaprastha (forest dweller), and sannyāsa (which see). A woman's āśramas involved moving from being the responsibility of her father to that of her husband and then of her sons.

Atharvans In the Vedic age, an ancient order of shamans who performed curative and protective rituals in Aryan homes. In time they won a role in performance of the aristocratic śrauta sacrifices.

Atharvaveda Vedic text produced by the Atharvans containing 565 metrical and prose hymns in 19 books. It includes both magical and ritual elements and systematic speculations on the meaning of the Vedic ritual.

ātman In Hinduism, the ultimate essence of a person, conceived of as an immaterial reality that provides consciousness.

Auru Mainyu The Zoroastrian personification of the spirit of evil; later known as Ahriman.

avatar In Vaishṇava thinking, a form assumed by the supreme being to undergo descent and birth on earth, to do deeds for the benefit of humanity. For example, Kṛishṇa is held to be an avatar of Vishṇu.

Avesta ("Book of the Law") The fragmentary and often obscure sacred book of the Zoroastrians.

baptism The Christian rite of initiation, involving prayers and the application of water by immersion, pouring, or sprinkling.

Bhagavadgītā The oldest scripture created by the Hindu Bhāgavatas, who worshiped Kṛishṇa Vāsudeva, a poem of 18 cantos preserved in the Hindu epic known as the Mahābhārata.

bhakti A spirit in Hindu interpersonal relations characterized by warm devotion and affectionate sharing.

bodhisattva-gaṇas In Buddhism, "congregations of future Buddhas" that grew up around certain stūpas. These loosely organized communities of monks and lay people played a significant role in the development of Buddhism.

Book of the Dead Sacred Egyptian text consisting of prayers written on papyrus scrolls, dating from the later periods of Egyptian history.

Brahman In the upanishads, the all-controlling power and single unifying essence of the universe.

brāhman The priestly caste, highest of Hindu society's four varṇas. Originally responsible for performing the Vedic sacrifices, the brāhmans later became teachers and performers of rituals.

brāhmaṇa A document belonging to the second phase of the historical development of Vedic scriptures, recording comments on the collection of hymns.

brahmasūtras A series of aphoristic Hindu texts on Brahman, the earliest of which dates from around 200 C.E.

Brāhmo Samāj ("Society of Believers in Brahman") A nineteenth-century organization for the reform of Hinduism by purging it of polytheism and social discrimination on the basis of caste, founded by Ram Mohan Roy in 1828. It was a powerful influence for change for nearly a century.

Buddha ("Awakened One") Name given to Śākyamuni, Gautama Siddhārtha, a spiritual master of the fifth century B.C.E. in northeastern India. The name came to be applied to all humans believed to have experienced and rediscovered the eternal truth (Dharma).

Buddha nature Late Buddhist doctrine that all sentient beings have within them something of the Buddha, inherently pure but apparently in an obscured and tainted state. Enlightenment lies in removing the taints, often through meditation and other ascetic techniques, to allow this inherently pure nature to shine forth. Characteristic especially of Chan (Zen) Buddhism.

buddhi In the traditional Hindu analysis of the psyche, a mental faculty that confers on an individual a personal self-consciousness and an intellectual ability to ponder information, make decisions, and formulate commands.

Cakravartin ("Turner of the Wheel") In Buddhism, a great, universal ruler.

caliph Any legitimate successor of Muḥammad; term derived from *khalīfa*.

Chan Any of several Buddhist sects emphasizing meditation, well known for their use of riddles, paradox, humor, and the rejection of any explicit philosophical system. Chan appealed especially to an urban elite. Known as *Zen* in Japan.

Chenyan East Asian Vajrayāna school that emphasized symbolic representation, the use of maṇḍalas, and the realization of the indestructible and immutable aspect of the enlightened mind. Known as *Shingon* in Japan.

Christendom An ideal of governance linking temporal and spiritual or ecclesiastical power in Europe following the reign of Charlemagne.

civil service examinations Long and difficult tests in the Confucian classics, first instituted in the Han dynasty, used to determine opportunities for social standing and economic prosperity in the Confucian state. They were required for literati status and a position in the government bureaucracy and sought to institutionalize the Confucian rule of merit.

coffin texts Sacred Egyptian texts consisting of inscriptions on the inner and outer lids of the coffins of the wealthy. The texts discuss the cult of the dead, temple rites, and religious myths.

Conservative Judaism One of the major forms of American Judaism today, midway between Reform and Orthodox Judaism with respect to the preservation of traditional Jewish law.

cosmogonic myths Myths accounting for the coming into being of the world or the universe.

cosmogony An account of the creation or origin of the universe.

cosmology An account of the character of the universe as a totality, often seeking to explain the processes of nature and the relationships among the various parts of the universe.

covenant A contract or treaty; in Judaism, a series of solemn agreements between the God of Israel and a number of founders of the nation, principally Abraham, Moses, and David.

dakhma Zoroastrian "tower of silence" built of stone with a circular well, in which corpses are exposed to the sun and to vultures.

Dao ("Way") The true, proper, and natural course of events. In Confucianism, the true way of life embodied in the teachings of Confucius; in Daoism, ultimate reality as well as the proper natural way of life humans must follow.

Dark Learning Philosophical side of Daoism popular among the literati during the period of Chinese disunity that emphasized the mysterious "dark" life of the cosmos and the immanent and transcendent aspects of the ultimate Dao.

de Sacred personal force, a kind of charisma or power by which some leaders attract devoted followers. Among Confucians, virtue, or the power of moral example; among Daoists, the mysterious power of the Dao.

deva Any deity of Hindu polytheism, conceived of as a radiant being dwelling in the sky, in the atmosphere, or on earth.

dharma In post-Vedic thinking, the cosmic principle of right behavior, expressed in codes of religious law. One's dharma is one's duty, the pattern of actions prescribed by sacred codes.

Dharma In Buddhist teaching, the eternal truth about reality. Over the centuries, Dharma came to encompass the principal doctrines of the three main schools of Buddhism.

dharmaśāstras Scriptures that record Hindu religious law in verse form, largely replacing the dharmasūtras.

dharmasūtras Prose works discussing Hindu social morality that began appearing in the fifth century B.C.E.

Diaspora (Greek, "dispersion") Jews living outside the land of Israel. Since the time of the Roman Empire, a majority of Jews in the world have lived in the Diaspora.

Digambaras The stricter party of the Jain religion whose "sky-clad" ascetics practiced nudity as part of their spiritual path.

divination Seeking to know about the divine or spirit realm, particularly with respect to present and future actions.

Dreaming In Aboriginal Australian religions, the time of the foundation of the world as recounted in myths; an original creative period when the primordial ancestors wandered the earth. Also known as the *Dream Time.*

druid ("very wise") A member of an ancient organized priesthood in ancient Gaul, Britain, or Ireland who performed elaborate ceremonies honoring many gods. The druids are said to have prophesied through their sacrifices and acted as judges. They later appeared in Irish and Welsh sagas and Christian legends as magicians and wizards.

Durgā In Hindu Śaivite mythology, a favorite personal form of the *śākti* (female aspect) of Śiva. Durgā is known particularly for having destroyed a demon named Mahisha.

ecumenism The movement to reunite Christian churches (from the Greek word for "world"), begun in the late nineteenth century when Christian missionaries from the United States and Great Britain sought to foster unity in overseas missions.

emergence Mythical account of the origin of human life. In Neoplatonic thought, the world emerged out of the divine; in some Native American myths, the first people emerged from subterranean dwellings. Emergence myths reflect the order or shape of this world.

enlightenment Freedom from ignorance; perceiving the ultimate truth about the nature of reality—the highest goal of many Daoist, Buddhist, and Hindu sects. Typically conceived of as a life devoid of selfishness and egocentrism and often described as a combination of a tranquil mind, deep insight, and action for the benefit of others.

Epic of Creation A Mesopotamian poem of the second millennium B.C.E. describing how the young god Marduk and his companions succeeded in vanquishing the forces of chaos before the formation of the world.

Epic of Gilgamesh A Babylonian poem from around 2000 B.C.E. that describes the haughty and harsh King Gilgamesh and the wild man Enkidu, fashioned by the gods to save the king's subjects. The epic focuses on the themes of destiny, immortality, and the quest for immortality.

Eucharist (Greek, "Thanksgiving") Name given to the meal and ceremony commemorating Jesus's Last Supper; also known as *Holy Communion.*

evolutionist theory The hypothesis, based on analogies with biological processes, that contemporary cultures could be placed on a continuum from simple to complex, primitive to modern. Simple societies and religions were thought to offer a window on the earliest societal and religious forms.

exclusivist sects Buddhist denominations that flourished in the Tang dynasty and thereafter became the dominant forms of Buddhism in China. The Pure Land schools offered a simple way to salvation that appealed especially to the laity; it postponed enlightenment *(nirvāṇa)* to the afterlife. Chan (Zen) emphasized an austere life dedicated to meditation within a monastery and enlightenment in this life.

excommunication Banishment from the church.

Fāṭimids A dynasty of Shīʿites and Ismaʿīlīs that ruled Egypt, founded Cairo in 969, and established an Islamic civilization that lasted until 1171.

fiqh ("jurisprudence") Science that deals with observance of Islamic religious law on the ritual, social, and theological levels.

Five Pillars The fundamental tenets or requirements of Islam: *shahāda,* affirmation of the one God; *ṣalāt,* ritual prayer; *ṣawm,* fasting; *zakāt,* almsgiving; and *ḥajj,* pilgrimage to Mecca.

fundamentalism A Christian movement in the United States in reaction to biblical criticism in the nineteenth century. Leaders sought to discredit the critics by laying down the "fundamentals" of the faith—the tenets that must undergird all Christian thought and practice.

gāthās Hymns attributed to Zoroaster, forming the oldest part of the Avesta.

gender roles Assignments of purportedly appropriate actions, feelings, and accomplishments depending on one's sex. These assignments differ among religions and cultures and are instilled in various, usually subtle ways.

Gnosticism A movement started in the second century C.E. in which groups of Christians claimed special knowledge (*gnosis* in Greek) of divine revelation.

Gopāla ("Cowherd") Epithet applied to the young and rambunctious Kṛishṇa, who spent his childhood among rural cowherds to escape the malice of a hostile king, to differentiate him from the knightly Kṛishṇa of the Bhagavadgītā.

gospels ("good news") Stories of Jesus's life and work collected by followers and the message of Jesus's resurrection from the dead and its implications; also, the body of teaching about Jesus that his followers preached.

grace In Christian theology, unmerited generosity or beneficence shown by God to humans; divine mercy as opposed to divine justice.

gṛihyasūtras Hindu texts defining rites and procedures for domestic *(gṛihya)* rituals as well as the principles of social and religious practices in general.

gudwara ("gate of the guru") A Sikh temple or sanctuary housing a copy of the Adi Granth.

guru A Hindu spiritual teacher selected by an aspirant, deemed to be an expert in mystical disciplines and an effective guide to the life of introspection.

ḥajj ("pilgrimage") Pilgrimage to Mecca, which all Muslims must make at least once, if possible.

haoma A plant whose juice provides a potent drink used in ritual. See also *soma.*

Hasidism A Jewish religious revival movement begun in eastern Europe by Israel Baal Shem Tov around 1760. Early Hasidism stressed the importance of prayer and religious joy and sought to reduce the importance of study and intellect. Today Hasidism is the most tradition-oriented branch of modern Judaism.

hijra ("emigration") Muḥammad's flight from Mecca to Medina in 622.

Hou Ji God of millet among the Chinese Zhou people and the first ancestor of the Zhou ruling house. Myths told of his discovery of agriculture and his gift of this knowledge to humans.

householders People in the second of the Hindu āśramas, who work, marry, and raise a family.

Huayan A sixth-century Chinese philosophical school of Buddhism that emphasized the harmony and interrelatedness of all phenomena. Known as *Kegon* in Japan.

humanism A school of thought with a high esteem for the individual and an emphasis on human possibilities, achievements, and reasoning. Applied to Greek culture and to Renaissance and later European culture.

ijmāʿ ("consensus") The consensus of the Muslim community *(umma).*

imām ("who stands before, model") Leader of Muslim congregational prayers; also, head of a community or school of law; also a title of honor. For Shīʿites, a predestined individual who is descended from the prophet's family through his cousin ʿAli and whose religious authority is beyond reproach.

immortals *(xian)* Wizardlike saints of popular Daoism known for their eccentric behavior and superhuman powers. They were humans who by good deeds and the arts of alchemy and meditation, and sometimes luck, achieved immortality.

Indo-Europeans People from around the Caspian Sea area assumed to have migrated both east and west starting around 2000 B.C.E. Because they had mastered bronze-tipped weapon making and the horse and chariot, they conquered many local peoples. They thus influenced many cultures in Asia and Europe, playing important formative roles in India, Iran, Greece, Rome, and northern Europe.

Indra A major deity of the Ṛigvedic pantheon; the ancient war god of the Aryas and in India also a champion against powers that withhold rain.

Indus civilization The civilization flourishing in northwestern India near the Indus River before the Aryan invasion (pre-1700 B.C.E.). Renowned for their highly consistent and well-organized cities. Main sites include Harappā and Mohenjo-Dāro.

initiation A ritual that marks a transition between physical states, coupled with a change in social status. Often a time when the esoteric meaning of religious myths, rituals, and symbols is revealed.

Inquisition A Christian crusade to expunge heretical thought and to enforce religious conformity that began in Spain in the thirteenth century.

Izanagi With Izanami, one of the primordial parents in Shintō mythology. Their actions illustrate the dynamic tension characteristic of Japanese religiosity.

Izanami See *Izanagi.*

Jacob The grandson of Abraham and the third patriarchal ancestor of the Jewish people; also called *Israel.*

Jātakas Folkloric stories of acts that the Buddha supposedly performed in his previous lives, in which the Buddha appears as an animal, a human being, or a deity. Jātaka collections began appearing around the start of the Common Era.

jātis Castes; groups bound to a hereditary occupation in the traditional Hindu social order.

Jerusalem The capital city of the ancient kingdom and the modern state of Israel. The ancient temples were located there.

Jina ("Victor") Name given to Nataputta Vardhamana (c. 599–527 B.C.E.), who gave Jainism its present form, held to have victoriously crossed the river of life, overcoming human misery. From this title Jainism derives its name.

***jingū-ji* system** "Shrine-temple" system whereby in the classical period most Shintō shrines also enclosed a Buddhist temple and vice versa.

jīva Life, soul, all that is living. Jains hold that jīvas mingle with particles of karma to determine an individual's destiny and character; when the jīva is freed from karma, liberation occurs, and the soul rises to the zenith of the universe, remaining motionless and free from suffering forever.

justification The act of making just or righteous. Christians maintain that God alone can make humans just but argue about the role humans must play in the process.

Kabbalah ("Received Tradition") The tradition of Jewish mysticism, concerned with secret knowledge of the divine regions and the secret meanings of the Torah. The greatest work of Kabbalah is the Zohar (Spain, c. 1275 C.E.).

Kabir Sant poet (1440–1518), teacher of Sikhism's founder, Guru Nanak.

kachinas Hopi name for supernatural beings or deities. Sacred narratives refer to kachinas as primordial heroes who aid humans in hunting and agriculture. They are often impersonated by masked dancers.

kalām ("speech") In Islam, the word of God, extended to mean scholastic theology, which discusses questions of religion dialectically.

Kālī A goddess of mercurial and often violent disposition, representing the uncertainties of nature in an agricultural land; loosely integrated into Hinduism as a consort of Śiva.

kami Sacred spirits or deities believed to dwell in Shintō shrines.

karma ("action") A social or ritual act that is morally significant by virtue of being part of one's dharma or religious duty. Also, a dangerous or beneficent energy generated by the performance of such acts. One's karma will inevitably bring appropriate retribution.

karmic matter Particles of karma, thought by Jains to mix with the soul *(jīva)* to determine an individual's destiny and character.

Kegon See *Huayan*.

khalīfa ("successor") In the Qur'ān, Adam as God's viceroy on earth; by extension, Muḥammad as a human ideal. See also *caliph*.

Khalsa ("Pure") The militaristic wing of Sikhism, begun by Gobind Singh (1675–1708). Members pledge themselves to an austere code of conduct, to wear special symbols, and to protect the religion. All members take the name Singh, "lion."

Khārijites ("Seceders") Muslim sect that arose in opposition to ʿAli at the Battle of Siffan (657), known for a puritanical outlook and harsh treatment of religious error. Today known as the Ibadites.

Kokutai "National Essence," the name given by the Japanese National Scholars to the unity of political and religious structure; also interpreted to mean the unique character of "Japaneseness."

Krishṇa Vāsudeva The Supreme Lord of the Hindu Bhāgavatas.

kshatriyas Members of the Vedic second varṇa, or warrior class; later, members of any of various military castes within the second varṇa.

kufr Unbelief in God; connotes deliberate and active resistance to the truth in its Qur'ānic sense. Also interpreted as "ingratitude."

lamas Religious leaders in Tibetan Buddhism.

li Ritual, decorum, propriety; one of the building blocks of Confucius's thought and the key to achieving universal harmony. All life should be regulated by it. Externally, it brings about a smoothly working society; internally, it manifests itself in *ren*.

Li Principle, a key term in Neo-Confucianism, in which it stood for ultimate reality, immanent in all things. Mystical experience of Li was the basis of the sage's enlightenment.

liṅgam In the iconography of Śaivism, the short, round-topped pillar that is the principal emblem of Śiva. Vaguely in the form of the male organ, it suggests to worshipers the generative power of Śiva in the creation of the universe.

Long March The 6,000-mile retreat of the Chinese Communist guerrillas in the 1930s that became the principal "salvation history" for the Maoist movement. Many exemplary Communist martyrs were made during this march.

Mahābhārata A vast Hindu epic containing the Bhagavadgītā.

mahāpurusha ("great man") Name Buddhists applied to Buddha and an enlightened bodhisattva. Comes to be applied to any great man.

Mahāvira ("Great Hero") Name given to Nataputta Vardhamana (c. 599–527 B.C.E.), the twenty-fourth and last Tīrthaṃkara, or ford finder; first practitioner of ascetic nudity and organizer of Jainism.

Mahāyāna One of the three main early schools of Indian Buddhism, today found primarily in Japan, Korea, and China.

Mahdi In Islam, the messianic imām of the future.

manas In Hindu thought, the lower mind. As used in Vedic texts, it is thought to include aspects of both mind and emotion.

maṇḍala ("circle") In Buddhism, a circular symbol, often enclosed in a square. Buddhist stūpas were maṇḍalas. The maṇḍala was especially important in Vajrayāna Buddhism, where it signified the dwelling or palace of a pure being such as a Buddha.

Manichaeism Religion founded by Mani (c. 216–276 C.E.) that emphasized the dualism between the forces of light and darkness and combined elements of Zoroastrianism, Buddhism, and Christianity. It influenced the Christian Saint Augustine and the Albigensians in medieval southern France.

mantra A sacred sound; originally a hymn of the Vedas, in Hinduism it came to signify the sound, often a one- or two-syllable word, used as the focus of meditation. In Vajrayāna Buddhism, Buddhas and bodhisattvas were thought to have their own seed mantras, their manifestation in sound; meditation on a seed mantra could intensify the figure's characteristics in the mind.

martyr (Greek, "witness") A believer who died in defense of the faith, especially one of the early Christians who were victims of systematic persecution. Martyrs are remembered with reverence, and their tombs are regarded as places of special holiness.

masks Headpieces and costumes worn by masqueraders who through gestures, mime, and dance impersonate ancestors, spirits, or divinities. They are taken as visual metaphors representing the dynamic cosmos.

matsuri Ritual celebrations held at Shintō shrines by priests on a regular basis. Most matsuri are public and include prayers, blessings, and a meal.

May Seventh schools Schools of the Maoist period in China, named for the date (May 7, 1966) of the directive that established them, requiring that all students devote six months to classroom study and six months to purifying labor in the countryside each year.

māyā The power of creation and illusion in Hindu philosophy. In the teaching of Śaṅkara, a deluding agency of mysterious nature that causes the human consciousness to perceive a universe of many persons and things, whereas the unity of all is the revealed truth.

Messiah ("Anointed One") Title of the expected redeemer who will arrive at the end of days and release humanity in general and the Jews in particular from the sorrows of their present existence. Came to be applied to Jesus.

miko Japanese female shamans who by entering a trance are able to be possessed by kami and other spiritual beings. When in the trance, their words are taken to be those of the kami.

Mishnah A compilation of rabbinic teaching (c. 200 C.E.), mostly legal, that forms the earliest part of the Talmud.

moksha Enlightenment, release, liberation, from the retributions ordinarily entailed by one's past deeds and thus from the necessity of further deaths and rebirths in the world. For most Hindus such liberation is the highest blessedness, salvation itself.

Moses The political and religious founder of the Israelite nation. According to tradition, Moses led the people of Israel during their struggle to escape from slavery in Egypt; when the liberated people had marched to Mount Sinai, Moses delivered to them the commandments of their God (the Torah) and initiated them into their national covenant with him.

Muḥammad ("Praised") Prophet and founder of the Islamic faith (c. 570–632), from the Ḥāshim clan of the Quraysh tribe of Mecca, through whom God transmitted his revelation to humanity, the Qur'ān.

Muslim One who surrenders to the will of Allāh and accepts his final revelation, the Qur'ān, and his final prophet, Muḥammad.

Muʿtazilites A rationalistic school of theology or *kalām* that used Hellenistic philosophy, prized dialectical argument, and asserted free will.

mystery religions Greek religious groups associated with Dionysus, Orpheus, and Demeter that conducted secret rites offering ecstasy to ordinary humans through eating, drinking, dancing, and sex.

Nanak Founder of Sikhism (1469–1539), who emphasized the unity between Islam and Hinduism and urged the contemplation of God and the singing of hymns.

National Scholars A group of intellectuals who in the late medieval period revived Japanese classical learning and instituted a Shintō renewal.

naturalness The proper way of life in Daoism. To be in harmony with the Dao, one had to learn to act spontaneously as a straightforward reflection of the Dao rather than as motivated by the promise of personal gain. See also *wu-wei*.

Nembutsu See *Nienfo*.

Nichiren A Japanese Tendai monk (1222–1282) whose name is also applied to the "Lotus lineage" school of Buddhism he founded. Militaristic and nationalistic, Nichiren emphasized devotion, the authority of the Lotus Sūtra, and the recitation of a sacred formula.

Nienfo The chant *"Namo Omito Fo"* ("Hail to the Buddha Amitābha") used in Pure Land Buddhism. Many lay people have thought it the only practice necessary to ensure rebirth in the Pure Land of Amitābha, just short of nirvāṇa. Known as *Nembutsu* in Japan.

nirvāṇa Enlightenment (literally, blowing out). The state gained by Buddha and by any being who is able to extinguish all attachments and defilements. Though gained in and through meditation, affects all of one's life. Said to be indescribable, though wonderful. At death, one who has gained nirvāṇa does not become reborn.

original sin The idea that human nature is indelibly tainted with the tendency to sin. Paul, an early Christian, held that humans are marked from birth by a sinful disposition inherited from Adam, the only cure for which is Jesus's sacrificial death.

Orthodox Judaism One of the major forms of American Judaism today, noted for its loyalty to traditional Jewish law and its resistance to modernization.

Osiris Egyptian agricultural deity believed to rule over the underworld and associated with the annual floodwaters, thought to bestow immortality and soil fertility.

outcastes In the Hindu social system, the caste not included in the four main varṇas. Its members handled polluting things, such as corpses and dirt.

parables Stories taken from everyday life intended to raise awareness and provoke thought. Jesus used many parables in his teaching.

Parousia Jesus's return at the end of the world; also known as the *Second Coming*.

Parsis Zoroastrians now living in India, mostly in the Bombay area.

Pārśva An early Jain teacher (872–772 B.C.E.) held to be the twenty-third Tīrthaṃkara, or ford finder.

Passover The annual celebration by Jews of their ancestors' escape from slavery in Egypt. Its distinctive features are the eating of unleavened bread *(matzah)* for a week and the elaborate and symbolic Seder meal.

penance The act of repenting for sins; part of a Christian rite whereby a sinner admits sinfulness, repents, confesses to a priest, performs some action to demonstrate reform (special prayers or an act of charity), and is absolved of the sin by the priest. This penitential system arose to permit readmission to the church of Christians who had weakened under persecution during the third century.

pietism A seventeenth-century religious movement in reaction to Lutheran orthodoxy that emphasized emotional experience, Bible study, and intense personal prayer.

polytheism The belief in or worship of many gods, typical of Egyptian, Vedic, Hindu, Greek, Native American, and other religious systems. Often these gods are considered to have powers over particular aspects of reality and to reflect a deeper underlying principle or essence.

prāṇa ("breath") The internal current of air that Hindus believe to be the fundamental animating principle of a living being.

pratītya samutpāda The doctrine of interdependent origination taught by the Buddha, holding that all elements of reality arise in conjunction with one another.

primordial beings Mythic creatures who came into being at the beginning of creation. Often ambiguous in shape, they have the power to change forms and to defy other rules of time and space that are part of the natural order that became established after them.

prophets People believed to carry messages between God and the people of Israel. Early prophets promoted monotheism; some were also important advocates of social justice.

pūjā A post-Vedic style of ritual, adapted to the worship of devas who have consented to dwell on earth in images or other material objects.

Pure Land Any of several Buddhist sects emphasizing faith and devotion to the Buddha Amitābha, leading to rebirth in his other-worldly paradise, the Pure Land. Begun in India, Pure Land became influential in rural China, where it centered on invoking the name of Amitābha (see *Nienfo*).

Purgatory In Roman Catholicism, a middle region of the cosmos, between heaven and hell, to which most humans go for purgation of sins before entering heaven.

pyramid texts Sacred Egyptian texts consisting of inscriptions on the walls of the pyramids built for certain pharaohs. The texts discuss funerary rites and details of the ruler's life in the hereafter.

Qur'ān ("Recitation") The holy scripture of Islam, revealed to humanity by Allāh through Muḥammad.

rabbi A master of Oral Torah, the great unwritten tradition of Judaism. After the destruction of the Second Temple in the first century C.E., Judaism came increasingly under the leadership of rabbis, respected for the breadth of their religious learning.

rājanyas Vedic name for the kshatriyas, or members of the warrior caste, who came to be the rulers of India.

Rāmāyana An epic poem composed by Valmiki around the fourth century B.C.E. about the career of Rāmacandra of Ayodhya. Any book on that theme can be called a Rāmāyana, however. One such is the great Hindi poem composed in the decade following 1574 C.E. by Tulsi Dās, which he titled the *Rāmcaritmānas* ("Pool of the Deeds of Rāma").

Reform Judaism An effort to modernize Jewish thought and practice that originated in Europe around 1800. Characterized by relative neglect of traditional Jewish law, it is one of the major forms of American Judaism today.

ren Humaneness, a basic building block of Confucius's thought; for a Confucian gentleman *(zhunzi),* love for humanity and a sense of obligation toward society, exercised primarily through *li.*

Ṛigveda The largest and ritually most important of the four Vedas, containing 1,028 hymns used in the Aryas' sacrificial rituals.

ṛita In the cosmology of the Vedas, the impersonal principle of righteousness and harmony that is operative in both the actions of virtuous human beings and the regularity of the movements of natural bodies.

rite of passage A ritual that effects a change in social status, as from youth to adulthood. Generally has three stages: separation from society, a transition or liminal phase, and reintegration into society as a member with a new status. Often plays on the theme of death and rebirth.

sacrifice The act of making an offering to a deity or spiritual being, often through the death of a victim on behalf of the sacrificers. In primal religions, sacrifice is thought to release the power of life force from the victim.

sage The ideal embodiment of the Dao. In old Confucianism, an impossibly high status reached by only a few ancient kings and other worthies. In classical Daoism, the perfect example of a person living naturally, in harmony with the Dao. In popular Daoism, the equivalent of an immortal *(xian),* a practitioner of alchemy and discoverer of immortality. Among Neo-Confucians, a realizable ideal that tended to replace the *zhunzi* as a goal of religious practice.

Śaivas Post-Vedic Hindu monotheists who believe that Śiva is the one Lord of the Universe.

Śāktas Hindus whose worship is directed toward one of the personifications of Śiva's *śākti,* or feminine aspect.

śākti The feminine aspect of Śiva, which created and controls the world, often personified as a mythical consort of Śiva, such as Durgā or Kālī.

samādhi A condition of intense mental concentration without awareness of thoughts or sensations, the culminating trance in Hinduism or Buddhism in which the saving insight is revealed.

Sāmaveda One of the four Vedas, a collection of songs of the sāmans, the cantors of Aryan sacrificial ceremonies, taken primarily from the ninth book of the Ṛigveda.

saṃsāra The cyclical world, characterized by the cycle of birth, life, death, and rebirth.

saṃskāras Hindu rites of the round of life. These ceremonies, usually performed in the home, mark important transitions among members of the three highest castes, including birth, initiation, marriage, and death.

sanctification The act of making holy, regarded by Christians as a divine act involving humans following justification.

sandhyās Personal Hindu meditations performed at daily solar transitions such as dawn, noon, and dusk.

Saṅgha ("Group") The order of Buddhist monks; the Buddhist clergy collectively.

sannyāsa In Hinduism, renunciation of desires or of worldly gains or worldly life itself. In this last sense, *sannyāsa* can entail a ritual departure from home and entry into the fourth āśrama of life, that of the *sannyāsī.*

sannyāsī A Hindu who has renounced worldly life.

Sant A Hindu devotional movement that influenced early Sikhism.

satī ("true one") A widow who carries out the medieval Hindu rite of immolating herself on the funeral pyre of her deceased husband; also, the practice of this rite.

satyāgraha ("holding on to truth") Mahātma Gāndhī's principle for the nonviolent attainment of social justice.

secondary divinities In African religions, beings that serve the Supreme Being as messengers and intermediaries, appealed to for both personal welfare and the group's protection. They are sometimes portrayed as the children of God, sometimes as refractions of God.

self-strengthening A nineteenth-century theory promoted by

Confucian bureaucrats that sought to borrow Western technology without Western cultural or religious values. Technology would strengthen China to resist foreign values.

shahāda The fundamental creed of Islam, the first and most important of the Five Pillars: "There is no god but God, and Muḥammad is his apostle."

shaman A priest-doctor who uses religious and magical techniques to cure the sick and reveal the hidden. Often uses trance-inducing techniques to "travel" to the spirit world to seek guidance in human affairs. Also called *medicine man.*

sharī'a ("to prescribe") The canonical laws of Islam as put forth in the Qur'ān, the sunna, and the opinions of the orthodox ʿulamā' of a recognized school of law.

shaykh ("elder") A venerable older man of authority; also used to refer to a superior of a Ṣūfī order.

Shīʿism A branch of Islam comprised of many groups who regard religious authority to emanate from the family of Muḥammad through his cousin ʿAli. The largest group, the Twelvers, so called for their reverence for 12 imāms, is located mainly in Iran. Zaydites, called Fivers, live mainly in Yemen. Ismāʿīlīs, known as Seveners, live mainly in India. The name *Shīʿite* is derived from *Shīʿa ʿAli,* "Party of ʿAli."

Shingon See *Chenyan* and *Vajrayāna.*

shirk ("association") In Islam, the ascription of partners of God; hence, polytheism.

siddha A sage in Hinduism or Vajrayāna Buddhism, often believed to be endowed with *siddhis,* or supernormal powers, such as levitation.

Śiva A high deity in post-Vedic Hinduism. To some polytheists he was the special god of destruction, but to montheists he became the one Lord of the Universe.

smṛiti ("remembered") A Hindu scripture that is deemed to be of second rank because of its post-Vedic human authorship and yet of much authority because it is believed reliably to reexpress the message of the Vedas.

soma An exhilarating drink poured as a libation in Vedic sacrifices and drunk by the priestly sacrificers. See also *haoma.*

śramana Any member of a broad class of ascetics in early India, characterized by the practice of extreme austerity and self-mortification.

śrauta An outdoor sacrificial ritual of the Aryas, performed by one, four, or sometimes a great number of priests and accompanied by the hymns of the Ṛigveda.

Śrauta Sūtras Easily memorized aphoristic prose outlines of the performance of the śrauta sacrifices that appeared after 600 B.C.E.

stūpa A burial mound, often said to contain some bodily relic of the Buddha.

śūdras The fourth and lowest varṇa, containing castes whose hereditary work is manual but not grossly defiling.

Ṣūfī A follower of the mystic way in Islam.

Ṣūfism Mystical Islam.

sun dance The central religious ceremony of the Native American Plains tribes, a dance rite in which warriors attach themselves to a central pole by long ropes and skewers through the muscles of their chests; they dance until the skewers tear through their flesh. The sun dance is understood as a sacrifice to the Great Spirit.

sunna ("tradition") In Islam, the customary way of behavior, especially that of the prophet Muḥammad.

Sunnis The predominant body of orthodox Muslims, who accept the legitimacy of the first four caliphs. The name derives from *sunna,* "tradition."

sūtra ("stitch") Short aphoristic Hindu text that states or summarizes a key doctrine or ritual act in easily memorizable form.

Svetāmbaras The more liberal ("white-clad") party of Jain ascetics.

Tai Ping Rebellion Mid-nineteenth-century movement that combined popular Daoist, folk religious, and Christian elements in an attempt to build a utopian, theocratic state in place of the faltering Qing (Manchu) dynasty. The rebellion was finally put down with Western help after millions of deaths.

Talmud A voluminous collection of ancient rabbinic teaching, loosely organized as a commentary on sections of the Mishnah. The Jerusalem or Palestinian Talmud (c. 425 C.E.) is of lesser status than the Babylonian Talmud (sixth century C.E.); the latter has served as the basis of Jewish law since the early Middle Ages.

Tāntrism A marginal Hindu tradition, taught in scriptures called *tāntras,* that holds the supreme deity to be feminine and insists that liberation *(moksha)* can be won through erotic practices. Influenced Buddhist Vajrayāna.

Tendai Buddhist sect that dominated religious life in Japan throughout the classical period. The founders of the medieval Pure Land, True Pure Land, and Nichiren sects began their religious careers as Tendai monks. Known as *Tiantai* in China.

Theravāda One of the three main early schools of Indian Buddhism, today found primarily in southern Asia. Also called *Hīnayāna Buddhism.*

Tian ("Heaven") Chief deity of the Zhou, to whom only kings (and later, emperors) could sacrifice. Later taken up by Confucianism as an impersonal guardian of the moral order, especially the Mandate of Heaven.

Tiantai See *Tendai.*

Tīrthaṃkaras ("ford finders") Jain saints who have found their way across to the other side of life and hence are liberated from the cycle of birth and death. Jains hold that Mahāvira, the founder of Jainism, was the twenty-fourth and last such ford finder.

Torah The Five Books of Moses, the first five books of the Hebrew Bible; also, the scroll on which these works are inscribed. Later the term was expanded to refer to the entire body of the rabbinic tradition as well.

totems Living creatures believed to share the life force of the deity with which they are associated.

trickster A mythic figure whose cunning and playful disobedience brings about changes in the shape of the world. A demiurge who introduces disorder into the cosmos. Often associated with divination.

Tripiṭaka The "Triple Basket" of the Buddhist sūtras, Vinaya, and Abhidharma texts that came to form the core of early Buddhist scripture. Each school of Buddhism developed its own authoritative Tripiṭaka and thus its own Dharma.

Twilight of the Gods In ancient German and Scandinavian mythology, the ever-present threat of the cataclysmic destruction of the universe. Would be foreshadowed by such events as civil wars, brothers warring with brothers, and outbreaks of incest. (In German, *Götterdämmerung.*)

ʿulamāʾ The learned scholars (clerics, lawyers) of the Muslim community *(umma).*

umma ("community") The greater body of Muslims, transcending political and ethnic barriers; the Islamic world.

universalist ("catholic") schools Buddhist denominations that flourished in the Tan dynasty, especially the Huayan and Tiantai schools. Though each was based on primary allegiance to a particular sūtra (for Tiantai this was the Lotus Sūtra), all tried to find an honored place for all Buddhist texts and practices.

upanishads ("secret teachings") A series of Hindu texts, the first appearing around 600 B.C.E., that focused on mystical knowledge. Of more than 100 written, 13 are held to be revealed scripture.

Vaishṇavas Post-Vedic Hindu monotheists who believe that Vishṇu is the one Lord of the Universe.

vaiśyas The third of the four varṇas and the lowest entitled to study the Veda; the modern varṇa includes merchants and clerical workers.

Vajrayāna One of the three main early schools of Indian Buddhism, today found primarily in Tibet and Mongolia. Also known as *Chenyan* or *Shingon.*

varṇa One of the four broad classes of traditional Hindu society, mentioned in late Vedas and used ever since to provide stratifications for placing the castes in a social hierarchy.

Varuṇa A major deity of the Ṛigvedic pantheon, the sky-dwelling guardian of *ṛita,* overseer of human moral behavior, and patron of kings.

Vedānta ("Veda's End") The upanishads and the teaching regarding Brahman that is essential to them.

Vedas The early religious literature of the Aryas, centered on four collections *(saṃhitās)* of ritual materials: Ṛigveda, Sāmaveda, Yajurveda, and Atharvaveda.

Vinaya The collection of Buddhist regulations that guided behavior in the monasteries.

Vishṇu Vedic deity associated with the sun, germination, growth, and the support of life. Considered the Lord of the Universe by certain believers (Vaishṇavas) in post-Vedic times.

vision quest Native American Plains ritual, an ordeal undertaken by an individual involving a physical trial of isolation, fasting, chanting, vigil, and exposure to the elements in order to contact the spirit world through a dream of a hallucinatory vision, often done under the direction of a shaman.

Vṛitra The demon fought and conquered by Indra in the Vedas.

Wahhābis A sect of radical Islamic reformers founded by Muḥammad ibn-ʿAbd-al-Wahhāb (1703–1792) in Arabia in the eighteenth century, violently opposed to pilgrimage to saints' tombs and the adoration of holy relics.

wu-wei ("nonaction") In classical Daoism, the proper way of desireless action characteristic of both the Dao and the sage. Opposed to *wei,* egotistic action typical of ordinary people. If one "acts with nonaction," one achieves naturalness and harmony with the Dao.

Yahweh The modern reconstruction of the name of God in the Torah. (Because for several centuries Jews avoided saying this name, the original pronunciation was forgotten.)

Yajurveda One of the four Vedas, consisting of short incantations *(yajuses)* used by the adhvaryus; about half the content is extracted from the Ṛigveda.

yang With *yin,* one of the dual principles or forces underlying all changes in both the natural and human realms, representing open and active power.

yin With *yang,* one of the dual principles or forces underlying all changes in both the natural and human realms, representing hidden and passive power.

yoga In Hinduism, any systematic discipline of meditation directed toward the realization of an arcane religious truth.

yogī A practitioner or master of yoga; a sage or wise man.

Yom Kippur The Jewish Day of Atonement, devoted to fasting and repentance; the holiest day of the Jewish year.

yoni In the iconography of Śaivism, the spouted plate, figuratively suggestive of the female organ, that surrounds the liṅgam. The yoni is understood to represent the *śākti* or feminine aspect of Śiva's divine nature.

Zarathustra Founder of Zoroastrianism. In Greek known as Zoroaster.

Zen See *Chan.*

zhunzi Superior man, true gentleman, true aristocrat—the attainable ideal of old Confucianism, conceived of especially as a government bureaucrat with high ideals of selfless service, in virtue less than the sage but similar in quality. One could not be born a *zhunzi* but could aspire to that status through study and conformity to *li.*

Zionism The modern Jewish movement of national revival. Zionism culminated in the reestablishment of the state of Israel in 1948.

BIBLIOGRAPHY

INTRODUCTION

Secondary Sources

Baird, Robert D. *Category Formation and the History of Religion.* The Hague, Netherlands: Mouton, 1971. An important study that defines religion as the ultimate human concern.

Barrett, David, ed. *World Christian Encyclopedia: A Comparative Study of Churches and Religions in the Modern World,* AD *1900–2000.* New York: Oxford University Press, 1982. Not limited to Christianity, this work is the most exhaustive demographic and statistical analysis ever done of religions (and unbelief too) around the globe.

Berger, Peter L. *The Sacred Canopy: Elements of a Sociological Theory of Religion.* Garden City, N.Y.: Doubleday, 1967. Religion as the overarching value structure of societies, as discussed by a leading American sociologist of religion.

Blasi, Anthony J., and Andrew J. Weigert. "Towards a Sociology of Religion: An Interpretative Sociology Approach," *Sociological Analysis* 37 (1976): 189–204. Levels of social analysis for the study of religion.

Durkheim, Emile. *The Elementary Forms of the Religious Life,* trans. Joseph Ward Swain. New York: Free Press, 1965. Originally published in France in 1912. Basic work by one of the founders of the sociology of religion.

Eliade, Mircea. *Rites and Symbols of Initiation: The Mysteries of Birth and Rebirth,* trans. Willard R. Trask. New York: Harper & Row, 1965. Symbolic interpretation of the ritual of rebirth as found in many cultures, by a well-known historian of religion.

———, ed. *The Encyclopedia of Religion* (16 vols.). New York: Macmillan, 1987. The first source to consult for the general study of religion.

Geertz, Clifford. "Religion as a Cultural System." In *Anthropological Approaches to the Study of Religion,* ed. M. Banton. London: Tavistock, 1963. Definition of religion as a cultural system of symbols, by a leading cultural anthropologist.

Larson, Gerald James. "Prolegomenon to a Theory of Religion." *Journal of the American Academy of Religion* 46 (1978): 443–463. Religion defined by stressing its analogical affinity to language.

Lessa, William A., and Evon Z. Vogt, eds. *Reader in Comparative Religion: An Anthropological Approach,* 4th ed. New York: Harper & Row, 1979. An excellent collection of essays both classical and recent on the anthropological approach to religious studies.

Melton, J. Gordon. *The Encyclopedia of American Religions,* 2nd ed. Detroit: Gale Research, 1987. A thorough descriptive taxonomy of American religions, listing over 1,300 denominations, sects, and cults and providing basic information on individual groups and the "families" they are related to. Supplementary volumes add hundreds of additional bodies.

Ray, Benjamin C. *African Religions: Symbol, Ritual, and Community.* Englewood Cliffs, N.J.: Prentice-Hall, 1976. Excellent survey of African traditional religions, arranged topically and based on case studies.

Sharpe, Eric J. *Understanding Religion.* New York: St. Martin's Press, 1983. A clear and concise introduction to the field.

Smart, Ninian. *The Phenomenon of Religion.* New York: Herder and Herder, 1973.

———. *The Science of Religion and the Sociology of Knowledge: Some Methodological Questions.* Princeton, N.J.: Princeton University Press, 1973. Two important examinations of methodological problems in the study of religion.

———, and Donald Wiebe. *Concept and Empathy: Essays in the Study of Religion.* New York: New York University Press, 1986. A helpful series of essays on the methodological problems in the study of religion.

Smith, Wilfred Cantwell. *The Meaning and End of Religion.* New York: Macmillan, 1962. Influential criticism of religions and isms as abstractions. Emphasis is on individual faith in relation to cumulative religious traditions.

Streng, Frederick J. "Studying Religion: Possibilities and Limitations of Different Definitions." *Journal of the American Academy of Religion* 40 (1972): 219–237.

———. *Understanding Religious Life,* 3rd ed. Belmont, Calif.: Wadsworth, 1985. Religion emphasized as the ultimate transformation, as seen from the perspective of the history of religion.

Turner, Victor W. *The Ritual Process: Structure and Anti-structure.* Ithaca, N.Y.: Cornell University Press, 1969. Important study of the structure of ritual processes and of the liminal phase of rituals.

Van Gennep, Arnold. *The Rites of Passage,* trans. Monika B. Vizedom and Gabrielle L. Caffee. Chicago: University of Chicago Press, 1976. Originally published in 1909 and still a very useful study.

Part One: Primal Religions and Religions of Antiquity

PRIMAL RELIGIONS

Secondary Sources

Brown, Diane DeGroat. *Umbanda: Religion and Politics in Urban Brazil,* ed. Conrad Phillip Kottack. Ann Arbor, Mich.: UMI Research Press, 1986. The best study available in English.

Douglas, Mary. *Natural Symbols: Exploration and Cosmology,* 2nd ed. London: Barrie & Jenkins, 1973. Reflections on the meaning of more technical ethnographic studies of primitive people.

Evans-Pritchard, Edward Evan. *Nuer Religion.* Oxford: Clarendon, 1956. A classic study of religion in a primitive society.

———. *Theories of Primitive Religion.* Oxford: Clarendon, 1965. A catalog of early theories of religion, focusing especially on the nineteenth century.

Griaule, Marcel, and Germaine Dieterlen. "The Dogon of the French Sudan." In *African Worlds: Studies in Social Values of African Peoples,* ed. Darylle Ford. London: Oxford University Press, 1954. In conjunction with the International African Institute. A brief summary of the findings of a French sociological field study.

Morton-Williams, Peter. "An Outline of the Cosmology and Cult Organization of the Oyo Yoruba." In *Peoples and Cultures of Africa: An Anthropological Reader.* Garden City, N.Y.: Doubleday, 1973. In conjunction with the American Museum of Natural History.

Turner, Harold W., ed. *Bibliography of New Religious Movements in Primal Societies,* vol. 1, *Africa.* Boston: Hall, 1978. Evidence of the enormous range of new movements in primal societies, indicating that primal religious movements are living and emerging.

EGYPT

Primary Sources

Allen, George, trans. *Book of the Dead, or Going Fourth by Day: Ideas of the Ancient Egyptians Concerning the Hereafter as Expressed in Their Own Terms,* ed. Elizabeth Blaisdell Hauser. Chicago: University of Chicago Press, 1974. A valuable collection of source materials.

Faulknot, R. O., trans. *The Ancient Egyptian Pyramid Texts.* Oxford: Clarendon Press, 1969. A careful translation.

Secondary Sources

Bleeker, C. J. *Egyptian Festivals: Enactments of Religious Renewal.* Leiden, Netherlands: Brill, 1967. Valuable study of ritual.

Breasted, James Henry. *The Dawn of Conscience.* New York: Scribner, 1933. An important, if slightly dated, study by a pioneer researcher.

Clark, R. T. Rundle. *Myth and Symbol in Ancient Egypt.* London: Thames & Hudson, 1959. A good introduction.

Frankfort, Henri. *Ancient Egyptian Religion: An Interpretation.* New York: Columbia University Press, 1948. A leading scholar's viewpoint.

Frankfort, Henri; Mrs. H. A. Frankfort; John A. Wilson; and Thorkild Jacobsen. *The Intellectual Adventure of Ancient Man: An Essay on Speculative Thought in the Middle East.* Chicago: University of Chicago Press, 1946. Available also in paperback under the title *Before Philosophy.* Baltimore: Penguin, 1949. Contains an excellent introduction to Egyptian religion by John A. Wilson.

Griffiths, J. Gwyn. *The Conflict of Horus and Seth: From Egyptian and Classical Sources.* Liverpool, England: Liverpool University Press, 1960. A detailed study of an important aspect of the Osiris myth.

Morenz, Siegfried. *Egyptian Religion,* trans. Ann E. Keep. Ithaca, N.Y.: Cornell University Press, 1973. A readable, scholarly, and comprehensive treatment.

Raymond, E. A. E. *The Mythical Origin of the Egyptian Temple.* Manchester, England: Manchester University Press, 1969. A readable and valuable account.

MESOPOTAMIA

Primary Sources

Mendelsohn, Isaac, trans. *Religions of the Ancient Near East: Sumero-Akkadian Ugaritic Epics.* New York: Liberal Arts Press, 1955. A useful collection of primary texts.

Sjöberg, Åke W., and Bergmanns, E., trans. *The Collection of the Sumerian Temple Hymns.* Locust Valley, N.Y.: Augustin, 1969. A collection of translations with commentary.

Secondary Sources

Frankfort, Henri; Mrs. H. A. Frankfort; John A. Wilson; and Thorkild Jacobsen. *The Intellectual Adventure of Ancient Man: An Essay on Speculative Thought in the Middle East.* Chicago: University of Chicago Press, 1946. Available also in paperback under the title *Before Philosophy*. Baltimore: Penguin, 1949. Contains an excellent introduction to Mesopotamia by Thorkild Jacobsen.

Jacobsen, Thorkild. *Toward the Image of Tammuz and Other Essays on Mesopotamian History and Culture,* ed. William L. Moran. Cambridge, Mass.: Harvard University Press, 1970. Interpretative material by one of the most respected scholars in this field.

———. *The Treasures of Darkness: A History of Mesopotamian Religion.* New Haven, Conn.: Yale University Press, 1976. A brilliant and readable interpretation.

Kramer, Samuel Noah. *From the Poetry of Sumer: Creation, Glorification, Adoration.* Berkeley: University of California Press, 1979. Translation of the poetry accompanied by a commentary by a well-known authority.

———. *Sumerian Mythology.* Philadelphia: American Philosophical Society, 1944. Introductory treatment with a careful commentary.

ZOROASTRIANISM

Primary Sources

Darmesteter, James, trans. *The Zend-Avesta, the Sacred Books of the East,* ed. F. Max Müller, vol. 3. New York: Scribner, 1898. A well-known scholarly work.

Henning, M., trans. *Avesta: The Hymns of Zarathustra.* Westport, Conn.: Hyperion Press, 1980. Originally published in 1952.

Secondary Sources

Boyce, M. *A History of Zoroastrianism* (2 vols.). Leiden, Netherlands: Brill, 1982. A detailed account of the development of the religion.

Duchesne-Guillemin, Jacques. "The Religion of Ancient Iran." In *Historia Religionum: Handbook for the History of Religion,* vol. 1, ed. C. Jouco Bleeker and Geo Widengren. Leiden, Netherlands: Brill, 1969. A useful introduction by a professor at the University of Liège.

———. *The Western Response to Zoroaster.* Westport, Conn.: Greenwood Press, 1973. A reprint of the 1958 edition, dealing with Israel and Greece as well as Iran.

Hinnells, John R. *Persian Mythology.* London: Hamlyn, 1973. Valuable for its illustrative materials.

Pangborn, C. R. *Zoroastrianism: A Beleagured Faith.* New York, Advent Books, 1983. The author raises the question of the contemporary status of the religion and its possibilities for survival.

Pavry, Jal D. *Zoroastrian Doctrines of a Future Life from Death to the Individual Judgment.* New York: Columbia University Press, 1929. Features careful scholarship and a useful bibliography.

Zaehner, R. C. *The Dawn and Twilight of Zoroastrianism.* New York: Putnam, 1961. A major historical study.

———. *The Teachings of the Magi.* London: Allen & Unwin, 1961. Text and commentary by the leading English-language scholar in the field.

———. *Zurvan: A Zoroastrian Dilemma.* London: Oxford University Press, 1955. A critical interpretation, including texts, of the later Zoroastrian teaching of the Sassanid period.

GREECE

Primary Source

Rice, David G., and John E. Stambaugh, eds. *Sources for the Study of Greek Religion.* Missoula, Mont.: Scholars Press, 1979. A wide range of materials from the Olympians to the mystery cults.

Secondary Sources

Grant, Frederick C., ed. *Hellenistic Religions: The Age of Syncretism.* New York: Liberal Arts Press, 1953. Materials (plus commentary) from the late period of Greek culture, including the traditional religion, cults, and philosophy.

Guthrie, William K. *The Greeks and Their Gods.* Boston: Beacon Press, 1950. Excellent, detailed, and critical study, ranging from Homer to Plato and Aristotle.

Harrison, Jane E. *Prolegomena to the Study of Greek Religion.* New York: Arno Press, 1975. Originally published in 1903. Insightful work, still valuable for its wealth of detail.

Murray, Gilbert. *Five Stages of Greek Religion.* Westport, Conn.: Greenwood Press, 1976. Originally published in 1925. An older work whose pattern of interpretation is still useful.

Nilsson, Martin P. *Greek Folk Religion.* New York: Columbia University Press, 1940. American Council of Learned Societies lectures by a leading scholar in the field.

———. *A History of Greek Religion,* trans. F. J. Fielden. Oxford: Clarendon Press, 1949. A standard work.

Otto, Walter F. *The Homeric Gods.* London: Thames & Hudson, 1979. Originally published in 1954. An insightful, comprehensive study.

ROME

Primary Source

Ferguson, John. *Greek and Roman Religion: A Source Book.* Park Ridge, N.J.: Noyes, 1980. A classic.

Secondary Sources

Bailey, Cyril. *Phases in the Religion of Ancient Rome.* Westport, Conn.: Greenwood Press, 1972. Originally published in 1932. A useful summary of many features of Roman religion, including magic, spirits, deities, mysticism, and syncretism.

Dumézil, Georges. *Archaic Roman Religion* (2 vols.), trans. Philip Krapp. Chicago: University of Chicago Press, 1971. A major study by a leading scholar.

Grenier, Albert. *Roman Spirit in Religion, Thought and Art,* trans. M. R. Dobie. New York: Cooper Square Press, 1970. Originally published in 1926. Changes in the religious ethos related to a wide range of cultural activities.

Kerenyi, Karoly. *The Religion of the Greeks and Romans.* Westport, Conn.: Greenwood Press, 1973. Originally published in 1962. The Greek and Roman worldviews compared and contrasted.

Ogilvie, R. M. *The Romans and Their Gods in the Age of Augustus.* London: Chatto & Windus, 1969. A comprehensive view of Roman religion at a crucial period of Roman history.

Wagenvoort, Hendrik. *Roman Dynamism: Studies in Ancient Roman Thought, Language, and Custom.* Westport, Conn.: Greenwood Press, 1976. Originally published in 1947. A creative philological-anthropological study.

THE SCANDINAVIANS

Secondary Sources

Branston, Brian. *Gods of the North.* New York: Vanguard, 1955. A readable and comprehensive interpretation.

MacCulloch, J. A. *The Celtic and Scandinavian Religions.* London: Hutchinson's University Library, 1948. An introductory work that summarizes the two traditions.

———. *Eddic Mythology,* ed. Louis Herbert Gray. New York: Cooper Square Press. Originally published in 1916. A useful overview.

Munch, Peter Andreas. *Norse Mythology: Legends of Gods and Heroes,* trans. Sigurd Bernhard Hustvedt. Detroit: Singing Tree Press, 1968. Originally published in 1926. Informative materials by a leading nineteenth-century scholar.

Turville-Petre, E. O. G. *Myth and Religion of the North: The Religion of Ancient Scandinavia.* New York: Holt, Rinehart & Winston, 1964. A description by a professor of ancient Icelandic at Oxford of the Scandinavian gods, heroes, cults, and temples.

PART TWO: RELIGIONS OF INDIA

HINDUISM

Primary Sources

Dimock, Edward, trans. *In Praise of Kṛishṇa: Songs from the Bengali.* Chicago: University of Chicago Press, 1981. Originally published in 1967.

Edgerton, Franklin, trans. *The Bhagavad Gītā.* Cambridge, Mass.: Harvard University Press, 1985. Literal and objective, useful for serious studies.

Embree, Ainslee T. *The Hindu Tradition.* New York: Random House, 1972. Brief selections from Hindu writings of all periods.

Doniger, Wendy, trans. *Hindu Myths: A Sourcebook.* New York: Penguin, 1975.

———, trans. *Ṛig Veda: An Anthology.* New York: Penguin, 1982.

———, and Brian K. Smith, trans. *The Laws of Manu.* New York: Penguin, 1992.

Goldman, Robert P., et al., trans. *The Rāmāyana of Vālmīki* (3 vols.). Princeton, N.J.: Princeton University Press, 1984–1992). A continuing translation of the critical edition.

Growse, F. S., trans. *Rāmāyana of Tulasidas.* Columbia, Mo.: South Asia Books, 1978. Originally published in 1877.

Hume, Robert E., trans. *The Thirteen Principal Upanishads,* rev. ed. New York: Oxford University Press, 1971. Originally published in 1931.

Secondary Sources

Adams, Charles J., ed. *Reader's Guide to the Great Religions,* 2nd rev. ed. New York: Free Press, 1977, pp. 106–155. Includes an annotated bibliography to 1977.

Carpenter, James Estlin. *Theism in Medieval India.* Livingston, N.J.: Orient Book Distributors, 1977. Originally published in 1921. Secondary survey, still useful for a general introduction to the field.

Davis, Richard. *Ritual in an Oscillating Universe: Worshiping Śiva in Medieval India.* Princeton, N.J.: Princeton University Press, 1991. Daily worship in a Śaiva temple and its meaning in Śaiva Siddhānta doctrine.

Dowson, John. *A Classical Dictionary of Hindu Mythology.* Columbia, Mo.: South Asia Books, 1987. Originally published in 1879.

Eliade, Mircea. *Yoga: Immortality and Freedom.* New York: Penguin, 1989. Originally published in 1958.

Farquhar, John Nicol. *An Outline of the Religious Literature of India.* Livingston, N.J.: Orient Book Distributors, 1984. Originally published in 1920. Still useful for identifying authors and documents and the traditions to which they belong.

Hiriyanna, M. *Essentials of Indian Philosophy.* Columbia, Mo.: South Asia Books, 1986. Originally published in 1949.

Keith, Arthur Berriedale. *The Religion and Philosophy of the Veda and Upanishads* (2 vols.). Livingston, N.J.: Orient Book Distributors, 1976. Originally published in 1925. A comprehensive manual, with evaluation of earlier interpretations.

Lingat, Robert. *The Classical Law of India.* Berkeley: University of California Press, 1973. Originally published in 1967. General introduction to Hindu codes and concepts.

Mitchell, George. *Hindu Temple: An Introduction to Its Meaning and Forms.* Chicago: University of Chicago Press, 1988. Originally published in 1978.

Pandey, Raj Bali. *Hindu Saṃskāras*. Columbia, Mo.: South Asia Books, 1987. Originally published in 1949. Provides information on the Hindu domestic rituals and their history.

Sivaraman, K. *Śaivism in Philosophical Perspective*. Livingston, N.J.: Orient Book Distributors, 1973. The doctrine of a major Śaivite monotheistic sect.

Whitehead, Henry. *Village Gods of South India*. Columbia, Mo.: South Asia Books, 1986. Originally published in 1921.

Zaehner, Richard C. *Hinduism*. New York: Oxford University Press, 1962. An introduction to the history of Hinduism, stressing selected periods and traditions.

Zimmer, Heinrich. *Myths and Symbols in Indian Art and Civilization*. Princeton, N.J.: Princeton University Press, 1971. Originally published in 1946.

JAINISM

Primary Sources

Ghoshal, Sarat C., ed. *The Sacred Books of the Jainas* (11 vols.). New York: AMS Press, 1917–1940.

Jacobi, Hermann, trans. *The Gaina Sūtras, the Sacred Books of the East*, ed. F. Max Müller. New York: Scribner, 1901, vol. 10. Originally published in 1884. The basic texts.

Secondary Sources

Casa, Carlo della. "Jainism." In *Historia Religionum: Handbook for the History of Religion*, ed. C. Jouco Bleeker and Geo Widengren, vol. 2. Leiden, Netherlands: Brill, 1971. An authoritative presentation by a professor at the University of Turin.

Jain, Muni Uttam Kamal. *Jaina Sects and Schools*. Delhi, India: Concept Publishing Company, 1975. A useful account.

Jaini, Padmanabh S. *The Jaina Path of Purification*. Berkeley: University of California Press, 1979. An excellent introduction that focuses on both the practice of the religion and its history.

Mehta, Mohan Lal. *Outlines of Jaina Philosophy: The Essentials of Jaina Ontology, Epistemology and Ethics*. Bangalore, India: Jain Mission Society, 1954. A careful presentation that contrasts Jainism with other religions and philosophies.

Roy, Ashim Kumar. *A History of the Jainas*. New Delhi: Gitanjali Publishing House, 1984. A useful recent study of Jain history that gives major attention to the different parties in the religion.

Schurbring, Walther. *The Doctrine of the Jainas*, trans. Walter Beurlen. Delhi: Banarsidass, 1962. A scholarly work by a professor at the University of Hamburg.

Stevenson, Mrs. Sinclair. *The Heart of Jainism*. London: Oxford University Press, 1915. A balanced view by a sympathetic Christian observer.

Zimmer, Heinrich. *Philosophies of India*, ed. Joseph Campbell. Chicago: University of Chicago Press, 1969. Originally published in 1951. The chapters on Jainism are especially valuable.

SIKHISM

Primary Source

Singh, Trilochan; Bhai Judh Singh; Kapur Singh; Bawa Harkishen Singh; and Khushwant Singh, eds. *Selections from the Sacred Writings of the Sikhs*, rev. George S. Fraser. London: Allen & Unwin, 1960. A useful collection of the basic documents.

Secondary Sources

Cole, W. Owen. *The Guru in Sikhism*. London: Darton, Longman & Todd, 1982. A careful, definitive study of the role of the succession of Sikh leader-teachers, well written and clear.

———, and Piara Singh Sambhi. *The Sikhs: Their Religious Beliefs and Practices*. London: Routledge & Kegan Paul, 1978. A useful, highly readable presentation by a lecturer at Leeds Polytechnic and the president of the Leeds Gudwara.

Khushwant, K. S. *A History of the Sikhs* (2 vols.). Princeton, N.J.: Princeton University Press, 1963, 1966. A major reference work by an authority in the field.

———. "Sikhism." In *Encyclopaedia Britannica*, 15th ed., vol. 16. A brief, well-organized account.

———. *The Sikhs Today*. Columbia, Mo.: South Asia Books, 1976. A sympathetic treatment of the faith by a member who brings a critical insight into his heritage.

McLeod, W. H. *Early Sikh Tradition: A Study of the Janam-Sakhis*. Oxford: Clarendon Press, 1980. An important and skillful study set in the context of the history of religions.

———. *The Evolution of the Sikh Community: Five Essays*. Oxford: Oxford University Press, 1976. A valuable and illuminating appraisal of the social dimension of Sikhism.

———. *Guru Nanak and the Sikh Religion*. London: Oxford University Press, 1969. A critical delineation of the founder's character and role.

PART THREE: BUDDHISM

Primary Sources

Beyer, Stephan, trans. *The Buddhist Experience: Sources and Interpretations*. Encino, Calif.: Dickinson, 1974. An anthology of texts from a wide variety of Buddhist traditions.

Cowell, E. B.; F. Max Müller; and Takakusa Junjirō, trans. *Buddhist Mahāyāna Texts*. New York: Dover, 1969. A collection that contains three basic texts (sūtras) of the Buddhist Pure Land tradition.

Davids, T. W. Rhys, trans. *Buddhist Sūtras*. New York: Dover, 1969. An old but still useful collection drawn from the *Sutta Pitaka* of the Pali Tripiṭaka. If only one text or set of texts can be read, this collection would be an appropriate choice.

Evans-Wentz, W. Y., trans. *Tibet's Great Yogī Milarepa,* 2nd ed. London: Oxford University Press, 1951. A fascinating hagiography that relates the life of a Tibetan yogī famed for his magic powers and his attainment as a living Buddha.

Freemantle, Francesca, and Chogyam Trungpa, trans. *The Tibetan Book of the Dead.* Berkeley, Calif.: Shambala Press, 1975. A distinctive presentation of the supposed transition from the moment of dying to the point of enlightenment or rebirth.

Hurwitz, Leon, trans. *Sūtra of the Lotus Blossom of the Fine Dharma.* New York: Columbia University Press, 1976. A rich and highly imaginative text important to East Asian Buddhism, particularly the Tiantai (Tendai) school of China and Japan and the Nichiren school and its offshoots in modern Japan.

Khoroche, Peter, trans. *Once the Buddha Was a Monkey: Arya Sura's Jatakamala.* Chicago: University of Chicago Press, 1989. A fine rendition of a highly literary text that recounts 34 stories from the previous lives of the Buddha.

Matics, Marion, trans. *Santideva's Entering the Path of Enlightenment.* New York: Macmillan, 1970. An influential devotional poem that represents the Indian Madhyamika tradition founded by Nāgārjuna.

Reynolds, Frank E., and Mani B. Reynolds, trans. *Three Worlds According to King Ruang.* Berkeley, Calif.: Lancaster & Miller, 1981. A Thai Buddhist treatise on cosmology and ethics that presents an important Theravāda perspective in which the philosophical and mythicosymbolic aspects of the tradition are joined.

Strong, John. *The Legend of King Aśoka: A Study and Translation of the Aśokavadana.* Princeton, N.J.: Princeton University Press, 1983. A superb interpretation and rendition of a popular hagiographic account that deals with Buddhist kingship and lay ideals.

Thurman, Robert, trans. *The Holy Teaching of Vimalakīrti.* College Park: Pennsylvania State University Press, 1976. An early Mahāyāna text that highlights the insight and skill of a lay bodhisattva.

Yampolsky, Philip B., trans. *The Platform Sūtra of the Sixth Patriarch.* New York: Columbia University Press, 1967. A basic text of Chan Buddhism that purports to recount the life and a famous sermon of the Chinese master Hui-neng (638–713).

Secondary Sources

Beyer, Stephan. *The Cult of Tārā: Magic and Ritual in Tibet.* Berkeley: University of California Press, 1973. A difficult book, but still unequaled as a study of Buddhist practice in Tibet.

Collins, Steven. *Selfless Persons: Imagery and Thought in Theravāda Buddhism.* Cambridge: Cambridge University Press, 1982. By far the best available introduction to Theravāda doctrine.

Foucher, Alfred. *The Life of the Buddha According to the Ancient Texts and Monuments of India,* trans. Simone Boas. Middletown, Conn.: Wesleyan University Press, 1963. An excellent reconstruction of the legend of the Buddha at the beginning of the Common Era.

Hardacre, Helen, and Alan Sponburg, eds. *Maitreya, the Future Buddha.* New York: Cambridge University Press, 1988. An intriguing collection of essays on Maitreya in different Buddhist cultures from India to Japan.

Holt, John Clifford. *The Buddha in the Crown: Avalokiteśvara in the Buddhist Tradition of Śrī Lanka.* New York: Oxford University Press, 1991. A very sophisticated account of aspects of Sinhalese Buddhism that involve processes of assimilation and change.

Kasulis, Thomas. *Zen Action/Zen Person.* Honolulu: University of Hawaii Press, 1985. Of the many books on Zen Buddhism, this one is unmatched for clarity and precision.

La Fleur, William. *The Karma of Words: Buddhism and the Literary Arts in Medieval Japan.* Berkeley: University of California Press, 1983. An important study of the pervasiveness of Buddhism in medieval Japanese culture.

Kitagawa, Joseph, and Mark Cummings, eds. *Buddhism in Asian History.* New York: Macmillan, 1989. An excellent, well-organized collection of essays that is appropriate for readers interested in further information on various aspects of Buddhism.

Reynolds, Frank E., et al. "Buddhism." In *Encyclopaedia Britannica,* 15th ed., vol. 15, pp. 263–305. An overview providing an advanced account of various Buddhist schools, doctrines, and literature.

Snellgrove, David, ed. *The Image of the Buddha.* London: Serindia Publications/UNESCO, 1978. A broad-ranging, well-illustrated survey of Buddhist art and iconography that covers all of the major Asian traditions.

Streng, Fredrick. *Emptiness: A Study of Religious Meaning.* Nashville, Tenn.: Abingdon Press, 1967. This study remains the most interesting discussion of the philosophy of Nāgārjuna.

Teiser, Stephen. *The Ghost Festival in Medieval China.* Princeton, N.J.: Princeton University Press, 1988. A comprehensive interpretation of a popular festival that has played a central role in the history of Buddhism in China.

Williams, Paul. *Mahāyāna Buddhism: The Doctrinal Foundations.* London: Routledge & Kegan Paul, 1989. A readable introduction to a very difficult and complicated subject.

PART FOUR: RELIGIONS OF CHINA AND JAPAN

CHINA

Primary Sources

Waley, Arthur, trans. *The Analects of Confucius.* New York: Random House, 1938. Extensive introduction and notes emphasizing the historical context of Confucius's thought.

———. *The Way and Its Power.* New York: Grove Press, 1958. Important for its explanatory materials and its emphasis on the mystical elements of Lao-zi's thought.

Watson, Burton, trans. *Chuang-tzu: Basic Writings.* New York: Columbia University Press, 1964. Best-balanced modern translation of this difficult work.

The I Ching or Book of Changes, trans. into German by Richard Wilhelm and into English by Cary F. Baynes. Princeton, N.J.: Princeton University Press, 1967. Extensive introduction and notes. The best attempt so far to render this enigmatic text intelligible to the modern reader.

Wing-tsit Chan, trans. and comp. *A Source Book in Chinese Philosophy.* Princeton, N.J.: Princeton University Press, 1963. A large selection of documents with short but useful introductions. If only one text can be read, it should be this one, but it needs to be balanced with sociological and anthropological materials.

Secondary Sources

Blofeld, John. *Beyond the Gods: Buddhist and Taoist Mysticism.* New York: Dutton, 1974. Engaging account of Buddhist and Daoist piety by an informed traveler in China in the 1930s.

Bredon, Juliet, and Igor Mitrophanow. *The Moon Year.* Shanghai: Kelly & Walsh, 1927. An encyclopedia of folk religion based on the yearly festival calendar.

Chang, Garma C. C. *The Practice of Zen.* New York: Harper & Row, 1959. Despite its title, an insightful and sober account of Chan Buddhism. Valuable for its translations of autobiographies of monks and other religious virtuosi.

Creel, H. G. *The Birth of China.* New York: Ungar, 1937. Popular account of life and attitudes in the Shang and Western Zhou periods. Draws heavily on archaeology.

de Bary, William Theodore, ed. *The Unfolding of Neo-Confucianism.* New York: Columbia University Press, 1975. A collection of scholarly articles emphasizing the religious dimension of Neo-Confucianism. A good balance to the purely philosophical approach.

Fingarette, Herbert. *Confucius: The Secular as Sacred.* New York: Harper & Row, 1972. Sensitive and very readable interpretation of Confucius as a social and religious reformer with insights still useful for modern people.

Levenson, Joseph R. *Confucian China and Its Modern Fate.* Berkeley: University of California Press, 1958. Sociological study of interaction of Confucian elite with political and cultural forces in Chinese history. Extensive discussion of the Confucian attempts and failure to meet the challenge of modernity.

Lifton, Robert Jay. *Revolutionary Immortality: Mao Tse-tung and the Chinese Cultural Revolution.* New York: Random House, 1968. Very readable interpretation of the Cultural Revolution from a psychological viewpoint.

MacInnis, Donald E., comp. *Religious Policy and Practices in Communist China.* New York: Macmillan, 1972. Collection of documents translated from Chinese and eyewitness accounts of religious life in China under Mao.

Overmeyer, Daniel L. *Folk Buddhist Religion.* Cambridge, Mass.: Harvard University Press, 1976. Valuable study of secret societies in Chinese history.

Saso, Michael R. *Taoism and the Rite of Cosmic Renewal.* Pullman: Washington State University Press, 1972. An anthropological account based on extensive fieldwork of contemporary folk Daoism as practiced in Taiwan. A needed corrective to the tendency to view Daoism as a purely philosophical and individual phenomenon.

Taylor, Rodney Leon. *The Cultivation of Sagehood as a Religious Goal in Neo-Confucianism: A Study of Selected Writings of Kao P'an-lung.* Missoula, Mont.: Scholars Press, 1978. Translations of writings showing Neo-Confucian meditation and other religious practices and attitudes.

Wright, Arthur F. *Buddhism in Chinese History.* New York: Atheneum, 1965. A short, popular account of Chinese Buddhism. Especially valuable in evaluating the impact of Buddhism on Neo-Confucianism and later Chinese culture.

Yang, C. K. *Religion in Chinese Society.* Berkeley: University of California Press, 1967. A historical study of traditional Chinese religious values and their social functions. A good one-volume companion to the Wing-tsit Chan collection.

JAPAN

Primary Sources

Aston, W. G., trans. *Nihongi: Chronicles of Japan from the Earliest Times to A.D. 697.* London: Allen & Unwin, 1956. Originally published in 1896. A continuous narrative constructed out of much of the same mythological material as in the Kojiki but with many variant tales and historical asides toward the end.

Phillipi, Donald L., trans. *Kojiki.* Tokyo: Tokyo University Press, 1968. Because of its extensive explanatory notes, this is the best introduction to Shintō mythology. Its nonstandard transliteration of Japanese names attempts to recover archaic forms.

———., trans. *Norito: A New Translation of the Ancient Japanese Ritual Prayers.* Tokyo: Institute for Japanese Culture and Classics, Kokugakuin University, 1959. If only one primary source can be read, it should be this collection of ritual texts, which contains much mythological material.

Tsunoda, Ryusaka; William Theodore de Bary; and Donald Keene, comps. *Sources of Japanese Tradition* (2 vols.). New York: Columbia University Press, 1958. Contains many useful documents (in vol. 2) relating to the Shintō revival in the Tokugawa period and the imperial restoration and ultranationalism of the modern period.

Secondary Sources

Aston, W. G. *Shintō: The Way of the Gods.* London: Longman, 1905. Old but still unsurpassed study of ritual and ethics based primarily on literary evidence.

Blacker, Carmen. *The Catalpa Bow: A Study of Shamanistic Practices in Japan.* London: Allen & Unwin, 1975. A cogent attempt to reconstruct the form and meaning of ancient shamanism through the study of more recent practices, folklore, and literary and archaeological sources.

Buchanan, Daniel C. "Inari, Its Origin, Development, and Nature," *Transactions of the Asiatic Society of Japan,* 2nd series, no. 12 (1935), 1–191. Dated but valuable study of this Shintō cult.

Earhart, H. Byron. *A Religious Study of the Mount Haguro Sect of Shugendo: An Example of Japanese Mountain Religion.* Tokyo: Sophia University Press, 1970. A detailed account of one of the survivors of the ancient *yamabushi* cults.

Hardacre, Helen. *Shintō and the State.* Princeton, N.J.: Princeton University Press, 1987. The best work concerning the important religion-state issues in Japan in the nineteenth and twentieth centuries.

Herbert, Jean. *Shintō: At the Fountainhead of Japan.* London: Allen & Unwin, 1967. A wealth of information valuable mainly as an encyclopedia of Shintō, marred by an apologetic and sometimes theological stance that tries to defend Shintō from "Westernized scholarship."

Hori, Ichirō. *Folk Religion in Japan: Continuity and Change,* ed. Joseph M. Kitagawa and Alan L. Miller. Chicago: University of Chicago Press, 1968. Essays by a leading Japanese scholar showing the enduring power of folk religion and its usefulness in understanding such phenomena as shamanism, the new religions, mountain religion, and Shintō-Buddhist amalgamation.

Kitagawa, Joseph M. *Religion in Japanese History.* New York: Columbia University Press, 1966. The most complete history of all the Japanese religious groups, showing their development and interactions. Especially valuable for the modern period.

McFarland, H. Neill. *The Rush Hour of the Gods: A Study of the New Religious Movements in Japan.* New York: Macmillan, 1967. Despite the title, a valuable and readable introduction to the new religious phenomenon including non-Shintō forms.

Matsumoto, Shigeru. *Motoori Norinaga, 1730–1801.* Cambridge, Mass.: Harvard University Press, 1970. Detailed study of the life and thought of this important "national scholar."

Muraoka, Tsunetsugu. *Studies in Shintō Thought,* trans. Delmer M. Brown and James T. Araki. Tokyo: Ministry of Education, 1964. Good source for modern trends in Shintō scholarship and theology.

Straelen, Henry van. *The Religion of Divine Wisdom: Japan's Most Powerful Movement.* Kyoto, Japan: Veritas Shōin, 1957. A detailed account of Tenrikyō.

Webb, Herschel. *The Japanese Imperial Institution in the Tokugawa Period.* New York: Columbia University Press, 1968. Important study emphasizing the significance of the emperor's religious dimension for an understanding of his function in modern Japanese history.

PART FIVE: JUDAISM

Primary Sources

Glatzer, Nahum, ed. *The Judaic Tradition.* North Vale, N.J., 1987. An anthology of representative quotations taken from every important period in the history of Judaism.

Marcus, Jacob R., ed. *The Jew and the Medieval World: A Source Book: The Years 351–1791.* New York: Harper & Row, 1965. Source materials that enrich our understanding of the period.

Montefiore, C. G., and H. Loewe, eds. *A Rabbinic Anthology.* New York: Schocken Books, 1974. Originally published in 1938. A first-rate collection of rabbinic materials not generally available elsewhere in translation.

Note that a complete translation of the Bible has been produced by the Jewish Publication Society of America, and complete translations of other Jewish classics (including the Talmud, the Midrash, and the Zohar) have been produced by the Soncino Press.

Secondary Sources

Blau, Joseph. *Modern Varieties of Judaism.* New York: Columbia University Press, 1966. A survey of the origins and distinctive character of the important movements in modern Jewish life.

Encyclopaedia Judaica (16 vols.). Jerusalem: Keter Publishing House, 1972. A good general reference work.

Glazer, Nathan. *American Judaism.* Chicago: University of Chicago Press, 1957. A useful brief survey of the history and distinctive features of Jewish life in the United States.

Goldberg, David, and John Rayner. *The Jewish People: Their History and Their Religion.* New York: Viking, 1987. A new compact introduction to Jewish history, literature, belief, and practice.

Hertzberg, Arthur, ed. *The Zionist Idea.* Garden City, N.Y.: Doubleday, 1959. A useful collection of writings by important Zionist thinkers, together with an excellent brief introduction to the background and the various goals of the Zionist movement.

Heschel, Abraham Joshua. *The Prophets.* New York: Harper & Row, 1962. A splendid analysis of the message and significance of biblical prophecy.

Idel, Moshe. *Kabbalah: New Perspectives.* New Haven, Conn.: Yale University Press, 1988. An illuminating book by the outstanding scholar in the field of Jewish mysticism.

Kaufmann, Yehezkel. *The Religion of Israel: From Its Beginnings to the Babylonian Exile,* trans. Moshe Greenberg. Chicago: University of Chicago Press, 1966. A stimulating interpretation of the biblical heritage.

Neusner, Jacob. *There We Sat Down.* Nashville, Tenn.: Abington Press, 1971. A depiction of the beliefs and activities of the Babylonian rabbis who shaped the classical Judaic tradition.

Rifkin, Ellis. *A Hidden Revolution: The Pharisees' Search for the Kingdom Within.* Nashville, Tenn.: Abington Press, 1978. A provocative and insightful interpretation of the Pharisees and the time in which they emerged.

Scholem, Gershom. *Major Trends in Jewish Mysticism,* 3rd ed. New York: Schocken Books, 1954. Originally published in 1941. The best available scholarly introduction to Jewish mysticism.

Seltzer, Robert M. *Jewish People, Jewish Thought: The Jewish Experience in History*. New York: Macmillan, 1980. A well-written, well-researched survey of Jewish intellectual history from the biblical period to the present.

Silver, Daniel Jeremy, and Bernard Martin. *A History of Judaism* (2 vols.). New York: Basic Books, 1974. A fine survey of Jewish history and literature.

Steinsaltz, Adin. *The Essential Talmud,* trans. Chaya Galai. New York: Basic Books, 1976. A helpful crystallization of the rabbinic mind by a contemporary master of talmudic literature.

Wiesel, Elie. *Souls on Fire: Portraits and Legends of Hasidic Leaders,* trans. Marian Wiesel. New York: Random House, 1972. A sympathetic interpretation of the Hasidic spirit by a contemporary Jew.

PART SIX: CHRISTIANITY

Primary Sources

Augustine: Earlier Writings, ed. J. H. S. Burleigh. *Augustine: Confessions and Enchiridion,* ed. Albert Cook Outler. *Augustine: Later Works,* ed. John Burnaby. Vols. 6, 7, and 8 in the Library of Christian Classics. Philadelphia: Westminster Press. A clarity seldom found in translations from this period.

Abbott, Walter M., and Joseph Gallagher, eds. *The Documents of Vatican II: With Notes and Comments by Catholic, Protestant, and Orthodox Authorities*. New York: Guild Press, 1966.

Ahlstrom, Sydney E., ed. *Theology in America: The Major Protestant Voices from Puritanism to Neo-Orthodoxy*. Indianapolis: Bobbs-Merrill, 1967.

Bettenson, Henry, ed. Selected Passages from the Canons of the Council of Trent found in *Documents of the Christian Church*. New York: Oxford University Press, 1963.

Calvin, John. *Institutes of the Christian Religion*. Philadelphia: Westminster Press, 1960. The foundation document of the Reformed tradition.

Dillenberger, John, ed. *Martin Luther: Selections from His Writings*. Garden City, N.Y.: Doubleday, 1961. A fine, balanced presentation with a good introduction.

Gaustand, Edwin Scott. *A Documentary History of Religion in America*. Grand Rapids: Eerdmans, 1982–1983.

Kidd, B. J., ed. *Documents Illustrative of the Continental Reformation*. Oxford: Clarendon Press, 1911. A good collection of key documents.

Peers, E. A., ed. *The Complete Works of Saint Teresa of Jesus*. New York: Sheed & Ward, 1946. A remarkable summation of the spirit of the Catholic Reformation as well as of contemplative life.

Pegis, Anton C., ed. *Introduction to St. Thomas Aquinas*. New York: Random House, 1945. One of many editions, but one of the best.

Richardson, Cyril C., ed. *Early Christian Fathers*. New York: Macmillan, 1970. The first volume of the Library of Christian Classics and the best of several such collections of the writings of the early fathers. Introduced by Richardson, the work initiates us into an alien world. The whole series merits the attention of serious students of the history of Christianity, and this particular volume is excellent for the beginner.

Ruether, Rosemary Radford, and Rosemary Skinner Keller. *Women and Religion in America*. San Francisco: Harper & Row, 1981–1986.

Secondary Sources

Ahlstrom, Sydney E. *A Religious History of the American People*. New Haven, Conn.: Yale University Press, 1972.

Bokenkotter, Thomas. *A Concise History of the Catholic Church*. Garden City, N.Y.: Doubleday, 1977.

Brown, Peter. *Augustine of Hippo: A Biography*. Berkeley: University of California Press, 1969.

Chadwick, Henry. *The Early Church*. New York: Viking Penguin, 1967.

Cochrane, Charles Norris. *Christianity and Classical Culture*. New York: Oxford University Press, 1970.

Cross, F. C., ed. *The Oxford Dictionary of the Christian Church,* 2nd ed. New York: Oxford University Press, 1977. An indispensable tool for both the fledgling and the seasoned historian of Christianity.

Ellis, John Tracy. *American Catholicism*. Chicago: University of Chicago Press, 1969.

Frazier, E. Franklin, and C. Eric Lincoln. *The Negro Church in America and the Black Church since Franzier*. New York: Schocken Books, 1974.

Frend, W. H. C. *The Rise of Christianity*. Philadelphia: Fortress Press, 1984.

González, Justo L. *A History of Christian Thought*. Nashville, Tenn.: Abingdon Press, 1970. An excellent treatment of a complex subject, though it stops far short of the present.

Grant, Robert M. *A Short History of the Interpretation of the Bible*. Philadelphia: Fortress Press, 1984.

Hudson, Winthrop S. *Religion in America*. New York: Scribner, 1981.

Latourette, Kenneth Scott. *A History of Christianity*. New York: Harper & Row, 1953. Probably the most esteemed general treatment. Very thorough and evenhanded.

MacHaffie, Barbara J. *Her Story: Women in the Christian Tradition*. Philadelphia: Fortress Press, 1986.

Neill, Stephen. *The Interpretation of the New Testament, 1861–1961*. New York: Oxford University Press, 1964.

Pagels, Elaine. *The Gnostic Gospels*. New York: Random House, 1979.

Ruether, Rosemary Radford, and Eleanor McLaughlin. *Women of*

Spirit: Female Leadership in the Jewish and Christian Traditions. New York: Simon & Schuster, 1979.

Schmemann, Alexander. *The Historical Road of Eastern Orthodoxy.* Chicago: Regnery, 1963.

Smith, Margaret. *An Introduction to Mysticism.* New York: Oxford University Press, 1977.

The Interpreter's Dictionary of the Bible. Nashville, Tenn.: Abingdon Press, 1976.

Tyson, Joseph B. *The New Testament and Early Christianity.* New York: Macmillan, 1984. A clear, readable account of the development of early Christian thought and practice as seen in the extant literature of the period, including the canonical scriptures.

Walker, Williston; Richard A. Norris; David W. Lotz; and Robert T. Handy. *A History of the Christian Church,* 4th ed. New York: Scribner, 1985.

Ware, Timothy. *The Orthodox Church.* New York: Viking Penguin, 1963.

PART SEVEN: ISLAM

Primary Sources

ʿAbduh, Muḥammad. *The Theology of Unity,* trans. Isḥāq Masaʿad and Kenneth Cragg. London: Allen & Unwin, 1966. The major theological work of the man who is often called the founder of Islamic modernism.

ʿAli, Sayyīd Amir. *The Spirit of Islam.* London: Methuen, 1965. Originally published in 1922. A classic of "liberal" modernism, particularly in its apologetic methodology and stance on major social issues.

Arberry, Arthur J., trans. *The Koran Interpreted* (2 vols.). London: Allen & Unwin, 1955. Arberry's translation weds scholarly precision with excellent literary quality. His work can be fruitfully compared with one or both of the following:

Dawood, N. J., trans. *The Koran,* 4th rev. ed. New York: Penguin, 1974.

Pickthall, Muḥammad M., trans. *The Meaning of the Glorious Koran.* New York: Mentor Books, 1953.

al-Ashʿari, Abu-al-Hasan. *Kitāb al-Ibānah ʿan Usūl al-Diyānh,* trans. Walter Klein. New Haven, Conn.: American Oriental Society, 1940. An annotated translation of a major theological work.

ibn-Bābawayhī, Abu-Jaʿfar Muḥammad. *A Shīʿite Creed,* trans. A. A. A. Fyzee. Calcutta, 1942. An important early statement of Twelver Shīʿite doctrines by a tenth-century Shīʿite theologian.

al-Hujwīrī, ʿAlī-ibn-Urhmān al-Jullābī. *Kashfal-Mahjūb,* 2nd ed., trans. R. A. Nicholson. London: Luzac, 1936. The oldest Persian treatise of Ṣūfism. Hujwīrī lived in the eleventh century.

Iqbal, Muḥammad. *Reconstruction of Religious Thought in Islam.* Lahore: Muḥammad Ashraf, 1962. A comprehensive rethinking of Islam by an original and often daring intellectual. The book grew out of a series of lectures delivered by Iqbal in 1928.

ibn-Isḥāq, Muḥammad ibn-Yasār. *The Life of Muḥammad,* trans. Alfred Guillaume. New York: Oxford University Press, 1955. Other than the Qur'ān itself, ibn-Isḥāq's work is the most important single source for the study of Muḥammad's life and thought.

al-Kalābādhī, Abu-Bakr. *The Doctrine of the Ṣūfīs,* trans. Arthur J. Arberry. Cambridge: Cambridge University Press, 1935. A general treatment of Ṣūfī doctrine written by a tenth-century Ṣūfī.

Rahman, Fazlur. *Islam,* 2nd ed. Chicago: University of Chicago Press, 1979. A critical interpretation of Islam by a contemporary Muslim intellectual.

The following anthologies contain a wide variety of Islamic literature in translation:

Arberry, Arthur J., ed. and trans. *Aspects of Islamic Civilization.* London: Allen & Unwin, 1964.

Jeffrey, A., ed. and trans. *A Reader on Islam.* The Hague: Mouton, 1962.

Schroeder, Eric, ed. *Muḥammad's People.* Portland, Maine: Bond Wheelwright, 1955.

Williams, John A., ed. *Islam.* New York: Washington Square Press, 1963.

Secondary Sources

Arberry, Arthur J. *Ṣūfism.* London: Allen & Unwin, 1950. The best of several available introductions to the Ṣūfī literature.

Coulson, Noel J. *A History of Islamic Law.* Edinburgh: Edinburgh University Press, 1964. A very readable introduction to a field that is often difficult for the beginner.

Cragg, Kenneth. *The House of Islam,* 2nd ed. Belmont, Calif.: Wadsworth, 1975. A sensitive introduction.

———, and R. Marston Speight. *Islam from Within.* Belmont, Calif.: Wadsworth, 1975. An anthology of texts designed to accompany *The House of Islam.*

Denny, Frederick M. *An Introduction to Islam.* New York: Macmillan, 1985. A new introduction with a good bibliography for further study.

Gibb, H. A. R. *Modern Trends in Islam.* Chicago: University of Chicago Press, 1947. Somewhat dated but still very useful.

———. *Mohammedanism,* 2nd ed. New York: Oxford University Press, 1953. An excellent general introduction to Islam, despite the old-fashioned title.

Holt, P. M.; Ann K. S. Lambton; and Bernard Lewis, eds. *The Cambridge History of Islam* (2 vols.). Cambridge: Cambridge University Press, 1977. Recommended for historical orientation and reference.

Jansen, G. H. *Militant Islam.* New York: Harper & Row, 1979. A provocative and readable presentation of the current "militant revival" in the Islamic world.

Lewis, Bernard, ed. *Islam and the Arab World.* New York: Knopf, 1976. A lavishly illustrated survey of Islam in its original heartland. The book is a compilation of articles by specialists in various fields.

Momen, Moojan. *An Introduction to Shīʿi Islam.* New Haven: Yale University Press, 1985. An excellent introduction to Twelver Shīʿism.

Smith, W. C. *Islam in Modern History.* Princeton, N. J.: Princeton University Press, 1957. Often wordy but careful, sensitive, and accurate.

Watt, W. M. *Islamic Philosophy and Theology.* Edinburgh University Press, 1962. In this short book Watt does for theology what Coulson does for law.

———. *Muḥammad at Mecca.* Oxford: Clarendon Press, 1953.

———. *Muḥammad at Medina.* Oxford: Clarendon Press, 1955. These two books are the best modern biography of Muḥammad available in English. Watt places heavy emphasis (perhaps too heavy) on the social and economic factors in the foundation of Islam. Watt has condensed the original two-volume biography into a single volume: *Muḥammad, Prophet and Statesman* (Oxford: Clarendon Press, 1961).

INDEX

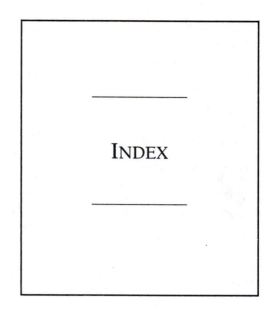

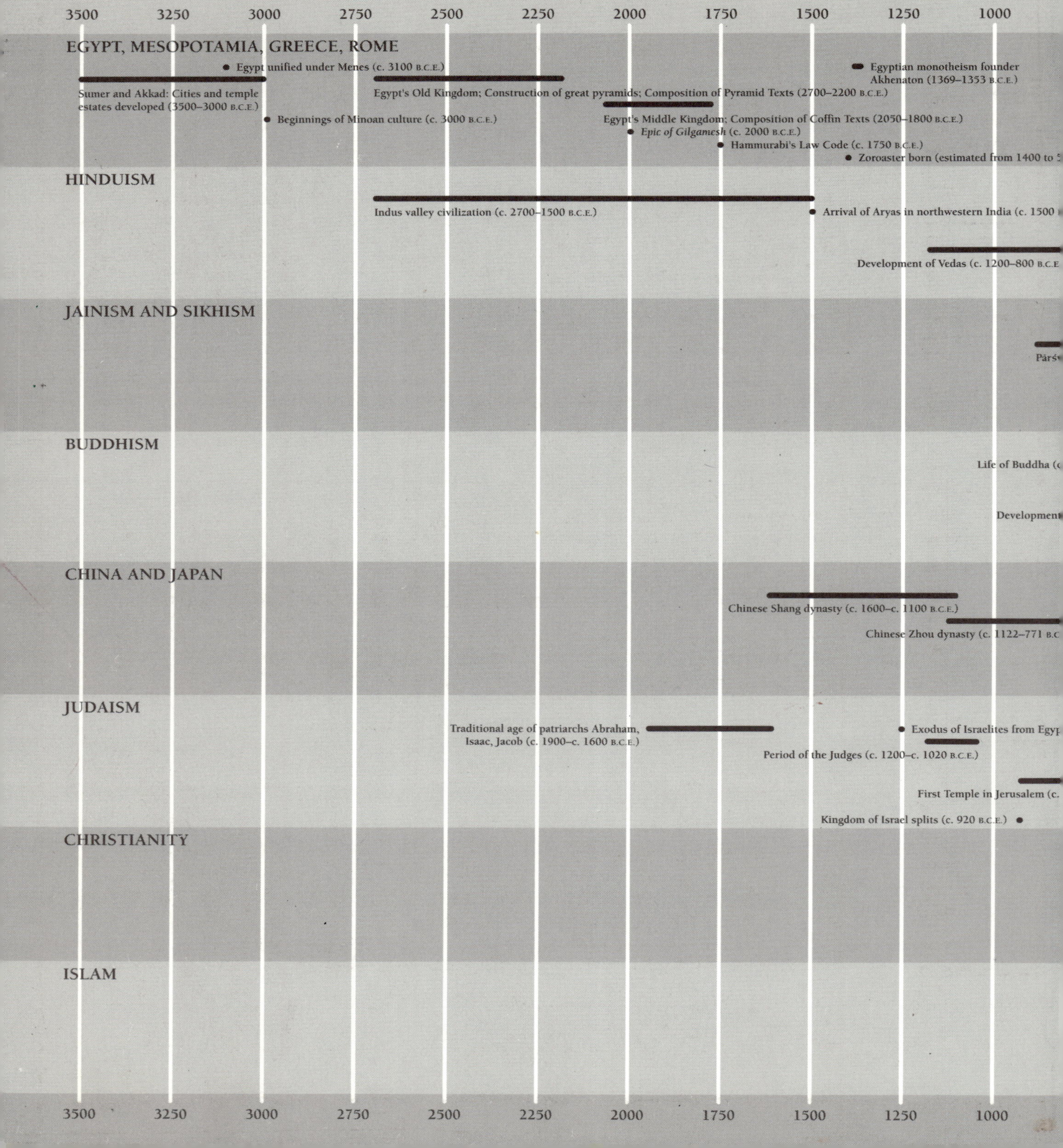

3500 3250 3000 2750 2500 2250 2000 1750 1500 1250 1000
EGYPT, MESOPOTAMIA, GREECE, ROME
Egypt unified under Menes (c. 3100 B.C.E.)
Egyptian monotheism founder Akhenaton (1369–1353 B.C.E.)
Sumer and Akkad: Cities and temple estates developed (3500–3000 B.C.E.)
Egypt's Old Kingdom; Construction of great pyramids; Composition of Pyramid Texts (2700–2200 B.C.E.)
Beginnings of Minoan culture (c. 3000 B.C.E.)
Egypt's Middle Kingdom; Composition of Coffin Texts (2050–1800 B.C.E.)
Epic of Gilgamesh (c. 2000 B.C.E.)
Hammurabi's Law Code (c. 1750 B.C.E.)
Zoroaster born (estimated from 1400 to
HINDUISM
Indus valley civilization (c. 2700–1500 B.C.E.)
Arrival of Aryas in northwestern India (c. 1500
Development of Vedas (c. 1200–800 B.C.E
JAINISM AND SIKHISM
Pārś
BUDDHISM
Life of Buddha (
Development
CHINA AND JAPAN
Chinese Shang dynasty (c. 1600–c. 1100 B.C.E.)
Chinese Zhou dynasty (c. 1122–771 B.C
JUDAISM
Traditional age of patriarchs Abraham, Isaac, Jacob (c. 1900–c. 1600 B.C.E.)
Exodus of Israelites from Egyp
Period of the Judges (c. 1200–c. 1020 B.C.E.)
First Temple in Jerusalem (c.
Kingdom of Israel splits (c. 920 B.C.E.)
CHRISTIANITY
ISLAM
3500 3250 3000 2750 2500 2250 2000 1750 1500 1250 1000